Children's Literature:
A Developmental Perspective

THE WILEY BICENTENNIAL—KNOWLEDGE FOR GENERATIONS

$\mathcal{E}$ach generation has its unique needs and aspirations. When Charles Wiley first opened his small printing shop in lower Manhattan in 1807, it was a generation of boundless potential searching for an identity. And we were there, helping to define a new American literary tradition. Over half a century later, in the midst of the Second Industrial Revolution, it was a generation focused on building the future. Once again, we were there, supplying the critical scientific, technical, and engineering knowledge that helped frame the world. Throughout the 20th Century, and into the new millennium, nations began to reach out beyond their own borders and a new international community was born. Wiley was there, expanding its operations around the world to enable a global exchange of ideas, opinions, and know-how.

For 200 years, Wiley has been an integral part of each generation's journey, enabling the flow of information and understanding necessary to meet their needs and fulfill their aspirations. Today, bold new technologies are changing the way we live and learn. Wiley will be there, providing you the must-have knowledge you need to imagine new worlds, new possibilities, and new opportunities.

Generations come and go, but you can always count on Wiley to provide you the knowledge you need, when and where you need it!

WILLIAM J. PESCE
PRESIDENT AND CHIEF EXECUTIVE OFFICER

PETER BOOTH WILEY
CHAIRMAN OF THE BOARD

To Our Readers

We are writing *Children's Literature: A Developmental Perspective* for pre-service and in-service teachers, students of English, library science majors, and young men and women who have chosen children's literature as an elective course. Such students share a growing responsibility in the education of today's children as the federal government has made a major commitment to improve the reading skills of our children. To achieve the goals outlined by the federal government, those who work with children need a wide and deep knowledge of children's literature. *Children's Literature*, through its developmental approach, provides a focus on what children need and are interested in at different developmental stages.

A Developmental Approach to Children's Literature

Our book takes a developmental approach to children's literature, thus providing a more meaningful and practical introduction to the subject. With an understanding of the developmental theory that explains a child's abilities, needs, and interests, future teachers are better prepared to meet the needs of individual children and to help them develop their literary skills. In this way, teachers can foster a lifelong love of reading. We believe that our book, combining children's literature with developmental psychology, offers professors and students a more sophisticated and in-depth approach to a subject sometimes referred to as "kiddie lit." In this book, *the underlying structure for children's book selection is based on a developmental framework.* To select the appropriate book for a child, the teacher, librarian, parent, or other adult needs not only to know children's literature, but also to understand the developmental level of the children they are serving.

What is the child like? Is she in the middle years, is she active, curious, and competitive? Or is he just learning to walk and talk, and is fascinated by sounds and colors? Perhaps the child is a dreamer and likes to create her own stories or spend hours building with a lego set. The secret to leading a child to the right book is not only to know the books, but to know the child. Only then is the concept of goodness-of-fit (the match between a child's developmental level and appropriate literature) complete. In this way, the traditional genres of children's literature become more meaningful when viewed through a developmental lens.

Although most readers of this text may be studying children's literature formally for the first time, they have been readers for many years. They may still quote Dr. Seuss or remember tearfully reading *Charlotte's Web*. These classics are still being read and reread, but thousands of other new, innovative books are also capturing the imagination of today's children. Harry Potter, for example, has taken the world by storm, just as *The Wizard of Oz* did at the beginning of the last century. By reading *Children's Literature: A Developmental Perspective*, students will learn what makes the most recently published books attractive to children while still recognizing the value of books that have held children's interest in the past.

Organizational Themes

The *first* of our organizational themes is the use of a biopsychosocial model — the biological, psychological, and social forces that drive development — to achieve our goal of matching children with appropriate literature. The key to selecting the appropriate book for a child not only is the knowledge the teacher, librarian, parent, or other adult has about children's literature, but also what they know about the developmental level of the children they are serving.

The *second* of our organizational themes is the use of genres. These are categories that help readers understand the various characteristics of the wide range of children's literature. In *Children's Literature: A Developmental Perspective*, we have selected eight genres — picture books, traditional literature, modern fantasy, poetry and drama, contemporary realistic fiction, historical fiction, biography and autobiography, and informational books — to help children understand the nature of children's literature.

The *third* of our organizational themes relates to the introduction of topical ideas that teachers and librarians will find valuable in comprehending the modern world of books. For example, we have not only included guidelines and models for children's literature to be used in the curriculum, but we have also examined such sensitive issues as privacy, censorship, and technology.

The text has a total of 14 chapters. Within each chapter, developmental characteristics of children of a particular age level are discussed and book suggestions for each genre are made based on these characteristics. We have also identified specific topics that are representative of the various developmental levels: gender issues, reluctant readers, bullying, death, peer relationships, fear and anxiety, obesity, etc. These stories encompass classical as well as the best of the current literature and stress the goodness of fit that we as professionals are seeking in our selection of books for young people. We believe this technique offers a fine balance of key elements, developmental characteristics, and strong content providing readers with a rich and deep sense of children's literature.

The 14 chapters are organized into four parts as follows. Part One provides an introduction to children's literature and development. Part Two provides the foundation of children's literature: the genres, selection, children's responses, illustration, and diversity. Part Three discusses the contents of children's literature based on developmental stages. Part Four concludes the text with a chapter on a science literature curriculum illustrating how children's literature reaches across the curriculum, and a chapter on issues related to children's literature about which teachers and librarians need to be aware.

PART ONE – INTRODUCTION
Chapter 1. Children, Literature, and Development: Interactions and Insights
Chapter 2. Children and Their Literature: Changes through the Years

PART TWO – UNDERSTANDING CHILDREN'S LITERATURE
Chapter 3. Genres in Children's Literature
Chapter 4. Analyzing, Selecting, and Responding to Children's Literature
Chapter 5. The Craft of Writing and Illustrating
Chapter 6. Diversity in Children's Literature

PART THREE – THE CONTENT OF CHILDREN'S LITERATURE
Chapter 7. Literature for the Early Years (Ages Birth–2)

Contents of the Chapters

Chapter 1: Children, Literature, and Development: Interactions and Insights
In Chapter One, we present a developmental perspective that describes the biopsychosocial characteristics of children, both typical and exceptional. This perspective will be used to analyze the interactions of children with literature, which should help teachers, librarians and parents to select appropriate stories. Developmental theories are briefly discussed and illustrated by appropriate children's stories. Following each discussion of a developmental theory is a section entitled *Strategies for Integrating (Name of Theory) Into Children's Literature*.

Chapter 2: Children and Their Literature: Changes through the Years
The theme guiding our work in this chapter is that stories about and for children reflect the prevailing view of children at any particular time. Our journey begins with the colorful tales passed on by oral tradition and continues with the literature of the Greeks. The appearance of the Gutenberg press dramatically increased the number of books available, which was accompanied by a steadily changing picture of children and the influence of such individuals as Randolph Caldecott and John Newbery. Such themes as the recognition of gender differences and the increasing popularity of fantasy testify to the status of children and children's books. As children's literature parallels the rapid societal changes of the twentieth and the twenty-first centuries, its themes reflect the conflicts and problems that modern children experience.

Chapter 3: Genres in Children's Literature
Chapter 3 is devoted to the scope of children's literature, ranging from the realistic to the fantastic. Genres, those characteristics that distinguish one form of literature from another, are at the heart of our discussion. We explain the following eight categories, offering extensive examples of each.

Picture Books (including Easy Readers)
   Traditional Literature (Folktales and Fairy Tales, Myths, Legends, Fables, and Parables)
Modern Fantasy (including Science Fiction)
Poetry and Drama
Contemporary Realistic Fiction
Historical Fiction
Biography and Autobiography
Informational Books

Chapter 4: Analyzing, Selecting, and Responding to Children's Literature

Chapter 4 focuses on how the selection and evaluation of many genres of children's literature should be made using our developmental model and several literary elements. Discussion of the criteria used to select books for various awards, including the Newbery and Caldecott Medals (and other awards), is also included. To assist our readers with selective and evaluative criteria, we have analyzed *Because of Winn Dixie* and *Belle Prater's Boy* by applying the literary elements presented in the chapter. In our discussion we have also incorporated the manner in which children respond to their literature by discussing the Reader Response theory of Louise Rosenblatt.

Chapter 5: The Craft of Writing and Illustrating

Our discussion in this chapter focuses on the personal backgrounds of outstanding authors and illustrators who have contributed and continue to contribute to children's literature. These authors and illustrators retain their magnetism for children because of style, subject matter, and their understanding of the developmental needs and interests of children. The various media and techniques artists use to make their illustrations appropriate and often award-winning are described in light of an author's choice of language to insure an appropriate goodness-of-fit.

Chapter 6: Diversity in Children's Literature

The importance and the need for an understanding of multiculturalism in children's literature are highlighted in Chapter 6. Although multiculturalism is the main theme of the chapter, examples of diversity appear in all chapters of the book. We have adopted Rudine Bishop's interpretation of diversity as our guide in this chapter: Multicultural refers to all those who have been marginalized by society. In this way, we hope to show how children's literature helps to eliminate prejudice, stereotypes, and value conflicts directed at those who differ in culture, social class, age, religion, special needs, or gender orientation. To accomplish this objective, we first trace the roots of multiculturalism in children's literature, and then stress the work of Lev Vygotsky, explaining how his ideas concerning cultural influence lead to a deeper understanding of cultural sensitivity. Finally, we explore the children's literature of four cultures: Latino, African American, Asian American, and Native American.

Chapter 7: Literature for the Early Years (Ages Birth–2)

NOTE: *In Discovering Children's Literature in the 21st Century, we have intentionally chosen to include literature appropriate for children not only from kindergarten through grade six or eight but from birth through high school. Including such a broad range of literature along with an increased understanding of child development from birth through adolescence is a unique component of our book. It provides readers with the opportunity of helping children select appropriate literature, whether they are having difficulty reading at the most primary level or are ready (biopsychosocially) to read at an adult level. Although certification specifications may limit teachers to work with children of a certain age, from our extensive research into child development and our teaching and library experience, we know that children's ability to read varies widely within every age range, We want the students who read this book to understand the outstanding developmental characteristics for all age levels. In this way, they will learn to be more understanding and knowledgable and more aware of the individual differences of the children with whom they work. Consequently, they will be more successful in helping young readers not only now but in the future.*

In Chapter 7 we have advanced suggestions for bringing children into the world of books as early as the prenatal days. We have turned to the latest developmental data about infancy — from brain research to pertinent environmental elements — to make a reading environment as attractive as possible to children as early as possible. By applying such developmental data to appropriate literature for these years (picture books, Mother Goose books, board books, etc.), we hope that our readers will acquire the personal tools that enable them to motivate children to become lifelong readers.

Chapter 8: Literature for the Preschool Years (Ages 2–4)

As the tremendous explosion of language continues during these years, young readers will appreciate the rhythms and nuances of music, poetry, and drama as they are portrayed in appropriate literature. Given children's tremendous receptivity for language, the preschool years present unparalleled opportunities for reading aloud and overcoming any lingering reluctance to derive pleasure from the written word. Family literacy and lap-time story hours are also discussed.

Chapter 9: Literature for the Early Elementary School Years (Ages 5–7)

These years, referred to by many psychologists as the time of the 5 to 7 shift, signal a major transition in children's thinking. Cognitive abilities are developing rapidly, and we believe teachers, librarians, and parents can aid thinking skills by questioning children on what they read. For example, the importance of blending developmental data with appropriate literature is dramatically demonstrated during these years by using easy readers and transitional books. Simply written informational books (including biography and autobiography) are included, since early elementary school children are eager to grasp facts as well as fiction. The importance of reading aloud and suggesting how families of non-English-speaking children can participate in their education are also emphasized.

Chapter 10: Literature for the Intermediate School Years (Ages 8–10)

The developmental characteristics of these years — more complex reasoning, broadening relationships, the growing evaluation of self — testify to the need for children to be familiar with the many genres of literature to meet these needs. Special topics that interest children include sports and activities (soccer, little league, writing diaries and journals). Children can be helped by stories that contribute to their understanding of such topics as competition, cooperation, winning and losing, getting along with their family and friends, and improving their thinking skills. How children's literature can be used across the curriculum is also discussed. To help our readers organize informational topics, we turn to the work of Howard Gardner and his Theory of Multiple Intelligences. In this way, teachers and librarians can present pertinent and important informational books in a meaningful manner.

Chapter 11: Literature for the Middle School Years (Ages 11–14)

Children of this age continue to sharpen their thinking skills and become good problem solvers, both in and out of the classroom. Simultaneously, their search for identity becomes more intense. Books for these years encompass fantasy, poetry, contemporary realistic fiction, historical fiction, and traditional literature. We continue to stress books that are appropriate for the reluctant reader and the successful use of picture books for older children. We also stress a wide range of biographical and informational books, again using Gardner's work as an organizing theme.

Chapter 12: Literature for the High School Years (Ages 14–18)

With the changes that young adults are experiencing, they are open to a wide range of interpretations that are reflected in the literature for this period. We have presented literature that should match their needs. For example, we have included a discussion of gay and lesbian literature as well as the crossover of adult books for young adults and the place of graphic novels in the curriculum. Since reading skills continue to evince serious concern, we have devoted a section of the chapter to reluctant readers and books that appeal especially to boys (our largest segment of nonreaders).

Chapter 13: Science Literature through the Grades: A Curricular Model

In this chapter we have selected one subject — science literature — as a model of how children's literature can be used in all subjects across the curriculum and for all grade levels. We draw extensively on Maslow's Theory of Needs to encourage and motivate students from kindergarten through high school. With its changing, dynamic subject matter, science affords young readers a glimpse of how inspiring, beneficial, and informative school subjects can be. In this way, we have attempted to demonstrate how the body of children's literature can enrich all subjects.

Chapter 14: Issues for Teachers and Librarians

In this, the final chapter, we have identified several topics we believe teachers and librarians should be aware of. The issue of censorship is a constant in the history of the printed word. Today, perhaps more than ever before, the need to understand and apply a set of guiding principles to deal with censorship is crucial, if not critical. Although our future teachers and librarians are computer literate, we have supplied a comprehensive list of websites that will aid them in their search for appropriate information about research topics and specific books or authors. Finally, the need for teachers and librarians to coordinate and cooperate in their efforts to ensure that young readers continue to grow in literacy is becoming steadily more apparent.

Teaching and Learning Features

Among the features that distinguish this book are the following.

• Each chapter begins with a detailed chapter outline followed by an opening vignette. Then comes a GUIDELINES FOR READING CHAPTER XXXX to help readers focus on important elements. In formulating these guidelines, we have integrated the evaluative criteria used to assess literature with developmental characteristics of the particular age group the chapter is analyzing. We ask our readers to be specific in their responses. (The evaluative criteria are discussed in detail in Chapter 4.) We believe this is another important feature in making *Children's Literature* an effective teaching tool.

• We have devised five types of interactive features, boxes that highlight a chapter's content. We believe these boxed features add interest and depth to the narrative of the chapter. These features are intended to encourage class discussion by having readers express their ideas about relevant and pertinent issues that involve children's literature. The titles of these boxes are:

What's Your View? These are designed to encourage readers to divulge their opinions on the matter under discussion.

Culture and Children's Literature   These features stress the role that any culture plays in its literature and the developmental effects it has on children.

Then and Now   Tracing the changes that occur in the interpretation of various issues (for example, the development of picture books) is a rich source of information for readers.

Spotlight On... Outstanding Authors and Illustrators   This feature is intended to demonstrate the background and talent of various outstanding individuals (Maurice Sendak, Virginia Hamilton, etc.)

Guidelines for Reading the Chapter   The chapter-opening *Guidelines* features help readers focus on the important elements of the chapter. In formulating these guidelines, we have integrated the evaluative criteria used to assess literature with developmental characteristics of the particular age group the chapter is analyzing. We ask our readers to be specific in their responses. The evaluative criteria are discussed in detail in Chapter 4.

• Each chapter includes appealing and relevant *Spinoffs*, classrooms and library-tested activities that help teachers and librarians enrich and extend children's enjoyment of the many genres of literature. *Spinoffs* also challenge children's imagination and encourage them to respond positively to the books that are being discussed. They often involve children in the use of technological aids to further their appreciation. These appear following major sections of each chapter.

• **DEVELOPMENTAL SUMMARY CHARTS**: Each of the genre chapters includes a summary of the developmental features of the period that highlight outstanding biopsychosocial characteristics. For example, we'll discuss attachment and relationships during the early years, play during the preschool years, thinking skills and problem solving during the intermediate and middle school years, and relationships in the high school years. These topics are then reflected in the children's literature discussed in the chapter.

• **CHAPTER-OPENING VIGNETTE**: Each chapter opens with a vignette. These vignettes act as *advance organizers*, which is a concept proposed by the educational psychologist David Ausubel. They are designed to prepare the reader for the material that is to come, thus encouraging meaningful learning. The characters in the vignettes also reveal the developmental topics presented in the chapter, thus helping teachers integrate development with the literature under discussion in the chapter.

• **RECOMMENDED CHILDREN'S BOOKS AND PROFESSIONAL BIBLIOGRAPHY**. Each chapter concludes with a listing of recommended titles (over 2000 in all the chapters). The literature we select is not only based on the quality of the book itself, but also on the child's individuality, personality, interests, and reading capabilities. The professional bibliography is designed to aid teachers' understanding of the age group of the chapter and to provide insights into the literature based on expert opinion.

• To conclude each chapter, we have formulated a *Chapter Checklist* section, which is designed to allow readers to test themselves on the reading of the chapter. This brief review is essentially a Student Guide that is built into the text. The Chapter Checklist is based on *Bloom's Taxonomy of Thinking Skills* and is written to guide teachers and librarians in selecting questions for students that will reveal their knowledge, comprehension, application, analysis, and synthesis of the chapter content.

• Each chapter contains an extensive bibliography of both classic and current children's books. These bibliographies contain more than 2000 references.

• Each chapter also contains a detailed list of professional references that offers a wide range of additional material to enrich the reader's understanding of the chapter's content.

Instructor resources can be found at www.wiley.com/college/travers.

Acknowledgments

Many individuals have contributed to the completion of this book. Professional colleagues working in the field of children's literature have been a continual source of both help and encouragement. Marie Benner of the Boston Public Library and the Waterville (ME) Public Library and Gerry Driscoll of the McCall Middle School Library Winchester (MA) deserve particular thanks. Martha Parravano, Executive Editor of The Horn Book offered both encouragement and support as did Dr. Lenore Parker, former Professor of Children's Literature at Lesley University, Cambridge, MA. and founder of the BCBC (Boston Children's Book Club), a small but active group of children's literature advocates.

We would be remiss if we did not recognize the importance of our association with the *Foundation for Children's Books* in selecting and analyzing current authors whom we have included in *Children's Literature: A Developmental Perspective*. The FCB is a nonprofit, educational organization that was organized in 1983 to assist the professionals who most directly influence young readers: teachers, librarians, and parents. The Foundation offers a dynamic speaker series, innovative conferences and workshops, as well as author visits and residencies in under-served schools.

We are particularly grateful for the suggestions of our many colleagues and in particular for the ideas expressed by Brendan Rapple, Collection Development Librarian at Boston College in his discussion of the Internet as a research tool. George Ladd, Professor of Science Education at Boston College and Director of the Science Poetry Annual Contest in the state of Massachusetts, provided excellent examples of the writings of many students. Our colleagues John Dacey and John Savage have been unstinting in their advice and support.

We are delighted to acknowledge and express our appreciation for the help that our many friends and colleagues at John Wiley offered us. In particular, we would like to mention the constant advice and reassurance that our editor Robert Johnston gave us. He was a constant source of motivation and shepherded our work from first idea to final words. He was ably assisted by Eileen McKeever, Katie Melega, Carrie Tupa, Nicole Repasky, Madelyn Lesure, Elle Wagner, and Suzanne Ingrao.

Finally, we should like to thank our family: Jane, Liz and Rob, Ellen and Kevin, John and Janice, for their constant encouragement to write *Children's Literature: a Developmental Perspective*. We are grateful to our four children: Liz, Ellen, John, and Jane who consider our book their fifth sibling and our seven grandchildren: Jackie, Gina, Zachary, Maddie, Joseph, Lindsey, and Nicholas to whom this book is dedicated. They never fail to answer our frequent question: *What are you reading?*

We are also deeply appreciative of the many reviewers who by their expertise and recommendations improved the quality of our work.

Karen Donnelly, *Louisiana State University*
Patricia P. Wiese, *Texas A&M University*
Steve Luebke, *University of Wisconsin—River Falls*
Debbie Mercer, *Fort Hays State University*
Betty Dean Newman, *Athens State University*
Louise Stearns, *Southern Illinois University*
Margaret A. Dietrich, *Austin Peay State University*
Kay G. Rayborn, *Henderson State University*
Laura Apol, *Michigan State University*
Cynthia Moles, *St. Josephs, Maine*
Bonnie Mackey, *University of Houston*
Geraldine Dougherty, *Colorado State University—Pueblo*
Sylvia Baer, *Gloucester Community College*
Ruth Brio, *Duquense University*
Alan Rouch, *University of North Carolina—Charlotte*
Sharron McEmeel, *University of Wisconsin—Stout*
Susan Merrifield, *Lesley College*
Margaret Bush, *Simmons College*
Geraldine A. Driscoll, *Winchester Public Schools*

Brief Contents

Contents

CHAPTER 5

The Craft of Writing and Illustrating 96

CHAPTER 6

Diversity in Children's Literature 120

CHAPTER 7

Literature for the Early Years (Ages Birth – 2) 146

CHAPTER 11

Literature for the Middle School Years (Ages 11 – 14) 250

CHAPTER 12

Literature for the High School Years (Ages 14 – 18) 282

Children's Literature:
A Developmental Perspective

CHAPTER 1

Children, Literature, and Development: Interactions and Insights

It was a warm July evening, the children were drowsy after a hectic day, and a stillness began to settle over the house. We had to finish some writing (this chapter) and were working on the computer when we sensed someone come quietly into the study.

Lindsey, carrying a heavy book, had slipped into one of the chairs, tucked her legs under her, and began to read J. K. Rowling's Harry Potter and the Chamber of Secrets, *a good challenge for an 8-year-old. Not wanting her to think she was being tested (especially in July!), we asked her to read a little for us. Obligingly, she moved her chair closer and began to read about Harry's latest adventure. She's a good reader and obviously enjoyed reading, even when tired. Both of us thought, "What a gift," to be immersed in the world of reading.*

The lucky children are those who love to read. Walk into any bookstore or library in the country and you will find children devouring books. This wonderful sight provides endless opportunities for teachers, librarians, and parents. What should children be reading? Why? Who selects the books for them, for their classrooms, for their school libraries, and for the children's section in the public library? What criteria do they use? And what about reluctant readers? What choices are best for them? Answers to these questions lie in the connections we make between children's levels of development—physical, psychological, social (biopsychosocial)—and the books they read. The goal of this book is to help you make those important connections.

Providing help for teachers, librarians, and parents that matches the developmental levels of children—their needs, desires, and interests—is a serious business, one that affects the lives and futures of millions of children each year. The world of books offers them an exciting, challenging kaleidoscope of adventure and information that can only enrich their lives. In this opening chapter, we explore the relationship between children's literature and development by examining key developmental issues, discussing the ideas of leading developmental theorists, and linking these developmental concepts to classic and current children's literature. We also illustrate how these developmental ideas appear in the books that your children are reading.

**HARRY POTTER AND THE
CHAMBER OF SECRETS**
*J. K. Rowling, Scholastic, Cover
Art by Mary GrandePre*

Guidelines for Reading Chapter 1

After you read Chapter One, you should be able to answer the following questions.

• In helping children with their book selections, can you explain why age alone is an inadequate guide?

• Can you give specific examples of the match between goodness-of-fit and appropriate literature?

• Are you able to identify the ideas of developmental theorists in the stories discussed in this chapter?

• How does knowledge about a biopsychosocial perspective of development help an adult in advising book selection for a particular child?

• How would you explain the manner in which developmental psychology helps teachers, librarians, and parents to understand a child's response to literature?

• Can you identify the themes of several of the stories mentioned in this chapter that reflect the ideas of particular theorists?

Children's Literature and Child Development

Children's Literature: A Developmental Perspective promises to unlock the secret of what happens in the interaction between a child and a book. Our goal is to help you discover what makes a young reader hungry to devour the contents of a book. For example, what makes Christopher Paul Curtis's *The Watsons Go to Birmingham—1963*, a Newbery Honor Book and also a Coretta Scott King Honor Book, popular with children in intermediate and middle school? The answer lies in the manner in which the author weaves humor into the steadily increasing tension of the story, the nature of the characters, and the setting of the story, which have made it a Readers' Choice for children in state contests throughout the country.

Examining the literary elements of a story isn't enough, however. We must be sure that a child's developmental level is adequate for the child to understand and enjoy the story's events and themes. The goal of working with children is to match their developmental characteristics with the appropriate literature, thus engaging children and ultimately improving their reading skills and inspiring in them a love of books. Consequently, we all share a growing responsibility for the education of today's children, a responsibility that demands an awareness of a child's total development as well as a wide and deep knowledge of children's literature.

Although you may be studying children's literature formally for the first time, you undoubtedly have been a reader for many years. You may still quote Dr. Seuss's *The Cat in the Hat* (1957) or remember tearfully reading E. B. White's *Charlotte's Web* (1952). These classics are still being read and reread, but thousands of other new, innovative books are also capturing the imagination of today's children. The many books about Harry Potter that J. K. Rowling began writing in 1998 (*Harry Potter and the Sorcerer's Stone*), for example, have taken the world by storm. Rowling has related the adventures of Harry at Hogwarts, the school for witches, beginning when he was 11 years old until his graduation at age 17. These books alone span many of the developmental years that we discuss here. By reading *Children's Literature: A Developmental Perspective*, you will learn what makes the most recently published books appealing to children and young adults while recognizing the value of books that have held their interest in the past.

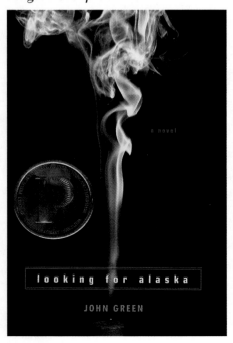

LOOKING FOR ALASKA
Used with permission of Penguin Group USA Inc.

Themes to Guide Our Work

To help you achieve the goal of integrating children's literature with current knowledge of developmental psychology, thus helping you match book with child, we have adopted a thematic approach. Our belief is that the themes, principles, and data of developmental psychology integrate seamlessly with the outstanding children's literature that authors and illustrators have created to attract their readers. For example, in the infancy chapter we'll discuss Jane Yolen's *The Lullaby Songbook* in light of an infant's growing perceptual ability. We continue in a similar manner through the high school years, when we analyze John Green's *Looking for Alaska* in view of the problems that many young adults experience with drugs and alcohol. We have identified the following three themes to guide our work.

1. IDENTIFICATION AND INTEGRATION of current and classic works of children's literature (*Goodnight Moon, The Penderwicks, Holes,* etc.) with the developmental level that best matches a child's needs.

2. A DEVELOPMENTAL FRAMEWORK that presents the outstanding characteristics of children of different developmental levels plus the behaviors most often recognized as typical of a particular level. For example, the appearance of distinctive personalities during the preschool years, which is nicely captured by Kevin Henkes in *Wemberly Worried*, or the bully who terrorizes victims during the middle school years, as seen in Jerry Spinelli's *Crash*.

3. BIOPSYCHOSOCIAL (BIOLOGICAL, PSYCHOLOGICAL, AND SOCIAL) INTERACTIONS today are recognized as the most effective means of understanding a child's development. We now know that these interactions reflect the forces that shape development: genetic, neural, behavioral, and environmental. For example, in infancy we can identify rapid physical growth, sensitivity to speech sounds, improved attention, increasing vocabulary, the social smile, and the appearance of attachment.

We turn now to the first of our themes, children's literature.

The Beauty and Appeal of Children's Literature

The jewel in the reading crown, of course, is meaning. How do children represent meaning, and how does that representation determine their comprehension? Here we turn to the interaction between children and literature, including both the developmental level of the child and the literary elements of the book, to explain a child's response to literature. How do children respond to books? On the surface it seems like a simple question with a simple answer: They respond in a manner that indicates whether they enjoy what they're reading or not. But if you're going to help them with their book selections, you must probe more deeply.

If enjoyment, thoughts, and emotions are intertwined in a reader's response, then your task becomes one of detecting *why* they enjoy, *what* they think, and *how* they feel about it. This takes us back to the interaction between child and book: developmental level, contextual pressures (parents, siblings, teachers, peers), features in the book that attract a reader's attention (color, illustrations), topics that naturally appeal to children of various levels (animals, mysteries, biographies), and many other considerations (male/female, peer influence).

We know now that children may not respond immediately to their reading. Thanks to the research of Albert Bandura (1997) on *observational learning* (often referred to *as modeling*), we understand that children may need time to wrestle with the meaning of what they're reading and *then* act on what they've thought about. To take us into the exciting world of authors' words and children's enjoyment, we turn to the ideas of Louise Rosenblatt.

The Work of Louise Rosenblatt

Louise Rosenblatt was for many years a professor at Barnard College and the University of Miami. In 1938 she published a book titled *Literature as Exploration*, which introduced the concept of reader response theory. This marked a transition in identifying and accepting the active role of the reader in the interaction between child and book. Her rationale for this (at the time radical) position is found in the following words (Rosenblatt, 1938, p. vi).

Through books, readers may explore their own natures, become aware of potentialities for thought and feelings within themselves, acquire clearer perspectives, develop aims, and a sense of direction.

This quote unmistakably represents a viewpoint that emphasizes the active and personal nature of the reading process as readers engage in either *efferent* reading (reading for information) and/or *aesthetic* reading (reading that captures the feelings and experiences of the reader).

Known as the *transactional theory* of reader response, Rosenblatt's ideas were widely acknowledged at the time, but failed to ignite the educational and literary community. In 1978, however, she published *The Reader, the Text, and the Poem*, which again brought her ideas to the forefront but now had immediate impact. How do we explain these different reactions to her work? The answer can be found in the changed intellectual climate: By the time Rosenblatt's 1978 book was published, teachers of reading were much more concerned with issues of cognitive development and comprehension than with rote memorization of study skills techniques.

During the 1970s several theories of the representation of meaning were formulated suggesting that if children couldn't understand what they were reading, they were failing to construct proper representations. Consequently, strategies for improving children's representations of what they read became popular. It was within this framework that Rosenblatt's explanation of how readers' responses could vary from child to child was eagerly received. The critical element in Rosenblatt's work is how a child experiences and reacts to a text.

Children and Response Theory

We cannot emphasize enough how valuable it is for you as a teacher or librarian to adapt Louise Rosenblatt's *transactional theory* reader response to your work with children's literature. Rosenblatt's theory is an excellent guide to how a child or a group of children will respond to whatever book that you provide them. Always remember that children bring to their reading the compilation of who they are biopsychosocially. In Spinoffs, the activities that we suggest for each developmental age throughout the book, we emphasize the various ways that children may respond to books. Considering, however, the thousands of books that are published each year, and the hundreds of children that you may serve, it certainly is not easy to know when this magical moment of offering the right book to the right child occurs. Only by children's responses do you know when they have internalized the book so that it has become a positive experience for them.

We'd like to give you an example of what we mean. As this text goes to press, twenty-five first- and second-graders in a nearby elementary school are preparing to present Kevin Henkes' *Chrysanthemum* to their classmates. Their teachers have already read *Chrysanthemum* to them; many parents have bought it for them so that they can picture who they will be on stage. They are familiar with all the characters and they know each by name: Sam, Victoria, Les, Kay Max, Sue, and of course Chrysanthemum.

They're also familiar with the classroom setting and with how Chrysanthemum, who at first loved her name, is now questioning its appeal. During lunch they talk about the play with each other; some of the children say they dream about it at night. Every Thursday after school they meet to practice their parts and to socialize with juice and cookies. In their imagination, they *are* the characters the director selects them to be. Years later, should they meet the director, they may recall the excitement of enacting a play from a book that they will never forget.

Rosenblatt knew what happens when a young child responds to a picture book like *Chrysanthemum*. At first, she may just examine the illustrations, noticing the various kinds of mice, each one different from the others. Then when she reads it or listens to someone read it to her, she brings her prior experiences to what she reads. She may already have read Numeroff's *If You Give a Mouse a Cookie*, or she may have a mouse doll that she takes to bed with her. Being in first or second grade, she also may have had social experiences that are similar to Chrysanthemum's: being teased or bullied or laughed at. Now, if her teacher reads the story with obvious enjoyment and understanding, the young child will respond *aesthetically* to the book and look forward to reading it by herself. Acting out the book for her is "the frosting on the cake." It reaffirms the meaning of the book and creates a lasting personal experience.

CHRYSANTHEMUM
Used with permission of HarperCollins Publishers

Another positive response to reading that would have pleased Louise Rosenblatt is the manner in which second-graders relate to Esther Averill's series *The School for Cats*, which has recently been reissued. Averill's love for cats is irrepressible, as reflected in her simple line drawings of the cats that meet under her streetlight at night. When a teacher reads or students themselves read about Jenny, the timid black cat with the red scarf, they listen. When she introduces students to the cats that surround Jenny, they easily assume their identities. Later, in language arts lessons, after reading *Jenny's Birthday Party*, for example, each child who becomes one of the cats mentioned in the books eagerly answers the teacher's questions: What is your cat's name? What color are you? What talent do you have that you will perform at Jenny's party? Whatever time the teacher schedules for her work with her class (aka *The Cat Club*) is beneficial not only for students' comprehension and understanding of Esther Averill's books, but for the pleasure that the students will remember forever.

As children advance in school and develop their critical thinking skills, teachers often challenge them to write their own versions of the books they read. Mysteries such as Donald Sobol's *Encyclopedia Brown* are a suitable challenge. Once the children have gotten to know the main characters, solved the mystery, and checked in the book to see if they reasoned correctly, their teacher encourages them individually or in small groups to create their own mystery. For example, in one classroom the portable blackboard disappeared. Children were filled with questions: Who had taken it? Why did they take it? What clues did the robbers leave that would help them to reclaim it? Then, after dividing into small groups, the children in each group wrote a version of *The Mystery of the Disappearing Blackboard*—not a bestseller, but a perfect response to their reading that helped develop their cognitive abilities, language arts, and social skills. They were so enthusiastic about the project that many worked together after school to complete it.

AESTHETIC AND EFFERENT READING　When studying Rosenblatt's transactional theory, we often encounter the words *aesthetic* and *efferent*. Both words connote differences in the way that children approach reading. Efferent reading is reading to seek information. Aesthetic reading is reading for pleasure. Aesthetic reading is an excellent description of how children become involved in their picture books, their fantasies, their traditional literature, their poetry, and contemporary and historical fiction. They read them with joy, with excitement, and with an awareness of "Wow, This is the best book I have ever read!"

Efferent reading involves facts, data, and theorizing. Those of you who believe that a classroom or library is not complete without dog-eared copies of almanacs and books like *The Guiness Book of World Records* can attest to the fact that many children

Spin Off

From Books to Plays

Below is a very abbreviated script for a classroom play "The School for Cats," adapted from the book by Esther Averill.

CHARACTERS: NARRATOR; TEACHER; JENNY, SMALL BLACK CAT WEARING A RED SCARF; PICKLES, A FIRE CAT WEARING FIREMAN'S HAT AND RIDING A FIRE ENGINE (A LARGE BOX PAINTED RED); THE CAT CLUB: ALL THE REST OF THE CHILDREN IN THE CLASS.

Setting: School room with a sofa or chair in the center.

ACT 1

NARRATOR: Every summer the Cat Club members go to school to learn good manners.

TEACHER: If you all learn your manners and do just as I say, then you all will have your catnip before jumping into bed.

CAT CLUB: Please, dear teacher. We promise if you do, we won't forget our manners. We'll be both kind and true.

NARRATOR: But Pickles does not have good manners. He likes to scare the cats with his hook and ladder.

PICKLES (RUNNING INTO THE CATS): Make way for the hook and ladder! Make way for the hook and ladder!

NARRATOR: Jenny is scared. She hides under the sofa.

CAT CLUB (TOGETHER): Shame on you, Pickles. You are a naughty cat. You do not please; you only tease. What kind of manners is that?

JENNY (FROM UNDER THE SOFA): When the cats go to bed, I'm going to run away.

(All the cats exit except Jenny)

End of Act I

ACT II

Setting: Outside

JENNY: I ought to go back. I will go back. I won't be afraid of that fresh cat, Pickles. I'll say to her . . . I'll say . . . What will I say?

(Jenny falls to the floor and starts to cry.)

All the cats except Pickles come on stage to comfort Jenny.

CAT CLUB (TOGETHER): Jenny, you are you. Six feet tall. You are not afraid at all. Brave and strong. Hum a song. Pickles won't be boss for long.

NARRATOR: Just then Pickles runs on stage toward Jenny with his fire truck.

PICKLES: Make way for the hook and ladder! Make way for the hook and ladder!

NARRATOR: Jenny jumps up. She faces Pickles.

JENNY (SHOUTING): PICKLES, MAKE WAY FOR THE BIGGEST FIRE ON EARTH!

NARRATOR: Jenny and Pickles tumble and roll over each other. Then they both stand up. Jenny wears Pickles' hat.

PICKLES (SHAKING HANDS—OOPS, PAWS—WITH JENNY): Jenny, you win. I promise never to chase little cats again.

CAT CLUB (CHEERING): Congratulations, Pickles. You are now a mannerly cat. You do not tease. You only please. And that's the beginning of your education.

Curtain closes as all the cats make a circle around Jenny and Pickles.

THE END

eagerly devour facts, especially strange facts. They, obviously, are efferent readers. They may also be aesthetic readers when the illustrations and the facts they uncover are stranger and more exciting than fiction. So aesthetic reading and efferent reading are not contradictory concepts; they are only opposite ends of the reading spectrum. Children are capable of simultaneously being efferent and aesthetic readers.

Before students are assigned a topic for efferent reading, the teacher or librarian, using knowledge of children's biopsychosocial development and their individual interests, suggests that they select one of a number of topics to explore. Teachers and librarians have only to become familiar with Howard Gardner's *Frames of Mind: The Theory of Multiple Intelligences* to offer children a choice of topics that are consistent with their interests and the kinds of intelligences they have demonstrated. (In later chapters of this text we offer many examples of outstanding books that appeal to the range of intelligences that Gardner believes are inherent in every child.)

Teachers and librarians can motivate their students to engage in both aesthetic and efferent reading and activities that reinforce such reading. They may also leave their students alone to experience the joy of reading in a quiet place without interruption. Whatever name or acronym (for example, SSR—Sustained Silent Reading) you devise to describe the time you allot in your classroom to reading silently, it is important that children have a consistent opportunity to respond privately to what they are reading.

Next we examine the second guiding theme of this book: a developmental framework.

The Importance of a Developmental Framework in Book Selection

The premise of this book is that *book selection should be based on a developmental framework*. The secret of selecting the appropriate book for a child is not only the knowledge that teachers, librarians, and parents have about children's literature, but also what they know about the developmental level of each child they are serving. What is the child like? Is she in the middle years, active, curious, and competitive? Is he just learning to walk and talk, and is fascinated by sounds and colors?

Is the child a dreamer who likes to create her own stories or spend hours building with blocks? What is the child's cultural background? Has the child had any major traumatic experiences? The secret to leading a child to the right book is not only knowing the books but also knowing the child. Only then can *goodness-of-fit* be achieved. (In our work, goodness-of-fit refers to the match between a child's developmental level and appropriate literature and is based on the concept originally developed by the child psychiatrists Stella Chess and Alexander Thomas (1987, 1999). It's a term we use throughout this text.) Consequently, the traditional genres (categories) of children's literature become more meaningful when viewed through a developmental lens.

We believe that understanding development provides teachers, librarians, and parents with a necessary depth of knowledge for selecting appropriate books for children. We also believe that grasping the range and application of developmental data provides insights into the problems and triumphs of the children depicted in the literature. In this way, teachers can assist young readers, as well as those in middle and high school, in understanding experiences that they have had or may later encounter in their own lives.

What Is Development?

The middle school child who avidly reads Richard Peck's *A Long Way from Chicago* is not the same child who, a few years earlier, was enthralled by Eric Hill's *Goodnight Spot*, a delightful picture book for preschoolers. She has changed dramatically—physically, psychologically, and socially—which is the meaning of development. Development is about change in all aspects of a child's life, and change is the key to understanding the relationship between books and children.

Today's developmental psychologists search for explanations of developmental change in the interactions among physical, cognitive, social, and cultural influences. This type of analysis has led to the insightful conclusion that a child's age tells us nothing about *why* a particular behavior appears at a specific time (Rutter, 2002). Consequently, age alone isn't the answer. The answer lies hidden in the interactions among the various developmental forces acting in and on a child, forces that are referred to as *biopsychosocial* interactions. We'll apply this insightful new approach to analyzing development in the coming sections, but first let's examine what is meant by "biopsychosocial."

It is no longer possible to talk about cognitive development, language development, and personality development as separate issues. Long lists of what children can do at various ages say nothing about how or why these behaviors have appeared or become integrated. By recognizing the significance of biopsychosocial interactions, you can better understand the complexity of development and use this knowledge as a guide in helping children select appropriate books that are both enjoyable and meaningful.

Knowing a child, knowing a book, and knowing developmental theory enables teachers, librarians, and parents to select books that match children's developmental needs. As you read this section, note how children's literature integrates nicely with developmental concepts, a condition we've identified as goodness-of-fit. As an example, let's briefly review the basic ideas of two well-known developmental theorists—Erikson and Piaget—in a way that will help you in selecting and analyzing children's literature.

Erikson and Society

Erik Erikson (1902–1994) is a leading proponent of the *psychosocial theory of development*. He believed that children interact with an ever-widening circle of individuals, beginning with their mothers and ending with humanity as a whole (Thies & Travers, 2001). In the process, they pass through a series of eight psychosocial stages. Each of these stages is marked by a developmental crisis that must be resolved so that the individual can move on. The resolution of these crises is necessary for one's continuing healthy psychological development.

STRATEGIES FOR INTEGRATING CHILDREN'S LITERATURE WITH ERIKSON'S THEORY   Knowledge of Erikson's psychosocial stages can be quite helpful to teachers, librarians, and parents as they work with children in the world of books. Here is a brief description of Erikson's five stages that pertain to childhood together with an appropriate work of literature that illustrates each stage.

1. **BASIC TRUST VERSUS MISTRUST (BIRTH TO $1\frac{1}{2}$ YEARS OLD).** In the first stage, infants derive security and comfort from warm relations with their parents, which leads to a strengthening of the attachment process. The picture book *Mama's Little Bears*, written and illustrated by Nancy Tafuri, is a gentle and loving story of three bear cubs who explore the unknown, but always under the watchful eye of their caring mother, who is pictured in each spread—ready to protect them from harm if need be.

2. **AUTONOMY VERSUS SHAME AND DOUBT ($1\frac{1}{2}$ TO 3 YEARS OLD).** At about $1\frac{1}{2}$ years old, children face this crisis. They begin to demonstrate independence, as seen in *Carry Me, Momma* by Monica Devine, which is a picture book about an Inuit child's determination to be independent. When it's time for her to walk, she does, but at bedtime she still pleads with her mother to carry her to bed.

3. **INITIATIVE VERSUS GUILT** (the preschool years). The third crisis, initiative versus guilt, typically begins when a child is about 3 years old. Building on the ability to control themselves, children now demonstrate responsibility and a sense of purpose as they begin to acquire the ability to master such tasks as learning to read. In Susan Cooper's short picture book *Frog*, appropriate for reading aloud to preschoolers, Little Joe cannot swim. "He just doesn't get it." When he sees a frog in distress in the family swimming pool, however, he puts aside his apprehension and, with a renewed sense of determination, swims out to rescue the frog.

4. INDUSTRY VERSUS INFERIORITY (THE EARLY ELEMENTARY AND INTERMEDIATE SCHOOL YEARS). Children of this age are immersed in the task of acquiring the needed information and skills of their culture. They expand their horizons beyond the family and begin to explore the neighborhood and school communities to develop new relationships. School becomes a proving ground, and some degree of success is necessary for personal adjustment and social acceptance. In Patricia Polacco's picture book *Thank You, Mr. Falker,* although Tricia (the heroine) looks forward to learning how to read, she meets with little success. Only when her fifth-grade teacher personally encourages and coaches her does she finally succeed.

5. IDENTITY VERSUS IDENTITY CONFUSION (ADOLESCENCE). As children begin the adolescent years, their main task is to achieve a state of identity. (See Chapter 12 for a more detailed discussion of adolescents and their literature.) Uncertainty produces identity confusion, and a bewildered youth may withdraw, run away, or turn to drugs or sex. The challenges are new, the tasks are difficult, and the alternatives are often overwhelming. Needless to say, adolescence, especially the first years, requires considerable patience and understanding. Jean Davies Okimoto sensitively portrays the identity confusion of 15-year-old Moonbeam Dawson, a biracial teenager in *The Eclipse of Moonbeam Dawson.* After moving out to live on his own at a Canadian resort, he changes his name, finds out about his native heritage, and discovers peace within himself. (Erikson's remaining stages—intimacy and solidarity versus isolation, generativity versus stagnation, and integrity versus despair—apply to the adult years.)

Here are several strategies to help integrate children's literature with Erikson's theory.

• During the early years (ages 0–2, trust versus mistrust), parents and caregivers should talk to infants and read them stories that illustrate the beauty and rhythm of language. A unique and beautiful book is *The Lullaby Songbook,* edited by Jane Yolen, with musical arrangements by Adam Stemple. "One of the most tender moments an adult and child can share is the lullaby and these are the songs that say to the listening child: Go to sleep now. I am here" (Yolen, 1986).

• As children move into the preschool years (ages 2–4), teachers, librarians, and parents should identify stories that emphasize and increase a child's spirit of initiative. For example, the classic picture book *Madeline,* the story of the independent and mischievous little French girl by Ludwig Bemelmans, continues to entertain children because the heroine has so many zany adventures with her compatriots.

• With the onset of the early elementary school years (5–7), children may seek stories that engage their sense of industry. Themes of positive peer relationships, a thirst for knowledge, and a desire to achieve are seen in Patricia Lee Gauch's charming picture book *Tanya and the Red Shoes,* illustrated by Satomi Ichikawa. It is an appealing story of a child's dream of being a ballerina coming true. Although Tanya often feels self-conscious and awkward walking across the floor, she finally realizes that it requires much practice, a helpful big sister, and many blisters to be a dancer with the red shoes.

• In the intermediate years, children (ages 8–11) also expand their interest in the world around them and become intrigued by adventure. In *Rowan and the Keeper of the Crystal,* the third book in an award-winning Australian fantasy series by Emily Rodda, Rowan overcomes his feelings of inferiority and demonstrates his sense of industry by pursuing the antidote that will cure his mother's illness.

- When children are in middle school (ages 12–14), they seek their own identity and relate to books such as Katherine Paterson's *Jacob Have I Loved*, in which Sara Louise analyzes her relationship with her twin sister and her entrance into the adolescent world.

- During their high school years (ages 14–18), young people continue to seek their identity—now as young adults. In *Shooter*, Walter Dean Myers seeks the connection through the use of documents such as newspaper articles, police and medical examiner's reports, and personal interviews that leads to the protagonists Cameron Porter and his co-conspirator, Carla Evans, becoming partners with Leonard Gray in a Columbine-like high school shooting. Yet the main thrust of the novel is the defining moment when the main characters acquire maturity and acknowledge the serious consequences of their actions.

Leaving the world of personality development and turning to explanations of cognitive development takes us first to the ideas of Jean Piaget.

Piaget and Thinking

Did you ever wonder why babies talk when they do? Or why they don't look for a toy that they *see* you hide behind a chair? Or why they think there's more milk in a tall, thin jar than in a short wide one, even though you pour the milk from one into the other right in front of them? The Swiss psychologist Jean Piaget (1896–1980) wondered about and sought to answer these questions by analyzing the *cognitive structures* of the intellect. How did Piaget explain cognitive development?

Piaget believed that intelligence matures as children develop increasingly complex cognitive structures that enable them to organize and adapt to their world as they pass through four stages: the *sensorimotor* (using their bodies to form cognitive structures), the *preoperational* (rapid language growth), the *concrete operational* (increase in abstract thinking), and the *formal operational* (reasoning with symbols) stages.

STRATEGIES FOR INTEGRATING CHILDREN'S LITERATURE WITH PIAGET'S THEORY   Piaget's stages of cognitive development still hold considerable appeal to those seeking an overview of a child's mental development. Here are several ideas you may find useful as a guide in helping children with their book selections.

- In Piaget's theory preschool children are still cognitively *egocentric*. Guide them to stories whose main themes emphasize relationships, for example, children playing and working together. Amy Schwartz, author and illustrator of the picture book *The Boys Team*, understands preschoolers when she writes about a group of three boys doing everything together: "building, climbing, eating, chasing." The illustrations match their activities, which take place in an exciting city environment.

- Since play is an important part of a preschool child's life, select stories that portray children playing constructively: asking questions, using make-believe play to understand their world, and learning to follow rules. In Peter Sis's *Madlenka's Dog*, children again meet Madlenka (introduced in the previous book, *Madlenka*). Or perhaps they meet her for the first time as she takes her invisible dog with the visible collar for a walk through her diverse New York City neighborhood. Later she and her best friend, Cleopatra, who has an imaginary horse, together play imaginative games.

• As children move into Piaget's concrete operational period, suggest stories that show how their thinking can solve problems. Encourage children to read stories that illustrate how they can mentally retrace their steps, how they should not be deceived by the appearance of things, and how they can combine ideas to solve problems. Mystery stories like the *Encyclopedia Brown* series (by Donald Sobol) are particularly challenging to children in Piaget's concrete operational period. Readers can match their wits with Encyclopedia Brown and find the relevant clues that lead to each solution.

• For those children sufficiently advanced to be identified at the formal operational level, abstract, logical thinking characterizes their behavior. For example, older children marvel at the maturity of Bobby in Andrew Clements' novel *Things Not Seen* when he wakes up one morning to discover that he is invisible. Although he mentions this problem to his parents, Bobby decides that he must solve his dilemma himself. By not attending school or keeping in touch with his old friends, he lessens the possibility that his condition will become front-page news. This also provides time for him to analyze what could have happened and to meet Alicia, a blind girl who is instrumental in helping him regain his visibility.

THINGS NOT SEEN
Used with permission of Penguin Group USA Inc.

The ideas of Erikson and Piaget are only two examples illustrating the close link between children's literature and developmental psychology. In the pages to come, we'll apply the theories, research, and speculations that come from centuries of hard-won gains in understanding human development to centuries of work by authors and illustrators reaching out to children, always trying to engage them at an appropriate developmental level. The result has been an intriguing mixture of science and art that has informed, enlightened, and fascinated children through the ages.

The Importance of Biopsychosocial Interactions

We come now to our third and final theme. As a result of recent findings, modern developmental psychologists have turned to an analysis of biopsychosocial interactions in their efforts to understand development. It is not enough to list developmental characteristics, which tell us nothing about the causes of behavior. To reach the roots of development, the search must take us into the *interactions* among biological, psychological, and social influences. (See Dacey & Travers (2009) for an extended discussion of biopsychosocial interactions.) Concentrating on the biopsychosocial interactions of children provides a guide for exploring cultural issues that greatly enrich the understanding of human development.

Table 1.1 identifies several features of the biological, psychological, and social aspects of interactions.

The elements of biopsychosocial interactions listed in Table 1.1 certainly aren't exhaustive but indicate numerous developmental features that affect growth during the life span. *More important, however, we would like you to think about the dynamic interactions that occur across the three categories and how these interactions affect development of the whole child.* For example, genetic damage (biological) may negatively affect cognitive development (psychological) and lead to poor peer relationships (social).

Spotlight On

Other Contributing Theorists

The theories we've discussed thus far fall neatly into the realm of developmental psychology. There are other theorists, however, who are not so easily classified as developmental, but who have made significant contributions both to development and to children's literature. We also trace their influence on children's literature throughout the book.

Abraham Maslow

Abraham Maslow (1987), a humanistic psychologist at Brandeis, proposed a theory of human needs that has remained with us to this day. Basic to his thinking was the belief that if we can convince children that they should—and can—fulfill their potential, they will embark on the path to self-actualization, which requires the satisfaction of a hierarchy of needs.

According to Maslow, there are five basic types of needs: physiological (hunger and sleep), safety (security, protection, stability, and freedom from fear and anxiety), love and belonging (need for family and friends), esteem (reactions of others to us as individuals, and also our opinions of ourselves), and self-actualization (feelings of restlessness unless we are doing what we think we are capable of doing). The needs at the base of the hierarchy (physiological and safety) are assumed to be more basic than the needs higher in the hierarchy. (See Chapter 13 for a more detailed discussion of the power of Maslow's motivational needs and their relationship to children's literature.)

Albert Bandura

An important theorist whom we'll discuss in the pages to come is Albert Bandura, with his theory of *social cognitive learning*. In his work Bandura has stressed the potent influence of *modeling* on personality development (Bandura, 1997). He called this *observational learning*. In a famous statement on *social (cognitive) learning* theory, Bandura and Walters (1963) cited evidence to show that learning occurs through observing others, even when the observers do not imitate the model's responses at that time and obtain no reinforcement. For Bandura, observational learning means that the information we acquire from observing and reading about other people, things, and events influences the way we act. We encourage teachers, librarians, and others to offer the biographies and autobiographies we review throughout the book as models for the children they serve.

The importance of models is seen in Bandura's interpretation of what happens as a result of observing others. For example, by observing others, children may acquire new responses, or strengthen or weaken existing responses. Finally, if children witness undesirable behavior that is either rewarded or goes unpunished, undesirable behavior may result.

Howard Gardner

Another theorist who has made major contributions to our knowledge of development is Howard Gardner (1983, 1991, 1993, 1997). Gardner has forged a tight link between thinking and intelligence with his theory of *multiple intelligences*. An especially intriguing aspect of Gardner's work is the insight it provides into those individuals who possess penetrating mathematical vision but are baffled by the most obvious musical symbols. Gardner attempted to explain this apparent inconsistency by identifying eight equal intelligences: linguistic, musical, logical-mathematical, spatial, bodily-kinesthetic, interpersonal, intrapersonal, and naturalistic. We discuss Gardner's work in greater detail in later chapters and suggest to teachers and librarians many books that reflect the intelligences of their students.

Lawrence Kohlberg

Among the more notable efforts to explain a child's moral development is that of Lawrence Kohlberg (1975, 1981). Using Piaget's ideas about cognitive development as a basis, Kohlberg's moral stages emerge from a child's active thinking about moral issues and decisions. Kohlberg formulated a sophisticated scheme of moral development extending from about 4 years of age through adulthood, and we constantly see his ideas come to life in the unfolding of children's stories, from *The Cat in the Hat* (Seuss) for preschoolers to *Understanding the Holy Land: Answering Questions about the Israeli-Palestinian Conflict* (Mitch Frank) for young adults.

Lev Vygotsky

No discussion of theoretical contributions would be complete without mentioning Lev Vygotsky. Since we devote a portion of Chapter 6 to his work on the zone of proximal development and scaffolding, we'll just briefly state here that Vygotsky believed that children's mental development depends on the interactions that they have with those around them. In other words, Vygotsky was one of the first to recognize the impact that the environment has on a child's development.

Table 1.1 ELEMENTS OF BIOPSYCHOSOCIAL INTERACTIONS

BIO/LOGICAL	PSYCHO/LOGICAL	SOCIAL/CULTURAL
Genetics	Cognition	Attachment
Fertilization	Information processing	Relationships
Pregnancy	Problem solving	Reciprocal interactions
Birth	Perception	School
Physical development	Language	Peers
Motor development	Moral	Television
Puberty	Self-efficacy	Stress
Disease	Personality	Family
	Emotions	Culture

A good example from children's literature about how children's interactions change with changing circumstances is found in the many picture book escapades of Marc Brown's aardvak, Arthur. In *Arthur's Eyes*, Arthur is unable to see the blackboard, or to score a basket when he plays ball (biological). He even stumbles into the girls' bathroom because he is unable to read the sign on the door. Although Arthur is reluctant at first to wear his glasses (psychological), when he finally does wear them, his whole world improves (social), and even his heartthrob Sue Ellen is impressed!

Another example from the literature for middle school students illustrates how genetic damage (biological) may negatively affect learning (psychological)

What's Your View?

The Great Brain

In *The Great Brain*, we witness a demonstration of attentive, intelligent behavior that takes different forms. When Tom was 10 years old and living in a rural Utah community, his father decided to install the first indoor toilet in the town. When the only plumber in town came around to dig a cesspool, Tom charged each of his friends a penny to watch. His little brother protested, but Tom told him that he had to keep thinking of new ideas so that his great brain would continue growing.

Next he decided to charge them to come into the house and flush the toilet. When his mother heard about it, she was furious and made Tom refund all the money. But after Tom gave back all the money he had collected, there were still twenty children demanding their money. He complained to his mother about all the "cheaters," but she made him use his own money to finish paying back everyone. Tom's brother looked at him and decided that Tom would carry this financial catastrophe to the grave.

Tom's next adventure turned out much more satisfactorily. When two of his friends were lost in the twists and turns of a series of caves, the entire town came to help find them. For two days and a night they searched but couldn't find the boys. Everyone feared they were lost for good, but Tom's great brain went to work.

His two lost friends had taken their dog, Lucky, with them. Lucky liked to play and romp through the fields with Tom's dog, Brownie. Tom convinced the adults to let him go into the caves with Brownie and a pound of liver. He thought his dog would have a good chance of finding his pal Lucky. He smeared the liver over rocks on the way in, knowing that Brownie would use the smell to lead them out. Tom found his friends, Brownie led them out, and Tom became the town's hero.

In what way does the problem-solving Tom demonstrates in his search for his lost friends illustrate how biopsychosocial interactions affect behavior? Do authors, as well as teachers, librarians, and parents, need to be aware of developmental change in their characters, or should they just concentrate on telling a story? What's your view?

THE GREAT BRAIN
Used with permission of Penguin Group USA Inc.

and lead to poor relationships (social). In Virginia Hamilton's novel *Sweet Whispers, Brother Rush*, 14-year-old Tree is responsible for caring for her beloved older retarded brother, Dab. When her brother dies, she talks to her mother about the family's relationships. It's only then that she understands how her brother's biological condition (an inherited blood disease called *porphyria*) affected all other aspects of family life, cognitive and social.

In John Fitzgerald's charming classic tale of *The Great Brain* (recently reissued), we see in fiction reissued for middle school students the playing out of many of the developmental issues we'll be discussing throughout the remainder of this book: thinking, problem solving, imagination, emotions, and others.

These, then, are the three themes that will guide us as we explore the pathways that lead us into the challenging and fascinating tapestry of children's literature: its history, the genres, techniques for selecting appropriate books, its diversity, how authors and illustrators work together, the developmental levels and suitable literature, the emergence of children's literature in all parts of the curriculum, and special topics of interest to teachers and librarians. First we trace the rich and revealing history of children's literature.

Chapter Checklist

Read the following items carefully. If you have difficulty responding to any of them, return to the chapter to review the material.

After reading this chapter, you can

1. Describe the necessity of understanding the relationship between a book and a child's level of development.

2. State the reasons why you can't depend on age alone to help children with their book selections.

3. Explain the biopsychosocial interactions that constitute development change and lead to changes in children's book selections.

4. Demonstrate how knowledge of developmental theory guides teachers and librarians in helping with a child's book selection.

5. Analyze the impact of both traditional and modern theories on our understanding of how children understand a book's themes.

6. Explain the significance of "goodness-of-fit."

7. Discuss how knowledge of developmental theory relates to the themes of children's literature, using several of the recommended stories mentioned in this chapter.

8. Identify specific books discussed in the chapter that illustrate the significance of developmental contextualism.

9. Explain how awareness of Erikson's psychosocial stages aids in book selection.

10. Describe how developmental theory and the search for appropriate children's literature are mutually supportive.

Children's Bibliography

Averill, Esther. (2005). *The School for Cats*. New York: New York Review of Books, Children's Collection.

Averill, Esther. (2005). *Jenny's Birthday Book*. New York: New York Review of Books, Children's Collection.

Bemelmans, Ludwig. (1939). *Madeline*. New York: Simon & Schuster.

Birdsall, Jeanne. (2005). *The Penderwicks*. New York: Knopf.

Brown, Marc. (1979). *Arthur's Eyes*. Boston: Little, Brown.

Brown, Margaret Wise. (1947). *Goodnight, Moon*. New York: Harper & Row.

Chesworth, Michael. (2002). *Alphaboat*. New York: Farrar, Straus, & Giroux.

Clements, Andrew. (2002). *Things Not Seen*. New York: Philomel.

Cooper, Susan. (2002). *Frog*. New York: McElderry.

Curtis, Christopher. (1995). *The Watsons Go to Birmingham—1963*. New York: Delacorte.

Devine, Monica. (2002). *Carry Me, Momma*. New York: Stoddard.

Fitzgerald, John. (1967, rev. 2004). *The Great Brain*. New York: Dell.

Frank, Mitch. (2005). *Understanding the Holy Land: Answering Questions about the Israeli-Palestinian Conflict*. New York: Viking.

Gauch, Patricia Lee. (2002). *Tanya and the Red Shoes*. New York: Philomel.

Green, John. (2005). *Looking for Alaska*. New York: Dutton.

Hamilton, Virginia. (1982). *Sweet Whispers, Brother Rush*. New York: Philomel.

Henkes, Kevin. (1991). *Chrysanthemum*. New York: Greenwillow.

Hill, Eric. (1998). *Goodnight Spot*. New York: G.P. Putnam's Sons.

Myers, Walter Dean. (2004). *Shooter*. New York: Amistad/Harper.

Napoli, Donna Jo. (1998). *Changing Tunes*. New York: Dutton.

Numeroff, Laura Jaffe. (1985). *If You Give a Mouse a Cookie*. New York: Harper & Row.

Okimoto, Jean Davies. (1997). *The Eclipse of Moonbeam Dawson*. New York: Tor.

Paterson, Katherine. (1980). *Jacob Have I Loved*. New York: Crowell.

Peck, Richard. (1998). *A Long Way From Chicago*. New York: Scholastic.

Polacco, Patricia. (1998). *Thank You, Mr. Falker*. New York: Philomel.

Rodda, Emily. (2002). *Rowan and the Keeper of the Crystal*. New York: Harper Trophy.

Rowling, J. K. (1998). *Harry Potter and the Sorcerer's Stone*. New York: A.A. Levine.

Rowling, J.K. (1999). *Harry Potter and the Chamber of Secrets*. New York: A.A. Levine.

Schwartz, Amy. (2001). *The Boys Team*. New York: Atheneum.

Seuss, Dr. (1957). *The Cat in the Hat*. New York: Random House.

Sis, Peter. (2002). *Madlenka's Dog*. New York: Farrar, Straus, & Giroux.

Sobol, Donald. (2003). *Encyclopedia Brown and the Case of the Jumping Frogs*. New York: Delacorte.

Spinelli, Jerry. (1996). *Crash*. New York: Random House.

Tafuri. (2002). *Little Bears*. New York: Scholastic.

White, E. B. (1952). *Charlotte's Web*. New York: HarperCollins.

Yolen, Jane. (1986). *The Lullaby Songbook*. New York: Harcourt Brace & Co.

Professional References

Bandura, A. (1997). *Self-efficacy: The Exercise of Control*. New York: Freeman.

Bandura, A., & Walters, R. (1963). *Social Learning and Personality Development*. New York: Holt, Rinehart & Winston.

Chess, S., & Thomas, A. (1987). *Know Your Child*. New York: Basic Books.

Chess, S., & Thomas, A. (1999). *Goodness of Fit: Clinical Applications from Infancy through Adult Life*. Philadelphia: Brunner/Mazel.

Dacey, John, & Travers, John. (2009). *Human Development across the Lifespan* (updated 7th ed.) New York: McGraw-Hill.

Gardner, Howard. (1983). *Frames of Mind: The Theory of Multiple Intelligences*. New York: Basic Books.

Gardner, Howard. (1991). *The Unschooled Mind*. New York: Basic Books.

Gardner, Howard. (1993). *Creating Minds*. New York: Basic Books.

Gardner, Howard. (1997). *Extraordinary Minds*. New York: Basic Books.

Kohlberg, L. (1975). The Cognitive-Developmental Approach to Moral Education. *Phi Delta Kappan*, 56: 670–677.

Kohlberg, L. (1981). *The Philosophy of Moral Development*. New York: Harper & Row.

Maslow, A. (1987). *Motivation and Personality*. New York: Harper & Row.

Rosenblatt, Louise. (1938). *Literature as Exploration*. New York: Noble and Noble.

Rosenblatt, Louise. (1978). *The Reader, the Text, and the Poem*. Carbondale: Southern Illinois University Press.

Rutter, M. (2002). Nature, Nurture and Development: From Evangelism through Science toward Policy and Practice. *Child Development*, 73(1): 1–21.

Thies, Kathleen, & Travers, John. (2001). *Growth and Development through the Lifespan*. Thorofare, NJ: Slack.

Vygotsky, L. (1978). *Mind in Society*. Cambridge, MA: Harvard University Press.

Children and Their Literature: Changes through the Years

The concept of childhood shifts constantly from period to period, place to place, culture to culture—perhaps even from child to child. The literature designed for childhood is going, therefore, to reflect this variety too. It takes a considerable mental leap to remember that the innocent schoolgirl intrigues of Angela Brazil or Enid Blyton in the 1940s were designed for the same age group as the sexually active and angst-ridden teenagers of Judy Blume in the 1970s.

(Hunt, 1995, p. ix)

Peter Hunt's words are an excellent introduction to the history of children's literature, since they emphasize the frustration of attempting to understand children's stories through the centuries apart from the context of the times. How does any society define "child"? Are they miniature adults, or youths with potential? What is appropriate for children? Before you embark on a detailed examination of children's literature, valuable insights into this fascinating subject can be gained by tracing its roots and following the paths that have brought it into the twenty-first century.

Doing this reveals an inescapable conclusion that will guide your reading and understanding of the history of children's literature: *stories about and for children reflect the prevailing view of children at a particular time.* As Heywood (2001) notes in his history of childhood, if historians wish to understand children of the past, they must first discover how adults viewed children in the past. Hunt (1995, p. ix) also emphasizes this theme when he states that the concept of childhood changes from period to period, place to place, culture to culture, and child to child. Viewing children as miniature adults (and treating them this way) is quite different from recognizing the significance of biopsychosocial interactions in a child's development.

Our journey into children's literature begins with the colorful tales passed on by oral tradition. Next, we encounter the more sophisticated literature of the Greeks and Romans. After Gutenberg's printing press appeared (about 1455), the number of books—as we think of books—multiplied rapidly, and a new picture of children gradually emerged. During the nineteenth century, scientific studies of children appeared in connection with the work of Darwin and Preyer. Authors began to address gender differences, and the increasing popularity of fantasy testified to the growing status of children and children's books.

As children's literature witnesses the rapid societal changes of the twentieth and twenty-first centuries, its themes reflect the conflicts and problems modern children experience—thus affirming the growing acceptance of the *goodness-of-fit* concept. The history of children's literature, therefore, has been intense, picturesque, and revealing—providing a child's-eye view of a breakneck journey through the years.

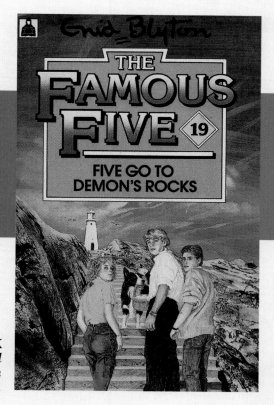

FIVE GO TO DEMON'S ROCK
Five Go to Demon's Rock by Enid Blyton. Reproduced by permission of Hodder and Stoughton Limited.

Guidelines for Reading Chapter 2

After you finish reading Chapter Two, you should be able to answer the following questions.

• How can the changing views of childhood be reconciled with the changing themes in children's literature?

• What views of childhood, expressed by classical Greek scholars, influenced their society's concept of children?

• What impact did theorists such as Darwin and Preyer have on children's stories?

• Do you agree with Peter Hunt's assessment that mainstream writing for children in the nineteenth century became more sophisticated?

• How did the nature of children's magazines change through the years? What is their current appeal?

• What role did *The Wizard of Oz* play in the development of twentieth-century children's literature?

• Which twentieth-century developmental theorists helped shape the direction of children's stories?

• What changes in twentieth century children's literature help explain its continuous growth and appeal?

• How has the nature of children's stories changed as we move into the twenty-first century?

• What is your reaction to the growing belief among publishers that "children are consumers?"

The Early Tradition

If childhood is indeed a fairly recent invention of the human mind, what can we say about its emergence from the dim and murky days of the past? Discovering and tracing the roots of children's literature takes us to the colorful and casual stories that were passed on by oral tradition. Here, we find the roots of children's literature embedded in the great stories of the past—stories not primarily intended for children, but colorful, often lurid, adventures that, no doubt, were eagerly overheard by children. Rare manuscripts, usually handwritten by monks or scribes, occasionally appeared that were available only to a small number of wealthy individuals. The oral transmission of stories, however, was the rule, and the occasional handwritten manuscript the exception.

Stories to Dream By

The audience for these stories, with their often bawdy and bloody themes, consisted of children and adults. Close your eyes and picture this scene: a mixed group of people, clinging together around a fire, listening to spellbinding tales of bravery and cowardice, heroes and villains, the damned and the saved. As warmth and security reached out from the fire, feelings of companionship and security permeated the children's consciousness. In this way they gradually absorbed the values and ideas of their culture. It's interesting, also, to speculate about the manner in which young people would have responded to these tales.

From these early forms of oral communication arose the contributions and influence of the Greeks and Romans.

Then and Now

Storytelling and the Oral Tradition

How many times have you been in a classroom or library and casually observed a children's storytelling hour? How often have you participated and become part of an art form that dates back to prehistoric times? Ancient storytellers, who usually possessed prodigious memories, were mainly responsible for preserving the traditions and values of bygone societies. What stories did they memorize and retell, shaping their tales to the needs and interests of their audiences? What criteria did they use to select their stories? What dramatic gestures, movements, and intonations did they use? What determined the pace of their stories? How did they fire the imagination of their audiences and bring them to a peak of suspense? These are only a few of the questions expert storytellers had to answer to establish a meaningful relationship with their listeners.

For stories, past or present, to arouse and sustain a child's attention, they must be presented in a manner calculated to entertain, excite curiosity, stimulate mental images, and perhaps even provoke feelings of anxiety and fear. We can only guess at what children in ancient times thought as they listened to stories, told as oral poetry which were not written down until many years later (Cahill, 2003). Yet . . . these tales were mentally stored and passed down from one storyteller to another, which helps to explain the changes seen in many similar stories (Ong, 2003).

We can only wonder what impact these captivating stories had on a child's development. What did the children take from them? Stories have a definite structure—often long and complex—that children must follow. This structure includes a setting, characters with varied and complex motivations, problems to be faced, and a resolution to be reached. And weaving its way through all these threads are the emotions generated in children: uncertainties, fears and anxieties, and the joy of imagining good triumphing over evil. With increasing cognitive maturity, children become more aware of the character's objectives and motives.

From our understanding of preliterary times, it seems safe to conclude that ancient storytellers—for the most part—were not particularly concerned about the children in their audiences. Consequently, we can conclude that since children lacked the skills to identify implications in a story's characters and themes, they did not comprehend a story in a manner similar to the way adults did (Gardner, 1982).

Today, however, many storytellers consciously structure their stories to the developmental needs of their young audiences. Allen Say, for example, the internationally renowned writer and artist, is recognized by many children as the man who uses a kamishibai (a portable stage once used by itinerant storytellers in Japan) when he demonstrates his award-winning story of the *Kamishibai Man* (2005).

Thousands have attended storytelling festivals throughout the world, such as the annual National Storytelling Festival in Jonesborough, Tennessee. This event, which lasts for three days, features performances by some of the world's greatest storytellers. Less famous storytellers weave their tales for children in local li-

braries and classrooms. Children themselves may appear as storytellers! Working together in the classroom, children often take turns orally relating stories from books they have been reading. In perfecting their presentation, they learn much about how stories are structured, how to modulate their voices to capture their classmates' attention, and how to emphasize dramatic scenes.

But the most effective storyteller for children today may be the compact audiobook. When used with earphones, it disturbs no one and can be taken almost anywhere. The only requirement is that children listen and use their imaginations. Outstanding books for children on audiotape are available in schools and libraries everywhere. These stories, expertly taped by sources such as Audio Bookshelf (audiobookshelf.com), are dramatically read by professional actors and leave children spellbound as their imaginations take them into the world of pretend. The imaginative ability of young children differs from that of older children, who believe imagining something differs from actually doing it. Remember that children grow in a social world, where attending to (listening, observing) and interacting with other people is a major force in their development (Siegler & Alibali, 2005).

Research has clearly established that young children (3 and 4 years old) can distinguish between imagining and doing, between reality and pretense. The distinction, however, is a shaky one that slowly becomes clarified as children grow older. As Bjorklund (2005, p. 247) notes, young children, even 6- and 7-year-olds, easily perceive imagination as reality, which helps explain the spell storytellers can cast over them. (These issues have considerable impact on stories dealing with fantasy, which we'll discuss later in the chapter.)

KAMISHIBAI MAN

ALLEN SAY

KAMISHIBAI MAN
Cover from KAMISHIBAI MAN by Allen Say. Jacket art © 2005 by Allen Say. Reprinted by permission of Houghton Mifflin Co. All rights reserved.

Epic Tales of Greek and Roman Days

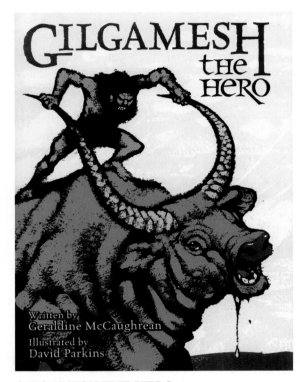

GILGAMESH THE HERO
*Reprinted with permission
of Wm. B. Eerdmans
Publishing Co.*

Given the obvious and oft-expressed views about the maximum development of body and mind, it's no surprise that Athenian scholars paid close attention to harmonious human development and the means for achieving it. Plato and Aristotle both emphasized the need for children to experience the interaction between a sound body and a sound mind. These great Greek philosophers identified and accepted the developmental characteristics of children that lead to individual differences.

It's hard to believe that most, if not all, children in ancient Greece and Rome were unfamiliar with the epic tales of Homer (*The Iliad, The Odyssey*), and Virgil (*The Aeneid*), which their cultures used to instill the goals of virtue and excellence in the young (Beck et al., 1999). For example, you can imagine the appeal to children listening to stories about a fierce hero such as Achilles, who, after overcoming his grief over the death of his friend Patroclus, returns to battle. Or the opening words of *The Aeneid* (*I sing of warfare and a man at war*) in which Virgil creates several scenes that could only entrance the children of his time (about 29 BC).

Proud though they were, the Roman conquerors of Greece recognized the value and utility of Greek thought and took for their own use much of Greek philosophy, literature, art, and science, including their views of children (Borstelmann, 1983). One interesting aspect of the suggested training procedures for children is the emphasis on good example, as is found in Virgil's *The Aeneid*. A focus on desirable behavior is a continuing feature in the history of children's literature, predating today's acceptance of the significance of observational learning. [See Bandura's work, especially *Self-Efficacy: The Exercise of Control* (1997).]

When contemporary authors Jane Yolen and Richard Harris undertook the daunting task of writing a series about young heroes, they adapted tales from ancient history, such as *Jason and the Gorgon's Blood* (2004) and *Odysseus in the Serpent Maze* (2001), to fulfill the desire of children to read (and hear) stories told long ago that remain an indispensable part of children's literature. Geraldine McCaughrean's retelling of the world's oldest written epic, *Gilgamesh the Hero* (2003), is another example of how past heroic exploits continue to be the basis for many contemporary adventures.

The Decline of Literature and Learning

Once the Romans were finally defeated, education and learning declined and a dark curtain of ignorance descended upon Europe. Communication largely remained oral, but as Christianity spread, a small number of schools came into existence. Yet no clearly formulated concept of education existed. During these long years, childhood was considered to end at age 7 because children had by then acquired their language abilities and were thought to be capable of adult behavior.

A new concept of childhood, however, was taking shape as a result of Gutenberg's invention of the printing press. Postman (1982, p. 19) colorfully described Gutenberg as "a goldsmith from Mainz, Germany who, with the aid of an old wine-press," gave birth to childhood.

The Dawn of Childhood

As we begin our passage through the pages of history, it's well to keep the date of 1455 in mind. It was about then that Gutenberg unveiled what we think of today as the first printing press. This, in turn, led to the *Gutenberg Bible*, the first full-sized book printed with movable type. Only forty-six copies of this bible exist today. Table 2.1 presents a chronology of several important dates in the history of the written word. Note that books were being produced in Asia and the Middle East centuries before their appearance in Europe.

Once Johannes Gutenberg's movable-type printing press appeared in the 1450s, printed books, such as the *Bible* and *Aesop's Fables*, rapidly proliferated. It is estimated that within fifty years following Gutenberg's invention, more than eight million books were printed (Postman, 1982). Before the Pilgrims arrived at Plymouth, English children had already grappled with the gloom and doom of John Foxe's *Book of Martyrs* (1563). Children were being taught psalms and prayers from the Bible, and the letters of the alphabet were being printed on hornbooks, paddle-shaped pieces of wood protected by transparent layers of animal horn. The battledore, a folded piece of cardboard, was an improvement over the hornbook and remained popular with young readers until the mid-nineteenth century (Avery, 1995, p. 4).

Literature in the Eighteenth Century

As the ideas of Locke and Rousseau gained acceptance, the concept of childhood began to change. Butts & Cremins (1953, p. 71) summarize these changes as follows.

Despite the prevailing attitudes toward child nature that led to the treatment of the child as a sinful though miniature version of the adult person, there were signs that a change in outlook was in the making in the educational thought of the eighteenth century.

Table 2.1 IMPORTANT DATES IN THE HISTORY OF THE WRITTEN WORD

DATE	ACCOMPLISHMENT
2700 BC	The Egyptians wrote books on papyrus scrolls.
1000 BC	The Chinese constructed books by writing on strips of bamboo.
300 AD	The Romans wrote on sheets of parchment (treated animal skin). These were then sewn together to form a book.
800 AD	Irish monks wrote and illustrated *The Book of Kells*.
1455 AD (APPROXIMATELY)	Gutenberg printed the first book on a printing press (Beck et al., 1999).

What's Your View?

Changing Views of Childhood

Throughout the late seventeenth and early eighteenth centuries, different views of child development appeared in both the United States and England. John Locke, in *Some Thoughts Concerning Education* (1693), presented a concept of childhood that was revolutionary for its time. He affirmed that school was not only for learning, but for play and pleasure as well.

Reading and writing I allow to be necessary, but yet not the chief business. . . . Not but I think learning a great help in well-disposed minds; but yet it must be confessed also, that in others not so disposed, it helps them only to be the more foolish, or worse men. (Locke, 1904, p. 142).

Locke adopted the concept of the mind as a *tabula rasa*, or blank slate. (Actually, he used the phrase "white paper void of all characters" (Pinker, 2002, p. 5). Parents and teachers determined what would be written on the blank slate by controlling the child's experiences. For children to develop desirable behaviors, Locke believed they must be subjected to drill and practice.

Jean Jacques Rousseau, on the other hand, was guided by the principle that man is good and it is society that makes him bad. Consequently, rather than depending on parents and teachers to structure a child's experiences, Rousseau looked to the forces of nature. In his famous treatise on education, *Emile* (1762), he recommended that experience alone rather than verbal lessons, should be a child's teacher (Rousseau, 1911).

The School of Good Manners, written in England, was adapted for children in New England by Eleazar Moody in 1715 (Avery, 1995). One of the New World's first publications for children, it stressed piety, neatness, honoring one's parents, and politeness above all else. In the early eighteenth century, views such as those of Rousseau aroused the ire of Cotton Mather and other Puritan ministers, who believed children should be ruled by absolute authority. The Puritans—champions of education, but under the influence of Mather—disapproved this gentle view of children. Further, they believed that all fiction belonged in Satan's library—since it was not true, it was a lie. Thus fear, obedience, and discipline were considered the essential ingredients of instruction. These concepts were incorporated into *The New England Primer*, probably the most noteworthy of 17th-century American children's books (MacLeod, 1995, p. 103).

Comenius's *Orbis Sensualism Pictus*, published in Nuremberg in 1638 and translated into Latin and English by Charles Hoople in 1659, is sometimes regarded as the first labeled picture book for children (Hunt, 2001; Ulich, 1950). Yet its graphic pictures of torture, death, and disease reflected society at large, more than a true picture of children.

As you consider these contrasting theories of education, which do you think has had the most lasting impact on children's reading? What's your view?

These changes appeared when children's books, as we understand them, slowly but steadily gained acceptance, thanks to the work of individuals such as Daniel Defoe and John Newbery.

DANIEL DEFOE   In 1719 Daniel Defoe wrote the original *Robinson Crusoe*, an adult adventure story about a man surviving on a deserted island after being shipwrecked. So many imitations of *Robinson Crusoe* appeared that they were called Robinsonades. In Switzerland, Johann David Wyss created a Robinsonade he called *The Swiss Family Robinson*, which was translated into English in 1814. Children eagerly read these books, as well as Jonathan Swift's adult adventure novel *Gulliver's Travels*, published in 1726. Cheap editions of fairy tales and folktales that had been popularized by the oral tradition were called *chapbooks*. Peddlers, or chapmen, during the late seventeenth and eighteenth centuries were familiar figures as they traveled throughout the British Isles selling chapbooks. It is said that as early as 1688, a chapbook printer had in stock at least one chapbook for every fifteen families in England (Kinnell, 1995, p. 40).

JOHN NEWBERY   John Newbery, for whom the Newbery Medal is named, was not only an English bookseller, but was the first publisher who concentrated on a class of children's books that could be seen as worthy of the kind of artistic and financial investment normally reserved for adult books. He recognized the "growing economic importance of children as the social base of the book market widened" (Avery, 1995, p. 15). In 1744 he wrote *A Little Pretty Pocket Book*, which was among the first, and undoubtedly one of the best loved, of the early books intended for "the instruction and amusement of children."

A lighthearted view of children was also revealed in *Little Goody Two Shoes* (1745), purportedly written by Oliver Goldsmith, who worked for John Newbery. Gradually, children were being accepted as children rather then as miniature adults. This changing concept was clearly visible in the marketplace, where parents bought rocking horses, baby clothes, and books. Especially in demand was *Tales of Mother Goose — or Tales of Past Times, Told by Mother Goose —* by Charles Perrault, published in Paris in 1697, then translated into English and published by John Newbery and his associates. Not until the sixth edition in 1772, however, were favorite stories such as *Cinderella* and *Little Red Riding Hood* retold in English without the French words alongside (Kinnell, 1995).

Literature in the New World

Often overlooked in this changing concept of childhood is an important article by Charles Darwin that appeared in 1877. Entitled *Biographical Sketch of an Infant*, it provided a scientific basis for studying children. When this was followed in 1882 by William Preyer's *The Mind of the Child*, childhood became firmly entrenched as a separate subject, deserving of study to answer the growing number of questions about human development. The nineteenth century was to prove remarkably fertile in studies of child development, particularly with the work of such individuals as Alfred Binet and his study of intelligence testing, and G. Stanley Hall's writings on childhood and adolescence.

The Nineteenth Century

In the United States, the years preceding and during the Civil War were fraught with political upheaval, but the literary scene was still lively and distinguished. During this time, Samuel Goodrich, founder of *Parley's Magazine* (1833) and *Merry's Museum*, was one of the most prolific and successful publishers of children's books, writing hundreds of books and selling millions of copies (Macleod, 1995).

Yet being a full-time children's author was still difficult. Children, especially those from the middle class, were reading books published in Britain and the United States, such as Charles and Mary Lamb's *Tales of Shakespeare* (1806), *The Brothers Grimm* (the first English version published in 1823), as well as the translation of Hans Christian Andersen's *A Danish Story Book, Danish Fairy Legends and Tales* (1846). These works were sufficiently rational to allay adult misgivings about fantasy, while satisfying children's persistent interest in folk and fairy tales. In America in the early 1800s, Christmas was not Christmas without a family reading of Clement Moore's *A Visit From St. Nicholas*, published in a Troy, New York newspaper in 1823 and better known now as *The Night Before Christmas*. Moore's

THE OWL AND THE PUSSY CAT
Used with permission of HarperCollins Publishers

appealing fantasy and Charles Dickens' A *Christmas Carol* (1843) are two holiday treats that continue to bring pleasure to children in the twenty-first century.

In the nineteenth century, Edward Lear's verses and limericks were immensely popular with children. In those stern and somber times, Lear did his best to make children smile as they read *The Book of Nonsense* (1846). Since his book of poetry, *Of Pelicans and Pussy Cats*, was reissued in 1990, today's children still have access to his limericks. *The Owl and the Pussy Cat* has also been adapted and exquisitely illustrated by Jan Brett (1992) and Anne Mortimer (2006).

Following the Civil War, the United States continued to evolve into an industrialized nation, with an exploding immigration of unskilled workers and an expanding middle class. Sales of domestic novels written for women skyrocketed. Education increased in importance as years of schooling were extended. Yet poverty in America's cities increased. The desperate living conditions of the poor became the focal point of many books and editorials.

Childhood was valued in and of itself, and juvenile novels clearly reflected this changed perception of childhood. In America, publishers successfully competed to produce outstanding reading materials for an expanding market. Mark

Spotlight On
Lewis Carroll

Time Life/Mansell/The Image Bank/Getty Images

Today, an adult has only to look at the photographs of children taken by Charles Dodgson (Lewis Carroll), a don at Oxford University, a photographer as well as a writer, to realize his intense interest in little girls. In a recent gallery exhibit, *Dreaming in Pictures: The Photography of Lewis Carroll*, at the International Center of Photography in New York, portraits of young girls comprise a majority of the seventy-two photographs. The pictures of Alice, the third child of the Liddell family and the child for whom Carroll wrote the fantasies *Alice's Adventures in Wonderland* and *Through the Looking Glass*, were particularly revealing. Art critic Mark Feeney commented that Carroll offered an idealized vision of childhood (Feeney, 2004).

Jackie Wullschlager, author of *Inventing Wonderland* (1995), a psychobiography of outstanding children's writers in Victorian England, mentions that Carroll was "adamant that in these friendships he was above reproach holding the Victorian view that contact with children was morally uplifting" (Wullschlager, 1995, p. 40). Carroll was 23, a mathematician at Oxford University, shy, slim, and handsome when he began to

write. Legend tells us that he and his friend Robinson Duckworth were picnicking with the three Liddell girls when Carroll began a story about Alice falling into a hole, which he proceeded to develop and expand. Alice pleaded with him to write out the tale for her. That night, he stayed up late and began writing the book that would become one of the most unusual and widely read fantasies in the history of children's literature.

Carroll's original manuscript was titled *Alice's Adventures Underground* and was sold to Macmillan in 1863. Later, he doubled its length and changed the title, because it sounded too much like a child lost in a mine. John Tenniel, the illustrator, enhanced Carroll's story, but their personality clashes delayed the publication of *Alice* for years. In 1864 Tenniel stopped working with Carroll, and he complained about the appearance of the illustrations when the book finally appeared in 1865. All copies of that first edition were recalled, and Carroll himself paid for a reprint (Wullschlager, 1995, p. 53). Gradually, through word of mouth, 160,000 copies were sold by the time Carroll died in 1898. And it has been selling well ever since!

Twain's *The Adventures of Tom Sawyer* (1876) and *The Adventures of Huckleberry Finn* (1884), each of which Samuel Clemens (Mark Twain) identified as a "boy's book" (Perry, 2004), were widely read by adults and children. Twain's characters were typically American rather than English. Their unbounded energy and optimism reflected the plain living and individualism of the new country (Avery, 1994). Twain's books, and those by other nineteenth-century authors such as Louisa May Alcott, Mary Mapes Dodge, Robert Louis Stevenson, and Rudyard Kipling, are now considered classics and continue to line the shelves of libraries and bookstores.

THE GROWING SUCCESS OF CHILDREN'S AUTHORS Successful American authors now were able to support themselves, and new writers came into the field of children's literature. In 1867 author Martha Finley created *Elsie Dinsmore*, an emotional, sentimental girls' novel that proved enormously successful. Finley went on to write twenty-eight more Elsie stories. Yet *Elsie Dinsmore* was only a harbinger of books to come. Readers enthusiastically and eagerly praised Louisa May Alcott as the author of *Little Women* (1868). In fact, she may well have been the best loved of all American children's writers in her time.

Books by English authors continued to be read by American children. Two of the most outstanding were the unique fantasies *Alice's Adventures in Wonderland* (1865) and its sequel, *Through the Looking Glass* (1871), written by Lewis Carroll (a pseudonym of Charles Dodgson) and illustrated by Sir John Tenniel.

Books from other European countries were also absorbing children's attention. We know that the translation of Hans Christian Andersen's *A Danish Story Book, Danish Fairy Legends and Tales, Wonderful Stories for Children* (1846) was more widely read in England and America than in Denmark. Johanna Spyri's *Heidi* (1954/1884) was translated into English, and C. Collodi's *The Adventures of Pinocchio*, originally written in Italian in 1883, appeared in an English version in 1891. Mary Mapes Dodge's re-creation of Holland as the setting for her *Hans Brinker* or *The Silver Skates* (1865) was so authentic that readers were amazed to learn she had never lived there.

TREASURE ISLAND *Reprinted with the permission of Atheneum Books for Young Readers, an imprint of Simon & Schuster Children's Division from TREASURE ISLAND by Robert Louis Stevenson. Copyright 1911 Charles Scribner's Sons; copyright renewed 1939 N.C. Wyeth.*

Color Captivates Children

In the last quarter of the nineteenth century, Edmund Evans, a London printer, invented the full-color printing process. Now that children's books could be embellished with color plates, publishers competed with one another to make the most attractive editions. Randolph Caldecott, the illustrator for whom the Caldecott Award is named, collaborated with William Cowper and Edmund Evans to produce *The Diverting History of John Gilpin* (Cowper, 1878) and at least two books each Christmas for years to come. An illustration from *The Diverting History of John Gilpin*, showing John Gilpin's ride, is memorialized on the Caldecott Medal. Between 1865 and 1898, Walter Crane also worked with Edmund Evans to illustrate "toy books" and other beautifully engraved precursors of today's picture books. Kate Greenaway was another outstanding illustrator whose first book, *Under the Window*, was printed by Evans in 1878.

Beatrix Potter's works, however, are seminal in children's literature. *Peter Rabbit* first appeared in a series of drawings in a letter Potter sent to a 5-year-old boy who was ill. She later asked to borrow it back and used them as the blueprint for *The Tale of Peter Rabbit*. Her understated text and black and white illustrations for *Peter Rabbit* (1901) were privately distributed before the book was printed in a colored edition by Messrs. F. Warne & Co in 1902 (Robinson, 1995). An English artist, Potter contributed much to the modern picture book by balancing the relationship between text and illustration. Although the characters in her later books were rabbits, mice, guinea pigs, kittens, and other small creatures, she flawlessly illustrated them—honestly, humorously, and without sentimentality. So concerned was she that her books be read by or to small children that she made certain they were printed in a small book format, in order to fit easily into little hands.

THE PLACE OF NINETEENTH-CENTURY PERIODICALS IN CHILDREN'S LITERATURE   Even before the mid-nineteenth century, periodicals such as *Youth's Companion* were popular in the United States. Often, editorials and stories described the plight of poor immigrant children, which appealed to more fortunate children who supported private groups like the Children's Aid Society with their pennies. Between 1850 and 1890, however, the growth of periodical publishing increased considerably. In the 1890s, for example, the circulation for *The Youth's Companion* was approximately 500,000. Part of its appeal was its annual rewards to current subscribers for enlisting new subscribers, and its roster of famous writers, such as Oliver Wendell Holmes, Harriet Beecher Stowe, and Jack London (Pool, 1995). Many of the mainstream books published at this time had been previously serialized in magazines. In 1873, when Mary Mapes Dodge became the editor-in-chief of Scribner's *St. Nicholas Magazine*, it became the best-known and most respected magazine of its time. It serialized the work of Louisa May Alcott, Frances Hodgson Burnett, Joel Chandler Harris, and Mark Twain, to name a few. Daring to be different, it strove for wide appeal. Well-known writers were pleased when their stories and articles appeared in *St. Nicholas Magazine*.

Some periodicals were published to counteract the influence of the cheap dime novels of the 1870s that were being churned out by steam-powered rotary presses. One such magazine was the British *The Union Jack*, edited by G. A. Henty, a well-known historical adventure writer. It serialized adventure stories that would later be picked up by Longman, Macmillan, and other prominent publishers. Another was *The Riverside Magazine for Young People*, printed in Boston. Establishing the periodical in 1867, its editor, Horace Scudder, was determined that the magazine be known for its literary excellence and lack of a didactic tone. Hans Christian Andersen was one of its contributors in the 1860s. Although Horace Scudder was sincerely interested in publishing a quality magazine, other editors were interested only in financial success (Hunt, 1995). Lack of interest, decreasing advertising revenues, and competition with other media caused a gradual decline in periodical publishing during the early part of the twentieth century.

The Recognition of Gender Differences

In the nineteenth century and early twentieth century, boys and girls read many books that appealed specifically to their gender. The role that gender plays (and has played) in the books that children enjoy has remained a central element in children's literature. Today, as authors and publishers have come to recognize gender as a powerful influence on a child's development, gender-oriented stories have become increasingly popular with both sexes.

THE APPEAL OF FEMININE CHARACTERS   Girls who liked *Little Women* also enjoyed *What Katy Did*, a series written by Susan Coolidge in 1871, whose heroine is an independent young lady with a spinal cord injury. They also found engrossing stories such as Frances Hodgson Burnett's *The Secret Garden* (1911) and *A Little Princess: Being the Whole Story of Sarah Crew* (1916), which are American in feeling, although the setting is English (Avery, 1994, p. 9). Stories like Margaret Sidney's *Five Little Peppers and How They Grew* (1881), Kate Wiggin's *Rebecca of Sunnybrook Farm*, (1903), Eleanor Porter's *Pollyanna* (1913), and Jean Webster's *Daddy Long Legs* (1912) appealed to readers' sense of family or their desire that suffering, orphaned, or abandoned characters might live happily ever after.

DIME NOVELS, PENNY DREADFULS, AND BOYS' SERIES   Boys, particularly, found dime novels attractive. Originally written as cheap and lurid adult novels, dime novels were mass-marketed and sold by the publishing firm of Beadle and Adams, beginning in 1860. As many as 65,000 copies of one dime novel were sold in a matter of months. Hack writers wrote these stories, which went with the soldiers into the military camps during the Civil War. Boys were fascinated by the dramatic appeal and the pulsating energy of these novels, and they sold furiously (MacLeod, 1995, p. 122).

Boys also enjoyed reading adventures like Robert Louis Stevenson's *Treasure Island* (1883) and *Kidnapped* (1886), and Howard Pyle's *The Merry Adventures of Robin Hood* (1883). But the works of Oliver Optic, the pseudonym for William Taylor Adams, were even more popular. Optic was a prolific writer and the editor and founder of many magazines during the 1850s, who developed the formula for boys' series books. His greatest accomplishment, however, was influencing Horatio Alger to write *Ragged Dick* (1868), the most popular "rags to riches" novel of its time.

Spin Off
Create a Magazine

Intermediate and middle school students in small groups welcome the challenge of creating magazines on their own. Using a magazine like *Cricket*, or others that we describe later in the chapter (see page 34), have your students examine back copies that they can borrow from the school or public library. Urge them to critically scan the table of contents and the format. After they have decided how many issues they would like to write, assign editors, artists, and writers so that the students work in small groups to develop stories, articles, letters to the editor, and whatever else they would like to include in their magazine. Once the magazines are complete and bound or stapled, make sure that they circulate and that the children take them home to show their families.

THE PETERKIN PAPERS
Cover from THE COMPLETE PETERKIN PAPERS by Lucretia P. Hale. Copyright © 1960 Houghton Mifflin Company, renewed 1988. Reprinted by permission of Houghton Mifflin Company. All rights reserved.

Alger's novels inspired boys of the nineteenth century to "rise in the world," making the name Horatio Alger a metaphor for success. American boys were also interested in tall tales about Kit Carson, Billy the Kid, and Jesse James, elevating them to folk heroes, since they found America's frontier was an adventure far more exciting than fantasy. On both sides of the Atlantic, books about boys at school appeared in inexpensive and flashy periodicals, often called penny dreadfuls (Hunt, 1995).

Listening to Lucretia Hale's short stories in *The Peterkin Papers* (1880) being read aloud was perfect entertainment for all members of the family. The Peterkin family, with their ridiculous problems resolved by the "Lady from Philadelphia," were gentle and humorous. Hale's story "The Lady Who Put Salt in Her Coffee" may not make today's children laugh like they do when they read the escapades of *Captain Underpants* (Dave Pilkey), but *The Peterkin Papers* were amusing to both boys and girls in the nineteenth century.

Both genders enjoyed reading Rudyard Kipling's *Jungle Book* (1894) and *Just So Stories* (1899), which explained how animals acquired special characteristics (how the camel got his hump, the leopard his spots, etc.). These books are still available in many different versions as well as on video. A book that is not so readily available in the twenty-first century, despite its appeal to children, is the controversial *Little Black Sambo* by Helen Bannerman, published in 1899. Fortunately, Julius Lester has written a much kinder edition, *Sam and the Tigers: A New Telling of Little Black Sambo* (1996), which has found favor with all races. (See further discussion in Chapter Thirteen.)

Fantasy and Traditional Literature in the Nineteenth Century

As you read this history of children's literature, you have probably realized how the concept of childhood had become so accepted in the nineteenth century that we can even speak and write of fantasy. If you think of what fantasy implies—in the graceful words of Dorothy and Jerome Singer (1990, p. 19), "the concept of what might be, being able to move in perception and thought away from the concrete given"—then this recognition of the reality of a child's imagination is staggering. Lewis Carroll's *Alice's Adventures in Wonderland* appeared in 1865 and has since been recognized as perhaps the most brilliant and original children's book of its century, perhaps of all time.

Children were also introduced earlier in the nineteenth century to traditional literature (fairy tales and folklore) that is now commonplace. The first English version of *The Brothers Grimm* was published in 1823 (Hunt, 1995, p. 140). Later, George MacDonald brought together known but not previously published fairy tales, in his popular book *At The Back of the North Wind* (1871). Andrew Lang edited the *Blue Fairy Book* (1889) and continued, presumably, to write eleven other collections although he later confessed that his wife was the real editor (Hunt, 1995, p. 140). Joseph Jacobs collected *English Fairy Tales* the following year.

Table 2.2 summarizes the contributions to children's literature by several outstanding scientists and authors.

Table 2.2 CONTRIBUTIONS TO NINETEENTH CENTURY CHILDREN'S LITERATURE

INDIVIDUAL	CONTRIBUTION	PUBLICATION
Charles Darwin (scientist)	Scientific study of children	*Biographical Sketch of an Infant*
William Preyer (scientist)	Development of mental abilities	*The Mind of the Child*
Alfred Binet (scientist)	Construction of intelligence test	*The Development of Intelligence in Children* (with T. Simon)
G. Stanley Hall (scientist)	Study of adolescence	*Adolescence* (2 volumes)
Charles Dickens (author)	Contributed to the emergence of children's literature	*A Christmas Carol*
Lewis Carroll (author)	Attracted children to fantasy	*Alice's Adventures in Wonderland*
Mark Twain (author)	Primarily boys' books, but both young and old enjoyed them.	*The Adventures of Tom Sawyer* *The Adventures of Huckleberry Finn*
Robert Louis Stevenson (author)	Popularized adventure stories for children	*Treasure Island*
Rudyard Kipling (author)	Wrote adventure stories that appealed to both boys and girls	*Jungle Book*

The Twentieth Century: Children's Literature Comes of Age

Fantasy continues to be popular with children in America and Great Britain into the twenty-first century. L. Frank Baum opened the twentieth century in America with *The Wonderful Wizard of Oz*, a fantastic tale involving the daring adventures of Dorothy, the Tin Man, the Cowardly Lion, the Scarecrow, and other unique characters. The book captivated children everywhere. (See Chapter Four.) Beatrix Potter's *Tales of Peter Rabbit* (1901, 1902), Hugh Lofting's *The Story of Dr. Dolittle* (1920), P. L. Travers' *Mary Poppins* (1924), and A. A. Milne's *Winnie the Pooh* (1926) each represented a literary feast for children of all ages. But J. R. Tolkien's *The Hobbit* (1937), the prequel to the adult-oriented fantasy *Lord of the Rings*, was especially well received, as was Kenneth Grahame's *The Wind in the Willows* (1908), because of its anthropomorphic approach to animals.

The Universality of Literature

Translations in the twentieth century, like that of Hungarian Felix Salten's *Bambi* (1926), French writer Antoine de Saint-Exupery's *The Little Prince* (1943), Jean de Brunhoff's *The Story of Babar, the Little Elephant* (1931), as well as Swedish author Astrid Lindgren's *Pippi Longstocking* (1959), also found their way into the list of favorite children's books. Before World War II, in Germany, Erich Kastner wrote the classic *Emil and the Detectives* (1931 translation).

Spin Off

Classics into Movies

Walt Disney Productions and other movie studios have adapted many of classics into children's movies, although the movie often bears little resemblance to the book. When E. B. White was approached for his consent to have a movie made of *Charlotte's Web*, he consistently refused. In 1969, however, seventeen years after its publication, he did write Ursula Nordstrom, his editor at Harper's, that "if Les Davis [a young filmmaker] wants to explore the possibilities he should get in touch with my agent" (White, 2006, p. 534). Up to this time, however, White would not sign a contract unless it gave him the right to see and approve the "general shape and appearance of the main characters, and the Hollywood big shots won't sign a contract that *does* give me this right" (White, 2006, p. 534).

Recently, however, Walden Media, part of the team that produced *Holes* (Sachar), *Because of Winn-Dixie* (Di Camillo), and *Bridge to Terabithia* (Paterson) maintain that their goal is to work with authors to maintain the integrity of the original story. They have also produced *The Chronicles of Narnia* (C. S. Lewis) and *The Giver* (Lowry), and have emphatically stated that their purpose in producing these beloved classics (and yes, *Charlotte's Web*) is to further children's reading (Kahn, 2005, p. 8).

• Discuss with your students whether they think that movies of books made by a company like Walden Media *do* promote reading. Why? Since many of these books contain illustrations by outstanding artists, do your students feel that by seeing only the movie they miss an important part of the experience? What role does imagination play in reading the book as contrasted with watching the movie?

• Suggest that they poll their classmates through the Internet or in person, to discover how many students prefer to see the movie rather than read the book, or vice versa. Make a list of the reasons they give for their answers. Then ask whether they prefer to see the movie first or read the book first. You may be surprised by the results, which can lead to further discussion.

As a writer and playwright, he wrote sensitive and timely works that were banned and burned during the Hitler regime. Isaac Bashevis Singer, a Polish-born American Yiddish author, displayed the ability to blend the real with the unreal in his National Book Award–winning *A Day of Pleasure: Stories of a Boy Growing Up in Warsaw* (1969).

Outstanding books by authors from other countries continue to demonstrate the universality of children's literature, such as Margaret Mahy's *The Haunting* (New Zealand). English writers such as Mary Norton (*The Borrowers*), Roald Dahl (*Charlie and the Chocolate Factory, The BFG*, etc.), Philip Pullman (his *Dark Materials* trilogy, 1996), David Almond (*Skellig*, 1999), and Diana Wynne Jones (*Charmed Life*, 2001) carry on the historic tradition of "books across the sea" for older readers. English writers and illustrators such as Anthony Browne, Shirley Hughes, and Helen Oxenbury offer picture books for children in the tradition of Randolph Caldecott.

Canadian novels, such as the popular *Anne of Green Gables* by L. M. Montgomery, introduced to American readers in 1908, are well represented today by middle school and young adult novels such as Polly Horvath's *The Canning Season* (2003) and Brian Doyle's *Angel Square* (1984). Kazumi Yumoto's *The Friends* (1998, Japan) and Cornelia Funke's *The Thief Lord* (2002, Germany) are books whose United States publishers were awarded the Mildred Batchelder Award, as the most outstanding books of the year in which they were translated. Jackie French's appealing picture book *Diary of a Wombat* (2003) and the young adult novel *Hitler's Daughter* (1999, Australia), for which she won the 2000 Australian CBC Young Readers Book of the Year Award, also contribute to children's greater understanding of the cultures of other countries.

Today, books for children and adolescents written by foreign authors command a significant readership in the United States. For the first time, in 2006, the Children's Book Council and the U.S. Board on Books for Young People (a division of the International Board on Books for Young People) selected books that "counteract cultural stereotypes, bridge cultural gaps, and build connections" (Isaacs, 2006), and included them in the Outstanding International Booklist. To the disappointment of the committee, no South or Central American books were submitted for consideration. Among the authors whose books were included in the first Outstanding International Booklist are Anthony Browne (Great Britain) for *My Mom*, Judith Clarke (Australia) for *Kalpana's Dream*, Lisa Heydlauff (India) for *Going to School in India*, Josef Holub (Germany) for *An Innocent Soldier*, and Joan de Deu Prats (Spain) for *Sebastian's Roller Skates*. (The complete list is available in the *School Library Journal*, Feb. 2006.)

Nothing, however, contributed more to the growing popularity of children's literature in the twentieth century than the work of Sigmund Freud and his emphasis on the early years as a decisive time in human development (Dacey & Travers, 2009). As we have seen in Chapter 1, Freud's ideas no longer dominate developmental psychology, but in more than 100 years of childhood studies, it's impossible to ignore the influence that the founder of psychoanalytic theory had on our concept of childhood.

Then and Now

Poetry Through the Years

Poets like Edward Lear (*The Nonsense Book*, 1846) and Lewis Carroll (*Jabberwocky*, 1855) are often credited with setting the standards for poetry for children. Other famous poets whose works have endured are Robert Louis Stevenson (*A Child's Garden of Verses*, 1863) and A. A. Milne (*When We Were Very Young*, 1926). In the early years of the twentieth century, Langston Hughes (*The Dream Keeper and Other Poems*, 1932) introduced idiomatic black speech in his poetry to reach the people he loved. During the mid-twentieth century, poets like David McCord (*Far and Few*, 1952), John Ciardi (*I Met a Man*, 1961), and Ogden Nash (*The Tale of the Custard Dragon*, 1959) challenged children with their word play, puns, and sly wit.

The 1960s and 1970s witnessed greater experimentation with poetic form, subject matter, and inclusion. Free verse, such as Karen Hesse's *Out of the Dust* (1997), became popular. Karla Kuskin wrote brief, sensitive poems like those found in her collection *Near the Window Tree* (1975). Some poets incorporated *social issues* into their poetry. Children became acquainted with topics such as poverty, crime,

and injustice by reading Eve Merriam's controversial *Inner City Mother Goose* (1969).

Also, for the first time, racial prejudice was explored in poetry. In 1969, in a collection titled, *Don't You Turn Back*, Langston Hughes wrote poetry that empathized with the plight of African Americans. Children were captivated in 1978 with the strong rhythm and personal observations of another African American poet, Eloise Greenfield, in her first poetry book, *Honey, I Love, and Other Love Poems*. Her poetry, including the award winning *Nathaniel Talking* (1988), is sensitive, warm, and endearing. Nathaniel is a 9-year-old poet who raps about his world (a musical rap that Greenfield learned as a child). With the publication of *Neighborhood Odes* (1992) by Garry Soto came stories about the Latino culture. Diversity was also eloquently expressed in the collection of native poems *Dancing Tepees, Poems of American Indian Youth* (1989) by Virginia Driving Hawk Sneve, and in the poetry, songs, and dances of American Indians by Hettie Jones in *The Trees Stand Shining*, first published in 1971.

Then and Now

The Continuing Role of Periodicals in Children's Literature

We previously noted the decline of periodical literature for children as the nineteenth century came to a close. Today, however, periodical publishing has reestablished itself as a successful commercial venture, serving the needs of today's children in a modern fashion. Once again, we see society's changing view of childhood and its understanding of a child's needs, based on Maslow's hierarchy (see Chapter One), contributing to the popularity of current publications.

Since its first issue in 1946, *Highlights for Children* has sold a billion copies. Founded by Garry and Caroline Myers, child development professionals, *Highlights* is geared to the younger child and is frequently moralistic in tone. By including cartoon characters like Goofus—the boy who always does the wrong thing—and his antithesis, Gallant—who is perfect—the editors present situations that stress Kohlberg's theory of moral development (see Chapter One) in a context to which youngsters can relate.

The publications of the Carus Publishing Company compare in literary quality with *St. Nicholas Magazine*. *Cricket*, Carus's first magazine, was launched in 1973. This was followed by *Ladybug*, *Spider*, and others. With the approval of a board of directors that includes outstanding children's authors and critics, magazines published by Carus, including *Cicada* for teens, provide children from ages 2 through the teen years with exciting articles, stories (often serialized), poetry, and artwork often submitted by young subscribers. Since 1920 Scholastic Inc. has offered school children *Scholastic Magazine*, which classroom teachers find useful to supplement their curriculums. *Ranger Rick* and *Your Big Backyard* are two additional magazines, published by the National Wildlife Federation, that are widely used in elementary schools to enhance environmental studies.

Another outstanding and informational magazine is *National Geographic Kids* (formerly *World*), established by the National Geographic Society in the 1980s. Extraordinary photography with short, informative captions pique children's curiosity about the world around them. The magazine also includes special sections like *Fun Stuff*, *World News*, and *Kids Did It*—featuring outstanding accomplishments of young people that certainly encourage role modeling.

Other magazines address gender interests. *Boys Life* (sponsored by the Boy Scouts of America) still captures the sense of adventure of the magazines of an earlier century, while *American Girl* (published by the Pleasant Company), although criticized for neglecting girls' physical development, includes stories and arts and crafts to strengthen their cognitive development. *American Girl* also offers girls the opportunity to develop their social skills by reading columns such as *Heart to Heart* and *The Whole You*.

In 1980 Cobblestone Publishing presented its first issue of *Cobblestone* magazine, which offers children additional data about the context of historical periods. Children find it an excellent source of information for history and social studies reports. *Faces*, another periodical by the same publisher, along with *Skipping Stones* and *Daybreak Star*, increase children's awareness of various cultures throughout the world.

In stories and articles that teenagers write for magazines such as *Teen Voices* ("because you're more than a pretty face"), adolescents explore their identity and identity confusion. (See the discussion of Erikson's theory in Chapter One.) Published by Women's Express Inc., *Teen Voices'* mission is to "further social and economic justice by empowering teenage and young adult women." Other teen magazines, such as *Career World* (Weekly Reader publication), *New York Times Upfront* (Scholastic), and *Young Money* (Education Foundation), are serious but well-written, attractively designed magazines for the thoughtful young adult. Publishers of magazines for contemporary children and teenagers, by appealing to their biopsychosocial development, arouse their curiosity and enhance their self-concept, thus providing readers with articles that treat them as individual personalities.

The Golden Age of Children's Literature

Between World War I and World War II, publishers, authors, reviewers, and literary associations, reacting to the elevated status of childhood posited by Freud, contributed to the publication of outstanding children's books in the United States. Publishers like the Macmillan Company made a major commitment to children's books and magazines and developed a new juvenile department in 1918 (Hunt, 1995). Other well-known publishers quickly followed. Frederick Melcher, managing editor of *Publishers Weekly*, along with others, promoted the founding of Children's Book Week in 1919. He also founded the Newbery Medal in 1922 through the American Library Association, to honor the author of the most distinguished book published in the United States the previous year. In 1924 Bertha Mahony Miller became the first editor–in–chief of *The Horn Book*, a highly respected magazine issued six times a year to review children's fiction and nonfiction and to inform its readers about issues of importance in the field of children's literature. *The Junior Book of the Month Club* and the *Junior Literary Guild* were both established in the 1920s to encourage and publicize children's literature.

THE IMPACT OF ILLUSTRATORS   When Randolph Caldecott, for whom the Caldecott Medal is named, began illustrating picture books like *Sing a Song of Sixpence* (1880), he paved the way for talented artists like Walter Crane, Beatrix Potter, and Wanda Gag to create books that capture and enrapture children visually and cognitively. Illustrators chose various techniques, such as drawing, painting, printmaking, collage, woodcuts, and photography. Walter Crane, for example, author and illustrator of more than forty books, created his *Absurd ABC* (1874) in bright red, black, and yellow Japanese block prints.

Ten years after Wanda Gag wrote and illustrated *Millions of Cats*, the American Library Association established the Randolph Caldecott Medal in 1938 to honor the illustrator of the most distinguished picture book published in the United States the preceding year. Among the group of outstanding artists who have received this award, or whose books have been selected as Caldecott Honor Books, are Marjorie Flack, *The Story of Ping* (1933); H. A. Rey, *Curious George* (1941); Ludwig Bemelman, *Madeline* (1939); Virginia Lee Burton, *Mike Mulligan and His Steam Shovel* (1939); Robert McCloskey, *Make Way for Ducklings* (1941); and Dr. Seuss's, *And To Think I Saw It on Mulberry Street* (1937). Although Margaret Wise Brown's picture book *Goodnight, Moon* (1947) never received this prestigious award, it is still widely read and fondly remembered. These illustrators made such an impression on later artists such as Maurice Sendak, Barbara Cooney, Chris Van Allsburg, Tomie de Paola, Ezra Jack Keats, Paul O. Zelinsky, and others, that the picture book continues to be one of the outstanding genres in children's literature.

FAMILY VALUES AND HUMOR IN CHILDREN'S LITERATURE   In the 1930s and 1940s, heroines like Caddie in Carol Ryrie Brink's *Caddie Woodlawn* (1935) and Laura in Laura Ingalls Wilder's *Little House in the Big Woods* (1932) were brave, adventurous, industrious, and definitely of pioneer stock. Their adventures were read by thousands of children. The idea of close-knit families, stoic self-sufficiency, and the support of helpful neighbors in times of hardship appealed to children. The Wilder books led to Eleanor Estes' *The Moffats* (1941), a poor but happy family in middle America. Her *Hundred Dresses* (1940) was the first story for children that dealt directly with prejudice, in which a group of children taunted another child because of her "funny" name. Lois Lenski, on the other hand, related family stories like *Strawberry Girl* (1945), which told about sharecroppers and immigrant workers. Carolyn Haywood's "chapter books" brought younger children into the friendly world of *Betsy and the Boys*, enabling them to share in their adventures.

During the twentieth and into the twenty-first century, children from preschool through high school have been able to enjoy many humorous stories. Beverly Cleary's hilarious exploits about Ramona, Beezus, and Henry Huggins and Judy Blume's telling of Fudge's zany experiences still captivate children in elementary and intermediate school. Jon Scieszka's *The True Story of the 3 Little Pigs* (1989) makes them laugh out loud. Lois Lowry's *Gooney Bird Greene* (2002), Barbara Park's slightly irreverent *Junie B., First Grader: One-Man Band* (2002), along with Daniel and Jill Pinkwater's *The Werewolf Club Meets Dorkula* (2001), also entertain young children who are beginning to read. Roald Dahl's many novels, including *The BFG* (1982), remain favorites with the middle school reader, while Louise Rennison's *Knocked Out by My Nunga-Nungas* (2002) amuses teenagers. Although these are only a few examples, humor is always welcome in contemporary children's literature.

WAR AS A TOPIC IN CHILDREN'S LITERATURE   Despite the popularity of humor, it was a serious Revolutionary War story by Esther Forbes (*Johnny Tremain*) that won the Newbery Medal in 1944. Even now, at the beginning of another century, World War II and the Holocaust continue to be the subjects of many historical novels. Nonfiction, such as Anne Frank's *Diary of a Young Girl* (1952), and popular movies about the period have brought World War II to this generation's attention. A widely read story is Lois Lowry's *Number the Stars* (1989), in which a young Danish girl escapes by outwitting the German soldiers who are on guard. Fiction about World War II has attracted more interest today than when the war was in progress. Perhaps World War II was too *real* at the time. Since the dreadful disaster of September 11, 2001, children's literature again contains references to war, especially the "War on Terror." Obliquely referred to in picture books like Mordecai Gertsein's *The Man Who Walked Between the Towers* (2003), the effects of this struggle are more fully developed in the trilogy of *The Breadwinner* (2000), *Paravana's Journey* (2002), and *Mud City* (2003) written by Deborah Ellis about Shauzia, a 14-old Afghani girl, who escapes from Kabul and hides out in Pakistan, disguised as a boy.

THE POPULARITY OF SERIES   Although outstanding literature like E. B. White's *Charlotte's Web* (1952) has attracted, and continues to attract, thousands of young readers, books in a series have also played an important role in the biopsychosocial development of children. Edward Stratemeyer, during the 1930s and 1940s, planned and assigned over forty different series, including *Nancy Drew, The Hardy Boys,* and *The Bobbsey Twins,* to a variety of writers. Over a thirty-eight–year period, the *Nancy Drew* books alone were printed in seventeen languages and, according to a published report, achieved sales of more than 30,300,000 copies. The assigned writer received $125 to $250 a story (Prager, 1969). For twenty-first–century readers, however, Nancy Drew has been subjected to an extreme makeover in *Without a Trace* (2004). She now drives a gas-electric hybrid automobile, her hair is strawberry blond, and the offensive racial and sexual stereotypes of the original stories have been removed (Benfer, 2004).

In addition to contemporary fiction series, biographies in a series often motivate children who have given themselves little time to prepare their reports. They provide brief facts about a wide range of people—statesmen, explorers, writers, artists, entertainers, sports figures, and others—that may not be readily available in individual biographies. Yet biographies like Marc Aronson's *Sir Walter Ralegh* (correct spelling) *and the Quest of El Dorado* (2000) and Russell Freedman's *Lincoln* (1987), emphasizing authenticity, scholarship, and research, are the models for today's children's biographies.

Now and the Future

American attitudes toward children continue to change as insights into the complexity of child development become clearer. No longer are children viewed as repositories of stimulus-response connections. As traced in Chapter One, children are now seen as the product of the interaction of genetic, biological, behavioral, and contextual forces (biopsychosocial elements). Research into developmental issues such as attachment, observational learning, and childhood stress is helping to explain children's behavior and is reflected in children's literature.

Dealing with Reality

Some teachers, librarians, and parents, however, feel that children's literature should be more restrained in dealing with the reality of problems like sex, violence, and drugs that pervade our culture. Thus, the pressure of censorship from groups who believe such problems should not be considered in children's literature is a constant concern for professionals whose responsibility is to select what is best for the children they serve. (We discuss this issue at length in Chapter Fourteen.)

Since the 1960s, when the novel *Harriet the Spy* (1964), by Louise Fitzhugh, was published (about a precocious child who did not get along with her parents), the treatment of realistic social problems has been a thread that runs through much of contemporary fiction for children. A good writer of contemporary fiction skillfully treats a troublesome situation in such a manner that the characters are able to gradually overcome the problem through developing maturity and understanding. Lois Lowry, for example, treats terminal illness without sentimentality in *A Summer to Die* (1977) and the brutality of war sensitively in *Number the Stars* (1989). Robert Cormier, whose books continue to be controversial, honestly addresses topics such as gangs (*The Chocolate War* (1974), attempted rape, and blackmail in his books for older children.

RECOGNIZING DIVERSITY   In the 1960s, federal grant money was made available to libraries through the National Defense Education Act. Consequently, publishers expanded their lists and began catering to school and public libraries, in addition to bookstores and the general public. The civil rights movement in the 1960s provided the impetus for publishers to consider the work of African American writers. Before that time, very few books contained black characters, and those that did featured stereotypes like those in *Nicodemus* (Inez Hogan), the long-running, popular series of the 1930s. But in 1962 Ezra Jack Keats won the Caldecott Medal for *The Snowy Day*, in which he illustrated the winter activities of a genuine, playful, and loving African American child.

More fiction and nonfiction about African Americans began to appear. Mildred Taylor's *Roll of Thunder, Hear My Cry* (1976), and *The Land* (2001) attracted considerable interest. Works by outstanding authors like Christopher Paul Curtis (*Bud Not Buddy*, 1999, *The Watsons Go to Birmingham*, 1963), and Walter Dean

Myers, who concentrates his talents as a writer on middle school children and young adults, are all worthy recipients of major awards.

With books about parallel cultures being published more frequently, it is important to mention the historical significance of the work of Scott O'Dell. Since his first book, *Island of the Blue Dolphins*, was published in 1960, until his death in 1989, he contributed to a greater historical understanding of the many cultures that now make up the United States. Children in America continue to gain a deeper understanding of Native Americans from the folktales, fiction, and nonfiction of Joseph Bruchac. Hispanic children are likewise enriched by the poetry, short stories, and novels of Gary Soto, while Asians benefit from the picture books, biographies, and novels of Allen Say and Lawrence Yep (*Dragon Wings*, 1975). Many other minorities are also included in books for children. (See Chapter Six for an extended discussion of diversity in children's literature.)

The Search for Quality

The modern history of children's literature is still in progress. Thousands of books are being sold on the Internet and by mammoth bookstore chains, as the small, community bookstore struggles to survive. Individual American publishing firms, once independent, are now dominated by eight large multinational corporations. Today's children are viewed more often as consumers—rather than readers—as the buzzwords in publishing are now "synergy," "licensing," and "big names" (Hade, 2002). Yet in spite of DVDs, televisions, and computers, children still find time in their busy lives to read the outstanding books we discuss in later chapters. Books by Newbery Medal winners like Susan Patron (*The Higher Power of Lucky*, 2006), Lynne Rae Perkins (*Criss Cross*, 2005), Kate DiCamillo (*The Tale of Despereaux*, 2004), Avi (*Crispin: The Cross of Lead*, 2003), Linda Sue Park (*A Single Shard*, 2002), Richard Peck (*A Year Down Yonder*, 2001), Christopher Paul Curtis (*Bud, Not Buddy*, 2000), Louis Sachar (*Holes*, 1999) Karen Hesse (*Out of the Dust*, 1998), E. L. Konisburg (*The View from Saturday*, 1997), Karen Cushman (*The Midwife's Apprentice*, 1996), and hundreds of other writers, continue to relate to their readers and offer them adventure, wisdom, and satisfaction.

INFORMATIONAL BOOKS   Informational books have attained a new level of excellence as expressed in the writings of Jim Murphy, author of *American Plague* (2003), *Blizzard* (2000), and *The Great Fire* (1995), among others. James Cross Giblin has written about unusual subjects in works such as *From Hand to Mouth: Or How We Invented Knives, Forks, Spoons and Chopsticks* (1987). Rhoda Blumberg has enriched young readers with her books about diverse topics, such as *Commodore Perry in the Land of the Shogun* (1985), *The Great American Gold Rush* (1990), and *Shipwrecked! The True Adventures of a Japanese Boy* (2000).

PICTURE BOOKS FOR OLDER READERS   Picture books for older readers are a recent trend and an excellent source of information. For example, Diane Stanley, who began to develop picture book biographies in 1986, continues to combine finely detailed illustrations with authentic and carefully researched events in the lives of outstanding men and women (e.g., Peter the Great, Charles Dickens, William Shakespeare, Good Queen Bess). She not only informs readers, but draws them into an exciting, true adventure, visually expressed using dramatic illustrations. Not only are picture books for older readers a visual feast, but they also encourage reluctant readers to read willingly with a feeling of genuine accomplishment.

WHAT LIES AHEAD?   To achieve the *goodness-of-fit* that we constantly stress throughout *Children's Literature: A Developmental Perspective*, teachers and librarians conscientiously analyze, select, and respond to outstanding books, as we'll see in Chapter Four. They are well aware of the importance of introducing their students to all genres. (We introduce these genres in Chapter Three and view them through a developmental lens in Chapters Seven through Twelve.) It's a continuous process as new categories of literature, such as graphic novels and hip-hop literature, emerge. We have only to witness the phenomenon of Harry Potter, however, to recognize the increased fascination of children with fantasy and science fiction. It proves that when children are invited to a literary feast, they will reserve a place at the table—if they like what's being served. Table 2.3 summarizes the outstanding events in children's literature.

Table 2.3 CHILDREN'S LITERATURE THROUGH THE YEARS

TIME	FORM	CONTENT
The Early Tradition (preliterate)	Oral storytelling	Tales of bravery and cowardice
Greeks and Romans (400 BC—600 AD)	Epic tales	*The Iliad, The Odyssey, The Aeneid*
The Gutenberg press (1455)	Stories in book form	Religious, educational, fables
The New World	Changing views of children, use of color	Fiction, nonfiction
Twentieth century	Increased role of children's literature, major role of illustrators, recognition of diversity, outstanding nonfiction	Stories of family, nature, war; expanding use of realism; more variety in young adult literature

Chapter Checklist

Read the following items carefully. If you have difficulty responding to any of them, return to the chapter and review the material.

After reading this chapter, you can

1. Describe how Greek and Roman literature affected the development of the youth of those times.

2. Explain the meaning of the expression, "the Dawn of Childhood."

3. Analyze the influence of the writings of John Locke and Jean Jacques Rousseau.

4. Evaluate the significance of the work of Charles Darwin and William Preyer for children's literature.

5. Demonstrate the causes, growth, and acceptance of children's literature in the nineteenth century.

6. Explain the enduring popularity of magazines in children's literature.

7. Identify the reasons for Mark Twain's enormous popularity.

8. Relate Sigmund Freud's ideas to the themes of children's literature.

9. Explain why the interval between the two World Wars is frequently referred to as "the Golden Age of Children's Literature."

10. Identify and evaluate the impact of topics such as realism and diversity on children's literature in the twenty-first century.

Children's Bibliography

Alcott, Louisa May. (1868). *Little Women*. Boston: Little, Brown.

Almond, David. (1999). *Skellig*. New York: Delacorte Press.

Andersen, Hans Christian. (1846). *A Danish Storybook, Danish Legends and Tales*. London: F. Warne and Co.

Aronson, Marc. (2000). *Sir Walter Ralegh and the Quest for El Dorado*. New York: Clarion Books.

Avi. (2002). *Crispin: The Cross of Lead*. New York: Hyperion.

Bader, Barbara. (1991). *Aesop and Company*. Boston: Houghton Mifflin.

Bannerman, Helen. (1899). *The Story of Little Black Sambo*. London: Chatto & Windus.

Baum, L. Frank. (1900). *The Wonderful Wizard of Oz*. New York: Morrow.

Bemelman, Ludwig. (1939). *Madeline*. New York: Macmillan.

Blume, Judy. (1972). *Are You There, God? It's Me, Margaret*. New York: Dell.

Blume, Judy. (2003) *Double Fudge*. New York: Puffin Books.

Blumberg, Rhoda. (1985). *Commodore Perry in the Land of the Shogun*. New York: Lothrop, Lee & Shepard.

Blumberg, Rhoda. (1990). *The Great American Gold Rush*. New York: Bradbury Press.

Blumberg, Rhoda. (2001). *Shipwrecked! The True Adventures of a Japanese Boy*. New York: HarperCollins.

Bond, Michael. (1960/2002). *Paddington Bear*. New York: HarperCollins.

Brink, Carol Ryrie. (1935). *Caddie Woodlawn*. New York: Macmillan.

Brown, Margaret Wise. (1947). *Good Night, Moon*. New York: HarperCollins.

Browne, Anthony. (2005). *My Mom*. New York: Farrar.

Bruchac, Joseph. (2006). *Jim Thorpe: Original All-American*. New York: Dial.

Burnett, Frances Hodgson. (1912). *The Secret Garden*. New York: HarperCollins.

Burnett, Frances Hodgson. (1916). *A Little Princess: Being the Whole Story of Sarah Crewe*. New York: Scribner.

Burton, Virginia. (1942). *The Little House*. Boston: Houghton Mifflin.

Burton, Virginia. (1939, 2002). *Mike Mulligan and More*. Boston: Houghton Mifflin.

Caldecott, Randolph, Illustrator (1880, 1998). *Sing a Song of Sixpence*. New York: Barron.

Carroll, Lewis. (1865). *Alice's Adventures in Wonderland*. New York: Macmillan.

Carroll, Lewis. (1872). *Through the Looking-Glass and What Alice Found There*. New York: Macmillan.

Carroll, Lewis. (1855/2003). *Jabberwocky*. Cambridge, MA: Candlewick.

Ciardi, John. (1961). *I Met a Man*. Boston: Houghton Mifflin.

Clarke, Judith. (2005). *Kalpana's Dream*. New York: Front Street.

Cleary, Beverly. (1999). *Ramona's World*. New York: Morrow.

Collodi, Carlo. (1892/1986). *The Adventures of Pinocchio*. Berkeley: U of California Press.

Comenius, J. (1659). *Orbis Sensualism Pictus*. Leipzig.

Coolidge, Susan. (1871/1968). *What Katy Did*. New York: Dutton.

Cormier, Robert. (1974/1994). *The Chocolate War*. New York: Knopf.

Cowper, William. (1878). *The Diverting History of John Gilpin*. Illus. Randolph Caldecott. London: G. Routledge.

Crane, Walter. (1981). *Absurd ABC*. New York: Metropolitan Museum of Art.

Curtis, Christopher Paul. (1995). *The Watsons Go to Birmingham—1963*. NewYork: Delacorte.

Curtis, Christopher Paul. (1999). *Bud, Not Buddy*. New York: Delacorte.

Cushman, Karen. (1995). *The Midwife's Apprentice*. New York: Clarion.

Dahl, Roald. (1964). *Charlie and the Chocolate Factory*. New York: Knopf.

Dahl, Roald. (1982). *The BFG*. New York: Farrar, Straus, & Giroux.

de Brunhoff, Jean. (1992). *The Adventures of Babar*. New York: Dean.

Defoe, Daniel. (1719/2003). *Robinson Crusoe*. New York: Atheneum.

De Saint Exupery, Antoine. (1943). *The Little Prince*. New York: Dell.

DiCamillo, Kate. (2000). *Because of Winn-Dixie*. Cambridge, MA: Candlewick.

DiCamillo, Kate. (2003). *The Tale of Despereaux*. Cambridge, MA: Candlewick.

Dickens, Charles. (1843) *A Christmas Carol*. London: Chapman & Hall.

Dodge, Mary Mapes. (1865). *Hans Brinker or The Silver Skates*. New York: James O'Kane.

Doyle, Brian. (1984). *Angel Square*. New York: Bradbury Press.

Ellis, Deborah. (2000). *The Bread Winner*. Toronto: Douglas & McIntyre.

Ellis, Deborah. (2002). *Paravana's Journey*. Toronto: Groundwood Books.

Ellis, Deborah. (2003). *Mud City*. Toronto: Groundwood Books.

Estes, Eleanor. (1941/1989). *The Moffats*. New York: Dell.

Estes, Eleanor. (1974/2002). *The Hundred Dresses*. New York: Harcourt Brace.

Finley, Martha. (1867/1977). *Elsie Dinsmore*. New York: Garland.

Fitzhugh, Louise. (1964). *Harriet the Spy*. New York: Harper & Row.

Flack, Marjorie & Wiese Kurt. (1933). *The Story About Ping*. New York: Viking.

Forbes, Esther. (1943). *Johnny Tremain*. Boston: Houghton Mifflin.

Frank, Anne. (1952/1958). *Anne Frank: The Diary of a Young Girl*. New York: Doubleday.

Freedman, Russell. (1987). *Lincoln: A Photobiography*. New York: Clarion.

French, Jackie. (2003). *Diary of a Wombat*. New York: Clarion Books.

French, Jackie. (2003). *Hitler's Daughter*. New York: HarperCollins.

Funke, Cornelia. (2002). *The Thief Lord*. New York: Scholastic.

Gag, Wanda. (1928). *Millions of Cats*. New York: Coward.

Gerstein, Mordecai. (2003). *The Man Who Walked Between the Towers*. Brookfield, CT.: Roaring Brook Press.

Giblin, James. (1987). *From Hand to Mouth*. New York: Crowell.

Goldsmith, Oliver. (1882). *Goody Two Shoes*. London: Griffin & Farran.

Grahame, Kenneth. (1908/1933). *The Wind in the Willows*. New York: Scribner.

Greenaway, Kate. (1900/1981). *Under the Window*. London: Bodley Head.

Greenfield, Eloise. (1978). *Honey, I Love, and Other Love Poems*. New York: HarperCollins.

Greenfield, Eloise. (1988). *Nathaniel Talking*. New York: Black Butterfly Children's Books.

Grimm, Jacob, & Grimm, Wilhelm. (2004). *The Annotated Brothers Grimm*. Maria Tatar, ed. New York: Norton.

Hale, Lucretia. (1880/1960). *The Peterkin Papers*. Boston: Houghton Mifflin.

Haywood, Carolyn. (1973/1978). *Betsy and the Boys*. New York: Harcourt.

Heydlauff, Lisa. (2005). *Going to School in India*. Boston: Charlesbridge.

Hesse, Karen. (1997). *Out of the Dust*. New York: Scholastic Press.

Hogan, Inez. (1939). *Nicodemus*. New York: Dutton.

Holub, Josef. (2005). *An Innocent Soldier*. New York: Scholastic.

Horvath, Polly. (2003). *The Canning Season*. New York: Farrar, Straus, & Giroux.

Hughes, Langston. (1969). *Don't You Turn Back*. New York: Knopf.

Hughes, Langston. (1932/1994). *The Dream Keeper and Other Poems*. Illus. Brian Pinkney. New York: Knopf.

Jacobs, Joseph. (ND). *English Fairy Tales*. New York: Putnam.

Jones, Diana. (2001/1977). *Charmed Life*. New York: Greenwillow.

Jones, Hettie. (1971). *The Trees Stand Shining*. New York: Dial.

Kastner, Erich. (1930/1959). *Emil and the Detectives*. New York: Scholastic.

Keats, Ezra Jack. (1962). *The Snowy Day*. New York: Scholastic.

Kipling, Rudyard. (1894/1991). *The Jungle Book*. New York: Longman.

Kipling, Rudyard. (1899/1993). *The Just So Stories*. New York: Viking.

Konigsburg. (1996). *The View from Saturday*. New York: Atheneum.

Kuskin, Karla. (1975). *Near the Window Tree*. New York: Harper & Row.

Lamb, Charles, & Lamb, Mary. (1806,1807). *Tales From Shakespeare*. New York: Crowell.

Lang, Andrew. (1889). *The Blue Fairy Book*. New York: Longmans, Green & Co.

Lang, Andrew. (1979). *Fairy Tale Treasury*. Cary Kaus, ed. New York: Avenel Books.

Lear, Edward. (1846). *Book of Nonsense*. London: T. McLean.

Lear, Edward. (1991). *The Owl and the Pussy Cat*. Illus. Jan Brett. New York: Putnam.

Lear, Edward. (2006). *The Owl and the Pussy Cat.* Illus Ann Mortimer. New York: HarperCollins.

Lenski, Lois. (1945/1988). *Strawberry Girl.* New York: Harper & Row.

Lester, Julius. (1996). *Sam and the Tigers: A New Telling of Little Black Sambo.* New York: Dial.

Lewis, C. S. (1950). *The Chronicles of Narnia.* New York: Macmillan.

Lindgren, Astrid. (1959). *Pippi Longstocking.* Trans., Florence Lamborn. New York: Scholastic Book Services.

Lofting, Hugh. (1920/1967). *The Story of Dr. Dolittle.* New York: Lippincott.

Lowry, Lois. (2002). *Gooney Bird Greene.* Boston: Houghton Mifflin.

Lowry, Lois. (1977). *A Summer to Die.* Boston: Houghton Mifflin.

Lowry, Lois. (1989). *Number the Stars.* Boston: Houghton Mifflin.

MacDonald, George. (1871/1977). *Complete Fairy Tales of George MacDonald.* New York: Schocken Books.

Mahy, Margaret. (1982). *The Haunting.* New York: Atheneum.

McCaughrean, Geraldine. (2003). *Gilgamesh the Hero.* New York: Oxford University Press.

McCloskey, Robert. (1941). *Make Way for Ducklings.* New York: Viking.

McCord, David. (1952). *Far and Few.* Boston: Little, Brown.

Merriam, Eve. (1969/1996). *Inner-City Mother Goose.* New York: Simon & Schuster.

Milne, A. A. (1926/1989). *Winnie the Pooh.* New York: Penguin.

Montgomery, L. M. (1908/2001). *Anne of Green Gables.* New York: Grosset & Dunlap.

Moore, Clement. (1823/1992). *A Visit from St. Nicholas.* Boston: Houghton Mifflin.

Murphy, Jim. (2003). *An American Plague: The True and Terrifying Story of the Yellow Fever Epidemic of 1793.* New York: Clarion Books.

Murphy, Jim. (2000). *Blizzard: The Storm That Changed America.* New York: Scholastic Press.

Murphy, Jim. (1995). *The Great Fire.* New York: Scholastic.

Nash, Ogden. (1959/1995). *The Tale of the Custard Dragon.* Boston: Little, Brown.

Newbery, John. (1764/1967). *A Little Pretty Pocket Book.* a Fascmile. New York: Harcourt.

Norton, Mary. (1953). *The Borrowers.* San Diego: Harcourt Brace.

O'Dell, Scott. (1960). *Island of the Blue Dolphins.* Boston: Houghton Mifflin.

Patron, Susan. (2006). *The Higher Power of Lucky.* New York: Atheneum.

Park, Barbara. (2002). *Junie B. First Grader: One-Man Band.* New York: Random House.

Park, Linda Sue. (2001). *A Single Shard.* NewYork: Clarion.

Peck, Richard. (2000). *A Year Down Yonder.* New York: Dial Books.

Perkins, Lynne Rae. (2005). *Criss Cross.* New York: Greenwillow.

Perrault, Charles. (1901). *Tales of Mother Goose.* Trans., Charles Welsch. Boston: D. C. Heath & Co.

Pilkey, Dave. (1999). *Captain Underpants.* New York: Scholastic.

Pinkwater, Daniel and Jill. (2001). *The Werewolf Club Meets Dorkula.* New York: Atheneum.

Porter, Eleanor. (1913). *Pollyanna.* New York: Farrar, Straus, & Giroux.

Potter, Beatrix. (1901). *The Tale of Peter Rabbit.* New York: Frederick Warne.

Prats, Joan de Deu. (2005). *Sebastian's Roller Skates.* LaJolla, CA.: Kanemiller.

Pullman, Philip. (1996). *The Golden Compass: His Dark Materials, Book One.* New York: Knopf.

Pyle, Howard. (1883). *The Merry Adventures of Robin Hood.* New York: Scribner.

Rennison, Louise. (2003). *Dancing in My Nuddy-Pants: Even Further Confessions of Georgia Nicolson.* New York: Harper.

Rey, Margret and H. A. (1941/1995). *Curious George.* Boston: Houghton Mifflin.

Sachar, Louis. (1998). *Holes.* New York: Farrar, Straus, & Giroux

Salten, Felix. (1923, English trans. 1929). *Bambi.* New York: Noble and Noble.

Say, Allen. (2005). *Kamishibai Man.* Boston: Houghton Mifflin.

Scieszka, Jon. (1989). *The True Story of the 3 Little Pigs.* New York: Viking.

Sendak, Maurice. (1963). *Where the Wild Things Are.* New York: HarperCollins.

Seuss, Doctor. (1937). *And to Think That I Saw It on Mulberry Street.* New York: Vanguard.

Sidney, Margaret. (1881). *Five Little Peppers and How They Grew.* Boston: Lothrop.

Singer, Isaac, B. (1969). *A Day of Pleasure: Stories of a Boy Growing Up in Warsaw.* New York: Farrar, Straus, & Giroux.

Sneve, Virginia Driving Hawk. (1989). *Dancing Tepees, Poems of Amercian Indian Youth.* New York: Holiday House.

Soto, Gary. (1992). *Neighborhood Odes.* New York: Harcourt Brace.

Spyri, Johanna. (1884/1954). *Heidi.* New York: Doubleday.

Stanley, Diane. (2002). *Saladin: Noble Prince of Islam.* New York: HarperCollins.

Stevenson, Robert Louis. (1886). *Kidnapped.* Akron, OH: Saalfield.

Stevenson, Robert Louis. (1883). *Treasure Island.* London: Cassell & Co.

Stevenson, Robert Louis. (1885). *A Child's Garden of Verses.* London: Longmans, Green, and Co.

Swift, Jonathan. (1726/1940). *Gulliver's Travels.* London: J. M. Dent & Sons.

Taylor, Mildred. (1976). *Roll of Thunder, Hear My Cry.* New York: Dial.

Taylor, Mildred. (2001). *The Land.* New York: Fogelman.

Tolkien, J. R. (1937). *The Hobbit.* Boston: Houghton Mifflin.

Tolkien, J. R. (1968). *The Lord of the Rings.* Boston: Houghton Mifflin.

Travers, P. L. (1924/1962). *Mary Poppins.* New York: Harcourt.

Twain, Mark. (1876). *The Adventures of Tom Sawyer.* San Francisco: A. Roman & Co.

Twain, Mark. (1884). *The Adventures of Huckleberry Finn.* New York: Harper & Row.

Warner, Susan. (1850/1987). *The Wild,Wild World.* New York: Feminist Press, City University of New York.

Webster, Jean. (1912). *Daddy Long Legs.* New York: Grosset & Dunlap.

White, E. B. (1952). *Charlotte's Web.* New York: Harper.

Wilder, Laura Ingalls. (1935). *Little House on the Prairie.* New York: HarperCollins.

Wiggin, Kate. (1910). *Rebecca of Sunnybrook Farm.* New York: Grosset & Dunlap.

Wyss, Johann. (1814/1954). *Swiss Family Robinson*. New York: Doubleday.

Yep, Lawrence. (1975). *Dragonwings*. New York: Scholastic.

Yolen, Jane & Harris, Richard, (2004). *Jason and the Gorgon's Blood*. New York: HarperCollins.

Yolen, Jane & Harris, Richard. (2001). *Odysseus in the Serpent Maze*. New York: HarperCollins.

Yumoto, Kazumi. (2002). *The Letters*. New York: Farrar, Straus.

Yumoto, Kazumi. (1998). *The Friends*. New York: Bantam Dell.

Professional References

Aristotle. (1926). *The Nicomachean Ethics*. Trans. H. Rackmam. Cambridge, MA: Harvard University Press.

Avery, Gillian. (1994). *Behold the Child: American Children and Their Books, 1621-1922*. Baltimore: Johns Hopkins University Press.

Avery, Gillian. (1995). "The Beginnings of Children Reading to c. 1700." In Peter Hunt (ed.), *Children's Literature*. New York: Oxford University Press.

Bandura, A. (1997). *Self-Efficacy: The Exercise of Control*. New York: Freeman.

Bechtel, Louise Seaman. (1955). *Books in Search of Children*. Boston: Houghton Mifflin.

Beck, R., Black, L., Naylor, P., & Shabaka, D. (1999). *World History: Patterns of Interaction*. Boston: Houghton Mifflin.

Bel Geddes, J. (1997). *Children and Childhood*. New York: Oryx Press.

Benfer, Amy. (2004). "Girl, Revised." In *New York Times* (OP.-ED). March 6, 2004.

Bjorklund, David. (2005). *Children's Thinking*. Belmont, CA: Wadsworth.

Borstelmann, L. (1983). "Children Before Psychology: Ideas About Children from Antiquity to the Late 1800s." In Paul Mussen (ed.), *Handbook of Child Psychology*. New York: John Wiley.

Butts, R. F., & Cremin, L. (1953). *A History of Education in American Culture*. New York: Henry Holt & Co.

Cahill, T. (2003). *Sailing the Wine-Dark Sea: Why the Greeks Matter*. New York: Doubleday.

Dacey, John, & Travers, John. in press. *Human Development Across the Lifespan* (7th ed.). New York: McGraw-Hill.

Darwin, Charles. (1877). "Biographical Sketch of an Infant". Mind, 2, 285–294.

Elliott, S., Kratochwill, T., Littlefield Cook, J., & Travers, J. (2000). *Educational Psychology*. New York: McGraw-Hill.

Feeney, Mark. (2004). "Carroll's Photographs Are Adventures in a Visual Wonderland." *Boston Globe*, August.

Ferrill, A. (1986). *The Fall of the Roman Empire*. New York: Thames and Hudson.

Gardner, Howard. (1982). *Developmental Psychology*. Boston: Little, Brown.

Hade, Daniel. (2002). "Storyselling: Are Publishers Changing the Way Children Read?" *The Horn Book Magazine*, September/October 509–517.

Heywood, C. (2001). *A History of Childhood*. Cambridge, UK: Polity Press.

Hunt, Peter. (2001). *Children's Literature*: Malden, MA: Blackwell.

Hunt, Peter, ed. (1995). *Children's Literature. An Illustrated History*. New York: Oxford University Press.

Isaacs, Kathleen. (2006). "It's a Big World After All." *School Library Journal*, February, 40–44.

Kahn, Joseph P. (2005). "Books Brothers." *Boston Globe*. April 21, D1, D8.

Kinnell, Margaret. (1995). "Publishing for Children." In Peter Hunt, ed. *Children's Literature: An Illustrated History*. New York: Oxford University Press.

Locke, J. (1904). *Some Thoughts Concerning Education*. Introduction and notes by R. H. Quick. New York: Macmillan.

MacLeod, Anne S. (1995). "Children's Literature in America from the Puritan Beginnings." In Peter Hunt, ed. *Children's Literature: An Illustrated History*. New York: Oxford University Press.

Odean, Kathleen. (2002). "The Return of Old Friends." *Book*. July–August, 32.

Ong, W. (2003). *Orality and Literacy*. London: Routledge.

Perry, Mark. (2004). *Grant and Twain*. New York: Random House.

Pinker, Steven. (2002). *The Blank Slate*. New York: Viking.

Pool, Gail. (1995). Magazines for Children. In Anita Silvey (ed). *Children's Books and Their Creators*. Boston: Houghton Mifflin.

Postman, N. (1982). *The Disappearance of Childhood*. New York: Dell.

Prager, Arthur. (1969). "The Secret of Nancy Drew." *Saturday Review*, January 25, ed. 18.

Preyer, William. (1882). *The Mind of the Child*. New York: Appleton.

Robinson, Lolly. (1995). "Potter, Beatrix." In Anita Silvey, ed. *Children's Books and Their Creators*. Boston: Houghton Mifflin.

Rousseau, J. (1911). *Emile*. Trans. Barbara Foxley. New York: Dutton.

Rudman, Masha, ed. (1988). *For the Love of Reading*. Mount Vernon, NY: Consumers Union.

Siegler, R. & Alibali, M. (2005). *Children's Thinking*. Upper Saddle River, NJ: Prentice Hall.

Silvey, Anita, ed. (1995). *Children's Books and Their Creators* Boston: Houghton Mifflin.

Singer, Dorothy, & Singer, Jerome. (1990). *The House of Make-Believe*. Cambridge, MA: Harvard University Press.

Ulrich, R. (1950). *History of Educational Thought*. New York: American Book Co.

Unger, R., & Crawford, M. (2000). *Woman and Gender: A Feminist Psychology*. New York: McGraw-Hill.

White, Martha, ed. (2006). *Letters of E. B. White*. (rev. ed.) New York: HarperCollins.

Wullschlager, Jackie. (1995). *Inventing Wonderland*. New York: Simon & Schuster.

Yolen, Jane. (1993). "How Children's Literature Has Evolved." In Masha Kabakow Rudman, ed. *Children's Literature: Resource for the Classroom*. Norwood, MA: Christopher-Gordon.

Genres in Children's Literature

The role of literature is to illuminate, to strengthen, to explain why some aspect of life is moving or terrible or sad or important or insignificant for people who might otherwise not understand so much or so well. Reading is experience, but it also enriches other experience (Solomon, 2004).

While reading Andrew Solomon's comments from The New York Times, *we come to realize that his words apply to children's literature. In all its manifestations, children's literature is vast and far-reaching, extending from the realistic to the fantastic, and addressing an audience that spans many developmental levels. A book such as* The Invention of Hugo Cabret *(Selznick), for instance, unfolds as a movie reel to include fantastic, historic, and graphic elements in one unique package.*

As we will see in the chapters ahead, there are as many styles, types, and kinds of children's books as there are children. So that all children from infancy through high school can enjoy this complex, fascinating body of literature more easily, we have divided it into *genres*, characterized by various features that distinguish one genre from another.

In this chapter, we will explore the role of genres in children's literature and then discuss, with numerous examples, eight major genres. From preschool through high school, young people read whatever genre excites them, and it's not unusual to find a middle school student devouring the information embedded in Steve Jenkins' *Hottest Coldest Highest Deepest*. Even though it's a picture book, it's filled with curious facts that children of this age are anxious to explore. An intermediate school child may be fascinated listening to the traditional tale *Sundiata* as retold by David Wisniewski. Initially, he may be attracted to the book because it is about a lion king, but then he is motivated to continue listening because of the dramatic manner in which Wisniewski presents Sundiata's strength in overcoming adversity and his courage in facing the enemy. Introducing children to all genres widens their interests and increases their knowledge. We begin our work by presenting an overview of the genres of children's literature. We analyze them developmentally in Chapters Seven through Twelve.

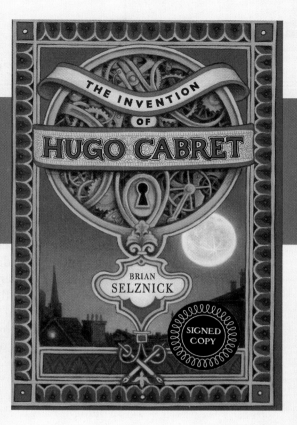

THE INVENTION OF HUGO CABRET
Book cover from THE INVENTION OF HUGO CABRET by Brian Selznick. Copyright © 2007 by Brian Selznick. Reprinted by permission of Scholastic Inc.

Guidelines for Reading Chapter 3

After you finish reading Chapter Three, you should be able to answer the following questions.

• Why are genres important in understanding children's literature?

• Identify the various types of genres and the characteristics that distinguish each.

• What defining features justify including picture books as a separate genre?

• What unique qualities of traditional literature account for its enduring popularity?

• Based on poetry's differentiating features and children's developmental characteristics, why does poetry appeal to children?

• The defining characteristics of fantasy identify it as a genre with great appeal to children. Why?

• What characteristics distinguish contemporary realistic fiction from historical fiction?

• What characteristics contribute to a "good" biography?

• Which criteria lead to an outstanding informational book?

Genres in Children's Literature

The eight genres of children's literature—*the picture book, traditional literature, modern fantasy, poetry and drama, contemporary realistic fiction, historical fiction, biography and autobiography,* and *informational books*—reflect the biopsychosocial development of children. Although other texts may use a different number of genres, the concept is similar: genres are a method for categorizing children's literature that enable children to become familiar with, have a goodness-of-fit in, and be free to experience all aspects of children's literature.

Table 3.1 illustrates the eight genres and their meaning.

We believe that combining developmental knowledge with genres is the key to organizing children's literature as we enter the twenty-first century. By recognizing the characteristics of a specific genre (biography or historical fiction, for example), we detect the major elements that make one book different from another. Often teachers and librarians urge children to select different genres to develop a specific theme. While studying Boston and its role in the American Revolution in social studies, children might read Jean Fritz's biography *And Then What Happened, Paul Revere?*; and historical fiction such as Esther Forbes' *Johnny Tremain,* about Paul Revere's apprentice; or Ann Rinaldi's *The Fifth of March,* an exciting story of the Boston Massacre. Poetry, such as Henry Wadsworth Longfellow's *The Midnight Ride of Paul Revere,* could be read aloud, while the picture book *Boston Then and Now,* about fifty-nine historic sites photographed by Peter Vanderwarker, and the informational book *Boston: The Way It Was,* by Lorie Conway, are available for students to complete theirresearch.

Here we see how five different genres offer insights into one unified theme. In the following chapters we continue to discuss how children at various developmental levels can widen their horizons by varying the genres they read, and can become consciously aware of how they may use books from various genres to develop themes across the curriculum.

Table 3.1 THE EIGHT GENRES

GENRE	MEANING
Picture book	Usually, the integration of words with illustrations; however, some picture books are wordless
Traditional literature	Stories and songs emerging from an oral tradition whose authors are unknown
Fantasy	Journeys into other, imaginative worlds
Poetry and drama	Language used in a unique manner to express beauty and excitement
Contemporary realistic fiction	Stories that could be true in the here and now
Historical fiction	Stories that could have been true in the past
Biography and autobiography	True accounts of a person's life, written about or by that person
Informational books (nonfiction)	Books containing verifiable facts

Genres and Thinking Skills

Not only will your understanding of genres help you to diversify your students' reading and expand their understanding of and interaction with the world, but it will also allow your young readers to strengthen their cognitive abilities. Children need to shape their facts to gain as much value from them as possible. By reading many genres of children's literature, children sharpen and refine their thinking skills, as well as improve their ability to classify, that is, group objects on the basis of a set of characteristics (Bjorklund, 2005). This skill helps them understand the characters, themes, plots, and other elements that appear in their readings.

In Chapters Seven through Twelve, we discuss why children, because of their biopsychosocial development, choose specific genres and why their preference for particular genres changes. For example, historical fiction is difficult for early elementary students to comprehend, because of their inability to understand the passage of time, but middle school children find it absorbing. Poetry, on the other hand, especially if it rhymes, is fun for preschoolers because of their innate sense of rhythm, yet high school students may find it boring because of the manner in which it was taught to them in lower grades. Teachers and librarians have the obligation to make children aware of *all* genres and to encourage them to read widely according to their level of development.

Now let's turn our attention to the picture book as a genre.

The Picture Book

What is a picture book? Marcus (2002, p. 31) defines it as "not merely an illustrated book where pictures are infrequently interspersed throughout the text but a dialogue between two worlds: the world of images and the world of words." Critics, however, question how the picture book can be considered a genre since it often includes other categories like biography, fantasy, traditional literature, and poetry. For example, Mary Pope Osborne's *Kate and the Beanstalk* (2000) is a picture book retelling by the author/illustrator of Andrew Lang's folktale *Jack and the Beanstalk* (1890). It belongs in the picture book genre because it is a dramatic and seamless integration of words and pictures. The *format* of the picture book, rather than its subject matter, identifies it as a genre. Writing and illustrating a picture book is a difficult and challenging task (as we discuss in Chapter Five). Graeme Base (1996), the internationally acclaimed Australian author and illustrator, admits that his picture book, *Animalia*, took him more than three years to complete.

Then and Now

The Place of Postmodernism in Picture Books

Most picture books for small children are comforting and predictable, ideal for reading aloud, and perfect for bedtime stories. Since the time of Randolph Caldecott (1846–1886), when children were thrilled by the artist's illustrations in *The Diverting History of John Gilpin* (1878), the first of his sixteen picture books, children have listened to and treasured what are now picture book classics. College students may still recall what happened in Bernard Waber's *Ira Sleeps Over* (1972), when Ira misses his teddy bear, and how they laughed at Bill Peet's *Pamela Camel* (1984). Their toys of Curious George, Madeline, or Babar were put aside a long time ago, but they still are fondly remembered.

Some picture story writers and illustrators, however, like David Macaulay in his *Black and White* (1990), are challenging conventional concepts of form and structure and are producing works that reflect the framework of postmodernism. Think of postmodernism as sheer skepticism about the actual existence of any form of com-

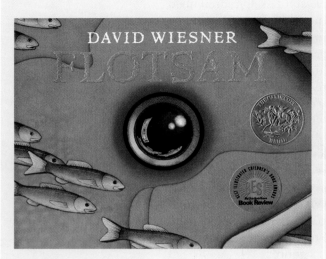

FLOTSAM
Cover from FLOTSAM by David Wiesner. Jacket illustrations copyright © 2006 by David Weisner. Reprinted by permission of Clarion Books, an imprint of Houghton Mifflin Company. All rights reserved.

plete explanation based on reality (Butler, 2002). The skepticism generated by postmodernists is captured neatly by Steven Pinker (2002) when he notes that the ideas contained in the language we use have no real relationship to things in the world, but are socially constructed. In other words, our ideas are figments of our imagination cloaked in language.

Anthony Browne offers today's children a postmodern literary experience when he inserts parodies of the Mona Lisa and the Laughing Cavalier into his picture book *Voices in the Park* (1998). Caldecott Medal winner David Wiesner successfully turns his story of *The Three Pigs* (2001) into a boisterous, lively, nontraditional escapade. The wolf blows the pigs right off the pages and into another universe, where they plop into other storybooks. The pigs even join the wolf for a ride on a paper airplane. Wiesner delights in creating exaggerated images that break boundaries and free him from literary restraint, as he does again in *Flotsam* (2006), another award-winning book. David Lewis (1996, p. 260) calls it "metafiction" (a kind of experimental or avant-garde writing and illustration), children call it "fun," and teachers and librarians call it a challenge to develop their students' critical thinking skills.

The Format of the Picture Book

The format of the picture book has evolved over the years, and among its many forms are the following.

THE *TOY BOOKS* of the nineteenth century are now the variously engineered, interactive, press-the-button, open the flap, sing-along picture books of the twenty-first century. Here are a few examples of toy books.

• **THE *POP-UP BOOK,*** such as the intricate *Wheels on the Bus* by Paul O. Zelinsky, and the fearfully realistic *Dinosaurs: Encyclopedia Prehistorica*, created by paper engineer Robert Sabuda and Matthew Reinhart (recommended only for children ages 5 and up). Pop-up books like these are so intricately structured that very young children find them difficult to manage by themselves, due to their lack of fine motor skills.

• **THE *BOARD BOOK*** is practically indestructible and the perfect form for small children not only to grasp, but also to chew. As we shall see in Chapter Seven, the board book is *the* book for children up to age 2.

• **THE *INTERACTIVE BOOK*** intrigues young children. When the quiet cricket in Eric Carle's *The Very Quiet Cricket* loudly chirps on the last page (a startling noise created by a computer chip), they are mesmerized.

THE *WORDLESS BOOK* tells a story without a written word. Pat Hutchins'classic *Changes* reveals in dramatic sequence how blocks can become whatever a child imagines them to be. In Barbara Lehman's *Museum Trip*, a young boy loses his class at the museum when he stops to tie his shoelaces. He becomes a part of the museum maze exhibit, works his way through the maze, and finally finds his way out to rejoin his class as they are about to leave. In David Wiesner's *Flotsam*, another curious young boy discovers an old camera at the beach that takes him on a fabulously precarious undersea adventure. Wordless books are an excellent source of information and entertainment for the child who cannot read; they are also absorbing for the child who cannot understand the language.

THE *ALPHABET BOOK* contains letters of the alphabet and pictures corresponding to each letter, such as Rosemary Wells' *Max's ABC*. Alphabet books range in complexity from the straightforward, large letters of the recently reissued *Animal ABC* (Garth Williams), to more cognitively complex books such as Peter Catalanotto's *Matthew A.B.C.*, in which a classroom of twenty-six Matthews are called Matthew A, B, C, and so on. Each Matthew has a distinctive characteristic. Matthew N, for example, is *nearly naked* and wears only briefs and a superhero cape, while Matthew X swallows a *xylophone*.

THE *COUNTING BOOK* presents number concepts by matching each number with a picture of its equivalent number of objects, e.g. *Count With Maisy* (Lucy Cousins), *Fish Eyes: A Book You Can Count On* (Lois Ehlert), and *Ten, Nine, Eight* (Molly Bang) where the numbers are reversed. Julia Donaldson has created the memorable rhyming counting book *One Ted Falls Out of Bed*. Yet only when children have mastered the notion of ordination will they relate biopsychosocially to counting books.

THE *CONCEPT BOOK* teaches young children about opposites, colors, sounds, the senses, and other major concepts, in books such as Ian Falconer's *Olivia's Opposites* and Chris Raschka's *Five Little Ones*. Both are authors and illustrators of many young children's books, and both are keenly aware of children's cognitive capabilities, especially the development of their sense of humor (see Chapter Ten). In the following chapters, concept books provide a goodness-of-fit for children's early development.

THE *PICTURE STORYBOOK,* which we are calling simply the picture book, tells a story by integrating words with pictures. It is our primary focus. In picture storybooks, the most frequent recipient of the Caldecott Medal, words may be minimal, as in David Wiesner's *Tuesday*, or of equal importance to the illustrations, as in Maurice Sendak's *Where the Wild Things Are*. Illustrators of picture books are often the first artists children know. Writers of picture books create scenes and characters that are frequently unforgettable. Jan Brett, the well-known author and illustrator of *The Mitten*, has created a picture book, *Honey . . . Honey . . . Honey . . . Lion*, that takes place in Africa and has characters such as the badger and the honey-guide, who are partners until one deceives the other. What happens then is believably humorous, while simultaneously offering small readers a lesson in trust.

PICTURE BOOKS FOR OLDER READERS   Because of their developmental value, as well as their value as a strong source of information, coupled with their visual impact, many picture books are attracting an increasing number of older readers who have become accustomed to gaining their facts through the Internet. Pam Munoz Ryan's picture book *When Marian Sang* (illustrated by Brian Selznick), about the modest contralto Marion Anderson, is an authentic and inspiring biography in picture storybook form for middle school children. Teachers and librarians often encourage the use of picture books as another genre to enhance the study of history, social studies, science, and biography in intermediate

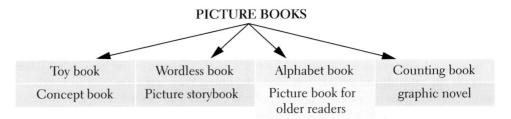

Figure 3.1 Subgenres of picture books.

and middle school. Don Brown's story of Albert Einstein, *Odd Boy Out*, for example, is a perfect segue into the study of mathematics and science.

THE GRAPHIC NOVEL   A recent addition to the picture book genre that is gaining a wide readership is the graphic novel, which is now being read by children from elementary through high school. Originally a comic book, the graphic novel has assumed the form of a paperback book and can be divided into three categories: for all ages, mainstream, and mature. The Japanese graphic novels—for example—*Manga*, are read from right to left. The impact of graphic novels on development is discussed in detail in Chapter Twelve. Additional picture books for older readers are reviewed throughout the book. Figure 3.1 illustrates the subgenres of picture books.

Traditional Literature

Traditional literature refers to those stories and songs of the beliefs, customs, and traditions from all parts of the world that have been passed down orally generation to generation from the beginning of time, and have no known authors. Much of traditional literature consists of folktales, fairy tales, legends, myths, fables, and parables, as well as rhymes, songs, and ballads. Contemporary writers like Cooper Edens, who has compiled an attractively illustrated edition of classic *Princess Stories* for children in grades 1 through 6 continue to keep traditional stories alive.

From a developmental perspective, by reading and listening to traditional literature children gain an ever-widening understanding of cultural differences. The heritage traced by traditional literature brings a sense of personal identification that is recognized and used by today's developmental psychologists. (For an excellent discussion of this topic, see the work of Nancy Eisenberg (1998).) The plots, motifs, (recurrent images), magical objects, spells, and transformations of traditional literature remain remarkably similar from country to country and throughout the world's various cultures.

Folktales

Among the most familiar forms of traditional literature is the *folktale*, the fictional account of events in the lives of humans, both good and evil, and of nonhuman characters as well. The craft of ogres and witches, who use magic objects to cast spells on the unsuspecting, is the basis of the folktale. The folktale itself is usually direct and to the point, dramatic and colorful, and especially effective when read aloud.

THE SETTING OF FOLKTALES has no specific time or place, and sometimes begins with "In the forest," "On a mountain top," or "Once upon a time." Such a setting is considered *symbolic* because the reader or listener is placed there without being provided with a detailed description to make the location believable (Norton, 1993). It may be as distant as the little house in the woods where Red Riding Hood lives; simple as a farm in Denmark where the little man, the nisse, strolls among the animals, or as pretentious as a castle in a far-off land, where lives the handsome prince.

TYPES OF FOLKTALES

- **THE *FAIRY TALE*** is a tale of magic (and sometimes fairies). It usually has a simple setting ("Once upon a time"), characters such as a beautiful heroine and a brave hero, and a problem that must be resolved before these characters can live happily ever after. The story of *Cinderella*, for example, has fascinated young readers for generations. It has hundreds of versions throughout the world, many of which have similar literary elements.

- **THE *TRANSFORMATION TALE*** changes a human into an animal, or an animal into a human, as in *The Frog Prince*.

- **THE *CUMULATIVE TALE*** uses repetition to build up the story, such as Verna Aardema's retelling of the West African tale *Why Mosquitos Buzz in People's Ears*.

- **THE *POURQUOI TALE*** answers the question why (*pourquoi*) a natural event occurs. In Julius Lester's *How Many Spots Does a Leopard Have?: and Other Tales*, children discover in this collection of folklore "Why The Sun and the Moon Live in the Sky," "Why Dogs Chase Cats," and "Why Monkeys Live in Trees." In *Beat the Story Drum, Pum-Pum*, Ashley Bryan rhythmically recounts "How Animals Got Their Tails" and "Why the Bush Cow and Elephant Are Bad Friends."

- **THE *BEAST TALE*** features talking animals and outlandish stories like *The Three Little Pigs*, *Henny Penny*, and *The Musicians of Bremen*.

- **THE *HUMOROUS TALE*,** or as it is sometimes called, the *noodlehead, droll, merry,* or *numbskull tale,* is a particularly attractive tale for children who love to laugh at the antics of a foolish character whose actions in the end make sense. Martha Hamilton and Mitch Weiss, in their collection *Noodlehead Stories*, offer children humorous tales from around the world, and give them tips so that they, too, can be storytellers.

NATIVE AMERICAN FOLKTALES This country's oldest stories come from Native American tribes and are based on the oral tradition. "An Indian agent, Henry Rowe Schoolcraft (*Algic Researches*, 1839), is credited with being one of the first to purposefully collect and translate Indian myths and stories into English" (Miller, 1995, p. 22). Even today, storytellers continue to pass on a tribe's oral traditions, which are then retold by such well-known writers as Joseph Bruchac and Paul Goble. Bruchac, of Abenaki Indian origin, relates the award-winning tale of *Gluskabe and the Four Wishes*, which is a version of the tale recorded in Charles Leland's *The Algonkian Legends of New England*, in 1884. Paul Goble, although English by birth, was adopted by the Sioux and Yakama tribes and developed his first stories from the narrative drawings on tipis and buffalo robes. He introduced children to the Plains spider trickster, Iktomi, in four humorous pourquoi tales sometimes called *trickster tales*. He also captivates readers with the transformational story about the Indian girl who becomes a mare in the Caldecott Medal story *The Girl Who Loved Wild Horses* (Goble, 1995).

Then and Now

Tall Tales, Needed Heroes

In the nineteenth century, as newcomers traveled west into pioneer territory, they created *tall tales*. These were exaggerated retellings of the daring exploits of men and a few women who became legends. like Daniel Boone and Davy Crockett Folk heroes who performed superhuman deeds served as the models in early America, when ordinary men and women performed extraordinary deeds to conquer the wilderness and establish a new country. Steven Kellogg (*Pecos Bill* and *Paul Bunyan*), and Julius Lester (*John Henry*) are among the writers and illustrators who humorously and dramatically captured the exploits of such heroes.

In the twenty-first century, Mary Pope Osborne retells another tall tale that is particularly relevant today. In *New York's Bravest*, she recalls the story of eight-foot-tall Mose, the nineteenth-century New York firefighter who disappears after rescuing residents from a burning hotel. The story ironically parallels the bravery of those firefighters who lost their lives during rescue operations in New York on September 11, 2001.

A picture book that is not literally a tall tale, but an outstanding retelling of heroic deeds done by ordinary men, is Maira Kalman's *Fireboat: The Heroic Adventures of the John J. Harvey*. In it, Kalman recalls the launching of the fireboat in 1931, and how it fell into disrepair and was later refurbished. Fortunately, it was fully equipped in time to supply water to the brave firefighters in the aftermath of the terrorist attack of September 11, 2001. For four days and nights, the crew of the *John J. Harvey* performed superbly. Both of these books reflect the acts of kindness that were offered to a community in terrible distress.

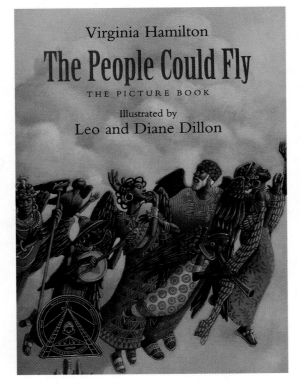

THE PEOPLE COULD FLY
Jacket cover by Leo and Diane Dillon, copyright ©2004 by Leo and Diane Dillon. From THE PEOPLE COULD FLY: THE PICTURE BOOK by Virginia Hamilton and Leo and Diane Dillon, illustrators. Used by permission of Alfred A. Knopf, an imprint of Random House Children's Books, a division of Random House, Inc.

TALES FROM DIVERSE CULTURES   Since America is composed of peoples from all over the world, it is not surprising that today's children are reading and listening to Latino, Hmong, Somalian, and Middle Eastern traditional tales to mention only a few. It will be surprising, however, if the traditional tales retold by recent immigrants do not evolve through time into a uniquely American literary tradition, as did the tales of the early settlers from the British Isles who established homes in the southern Appalachian Mountains. These settlers retold stories that combined their local dialect with the Anglo-Saxon expressions they had brought to their new world. Richard Chase captured the essence of these tales in his collections of *The Jack Tales*, reissued in 2004. Jack's adventures are retold with a definite Appalachian mountain flavor.

THE AFRICAN TRADITIONS   African American folklore stems from the deep and rich oral traditions of the African culture. Today, children delight in Julius Lester's retelling of stories about Brer Rabbit in the *Tales of Uncle Remus*, and the adventures of Anansi, the *trickster* spider of the Ashanti people, as told by Gerald McDermott. Ashley Bryan's melodic *Beat the Story Drum, Pum-Pum*, is only one of his African American stories, while John Steptoe's *Mufaro's Beautiful Daughters*, a Caledcott Honor Book, is an exquisitely illustrated version of *Cinderella*. Virginia Hamilton, in *The People Could Fly: American Black Folktales*, retells talking-animal stories, as well as tales that include the supernatural. Renowned artists Leo and Diane Dillon, in honor of the late Virginia Hamilton, have recently retold stories selected from *The People Could Fly* in picture book format for younger children.

Although the original authors of folktales remain un-known, we are indebted to collectors like the following, who have contributed so much to children's enjoyment of traditional literature throughout the world.

Charles Perrault (1628–1703)

In 1697 Charles Perrault, a Frenchman, published *Little Red Riding Hood, Cinderella, Sleeping Beauty, Tom Thumb, Bluebeard, Puss in Boots, The Fairies,* and *Ricky of the Tuft*—eight famous tales that had never before been printed. (Mother Goose was first associated with these eight folktales.) Although he heard these tales from many sources, such as nannies and other storytellers, his interpretation was such that "he made the leap from collecting folklore to writing what has been termed the first true literature for children" (Kvilhaug, 1995, p. 516).

The Grimm Brothers: Jacob (1785–1863) and Wilhelm (1786–1859)

The Grimm brothers, in the early nineteenth century, collected and published in Germany over 200 folktales, officially entitled *Nursery and Household Tales,* but popularly known as *Grimm's Fairy Tales.* Originally assembled as a part of a scholarly history of Germany, the first edition (1812) was published without illustrations and directed at adults. A subsequent edition was published in England (1823) and illustrated by the famous artist George Cruishank. In it were such popular tales as *Hansel and Gretel, The Frog Prince, Rumpelstilskin,* and *Snow White and the Seven Dwarfs.* Although some critics considered the stories dull, uninviting, and certainly not scholarly, the tales were enthusiastically received throughout Europe and have withstood the test of time (Loer, 1995, p. 286).

Hans Christian Andersen (1805–1875)

Hans Christian Andersen, born in Denmark, was not only a collector of fairy tales but a writer of *literary fairy tales* as well. In his first collection, *Fairy Tales Told for Children* (1835), he wrote only one original tale, *Little Ida's Flowers;* the remaining stories were based on Danish folktales he had heard as a child (*The Tinder Box, Little Claus and Big Claus,* and *The Princess and the Pea*). Andersen, however, continued writing original stories and is now considered to be the most distinguished author of the *modern literary fairy tale. The Snow Queen, The Nightingale, The Steadfast Tin Soldier,* and at least 100 others originated in his creative mind rather than being drawn from oral tradition. Twenty-two of his tales, both those he created and those he retold, are included with the original nineteenth-century illustrations in the *The Stories of Hans Christian Andersen* (2004), translated from the Danish by Diana Crone Frank and Jeffrey Frank. These stories are considered "less Germanic and more Scandinavian than its predecessors, lighter, more buoyant, conveying the energy and freshness of this most peculiar author." Liz Rosenberg honors *The Stories of Hans Christian Andersen* as "our best English version yet" (Rosenberg, 2004, p. 27).

Iona (1923–) and Peter Opie (1918–1982)

Peter and Iona Opie, an English couple, wrote a definitive study of the origin and meaning of nursery rhymes in 1951 entitled *The Oxford Dictionary of Nursery Rhymes.* They have gathered early and rare children's literature into what is the most outstanding collection of its kind, containing well over 12,000 bound volumes. It is housed in the Bodleian Library in Oxford, England, the site of their original research (Opie, 1988).

It is exciting to think that the folklore of America and the world continues to be carefully translated into other languages and authentically adapted so that children of all ages and cultures can have access to them. Children learning about their own and other people's folklore is truly the beginning of their understanding of the universality of people, and marks as well the beginning of modern literature in form and theme.

Myths

Myths, unlike secular folktales, are religious in nature. They are universal and timeless stories, drawn from incidents based on the lives of supernatural beings (the gods and goddesses) that served to demonstrate how their believers should behave.

"It was an early form of psychology. The stories of gods or heroes descending into the underworld, threading through labyrinths and fighting with monsters, brought to light the mysterious workings of the psyche, showing people how to cope with their own interior crises" (Armstrong, 2005, p. 11).

Mythology continues to fascinate even early elementary school children, who find reading or listening to *King Midas and the Golden Touch*, retold by Charlotte Craft, and Aliki's *The Gods and Goddesses of Olympus*, an exciting experience. Students 9 years old and older find an unequaled source of information in Robert Graves' classic two-volume work, *The Greek Myths*, and *Macmillan's Book of Greek Gods and Heroes*, by Alice Low.

Other ancient cultures, such as China, Africa, and Scandinavia, have their own mythology. In *Gods and Goddesses: In the Daily Life of the Ancient Egyptians*, Henrietta McCall offers readers from grades 4 through 8 detailed illustrations and short descriptions of the deities that ruled Egypt and influenced the day-to-day experiences of their followers. Kevin Crossley-Holland challenged high school students in his narrative *The Norse Myths* to find connections between these characters and those in popular fantasies such as *The Lord of the Rings*.

Legends

Legends have a historical basis (often mixed with fantasy), and their settings are less distant and more realistic than those of myths. Sherwood Forest, for example, where *The Legend of Robin Hood* allegedly took place, is an actual location in England. Not only do English legends relate the adventures of human heroes with extraordinary characteristics, such as King Arthur and Robin Hood, but legends from other countries also capture children's interest. Hungarian legends about Attila the Conqueror cast their spell on the reader. Danish legends such as that of Ogier, and French legends such as the Song of Roland boast about the exploits of these national heroes.

Fables

Presumably, Aesop, the most famous fabulist, lived as a slave on the island of Samos in the sixth century BC (Lewis, 1988). His fables were translated by Caxton into English in the fifteenth century. Whether or not all fables originated with him, we know that Aesop's fables demonstrate "worldly wisdom, presence of mind, trimming one's sails to circumstance, and above all, caution. And, as in the beast legends of most cultures, cunning and guile play a prominent part" (Hunt, 1995, p. 14). His animal characters often demonstrate that they (and their readers) can get along more easily if they consider each other's abilities and do not play jokes on each other.

Another fable maker, Jean De La Fontaine, published twelve volumes of *Fables* in France between 1668 and 1694, some of which were suggested by Aesop, while others were his own work. Children continue to be entertained by his fables, especially the story of the race between the hare and the tortoise. This fable and many others can be found in a collection by Ranjit Bolt (*The Hare and the Tortoise and other Fables of La Fontaine* illustrated by Giselle Potter). Other award-winning authors such as Barbara Bader in her *Aesop & Company: Scenes from His Legendary Life* and Jerry Pinkney (*Aesop's Fables*), retell fables for children who enjoy their brevity, sly humor, and moral tone. A Spanish translation, *Little Book of Fables*, written by Veronica Tetel Uribe and attractively illustrated by Constanza Bravo, reveals the humor and moral lessons of twenty of the most famous fables of all.

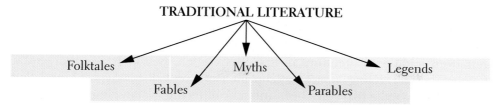

Figure 3.2   The Subgenres of Traditional Literature

Parables

A *parable* is a short, moralistic story that is similar to a fable, but it is usually religious in nature and has human characters. Since biblical days, parables have provided the basis for homilies, which teach us to tell right from wrong and good from evil. We have only to recall what happened in the parable of the sower who went out to sow his seed, to realize how significant a brief, didactic story can be: the seed sown on good ground bore fruit, but the seed sown on bad ground perished. Figure 3.2 illustrates the subgenres of traditional literature.

Modern Fantasy

Fantasy is my country. My imagination lives there . . . There's a secret garden there, and a midnight garden, a phoenix, a carpet, a cauldron and a land that can only be reached through the back of a wardrobe. There are dragons and magicians and hobbits, a great deal of music, the paintings of David and Claude and Chagall, and at night a starlit sky filled with comets and auroras. And every journey through that country is a quest.

(Cooper, 1995, p. 169)

The "midnight garden" mentioned above is a reference to *Tom's Midnight Garden* written by Phillipa Pierce. The cauldron cited by Cooper plays a significant role in Taran's quest in *The Black Cauldron, Book Two*, written by Lloyd Alexander as part of the *Prydain Chronicles*. Magic, magicians and dragons spill over into the fantasies of Ursula LeGuin's *A Wizard of Earthsea* and Robin McKinley's Newbery Medal book, *The Hero and the Crown*.

Fantasy is an extraordinary world in which readers who are willing to suspend disbelief are transported to another time and place, where they meet compelling characters who are typically on a quest that involves their readers in a struggle between good and evil. As we begin our analysis of fantasy in this chapter (and continue it in Chapters Seven to Twelve), remember that a child's interest in fantasy follows a clear developmental path that is tightly linked to a growing, symbolic maturity. In many ways, immersion in the world of fantasy illustrates Vygotsky's zone of proximal development in which children, with the help of teachers and librarians, move to higher levels of mental functioning. As memory improves, the circumstances of the story demand constant language facility. Again, we see a close tie between children's literature and cognitive development. As children develop the ability to read they move from the simple to the complex—from the easy reader to the transitional reader to the chapter book. Susan Cooper, using a simple vocabulary, draws the beginning reader into fantasy in her story of *The Magician's Boy*, in which a puppet disappears and the boy in his search meets and helps fairy tale characters.

Fantasy and Its Authors

Although fantasy writers often allude to stories from the oral tradition, fantasy differs from traditional literature in that it is written by a known author. Susan Cooper's *Dark is Rising* quintet may contain references to the *Legend of King Arthur*, and Lloyd Alexander may have been influenced by the Mabinigion (a Welch legend) in writing his *Prydain Chronicles*, but both authors are fantasy writers. Other fantasy writers include L. Frank Baum, who at the turn of the twentieth century wrote *The Wonderful Wizard of Oz*, and Lewis Carroll who wrote *Alice's Adventures in Wonderland*. Later, two friends, J. R. R. Tolkien and C. S. Lewis, both dons at Oxford University, wrote fantasies that are considered classics. The former captured and continues to engage the interest of both adults and children in the *little men who inhabit the Middle Earth* (*The Hobbit*, 1937), and the latter draws readers into a world that can be reached only through *the back of a wardrobe: The Lion, The Witch and the Wardrobe*, Book Two of *The Chronicles of Narnia* (1950).

Since J. K. Rowling's first book, *Harry Potter and the Sorcerer's Stone*, was published in 1998, this series has swept through the country and the world (over 190 million books are in print, in fifty-five languages and in 200 countries). Middle school and high school students have transferred their interest in Harry Potter to other modern fantasies written as a series, such as the complex trilogy *Dark Materials* by English author Philip Pullman, which includes the books: *The Golden Compass, The Subtle Knife*, and *The Amber Spyglass* (2000). Tamora Pierce's *The Will of the Empress* relates the adventures of Sandry and her friends, who unite to escape a trap planned by her cousin, the Empress of Wamorn. Young adults reluctantly accepted *Ptolemy's Gate* as the final volume of Jonathan Stroud's *The Bartimaeus Trilogy*, which has attracted them to the adventures of the acerbic-tongued 5,000-year-old djinn Bartimaeus, since the first volume.

Animal Fantasy (Anthropomorphism)

Very small children eagerly read and listen to fantasy. They may be at Piaget's level of preoperational cognitive development (*animism*), where they consider objects to be alive and conscious (Dacey & Travers, 2009). They readily accept the fact that the characters in Arnold Lobel's *Frog and Toad* converse like friends, and that the title characters of Leo Lionni's *Frederick* is a mouse that offers them stories to treasure. As transitional readers, they advance quickly to Avi's story about *Poppy*, the mouse heroine, and her first love, Ragweed. They continue to be intrigued by its sequel, *Poppy and Rye*, in which Poppy finds Ragweed's family in the midst of a crisis that leads to a desperate battle with some beavers.

As they grow older, children readily suspend their disbelief and accept the fact that in fantasy animals are often *anthropomorphic* (talking like people and assuming a human form or personality). Charlotte, Wilbur, and other animals in the barnyard continually chat in *Charlotte's Web* (E. B. White). In the *Redwall* series, storyteller Brian Jacques invents mice who arouse their friends to take up arms against the rats, a theme that continues in several of his books.

Why do children read fantasy? One view is that it's more satisfying because it is more intellectually demanding. Fantasy draws on the imagination of the reader. Tamora Pierce (1996), author of many fantasies, including *The Song of the Lioness* quartet and more recently *Trickster's Choice*, calls fantasy the "literature of possibilities that opens the door to the realm of WHAT IF? It challenges readers to see beyond the concrete universe and to envision other ways of living and alternative mindsets" (Pierce, 1996, p. 180).

MODERN FANTASY

Animal fantasy | Science fiction | Time travel

Figure 3.3 The Subgenres of Modern Fantasy

Science Fiction and Time Travel

Science fiction, a subgenre of fantasy, emphasizes the depiction of events that could happen. It encourages us to use our imagination and accept the unbelievable. With our increasing knowledge about space, we can suspend disbelief and read stories about life on another planet. It is also possible for us to accept what is known about DNA and imagine how it could be mishandled. The *Fourth World* by Kate Thompson is the first book in a science fiction trilogy, in which three young boys and a homeless girl, along with a sheepdog and a starling who talks, make their way across Britain into the fourth world, where they encounter strange, human-animal genetic manipulations.

FANTASY AND THE RELUCTANT READER   Time travel books are especially popular with younger children (early elementary and intermediate school). These books prove invaluable to teachers who are searching for creative ways to encourage reluctant readers to connect with their social studies. Mary Pope Osborne, in her extensive *The Magic Treehouse* series, captivates young children and draws them into many historical periods (e.g., *Viking Ships at Sunrise*). Another popular writer, Dan Gutman, author of *Babe & Me*, *Honus & Me*, and *Jackie & Me*, with the magic flip of a baseball card whisks his readers back to the time when these sports figures lived.

Jon Scieszka, known to children for *The Stinky Cheese Man*, has created a nine-book series (and recently, a television series) about *The Time Warp Trio*. In *See You Later, Gladiator*, Sam, Fred, and the Narrator find themselves in Italy, face to face with Roman gladiators. Written almost entirely in snappy dialogue, these books are especially entertaining for the reluctant, as well as the beginning, reader, because of their believable characters and lively plots. Figure 3.3 illustrates the subgenres of modern fantasy.

Poetry

It is a species of magic, the secret of which lies in the way the words lean upon each other, are linked and interlocked in sense and rhythm, and thus elicit from each other's syllables a kind of tune whose beat and melody varies subtly and which is different from that of prose.

(Cuddon, 1998, p. 678)

Poetry, with its richness, diversity, and linguistic playfulness, deserves a central role in every classroom from preschool through high school. Poetry thus becomes a vehicle for the expression and interpretation of ideas. Poetry, defined here as a genre, is discussed extensively in relation to a child's development in later chapters. Like other categories of children's literature, poetry is divided into various subcategories, including narrative, lyric, free verse, sonnet, haiku, concrete, and acrostic.

Forms of Poetry

NARRATIVE   Narrative poems are long, story telling poems, such as Longfellow's *The Midnight Ride of Paul Revere* and Ernest Lawrence Thayer's *Casey at the Bat*. Both of these have been recently illustrated by Christopher Bing and contain the literary and dramatic elements that appeal to children: an exciting setting, convincing characters, a dramatic event, and an unusual adventure presented in a unique style of illustration.

FREE VERSE   Poetry written in free verse—that is, verse free of a regular meter (also called *open form*)—is gaining in popularity, especially among middle school and high school students. Karen Hesse has written entire books in free verse, such as *Out of the Dust*, as has Virginia Euwer Wolff, who wrote *True Believer*. Children are discovering that free verse enhances their enjoyment of books as well as individual poems. Attracted initially by the apparent simplicity of each page (which contains much white space), middle school and high school students gradually become immersed in the stories these poems tell.

LYRIC   Lyric poetry includes short, expressive, non-narrative poems that are especially attractive to young children, because of their sing-song rhythm. Lyric poetry, however, is more deeply understood by older children because of their growing emotional maturity. Contemporary poets such as Barbara Esbensen (*Who Shrank My Grandmother's House?*) and Eloise Greenfield (*Honey, I Love*) are discussed later as poets who offer a goodness-of-fit for children in various developmental stages.

CONCRETE   Poetry can also be *visual* (as in concrete and acrostic poetry) with physical contours affecting the meaning of the poem. An example is the poem Karla Kuskin shaped into a tree in her collection *Any Me I Want to Be*. Another example is J. Patrick Lewis's *Doodle Dandies: Poems That Take Shape*. In this book, each of the nineteen poems is worked into a striking collage. A more scientific group of concrete poems is *Flicker Flash* by Joan Bransfield Graham, a book especially valuable for introducing the properties of light into the science curriculum. *Acrostic poems* can be easily identified, with the first letter of each line, when reading down, joining to spell a word. *Spring: An Alphabet*, by Steven Schnur, encourages children to write acrostic poems using the letters of their own names.

A WREATH FOR EMMET TILL
Cover from A WREATH FOR EMMET TILL by Marilyn Nelson, illustrated by Philippe Lardy. Jacket Painting © 2005 by Philippe Lardy. Reprinted by permission of Houghton Mifflin Company. All rights reserved.

SONNET   The sonnet consists of fourteen lines and is of three types: *Italian, Shakespearean,* and *Spenserian. The Shakspearean sonnet* is the most familiar type read by older children. A memorable example of this form of poetry is Marilyn Nelson's A *Wreath for Emmet Till*. Using the genre of the picture story book, Nelson weaves the agonizing story of a black boy's murder by white racists in 1955, into a group of fifteen interconnecting sonnets.

HAIKU   The Japanese haiku is a single-stanza, three-line lyric poem, of seventeen syllables on a single subject. Myra Cohn Livingston's collection *Cricket Never Dies* demonstrates that haiku is deceptively simple to read, but difficult for students to write.

Spin Off
Drama Enriches Poetry

Drama, a story with a plot, a setting, and characters, is written to be performed on stage and is an integral part of the poetry genre. Students can be encouraged to combine many forms of poetry into the two major categories of drama: comedy and tragedy. Choral singing, acting, pantomime, and Readers' Theatre (see Chapter Four) are a natural response to a child's love of poetry.

Narrative Poetry

Casey at the Bat works well as a choral reading, with groups arranged in an outfield formation, as suggested by Judy Freeman (2002). Wearing baseball caps and pretending to eat popcorn, the performers easily bring this narrative to life. Paul Fleishman's Newbery Medal book, *Joyful Noise: Poems for Two Voices*, is frequently presented by groups of elementary and middle school students, who alternate reading it aloud. It provides children with options of what insects they would prefer to be, and in what voice they would like to present it.

Humorous Verse

Humorous poems that can be read aloud are ideal tools to motivate your students to enjoy poetry. The children's Poet Laureate Jack Prelutsky's *A Pizza the Size of the Sun* (1996), contains so many witty poems that each member of the class can select one to read aloud.

Construct a "Laugh-o-meter" (using your imagination) to determine whose recitation is the funniest, with the most expression.

To motivate middle school and high school students to understand all forms of poetry, we recommend Paul Janeczko's *A Kick in the Head: An Everyday Guide to Poetic Forms*. It joyously leads the reader to an appreciation for all kinds of poetry.

Short poems such as "The Snowman," included in *You Read to Me, I'll Read to You: Very Short Stories to Read Together*, by Mary Ann Hoberman, are fun for primary school children to pantomime. For example:

His mouth can be an apple slice / An apple slice / Will turn to ice. / I'm getting pretty icy too / You do look icy / So do you. / Let's go inside / And get a drink / Some cocoa would be good, I think. / And while we're in / What shall we do? / You read to me. I'll read to you.

Mother Goose Rhymes, Jump Rope Songs, Lullabies, Ballads

Actually a part of the genre of traditional literature (because they have no known authors), rhymes like these are often considered poetry that groups of pre-primary and primary school children spontaneously recite. With just the slightest encouragement, children will enjoy drawing them, singing them, or acting them out.

The Language of Poetry

Poetry has its own language, and its images are employed to evoke emotion. Figures of speech, such as personification, simile, and metaphor, and figures of sound, like alliteration, assonance, and onomatopoeia, create the atmosphere the poet desires. For example, Karla Kuskin (*Any Me I Want to Be*) makes a strawberry come to life (personification): "Being a strawberry isn't all pleasing. / The morning they put me in ice cream. I'm freezing." And she makes a comparison using *like* or *as* (simile) when she warns: "All my scales are shaped like arrows. / They will hurt you if you touch". Russell Hoban in his poem *The Friendly Cinnamon Bun*, creates assonance by using the same vowel ("i") sounds in several words in the same line, "shining in his stickiness and glistening with honey," and by alliteration using ("s") as the initial consonant (Hoban, 2004, n. p.).

Along with the poetry of Jack Prelutsky and Shel Silverstein, elementary school children enjoy listening to the poetry of Douglas Florian (*Omnibeasts*) and selections from Caroline Kennedy's *A Family of Poems*. They learn the mechanics of poetry by studying the patterns of rhythm, rhyme, physical form, and the subject, but they learn to appreciate its beauty from teachers who transfer their own enthusiasm for poetry to their students.

In Sharon Creech's small book *Love That Dog*, teachers may find the magic method for introducing the poetry genre to their intermediate and middle school students. Once they have read, either independently or together, the story of Jack, the protagonist who "dislikes reading or writing poetry," but who then writes a touching poem about his dog, both students and Jack become "hooked" on poetry. Creech also refers to poems by Robert Frost, Valerie Worth, and Walter Dean Myers in order to capture the students' attention. By using Creech's book, you, too, may subtly introduce your students to poets to whom they can relate. This book may also motivate the most reluctant readers to write poetry themselves.

Figure 3.4   Kinds of poetry

Middle school students who read English and those who read Spanish are drawn together by Francisco X. Alarcon's *Poems to Dream Together*. Teenagers also relate to the poetry of contemporary writers such as Paul Janeczko, who has successfully written and collected many poems that deal with adolescence, and Nikki Grimes, a prolific author and poet who skillfully juggles the thoughts, feelings, and questions of eighteen Bronx high school students in *Bronx Masquerade* (2002) as they read aloud their poems at an Open Mike Night.

Contemporary Realistic Fiction

Real stories that could happen here and now are categorized as *contemporary realistic fiction*. The author attempts to weave a story based on believable characters, a plausible plot, and a recognizable setting so that young readers, who may not have experienced what the book's characters are experiencing, can vicariously live through the story's characters while they read.

In Katherine Paterson's novel *The Same Stuff as Stars*, for example, 11-year-old Angel recognizes her mother's alcohol problem, accepts the fact that her father is imprisoned, and realizes her mother has abandoned her and her little brother. When, however, her younger brother is "kidnapped" from elementary school in the Vermont town where they are forced to live with their great-grandmother, Angel's resiliency wavers. She is no longer emotionally in control of herself, her great-grandmother, or her little brother. Only when she receives help from a kind librarian, and strength from an amateur astronomer who lives in a trailer on her great-grandmother's land, does she regain her former self-assurance that her brother calls her "bossiness."

Themes of Contemporary Realistic Fiction

Although reality in its harshest dimensions is often portrayed in the genre of contemporary realistic fiction, the themes of kindness and generosity, as well as humor and love, continue to permeate children's fiction. Lois Lowry's *Gooney Bird Greene*, for example, is written with the same warmth and entertaining style that Beverly

Cleary develops in her books, such as *Ramona's World*. Even though Cynthia Rylant's Newbery Award book, *Missing May*, concerns the impact of May's death on her family, it is also laced with humor. Brian Robertson's struggle to survive when the small plane he is in crashes in the wilderness is the plot of Gary Paulsen's *Hatchet*, but it is his personal endurance and his ability to face the fact of his parents' divorce that are most admired. The complications and ramifications of being handicapped are expressed in Jack Gantos' series about Joey, where Joey elicits the sympathy of the reader as he wrestles with his ADHD. Young readers may choose among a wide variety of contemporary fiction, ranging from books about animals, mysteries, sports, school, family, and adventure (all of which we discuss at length in later chapters), that will bring them enjoyment and satisfaction.

Then and Now

Series Books Finally Accepted

In the past, librarians reluctantly accepted series books (such as *Nancy Drew*) in their libraries, and teachers often found them unacceptable for book reports. Series books such as the *Babysitter* and *Sweet Valley High* were distinguished "more by their numbers than the writing" (Yolen, 1993, p. 14). Considered as a group, series were easily identified by their predictable plots and one-dimensional characters. Whatever the Stratemeyer Syndicate produced (e.g., *Nancy Drew, The Bobbsey Twins, The Hardy Boys*, etc.) were scorned because they lacked real authorship. And yes, series were also accused—sometimes rightly—of being racist.

Today, however, teachers and librarians agree that books in a series succeed not only in engaging the reluctant reader, but also the avid reader at various developmental levels. From Barbara Park's *Junie B., First Grader*, to Mary Pope Osborne's *The Magic Treehouse*, Brian Jacques' *Redwall*, Lemony Snicket's *A Series of Unfortunate Events*, and Ann Brashares' *The Sisterhood of the Traveling Pants*, children and young adults are reading series books from preschool through high school and beyond. They gain self-assurance by becoming familiar with the characters and anticipating the plots and themes that relate to their personal interests. Teachers and librarians may prefer that students not limit their reading to books in a series. Yet series by authors such as Cynthia Rylant (*Henry and Mudge*) and Kate DiCamillo (*Mercy Watson*) are well written and offer beginning readers episodic stories that they need at this level. Author Hilary McKay's fans are children in the intermediate and middle school range, who eagerly anticipate each adventure of the Casson family. (*Caddy Ever After*, the fourth book in this series, is comparable to enduring family stories from other times.)

Today, some librarians "place paperback series on standing order" (Barstow, 1999, Foreword) to anticipate their readers' requests. Adults, however, who are responsible for selecting and purchasing a specific se-

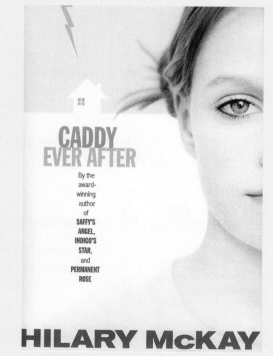

CADDY EVER AFTER
Getty Images

ries should be aware of the quality and literary elements of each book in the series. (See Chapter Four for a discussion of literary elements.)

Often children purchase their favorite paperback series and then trade books with their friends, much like their grandparents may have done with the Nancy Drew series. As they exchange ideas about their books, they unwittingly practice what Vygotsky would call "social interaction." Although some series books may be unable to withstand the test of time, others satisfy the needs and interests of many children, and often lead children to more thought-provoking literature.

DIVERSE CULTURES Contemporary realistic fiction includes novels about the experiences of children from diverse backgrounds, and will be discussed in greater depth in Chapter Six. As we know from the history of children's literature (see Chapter Two), African Americans were stereotyped in early children's literature until the civil rights activism of the 1960s. The Coretta Scott King Awards of the 1970s have made us more aware of books written by African Americans, who make an outstanding contribution to children's literature. Authors who have been honored include Mildred Taylor (*The Friendship*), Walter Dean Myers (*Fallen Angels*), Virginia Hamilton (*Sweet Whispers, Brother Rush*), and Christopher Paul Curtis (*Bud, Not Buddy*).

Fortunately, children from other cultures also recognize themselves and their experiences in contemporary fiction. Recent writers, including Carolyn Marsden, who wrote *The Gold-Threaded Dress*, about Oy, a little girl from Thailand and her experiences in an American school, and Candace Fleming, who wrote *Lowji Discovers America*, the sometimes touching and often humorous story of Lowji, an Indian boy who, on his arrival in Hamlet, Illinois, encounters an obnoxious landlady, a mysterious stranger, and a pig named Blossom. Authors like these write novels that portray their characters honestly, without resorting to stereotype.

THE SHORT STORY AS LITERATURE Another solution to a student's reluctance to read a whole book is the short story. Short story collections especially written for middle school and high school readers are proliferating. Chris Crutcher's *Athletic Shorts: Six Short Stories*, Gary Soto's short stories (including *Local News*, thirteen stories about the trials and tribulations of Latino children), and Graham Salisbury's *Island Boyz* about Hawaiian boys and girls, are an engrossing goodness-of-fit for adolescents who seek the personal satisfaction of reading a "good book."

Historical Fiction

Historical fiction has been a popular genre for students since Sir Walter Scott's *Ivanhoe* was published in the nineteenth century. Children find historical fiction adventurous, exciting, and a wonderful introduction to experiences they only can dream about.

Defining Historical Fiction

What is historical fiction? The answer is arbitrary. More than likely, if you asked senior citizens, they would give you a different answer than would children in elementary or middle school, for whom yesterday is history. For our purposes, we place historical fiction in any period of history through the Vietnam War. Whether the novel is set in ancient times (Julius Lester's *Pharaoh's Daughter*), medieval times (Karen Cushman's *The Midwife's Apprentice*), or more recent times, such as the American Revolutionary War (Esther Forbes' *Johnny Tremain*) or the American Civil War (Patricia Polacco's *Pink and Say*) characters, fictional or factual, must be convincing.

The setting has to be accurate and integrated into the plot. The historical novelist must make not only the setting but also the events and sensibilities of that place as true to the period as possible. Katherine Paterson, author of many historical novels, including *Lyddie*, noted that the author "must create living characters and tell a story about them that really might have happened to people who lived in that world" (Paterson, 1996, p. 347). Below are examples of outstanding novelists whose works we discuss here and in later chapters.

Scott O'Dell, a well-known historical fiction writer, has pioneered the skill of writing with sensitivity and understanding about the settlement of the West and the diaspora of Native Americans. In *Sing Down the Moon* he makes his readers aware of the displacement of the Navajos. Mildred Taylor's focus is the African American family. *Roll of Thunder, Hear My Cry* is her classic story about the Logans, an African American family who endured harrowing experiences during the 1930s. Episodes of their lives continue in the books *Let the Circle Be Unbroken, The Road to Memphis,* and *The Land.* Karen Cushman, in the context of medieval times, creates stories as if the reader were there and the characters were real. Her feminine characters in stories such as *The Midwife's Apprentice* and *Catherine Called Birdy* may be more liberated than those times would suggest, but they are exciting, resourceful, and accomplished.

Exploring History

An author of historical fiction must explore history, as Patricia MacLachan does in *Sarah, Plain and Tall,* but without exploiting it. Her story of Sarah is the short, sensitive story of a young woman who left her home to help children preserve theirs. The ability of the author to create a story that comes to life for the reader is important. Very young children may find it difficult to fully grasp the significance of a historical moment because of their lack of experience. But, they find picture books and easy readers more meaningful and a pleasure to read when the teacher or librarian offers them a short explanation before they begin the story.

Marie McSwigan's World War II story *Snow Treasure* became historical fiction, but at the time it was written (1940s) it was contemporary fiction. Most stories, however, are deliberately written about the past and require extensive research to make them authentic. A recent story about World War II is Dean Hughes' historical novel *Soldier Boys,* in which two young boys prepare for war, but from opposing sides. One is a 16-year-old Mormon from Utah, who is learning to be a paratrooper. The other is a 15-year-old who is promoted from the Hitler Youth into the German army. Their wartime encounter on a mountaintop in Germany is a tragic metaphor on what war is all about.

Historical Fiction Across the Curriculum

Historical fiction plays a major role in motivating students to understand and appreciate their study of history, social studies, and current events. By reflecting on grim events in *Out of the Dust,* Karen Hesse's Newbery Award book, students more keenly realize the tragedy of the Great Depression. They become more aware of the Japanese internment during World War II, when they read historical fiction such as Cynthia Kadohata's *Weedflower,* which empathizes with Sumiko, who is only 12 years old when she and her family are forced to live in a Japanese internment camp in Poston, Arizona. Allen Say's *Home of the Brave* teaches readers that over 120,000 Japanese Americans were interned in ten camps in six western states (Say, 2002). Historical fiction often helps readers become more sensitive to injustices endured through the years, while helping them sympathize with those who have been affected.

Biography, Autobiography, Memoir

At that time (1964) the biography market for young readers was dominated by the Landmark series, books replete with invented dialogue and undocumented incidents and designed largely to inspire patriotism, good character and hard work.

(Saul, 2001, p. 433)

Although invented dialogue and undocumented incidents were prevalent in many earlier biographies written for children, they are now generally considered unacceptable standards of good biography. Russell Freedman's biographies *Franklin Delano Roosevelt* and the Newbery Award book *Abraham Lincoln*, for example, contain extensive bibliographies, maps, and actual photography. He continues to be accurate and authentic in his recent outstanding biography, *The Voice That Challenged a Nation: Marian Anderson and the Struggle for Equal Rights*. Carefully selected photographs, appended source notes, a bibliography, and a discography thoroughly document his research. Children reading his books develop a sense of historical accuracy as they become captivated with the story. Marc Aronson, nonfiction winner of the Boston Globe–Horn Book Award for *Sir Walter Ralegh and the Quest for El Dorado*, exhorts authors of nonfiction "to experiment, take risks, try out all sorts of new narrative forms—none of which require any kind of invented dialogue or made-up interior dialogues with new narrative forms" (Aronson, 2001, p. 52).

Through reading biography, children learn about prominent figures from all walks of life. They may also be influenced by Bandura's theory of modeling and the important role it plays in their development. (See Chapter One.) By introducing your students to stories about musicians such as, for example, Mordicai Gerstein's *What Charlie Heard*, the life story of Charles Ives, or Andrea Davis Pinkney's, *Ella Fitzgerald: The Tale of a Vocal Virtuosa*, or Elizabeth Partridge's *This Land Was Made for You and Me: The Life and Songs of Woody Guthrie*, you may be fostering a child's musical career. The life stories of musicians is only one area that the biography genre encompasses.

Types of Biographies

Included in the biography genre are the autobiography and memoir. An *autobiography* is an account of the life (or excerpts from the life) of the person who is telling the story. The author and illustrator, Tomie de Paola, for instance, has completed *What a Year*, the third book about his childhood on 26 Fairmont Avenue. His first-person narrative for young readers contains details that are concrete and humorous, qualities that ensure it will be well remembered. For older readers, a *memoir* such as Lois Lowry's *Looking Back* is similar to an autobiography in that it is a book of her memories, some of which are painful to remember, such as the deaths of her son and her sister.

The Informational Book

Children want to read nonfiction, informational books not only for the facts they convey, but for the manner in which the author conveys them. (We discuss informational books—nonfiction—throughout this text.) Jane Goodall's *The Chimpanzees I Love: Saving Their World and Ours* is a good example. Not only does Goodall describe in detail the chimpanzees and their behavior, but her affection for them is clearly evident from the photographs she took at the Gombe National Park. David Macaulay's books, such as *The Way Things Work* and *Mosque*, are filled with facts and pen and ink sketches. Children turning the pages of these books not only become informed, but may also be inspired.

A book that conveys information is strengthened by bibliographical additions such as an index, a glossary, a timeline, and documentation that verifies its contents. The structure of an informational book, whether enumerative, sequential, chronological, or comparative, demands that it be accurate, well organized, appropriately and attractively designed, and clearly written. Susan Campbell Bartoletti's *Hitler Youth: Growing Up in Hitler's Shadow*, written for middle school students about what it was like to live in Germany during World War II, fulfills these requirements. *The Journey That Saved Curious George: The True Wartime Escape of Margaret and H. A. Rey*, written by Louise Borden for middle school students, has a similar setting but a less complex plot. Yet it, too, is an excellent informational book. Betty Carter (2000) used nonfiction as an example of how books and the Internet differ in the way they present information. While the Internet offers needed, specific information, usually in response to a specific question, informational books have a much wider range. Outstanding informational books encourage readers to think, solve problems, and engage in creative exploration. Consequently, as Carter (2000, p. 707) noted, nonfiction will survive the impact of the Internet, but will experience inevitable change. For children who have easy access to the Internet, a book must offer them information far more attractive, more reliable, and more geared to their developmental stage, than what they may discover on the computer.

Informational Books for the Early Elementary School Student

Young children seek informational books that are accurate, attractively illustrated, and easy to read. Children who are developmentally attuned to asking questions, seeking information, and becoming more curious about the world around them are amazed and excited by how much they discover in books such as Steven Jenkins' *Actual* Size, in which the sizes and weights of various animals and parts of animals are illustrated. Deborah Chandra and Madeleine Connors's *George Washington's Teeth*, and Katherine Gibbs Davis's *The Wackiest White House Pets* (from a grizzly bear to an alligator) hold them spellbound. As Betty Carter writes, "adults who are concerned with children and their reading, owe young readers and listeners opportunities to feed that non-fiction habit rather than relegate it to the Internet—or ignore it altogether" (Carter, 2000, p. 699).

Chapter Checklist

Read the following items carefully. If you have difficulty responding to any of them, return to the chapter to review the material.

After reading this chapter, you can

1. Explain the powerful role of genres in children's literature.

2. Identify the genres discussed in *Children's Literature: A Developmental Perspective*.

3. Specify the link between the use of genres and the development of thinking skills.

4. Explain the meaning of a picture book's deceptive simplicity.

5. Demonstrate how traditional literature reflects a culture's tradition.

6. Illustrate how poetry creates different moods while using the same language as prose.

7. Explain why the Harry Potter stories are so popular.

8. Specify how contemporary realistic fiction differs from historical fiction.

Children's Bibliography

Aardema, Verna. (1975). *Why Mosquitoes Buzz in People's Ears.* (Illus. Leo & Diane Dillon). New York: Dial.

Alarcon, Francisco X. (2005). *Poems to Dream, Together/Poemas ara sonar juntos.* New York: Lee and Low.

Alexander, Lloyd. (1965). *The Black Cauldron.* New York: Holt

Aliki. (1994). *The Gods and Goddesses of Olympus.* New York: HarperCollins.

Aronson, Marc. (2000). *Sir Walter Ralegh and the Quest for El Dorado.* New York: Clarion Books.

Avi. (1995). *Poppy.* New York: Orchard Books.

Bader, Barbara. (1991). *Aesop & Company: with Scenes from His Legendary Life.* Boston: Houghton Mifflin.

Bang, Molly. (1983). *Ten, Nine, Eight.* New York: Greenwillow.

Bartoletti, Susan Campbell. (2005). *Hitler Youth: Growing Up in Hitler's Shadow.* New York: Scholastic.

Base, Graeme. (1986). *Animalia.* New York: Harry N. Abrams.

Baum, L. Frank. (1900). *The Wonderful Wizard of Oz.* New York: Morrow.

Bemelmans, Ludwig. (1939) *Madeline.* New York: Viking Press.

Bolt, Ranjit. (2006). *The Hare and the Tortoise and other Fables of La Fontaine.* Cambridge, MA: Barefoot Books.

Borden, Louise. (2005). *The Journey That Saved Curious George: The True Wartime Escape of Margaret and H. A. Rey.* Boston: Houghton Mifflin.

Brashares, Ann. (2001). *The Sisterhood of the Traveling Pants.* New York: Laurel Leaf Books.

Brett, Jan. (2005). *Honey . . . Honey. . . Lion!* New York: Penguin Putnam.

Brown, Don. (2004). *Odd Boy Out: Young Albert Einstein.* Boston: Houghton Mifflin.

Browne, Anthony. (1998). *Voices in the Park.* New York: DK Publishing.

Bruchac, Joseph. (1995). *Gluskabe and the Four Wishes.* New York: Penguin.

Bryan, Ashley. (1980). *Beat the Story Drum, Pum-Pum.* New York: Atheneum.

Burton, Virginia Lee. (1942) *The Little House.* Boston: Houghton Mifflin.

Caldecott, Randolph. (1941). "The Diverting History of John Gilpin". In *R. Caldecott's Picture Books.* London: Frederick Warne.

Carle, Eric. (1990) *The Very Quiet Cricket.* New York: Philomel.

Carroll, Lewis (1965). *Alice's Adventures in Wonderland.* New York: Puffin.

Catalanotto, Peter. (2002). *Matthew A.B.C.* New York: Atheneum.

Chandra, Deborah, & Connors, Madeleine (2004). *George Washington's Teeth.* New York: Farrar, Straus, & Giroux.

Chase, Richard. (2004). *Jack Tales.* Boston: Houghton Mifflin.

Cleary, Beverly (1999). *Ramona's World.* New York: HarperCollins.

Cooper, Susan. (1973). *The Dark Is Rising.* New York: Aladdin.

Cooper, Susan. (2005). *The Magician's Boy.* New York: Margaret McElderry.

Cousins, Lucy. (1997). *Count with Maisy.* Cambridge. MA: Candlewick.

Craft, Charlotte. (1999). *King Midas and the Golden Touch.* New York: Morrow.

Creech, Sharon. (2001). *Love That Dog.* New York: Harper-Collin.

Crutcher, Chris. (1991). *Athletic Shorts: Six Short Stories.* New York: Greenwillow.

Curtis, Christopher Paul. (1999). *Bud, Not Buddy.* New York: Delacorte.

Cushman, Karen. (1994). *Catherine Called Birdy.* New York: Clarion.

Cushman, Karen. (1995). *The Midwife's Apprentice.* New York: Clarion.

Davis, Katherine Gibbs. (2004). *Wackiest White House Pets.* New York: Scholastic.

De Brunhoff, Jean. (1933). *The Story of Babar.* New York: Random House.

de Paola, Tomie. (1999). *26 Fairmount Avenue.* New York: G. P. Putnam's Sons.

de Paola, Tomie. (2002). *What a Year.* New York: Putnam.

DiCamillo, Kate. (2005). *Mercy Watson to the Rescue.* Cambridge, MA: Candlewick.

Donaldson, Julia. (2006). *One Ted Falls Out of Bed.* New York: Holt.

Edens, Cooper, ed. (2004). *Princess Stories: A Classic Illustrated Edition.* New York: Chronicle.

Ehlert, Lois. (1992). *Fish Eyes: A Book You Can Count On.* New York: Harcourt Brace.

Esbensen, Barbara. (1992). *Who Shrank My Grandmother's House?* New York: HarperCollins.

Falconer, Ian. (2002). *Olivia Counts.* New York: Atheneum.

Falconer, Ian, (2002). *Olivia's Opposites.* New York: Atheneum.

Fleming, Candace. (2005). *Lowji Discovers America.* New York: Atheneum.

Fleming, Denise. (2002). *Alphabet Under Construction.* New York: Holt.

Fleischman, Paul. (1988). *Joyful Noise: Poems for Two Voices.* New York: Harper & Row.

Florian, Douglas. (2004). *Omnibeasts.* New York: Harcourt.

Forbes, Esther. (1943). *Johnny Tremain.* Boston: Houghton Mifflin.

Fox, Mem. (2002). *The Magic Hat.* New York: Harcourt.

Frank, Diana Crone, & Frank Jeffrey trans. (2004). *The Stories of Hans Christian Andersen.* Boston: Houghton Mifflin.

Freedman, Russell. (1987). *Lincoln: A Photobiography.* New York: Clarion.

Freedman, Russell. (1990). *Franklin Delano Roosevelt.* Boston: Little, Brown.

Freedman, Russell (2001). *In The Days of the Vaqueros: American's First Cowboys.* New York: Clarion.

Freedman, Russell. (2004). *The Voice That Challenged a Nation: Marian Anderson and the Struggle for Equal Rights.* New York: Clarion.

Fritz, Jean. (1973). *And Then What Happened, Paul Revere?* New York: Coward.

Funke, Cornelia. (2004). *Dragon Rider.* New York: Scholastic.

Gantos, Jack. (1998). *Joey Pigza Swallowed the Key.* New York: HarperCollins.

Gerstein, Mordicai. (2002). *What Charlie Heard*. New York: Farrar/Foster.

Goble, Paul. (2001). *The Girl Who Loved Wild Horses*. New York: Atheneum.

Goodall, Jane. (2001). *The Chimpanzees I Love: Saving Their World and Ours*. New York: Scholastic.

Graham, Joan Bransfield. (1999). *Flicker Flash*. Boston: Houghton Mifflin.

Grimm Brothers. (2004). *The Annotated Brothers Grimm*. New York: W. W. Norton.

Gutman, Dan. (1997). *Honus and Me*. New York: Harper.

Gutman, Dan. (1999). *Jackie and Me*. New York: Avon.

Gutman, Dan. (2000). *Babe and Me*. New York: Avon Books.

Hamilton, Martha, & Weis, Mitch. (2000). *Noodlehead Stories*. Little Rock, AR: August House.

Hamilton, Virginia. (1982). *Sweet Whispers, Brother Rush*. New York: Philomel.

Hamilton, Virginia. (1985). *The People Could Fly: African American Folktales*. New York: Knopf.

Hamilton, Virgina. Leo & Diane Dillon, illus. (2004). *The People Could Fly. The Picture Book*. New York: Knopf.

Hesse, Karen. (1997). *Out of the Dust*. New York: Scholastic.

Hoban, Russell. (2004). "The Friendly Cinnamon Bun." In Neil Philip ed. *Hot Potato*. New York: Clarion.

Hoberman, Mary Ann. (2001). *You Read to Me, I'll Read to You*. Boston: Houghton Mifflin.

Hughes, Dean. (2001). *Soldier Boys*. New York: Atheneum.

Hutchins, Pat. (1971). *Changes, Changes*. New York: Macmillan.

Jacques, Brian. (1987). *Redwall*. New York: Philomel.

Jacques, Brian. (2001). *Castaways of the Flying Dutchman*. New York: Philomel.

Jenkins, Alvin. (2004). *Next Stop Neptune*. Boston: Houghton Mifflin.

Jenkins, Steve. (1998). *Hottest Coldest Highest Deepest*. Boston: Houghton Mifflin.

Janeczko, Paul B. sel. (2005). *A Kick in the Head: An Everyday Guide to Poetic Forms*. Cambridge, MA: Candlewick.

Kadohata, Cynthia. (2006). *Weedflower*. New York: Atheneum.

Kalman, Maira. (2002). *Fireboat: The Heroic Adventures of the John J. Harvey*. New York: Putnam.

Kellogg, Steven. (1984). *Paul Bunyan*. New York: Morrow Junior Books.

Kellogg, Steven. (1986). *Pecos Bill*. New York: Wm. Morrow Co.

Kennedy, Caroline. (2005). *A Family of Poems*. New York: Hyperion.

Kerrod, Robin. (2001). *Exploring the Universe*. New York: Raintree.

Kuskin, Karla. (1972). *Any Me I Want to Be*. New York: Harper & Row.

Le Guin, Ursula. (1968). *A Wizard of Earthsea*. New York: Parnassus Press.

Lehman, Barbara. (2006). *Museum Trip*. Boston: Houghton Mifflin.

Lester, Julius. (1987). *Tales of Uncle Remus: The Adventures of Brer Rabbit*. New York: Dial.

Lester, Julius. (1989). *How Many Spots Does a Leopard Have: And other Tales?* New York: Scholastic.

Lester, Julius. (1994). *John Henry*. New York: Dial.

Lester, Julius. (2000). *Pharaoh's Daughter*. San Diego: Harcourt.

Lewis, C. S. (1950) *The Chronicles of Narnia*. New York: Macmillan.

Lewis, J. Patrick. (1998). *Doodle Dandies: Poems That Take Shape*. New York: Atheneum.

Lewis, Naomi. (1988). *Cry Wolf and Other Aesop's Fables*. New York: Oxford University Press.

Lionni, Leo. (1967). *Frederick*. New York: Pantheon.

Livingston, Myra Cohn. (1997). *Cricket Never Dies: A Collection of Haiku and Tanka*. New York: Simon & Schuster.

Lobel, Arnold. (1972). *Frog and Toad Together*. New York: HarperCollins.

Longfellow, Henry Wadsworth. (2001). *The Midnight Ride of Paul Revere*. Christopher Bing, illus. New York: Handprint.

Low, Alice. (1985). *The Macmillan Book of Greek Gods and Heroes*. New York: Macmillan.

Lowry, Lois. (1989). *Number the Stars*. Boston: Houghton Mifflin.

Lowry, Lois. (1993) *The Giver*. Boston: Houghton Mifflin.

Lowry, Lois. (1998). *Looking Back*. Boston: Houghton Mifflin.

Lowry, Lois. (2002). *Gooney Bird Greene*. Boston: Houghton Mifflin.

Macaulay, David. (1990). *Black and White*. Boston: Houghton Mifflin.

Macaulay, David. (1988). *The Way Things Work*. Boston: Houghton.

Macaulay, David. (2003). *Mosque*. Boston: Houghton Mifflin.

MacLachan, Patricia. (1985). *Sarah, Plain and Tall*. New York: Harper.

Marsden, Carolyn. (2002). *The Gold-Threaded Dress*. Cambridge, MA: Candlewick.

McCord, David. (1977). *One At a Time: Collected Poems for the Young*. Boston: Little, Brown.

McKay, Hilary. (2006). *Candy Ever After*. New York: Margaret McElderry.

McDermott, Gerald. (1973). *Anansi the Spider: A Tale from the Ashanti*. New York: Holt.

McKinley, Robin. (1984). *The Hero and the Crown*. New York: Greenwillow.

McSwigan, Marie. (1942/1958) *Snow Treasure*. New York: Scholastic.

Myers, Walter Dean. (1988). *Fallen Angels*. New York: Scholastic.

Nelson, Marilyn. (2005). *A Wreath for Emmett Till*. Boston: Houghton Mifflin.

O'Dell, Scott. (1970). *Sing Down the Moon*. Boston: Houghton Mifflin.

Opie, Iona. (1984). *Oxford Book of Children's Verse*. New York: Oxford University Press.

Osborne, Mary Pope. (1998). *Viking Ships at Sunrise*. Magic Treehouse series. New York: Random House.

Osborne, Mary Pope. (2000). *Kate and the Beanstalk*. New York: Atheneum Books.

Park, Barbara. (2007). *Junie B., First Grader: Aloha-Ha-Ha!*. New York: Random House.

Partridge, Elizabeth. (2002). *This Land Was Made for You and Me: The Life and Songs of Woody Guthrie*. New York: Viking.

Paterson, Katherine. (1991). *Lyddie*. New York: Dutton.

Paterson, Katherine. (2002). *The Same Stuff as Stars*. New York: Clarion.

Paulsen, Gary. (1987). *Hatchet*. New York: Bradbury Press.

Peet, Bill. (1984). *Pamela Camel*. Boston: Houghton Mifflin.

Perkins, Lynne Rae. (2005). Criss Cross. New York: Greenwillow.

Pierce, Phillipa. (1958). *Tom's Midnight Garden*. New York: HarperCollins.

Pierce, Tamora. (2003). *Trickster's Choice*. New York: Random House.

Pierce, Tamora. (2005). *The Will of the Express*. New York: Scholastic.

Pinkney, Andrea Davis. (2002). *Ella Fitzgerald: The Tale of a Vocal Virtuosa*. Brian Pinkney, illus. New York: Hyperion.

Pinkney, Jerry. (2000). *Aesop's Fables*. New York: Seastar.

Polacco, Patricia. (1994). *Pink and Say*. New York: Philomel.

Prelutsky, Jack. (1996). *A Pizza the Size of the Sun*. New York: Greenwillow.

Prelutsky, Jack. (2002). *The Frogs Wore Red Suspenders*. New York: Greenwillow.

Pullman, Philip. (1996). *The Golden Compass*. New York: Random House.

Pullman, Philip. (1997). *The Subtle Knife*. New York: Random House.

Pullman, Philip. (2000). *Amber Spyglass*. New York: Alfred Knopf.

Rackham, Arthur. (2001). *Grimm's Fairy Tales*. New York: Seastar.

Raschka, Chris. (2006). *Five for a Little One*. New York: Atheneum.

Rinaldi, Ann, (1993). *The Fifth of March*. New York: Harcourt.

Rowling, J. R. (1998). *Harry Potter and the Sorcerer's Stone*. New York: Scholastic.

Ryan, Pam Munoz. (2002). *When Marian Sang*. New York: Scholastic.

Rylant, Cynthia. (1992). *Missing May*. New York: Orchard Books.

Rylant, Cynthia. (2006). *Henry and Mudge and the Big Sleep-over*. New York: Simon & Schuster.

Sabuda, Robert, & Reinhart, Matthew. (2005). *Dinosaurs: Encyclopedia Prehistorica*. Cambridge, MA: Candlewick.

Salisbury, Graham. (2002). *Island Boyz*. New York: Random House.

Say, Allen. (2002). *Home of the Brave*. Boston: Houghton Mifflin.

Schnur, Steven. (1999). *Spring: An Alphabet Acrostic*. New York: Clarion.

Sciezka, Jon. (1989). *The True Story of the 3 Little Pigs*. New York: Viking.

Scieszka, Jon. (2000). *See You Later, Gladiator*. New York: Viking.

Sendak, Maurice. (1963). *Where the Wild Things Are*. New York: Harper Collins.

Silverstein, Shel. (1974). *Where the Sidewalk Ends*. New York: HarperCollins.

Snicket, Lemony. (1999). *The Bad Beginning*. New York: HarperCollins.

Soto, Gary. (1993). *Local News*. New York: Scholastic.

Spires, Elizabeth. (2001). *I Am Arachne*. New York: Foster Books.

Steptoe, John. (1987). *Mufaro's Beautiful Daughters: An African Tale*. New York HarperCollins.

Stroud, Jonathan. (2006). *Ptolemy's Gate*. New York: Hyperion.

Taylor, Mildred. (1976). *Roll of Thunder, Hear My Cry*. New York: Dial.

Taylor, Mildred. (1981). *Let the Circle Be Unbroken*. New York: Dial.

Taylor, Midred. (1987). *The Friendship*. New York: Dial.

Taylor, Mildred. (1990). *The Road to Memphis*. New York: Dial.

Taylor, Mildred. (2001). *The Land*. New York: Phyllis Fogelman Books.

Thayer, Ernest Lawrence. (2000). *Casey at the Bat: A Ballad of the Republic Sung in the Year 1888*. Christopher Bing, illus. New York: Handprint.

Thompson, Kate. (2005). *Fourth World*. New York: Bloomsbury.

Tolkien, J. R. R. (1937). *The Hobbit*. Boston: Houghton Mifflin.

Uribe, Veronica Tetel. (2004). *Little Book of Fables*. Susan Ouriou, trans. Toronto: Douglas & McIntyre.

Waber, Bernard. (1972). *Ira Sleeps Over*. Boston: Houghton Mifflin.

Vanderwarker, Peter. (1982). *Boston Then and Now: 59 Boston Sites Photographed in the Past and Present*. New York: Dover.

Wells, Rosemary. (2006). *Max's ABC*. New York: Viking.

White, E. B. (1952). *Charlotte's Web*. New York: HarperCollins.

Wiesner, David. (1991). *Tuesday*. New York: Clarion Books.

Wiesner, David. (2006). *Flotsam*. New York: Clarion.

Wiesner, David. (2001). *The Three Pigs*. New York: Clarion.

Williams, Garth. (2005). *Animal ABC*. New York: Golden.

Wisniewski, David. (1992). *Sundiata*. New York: Clarion Books.

Wolff, Euwer Virginia. (2001). *The True Believer*. New York: Atheneum.

Zelinsky, Paul O. (1990). *The Wheels on the Bus*. New York: Dutton.

Professional References

Armstrong, Karen. (2005). *A Short History of Myth*. Edinborough: Canongate.

Aronson, Marc. (2001). "Fanfare 2001. The Horn Book Honor List." *The Horn Book* January/February, 49–50.

Barr, Catherine, ed. (1999). *Reading in Series*. Westport, CT: Libraries Unlimited Bowker.

Barstow, Barbara. (1999). "Foreword." In *Reading in Series*. Mew Providence, NJ.

Beckett, Sheila. (2001). "Parodic Play with Paintings in Picture Books". In J. Pfeiffer & E. Keyser, eds. *Children's Literature*. Vol. 29. New Haven CT: Yale University Press.

Beram, Neill. (2004). "The Beaten Path." *The Horn Book*. January/February, 53–59.

Bjorklund, David. (2005). *Children's Thinking*. Belmont, CA: Wadsworth.

Bloom, L. (2000). "Language Acquisition in Its Developmental Context." In W. Damon (series ed.), D. Kuhn & R. Siegler (volume eds.): *Handbook of Child Psychology: Volume 2: Cognition, Perception, and Language*. New York: Wiley.

Butler, C. (2002). *Postmodernism*. London: Oxford University Press.

Carter, Betty. (2000). "A Universe of Information: The Future of Nonfiction". *The Horn Book*. November/December, 697–707.

Conway, L. (1996). Boston: The Way It Was. Boston: WGBH.

Cooper, Susan. (1995). "Voices of the Creators." In Anita Silvey, ed. *Children's Books and Their Creators*. Boston: Houghton Mifflin.

Cuddon, J. A. (Rev. Preston C. E.). (1998). *Literary Terms and Literary Theory*. London: Penguin.

Dacey, John & Travers, John. (2009). *Human Development Across the Lifespan*. New York: McGraw-Hill.

Dukes, Carol Muske. (2002). "A Lost Eloquence." (op-ed). *New York Times*. December 29, 2002.

Eisenberg, Nancy. (1998). "Introduction." In W. Damon (series ed.), D. Kuhn & R. Siegler (volume eds.). *Handbook of Child Psychology Volume 3: Socioemotional, and Personality Development*. New York: Wiley.

Freeman, Judy. (2002). *What's New in Children's Literature*. Bellevue, WA: Bureau of Education and Research.

Greenlaw, M. Jean. (1995). "Science Fiction." In Anita Silvey (ed.). *Children's Books and Their Creators*. Boston: Houghton Mifflin.

Hunt, Peter (ed.). (1995) *Children's Literature: An Illustrated History*. New York: Oxford University Press.

Kellman, P. & Banks, M. (1998). "Infant Visual Perception". In W. Damon (series ed.) & D. Kuhn & R. Siegler (volume eds.), *Handbook of Child Psychology; Volume 4: Child Psychology in Practice*. New York: John Wiley.

Kvilhaugh, S. (1995). Perrault, Charles. In Anita Silvey (ed.). *Children's Books and Their Creators*. Boston: Houghton Mifflin.

Lewis, David. (1996). "The Constructedness of Texts: Picture Books and the Metafictive." In S. Egoff (ed.). *Only Connect*. New York: Oxford University Press.

Loer, Stephanie. (1995). "Mother Goose." In Anita Silvey (ed.). *Children's Books and Their Creators*. Boston: Houghton Mifflin.

Lowry, Lois. (2002). "The Remembered Gates and the Unopened Door." *The Horn Book*. March/April.

Marcus, Leonard S. (2002). *Ways of Telling*. New York: Dutton.

Meltzer, Milton. (2001). "Wilder Medal Acceptance." *The Horn Book*. July/August, 425.

Miller, Sara. (1995). "American Folklore." In Anita Silvey (ed.). *Children's Books and Their Creators*. Boston: Houghton Mifflin.

Myers-Shaffer, Christine. (2000). *Principles of Literature*. New York: Barron's Educational Series.

Norton, Donna. (1993). "Genres in Children's Literature: Identifying, Analyzing, and Appreciating." In M. Rudman (ed.). *Children's Literature*. Norwood, MA: Christopher-Gordon.

Opie, Iona, & Opie, Peter, eds. (1988). *Tail Feathers from Mother Goose*. Boston: Little, Brown.

Opie, Iona. (2002). *The Very Best of Mother Goose*. Cambridge, MA: Candlewick.

Paterson, Katherine. (1995). "Voice of the Creators: Katherine Patterson." In Anita Silvey, ed. *Children's Books and Their Creators*. Boston: Houghton Mifflin.

Pierce, Tamora. (1996). "Fantasy: Why Kids Read It, Why Kids Need it." In Sheila Egoff, et al. *Only Connect*. New York: Oxford University Press.

Pinker, S. (2002). *The Blank Slate*. New York: Viking.

Rosenberg, Liz. (2004). Old Fables in a New Guise. *Boston Globe*, March 14.

Saul, Wendy. (2001). "Milton Meltzer." *The Horn Book*. July/August 431.

Shulevitz, Uri. (1996). "What Is a Picture Book?" In Sheila Egoff, ed. *Only Connect*. New York: Oxford University Press.

Solomon, Andrew. (2004). "The Closing of the American Book." op-ed, *New York Times*, July 10, 2004.

Wiesner, D. (2002). "Caldecott Medal Acceptance." *The Horn Book*, LXXVIII (4).393–399.

Yolen, Jane (1993). "How Children's Literature Has Evolved." In Masha Kabakow Rudman (Ed.). *Children's Literature*. Norwood, MA.: Christopher-Gordon Publishers, Inc.

Analyzing, Selecting, and Responding to Children's Literature

When Mars Bar, a tough character in Jerry Spinelli's Newbery Award book Maniac Magee, *grabs Amanda's book from Maniac, Maniac is distraught. He gets the book back but one page is destroyed. "Maniac uncrumpled the page, flattened it out as best he could. How could he return the book to Amanda in this condition? He couldn't. But he had to. It was hers. Judging from that morning, she was pretty finicky about her book" (Spinelli, 1990, p. 38).*

Maniac was the only outsider that Amanda let read her books. He even tried to tackle her A volume encyclopedia. "Problem was, Amanda was always reading it. And she vowed she wasn't giving it up, not even to Maniac, til she read everything from Aardvark to Aztec. To make matters worse, the supermarket offer had expired, so there were no other volumes" (Spinelli, 1990, p. 56).

The more Amanda refused to let go of volume A, the more Maniac wanted it. Even when she tried to hide it, he would always find it. He would get up earlier in the morning, read it by flashlight for awhile, and then sneak it back. Obviously, Amanda and Maniac loved to read, and although they had little funds to buy books, they treasured the few books that were available to them. If they were your students, how do you think they would answer a question we ask in this chapter: What is a good book?

A good book satisfies the needs of the reader, which Amanda's books do. If you recall Maslow's needs hierarchy in Chapter One, what could be more helpful for children's goodness-of-fit than that they choose books that satisfy their needs? Children have the need to feel competent, to play and belong, and especially to feel emotionally and physically secure. A good book recognizes these needs as well as others. A good book also introduces a child to beauty in its various forms, which Maniac and Amanda instinctively knew. They would undoubtedly find their reading even more rewarding if they understood a book's *literary elements*. Understanding what makes a book work—the literary elements of setting, characters, point of view, plot, style, and theme—would be like Maniac's and Amanda's understanding what makes Maniac run: is it his shoes, his strong legs, his determination, or a combination of all three?

In this chapter, to help you become more familiar with the literary elements of a book, we will analyze Kate DiCamillo's *Because of Winn-Dixie* and Ruth White's *Belle Prater's Boy*, which are different, yet in many aspects surprisingly similar. We'll also explain how books are selected and organized, discuss the outstanding resources available for reviewing children's literature, and introduce various literary awards that aid in selection. Finally, we'll carefully look at the many ways children respond to books, using Louise Rosenblatt's seminal work, *the Reader, the Text, the Poem,* as a guide that we explained in Chapter One.

MANIAC MAGEE
*Reprinted with permission
from Little, Brown and
Company*

Guidelines for Reading Chapter 4

After reading Chapter Four, you should be able to answer the following questions.

• What are the major literary elements children should use as a guide for their reading?

• What is the significance of setting to a story's development?

• If you were to write a story, would you, like Lois Lowry, create your characters before anything else? Why?

• Should the use of conflict in a story's plot reflect developmental characteristics? Why?

• What role does *The Wonderful Wizard of Oz* play in the controversy concerning the best means of selecting a "good" book?

• Do you believe in the system of literary awards? Do you think it helps or hinders teachers, librarians, and parents in their book selections?

• Will you be influenced by literary awards in your selection of children's literature?

• Can you suggest techniques that would help young readers in their literary responses?

• What is the main argument in Rosenblatt's transactional theory of reader response?

Analyzing Children's Literature: The Literary Elements

When children analyze a story whose hidden elements need to be discovered before it can be fully appreciated, they are using and developing their cognitive skills. As young readers develop and mature, they interact successfully with their environment according to their ability to organize information. Helping children master the concepts embedded in stories and texts, which are vital to perceiving relationships, thinking, and reasoning, is a sure way to improve their competence in selecting and analyzing their reading. Understanding the substance and use of literary elements that are present not only in contemporary and historical fiction, but also in books of other genres, contributes to the refinement of their cognitive skills and increases their joy of reading and their ability to discuss what they read with others. Remember, however, that *meaning is basic to learning*; this is the key to how children analyze their literature. For example, with development:

- Cognitive processes such as attention, memory, problem solving, and creativity steadily improve.

- Children's responses to literature become more focused.

- Their emotional reactions are more intimately linked to what they are reading.

This steady enrichment over the years, when coupled with a deeper understanding of the literary elements you're about to study, work to produce readers who remain entranced with reading throughout their lives. Table 4.1 summarizes the *Literary Elements* we'll discuss in this chapter.

As we mentioned in the introduction, to illustrate the importance of literary elements in children's literature, we selected for analysis two books of contemporary fiction: Kate DiCamillo's *Because of Winn-Dixie* and historical finction, Ruth White's *Belle Prater's Boy*. We chose these award-winning books because children in the intermediate and middle school grades have consistently selected them as their favorites in Children's State Awards Programs across the country. Before we undertake our literary analysis, however, we will turn our attention to the authors, Ruth White and Kate DiCamillo.

Ruth White

One only has to read *Belle Prater's Boy* to understand that Ruth White must have had personal knowledge of the area where the story takes place, because she writes about it with such authority. Actually Ruth White was born in western Virginia.

Table 4.1 THE LITERARY ELEMENTS

LITERARY ELEMENTS	MEANING
Setting	Time, place, mood
Characters	Protagonist, antagonist, supporting characters
Point of view	Perspective: first person, third person
Plot	Action: progressive, episodic
Style	Unique method of story presentation
Theme	The story's lesson

She grew up there in the 1950s during the time in which *Belle Prater's Boy* takes place. Her family was poor; her father was a coal miner and her mother worked as a hospital food server. She was a thoughtful little girl who often must have wondered what the future held for her and her friends. When she became a young woman, she taught school, worked as a librarian, and became more aware of the young people with whom she came in contact. How did *they* see themselves and how would *they* face their reality?

These questions must have prompted her, in 1996, to write the poignant story of Woodrow and Gypsy, the main characters in *Belle Prater's Boy*. When Woodrow's mother suddenly disappears, how does Woodrow cope? Leaving the cabin he shared with his father, he moves to Coal Station to be with his grandparents and his cousin Gypsy. He must adjust to a new school, new friends, and a more formal lifestyle than the one he had previously. Slightly cross-eyed and poorly dressed, but with his sense of humor intact, he depends on Gypsy, who is searching for her identity, to show him how to look at the world in a new way. He never stops hoping, however, that he will see his mother again.

In 2003, White wrote *Tadpole*, a story whose main character, thirteen-year old Tadpole, is similar to Woodrow: talented, kind, and concerned. He wants to make sure that his youngest cousin will discover for herself who she really is and what makes her so special. He, like Woodrow, is poor and shoeless, until the neighbors bring him a new pair of shoes. They also rally around him to protect him from an abusive uncle. This story takes place in the Kentucky hills, and again White writes a 1950s description of life that resonates with realism.

In 2004 she wrote the tender, thought-provoking story *Buttermilk Hill*, whose plot revolves around a young girl, Piper Berry, who collects words like others collect coins. She tries to fit into her new family when her father remarries, but she resents her mother's new social life. White personally understood the anxieties and upsets of divorce because she had experienced the heartbreak of family separation.

In 2005 White returned to *Belle Prater's Boy* when she wrote the sequel *The Search for Belle Prater*. An anonymous phone call to Woodrow on New Year's Eve, thirteen years from the day he was born, initiates the search for Belle Prater that takes Woodrow, his new classmate Cassie, and Gypsy away from Coal Station. This time, they are determined that they will be successful. A dedicated and accomplished author, Ruth White clearly reveals the thoughts and emotions of the characters about whom she writes and makes them come alive for her readers.

Kate DiCamillo

As Kate DiCamillo said in her acceptance speech after winning the 2004 Newbery Medal for *The Tale of Despereaux*, "We readers form a community of unlikely heroes. We are all stumbling through the dark. But when we read, we journey through the dark together. And because we travel together, there is the promise of light" (DiCamillo, 2004, p. 397). It is significant that she referred to "unlikely heroes," because Despereaux, the tiny mouse with the big ears, was certainly an unlikely hero. Only when he read the story of a courageous knight who must make a difficult decision did he decide that he too must act bravely in spite of his misgivings. Opal, the young heroine in *Winn-Dixie*, is also an unlikely hero in her own way. She overcomes her loneliness of being motherless and turns her grief into helping others. In the small Florida town of Naomi, she gathers together in friendship a mixed group of people, young and old, who otherwise would never have become acquainted to provide emotional support for each other.

Kate DiCamillo moved to the small town of Clermont in central Florida in 1968. Like Opal in *Because of Winn-Dixie*, she loved going to the library. In her Newbery acceptance speech, she told her audience that the words of encouragement the librarian said to her—"Kate is a True Reader!"—are "a part of the miracle of my presence here tonight" (DiCamillo, 2004, p. 395). Although she has traveled through the darkness and into the light, she acknowledged that "we cannot act against the darkness until we admit that it exists" (DiCamillo, 2004, p. 397). She has always been interested in reading and writing, but it was only after she graduated from the University of Florida and was working in the Bookman, a book warehouse, that she seriously considered writing for publication. At Bookman she met a representative from Candlewick Publishing, who showed her manuscript to an editor, which launched her writing career.

Jane Resh Thomas (2004), DiCamillo's friend, commented that "Kate never writes the same book twice" (p. 403). Fortunately for her readers, DiCamillo has written well in many genres. First, she captivated them with the contemporary realistic novel *Because of Winn-Dixie (2000)*, which was selected as a children's favorite book in many states throughout the country. Then she wrote a more somber book, *The Tiger Rising* (2001), a National Book finalist that also takes place in Florida. The main character is Robert Horton, a 12-year-old who does not admit that darkness exists. He has an absent mother, a quiet, uncommunicative father, and a caged tiger that serves "as this novel's central metaphor (but) never seems more than a paper tiger" (Sieruta, 2001, p. 322).

Following the publication of *The Tale of Despereaux* (2003), a fantasy that captured a Newbery Award, she is now motivating beginning readers with a series of transitional books about the porcine wonder, *Mercy Watson* (2005). In addition to these, she has written another fantasy, *The Miraculous Journey of Edward Tulane* (2006), about a narcissistic toy rabbit that develops an understanding for others only after he is separated from his adoring owner and encounters others as he travels across the country. Kate DiCamillo is a writer whose large retinue of fans is waiting excitedly for her next genre adventure.

Now, we turn to the literary element *setting* to see how it is defined generally and specifically in *Because of Winn-Dixie* and *Belle Prater's Boy*.

Setting

The setting of a story must be convincing because it establishes the time, place, and mood for the action that is to unfold. It's the where and when of the story, and it often plays a leading role in the story (Cuddon, 1998, p. 66). In *Because of Winn-Dixie*, the setting is Naomi, a warm and sunny small town in South Florida, where Opal, the main character and first person narrator, lives with her father, who is the new preacher at the Open Arms Baptist Church (an abandoned store without pews). As Opal and her father settle into the friendly Trailer Park, she is still mourning her mother who has disappeared. The author succeeds, however, in counterbalancing Opal's loss by creating an inviting setting—a main street filled with small shops and a library that provides Opal the opportunity to make friends with a wide variety of characters.

Accompanied by Winn-Dixie, the smiling, stray dog she rescued, the lonely little girl makes friends up and down Naomi's main street. She especially likes to visit Miss Franny Block at the Herman W. Block Memorial Library and Otis at the Gertrude Pets store. The setting remains bright and cheerful, until the author describes a horrific thunder and lightning storm that terrifies Winn-Dixie. The sun is shining when Opal, Winn-Dixie, and her new friends gather in Gloria Dump's backyard. The backyard is described in minute detail: the jungle-like area with every kind of thing growing and the bottles hanging from the branches. Opal's friends bring gifts of food—egg salad sandwiches, pickles, Littmus sweet and sour lozenges—and are enjoying the party, when the setting suddenly changes. A fierce thunderstorm chases everyone inside. Winn-Dixie is missing! In harsh rain, the hunt for the dog begins.

The setting for Ruth White's historical fiction *Belle Prater's Boy* is Coal Station, a dingy mountain town built at the convergence of Black River and Slag Creek in the Appalachian mountains of Virginia. The reader learns that there are only two major streets in Coal Station: Main Street, where all the businesses are located, and Residence Street the only place in town where houses can be built on solid ground. This is where Gypsy (the narrator) lives with her beautiful mother and stepfather in a modern, one-story ranch with white shutters, a front porch, and the only picture window in town. They have a telephone, two radios, a phonograph, a refrigerator, an upright freezer, and an electric stove. Next door is the two-story house with the wrap-around porch where Woodrow (Belle Prater's boy and Gypsy's cousin) comes to live with their grandparents when his mother disappears.

The time is the fifties. Movies such as *Tarzan* and *Rear Window* are playing at the neighborhood theater. Kate Smith is singing *When the Moon Comes Over the Mountain* on the radio. Events like hot dog roasts and birthday parties create a carnival-like atmosphere, and the upbeat mood binds Woodrow, his grandparents, his cousin Gypsy, and her family together, until the setting changes dramatically. Although *most* of the inhabitants of the town are friendly, others confront Woodrow with questions about his mother's disappearance, which causes him to become angry and depressed.

Characters

Characters bring a story to life, and outstanding authors make us want to know more about them. Readers empathize with the characters and often imagine what a sequel—or even a movie—involving them would be like! The notion of "character' can be traced back to the seventeenth century, when individuals such as Francis Bacon and Walter Raleigh thought of humans as models of the world (Cuddon, 1998, p. 127). Memorable, three-dimensional characters come alive for the reader. The protagonist, who is the main character, the antagonist, who is the opposing force, and the supporting characters all contribute to the development of the plot. The author lets the reader know what the characters are like, not only from what they say, but also by what they do, how they dress, and how they communicate with each other. Through the literary skills of the author, readers form opinions about the characters. The characters, in turn, evoke emotions from their readers, such as sympathy and admiration, or distaste and disgust. It is the true measure of a book that readers are sorry when the story ends.

The noted children's author Lois Lowry (2002), discussing how she writes a story, admits that she always goes about the creation of a character first. "I then set a series of events in motion starting usually with one precipitating

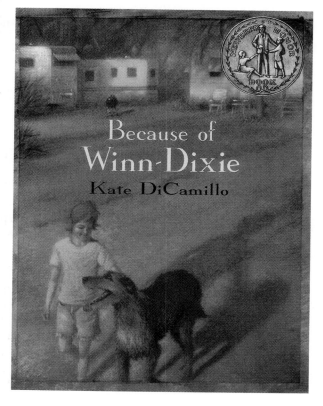

incident. I move the character through those events, and the character responds the way that character would. Each response triggers new events—and the character again responds the way that character would. . . . It is only after such a series of controlled surprises that a story finds its way to an ending" (p. 161).

Opal, the protagonist in *Because of Winn-Dixie*, is a sympathetic character, and young readers' attachment to her borders on sentimentality. Despite being lonely, she is determined to make friends. She introduces herself (and her readers) to supporting characters like Franny Block, who takes care of the small, private library, and Otis, the former criminal who works in a pet shop and plays his guitar for the animals. With the help of Winn-Dixie, whom she describes as "big and ugly" but always smiling, Opal becomes acquainted with the "pinched faced" Amanda Wilson, the 5-year-old Sweetie Pie Thomas, and the Dewberry brothers. She also becomes adept at bringing people of diversity together. She patiently listens to the librarian's stories, applauds Otis when he plays his guitar, and skillfully eases her father's sorrow. In so doing, she faces her own loss. She is not perfect, however, which raises her status in the eyes of her young readers, who like characters with flaws because they are easy to identify with.

Readers become acquainted with the protagonist Woodrow in *Belle Prater's Boy*, not only from what he says but from what he does. They know he likes riddles and puzzles, and playing tricks on his friends (and enemies). He is humorous, quick-witted, understanding, and sincere. When he first arrives at Coal Station, Gypsy, his cousin who introduces him to his sixth grade class, where she is also a student, feels sorry for him because of his mother's disappearance, his father's alcoholism, and his shabby clothes. Yet in spite of his crossed eyes and his recent arrival in Coal Station, Woodrow develops many warm relationships in the small community. Some prominent members of the community, however, become overly inquisitive about his mother's disappearance, and that antagonizes Woodrow.

Gypsy, who is also a protagonist, is concerned not only about Woodrow, but about herself. She wonders how others view her, or whether she is invisible under her long, flowing hair. Readers know she is a sensitive young girl who suffers frequent nightmares because of the manner in which her father died. Her father's death not only haunts her, but causes her to reject her stepfather, one of the supporting characters. At the climax of the story, however, she finds out the circumstances of her father's death and discovers that her stepfather has always loved her.

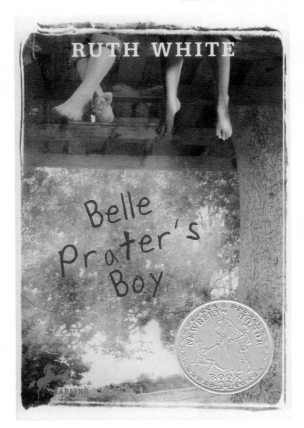

BELLE PRATER'S BOY
Jacket Cover from BELLE PRATER'S BOY by Ruth White. Used by permission of Random House Children's Books, a division of Random House, Inc.

Point of View

Point of view is the perspective from which a story is told. A *first person narrator*, who is indicated by the use of I, limits the events of the story to what he or she sees or hears. A *third person narration* is related by the author using the pronouns *he, she, it, they*, or *them*. In *Belle Prator's Boy*, we discover through Gypsy's point of view as a *first person narrator* how much Woodrow misses his mother. Gypsy tells the reader how she finds Woodrow scanning the classified ads in the Sunday newspaper, hoping to find a message from her there. But no matter how hard he tries, his mother never gets in touch with him. Gypsy knows, too, when Woodrow mistakenly believes his mother is the woman in his father's car. Throughout the book, she is Woodrow's sympathetic and loyal friend, who succeeds in making the readers support him.

In *Because of Winn-Dixie*, readers discover through Opal's point of view as *first person narrator* that she gradually draws closer to her father. She comes to realize that her father is lonely. She misses her mother, but begins to understand her situation when Gloria Dump tells her "There ain't no way you can hold on to something that wants to go, you understand?" (p. 159). As Opal continues to confide her innermost thoughts to her readers, they in turn accept her confidences and become her staunch friends. (Many readers actually belong to Opal's fan club.)

Plot

The plot is the action of a book beginning with a problem, rising to a climax (turning point), and descending to the solution (the outcome). As E. M. Forster (1927) wrote in his classic *Aspects of the Novel*, a plot is a narrative of events with the emphasis placed on *the causes of the events*. For example, "the king dies and then the queen died," tells a story. "The king died and then the queen died of grief" is a plot. Note how the sequence of events is similar in both cases, but the queen dying of grief focuses on causation. Plot can also be labeled as *progressive* or *episodic*.

PROGRESSIVE PLOT   With a progressive plot, the ending should grow naturally from the events of the story and be inevitable. Both of the books we are discussing in detail (*Because of Winn-Dixie* and *Belle Prater's Boy*) have *progressive* plots that proceed chronologically with a beginning, a middle, and an end. The beginning reveals the time, the place, the characters, and even the mood of the story. The middle is where the action takes place. The end contains the *denouement* (the unraveling of the plot's complications) where the story comes to an appropriate conclusion. *Belle Prater's Boy* is more complex than *Because of Winn-Dixie* because it has a *parallel* structure—two progressive plots that develop simultaneously. In every story the technique of *foreshadowing* (arranging events and information in such a way that later events are prepared for or shadowed beforehand) is used, and *flashbacks* are often inserted to show events that happened earlier.

In *Because of Winn-Dixie*, the plot develops from the first encounter Opal has with the stray dog *Winn-Dixie*, whom she rescues from the wrath of the supermarket manager, to her interactions with characters who help assuage her loneliness. The reader finally realizes that Opal's mother will not return, in the scene where Opal addresses the bottles hanging on the tree in Gloria Dump's yard: "Mama, I know ten things about you, and that's not enough . . . But Daddy is going to tell me more. . . . He misses you and I miss you but (my) heart doesn't feel empty anymore. It's full all the way up" (pp. 177–178).

The plot of *Belle Prater's Boy*, in which Woodrow searches for his mother, parallels a second plot involving his cousin Gypsy, who is seeking her own identity. Besides being the *first person narrator* of the story, Gypsy has personal problems that she must resolve. Even by the end of the story, Woodrow's main wish is unfulfilled. Yet many of his and Gypsy's problems are resolved. Woodrow gets his second wish (a chance to have his eyesight corrected) and Gypsy finds out her nightmares are connected to her father's suicide. She also has a chance to perform a piano recital. As the story concludes, Gypsy and Woodrow are at peace with themselves and their family, who accept them as they are.

Figure 4.1

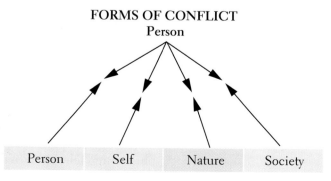

FORMS OF CONFLICT

EPISODIC PLOT   *Episodic* plots are apparent in books for younger readers, such as Beverly Cleary's *Ramona's World*, where each chapter is a story by itself, with setting, characters, plot, and resolution. In the chapter "Ramona Sits," for example, Ramona assumes the care of the neighbor's cat, Clawed. Thinking that all she must do is pat and cuddle the cat, she discovers that she must feed him, brush him, and change his litter box as well. One event follows another: he escapes from the basement during the night and awakens the entire house; he begins to choke on a hair ball while she is in charge of her little sister; her little sister Roberta then climbs into the cat condo and can't get out. Luckily, Ramona releases her little sister minutes before her mother returns and the episodic plot is complete.

CONFLICT   Without conflict there is no plot. Lukens (1990) has identified four types of conflict, which may take several forms as seen in Figure 4.1.

In the above diagram, conflict arises from four sources:

1. *Person versus person* (conflict between the character and a rival)
2. *Person versus self* (conflict within a character)
3. *Person versus nature* (conflict between a character and the environment)
4. *Person versus society* (conflict between a character and prejudice, segregation, etc.)

Examining Figure 4.1 helps to explain why psychologists believe that conflict results from competing motives, some external (another person, battling to survive a storm), some internal (forced to choose between eating cake or not putting on weight). For a thoughtful discussion of frustration and conflict, see Maslow (1987).

In *Because of Winn-Dixie*, Opal's conflict is person versus person, that is, Opal versus her father, who fails to communicate with her and continues to withdraw into his own thoughts. In *Belle Prater's Boy*, Woodrow's conflict is person versus society, that is, Woodrow versus the attitudes he encounters in the community. Gypsy's conflict is also person versus person, that is, Gypsy versus her stepfather. She is in conflict with herself when she reacts violently in the movie theater while watching *Rear Window*. Only then does she begin to resolve her problems.

Style

Style is the author's unique way of creating a story by using words, images, and figures of speech; it is how a writer says things (Cuddon, 1998, p. 872). Kate DiCamillo sprinkles so many literary expressions across the pages of her novel *Because of Winn-Dixie* that the reader could imagine how the characters look even without the illustrations. When Opal compares her father to "a turtle hiding inside its shell in there thinking about things and not even sticking his head out into the world," the reader immediately visualizes a quiet, shy, and lonely man. When Opal describes Winn-Dixie as looking like "a big piece of old brown carpet that had been left out in the rain," the reader knows the dog's fur is matted and neglected. Gloria Dump, her friend, listens to Opal's story *with her heart* because her eyesight is so poor. When Otis mesmerizes the animals with his guitar, Opal thinks he is some kind of snake charmer, the way he could play his guitar and make all the animals turn to stone. Children identify with Opal. They admire her determination and friendly good humor, and are particularly fond of her dog Winn-Dixie because of DiCamillo's style of writing.

Ruth White, the author of *Belle Prater's Boy*, on the other hand, draws on her knowledge of Appalachia to authenticate Gypsy and Woodrow, who constantly use phrases and tell stories that reflect their mountain heritage. Readers visualize them as they must have listened to *their* parents and grandparents tell stories in context. How else would they have known the story of how Buck Coleman swallowed the tape worm, or how Ed Morrell fell into the water in his strait jacket, or why Aunt Millie came back from the grave? It is this kind of humor that children enjoy, and the choice of words, the use of figurative speech, and even the length of the sentences reflect the style of the author.

Theme

Theme is the lesson the story tells, the central idea of the story (Cuddon, 1998, p. 913). When asked what does *Because of Winn-Dixie* really mean, children are often puzzled and give various answers. Some think the theme is expressed when Gloria Dump says she is listening to Opal's story with her heart. All agree, however, that *Because of Winn-Dixie* is a warm, heartfelt story of a lonely little girl searching for love and acceptance.

In *Belle Prater's Boy*, the theme is couched in the quotation from Antoine de Saint-Exupery's *The Little Prince* that introduces the narrative: "It is only with the heart that one can see rightly; what is essential is invisible to the eye." The underlying theme of *Belle Prater's Boy* seems to be the developing friendship between Woodrow and Gypsy, the union of their thoughts, dreams, and emotions. Although *Because of Winn-Dixie* and *Belle Prater's Boy* are different, we discover in each story that no matter how a character appears, it is the person within that is most important.

Literary Elements in Other Genres

Literary elements also underlie books of genres besides contemporary and historical fiction. A book of outstanding merit is as important to the development of a child in kindergarten, who is looking at a picture book for the first time, as it is to the development of middle and high school students who are engrossed in a fantasy like *Harry Potter*. For example:

• **PICTURE BOOKS**. Outstanding picture books for young children contain literary elements such as setting, plot (not too complex), characters that children can relate to, a definite point of view, and a distinctive style. Without a riveting story, children will not listen to or read a picture book again and again. In *Miss Nelson Is Missing*, author Harry Allard's point of view enables young readers to experience the sometimes tense, but humorous, plot. When first grade teacher Miss Nelson disappears, her class is distraught. When the witch Miss Viola Swamp arrives as her substitute, the class is devastated and become determined to bring Miss Nelson back.

Picture book author William Steig has produced books for children that even adults are proud to own, because they are written in his unique style. His books are often magical and replete with language that is rhythmic and fluid. In *Wizzil*, he introduces the reader to Wizzil the witch through continuous alliteration. Wizzil's parrot challenges her to go to the Frimp Farm to make the Frimp family—DeWitt Frimp, Fred Frimp, and Fred's wife, Florence—suffer. Wizzil turns herself into a household fly (*Musca domestica*) to irritate DeWitt, who springs up and swishes his swatter wherever he can swish it—but misses the Witch. Then Wizzil turns herself into a glove. The parrot cheers: That's the way, Wizzil. Make him sizzle!" And the story goes on, much to the delight of children who listen. Steig's numerous stories display his ability to paraphrase a thought or an emotion perfectly suitable to the situation, as in *Amos & Boris*. When Boris the whale is beached, Amos the mouse comes to his rescue by bringing two elephants to push him into the ocean. Boris muses, "You have to be *out* of the sea really to know how good it is to be *in* it."

A WRINKLE IN TIME *Used by permission of Farrar, Straus, and Giroux, LLC. Jacket design by Leo and Diane Dillon from A WRINKLE IN TIME by Madeleine L'Engle.*

• **FANTASY.** The literary elements previously mentioned also appear in fantasy. *Setting, characters, point of view, plot, style,* and *theme* retain their importance, but it is the element of *time* that is often stressed in fantasy. For example, in Natalie Babbitt's *Tuck Everlasting*, Winnie encounters the Tuck family, who live forever. William Sleator (1990, pp. 206, 207), author of many science fiction novels such as *The Boy Who Reversed Himself*, explains that "science fiction literature is about something that hasn't happened, yet might be possible someday." He continues by giving us his idea of time and time travel: "Time travel is out of the question, scientifically. However, spinning black holes might make time travel possible after all."

The setting in fantasy may be another world, as in Madeline L'Engle's *A Wrinkle in Time*, the Newbery Medal book that legitimized science fiction for children. Authors like Tolkien, Lewis, and Pullman draw the reader into *two* worlds: the first, or primary, world and a secondary world. These worlds, described in detail, often have their own flora and fauna, their own government, and strange inhabitants. Only when these worlds are integrated into the story (a map may be included in the book), however, will the reader believe they are logical and real. In a work of fantasy, the human characters are usually well-developed, but they must be believable even when they become involved in out-of-this-world experiences.

• **TRADITIONAL LITERATURE.** In traditional literature the setting is symbolic and the characters are flat and undeveloped. They rarely show improvement in the course of the story. Other than being naughty (the witch, the ogre, the giant, the wolf) or nice (the fairy godmother, the beautiful heroine, or the kind young man), the personality of the characters is seldom revealed to the reader. Small creatures, as well as giants, appear in folklore. Although there is variety in their tales, there is also similarity. The leprechaun from Ireland, the nisse from Norway, the tomte from Sweden, the kobold of Germany, the brownie of Scotland, the hobgoblin of England and other household spirits of northern Europe are helpful to humans, but only to those who treat them with kindness.

• **INFORMATIONAL BOOKS.** Many informational books, in addition to containing all the elements requisite for their genre mentioned in Chapter Three, have other literary elements that are necessary for good literature. In informational books such as Brenda Guiberson's *The Emperor Lays an Egg,* the characters, a female and male penguin, are sympathetically portrayed. We discover a plot when the male, after the female gives him the egg, concentrates all his efforts during the next two months to protect it. Both the male and female undergo hardships, as they go weeks without food and make little movement, so that their young will be protected against freezing. The setting is appropriate and highlighted by hand-painted paper collages and italicized sound-words that help explain the story.

Figure 4.2 illustrates how literary elements work together to produce outstanding literature, whether it is contemporary or historical fiction, fantasy, traditional literature, or informational books.

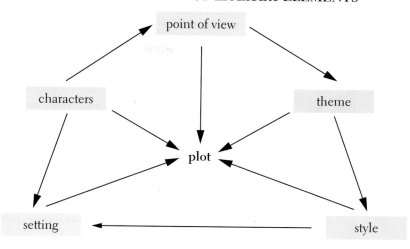

THE INTERACTION OF LITERARY ELEMENTS

Figure 4.2

Selecting Children's Literature

Knowledge of the genres and literary elements that are inherent in quality books helps adults who select children's literature to choose outstanding and appropriate literature for children. They must be aware of the biopsychosocial development of the children for whom they are making their selections, in order to ensure a goodness-of-fit between the book and the child.

Sources for Book Reviews

Many literacy resources are avaible to teachers, librarians, and parents to aid them in their selection of the best children's book. Teachers, librarians and others who are responsible for selecting children's books should become acquainted with outstanding books that have been recognized nationally and internationally and are listed in the Appendix of Children's Literature: A Developmental Perspective. The following journals will also keep professionals informed about what is current and up-to-date:

Book Review Journals

- *School Library Journal* (www.slj.com)
- *The Horn Book* (www.hbook.com)

- *The Bulletin of the Center for Children's Books* (University of Illinois; www.lis.uiuc.edu/puboff/bccb)
- *Booklist* (www.ala.org/booklist)

Annual lists of outstanding books are reviewed in:

- **Notable Children's Books** and **Best Books for Young Adults** chosen by American Library Association committees are available on the web (www.ala.org). These may also be ordered in pamphlet form from the ALA offices: 50 Huron Street, Chicago, IL and are found in *Booklist* (March edition).

A SELECTOR'S QUALIFICATIONS   When addressing the issue of selecting books for children, one should remember that book selection involves problem solving and deserves the same thought and attention that educators, philosophers, and psychologists devote to critical thinking, decision making, and problem solving. In book selection, several topics should guide adults in their decision making:

- Is *this* book appropriate for *this* stage of the child's development? In Chapter One we promised our readers that three themes would integrate our work: the search for the best children's literature (both classical and contemporary), the discussion of this literature within a developmental framework, and the use of biopsychosocial interactions to help us in making age-appropriate selections. For adults charged with the responsibility of selecting books for children, these should be only the *first* of their considerations. *They must understand the biological and psychosocial characteristics of children.*

- The second step selectors must take is to understand, clearly and with creditable knowledge, the cultural context of the children for whom they are making this choice. Is it for the typical middle school student, who has a normal but wide range of intelligence? Or is it for a unique group of children who have many and varied problems? Adults must also weigh issues such as diversity, socioeconomic status, reading levels, and emotional maturity, among others. Once they have reached decisions based on these factors, they must turn their attention to key ideas such as the literary elements we have identified in this chapter. For example, would the disappearance of Winn-Dixie appeal to the animal loving nature of children? Would they understand the role the dog plays in the story?

- Next, selectors must step back and evaluate their choices in light of the nature of the story and the characteristics of its potential readers. Is the match between story and readers appropriate? Will children understand, enjoy, and find comfort in the unfolding of the plot?

- Finally, selectors should discuss their conclusion with each other and be open to any overlooked ideas that would help ensure the best possible choice for their readers.

Organizing Books: The Dewey Decimal Classification System

Once books have been carefully selected and are ready to be placed in the classroom or on a library shelf, they must be organized in a way that makes them readily available for children to browse through and select for that goodness-of-fit we have emphasized throughout this text. One time-honored method for organizing books is the *Dewey Decimal Classification System*, named after its originator Melville Dewey (1851–1931), who wisely organized all information from 000 for general knowledge—(encyclopedias, almanacs, atlases)—to the 900s (history and geography). Table 4.2 lists the subject areas, along with examples of each.

By learning how books are organized, children become independent library users. When they understand a classification system such as the Dewey Decimal System, or a classification system that is accepted in their locale, they gain confidence and experience the pleasure of purposeful browsing by examining and selecting books on whatever subjects interest them. The library then becomes not just a reading room, but a place that fosters their joy of reading.

Table 4.2 THE DEWEY DECIMAL SYSTEM

000 General Knowledge	Encyclopedias, almanacs, atlases, museums, newspapers
100 Philosophy and Psychology	Death, ethics, superstition, relationships, perception, thinking
200 Religion and Mythology	Individual religions, myths
300 Social Science	Families, environment, government, education, folktales, fables, legends
400 Language and Grammar	Various languages, codes, Braille
500 Natural Science and Mathematics	Math, chemistry, biology, animal kingdom, plant life
600 Applied Science, Technology	Health, nutrition, medicine, computer technology
700 Arts and Recreation	Painting, drawing, music, sports, games
800 Literature and Poetry	Plays, poetry, Shakespeare (general literature appears in a separate section)
900 History and Geography	Countries, states, civilizations, history (biography appears in a separate section)

What's Your View?

Standard Classifications versus Leveling

Today some school libraries are organized by Accelerated Reader (AR) scores or other forms of leveling. Irene Fountas and Gay Su Pinnell have leveled over 2,000 books for children from K–6. Yet as helpful as leveling is in the classroom, it should not be the basis for classifying books in the school library. *Accelerated Reader* scores and other popular leveling schemes, are useful when teachers select books to teach their students specific reading strategies. But it is difficult for children to learn their own strategies and make independent judgments for choosing their reading material when these scores are the basis of their school library's organization (Shannon, 2004).

Leveling is occurring in more than just a few isolated school libraries. One librarian admits that when she first became the administrator of a school library organized according to leveling scores, she found it almost impossible to find a particular title for a teacher—much less for the students. *First, because she had to find the level of the book, then go to the shelf and search through countless others* (Pappas, 2004). Teachers and librarians can better use their time by providing a rich and enjoyable reading experience that leads to the goal of a child becoming a lifelong reader.

As we learn about children's distinctive differences and their biopsychosocial development, we believe it is difficult to restrict their access to books to a particular level. Lucy Calkins (2001), author of *The Art of Teaching Reading*, argues that teachers and librarians should trust themselves and their knowledge of individual children rather than accept levels as absolute. What's your view?

Spin Off
The Pickpocket

To circulate books in classrooms where computer use for checkout is not feasible, we recommend using a *Pickpocket* (devised by one of the authors). The classroom teacher pastes a library card and pocket inside each book, listing the name of the author and title. The student signs out the book by writing her name on the card and placing it in the *Pickpocket*, which is a rectangular piece of cardboard large enough to hold a library pocket with the name of each student. (Ask your school librarian to provide you enough pockets for your class.) When the student returns the book, she slips the card into the book and places it correctly on shelf. The *Pickpocket* has also been successfully used as a record keeper and a key to what a child is reading. By glancing at the *Pickpocket*, teachers and librarians readily discover what books are most popular (genre, age level, fiction or nonfiction, etc.) and can suggest how students can improve their reading, diversify their selections, and increase their knowledge.

Teachers and librarians who understand their students' biopsychosocial development help them select the genres of literature that are most appropriate for them at their developmental level. We know that a child's brain development, coupled with their experience, maturation, peer interactions, and education, produces a distinct set of needs at different ages. When teachers and librarians are aware of these needs they will undoubtedly help their students make more informed book selections.

THE CLASSROOM LIBRARY   Classroom libraries should be attractive and bright so that students will be motivated to read independently in school and at home. Even a small area for a library can be made distinctive from the rest of the classroom, by the addition of posters and colorful book covers pinned on a bulletin board and comfortable furniture, such as a beanbag chair or a cozy cushion or two on the floor. Books should be arranged on the shelves alphabetically, by the author's last name. They may also be grouped according to subject (mystery, sports, animal stories, etc.), or divided into fiction and nonfiction. Special titles could lie flat on shelves with their covers facing up for additional appeal, or on window-sills (which can serve as shelves, provided heavy book ends are used). The school librarian could offer a larger deposit of books from the school library and periodically coordinate special book themes with the classroom teacher in order to highlight the collection. Scattered on the table(s) could be popular paperback books and magazines in a variety of reading levels, to suit not only the eager but also the reluctant reader. Even newspaper clippings, pamphlets, copies of students' outstanding writing—anything that pertains to the curriculum, as well as small boxes for students to deposit their book suggestions and short personal recommendations—should be available in the classroom library.

The Wonderful Wizard of Oz—A Story of Controversy

An important aspect in selecting and organizing a library is determining what books should be included. As we have mentioned in the introduction to this chapter, a child's idea of a "good book" may differ from what is considered a good children's book by professional librarians, teachers, and other adults. But children's choices are not necessarily wrong, nor are adult choices necessarily right. Today, children's voices are being heard throughout most states as they vote for the books they believe are "the best"—unlike one hundred years ago when *The Wonderful Wizard of Oz* was discovered by children but ignored by librarians. The history of this book is an excellent example of the difficulty involved in selecting a "good book."

When L. Frank Baum wrote *The Wonderful Wizard of Oz* it was an immediate success with children and was recognized as a milestone in children's literature. In the introduction, Baum dedicated his book to children who sought only enjoyment and entertainment. He could not have anticipated how reluctant professionals would be to accept his story as a good book.

THE OPPONENTS   Although it was an immediate best seller, *The Wonderful Wizard of Oz* was not included in many large city library book lists. In 1902 Anne Carroll Moore, an influential librarian and later the first children's librarian at the New York Public Library, was highly critical of the quality of any book written by Baum. Taking their cue from Moore, other librarians hesitated to include his books in their collections. Consequently, it was difficult for children to find *The Wonderful Wizard of Oz* in many libraries throughout the country (Hearn, 2001).

The controversy surrounding *The Wonderful Wizard of Oz*—whether it was good literature or not—continued throughout the century and is still being debated. In the past, children read it and requested more stories about Oz, but many librarians refused to blemish their collection by including Baum's books and other series in their collections. The story circulated that in 1929, when a parent asked to see the Oz books in a local library, the librarian informed her, "We don't keep the Oz books any more. They are considered too fantastic for children." This ban on the Oz books infuriated the public. Yet professionals defended the librarians who believed that a book's popularity did not prove it was a good book.

THE PROPONENTS   On the other hand, many authors and illustrators of outstanding children's books confess that when they were children they were captivated by *The Wonderful Wizard of Oz*. It inspired them and helped to shape their imaginations (Glassman, 2000). Madeleine L'Engle, winner of the Newbery Medal for *A Wrinkle in Time*, recalls how pleased she was to learn that she could be as brave as the Scarecrow. Tomie de Paola, the beloved author and illustrator of *Strega Nona*, imagined himself walking down the yellow brick road instead of Dorothy. Uri Shulevitz, author and illustrator of the Caldecott Medal book *The Fool of the World and The Flying Ship*, even remembers where he was when he encountered *The Wonderful Wizard of Oz*: in Russia, where his family had fled to escape the Nazis. A young friend read it to him in Russian each week, chapter by chapter. Writer and illustrator of *Starry Messenger*, Peter Sis, remembers that he was not allowed to read *The Wonderful Wizard of Oz* as a child in Moravia because it was "ideologically incorrect." Only when he moved to New York could he explore the delights of Oz with his two children (Glassman, 2000).

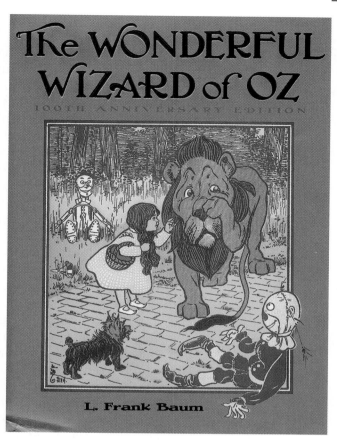

THE WONDERFUL
WIZARD OF OZ
*Used by permission of
HarperCollins Publishers*

Today, *The Wonderful Wizard of Oz* still evokes pleasure from children who read it. Paperback editions of all the Oz books, even later titles *not* written by L. Frank Baum, are in demand, and bookstores continue to stock them. Perhaps its popularity is in some measure due to the various amateur musicals about the book, and the appeal of the movie starring Judy Garland. Or perhaps its popularity is due to its sympathetic characters, its setting, and its espousal of universal themes.

As we discussed the history of children's literature in Chapter Two, we discovered that our view of children and who they are has changed throughout the centuries and continues to do so. So, too, have our opinions of what is good, best, or harmful for children to read. Professionals in the field of book selection still have the responsibility to choose the most qualified, most carefully written, and most attractive books for their young clientele.

To help them select books that are appropriate for the students in their care, teachers and librarians not only turn to magazines that review new books, but often turn to lists of books that have received a particular award. Among the most popular of these are the Newbery and Caldecott lists that have been a reliable source of what is good in children's literature. Intelligent, conscientious, and objective members of selection committees from respected groups such as the American Library Association make these awards to authors and illustrators whose books are considered to be among the most outstanding published in the United States and elsewhere. It is only fitting that teachers and librarians consider these lists of awards when making their book selections. A comprehensive list of these awards is included in the Appendix of this book. But how unanimous are professional opinions about the books that have been selected for awards? To answer this question, let's turn to the role that literary awards play in book selection.

Literary Awards

Although award-winning books should be considered seriously for inclusion in every school and public library, it is interesting to note that through the years the standards, rules, and choices of the various book award committees and their governing bodies have sometimes been subjects of controversy. *The Horn Book* Magazine has frequently served as a forum where writers, librarians, and others with a deep interest in children's literature express their opinions about various awards, especially those sponsored by the American Library Association, such as the Newbery, the Caldecott, the Coretta Scott King, and the Pura Belpré Awards (Table 4.3).

The Newbery Medal

The Newbery Medal was established in 1922 and named for the British bookseller, John Newbery. (See discussion in Chapter Two.) It is the longest active award in the United States, stamping its gold seal of approval on the most distinguished children's book written by an American author and published the previous year. Books by authors who win the Newbery Award continue to be in demand for years. Yet this illustrious award is not without its critics. The first recipient of the medal in 1922 was Hendrik Willem van Loon, author of *The Story of Mankind.* Today, his book might not have been considered for such an honor because critics could rightly say it is tediously written, overly long (500 pages), filled with dated information, contains no discussion of the history of Africa and little on the cultures of Asia, and lacks an index (Giblin, 2000).

Table 4.3 SELECTIVE LITERARY AWARDS ESTABLISHED BY THE AMERICAN LIBRARY ASSOCIATION

AWARD	ACHIEVEMENT
Newbery	Most distinguished children's book written by an American author the previous year—named after John Newbery
Caldecott	Most distinguished picture book published in the United States—named after Randolph Caldecott
Coretta Scott King	Two awards, one for outstanding writing and one for outstanding illustration presented annually to an African American author and illustrator whose work(s) promote world peace and unity—named after Coretta Scott King and dedicated to the life and work of Martin Luther King
Pura Belpré	Presented biannually to a writer or illustrator from any of the Spanish-speaking cultures of the Western Hemisphere—named after Pura Belpré, the first Latina librarian for the New York Public Library

QUESTIONS CONCERNING THE NEWBERY MEDAL   In 1952, when *Charlotte's Web*, a classic for all time, was published, many librarians were disappointed that it did not win the Newbery medal for 1953, although it was an Honor book. Laura Ingalls Wilder's books have never received the medal award although they, too, were considered Honor books. (As a consolation prize, however, when the Laura Ingalls Wilder Award was established in 1954, Laura Ingalls Wilder was its first recipient.) Other questions often address the lack of Newbery medals for books about or by African Americans. (We look at reasons why this is so in the discussion of diversity in Chapter Six.)

Milton Meltzer's question, *Where Do All the Prizes Go?* (Meltzer, 1976), became a wake-up call for librarians, teachers, and other professionals to the importance of nonfiction as children's literature. Since then, awards such as *The Boston Globe–Horn Book* Award for Nonfiction, The Golden Kite Award for Nonfiction (given by the Society of Children's Book Writers and Illustrators), The Orbis Pictus Award by the National Council of Teachers of English, and the *Washington Post* Children's Book Guild Award have been established to honor outstanding informational books or a nonfiction writer's body of work.

Yet nonfiction continued to be overlooked by the Newbery selection committees. Marc Aronson, writer and editor, in his acceptance speech as the recipient of the 2000 *Boston Globe–Horn Book* Award for Nonfiction, was critical of the Newbery committee for this omission. He believed "that nonfiction is a kind of sad stepsister that would rather be a novel but can't quite get there. . . . If you look beyond the awards, you see a mindset characterized more by prejudice than judgment" (Aronson, 2001, p. 50).

The Caldecott Medal

The Randolph Caldecott Medal has also received its share of criticism. Established in 1938, ten years too late to honor *Millions of Cats* (Wanda Gag) for its outstanding illustrations, it has recognized such distinguished illustrators as Robert Lawson for *They Were Strong and Good* (1941), Robert McCloskey for *Make Way for Ducklings* (1942), and Virginia Lee Burton for *The Little House* (1943), but it has neglected to honor such talented artists as Eric Carle. Inaugurating what is sometimes considered the "golden age" of picture books, the Caldecott Medal continues to acknowledge talented artists who dedicate themselves to children's book illustration.

QUESTIONS CONCERNING THE CALDECOTT MEDAL   Well-known children's book reviewer Peter Neumeyer questions why *So You Want to Be President* (illustrated by David Small) won the Caldecott Medal in 2001, when the text by Judith St. George "is randomly informative, sometimes exhortative and basically uninspired" (Neumeyer, 2001, p. C2). Concerned about whom the Caldecott Medals are intended for, he believes that readers don't separate the illustrations from the text in books they love. He points out that in the finest books, words and pictures are integrated. In Beatrix Potter's *The Tale of Peter Rabbit*, or Maurice Sendak's *Where the Wild Things Are*, one doesn't make sense without the other. Speculating about the 2001 Caldecott medal award's unconvincing selection of *So You Want To Be President*, he wonders if it is really "more a sales device than a helpful appraisal of a book" (Neumeyer, 2001, p. C2).

In 2005 Neumeyer wrote again about his concerns concerning the Caldecott awards. Although many outstanding picture books were published, he believed the selection committee had "viewed the whole rich panorama through a keyhole" (Neumeyer, 2005, p. F9). He continued his criticism by pointing out that neither Eric Carle nor Ashley Bryan had ever won a Caldecott Medal, "and to me it is unaccountable that one of the most glorious books ever like Lois Ehlert's *Pie in the Sky*, Douglas Florian's *Omnibeasts*, and Steve Jenkins' *Actual Size* was not selected" (Neumeyer, 2005, p. F9).

The Coretta Scott King Awards

Established in 1969, The Coretta Scott King Awards commemorate the life and work of Martin Luther King and the work of Coretta Scott King in advancing the goal of brotherhood. Presented annually by the American Library Association to an African American author and illustrator whose works are outstanding, they serve as an inspiration for young people to achieve their goals.

QUESTIONS CONCERNING THE CORETTA SCOTT KING AWARDS Marc Aronson, again writing in *The Horn Book* (2001), agrees that every person in the field of children's literature supports diversity, but he is convinced that creating awards "based on the race or ethnicity of its creators is a mistake" (Aronson, 2001, p. 277).

The Pura Belpré Award

This award, presented biannually by the American Library Association, specifies that the winner of the Pura Belpré must descend from any of the Spanish-speaking cultures of the Western Hemisphere. The award honors Pura Belpré, the first Latina librarian at the New York Public Library, a storyteller who spent her childhood in Puerto Rico. Many stories about her heritage have been compiled into the collection *The Tiger and the Rabbit* (1946). She has also written the folktale *Perez and Martina* for Viking that appeared in 1932 and was reissued in 1991.

QUESTIONS CONCERNING THE BELPRÉ AWARD   "The Spanish requirement is one problem with the Belpré Award because it excludes citizens of and émigrés from Brazil who speak Portuguese. But the idea of being Latino itself is another" (Aronson, 2001, p. 276). Aronson writes that Latino has no precise meaning. Writers who do not use that term to define themselves no matter how knowledgeable they are of their subject, cannot win the prize. "How can a requirement that is both ludicrously capacious and blindly restrictive make any sense?" (Aronson, 2001, p. 276). Aronson believes we should keep the Coretta Scott King and the Belpré awards, but modify them to honor content alone, rather than identity (Aronson, 2001, p. 278).

Criticism of the Awards

The many replies to the controversy ignited by Marc Aronson's article ("Slippery Slopes and Proliferating Prizes", 2001) were remarkable. For example, Andrea Davis Pinkney (then editorial director of Hyperion Books for Children and founder of the imprint *Jump at the Sun,* a line of books celebrating the richness and diversity of black life) defended the value of these awards in a response to Aronson's article. She argued that awards are "essential to the ALA tapestry. To allow white authors to become eligible for these awards is to turn that tapestry into the monochromatic blanket it used to be" (Pinkney, 2001, p. 539).

Adults concerned with fairness and equality wrote letters in large numbers to *The Horn Book.* Virginia Hamilton, the well-known and respected author who has since died, wrote that there is a difference in how a member of a Parallel Culture writes about the culture, versus how one outside of the community might write about it. Carol Edwards, membership chair of the Coretta Scott King Task Force, at the time reaffirmed the idea that all children need and want quality books and she feels that writers and illustrators who are African American are underrepresented.

What's Your View?

Replying to the Literary Awards

As a student of children's literature:

You have read the comments surrounding The Newbery Medal for not recognizing outstanding nonfiction.

You know that a reviewer criticized The Caldecott Medal for not considering the "syncopation" of art and text in the Caldecott Medal book for 2001.

You are aware of the controversy about the Coretta Scott King Awards committee for restricting its award to writers and illustrators who are African American.

You know that restricting the Pura Belpré Award to Hispanic Americans is controversial.

So how would you answer the following questions?

1. Do you believe additional national awards are necessary to encourage works by authors of parallel cultures? Why?

2. Can you think of books written by authors of Black and Hispanic cultures that you think should have received awards?

3. What would be your primary basis for considering a book: the author's heritage or the book's outstanding qualities? Why?

4. Would you establish an award permanently or would you review it every few years?

5. Do you agree with the late Virginia Hamilton, the beloved black author, when she said, "There is nothing wrong with having an award based on African-American experience?"

6. Do you believe the Coretta Scott King Awards limit the number of children who will read books by black authors?

7. What is your opinion of awards in general? Do you think they offer a valuable service to teachers, librarians, and especially to children? What's your view?

Responding to Children's Literature

An age-old question that appears and disappears on the pages of those who analyze children's literature is this: How do children respond to books? In Chapter One, we introduced Louise Rosenblatt's seminal work *The Reader, the Text, the Poem*, where she attempts to answer this question. Explaining how readers' responses vary from child to child, she argued that the meaning of a book depends on the transactions between children, with their perspective and prior knowledge, and the text itself, which expresses the author's ideas. This two-way process involves a reader and a text at a particular time and under particular circumstances (Rosenblatt, 1982). In other words, a child must be developmentally ready for a particular story or particular information, in order to have a goodness-of-fit between the two. The critical element in Rosenblatt's work is known as the *Transactional Theory of Reader Response*, which describes how a child experiences and reacts to a text. Readers engage in *efferent* reading (reading for information) or *aesthetic* reading (reading that captures the feelings and experiences of the reader). A reader can also engage in both efferent and aesthetic reading.

Strategies for Enriching Children's Responses to Their Reading

How do you actively encourage the interactions that lead to these responses? Using Rosenblatt's transactional theory as a guide, here are several suggestions for enriching children's responses to their reading. Other strategies are discussed in Appendices A and B.

A. Reading Aloud

Answering these questions will help you with your reading aloud technique.

• When you read a book aloud, do you select it by considering its developmental level, the features in it that attract a reader's attention (color, illustrations, etc.), or topics that naturally appeal to children of various interest levels (animals, mysteries, etc.)?

• As you read aloud, do you observe your students' listening response? Are they actively listening or are they distracted? Where does each child want to sit? Does every child eagerly and spontaneously participate in the laughter and reply to questions relating to the reading? Is reading aloud a joyous experience for you and your listeners?

B. Group Discussions

Here are several ideas for organizing small-group reading discussions. As Rosenblatt often reiterates, literature conversation groups are a transactional process in which students bring meaning to and take meaning from the books they read and discuss together (Rosenblatt, 1982).

• **THE GRAND CONVERSATION.** Originally called *literature circles* (Harste, Short, & Burke, 1988), the *grand conversation* describes children seated closely in a small group who discuss a book in a quiet conversational tone while the teacher offers open-ended questions to further the discussion. In such a setting, students reveal their excitement about and comprehension of the story (Peterson & Eeds, 1997). The freedom necessary for genuine reader response is basic to the success of the Grand Conversation (Daniels, 1994).

• **THE LITERARY LUNCH BUNCH.** A group composed of adults and students, meeting monthly to discuss a book such as *Because of Winn-Dixie*, as they share pizza and cold drinks, is called a *Literary Lunch Bunch* (Travers, 2000). One middle school teacher recently described his students' response when adults joined his sixth graders in a Literary Lunch as a truly different kind of experience for the children. Students described it as "awesome" and "great." Adults who participate in lunch bunches are impressed by the intelligence and respect of the students; the students enjoy the opportunity to express themselves and offer their ideas to adults who listen nonjudgmentally.

• **BOOK CLUBS.** When Shireen Dodson published *The Mother-Daughter Book Club* in 1996, she captured national attention with the idea of a mother-daughter club that parents nationwide are now making a common occurrence. (*mother-son* clubs are also becoming popular.) Through discussions of plots, characters, and authors' writing styles, members learn how to analyze an idea and take it apart (an excellent exercise in problem solving). By reading and talking together, the relationship between parents and children is also enriched (Dodson, 1996).

Kathleen Odean, in her *Great Books for Boys* (1998), discusses the kinds of books boys and their parents have found fun to share—not only humorous books, but also adventure and sports (preferably, non-stereotypical). She also points out the importance of selecting books that stress the positive influence of a father in a boy's life (Odean, 1998).

C. Special Events

Children like to participate in special activities that actively support their reading and writing activities. Here are several ideas to try.

• **LITERARY TEA.** Youngsters as young as first graders enjoy being "distinguished writers." For example, on a warm, sunny day recently, forty young writers, after sharing stories from the books each had worked on throughout the year, dressed up for tea served to them in porcelain cups from silver teapots. Parents had worked with the children every Friday morning in a writer's workshop, helping them articulate their ideas into books, editing with them as they wrote, and illustrating their stories. First grade teachers began this tradition eight years ago as a way to celebrate the efforts of the writers, and now it is an annual event (*Arlington Advocate*, June, 2003).

• **MEET THE AUTHOR.** Inviting an author to visit is an exciting event for children, but it is often costly. Active parent-teacher organizations and community associations, however, frequently contribute to the cost. An author or illustrator who lives locally may be willing to visit the school for a small honorarium. The innovative web site teachingbooks.net, lets students invite authors and illustrators into their classroom. (Minkel, 2003, p. 60). Publishers and multimedia companies distribute a wide range of videos to introduce students to outstanding authors and illustrators.

D. Dramatic Activities

For teachers and librarians to continue to generate reader reaction they must offer students creative opportunities to express their emotional responses to literature in a variety of ways:

• **READERS THEATER** can be spontaneous or previously rehearsed. When a first grade teacher notices two children reading the same book, such as Chris Raschka's *Yo! Yes?*, and suggests they take turns reading each line aloud to the class, it becomes a spontaneous dramatic presentation. Their voices rise and fall with the short lines as they continue alternating their reading until the last page is reached. When another primary grade teacher takes time to make puppets, write a script, and rehearse her students to read incidents from the stories in Arnold Lobel's *Frog and Toad* series, the readers' theater is more carefully planned.

As children advance in school, they select more complicated plots to be developed into Readers Theater, yet their enthusiasm remains high. Second and third graders have had much success presenting Harry Allard's *Miss Nelson Is Missing* (and adding music) for the enjoyment of their classmates, and fifth graders have adapted Barthe DeClementis's *Nothing's Fair in Fifth Grade* into an equally successful play.

• **TELEVISION BOOK COMMERCIALS.** Local cable stations are often willing to offer television time to elementary classes to promote reading, especially during Children's Book Week. Besides acting out commercials for their favorite books, children are often videotaped reviewing books they have read and enjoyed.

E. Book Readings, Competitions, and Reviews

• **BOOK REVIEWS.** Book reviews written by students can be offered to the local newspaper and included in the school news. Teachers may also encourage students to submit their work to national children's magazines (like *Cricket*) that publish students' work.

• **BOOKWORM BAFFLERS OR THE BOOK BOWL.** Good-natured competition is generated when children in the same grade in a school district are divided into teams and meet at a central location to answer questions about books they have read. Excitement is increased when those who participate are given tee shirts, the competition is reported on local television, and prizes are awarded.

• **SCHOOL READ.** A school read is similar to a community read where members of the community (old and young) read the same book and then discuss it at a central place (e.g., the main library, the town hall). Middle school or high school members read a segment of a book such as *The Seedfolks*

(Fleishman) for a designated time each day, then the school television is turned on while they continue to read another segment. When their reading is finished and the television is turned off, members of each class discuss what they have heard.

• **CHILDREN AS CRITICS.** When proprietors of an independent bookstore were knee-deep in advance copies of soon-to-be-published books, they loaned copies to interested middle school children and asked them to write reviews. They discovered that children are very opinionated about what they like and don't like. And their opinions are valuable to other children and adults who are shopping for books. More than fifty children work as critics, earning a small financial credit toward each book they read and write about, and their reviews are tacked onto a bulletin board in the children's section (Mulkerin, 2003).

F. Further Suggestions

These are only a few suggestions to encourage children to respond to their reading. Books like *Making Meaning in the Response-Based Classroom* (Margaret Hunsberger & George Labercane) and *Motivating Recreational Reading and Promoting Home-School Connections* (Timothy Rasinski) offer teachers and librarians many more strategies. As Madeleine L'Engle has so aptly written in *Walking on Water: Reflections on Faith and Art*, children must come to a place where "reader and author meet on the bridge of words" (L'Engle, 1980, pp. 37–38). With Rosenblatt's ideas in mind, it is exciting to consider the great possibilities of increasing a child's enjoyment and knowledge, not only by the solitary process of reading a book, but by sharing its contents with others.

Chapter Checklist

Read the following items carefully. If you have difficulty responding to any of them, return to the chapter to review the material.

After reading this chapter, you can

1. Describe how libraries—both school and public—organize their books.

2. List and define the literary elements of a book.

3. Provide examples of the literary elements in stories of your choice.

4. Give examples of techniques you could use to organize a classroom library.

5. Evaluate the controversy surrounding the meaning of a "good book."

6. Analyze the role that literary awards play—or should play—in book selection.

7. Suggest ways in which children can respond to a book.

Children's Bibliography

Allard, Harry, (1977). *Miss Nelson Is Missing*. Boston: Houghton Mifflin.

Ahlberg, Janet, & Ahlberg, Allan. (1986). *The Jolly Postman*. Boston: Little, Brown.

Aronson, Marc. (2000). *Sir Walter Ralegh and the Quest for El Dorado*. New York: Clarion Books.

Babbitt, Natalie. (1975). *Tuck Everlasting*. New York: Farrar, Straus, & Giroux.

Baum, L. Frank. (1900). *The Wonderful Wizard of Oz*. New York: Morrow.

Bemelmans, Ludwig. (1939). *Madeline*. New York: Macmillan.

Belpré, Pura. (1946). *The Tiger and the Rabbit*. Boston: Houghton Mifflin.

Belpré, Pura. (1991). *Perez and Martina*. New York: Viking.

Burton, Virginia Lee. (1942). *The Little House*. Boston: Houghton Mifflin.

Cleary, Beverly. (1999). *Ramona's World*. New York: Morrow.

de Paola, Tomie. (1975). *Strega Nona*. Englewood Cliffs, NJ: Prentice Hall.

DeClementis, Barthe. (1990). *Nothing's Fair in Fifth Grade*. New York: Puffin.

DiCamillo, Kate. (2000). *Because of Winn-Dixie*. Cambridge, MA: Candlewick.

DiCamillo, Kate. (2001). *The Tiger Rising*. Cambridge, MA: Candlewick.

DiCamillo, Kate. (2003). *The Tale of Despereaux*. Cambridge, MA: Candlewick.

DiCamillo, Kate. (2005). *Mercy Watson to the Rescue*. Cambridge, MA: Candlewick.

DiCamillo, Kate. (2006). *The Miraculous Journey of Edward Tulane*. Cambridge, MA: Candlewick.

Fleishman, Paul. (1997). *Seedfolks*. New York: HarperCollins.

Gag, Wilma. (1928). *Millions of Cats*. New York: Coward-McCann.

Guiberson, Brenda Z. (2001). *The Emperor Lays an Egg*. New York: Holt.

Kunhardt, Dorothy. (1940). *Pat the Bunny*. New York: Golden, Western.

Lawson, Robert. (1940). *They Were Strong and Good*. New York: Viking.

L'Engle, Madeleine. (1962). *A Wrinkle in Time*. New York: Farrar, Straus.

Lobel, Arnold. (1972). *Frog and Toad Together*. New York: HarperCollins.

McCloskey, Robert. (1941). *Make Way for Ducklings*. New York: Viking.

Potter, Beatrix. (1902). *Peter Rabbit*. New York: Frederick Warne.

Raschka, Chris. (1993). *Yo! Yes?* New York: Orchard Books.

Sendak, Maurice. (1963). *Where the Wild Things Are*. New York: Harper & Row.

Sis, Peter. (1996). *Starry Messenger*. New York: Farrar, Straus, & Giroux.

Sleator, William. (1986). *The Boy Who Reversed Himself*. New York: Dutton.

Sobol, David. (1990). *Encyclopedia Brown and the Case of the Disgusting Sneakers*. New York: Morrow.

St. George, Judith. Illus. David Small. (2000). *So You Want to Be President*. New York: Philomel.

Shulevitz, Uri. (1998). *Snow*. New York: Farrar, Straus, & Giroux.

Spinelli, Jerry. (1990). *Maniac Magee*. Boston: Little, Brown.

Steig, William. (2000). *Wizzil*. New York: Farrar, Straus, & Giroux.

VanLoon, Hendrik. (1921/1984). *The Story of Mankind*. New York: Liveright.

White, Ruth. (1996). *Belle Prater's Boy*. New York: Bantam, Doubleday, Dell.

White, Ruth. (2003). *Tadpole*. New York: Farrar.

White, Ruth, (2004). *Buttermilk Hill*. New York: Farrar.

White, Ruth. (2005). *Search for Belle Prater*. New York: Farrar.

Professional References

Aronson, Marc. (2001). "Slippery Slopes and Proliferating Prizes." *The Horn Book*. May/June, 271–279.

Aronson, Marc. (2001). "Nonfiction Award Winner." *The Horn Book*. January/February. 49–52.

Calkins, Lucy McCormick. (2001). *The Art of Teaching Reading*. New York: Longman.

Cuddon, J. A. (1998). *Literary Terms and Literary Theory*. New York: Penguin.

Daniels, Harvey. (1994). *Literature Circles: Voice and Choice in a Student-Centered Classroom*. York, ME: Stenhouse.

DiCamillo, Kate. (2004). "Newbery Medal Acceptance." *The Horn Book*. July/August. 395–400.

Dodson, Shireen. (1997). *The Mother-Daughter Book Club*. New York: Harper Perennial.

Forster, E. M. (1927). *Aspects of the Novel*. New York: Harcourt Brace & World.

Fountas, Irene C., & Su Pinnell Gay. (2001). *Guiding Readers and Writers (Grades 3–6)*. Portsmouth, NH: Heinemann.

Giblin, James. (2000). "More Than Just the Facts." *The Horn Book*. July/August.

Glassman, Peter, ed. (2000). *Oz: The Hundredth Anniversary Celebration*. New York: HarperCollins.

Hearn, Michael. (2001). "Toto, I've a Feeling We're Not in Kansas City Anymore. . . Detroit or Washington D. C." *The Horn Book*. January/February. 16–34.

Hunsberger, Margaret, & Labercane, George. (2002). *Making Meaning in the Response-Based Classroom*. Boston: Allyn & Bacon.

L'Engle, Madeleine. (1980). *Walking on Water: Reflections on Faith and Art*. Wheaton, IL: H. Shaw.

Lowry, Lois. (2002). "The Remembered Gate and the Unopened Door." *The Horn Book*. March/April. 159–177.

Lukens, R. (1990). *A Critical Handbook of Children's Literature*. Glenview, IL: Scott, Foresman.

Maslow, A. (1987). *Motivation and Personality*. New York: Harper & Row.

Meltzer, Milton. (1976). "Where Do All the Prizes Go? The Case for Nonfiction." *The Horn Book*. January/February. 17–23.

Minkel, Walter. (2003). "An Author in Every Classroom." *School Library Journal*, March.

Mulkerin, Mary. (2003). "Bookshop Lets Children Have First Word." *Boston Sunday Globe*. September 14.

Neumeyer, Peter. (2001). "Watering Down the Caldecott." *Boston Globe*. March 4, C2.

Neumeyer, Peter. (2005). "Moonlit Meanderings, Wordless Wonders." *Boston Globe*. February 13. F9.

Odean, Kathleen. (1998). *Great Books for Boys*. New York: Ballantine.

Pappas, Marjorie. (2004). "On My Mind." *Knowedge Quest*. November/December.

Peterson, Ralph, & Eeds, Maryann. (1990). *Grand Conversations: Literature Groups in Action*. Richmond Hill, ON: Scholastic.

Pinkney, Andrea. (2001). "Awards that Stand on Solid Ground." *The Horn Book*. September/October. 535–537.

Rasinski, Timothy, et al. (2000). *Motivating Recreational Reading and Promoting Home-School Connections*. Newark, DE: International Reading Association.

Rosenblatt, Louise. (1978). *The Reader, the Text, the Poem*. Carbondale, IL: Southern Illinois Press.

Rosenblatt, Louise. (1982). "The Literary Transaction: Evocation and Response." In K. Holland, R. Hungerford, & S. Ernst (eds.), *Journeying: Children Responding to Literature*. Portsmouth, NH: Heinemann.

Shannon, Donna. (2004). "The School Library Media Specialist and Early Literacy Programs." *Knowledge Quest*. November/December. 15–19.

Sieruta, Peter. (2001). "Kate DiCamillo. The Tiger Rising." *The Horn Book*. 321–322.

Silvey, Anita. (1995). *Children's Books and Their Creators*. Boston: Houghton Mifflin.

Sleator, William. (1996). "What Is It About Science Fiction?" In Egoff, Sheila. ed. *Only Connect*. Third Ed. New York: Oxford University Press. 206–212.

Thomas, Jane Resh. (2004). "Kate DiCamillo." *The Horn Book*. July/August. 401–404.

Travers, Barbara & Driscoll, Gerry. (2000). "The Literary Lunch Bunch: An Intergenerational Book Club." Presentation at MSLA Annual Conference, November 6.

The Craft of Writing and Illustrating

M. T. Anderson, a writer usually associated with young adult novels such as the Newbery Medal book, The Astonishing Life of Octavian Nothing, Traitor to the Nation, Volume 1: The Pox Party, *has written an outstanding picture book that defies the image of picture books being written only for young children.* Handel, Who Knew What He Liked, *illustrated by Kevin Hawkes, is a book written for all ages. Although in picture book format, it is an extensive and authoritative biography of one of the world's best-loved composers.*

Illustrator Kevin Hawkes has written and illustrated many books for children, including Weslandia, The Librarian Who Measured the Earth, *and* Painting the Wind: A Story of Vincent Van Gogh. *But illustrating* Handel, *presented a challenge to Hawkes. Although he loved illustrating this book, he wondered if he had done Handel justice. Readers agree, however, that his illustrations enhance the story. Wishing to portray the dramatic operatic presentation of Handel's* Messiah, *for example, he created a full-page acrylic painting of over fifty singers, individually portrayed in black and white.*

In this chapter we'll probe the strategies that authors and illustrators, such as those mentioned above, use to blend artistry and meaningful language into their stories, while simultaneously tapping into the rich vein of developmental data. This in itself is no easy task, but the effort is richly rewarded when children acquire awareness and begin to discern meaning in their reading and listening. To accomplish this goal, we'll introduce Newbery Medal authors, Caldecott Medal illustrators, and others who have contributed to making children's literature memorable.

Leonard Marcus (2002, p. 6) captured the sense of mystery surrounding the success of outstanding books when he noted that "artists and writers need not know why they work as they do—why, for instance, they prefer pen-and-ink or watercolor?" Why do certain ideas rather than others lodge in their memories and lead them on their journeys? We agree with Marcus, but still retain a suspicion that the solution to these riddles lies in the interaction among author, artist, and reader. And, if we dig even more deeply into these interactions, we suspect that we'll find our answers in the developmental characteristics of readers.

Anne Hoppe (2004, p. 41) expressed the magnitude of the challenge facing us in this chapter when she noted:

The two oldest forms of storytelling—words and images—meet and merge in picture books. A well-placed word can leave you elated or it can break your heart.

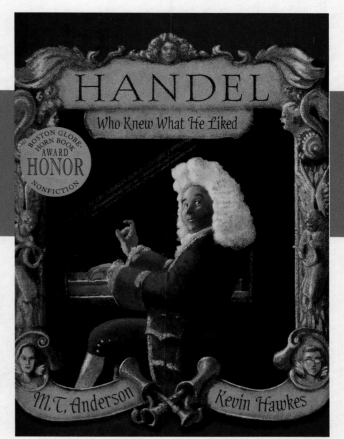

HANDEL, WHO KNEW WHAT HE LIKED
Text copyright © 2001 by M.T. Anderson. Illustrations copyright © 2001 by Kevin Hawkes. Reproduced by permission of the publisher, Candlewick Press Inc., Cambridge, MA.

Pictures can invoke peals of laughter or cries of outrage. A fundamental, some would argue inherent, understanding of both of these methods of telling stories is hard-wired into our humanity. And when the two forms come together, as they do in picture books, the whole is so very much greater than the sum of the parts. At its best and most successful, the skillful joining of words and pictures is nothing short of magical.

To help you understand the intricate and essential interplay between words and images that define the successful book, we'll first explore the manner in which children develop language. Next, we'll see how authors use appropriate language in their texts, and we'll attempt to discover how they build the structure of their story with developmentally appropriate and colorful words. We'll then begin our search for clues to the appeal of illustrations by examining children's own drawings. Our rationale is that their personal art reflects those objects, characters, lines, circles, and colors that most appeal to their senses. Following this discussion, we'll note several outstanding illustrations that capture those features and, knowingly or not, match children's developing senses, especially vision. Finally, we'll consider award-winning authors and illustrators who through their skill and talent have helped create literature for children that has endured throughout the years, and promises to stretch far into the future.

From our opening vignette about *Handel, Who Knew What He Liked*, you can discern that in our discussion we do not confine ourselves to picture books written only for young children. A movement to make nonfiction books more visual grew and spread in the 1980s, and this tendency is now apparent in books for older children (Giblin, 2000). Our focus, therefore, will be on both text and illustrations, since we can be sure of the continued and widespread use of art and pictures in books for all ages. Remember that our goal is to gain a deeper understanding of how the various features of children, text, and illustrations come together to produce an engaging, colorful, and meaningful story.

Guidelines for Reading Chapter 5

After you finish reading Chapter Five, you should be able to answer the following questions.

• What is the relationship between a child's language development and an author's use of text?

• How do authors and illustrators work together to aid a reader's search for meaning?

• How can the influence of children's artistic development on a text's illustrations be demonstrated?

• What are several perceptual principles that appear in a text's illustrations?

• Are there milestones in a child's perceptual development that both authors and illustrators must take into consideration?

• How do authors and illustrators combine their talents to represent as well as tell? Give examples from your readings.

• What basic principles help explain the integration of text, illustration, and development?

• Can you select a story that demonstrates the integration of the principles discussed in this chapter?

Language and Children

When authors set themselves the goal of spinning an irresistible tale, one of the first challenges they face is writing in a language their audience will understand. This takes us into the world of children's language development. Many psychologists—as well as parents, teachers, and librarians—believe one of a child's most amazing developmental triumphs is the beginning of actual speech. Think of it this way: with no formal training, children learn words, meanings, and how to combine them in a logical, purposeful manner (Dacey & Travers, 2009). In her fascinating book on brain development, Lise Eliot (2000) noted that we're probably safe in saying that our genes propel us into a language world. Our brains, however, direct this process—and this is a major point—children's experiences shape the final outcome.

Given this drive toward language and children's acquisition of their own language in a remarkably similar manner, we begin to suspect that nature plays a critical role in the process, which leads us to consider the brain's function. In other words, children in all parts of the world go through a process in which they first emit sounds, then single words, then two words, and finally, fairly complex sentences. By the time they are about 5 years of age, they have acquired the basics of their language. It's an astonishing achievement, when you consider that they do it mainly through their own development.

The Path of Language Development

Almost all children acquire the basics of their language so easily that it seems they have an innate tendency toward language acquisition. No matter how much trouble they may have with mathematics, for example, they move into their linguistic

Table 5.1 THE SEQUENCE OF LANGUAGE DEVELOPMENT

AGE	ACCOMPLISHMENT
Approximately 3 months	Children use intonations similar to those of adults.
About 1 year	They begin to use recognizable words and repeat sounds to express emotion.
About 4 years	They have acquired the complicated structure of their native tongue.
At approximately 5 years of age	Children use adultlike language, that is, they form sentences. Naming and counting are important to them.
At 6 or 7	Children now speak and understand sentences they have never previously used or heard.
From 8 to 10 years	Children begin to use their vocabulary skillfully (for example, not hesitating to use synonyms) and their conversational strategies noticeably improve.
From 11 to 13 years	Their speech closely resembles that of an adult.

world with comparative ease. This is not to say, of course, that all children reach the heights of eloquent expression. Remember: experience helps determine the final outcome. As you become aware of the beauty, appeal, and sheer power of children's literature, you realize the vital role it plays in the various aspects of children's language development: phonological development (sounds), semantic development (meaning), syntactic development (structure), and pragmatic development (conversational rules). To help you in your work with children of all ages, and to show how authors must write their story with appropriate vocabulary, Table 5.1 presents a brief overview of language development.

With these basic ideas about language development in mind, note the following general recommendations.

1. A CHILD'S ENVIRONMENT INFLUENCES THE NUMBER OF CONNECTIONS MADE IN THE BRAIN. Consequently, adults who speak *to*, rather than *at* children and read to them immediately after birth (perhaps during even the final prenatal weeks) provide an enriched language environment for children. (Note the lasting effects of *The Cat In The Hat* in Chapter 7, *Literature for the Early Years*.)

Phyllis Reynolds Naylor attributes her own writing success to her parents, who read aloud to her every night for as far back as she can remember. In her acceptance speech for winning the Newbery Medal for *Shiloh*, she thanked them for the "drama" in their voices, as they recounted adventures such as *Tom Sawyer*, *Huckleberry Finn*, *The Prince and the Pauper*, and *Alice in Wonderland*. She confesses that she was never interested in the authors—"it was the story that was important" (*Newbery and Caldecott Medal Books*, 2001, p. 168).

2. THE TYPE OF STIMULATION YOU USE MUST BE APPROPRIATE FOR THE CHILD'S AGE AND ABILITIES. Merely exposing children to language is remarkably ineffective. For example, a baby propped up before a television set does-n't necessarily form connections in the language areas of the brain. But when you in-troduce a child to a Caldecott picture book, such as *Hey, Al*, written by Arthur Yorinks and illustrated by Richard Egielski, the child will listen. As you read aloud how Al and his dog Eddie are transformed into birds and rise into the air by furiously flapping their wings, you stimulate the child's imagination as your words convey a sense of rhythm and sound. Books like *Hey, Al* are a powerful and positive tool for language development.

3. REMEMBER THAT CHILDREN'S EMOTIONS ARE AS INVOLVED IN LANGUAGE DEVELOPMENT AS IS THEIR ABILITY TO FORM WORDS AND MOVE THEIR LIPS AND TONGUE. From birth, children are remarkably sensitive to *how* they are spoken to and treated, especially during their early years. For example, in the Newbery Medal book *Missing May*, Cynthia Rylant under-stands the importance of words and the effect they create. She reveals her under-standing of the significance of the tone and texture of words, when she decides that Summer, the narrator of the story, will use language that reveals her sensitivity and sympathy toward the troubles of others. When Summer visits Cletus at his house for the first time, she knows in an instant

that this was not the same boy who had been coming to us with his battered old suitcases all these weeks. This was a different boy, and I knew, even before I set one foot inside his house, that here in this place, he was a much-loved boy. It's funny, how you can know something like that right away.

(Rylant, 1992, p. 60)

The characters that Cynthia Rylant portrays in *Missing May* may have painful ex-periences, but she conveys the message that these people count and should be ad-dressed with gentleness.

4. LISTEN CAREFULLY TO A CHILD'S SPEECH, BEGINNING RIGHT AFTER BIRTH. You must learn to be a good observer or you'll miss much of what children are trying to tell you in different ways. This is as true in infancy as in adolescence. Children typically leave a trail of clues—at all ages—that point to definite behaviors as clearly as an arrow seeking its target. Respond to them with supportive speech and stories.

In Lois Lowry's *The Silent Boy*, Katy, the narrator, offers Jacob, the "touched boy," her understanding, although he is unable to speak one word. She knows there must be meaning in the sounds he makes, and she tries very hard to figure out what it is. One time, she finds him in their stable and hears his voice. She likes the sound he makes since it seems like a kind of singing. But it was

a kind of singing that wasn't real singing at all. I wondered if he would mind my join-ing in so I watched his face, tried to catch onto the same note, and kept at it when I saw that it didn't make him uneasy.

(Lowry, 2003, p. 49)

5. AS CHILDREN GROW OLDER, ENGAGE THEM IN CONVERSA-TION IN WHICH YOU LISTEN AS WELL AS TALK. If you're willing to be an in-terested listener, you'll be amazed how much you'll learn about a child's life. Children, in turn, learn the skill of exchanging ideas and the give-and-take of conversation, while building new connections in many areas of the brain: language, thinking, listening, and emotional. Reading and discussing suitable and beguiling stories, at various ages, pro-vide a marvelous opportunity to encourage children to express their feeling about the story, and perhaps other issues that concern them. In Jerry Spinelli's *Maniac Magee*,

Maniac found a listener in Grayson, the park attendant who rescued him when he was only a "body clumped outside the buffalo pen." As they became friends, Maniac also found Grayson to be a great storyteller.

Beatrix Potter knew. She may have had her watercolors at hand, but she knew that *first came the words* (Bader, 2004, p. 633). As you become aware of the beauty, appeal, and sheer power of children's literature, you realize the vital role it can play in children's language development. Understanding the richness of language development, you can comprehend and sympathize with authors who strive to reach the young and attract older children into the reading world.

Authors face a daunting task. As they struggle to unravel the puzzle of successful storytelling they face the following three challenges.

1. How to transmit their ideas.
2. How to make each word count.
3. How to match the story's vocabulary and illustrations with the child's level of language development.

Addressing these challenges today are a number of talented authors who possess the insight, imagination, and ingenuity to produce books that enthrall, captivate, and charm their readers. Among them are the following.

Award-Winning Authors

In the last decade of the twentieth century, authors Karen Hesse, Jerry Spinelli, Cynthia Rylant, Karen Cushman, and Lois Lowry have won the Newbery Medal, the most distinguished award in children's literature. How they rose to meet the challenges associated with writing an award-winning book provides us with fascinating insights and gives us a glimpse into what children's literature will be like in the twenty-first century.

KAREN HESSE   Karen Hesse, for example, relates *Out of the Dust* in first person, free-verse poetry. She gives the reader a sense of the tragedy about the Great Depression of the 1930s by having Billie Jo Kelby, the 14-year-old narrator, describe a series of disastrous incidents that she, her family, and neighbors experienced in the Oklahoma panhandle. The use of blank verse not only provides Hesse with a successful method for presenting tragedy in small portions, but it also succinctly reveals the hardships Billie Jo endured and the forgiveness Hesse wants to express, between the characters and "between the people and the land itself."

How does Karen Hesse appeal to her readers? Writing in poetic form forced her to select her words carefully. Yet she never attempted to write *Out of the Dust* any way other than in free verse. In her acceptance speech for the Newbery Medal, she explained "that the frugality of the life, the hypnotically hard work of farming, [and] the grimness of conditions during the dust bowl demanded an economy of word" (Hesse, 2001, p. 300). Hesse stresses that children often suffer pain and sorrow, as well as joy. The question she asks is: should we accept that pain without trying to find a way to transcend it? In *Out of the Dust*, she answers her question by developing characters that grow, transform, and ultimately overcome their pain.

JERRY SPINELLI   Jerry Spinelli, author of *Maniac Magee*, weaves a story for adolescents that is part realism and part myth. He develops a character—a freedom-seeking, athletically–competitive young boy—who readily appeals to his audience. Because he is homeless, he is forced to be street-wise. Although outwardly brash, deep in his heart he longs for a home, a family, and a school life.

Spinelli's editor, John Keller, has written that Jerry listens and observes, but that his observations have not always endeared his work to adult readers. Yet he believes *Maniac Magee* is the best realized of Spinelli's characters. Maniac still does not fully understand his place in the world. "He roams from the darkness of his troubles, but he runs toward the light he sees shining from the decent people he encounters" (Keller, 2001, p. 150). Children gravitate toward *Maniac Magee* and often recall his story many years later.

How does Jerry Spinelli appeal to his readers? Spinelli transmits ideas using language familiar to the children with whom he communicates daily. In his talks with students, he often tells them that his ideas come from his own children. He sees children as funny and fascinating, elusive and inspiring, promising and heroic, and—sometimes—maddening.

CYNTHIA RYLANT   In *Missing May*, a story of grief and loss not unlike *Maniac Magee*, Cynthia Rylant transmits her ideas in prose that is lyrical and uplifting. The narrator is twelve-year-old Summer, who has been left an orphan and has been in many foster homes before Aunt May and Uncle Ob bring her to live with them. She loves them dearly and is heartbroken when Aunt May dies. Putting aside her own grief, she tries to console Ob with help from Cletus.

How does Cynthia Rylant appeal to her readers? Using language filled with gentle humor, Rylant reveals a tremendous talent for describing characters whose peculiarities become endearing to her audience. She understands "simple folk," and that people have a right to lead a lifestyle that suits them. "Through her own experiences, she creates her stories and has a deep love for people who are trying their best while they continue to be kind" (Ward, 2001, p. 197).

KAREN CUSHMAN   In *The Midwife's Apprentice*, Karen Cushman challenges not only herself, but also her readers to understand her story about medieval England and a homeless girl (Beetle) who was "unnourished, unloved, and unlovely." When the midwife, Jane Sharp, rescues her from a dung heap, she takes Beetle home to be a servant. But as Beetle's, self-confidence grows, she gradually learns that she can be a midwife. After changing her name to Alyce and becoming more accepted by the villagers, she is on the road to becoming self-reliant.

Cushman's husband Philip tells us that she was discouraged from writing *The Midwife's Apprentice* because friends said a history book might not sell, adolescents probably would not understand the concept of the past, and boys would never read a novel with a girl as the main character (Cushman, 2001, p. 254). Cushman's persistence, however, resulted in a historical novel that will long be remembered by girls and boys.

How does Karen Cushman appeal to her readers? Cushman worked hard to research her story in order to make her characters come alive. Through her talent of writing humorously and using words that are filled with meaning, she has successfully transmitted her ideas and captivated an audience, some of whom may never have read a historical novel before reading *The Midwife's Apprentice*. She admits that she does not start a book by thinking of the listener or the reader.

I just climb inside a story and write it over and over again until I know what it's about. Then I try to write as clearly and honestly as I can.

(Cushman, 2001, p. 246)

LOIS LOWRY (PICTURE)   In accepting her second Newbery Medal (her first was for *Number the Stars*) for the science fiction novel, *The Giver* (the first book in a trilogy that includes *Gathering Blue* and *Messenger*), Lois Lowry mentions that the

Giver passed along to the boy Jonas: knowledge, history, memories, color, pain, laughter, love, and truth (Marcus, 2002). Yet ironically, some adults think *The Giver* is nothing but a chronicle of evils. It is on the American Library Association's list of the ten most challenged books of the 1990s, which means libraries were frequently asked to remove it from their shelves. The incident in the book most criticized is when an adult kills a baby. But as startling and upsetting as this may be, it is this incident that makes Jonas see how futile and immoral his society is, and how he must muster his courage to escape "Elsewhere."

After mentioning what the Giver passed along to Jonas, Lowry concluded her Newbery Medal acceptance speech with the analogy that every time

they place a book in the hands of a child, they do the very same thing. It is very risky. But each time a child opens a book, he pushes open the gate that separates him from Elsewhere. It gives him choices. It gives him freedom. Those are magnificent, wonderfully unsafe things.

(Lowry, 2001, p. 216)

How does Lois Lowry, who has also received the Margaret A. Edwards Award for lifetime achievement in writing for young adults, appeal to her readers? By provoking powerful discussions in the classroom and library about justice, morality, humanity, memory, and other issues, she touches on topics that reach into the daily lives of young readers. And although she does not seek controversy, she does not shy away from writing about difficult topics she thinks worth discussing. She believes that telling about things is the way we learn to live with them (Kennedy, 2003).

THE SILENT BOY
Cover from THE SILENT BOY by Lois Lowry. Cover photograph © 2003 by Lois Lowry. Reprinted by permission of Houghton Mifflin Company. All rights reserved.

Authors and Illustrators

Although the Caldecott Medal is awarded only to artists for their distinguished illustrations, authors who write the texts of Caldecott books, such as Chris Van Allsburg, Arthur Yorinks, Peggy Rathmann, Paul O. Zelinsky, and David Macaulay, play a major role in making these picture books medal winners. They breathe life into the story by their use of language that makes the illustrations more meaningful.

CHRIS VAN ALLSBURG   On board *The Polar Express* on Christmas Eve is the narrator, a young boy in pajamas, who is heading for the North Pole on a train wrapped in steam, with other boys and girls still in their night clothes. Chris Van Allsburg paces the story slowly and mysteriously: the sound of the rumbling wheels as the train slides through mountains "where lean wolves roamed" and "white tailed rabbits hid from the train as it thundered through the quiet wilderness." When the train reaches the North Pole, the pace quickens and we sense the excitement when the children see an array of lights that look "like the lights of a strange ocean liner sailing on a frozen sea."

There, the boy meets Santa and his elves in a huge city that Van Allsburg vividly describes as standing alone at the top of the world, filled with factories where every Christmas toy was made. Van Allsburg uses words to create the pleasure the narrator feels when he receives a silver bell, "the first gift of Christmas." And he describes the narrator's dismay when he discovers he has lost his silver bell from Santa's sleigh. Surprise grips the reader and it is not until the boy opens his gifts on Christmas day that he finds the silver bell, with a note from Santa "to fix that hole in your pocket." The narrator concludes his story by saying "Though I've grown old, the bell still rings for me as it does for all who truly believe." In *The Polar Express*, Van Allsburg has created an enchanting picture book that completely integrates his writing with his illustrations.

How does Chris Van Allsburg appeal to his readers? For Chris Van Allsburg illustrating a story does not have the same quality of discovery as writing it. As he said during his Caldecott Medal acceptance speech:

As I consider a story, I see it quite clearly. Illustrating is simply a matter of drawing something I've already experienced in my mind's eye. Because I see the story unfold as if it were on film, the challenge is deciding which moment should be illustrated and from which point of view.

(Allsburg, 2001, pp. 29, 30)

ARTHUR YORINKS   Arthur Yorinks faced a different challenge than did Chris Van Allsburg, who is both an author and illustrator. Since he is not an artist, when Yorinks sets out to write a picture book, he must set his own pace without knowing the intent of the illustrator. He does this brilliantly. His friend, illustrator Richard Egielski, agrees that it is challenging to write a true picture-book text that tells the story and "still has the power to inspire a series of exciting images" (Egielski, 2001, p. 40). Yorinks successfully breathes life into the award-winning *Hey, Al*, and through his choice of words, allows Egielski's imagination to run free and create illustrations that turned his story into a picture book.

How does Arthur Yorinks appeal to his readers? His phrase "ripe fruit soon spoils" implies that Al and his dog Ed are getting bored living in their tropical island. Although Yorinks has predictably portrayed the life Al and Ed experience on their tropical island, he offers readers a surprise when he brings Al and Ed back to earth because they are having too much of a good time. His statement "Paradise lost is sometimes Heaven found," succinctly concludes Al and Ed's escapade and reveals that they are ready to accept themselves as they really are.

PEGGY RATHMANN   In *Officer Buckle and Gloria*, Peggy Rathmann weaves a story that delights children and illustrates the text so humorously that children in the audience laugh out loud at the antics of Gloria the police dog, who accompanies Officer Buckle on his school talks. Rathmann cleverly lets her readers in on the *big* secret, and they laugh with delight when Gloria acts out Officer Buckle's safety tips behind his back. Officer Buckle is totally unaware of what is occurring until he views a video of his talk. Then, he is chagrined and refuses to give any more safety talks. Instead he sends Gloria to the schools alone. But she will not perform without Officer Buckle. They need each other to make a winning team. Rathmann's safety tip #101 on the last page says it all: *always stick with your buddy.*

How does Peggy Rathmann appeal to her readers? Her ability to integrate a humorous text with the vitality of cartoonlike line drawings is the winning combination. Like Officer Buckle and Gloria, her text and drawings cannot get along without each other. In her Caldecott acceptance speech, she confesses that all her stories are based on family secrets, including the family dog's secrets. Rathmann's inherent humor fills the pages of this picture book and makes children, and adults, grateful for her artistic and writing talent that can transfer her humor into words and illustrations.

DAVID MACAULAY   In *Black and White*, David Macaulay deliberately mystifies his audience. Warning them that *Black and White* (which is also colored blue and green) appears to contain a number of stories that do not necessarily occur at the same time (or) may contain only one story, puts the reader immediately on guard.

Only by taking the author's advice to carefully inspect both words and pictures, will the reader comprehend what is taking place in this postmodern picture book. In his drawing and illustration classes, Macaulay constantly encourages students to ask themselves why things look the way they do. He believes that seeing necessitates thinking. "Nothing can be intelligently or intelligibly recorded on a piece of paper unless true seeing occurs. First on the part of the person making the picture and then on the part of the person reading it" (Macaulay, 2001, p. 130).

Macaulay moves from the beginning of one story to another (two to each page) in a logical order. The appeal of his language is clearly evident, as when the young narrator describes herself and her brother as "rejects from some origami zoo." Macaulay's four stories are entirely unpredictable. The robber hiding among the cows, the passengers who toss their newspapers to the winds while waiting for the train, the parents who come home dressed in newspapers, and the children who are amazed by their parents' behavior may all be performers in the theatre of the absurd. In *Black and White*, Macauley welcomes us into their world.

How does David Macaulay appeal to his readers? His creativity is unquestioned. In his acceptance speech for the Caldecott Medal, he defined his idea of the creative process as "that sequence of actions, erratic and unpredictable, by which the creative processor sets out to bring order and extract

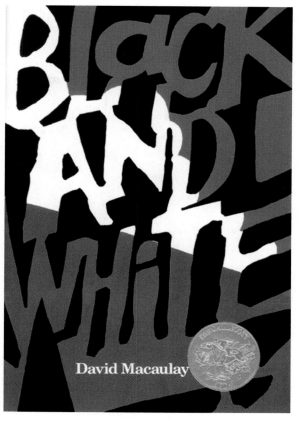

BLACK AND WHITE
Cover from BLACK AND WHITE by David Macaulay. Copyright © 1990 by David Macaulay. Reprinted by permission of Houghton Mifflin Company. All rights reserved.

Spotlight On
Paul O. Zelinsky

In his thought-provoking and insightful Zena Sutherland lecture, Paul O. Zelinsky beautifully summarized the ideas we've been discussing in this chapter. Perhaps he best stated the importance of integrating text and illustrations when he said: "My theory is that seeing is a form of thinking" (Zelinsky, 2003. p. 523).

Musing on how neuroscientists study visual perception, he noted that the instant light hits the retina, we begin processing information. Edges, which he believes are the basis of visual literacy, fascinate him. Noting that the goal of sight is constancy, he turned his attention to the figure-ground relationship (discussed in this chapter) and argued that this relationship keeps us from being flooded by unnecessary sensations.

For the artist, it's important to remember that visual perception is not merely a single thing. It's a collection of separate sensations that enable the identification of shape, movement, color, and objects. Although we respond to objects in our environments as integrated wholes, visual information comes from distinct subsystems. (See Gazzaniga, Ivry, & Mangun, 1998.)

As Zelinsky noted (2003, p. 535), the more you draw, the more you see. As an example of how ideas concerning visual perception come together for the artist, consider how he illustrated the frenzy of the prince in *Rapunzel*.

the shapes show it along with the characters: the prince's straight lines jutting forward and Rapunzel's curves wheeling out of their way. To the degree that I succeed, form and content of the picture will become one thing, and you'll find it in your thought-heart (Newbery and Caldecott Medal Books, 2001, p. 284).

Thought-heart is the expression Zelinsky often uses to denote emotion of thought and the logic of feeling. "It lies deep inside all of us, I am certain."

RAPUNZEL
Reproduced with permission of Penguin Group USA Inc.

meaning from a conglomeration of parts and elements which are without order or connection" (Macaulay, 2001, p. 137). *Black and White* took seven years for Macaulay to write; it had not been a "speedy journey." Yet for readers, *Black and White* is an entertaining challenge to which they may return again and again.

PAUL O. ZELINSKY   Paul Zelinsky's *Rapunzel* is more than a picture story book — it is a work worthy of Renaissance art. In his Caldecott acceptance speech (*Newbery and Caldecott Medal Books*, 2001), Zelinsky stated that if he had let himself think realistically about what he was getting into, he may have put Rapunzel off for another decade. But he continued to research and authenticate every detail of each illustration in the book — from sixteenth century scissors, to the features of a Tuscan village.

How does Paul O. Zelinsky appeal to his readers? To recreate a well-known fairy tale like Rapunzel, Zelinsky tells the story through pictures. This is evident in his portrayal of the sorceress, when she takes the baby Rapunzel from her parents. When children see this picture they notice the gentleness in her face. And they later shiver at her look of horror when Rapunzel says that her dress "doesn't want to fit me any more." As children's perceptual awareness increases, and as they read and reread this picture book, they discover details they may not have seen previously.

What makes a child respond to a picture in a book? Is it accuracy of depiction? Is it photographic realism? Or is an instinctive button being pushed, activated by bright colors or appealing animals? Whatever it is, it's a compelling form. It seems clear, then, that the blending of words and illustrations help young readers in their search for meaning.

The Search for Meaning

Before beginning our examination of the techniques illustrators use to reach children and help them gain knowledge and meaning, we should examine the role children's own drawings play in the process. Children's authors and illustrators skillfully use perceptual principles to attract young readers and to help them discover meaning in their stories. Well-written books force children to search for hidden facts that may be lying within the words or objects they are observing. Game books, such as Martin Handford's *Where's Waldo* series, address this problem directly when the author hides Waldo on every page, challenging children to find him. By concentrating, they can spot him in the various situations in which he is drawn.

Author and illustrator Anthony Browne, for example, is a skillful, well-known master of the art-game book technique. But his books are more than game books. In his *The Shape Game* (2003), he tells the fascinating story of an English family's experiences in the Tate Gallery in London, while placing real artwork within his own illustrations. Having the family compare and discover what are reproductions and what are his own pictures, Browne integrates this family with the pictures and, more importantly, helps them to make a meaningful connection between art and life.

Children and Perception

Why are children intrigued by Eric Carle's *The Very Quiet Cricket*? What is it about Carle's use of perceptual principles that fascinates children? To answer these questions, we must first consider the more basic question of how children learn to draw information from their environment and obtain meaning from what they observe.

The initial pathway by which information enters a child's system is through the senses—vision, hearing, smell, taste, touch—but how do children derive meaning from what they experience? Siegler and Alibali (2005) argue that regardless of the sense involved, perception involves the following three tasks:

1. Children must *attend* to what they think is important or to what attracts them because of color, intensity, and so on. In Carle's book, for example, the cover itself attracts attention by its implied action.

2. Children must learn to *identify* what they attend to. *The Very Quiet Cricket*, for example, effectively identifies darkness with night and brightness with day.

3. Children must *locate* the object of their attention—that is, they must determine how far away it is and where it is. Note how Carle cleverly positions the cricket and other objects on his pages.

USING PERCEPTUAL PRINCIPLES   When someone asks you what time it is, do you scrutinize all the minute markings on your watch? No. Your past experience enables you to ignore the irrelevant and concentrate on the significant, namely, the hands and numbers. *Children function in exactly the same manner as they search for meaning.* They organize the relevant stimuli—relevant, that is, to their developmental level—ignore the irrelevant, and move it into the background, thus creating a meaningful figure/ground relationship.

Since children have a basic drive to organize and structure their world, authors and illustrators capitalize on a child's tendency to group stimuli by frequently using the following principles.

1. CHILDREN TEND TO GROUP BY FAMILIAR OBJECTS. What do you see in the following figure?

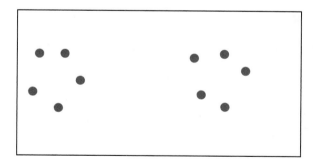

You see two groups of circles, rather than ten isolated figures.

In the Caldecott Medal book *Joseph Had a Little Overcoat*, author-illustrator Simms Taback carefully groups his figures throughout the book, making it easier for his young audience to follow the story. On the left-hand page of the centerfold, for example, Joseph stands with one hand extended, while his other hand holds his suitcase with a bunch of flowers under his arm. The reader's eyes are drawn first to Joseph, then across to the right-hand page where Joseph's smiling sister and her husband are raising their hands in greeting.

2. OBJECTS THAT ARE SIMILAR FORM NATURAL GROUPS. What do you see in the following figure?

```
XXXXXXXXXXXX
XXXXXXXXXXXX
XXXOOOXXXXXX
XXXXXXXXXXXX
```

You would undoubtedly answer that you saw three OOOs and the rest Xs.

In Eve Bunting's picture book *The Wall*, illustrated by Ronald Himler, the Wall is the Vietnam Veterans Memorial in Washington D. C., which honors the men and women of the U. S. armed forces who served in the Vietnam War. On it are the names of those who died or are "missing in action." In front of the many illustrations of the Wall stands a young boy (the narrator) and his father, trying to read the names. Beside them, on various pages, appear other people—an older man and his wife, a veteran in a wheel chair, and a class of school children. They are all grouped together to make it easier for children to organize the images of the different kinds of people who come together to honor the veterans.

Helping Children Discover Meaning

We cannot overemphasize the importance of having children find meaning and structure in whatever they are reading. Fortunately, authors and artists who produce outstanding children's books such as J. Briggs Martin, Jan Brett, and Michael Rosen, assist children by

- Using the familiar to introduce the unfamiliar
- Relating new material to a structure children already possess
- Stressing meaningful relations within the material

J. BRIGGS MARTIN   Author J. Briggs Martin and Caldecott Medal illustrator Mary Azarian (*Snowflake Bentley*) use children's past experiences to bring meaning to what the readers see on the pages of their book. By a beautiful blend of text and art, they introduce an unfamiliar topic (the biography of Wilson Bentley) by capitalizing on children's familiarity with snow and snowflakes. Illustrator Azarian enhances the topic, lyrically presented by Martin, by using woodcuts tinted with watercolors, to which the publisher has added snowflake-touched factual sidebars that give information about Wilson Bentley.

JAN BRETT   Jan Brett writes and illustrates her picture books so that children will have no difficulty understanding what the story is about. In *The Mitten*, for example, Nicki, a young boy, loses his mitten—something that often happens to young children. What is surprising, however, is how the woodland animals seek shelter in the mitten. Brett uses the borders of each page to help children anticipate what kind of animal will be entering the mitten next. The mitten-shaped borders

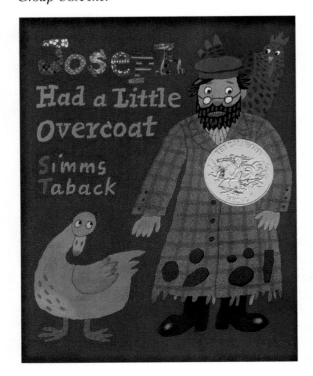

JOSEPH HAD A LITTLE OVERCOAT
Reproduced with permission of Penguin Group USA Inc.

help children follow Nicki in his walk through the woods, as he slides, climbs, makes snowballs, and finally finds his mitten, much to the delight of his grandmother.

MICHAEL ROSEN (PICTURE)   Children of all ages often experience trouble discovering and finding meaning in unfamiliar subjects. In *Shakespeare, His Work and His World*, author Michael Rosen and illustrator Robert Ingpen, a winner of the Hans Christian Andersen Medal, help older children learn about the world in which Shakespeare lived by asking them specific questions about *familiar* words: Have you ever described someone as *tongue-tied* or as *dull as dishwater?* Have you ever heard people say that they have *seen better days?* All of these phrases are found in Shakespeare's plays. Rosen tantalizes his readers' imaginations by entitling his first chapter *The Plot!* Other chapters that summarize outstanding plays are dramatically labeled and summarized in conversational prose.

Robert Ingpen portrays Shakespeare's world in extraordinary, two–page, full-color spreads that are equally attractive. Children with no knowledge of Shakespeare are drawn to this book. The author and illustrator use the familiar to relate new information to a structure children already possess. The text is also reinforced with a six-page, four-column timeline, as well as a detailed index and bibliography.

Now let's see how these ideas about perception and meaning impact book illustrators, as they attempt to make stories come alive for children.

Children and Their Drawings

An interesting question arises: how much do children's own drawings influence the meaning they obtain from the stories they read? Children love to draw and are fascinated by the illustrations in the books they read. Todd Parr is an illustrator who has incorporated children's drawings into his own art in *The Feel Good Book*, which contains illustrations that resemble the primitive drawings of young artists.

Another illustrator whose art work resembles children's art is Lois Ehlert. Her book *In My World* is a Caldecott Honor book. Ehlert uses bright, primary-colored geometric shapes to create letters and objects of nature in her books that she calls her "little love notes to children" (Ehlert, 1995, p. 221). Trained as a graphic artist, Ehlert brings to the art of the picture book a unique sense of color and the ability to make her intricate and time-consuming collages, which use a variety of papers, watercolors, inks, and real objects, appear as simple as a child's drawing. In *In My World*, for example, each page contains a vivid color and each object (a bug, a worm, a fish, the sun, or the stars) is cut out in the middle of the page. As the cutouts are overlayed, the reader discovers a different object on each page. Ehlert writes that "If there is a simple thread that weaves its way through all of my books, it is a colored thread" (Ehlert, 1995, p. 221). When she accepted the Boston Globe-Hornbook Award for her *Leaf Man* (*Horn Book*, Jan. /Feb. 2006), she explained how she collected leaves during her travels, gathered them in plastic bags, arranged them on the copier glass at Kinko's, pressed the start button, and soon had a stack of paper leaves that she used to construct her art for *Leaf Man*. "A little boy wrote and told me that he wanted to grow up to be like me, and make nothing out of something. I knew what he meant" (Ehlert, 2006, p. 32).

For reasons ranging from the artistic to the psychological, children's artwork has long attracted the attention of scholars. (For an interesting discussion of this topic see Milbrath, 1998; Matthews, 2003; Willats, 2005.) A famous example of this interest appeared as far back as 1857, when John Ruskin published *The Elements of Drawing*.

LEAF MAN
Reproduced by permission of Harcourt Trade Publishers

Those of us interested in the relationship between children's picture books and child development search for clues that explain the link between book illustrations, children's drawing ability, and the content of their pictures.

With regard to children's drawings, children instinctively follow a finely tuned sequence, moving from the pincer movements of infancy, to random scribbles to skillful creations. This artistic evolution suggests that children discover increasingly complex and powerful representational rules (Willats, 2005). As their skills develop, certain questions arise: And why do children scribble? What are they trying to say in their art? Does this carry over to their selection of books? And why do they lose their enthusiasm? In analyzing children's art, it's important to remember that their drawings express *what they are capable of doing*. Children are limited in eye-hand coordination, motor ability, and manual dexterity. But their drawings, as crude as they may be, tell us much about a child's personality, interests, attitudes, and emotional state.

Stages of Artistic Development

Rhoda Kellogg (1970), who taught preschool children for many years, collected over one million children's drawings and paintings done by thousands of children. You would enjoy reading Kellogg's discussion of children's art. Especially insightful is her belief that the basic line formation and motifs that appear in children's art are *also found in the art of adults* (Kellogg, 1970, p. 44). She believes children's art passes through four stages:

1. PLACEMENT, which refers to where on the paper the child places the drawing (2 to 3 years)

2. SHAPE, which refers to diagrams with different shapes (about 3 years)

3. DESIGN, which refers to a combination of forms (about 3 to 4 years)

4. PICTORIAL, which refers to representations of humans, animals, buildings, and other things (about 4 to 5 years).

By 2 years of age, children have achieved seventeen placement patterns, At 3 years, they're using circles, crosses, squares, and rectangles. By the time children are 4 years of age they enter the pictorial stage. As well-known artist Mitsumasa Anno points out, children as young as 2 years old *understand* when shown a simple drawing with circles for heads, rectangles for bodies, and single lines for arms and legs that "This is

What's Your View?

Children's Love of Drawing—What Happens?

Children love to draw, but explaining the developmental path of this skill remains extremely difficult. Noting how drawings appear, change, and disappear—from the scribbles of the 2 year old, to the 3 year old's interest in design, to the 4 and 5 year old's drawing representations—Gardner (1980, 1982) draws attention to the liveliness and enthusiasm of their work. And then suddenly, it stops! Usually, by age 9 or 10 years at the latest, most children simply give up drawing (Edwards, 1999). Why?

After the peak of creativity has been reached, children often limit their artistic efforts to copying forms or cease drawing altogether. This "reach for realism" is a critical stage of development during which children reflect their cognitive level by following rules and obeying the dictates of convention. With growing cognitive ability and a decrease in egocentrism, children may compare their efforts with those of others, become discouraged—their work just isn't as good—and lose interest.

Peter Reynolds, a young writer and illustrator, understands the insecurity children experience when they begin to draw. In *The Dot*, the young child Vashti, who is discouraged because she can't draw, is motivated by her teacher to "Just make a mark and see where it takes you." As the teacher builds Vashti's self-confidence by asking her to sign her name, Vashti, in turn, encourages another little boy to sign his squiggle. In *Ish*, Reynolds writes about how young Ramon stops drawing because his older brother criticized the vase he drew. His younger sister Marisol, however, saves his discarded drawings and tells him that the vase looked *vase*-ish, making Ramon see his drawings in a new way. When Reynolds visits schools, he insists that "when it comes to expressing yourself, you can change the rules, stretch them, or ignore them and dive headfirst into the unknown" (Reynolds, 2003).

It isn't until adolescence, however, that a small number of children again manifest a creative spark. At this time, inborn talent and a supportive environment help them develop the skills needed to withstand immersion in rules and correct thinking.

It is in the activity of the young child—the preconscious sense of form, the willingness to explore and to solve problems that arise, the capacity to take risks, the affective needs which must be worked out in a symbolic realm—that we find the crucial seeds of the greatest artistic achievements (Gardner, 1980, p. 269).

We can agree, then, that children like to draw, paint, and express themselves through their artistry. They lose interest, however, when they see no goal, or when making patterns no longer fascinates them. With no new objectives and challenges, their enthusiasm vanishes, their interest evaporates, and they turn their attention to other fields. How would you explain this phenomenon? What's your view?

Father, this is Mother." As Marcus (2002) notes, this is one of a child's first steps toward abstract understanding. After analyzing children's drawings, Kellogg concluded "that child art contains the aesthetic forms most commonly used in all art." As we continue our search in children's literature for evidence that explains the powerful allure of outstanding artists and authors, we would do well to use Kellogg's words as a guide.

If you would like to have a more informed view on this issue, you may want to read one or more of the references in this chapter, such as Kellogg's (1970) classic work.

Illustrating for Children

As we have learned thus far, memorable children's literature—the books that entertain, entrance, and inform—is that in which authors and illustrators have interwoven developmental principles throughout the story. They have searched for ways to captivate their readers through words and pictures that bring meaning and excitement into the reading world of children. For example, as children age they prefer curved lines to straight, they find color appealing, and they are drawn to as much complexity as they are capable of understanding. A good model of these perceptual principles can be found in *The Hello, Goodbye Window*, a Caldecott Medal book by Norton Juster and Chris Raschka, which reaches out from its pages to appeal to young readers with dazzling colors, a multitude of straight and curved lines, and an array of changing facial expressions.

Understanding a child's development enables illustrators to charm, as well as communicate knowledge. Eisner (2002, p. 10) described the process this way:

A Monet landscape or a Paul Strand photograph makes possible new ways of seeing: Monet's shimmering color gives us a new way to see light. Paul Strand's photographs provide a new way to experience the geometry of industrial cities.

Understanding perceptual principles and children's emergence into the artistic world, enables illustrators to represent as well as fascinate. Eisner (2002, p. 10) continues:

The arts liberate us from the literal; they enable us to step into the shoes of others and to experience vicariously what we have experienced directly.

These two statements aptly convey the goal of the illustrator: to further a reader's search for meaning.

Development and Illustrations

Combining the developmental characteristics discussed in the preceding chapters with those features of children's drawings just described, you can begin to discern a pattern that influences the choices facing illustrators. As their cognitive ability improves, children are gradually able to detect more complex patterns and pictorial cues, and show an ability to perceive and react to emotional expressions. The most memorable books in children's literature have been those that match children's growing perceptual and cognitive maturity.

Think, for example, of the tissue paper collages of Eric Carle, the writer and illustrator of *The Very Hungry Caterpillar*. The psychologically charged and surrealistic pencil and ink drawings of Chris Van Allsburg, as seen in his books such as *The Polar Express, Jumanjii, Zathura,* and *Probuditi!*, define his style. The strong geometric designs of D. B. Johnson's *Henry Builds a Cabin* emphasize the sturdiness of the main character (a bear), as well as the book's theme: the strength and balance of Henry David Thoreau's personality. Barbara Cooney reveals her talent for folk art in her illustrations of picture books that include the Caldecott winner *The Ox-Cart Man* (Hall, 1979). And Tomie dePaola's line drawings of his folk characters, Strega Nona and Big Anthony, identify his unique style.

In *Joseph Had a Little Overcoat* by Simms Taback, the Caldecott illustrator uses a combination of watercolors, gouache, pencil, ink, and collage to create a picture book of a Yiddish folktale that is filled with humorous characters and small details such as miniature photographs on the walls. He also uses die cut holes to foreshadow what Joseph will make out of his old clothing. (Die cut holes are a popular device allowing the very young to slide their finger into a small hole cut into each page of books such as *Pat the Bunny* by Dorothy Kunhardt, *The Very Hungry Caterpillar* by Eric Carle, and *Madlenka* by Peter Sis. Taback concludes his story of Joseph's overcoat with the words and music of an original song. His style is readily recognizable as "old world," similar in setting and clothing design to *Fiddler on the Roof.*

Ed Young's brushstrokes and soft pastel oriental panels bring to life *Lon Po Po*, a Chinese version of *Little Red Riding Hood*. Gerald McDermott includes stylized Pueblo wall paintings and the colors of the southwest in his *Arrow to the Sun*. Illustrators Leo and Diane Dillon received the Caldecott Medal for their African batik, fragmented forms in *Why Mosquitos Buzz in People's Ears* (Aardema, 1975). The Dillons modeled the wood block prints in their illustrations for Katherine Paterson's retelling of *The Tale of the Mandarin Ducks* (1990), after the Japanese art of ukiyo-e.

Development, Perception, and Illustrators

As we describe the work of well-known artists such as Chris Raschka, Ashley Bryan, Tomie De Paola, Robert McCloskey, Jerry Pinkney, and Mitsumasa Anno, and trace their illustrations from the simple to the complex, we need to reconsider the perceptual data that we have discussed—vision, hearing, touch, feeling—and remember that the goal of perception is to obtain information about the world and our place in it (Gibson & Pick, 2000). Remember: *Children are drawn to as much complexity as their developmental status permits.*

They determine satisfactory levels of complexity in three ways:

1. By attending, which helps them to decide what information is worth concentrating on and processing

2. By identifying, which helps them to decide what they are paying attention to

3. By locating, which helps them to decide how far away the object or event is and what is its direction (Siegler & Alibali, 2005)

By using these three guidelines, children establish a pattern of preferring objects or events that represent moderate complexity for their developmental level (Siegler & Alibali, 2005). Astute authors and illustrators use these principles in an appropriate manner to attract readers. Here are several who have mastered these techniques.

CHRIS RASCHKA *The Hello, Goodbye Window*, illustrated by Chris Raschka, is a Caldecott Medal winner and a stunning visual interpretation of Norton Juster's story of how a small girl spends time at her grandparents' house. The skills we have been discussing, which an illustrator should use to infuse meaning into a children's story, are present here. Raschka's drawings, whether they are watecolors mixed with pastel crayons or thin black lines, are like those of a child. His art portrays objects inside and outside the grandparents' house that are significant to the granddaughter. Even the small, harmless tiger lurking in the garden is shown.

As an author *and* illustrator, Raschka's work is deceiving in its simplicity. In *Yo! Yes?*, for example, his message is complex and universal: two lonely boys, who are strangers to each other, communicate the message that although one is black and the other is white, they can still be friends. Single-syllable words such as *yo*, *yes*, *me*, and *you* are as large as the illustrations and explode on the last page into a "WOW," as the two boys set off together.

ASHLEY BRYAN Children may be initially attracted by the vibrant colors of Ashley Bryan's picture book *Beautiful Blackbird*, but they are soon swayed by the rhythm of his words and by the universal truth that true beauty comes from within. His book *Let It Shine: Three Favorite Spirituals*, overflows with even greater vibrancy of color and imagery. The lyrics to "This Little Light of Mine," "When the Saints Go Marching In," and "He's Got the Whole World in His Hands," beg to be sung with joy and exuberance. This author, illustrator, folklorist, storyteller, and art teacher discovered early in his career that young children love to go on and on with what they are doing. "If a child didn't have an idea, I might say, 'Maybe there were some horses. . .' And right away the child would say, 'Don't tell me, don't tell me. I know what I want to do'" (Marcus, 2002, p. 26). This is a response that needs to be constantly encouraged.

TOMIE DEPAOLA Author and illustrator of many books for children, Tomie dePaola's folklike illustrations are easily recognizable. His stories of *Strega Nona* and *Big Anthony*, his short autobiographical sketches, and his retelling of traditional folklore are very familiar, being among the first picture books adults read to children. As children become developmentally able to comprehend his stories, humor, and delightful illustrations, they frequently ask to read his books independently.

ROBERT MCCLOSKEY   Winner of two Caldecott Medals, for *Make Way for Ducklings* and *Time of Wonder*, Robert McCloskey's stories are picture book classics. The illustrations of the ducklings who find a home with their mother in the Boston Public Garden appeals to children's perception. As McCloskey admitted, he tried every trick he could to get as much into the pictures as possible. He paced the illustrations and gave them a variety of viewpoints—aerial views and others—to create a sense of space, movement, and the feel of something going on (Marcus, 2002). Children are quick to sense the nuances of his art; if they ever visit Boston, they feel a sense of *deja vu,* and are eager to search for the ducklings.

The true story of the ducklings first appeared in the Boston newspapers. Later, McCloskey saw them crossing the street to the Public Garden (although not with the police and everyone watching as in his story). To prepare for his story, McCloskey bought live ducks and kept them in his bathtub in order to study them. He felt a great responsibility for the book after receiving letters from children all over the world, "along with lots of pictures of ducks."

JERRY PINKNEY   Jerry Pinkney, the only illustrator to win the Coretta Scott King Award and the Caldecott Honor Medal five times each, has illustrated many traditional tales. In *The Talking Eggs* (San Souci, 1989), his two-headed cow with its twisted horns is convincingly realistic. In *The Little Red Hen*, he dresses the hen in a snappy straw hat and brightly colored shawl. When the barnyard animals decline to help her plant seeds, she and her chicks later refuse to share their loaf of bread with them. Small children enjoy the repetition of her question "Who will help me?" and the response of each animal, "Not I." Pinkney has colorcoded the words for the animals in order to help beginning readers identify them more easily.

His illustrations for Patricia McKissack's *Goin' Someplace Special* address older children who are developing their perceptual awareness and increasing their knowledge of the world around them. His drawings not only anticipate the hazards Tricia Ann encounters as she takes the trolley to the library, but they notice her face, her pleasure, and the way she clasps her hands as Mama Frances ties the bow on her best dress. "Squaring her shoulders," she walks puzzled and resentful to the back of the bus where she sees a sign that says "COLORED SECTION." "Her face falls" when she sits on a bench "FOR WHITES ONLY." Through Pinkney's illustrations, readers with a deepening understanding perceive the disappointments and discouragement of the book's black characters. Tricia Ann, however, continues "real determined–like on her way," until she arrives at her special place.

As Pinkney explained in an interview with Leonard S. Marcus (*Ways of Telling*), watercolors allow him to bring freshness to drawing that, in fact, was carefully planned. He believes that the surface of the paper plays a role in the look and feel of the picture. It allows the viewers, in a sense, to step into the picture and finish it, seeing it with their mind's eye (Marcus, 2002, p. 151). Children who read the story and observe the illustrations of *Goin' Someplace Special* increase their perceptual awareness and empathy for the injustices around them.

MITSUMASA ANNO   In another interview with Leonard Marcus (2002, p. 7), Mitsumasa Anno, whose picture books are also known throughout the world, stated:

When I was a child I pictured the world-is-round concept as a rubber ball turned inside out with the people of the different continents living inside the ball. Of course, it was a boy's way of imagining. But this kind of imagination is another sort of eye for perceiving what things really are. And it is the source of all my books.

(Marcus, 2002, p. 7).

Young children seeing the images in Anno's Alphabet, Anno's Journey, and Anno's Counting Book may be puzzled by many of his references, but they are elated when they find an illustration they recognize. In Anno's Journey, for example, children are asked to look for details from paintings by Courbet, Millet, Renoir, and others. Anno believes that when a small child first sees the illustration of peasant women working in a field, he may not know that the source is Millet's The Gleaner, but he can make up a story about them—who they are, what they are thinking, and so on. Later, however, with developing perceptual and cognitive maturity, he may see the Millet painting and remember the women (Marcus, 2002, p. 11).

We know that children can be taught things in the traditional manner, but it is Anno's belief "that children's joy is always much greater when they make the discovery themselves without having to be taught" (Marcus, 2002, p. 16). (Bradford Washburn, late director of the Boston Museum of Science, reiterated this principle when he remarked that the top of Mount McKinley was thrilling, but "there's nothing on earth more exciting than the eyes of a youngster at the instant of discovery.") Anno provides conditions that allow children to learn for themselves. He relates the story of the little boy who excitedly showed his teacher the Superman picture in *Anno's USA*, and the teacher's feigned surprise that allowed the child to feel the joy of a personal discovery.

A museum much like Eric Carle's Museum in Massachusetts was established in March 2001 in Anno's home town of Tsuwano, Japan, to showcase his work. He has also been honored with the Hans Christian Andersen Medal in recognition of his "unique gift for communication to both East and West."

Authors and Illustrators—The Integration

With these ideas as background, let's turn to the way that perception, text, and art seamlessly come together to captivate young readers. Perhaps the best approach is to take the topics we've discussed thus far and apply them to a book such as Eric Carle's *The Very Quiet Cricket*, which reflects developmental data indicating that auditory and visual perceptual systems are the earliest to be used in obtaining information about the world (Gibson & Pick, 2000).

Carle's book contains all the vital ingredients of the successful story: attractive packaging, delightful illustrations, and charming narration. When we move beyond these superficial observations we note that the lines on the cover convey the messages of action and movement. On each page, the cricket and the insects it meets, create the sense of motion. Carle's use of curved shapes to form natural objects gives the feeling of actually observing the meeting between the cricket and the moth. His insertion of lines and dots on the surface of his creatures implies the texture of their surfaces. The combination of colors reaches out from the pages and tugs us into the cricket's world, from sunrise to darkness.

The pictorial cues tell us that the cricket is at ease in nature and that the insects it encounters are not threatening. In his subtle style Carle entices young readers

What's Your View?

Maurice Sendak

No discussion of authors and illustrators would be complete without describing the impact Maurice Sendak has had on contemporary outstanding illustrators and the children who read his books. Representing all the visual elements we have discussed, Sendak's work would receive a resounding *Yes!* to each of the questions mentioned above.

Maurice Sendak could be called an illustrators' illustrator because of the impact he has had on illustrators of picture books. Before his illustrations appeared in books such as *A Hole Is to Dig* (1952) and a *Very Special House* (1953), children in picture books were stereotypical: fair-haired and joyful, with few emotions, other than happiness, ever crossing their faces or affecting their demeanor. Sendak, however, insisted that young children wanted—even needed—to see a broader range of emotional experiences reflected in books. "He did more than anyone to free the picture book from its sentimental past" (Marcus, 2002, p. 165).

Before winning the Caldecott Medal for *Where the Wild Things Are* (1963), Sendak had illustrated over fifty books, authored seven, and received five Caldecott Honors. His work has been a model for many successful artists, including at least two Caldecott Medal winners. Paul O. Zelinsky, for example, calls Sendak "a master of form," and admits that he was his first and only illustration teacher.

Richard Egeliski, author and friend of Arthur Yorinks, mentions that Sendak was instrumental in leading Caldecott winner Yorinks to children's books. It was in Sendak's class at Parsons School that Yorinks discovered picture books and the artistic possibilities of book illustration. In an interview with Leonard Marcus, Sendak reveals that *Where the Wild Things Are* was based on a theory of picture book making that he formulated himself.

That device is a way of dramatically picturing what's going on: As Max's rage engorges him, those pictures fill the page. When his anger turns to a kind of wild jungle pleasure, the words are pushed off the page altogether. And then he deflates like any normal child; he's getting hungry, he's getting tired, and he wants to go back home. (Marcus, 2002, p. 168)

After writing *Where The Wild Things Are*, Sendak envisioned a trilogy of books. The second became *In the Night Kitchen*, and the third would be *Outside Over There*, which he believes is "the most beautifully structured book he has written." The kidnapping in *Outside Over There* recreates the Lindbergh baby kidnapping, which was very traumatic to Sendak as a child. The three books are connected because they're all about one minute's worth of distraction. "One temper tantrum, one wrong word causes all of the Wild Things to happen; one noise in the kitchen has Mickey doing a weird thing. One minute's dreamy distraction allows the kidnapping in *Outside Over There* to occur" (Marcus, 2002, p. 171).

Sendak told Tony Kushner, author of *The Art of Maurice Sendak: 1980 to Present*, that the themes of these books have specific titles. It's like looking for a place to go or finding a place to be (Gussow, 2003). When they discussed the images and motifs that reoccur in his books, Sendak admitted that milk remains a constant. Kushner and Sendak have since collaborated on a picture book, *Brundibar*, based on an opera written in 1938, which had fifty-five performances in a Nazi concentration camp in Czechoslovakia. It tells the story of two small children in Prague who try to get milk for their sick mother. Brundibar, the villain of both the opera and the book, is commonly thought to represent Hitler. He is finally driven from the city, and good triumphs in the end.

Although Sendak acknowledges (Marcus, 2002) that some people say you shouldn't frighten children, he believes children are already frightened by what has happened. All you can do at that point is console them. In his illustrations for *Mommy?*, his first pop-up book written by Arthur Yorinks and engineered by Matthew Reinhardt, Sendak assumes his young readers will not be alarmed when a small boy who is lost in a mad scientist's laboratory, discovers gruesome, in-your-face movie monsters (like Frankenstein) as he searches for his mother. Disturbing? Unsettling? The senior editor of *The New York Times Book Review* calls it "a remarkable body of work; it's a masterpiece of the genre, and it's got a force all its own" (Garner, 2006, p. 48). But does *Mommy?* provide a goodness-of-fit and developmentally appropriate illustrations for small children? What's your view?

into a sense of harmony with nature. When you read this book with children, note his clever use of the design stage—his introduction of circles, ovals, rectangles, and lines—which children find fascinating, as we have seen in their own drawings.

With regard to text, the continued repetition of certain lines has an hypnotic effect on young readers. Beginning on the second page, the first two lines of each page introduce the insect the cricket meets, after which follow the lines:

The little cricket wanted to answer,
so he rubbed his wings together.
But nothing happened. Not a sound.

The skillful use of surprise captures readers' attention and positions them for the ending when the cricket is finally able to chirp. This ending is enhanced when the reader turns to the final page and discovers. . . . But why spoil your pleasure; read it yourself!

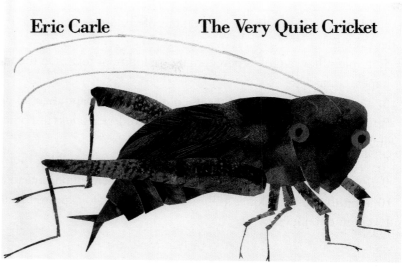

Eric Carle   **The Very Quiet Cricket**

THE VERY QUIET CRICKET
Reproduced with permission of Penguin Group USA Inc.

The techniques that Carle employs fit beautifully into the developmental sequence traced in this chapter. Particularly noteworthy are the means he uses to attract and hold his reader's attention. We have previously commented on his clever use of lines, and we find the same degree of thought and care put into his ingenious treatment of color. As we move from sunrise to darkness, the reader is swept up in a steady evolution from bright sunlight, to twilight, to evening darkness. In our discussion of Rhoda Kellogg's work we noted how childrens' art work utilizes properties such as shapes, designs, and pictorial formations—which Carle carefully builds into his illustrations.

Finally, Carle's application of perceptual principles could be used as a case study on perceptual development. Many of the perceptual principles we have discussed are obvious in his illustrations. For example, when our friend the cricket meets the mosquitoes, it reflects the grouping of familiar objects. But Carle also injects another comforting and familiar note in the same illustration by how he groups the stars in the background. Complexity is gradually introduced in a way that does not overwhelm; the lunar moth and dragonfly, for instance, are presented within the context of the familiar. *The Very Quiet Cricket* integrates the principles we have covered in this chapter in a way that demonstrates why some books, some authors, and some illustrators retain their appeal to readers over the years. Their enduring work has displayed a unique talent for integrating text and illustrations in a manner developmentally and engagingly appropriate for their intended readers.

‖ Chapter Checklist

Read the following items carefully. If you have difficulty responding to any of them, return to the chapter to review the material.

After reading this chapter, you can

  1. Evaluate an author's need to recognize the relationship between a reader's level of language development and a story's text.

  2. Describe how the skillful use of language in a story's text affects a reader's emotional response.

  3. Explain why patterned language, predictability, and pace are the building blocks of good writing for children.

4. Identify the clues in the illustrations of children's books that have their roots in children's artistic development.

5. Explain how a child's perceptual development relates to the manner in which an artist uses lines, shapes, colors, etc.

6. Demonstrate how an artist's use of illustrations capitalizes on a child's search for meaning.

7. List several reasons that indicate how children's books are powerful forces in furthering cognitive and language development.

8. Specify how a story's illustrations explain and expand the theme of the text.

9. Evaluate how the critical aspects of language, perception, and art come together to form a successful book.

10. Identify the techniques authors and artists use to capture the attention of children at the various developmental levels.

Children's Bibliography

Aardema, Verna. (1975). *Why Mosquitos Buzz in People's Ears.* New York: Scholastic.

Anderson, M. T. (2001). *Handel, Who Knew What He Liked.* Cambridge, MA: Candlewick.

Anderson, M. T. (2006). *The Astonishing Life of Octavian Nothing, Traitor to the Nation, Volume 1: The Pox Party.* Cambridge, MA: Candlewick.

Anno, Mitsumasa. (1977). *Anno's Journey.* New York: Putnam.

Anno, Mitsumasa. (1983). *Anno's U.S.A.* New York: Philomel.

Anno, Mitsumasa. (1992). *Anno's Counting Book.* New York: HarperCollins.

Brett, Jan. (1989). *The Mitten.* New York: G. P. Putnam's Sons.

Brown, Margaret Wise. (1942). *Indoor Noisy Book.* New York: Harper & Row.

Browne, Anthony. (2003). *The Shape Game.* New York: Farrar.

Bryan, Ashley. (2003). *Beautiful Blackbird.* New York: Atheneum.

Bryan, Ashley. (2007). *Let It Shine: Three Favorite Spirituals.* New York: Atheneum.

Bunting, Eve. (1990). *The Wall.* New York: Clarion.

Carle, Eric. (1990). *The Very Quiet Cricket.* New York: Philomel.

Cushman, Karen. (1995). *The Midwife's Apprentice.* New York: Clarion.

dePaola, Tomie. (1975). *Strega Nona.* New York: Simon & Schuster.

dePaola, Tomie. (1998). *Big Anthony: His Story.* New York: Putnam.

Ehlert, Lois. (1989). *Color Zoo.* New York: Lippincott.

Ehlert, Lois. (2002). *In My World.* New York: Harcourt.

Ehlert, Lois. (2005). *Leaf Man.* New York: Harcourt.

Hall, Donald. (1979). Barbara Cooney, illus. *Ox-Cart Man.* New York: Viking.

Handford, Martin. (1987). *Where's Waldo.* Boston: Little, Brown.

Hesse, Karen. (1997). *Out of the Dust.* New York: Scholastic.

Johnson, D. B. (2002). *Henry Builds a Cabin.* Boston: Houghton Mifflin.

Juster, Norton, & Raschka, Chris. (2005). *The Hello, Goodbye Window.* New York: Hyperion.

Kushner, Tony. Maurice Sendak, illus. (2003). *Brundibar.* After the opera by Hans Krasa & Adolf Hoffmeister. New York: Michael di Capua Books.

Kunhardt, Dorothy. (1968). *Pat the Bunny.* Racine, WI: Golden Press.

Lowry, Lois. (1993). *The Giver.* Boston: Houghton Mifflin.

Lowry, Lois. (2000). *Gathering Blue.* Boston: Houghton Mifflin.

Lowry, Lois. (2003). *The Silent Boy.* Boston: Houghton Mifflin.

Lowry, Lois. (2004). *Messenger.* Boston: Houghton Mifflin.

Macaulay, David. (1990). *Black and White.* Boston: Houghton Mifflin.

Martin, Bill Jr., & Archambault, John. Lois Ehlert, illus. (1986). *Chica Chica Boom Boom.* New York: Alladin.

Martin, J. Briggs. Azarian Mary Illus. (1998). *Snowflake Bentley.* Boston: Houghton Mifflin.

McCloskey, Robert. (1969). *Make Way for Ducklings.* New York: Viking Press.

McDermott, Gerald. (1974). *Arrow to the Sun.* New York: Viking.

McKissack, Patricia. Pinkney, Jerry, illus. (2001). *Goin' Someplace Special.* New York: Atheneum.

Naylor, Phyllis. (1991). *Shiloh.* New York: Atheneum.

Parr, Todd. (2002). *The Feel Good Book.* Boston: Little, Brown.

Paterson, Katherine. (1989). *The Tale of the Mandarin Ducks.* New York: Lodestar.

Pinkney, Jerry. (2006). *The Little Red Hen.* New York: Dial/Penguin.

Raschka, Chris. (1993). *Yo! Yes?* New York: Orchard Books.

Rathmann, Peggy. (1995). *Officer Buckle and Gloria.* New York: G. P. Putnam.

Reynolds, Peter H. (2003). *The Dot.* Cambridge, MA: Candlewick.

Reynolds, Peter H. (2004). *Ish.* Cambridge, MA: Candlewick.

Rosen, Michael. (2001). Ingpen, Robert, illus. *Shakespeare: His Work and His World.* Cambridge, MA: Candlewick.

Rylant, Cynthia. (1992). *Missing May.* New York: Orchard.

San Souci, Robert. Pinkney, Jerry, illus. (1989). *The Talking Eggs: a Folktale from the American South.* New York: Dial.

Sendak, Maurice. (1963). *Where the Wild Things Are.* New York: Harper.

Sendak, Maurice. (1970). *In the Night Kitchen.* New York: Harper & Row.

Sendak, Maurice. (1981). *Outside Over There.* New York: Harper & Row.

Sis, Peter. (2000). *Madlenka*. New York: Farrar, Straus, & Giroux.

Spinelli, Jerry. (1990). *Maniac Magee*. Boston: Little, Brown.

Taback, Simms. (1999). *Joseph Had a Little Overcoat*. New York: Viking.

Van Allsburg, Chris. (1985). *The Polar Express*. Boston: Houghton Mifflin.

Van Allsburg, Chris. (2002). *Zathura*. Boston: Houghton Mifflin.

Van Allsburg, Chris. (2006). *Probuditi!* Boston: Houghton Mifflin.

Yorinks, Arthur. (1986). *Hey, Al*. New York: Farrar, Straus, & Giroux.

Yorinks, Al. Sendak, Maurice, illus. included. (2006). *Mommy?* New York: Scholastic.

Young, Ed. (1989). *Lon Po Po*. New York: Philomel.

Zelinsky, Paul O. (1997). *Rapunzel*. New York: Dutton.

Professional References

Anno, Mitsumasa. (2002). In Marcus, Leonard. *Ways of Telling*. New York: Dutton.

Bader, B. (2004). "The Difference Words Make." *The Horn Book*. November/December. 633 – 644.

Bornstein, M., & Arterberry, M. (1999). "Perceptual Development." In M. Bornstein and M. Lamb (eds.), *Developmental Psychology: An Advanced Textbook*. Mahwah, NJ: Lawrence Erlbaum.

Bryan, Ashley. (2002). In Marcus, Leonard. *Ways of Telling*. New York: Dutton.

Cole, M., & Cole, S. (2001). *The Development of Children*. New York: Worth.

Cushman, Karen. (2001). "1996 Newbery Acceptance Speech." *The Newbery and Caldecott Medal Books 1986–2000*. Chicago: American Library Association.

Cushman, Paul. (2001). "Karen Cushman." *The Newbery and Caldecott Medal Books 1986–2000*. Chicago: American Library Association.

Dacey, John & Travers, John. (2004). *Human Development Across The Lifespan*. New York: McGraw Hill.

Edwards, Betty. (1999). *The New Drawing On The Right Side of The Brain*. New York: Penguin Putnam.

Egielski, Richard. (2001). "1987 Caldecott Acceptance Speech." *The Newbery and Caldecott Medal Books 1986–2000*. Chicago: American Library Association.

Ehlert, Lois. (1995). "Voices of the Creators." In Anita Silvey, ed. *Children's Books and Their Creators*. Boston: Houghton Mifflin.

Ehlert, Lois. (2007). "Picture Book Award Winner." *The Horn Book*, January/February, 19.

Eisner, Elliot. (2002). *The Arts and The Creation of Mind*. New Haven, CT: Yale University Press.

Eliot, L. (2000). *What's Going On In There?* NY: Bantam.

Fantz, R. (1961). "The Origins of Form Perception." *Scientific American*. 204(5), 66–72.

Gardner, H. (1980). *Artful Scribbles: The Significance of Children's Drawings*. New York: Basic Books.

Gardner, H. (1982). *Art, Mind, and Brain*. New York: Basic Books.

Garner, Dwight. (2006). "Coming at You." In *New York Times Book Review*. November 12, 48.

Gazzaniga, M., Ivry, R., & Mangun, G. (1998). *Cognitive Neuroscience*. New York: Norton.

Giblin, James, C. (2000). "More Than Just the Facts: A Hundred Years of Children's Nonfiction." *The Horn Book*, July/August, 413–424.

Gibson, Eleanor, & Pick, Anne. (2000). *An Ecological Approach to Perceptual Learning and Development*. New York: Oxford.

Gussow, Mel. (2003). "Sendak and Kushner Let Humor Get Through." *New York Times*. October 28.

Hoppe, Anne. (2004). "Half the Story: Text and Illustration in Picture Books. "*The Horn Book*. January/February, 41–50.

Keller, John. (2001). "Jerry Spinelli." *The Newbery and Caldecott Medal Books 1986–2000*. Chicago: American Library Association.

Kellogg, R. (1967). *Understanding Children's Art*. Del Mar, CA: CRM Publishing.

Kellogg, R. (1970). *Analyzing Children's Art*. Palo Alto, CA: National Press Books.

Kennedy, Louise. (2003). "Lighting the Way." *Boston Globe*. April 28, 2003.

Kushner, Tony. (2003). *The Art of Maurice Sendak: 1980 to the Present*. New York: Henry N. Abrams.

Kotulak, R. (1997). *Inside The Brain*. Kansas City, MO: Andrews McMeel.

Lowry, Lois. (2001). "1994 Newbery Acceptance Speech." *The Newbery and Caldecott Medal Books 1986–2000*. Chicago: American Library Association.

Macaulay, David (2001). "1991 Caldecott Acceptance Speech." *The Newbery and Caldecott Medal Books*. 1986–2000. Chicago: American Library Association.

Marcus, Leonard. (2002). *Ways of Telling: Conversations on the Art of the Picture Book*. New York: Dutton Books.

Matthews, J. (2003). *Drawing and Painting: Children and Visual Representation*. London: Chapman.

Milbrath, C. (1998). *Patterns of Artistic Development in Children*. Cambridge, England: Cambridge University Press.

Ratey, J. (2001). *A User's Guide To The Brain*. New York: Pantheon.

Restak, R. (2001). *The Secret Life of the Brain*. Washington, DC: The John Henry Press.

Ruskin, John. (1857). *The Elements of Drawing*. London: Smith, Elder

Sendak, Maurice. (2002). In Marcus, Leonard. *Ways of Telling*. New York: Dutton.

Siegler, R., & Alibali, M. (2005). *Children's Thinking*. Upper Saddle River, NJ: Prentice Hall.

Van Allsburg, Chris. (2001). "1986 Caldecott Acceptance Speech." *The Newbery and Caldecott Medal Books 1986–2000*. Chicago: American Library Association.

Ward, Diane. (2001). "Cynthia Rylant." *The Newbery and Caldecott Medal Books 1986–2000*. Chicago: American Library Association.

Willats, J. (2005). *Making Sense of Children's Drawings*. Mahwah, NJ: Lawrence Erlbaum.

Zipes, J. Paul, L. Vallone, P. Hunt, and G. Avery, eds. (2005). *The Norton Anthology of Children's Literature: The Traditions in English*. New York: Norton.

CHAPTER 6

Diversity in Children's Literature

What is it like to be an outsider?
What is it like to sit in the class where everyone has blond hair and you have black hair?
What is it like when the teacher says, "Whoever wasn't born here, raise your hand."
And you are the only one.
Then, when you raise your hand, everybody looks at you and makes fun of you.
You have to live in somebody else's country to understand.

(This poem was written by Noy Chou, a student from Cambodia, while she was in a suburban school in the Boston area.)

This first verse of Noy Chou's poem "You Have to Live in Somebody Else's Country to Understand" echoes the sentiments found in many other books, including Gene Luen Yang's *American Born Chinese*, the first graphic novel to win a Printz Award. Experiences such as those found in the books we discuss are a poignant reminder of the difficulties many children face as they struggle to adjust to a new society. With growing cognitive maturity, however, they often find relief reading these stories. Consequently, we will adopt a dual approach to the study of this subject. First, this chapter focuses on the "multiethnic literature" (Yokota, 2001) of Latinos, African Americans, Asian Americans, and Native Americans. (Children's literature rooted in other cultures—Jewish American, Arab American, Euro American, etc.—is presented elsewhere in this book.)

Second, multiple examples of diversity are included throughout this book, to reflect Bishop's (1997) belief that multiculturalism, in its broadest sense, includes those who have been marginalized by society. In this way, we hope to help young readers recognize, accept, and appreciate those who differ from them, whether in culture, social class, age, religion, special needs, or gender orientation. Accordingly, culturally neutral literature and culturally specific children's literature have been incorporated throughout this work, enabling us to include those traditionally ignored in children's literature.

In order to identify some of the key issues in the world of multiculturalism and how it plays out in children's literature, we'll first trace the path of multiculturalism in children's literature and give examples of its influence on a child's life. Then, we'll turn to Lev Vygotsky, whose work for many years has been a beacon of clarity in portraying how context exercises both a positive and negative influence in all aspects of a child's life. We'll then look at the children's literature of four cultures—Latino, African American, Asian American, and Native American—to discover how contemporary authors explore the trials and triumphs of today's children.

AMERICAN BORN CHINESE
Copyright 2006 by Gene Yang.
Reprinted by permission of Henry
Holt & Company.

Guidelines for Reading Chapter 6

After you read Chapter Six, you should be able to answer the following questions.

• Do you agree with the theme of Noy Chou's poem that many children have serious problems adjusting to a new society? Explain your answer in light of cultural differences.

• How does recognizing, accepting, and using diversity in children's literature benefit children?

• What are the major features in the history of multiculturalism in children's literature?

• What examples from children's literature illustrate how an author does or does not understand a particular culture at a significant level?

• What characteristics of various cultures would help teachers and librarians in their interactions with children?

• What are some ways Vygotsky's zone of proximal development can be used to encourage children's love of reading?

A Diverse Society

Americans pride themselves on living in a culturally diverse nation that encourages newcomers to share their way of life. Yet even under the best of conditions, this goal can be difficult for many children. The feeling of sadness at leaving a familiar and beloved setting is movingly portrayed in Frances and Ginger Park's *Good-bye, 382 Shin Dang Dong*, in which 8 year-old Jangmi leaves her Korean home and moves with her family to Massachusetts. How she adjusts to her new society and gradually comes to believe she may some day love her new country as much as her homeland is a theme that touches many children with similar experiences. Recognizing and understanding the impact of diversity on children are crucial in children's literature. The beauty of your work with young readers is that you can use the world of books to help them see others with similar challenges, goals, and hopes. When you genuinely display understanding and appreciation for people from other cultures, children will be encouraged to imitate your behavior. You thus enrich your own and your students' lives.

The Impact of the Cultural Climate

Librarians and teachers who are aware of the differences between a child's home culture and surrounding environment can do much to ensure that the child succeeds academically and personally (Greenfield & Suzuki, 1998). A good example of this can be seen in Kim's (1990) description of a group of Hawaiian children whose school experiences were not always positive. Yet these same children demonstrated considerable initiative and a high performance level at home—cooking, cleaning, and taking care of their brothers and sisters.

The competence and initiative of these Hawaiian children are nicely displayed in Graham Salisbury's book of short stories, *Island Boyz*. A native of the Hawaiian Islands, Salisbury identifies these traits in the story "Angel-Baby". Tina Marie Angel-Baby Diminico is the name of the story's heroine. Despite being fiercely teased by the boys in her class — especially Izzy — during her early elementary years, she more than holds her own.

In the fourth grade, she and Izzy have a fight, after which they slowly become friends. When they're in the sixth grade, Tina cooks Izzy a special treat for his birthday: a Hawaiian coconut pudding cake called *haupia*. They also survive a harrowing boat trip in a wild storm that demanded all the skills and cooperation they can muster. In telling the story of "Angel-Baby," Salisbury translates the abilities of Hawaiian children into a fascinating story of relationships.

Then and Now

Exceptional Children

For those of us who work with children, the concept of individual differences is part of our daily planning, which reflects Bishop's (1997) suggestions concerning the totality of diversity. Here we would like to call your attention to the needs of exceptional children. Knowledge of developmental characteristics can guide us in choosing materials that offer appropriate support for children who are exceptional.

The policy toward exceptionality has changed dramatically in recent years. At one time children with disabilities were either refused admission to public schools or educated in separate locations. Today, however, our belief is that children with special needs should be educated in *the least restrictive environment* possible. In 1990, Congress passed *the Individuals with Disabilities Act (IDEA)*, a revised version of *Public Law 94-142*, which mandated that all children with disabilities receive a free, appropriate education. These measures led to efforts to educate children with disabilities on a full-time basis in regular classrooms. This procedure is referred to as *inclusion*. (You may be more familiar with the term *mainstreaming*.)

Although you may have seen several methods for classifying exceptional conditions, the following are the most common categories of exceptionality. To illustrate how children with special needs successfully adapt to their environment, and how their peers respond to them, we urge you to read the following stories associated with the various categories of exceptionality.

- *Sensory and physical disorders* (visual, hearing, and orthopedic impairments). William Roy Brownridge's *The Final Game* is the inspiring story of Danny, a young hockey player who wears moccasins as goalie because a crippled leg and foot prevent him from wearing ice skates. When teammates taunt him, his brother, an outstanding hockey star, comes to coach the team and also teaches them the importance of team cooperation.

- *Mental retardation* (problems with intellectual functioning). Betsy Byars' Newbery Medal winner *Summer of the Swans* nicely demonstrates how normal activity surrounds children who are exceptional. It deals with a 14-year-old's relationship with her much younger, retarded brother. When he is lost, her desire to find him and her feelings for a boy who offers to help in the search arouse conflicting emotions.

- *Communication disorders* (speech and language disorders). Claire Blatchford's *Going with the Flow* details how fifth grader Mark, who is deaf, connects with his classmates on the basketball court. As a good-natured gesture, his friend Keith trips Mark—nonverbal communication—whenever Mark starts to monopolize the ball.

- *Learning disabilities* (difficulty with academic subjects with no specific mental or physical cause). *Just Kids: Visiting a Class for Children with Special Needs* is a fictional account written by Ellen Senisi about Cindy, whose experience helping in a special needs classroom increases her understanding of those who have trouble learning—a group she once mocked.

- *Emotional and behavioral disorders*. In *Al Capone Does My Shirts*, Gennifer Choldenko sensitively reveals how Moose Flanagan deals with the stress of caring for his autistic sister who lacks social interactions and an orderly sense of communication.

- *Children who are gifted and talented*. The gifted are appealingly described in E. L. Konigsburg's *The View from Saturday*. A group of witty, intelligent, and astute sixth graders participates in the academic bowl team and wins the state finals.

As we discuss the children's literature that represents the range of multiculturalism and diversity mentioned earlier, we'll present outstanding books, mainly written by native authors, to illustrate each culture. To do this, we will follow the selection criteria suggested by Yokota (2001):

- Is the book quality literature?

- Do the authors and illustrators offer culturally appropriate perspectives?

- Are the multidimensions of the culture presented?

- Are cultural details integrated naturally?

- Are the cultural details accurate and are interpretations current?

Multiculturalism in Children's Literature

We are a country of Muslims, atheists, Jews, Christians, Hindus, and devout spiritualists without a specific religious affiliation. We celebrate the winter solstice, Hanukkah, Christmas, Kwanza, and Ramadan. We brought longstanding cultural traditions and rites of passage from Haiti, Laos, Ghana, El Salvador, France, Germany, England, and Samoa, among countless others. Many of our children are taken through rites of passage that include bar mitzvahs, inceneros, debutante balls, and gang initiations.

(Muse, 1997, p. 285)

In her painstaking analysis of the path of multiculturalism in children's literature, Barbara Bader (2002, 2003a, 2003b, 2005) used the books *Little House in the Big Woods* by Laura Ingalls Wilder (originally published in 1932) and *Roll of Thunder, Hear My Cry* by Mildred Taylor (originally published in 1976), to emphasize the changing themes in children's stories. Reflecting a restless and evolving society, these stories move from a description of covered wagon days and the stereotypical image of Indians as "bloody savages" (*Little House in the Big Woods*), to the grim reality of segregation in the rural South (*Roll of Thunder, Hear My Cry*).

The Search for Minority Authors

Although many believe multiculturalism came about because of the changing nature of American society in the 1960s, and the rise of the civil rights movement in particular (Bishop, 1997), Payne and Welsh (2000) trace its roots to a torturous 2,500-year struggle. They believe the battle for equality, freedom, and dignity reaches back to the Code of Hammurabi (1750 BC), the Magna Carta (1215 AD), and the British Bill of Rights (1689 AD). Banks (1995) and Harris (1997) argue that multiculturalism has deep roots in the African American scholarship of the nineteenth and early twentieth century, which produced knowledge about African Americans that was later used in school and college curricula.

A major impetus came from Nancy Larrick's 1965 article "The All–White World of Children's Books," which appeared in the *Saturday Review of Literature*. Beginning with a question posed by a 5-year-old African American girl—"Why are they always white children?"—Larrick stunned readers with her hard-hitting analysis of the menial and negative images of African Americans in children's books. The move for a more positive depiction of people of color received a powerful boost from Larrick's portrayal of the limited scope of children's literature. As Harris (1997, p. 25) notes, from this time on children's literature depicting blacks showed a decided renaissance. Virginia Hamilton's *Zeely* (1967), for example, marked the turning point as books by black authors increasingly reflected realism, creativity, and excellence.

Following the formation of the *Council on Interracial Books for Children* (CIBC) in 1965, pressure intensified for minority authors to portray minority subjects realistically. Its publication, *Interracial Books for Children*, a quarterly bulletin, began to question such well-known books as Hugh Lofting's *The Story of Doctor Dolittle*, William Armstrong's *Sounder*, and Theodore Taylor's *The Cay* for their hidden, but inherent racism.

Gradually, black-authored books with a real sense of black culture began to appear. The writings of Virginia Hamilton (*Zeely*, *The House of Dies Drear*, *The Planet of Junior Brown*), John Steptoe (*Stevie*, *Mufaro's Beautiful Daughters*), and Julius Lester (*To Be a Slave*, *Black Folktales*), to name a few, signaled that a new era of writing about minorities had commenced. June Jordan's *Civil Wars*, the touching stories of Sharon Bell Mathis (*Sidewalk Story*, *Teacup Full of Roses*, *The Hundred Penny Box*), and the moving tales and poetry of Eloise Greenfield (*Good News*, her first picture book, followed by *She Come Bringing Me That Little Baby Girl*, and books of poetry such as *Honey, I Love* and *Nathaniel Talking*) all testified to the changing complexion of minority literature. The emergence of African American literature with its own voice, which began with the Crowell Biography series of picture books, set the stage for other, non-black minority writers who wanted their children to be proud of the achievements of their people (Bader, 2002).

The Widening Scope of Minority Books

Increasingly, a more widespread multiculturalism began to make its impact felt, and books depicting other underrepresented groups and topics began to appear. (For a more detailed discussion of this topic, see Bader, 2003a; Cai, 2002; Muse, 1997.) For example, the Japanese author Uchida Yoshiko—*The Dancing Kettle* (1949), *Journey to Topaz* (1971), *Journey Home* (1978)—displays an author's transformation as multiculturalism became a more accepted and expected part of children's literature. In *Journey Home*, Uchida revealed her deep-seated resentment at the internment of Japanese-Americans during World War II, feelings she had previously kept hidden. In her later stories, Uchida's writings give us a more genuine and moving account of what Japanese-American origins really mean.

During the 1970s efforts were made to diversify children's books (Muse, 1997). While CIBC was fighting heated battles against racism in these years, other wars were being fought—and won—in different venues and at different levels. In the continuing and intense struggle against racism, no one better promoted multiculturalism in older children's books than Walter Dean Myers (Bader, 2003a, p. 150). With a series of books that can only be described as captivating—*The Young Landlords*, *Hoops*, and *Fallen Angels* among others—Myers forged a trail of outstanding books that dealt with contempory scorching issues that included truth, honesty, racism, responsibility, and Vietnam. In so doing, he created a lasting place for multiculturalism in children's literature.

The Role of Independent Publishers

As the 1970s drew to a painful close, a sharp decline in the number of black-authored books occurred, and the gains of recent years were being lost. Muse (1997) commented that major trade publishers were reluctant to enter the field, because they believed multicultural books were a financial risk. It was during these years that the idea of a national award for a minority author and illustrator was first broached. After several years of a persistent struggle, the American Library Association presented the first Coretta Scott King Award in 1970 to "commemorate and foster the life, works and dreams of the late Dr. Martin Luther King Jr. and to honor Mrs. Coretta Scott King for her courage and determination to work for peace and world brotherhood." Lillie Patterson was the first African American author to receive the award for her book, *Martin Luther King Jr.: Man of Peace*. Yet by 1985, only eighteen books by African American authors had been submitted to the Coretta Scott King jury.

Other changes were also occurring during these years. Smaller, independent publishers appeared and gave a needed impetus to multicultural children's books with texts about Latin American issues, Native American traditions and settings, feminist struggles, gender issues, homelessness, and other topics. A leader in this movement was the *Children's Book Press* of San Francisco, which initiated a novel series of books entitled *How We Came to the Fifth World*. The series included stories such as *The Little Weaver of Thai Yen Village* (the story of a Vietnam war refugee), *My Aunt Otilia's Spirits* (a Puerto Rican ghost story), and the Native American history, *The People Shall Continue*. With the acceptance and success of books such as these, and with the popularity of the television program *Reading Rainbow*, multicultural children's literature was again on the fast track (Bader, 2003a).

The Changing Literary Scene

Beginning in the mid-1980s, a dramatic increase in sales about stories relating to African American children occurred. As black authors portrayed the theme of family pride and multifaceted complexity in their stories and emphasized the richness of their history, a sense of realism, both verbal and pictorial, leapt from the pages (Harris, 1997). The outstanding example of this is Valerie Flournoy's *The Patchwork Quilt*, which is the story of a grandmother's legacy and a granddaughter's dedication. This book, written in 1985, is realistically illustrated by Jerry Pinkney. Pinkney, who created a style of illustration that is identifiable in all his books, is able to make his characters stand out as unique individuals. In other books he has illustrated, such as Patricia McKissack's *Mirandy and Brother Wind* and Julius Lester's retelling *of The Tales of Uncle Remus*, he fills the pages with light and energy through his skillful use of watercolors.

By the end of the 1980s, the number of black-authored and black-illustrated books had increased substantially (the peak would come in 1995 with 100 books published), and the acceptance of black authors and illustrators had increased impressively. The Coretta Scott King Award for outstanding illustration was given in 1981 to Ashley Bryan for *Beat the Story Drum, Pum-Pum*, and Tom Feelings was selected in 1979 and 1994 for *Something on My Mind* (Nikki Grimes) and *Soul Looks Back in Wonder*. Eloise Greenfield's *Under the Sunday Tree* was illustrated by the black folk artist Amos Ferguson, while Faith Ringgold was author and illustrator of *Tar Beach* and *Aunt Harriet's Underground Railroad in the Sky*. African American children's literature had come full circle: being black in America was a rich and diverse experience.

Table 6.1 presents several highlights in the development of multicultural children's literature.

Culture and Children's Literature

The Steady Advance of Multiculturalism

As the themes, plots, and settings of stories featuring African American children became firmly entrenched in children's literature, the steady growth of stories about children in other cultures likewise expanded. An enormous and growing market for stories on diversity appeared. For example, in 1993 the newly established firm of Lee and Low (Philip Lee and Thomas Low, both Chinese Americans) published multicultural stories about Asian Americans. Their first book by Ken Mochizuki (illustrated by Dom Lee) was set in the painful context of the World War II internment camps. *Baseball Saved Us* is a sensitive account of Shorty, a Japanese-American boy, who determined to succeed in baseball while he and his family were interned. *Heroes*, by Mochizuki, is about Donnie Okada, who was teased in the 1960s for being the enemy until his father and uncle, who had been in the armed forces, taught his tormentors a lesson. (For an excellent discussion of this topic, see Yamate, 1997.)

Another example of the growing role of multiculturalism in children's literature can be seen in the rapid increase of Latino children's books, which was encouraged by the establishment of the Pura Belpré award in 1996. It is a biannual honor given by the American Library Association in conjunction with REFORMA, The National Association to Promote Library and Information Services to Latinos and the Spanish speaking. It is awarded to the Latino/Latina writer and Latino/Latina illustrator whose works best represent Latino culture.

Authors such as Gary Soto (*Taking Sides, Pacific Crossing*, and *Jesse*) have the ability to write stories and poems that colorfully and tastefully demonstrate that to be Latino is a way of being American (Bader, 2003b, p. 280). It is interesting to note that the requests for Spanish and bilingual titles of children's books have increased so much that the *Library Journal*, the *School Library Journal*, and *Publishers Weekly* have combined to publish *Criticas*, a bimonthly, annotated English Speaking Guide to the latest Spanish language titles in adult and children's literature. Teachers and librarians now have another resource from which to select books for their Latino students.

Native American children's literature has made slower inroads into the mainstream of children's literature. Bader (2003b) details the interesting story of how, in 1970, the *Council on Interracial Books for Children* decided to expand its awards contests for new African American writers, to include separate categories for Hispanic, Asian American, and Native American entries. No substantial body of literature emerged from any of these groups. The many tribes, and books by whites such as Holling Clancy Holling (*Tree in the Trail*), Elizabeth George Speare (*The Sign of the Beaver*), Jean Fritz (*The Double Life of Pocahontas*), and David Wisniewski (*The Wave of the Sea-Wolf*), among others, who wrote about the Native American culture across many genres, impeded writing by Native American authors.

Today, however, many Native American authors, such as Louise Erdrich (*The Birchback House*), Cynthia Leitich Smith (*Rain Is Not My Indian Name*), and Joseph Bruchac (*Crazy Horse's Vision*), have made substantial contributions to children's literature. It is interesting to note that when Kathleen Odean, writer, librarian, and chairperson of the Newbery Award Committee (2001), surveyed fourteen members of the Committee throughout the country on what they see as the most important shift in children's literature, one of the two themes they emphasized was *the emergence of more authentic voices from different cultures.* Junko Yokota, a professor at National-Louis University in Evanston, Illinois, and editor of *Kaleidoscope, A Multicultural Booklist for Grades K-8,* emphasized the sensitivity of book creators to represent cultures with honest, even if not always positive, portrayals (Odean, 2001).

Table 6.1 HIGHLIGHTS IN THE DEVELOPMENT OF MULTICULTURAL CHILDREN'S LITERATURE*

1887—Amelia Johnson founded *The Joy,* a periodical for African American children.	1968—Walter Dean Myers publishes his first children's book, *Where Does the Day Go.*
1920—W. E. B. DuBois began Brownie Books, a monthly children's magazine.	1969—The annual Coretta Scott King Award for African American illustrators is established.
1929—Bruno Lasker is the author of *Race Attitudes in Children.*	1972—Christopher Jenck's *Inequality: A Reassessment of the Effect of Family and Schooling in America* appears.
1933—Elizabeth F. Lewis' *Young Fu of the Upper Yangtze* wins the Newbery Award; author Charles Dawson publishes *ABC's of Great Negroes.*	1973—Johana Reiss's *The Upstairs Room* gains a Newbery Honor.
1942—Lois Lenski wins a Newbery Honor for *Indian Captive: The Story of Mary Jemison.*	1974—Virginia Hamilton's *M. C. Higgins* wins the National Book Award and the Boston Globe-Horn Book Award.
1944—Gunnar Myrdal's *An American Dilemma* is published; Shirley Graham's series of biographies for children begins with the Julian Messner Co.'s publication of *George Washington Carver.*	
1946—Mine Okubo publishes the first book depicting life for Japanese Americans in the internment camps.	1975—Virginia Hamilton becomes the first person of color to receive the Newbery Medal for *M. C. Higgins.*
1951—The Japanese American writer Yoshiko Uchida publishes the first book for children describing conditions in the internment camps.	1983—*Ways with Words: Language, Life, and Work in Communities and Classroom* is published by Shirley Brice Heath.

Table 6.1 CONTINUED

1954—Gordon Allport's *The Nature of Prejudice* is published; the Supreme Court hands down its *Brown v. Board of Education* decision; Joseph Krumgold's *And Now Miguel* wins the Newbery Medal.

1956—Arna Bontemps wins the Jane Addams Children's Book Award for the *Story of the Negro*, thus becoming the first person of color to be so honored.

1957—The New York Public Library, for the first time, publishes the annual, annotated bibliography *Books about Negro Life for Children*. In 1963 the title was changed to *The African American Experience in Children's Books*.

1965—The American psychologist Benjamin Bloom and his colleagues publish *Compensatory Education for Cultural Deprivation*. Nancy Larrick's searing article "The All-White World of Children's Books" appears in the *Saturday Review of Literature*.

1966—*Equality of Educational Opportunity*, James Coleman's penetrating analysis of the effects of the composition of a school's student population, is published. The Council on Interracial Books for Children begins publication. (See p. 124 in this chapter.) Elizabeth B. de Trevino's *I, Juan de Pareja* wins the Newbery Medal.

1990—Of the approximately 5,000 children's books published this year in the United States, only fifty-one were written/illustrated by African Americans. Lois Lowry wins the Newbery Medal for *Number the Stars* and Suzanne F. Staples wins the Newbery Honor for *Shabanu, Daughter of the Wind*.

1992—Octavio Paz wins the Nobel Prize for literature.

1995—Virginia Hamilton is the first author of color to receive the Laura Ingalls Wilder Award for an "author's collected works and contributions to children's literature"; Sharon Creech wins the Newbery Medal for *Walk Two Moons*.

2000—The Children's Book Guild and the *Washington Post* name Diane Stanley as the recipient of the 2000 Award for Nonfiction.

2005—Cynthia Kadohata, the author of *Kira-Kira*, the story of a Japanese family's move from Iowa to Georgia, is awarded the 2005 Newbery Medal.

2005—Toni Morrison receives the 2005 Coretta Scott King Award *for Remember: The Journey to School Integration*.

2007—Gene Yang receives the Michael Printz Award, an "annual award for literary excellence."

* Based on data from Banks & Banks (1995), Warder (1997), Norton (2001), and Cai (2002).

The Contribution of Lev Vygotsky

No discussion of diversity would be complete without mentioning the thinking and research of the Russian psychologist Lev Vygotsky (1896–1934). Emphasizing the influence of social and cultural processes on development, Vygotsky realized that adults interact with children in a way that a culture values. Here is a concept of enormous importance that is particularly pertinent today due to the increasing number of non-native English-speaking children and the growing realization that the most effective means of reaching these potential readers is in a cultural context.

But what does this mean for your work with children? To answer this question, let's turn to Vygotsky's notion of the *zone of proximal development*.

Spin Off
Vygotsky in the Classroom

Understanding and using Vygotsky's ideas can provide teachers and librarians with guidelines for helping children improve their understanding of children's literature. For example, in their analysis of the suggestions for *scaffolding* that emerge from Vygotsky's theory and research, Berk and Winsler (1995) detail a method such as the following for helping struggling readers.

A middle-school teacher organizes a learning group in which each member takes a turn leading a discussion that assists children in understanding the text that they are reading. In our example, the teacher and students are reading Chris Lynch's *Gold Dust*. The teacher's role is to facilitate scaffolding, that is, to encourage all the children to participate in the discussion. Four cognitive strategies are involved: *questioning, summarizing, clarifying*, and *predicting*. Initially, the teacher explains and models the strategies to bolster the children's confidence and participation in the discussion. Here is an example of the process.

• *Questioning*. First the teacher, and then a reader, asks questions about the story's content. What is the setting? (*Boston*, 1975.) How important is the setting to the story? (*It is a time of racial unrest in Boston.*) Who are the main characters (the protagonists)? (*Richard, an outgoing white boy, who takes Napoleon, a cultured black from Dominica, "under his wing."*) Are the characters stereotypical? (*No. Richard is poor and has no mother. He lives in a flat in a broken-down neighborhood. Napoleon's father is a visiting professor at Boston University and is well educated.*) One of the members challenges the answer that the boys are not stereotypical. So the reading group returns to the book to find an example of how ill at ease Richard is when he and Napoleon are dining at an exclusive restaurant. Napoleon, however, is comfortable and selects from the menu with confidence. The members of the group then agree that the boys come from different backgrounds.

• *Summarizing*. Next, the group leader summarizes what he or she thinks is the substance of the reading. *Even though Richard and Napoleon live in the middle of a racist atmosphere, they are friends, but Richard will never be able to make Napoleon a baseball player like he is.* Discussion follows within the group. *One reader thinks if Richard practiced more with Napoleon, he could make Napoleon a better baseball player. Another member of the group believes that Napoleon does not want to play baseball, but prefers to play rugby and cultivate his love of music. The group agrees that Napoleon's wishes should be respected.*

• *Clarifying*. Any confusing terms or ideas are discussed so that all members are clear on the passage that was read.

• *Predicting*. The leader encourages the group members to try to predict what will happen next, based on what has happened thus far in the story. *Until this point in the story, Napoleon and Richard are certain of their friendship. But, what will happen if Napoleon is confronted with racist threats; will Richard still be his friend?*

You can see how children learn that knowledge gained in one setting can be applied to another ("transfer of learning"). This is only one example of how Vygotsky's ideas about children's social processes translate into classroom practice.

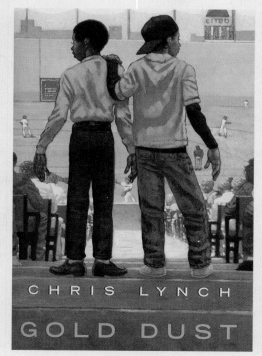

GOLD DUST
Used with permission of Harper-Collins Publishers

The Zone of Proximal Development

Vygotsky (1978) argued that adults (teachers, librarians, parents) working with children must be aware of a child's developmental level in order to recognize and accept the outer limits of that child's ability. To help guide teachers, he introduced his notion of the *zone of proximal development*, which is the distance between a child's actual developmental level and the child's level of potential development with adult guidance, or in collaboration with more capable peers. In other words, it's the difference between what children can achieve with guidance and what they can achieve through individual effort (Valsiner, 1998). Vygotsky's ideas on what constitutes the kind of assistance that should be given children, to move them to the upper limits of their zone of proximal development, were general in nature: demonstration, leading questions, introducing the beginning elements of the solution, etc. (Vygotsky, 1978).

Vygotsky believed that teachers, librarians, and parents encourage learning when their efforts awaken those developmental functions that are already maturing and that are in the zone of proximal development. The social environment surrounding children becomes the vital scaffolding, or support system, that parents, teachers, and librarians can contribute to the cognitive improvement of young readers in order to help them rise above their present level of functioning. Tragically, tuberculosis claimed Vygotsky's life in 1934. But his work, because of its cultural emphasis, is more popular today than it was when he died. Table 6.2 summarizes Vygotsky's major ideas.

Table 6.2 VYGOTSKY AND CULTURAL PROCESSES

KEY THEMES	MEANING	APPLICATION
Perspective	Child's cognitive development progresses by social interaction with others	Patricia McKissack's *The Honest-to-Goodness Truth* depicts cognitive and moral development, as a young child interacts with her mother.
Psychological mechanism	Social interactions with skilled others	Valerie Flournoy's *The Patchwork Quilt* demonstrates how social interactions shape development.
Language	Preintellectual speech develops into inner speech and helps with cognitive development	Virginia Driving Hawk Shreve's *Enduring Wisdom* discloses the power and beauty of language as a force in children's development.
Learning	Results from elementary processes and sociocultural interactions	By interacting with teachers and librarians, children learn about Japanese culture by reading *How My Parents Learned to Eat* by Ina Friedman.
Problem solving	Speech guides planful behavior; joint effort with others	Graham Salisbury's *Island Boyz* illustrates the independence and problem-solving abilities of children in their own cultures.

Reflections of Diversity in Children's Literature

In her thoughtful analysis of children's thinking and its relationship to culture, Barbara Rogoff (2003), a leading commentator on the influence of culture on development, noted that in a scientific age it's well to remember that we can only understand development in light of cultural practices and circumstances. Her powerful affirmation of culture's role in the lives of children summarizes our goal in this chapter: recognizing and accepting the significance of culture in a child's life.

Understanding Culture

If you think of *culture* as the customs, values, and traditions inherent in one's environment (Sue & Sue, 1991), you'll quickly realize that different cultures have different educational and developmental expectations for their children. *Asian* children, for example, are encouraged to avoid emotional displays, a characteristic that does not necessarily apply to *Asian American* children. Appreciating children's behavior demands an understanding of their cultures on at least three levels.

1. You understand at a *superficial* level; that is, you know the facts that make up a child's cultural history.

2. You understand at an *intermediate* level; that is, you understand the central behaviors that are at the core of children's psychosocial lives.

3. You understand at a *significant* level; that is, you grasp the values, beliefs, and norms that structure a child's view of the world and how to behave in that world. In other words, you change psychologically as you acquire information about, and interact with, a different culture (Casas & Pytluk, 1995).

But what does this understanding of culture mean for your work with children?

In a penetrating analysis of ethnic and racial identity, Cole & Cole (1996) note that by the time children are about 4 years old, they're aware of ethnic and racial differences. Significantly, their attitudes toward their own and other's ethnicity depend *on the attitudes of the adults around them.* Therefore, how teachers and librarians react to children from different cultures, how they work with them, and the literary vistas they open for them will broaden the cultural horizons of both adults and children.

Children begin learning from their teacher how to understand each other as early as preschool. By reading aloud stories such as *How My Parents Learned to Eat*, for example, teachers and librarians may invoke a discussion with their young students about Japanese culture. Rituals such as Japanese courtship and eating with chopsticks are related by the author, Ina Friedman, whose father, a sailor stationed in Japan, married her mother, a very proper, dignified Japanese young lady.

Latino Children and Literature

What does it mean to be Latino in this country? Today, Latinos/Latinas are thought to be those who trace their roots to the Spanish-speaking countries of Latin America or Spain (Marin, 1994). Although there are wide variations among this population, as with any other group, they possess a unique set of cultural beliefs that distinguish them from Asian Americans or African Americans. Brazilians, for example, consider themselves Latin American, although their language and literature is Portuguese rather than Spanish. They do in fact reflect Latin American culture. Many of their classics have been translated into Spanish, and with the passage of time, more of their children's literature will also be translated into English.

Early elementary school children find many cultural clues about their Latino/Latina friends when they read *My Name Is Maria Isabel*, a short book written by Alma Flor Ada, who has written more than 100 books (many in Spanish), and is director of the Center for Multicultural Literature at the University of San Francisco. The main character in this story is Maria Isabel Salazar Lopez, the new girl in class, who comes from a loving Latino family. Her first day in school, however, is marred because the teacher chooses to call her another name. Later in the year, the teacher, misunderstanding Maria's attitude, does not select her to sing at the Winter Festival. How Maria solves her problem, increases her teacher's understanding, and wins the support of her classmates makes for a sympathetic story.

Alma Flor Ada has also coauthored *Pio Peep!* with F. Isabel Campoy. Traditional Spanish nursery rhymes are presented in both English and Spanish to

Spotlight On

Gary Soto (1952 –)

Gary Soto, born and raised in Fresno, California, has never forgotten his Mexican American childhood. His novels, short stories, and poetry for adults, teenagers, and young children are frequently drawn from his memories—particularly from the street where he lived growing up. "These are the pictures that I take into my work, both in poetry and prose, pictures that stir the past, which I constantly haunt with an inventory list" (Soto, 1995, p. 614). Readers familiar with his novels *Taking Sides* (1991), *Pacific Crossing* (1992), and *If the Shoe Fits* (2002) learn a great deal about a Mexican American culture that emphasizes friendship, loyalty, and winning. Readers also learn about the stress that racial prejudice places on minority children.

Courtesy Gary Soto

Soto seems to have total recall of the small but vivid details of everyday life.

Although Soto has written over twenty-one autobiographical short stories, he is a poet at heart and today teaches poetry at the university level, even though he came from an illiterate family. He writes poetry for all ages such as *A Fire in My Hands: A Book of Poems* (1999), and *Neighborhood Odes* (1992), and he encourages the young people he meets to read and appreciate it. To encourage children to read, he often includes a glossary of the Spanish words and phrases sprinkled throughout his books. In spite of the fact that the characters may be Mexican American and disadvantaged, his stories have a wide appeal because of the universality of his topics.

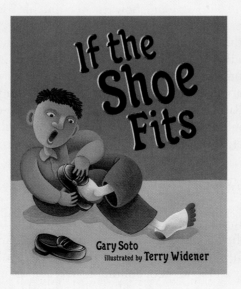

If the Shoe Fits

Gary Soto
illustrated by **Terry Widener**

IF THE SHOE FITS
Reproduced by permission of Penguin Group USA Inc.

simplify the transition from one language to the other. Drawn from the oral tradition of Latin America and the American Southwest, the verses are popular in the Spanish-speaking world and are well known for their rhythm and lyricism. Intermediate school readers will enjoy reading *How Tia Lola Came to (Visit) Stay* by Julia Alvarez, which about is a flamboyant aunt who travels from the Dominican Republic to Vermont for a short visit. Children quickly pick up the brief snatches of Spanish conversation randomly scattered throughout the book.

Mexican author Antonio Hernandez Madrigal has written an enchanting story, *Erandi's Braids*, for primary school children, adapting his story from the custom of Tarascan women in Mexico who sell their black braids when they need money. Erandi is willing to sell her hair to help her parents financially. The well-known Tomie dePaola, who illustrated this story, has illustrated folktales from many countries such as the Native American tale *The Legend of the Blue-Bonnet*, and other Mexican tales such as *The Legend of the Poinsettia* and *The Lady of Guadalupe*.

OTHER LITERARY FORMS   Journal writing is another literary form being used more frequently in contemporary fiction. Irma Amada Perez has written a bilingual diary for primary grades, *My Diary from Here to There/Mi diario de aqui hasta alla*, based on the author's journey from Mexico to Los Angeles, and illustrated in flaming colors by Maya Christina Gonzalez. Scholastic has introduced a new series of First Person Fiction (Orchard Books) to give a narrative life to the American immigrant experience. Included are authors such as Edwidge Danticat who has written the diary *Behind the Mountains*, and Ana Veciana Suarez who has written the diary *Flight to Freedom*. Both have made a smooth transition from writing adult novels to writing for middle school children.

Poetry is also popular with Latino children. Francisco X. Alarcon, for example, has written many whimsical poems about his Mexican childhood: both *From the Bellybutton of the Moon and Other Summer Poems/Del ombligo de la luna y otros* and *Laughing Tomatoes and Other Spring Poems/Jitomates risuenos y otros poemas de primaver* are Pura Belpré Honor Books. As we have seen, Gary Soto, who was born in the United States, continues to write both fiction and poetry about his Mexican American childhood experiences.

African American Children and Literature

Although children react to both the physical and social aspects of their environments, they are usually influenced more by one than the other, and their preference depends on the guidelines of their culture (Banks & Banks, 1993). The urban environment and the social milieu in which most African American children develop seem to predispose them toward the social elements of their environment, which then affects their school performance.

Author Jacqueline Woodson is popular with older children from many cultures because she has written sensitively and universally about children torn by trouble, who eventually leave their troubles behind. For example, *Miracle Boy* is a Coretta Scott King Award winner that details the struggle of three brothers successfully coping with the death of their parents. She has also written *Last Summer with Maizon*, the story of 11-year-old Margaret who is devastated when her father dies and her friend Maizon leaves her to go to boarding school. In *Hush*, when Toswiah Green's father agrees to testify against two fellow policemen, the family is placed in the witness protection program, where they learn to overcome loneliness with hope.

Pictures in African American homes are often those of the people they most admire, such as Martin Luther King, Jr., Jesse Jackson, and John and Robert Kennedy. In her book *Remember: The Journey to School Integration*, Pulitzer Prize winner Toni Morrison offers children a series of photographs recalling what happened before and after school segregation and expresses what she imagines were the thoughts and feelings of some of the people in the photographs. Pictures also play a large part in Christopher Paul Curtis's Newbery Medal book, *Bud, Not Buddy*. In this moving story, young Bud begins his touching, humorous, and determined search for his father, whom he knows only from pictures his mother gave him before she died.

This emphasis on the personal offers ideas for working with African American children. Children learn better, for example, when you involve them in activities that require interacting with others and when your attitude and the stories you recommend reflect the positive aspects of their culture. Interpersonal relationships within the family—often involving aunts, uncles, and grandparents—play a large role in the socialization of African American children, with the ultimate goal of helping them function independently within and without the family (Banks, 1995).

Patricia McKissack's tone when writing about African American children is warm and loving. Her book for ages 5–9, *The Honest-to-Goodness Truth*, relates how the young child Libby struggles to tell the truth and is heartbroken when her mother catches her telling a lie. From that moment on, she promises herself to tell the truth—no matter what it costs or whom it hurts—until everyone becomes upset with her. Her mother explains that "sometimes the truth is told at the wrong time. . . and that can be hurtful. But the honest-to-goodness truth is never wrong." Libby learns a difficult lesson about life through the support of her Mama.

Spotlight On
Virginia Hamilton (1936–2002)

Scholastic Inc.

The vibrant African American author Virginia Hamilton will be forever connected to *Zeely* (1967), her first novel, which established new standards for the contemporary era of African American literature. Although she has written many juvenile novels such as *The Planet of Jr. Brown* (1971) (selected by *School Library Journal* as a Best Book), *M. C. Higgins the Great* (1976) (the first book by a black writer to win a Newbery Medal), *Sweet Whispers* (1982), *The House of Dies Drear* (1968), and the *Mystery of Drear House* (1987), in celebrating Zeely's African elegance Hamilton declared that "black is beautful" without raising a fist (Bishop, 2002).

Rudine Sims Bishop (2002, p. 631) noted that Hamilton's books are "illuminations of what she called the American *Hopescape*, and in particular, the distinctiveness of African American experiences." For Virginia Hamilton, the African American experience was always a driving force within her. She often said that what personal self she had is in her books and that her stories are little pieces of herself (Apseloff, 1983).

Many of these experiences grew from the conversations Hamilton had with her extended family in Ohio, where she grew up. She often mentioned her storytelling mother, but it was her father whom she called "her sun." The family revolved around him—a musician who was moody at times, and who was interested in politics and reading. As she grew older, Hamilton yearned to go to New York, but a scholarship she received to Antioch College kept her in Ohio a while longer. Later, she attended the New School in New York where she met many people who influenced her intellectually and politically. Yet, *Zeely*, her first book, was begun while she was at Antioch, where she had amassed a large collection of African material. It was after her move to New York, however, that the Macmillan Company accepted it for publication.

Since that time she has become an esteemed author who is respected internationally for her contributions not only to African American culture, but to world cultures. She has been the recipient of many prestigious awards, including the Newbery Medal, the *Boston Globe–Horn Book* Award, the National Book Award, the Coretta Scott King Award, the Hans Christian Andersen Medal, the Laura Ingalls Wilder Award, and the first MacArthur "Genius" Award, granted to exceptionally talented and creative people.

Two phrases Hamilton has coined here reverberated throughout the literary world. One is *hopescape*, the dream of freedom that African Americans have in their travels across America. They are constantly moving to find a better place. She visualizes the black American in her literature as being speculative, symbolic, and brooding (Hamilton, 1981). The other phrase is *parallel culture*, which pertains to minorities who feel uneasy because of their ideological differences with the majority. Underlying Virginia Hamilton's writings is the dream of a freedom that is not quite attainable (Hamilton, 1981).

In her adolescent novels, she has always tried to put literary considerations before what she calls "sociological/ didactic ones." She has frequently commented that we expect novels for adolescents to answer the questions that "typically plague them at this time of their lives," but she has opted, instead, for emphasizing the literary ele-

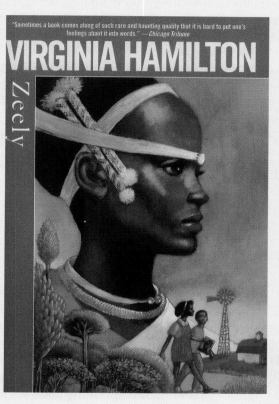

"Sometimes a book comes along of such rare and haunting quality that it is hard to put one's feelings about it into words." —*Chicago Tribune*

VIRGINIA HAMILTON

Zeely

ments of a dramatic setting, believable characters, and tensely engaging plots as in her *House of Dies Drear* and the *Mystery of Drear House.*

Her writings have not been limited to fiction. She has continually researched history to tell the authentic stories of her people as in her nonfiction *The People Could Fly* (1985), a collection of black folk tales. In her Coretta Scott King acceptance speech (*Horn Book*, 1986), she explained that folktales offered comfort and strength in hard times. Slaves could only sit down and tell stories under cover of darkness. Their meetings were so secret that they dared not use their own names lest news of their meetings reached the ears of the overseer.

Through all her works, Hamilton weaves the thread of unity: from teller to reader there is the unbroken communication that *we are all together.* In her 1993 Arbuthnot lecture, she noted that her first novel, *Zeely*, had been in print continuously for twenty-six years. (Today, it's still in print after forty years.) She has left us more than thirty books, and in the wake of her passing in February 2002, we can all take comfort in the knowledge that not only *Zeely*, but the treasure that is the body of her work, lives on (Bishop, 2002).

ZEELY
Cover illustration by Leo and Diane Dillon. Reproduced with permission.

FAMILY STRENGTHS A discernible shift has taken place in the African American family research that has resulted in a decided emphasis on the strength and resiliency of the African American family. For example, current studies have focused on the function of grandmothers and other extended family members in a child's development, as well as the presence of fathers in the household (Parke & Buriel, 1998). *In My Momma's Kitchen* by Jerdine Nolen, features a young narrator who stresses the happy extended-family events that occur in Momma's kitchen, especially when Daddy cooks corn pudding. He sometimes awakens the whole family in the middle of the night, so they can "sit around the table talking and singing and laughing just like that's what everybody does in the middle of the night." When daughter Nadene learns that she has been accepted to college on a music scholarship, Daddy hugs Momma and sings a made-up song as they all do a dance around Nadene.

Thus, family members strive to provide a set of guidelines for behaving in situations outside the home that reflect the network of connections and kinship functions with which children are most comfortable. When the Diakite family in *I Lost My Tooth in Africa*, by Penda Diakite, visits Mali, the ancestral home of the author, they discover they share common interests with their extended family, even though they live worlds apart. When Amina, for example, loses her tooth, her African relatives tell her that losing a tooth is a special event in their country, too. Her father promises her a chicken from the African tooth fairy if she puts her tooth under a gourd. When she finds a rooster and a hen there, she is excited and becomes concerned that she will have to leave Africa before the eggs hatch.

The more familiar teachers and librarians are with children's backgrounds, the greater success they will have interacting with them. For example, in the first years of schooling, children bring with them a cluster of experiences that affect, for better or worse, the outcomes they'll achieve later in life. The attitudes, interests, and parenting practices mothers and fathers demonstrate, reach into the classroom and affect school attainment, especially in subjects such as mathematics and reading. As McAdoo (2002) stressed, the parents' actions at home far outweigh all other school influences. Consequently, the roles that teachers, librarians, and parents play in the development of critical skills have far-reaching and decisive effects (Tucker & Herman, 2002).

Commenting on the influence that African American kinship systems have on child rearing, Parke & Buriel (1998) note the following:

- A sense of psychological and geographical closeness
- A strong sense of family obligation
- A willingness to absorb relatives within the family boundaries
- Frequent interactions with relatives
- Numerous family get-togethers
- A persistent pattern of mutual aid

Finally, recent research has disclosed that in their family interactions, the parents of the most successful African American children emphasize the ideas of ethnic pride, which children can gain by reading biographies about famous African Americans, such as George Washington Carver in Marilyn Nelson's *Carver: A Life in Poems*. Other examples include Alice McGill's brilliantly illustrated biography of Benjamin Banneker's grandmother, *Molly Bannaky*, or Mahalia Jackson in Roxane Orgill's *Mahalia*. In this appealing book, middle-school children almost hear Mahalia's soulful voice singing gospel hymns that touched everyone who listened to her, or saw her sway and clap her hands to make every word she sang a prayer. Though born poor, she made hit records, appeared in concerts before thousands, and inspired others to join Martin Luther King, Jr. in protest marches across America in the 1960s, while never losing her faith in God.

Asian American Children and Literature

Shaping strategies to the cultural needs of students is nothing new. Good teachers and librarians have been doing it for years, but with a growing and diverse population, the need has become more acute. For example, among our Asian American students we have heard the same story so frequently that it bears retelling. A young Korean girl, let's call her Lee, is adopted by a white, middle-class American couple and raised in a culture reflecting their values: suburban schools, regular church attendance, a busy schedule of after school activities, parties, and the agonies and ecstasies of a typical adolescence. Thinking of herself as an American adolescent, she is jolted when an acquaintance asks her how long she has been in America. On another occasion, a fellow student says. "Ask Lee, she's Japanese." These experiences mirror many of those related by An Na in her first novel *A Step From Heaven* (the Michael Printz Award Winner), about the difficulties she herself experienced living in the United States as a young girl born in Korea.

Lensey Namioka has written a humorous, insightful series about a Chinese American family that lives in Seattle. The fourth in this series, *Yang the Eldest and His Odd Jobs*, is narrated by his younger sibling Third Sister (a clone of Beverly Cleary's Ramona). She relates how Yang, the Eldest Brother, needs money to buy a new violin and wonders if he likes making money more than making music. The Yangs' life in the United States parallels Bette Bao Lord's story *In the Year of the Boar and Jackie Robinson*. When Shirley Temple Wong comes to New York knowing very little English, she is determined to become Americanized through baseball, at the same time Jackie Robinson is playing for the Dodgers. *Dragonwings*, written in 1975 by Laurence Yep, weaves a story of the complex relationship between a boy and his father as they build a flying machine together.

The Japanese American internment during World War II continues to be an engrossing topic of discussion for children as they continue to read, both fiction and nonfiction, about the hardships endured by more than 120,000 Japanese Americans

Spotlight On
Allen Say

Penny Wolin/Getty Images

Allen Say is widely read for the books he has written and illustrated about Japanese culture. His Caldecott Medal book *Grandfather's Journey* is an especially poignant autobiography of a child torn between two cultures: Japan and the United States. Born in Yokohama, Japan, in 1937, Say developed a talent for drawing at an early age. Although the well-known Japanese cartoonist Noro Shinpei took him under his wing and encouraged his talent in sketching with pen and ink, his parents preferred that he be a businessman. When he was sixteen, Say immigrated to the United States, attended several art schools, and eventually chose a career in commercial illustration. In 1989, while working on illustrations for a book about Billy Wong, a Chinese bullfighter, he admits that he "began to think with Billie Wong's mind and feel with his heart." When Billie Wong put on his bullfighting costume, he said that for the first time people were taking notice of him. To Say that was magic. As an immigrant to the United Sates, Say, who felt both visible, because he looked different, and invisible, because he did not belong in this country, understood exactly what Billie Wong meant (Say, 1995, p. 576).

Writing and illustrating children's books—particularly Japanese folktales—continued to capture his imagination. *The Boy of the Three-Year Nap* (1988), written by Dianne Snyder, which Say illustrated, was selected as a Caldecott Honor Book and a *Boston Globe-Horn Book* Award. Say's techniques were now changing. His illustrations, rendered in "brush line and vibrant color, recall the work of traditional Japanese painters while incorporating humor through exaggerated gestures" (Behr, 1995, p. 575). His style of illustration conveys his consummate artistic skill and is uniquely his own.

In *Home of the Brave* (2002), a picture book for older children, Say describes the experience of being in a Japanese American camp during World War II, in dreamlike sequences. He symbolizes hope for the future, while simultaneously grieving that such a tragedy occurred, by drawing the isolation and bewilderment of a man surrounded by children with their name-tags scattered into the wind. Say only wrote about the internment when the statistics took on a human face with personal meaning (*Afterword*, Say, 2002).

in ten camps in six western states. One of the families interned at the Manzanar camp in the California desert was that of Jeanne Wakatsuki Houston. Her classic memoir *Farewell to Manzanar*, written with her husband James D. Houston, has recently been reissued. In it, she details the many difficulties, resourcefulness, and dignity of the Japanese American families during their years of confinement.

As mentioned previously, Yoshiko Uchida also fictionalized her experiences in a Japanese American camp in *Journey to Topaz* for middle school students and *Journey Home*. An unusual book, however, that describes this experience in a surrealistic, haunting manner is Allen Say's *Home of the Brave*, a picture book for older children.

Linda Sue Park, the Korean-born author of *A Single Shard*, is the first Asian American in seventy-five years to receive the Newbery Medal (awarded her in 2002). In her Newbery acceptance speech, she commented how important it is for young people to see themselves reflected in positive images from the culture around them. "And I think," she said, "it is even more important for those in the majority to see images of people of color in a variety of contexts, to move away from seeing them as 'other'" (Park, 2002, p. 383). Throughout her speech she frequently used the word "include," which for her has special meaning. By broadening the experience of children through books they might not have chosen for themselves, she hopes they will find their own connections with the pages. "So Connect! Include!" (Park, 2002, p. 384).

Native American Children and Literature

We, the American Indians and Alaska Natives, are the original inhabitants of America. Our land was once a vast stretch of forest, plains, and mountains extending from the Atlantic to the Pacific Ocean and from the Arctic Circle to the tip of South America. In many American Indian and Alaska Native lands across the country, we still hunt, fish, and gather from the land, rivers, and seas, much as we have for thousands of years

(We, the First Americans, 1993).

Any discussion of Native American children's literature inevitably includes statements deploring the limited number of stories available to children; see, for example, Savage (2000) and Smith (2002). Kirkpatrick Hill, however, who was raised in Alaska and taught many years in multigrade classrooms or one-room school houses in the Alaskan wilderness, knows the Athabascan children well. In *The Year of Miss Agnes* she not only reveals the difficulties of living in the small Athabascan village on the Koyukuk River, but also demonstrates how skillfully the beloved teacher, Miss Agnes, encourages their individual talents and intelligence.

Many reasons may explain this void in children's literature, but one stands in the forefront: the relatively small number of Native Americans (about 2 million, including Eskimos and Aleuts; it is estimated that this number will increase to about 4.6 million by 2050). These relatively small numbers demand that publishers scrutinize Native American stories with a considerable degree of caution to ensure as wide an appeal as possible—a hurdle that may not exist for other cultural settings. This possible explanation for the small number of Native American stories has its positive side, as those stories that are published are of high quality.

Cynthia Leitich Smith, author of *Rain Is Not My Indian Name*, *Jingle Dancer*, and *Indian Shoes*—named 2001 Writer of the year by Wordcraft Circle of Native Writers and Story Tellers—is encouraged by the increasing number of books being published by Native American writers. Musing that when Native American writers follow traditional guidelines, they are more likely to be accepted, she nevertheless worries that what gets lost is the actual voice and heart of the Native American authors

(*Horn Book*, July/August 2002, p. 409). She refers especially to the storytelling rhythms, the music of the language, and the Native American humor that are scarcely recognized. She cautions mainstream "gatekeepers" that to not recognize the difference in the style of native writing is to continue to characterize those differences as weaknesses. Yet she optimistically believes that inclusiveness is slowly winning out.

THE NEED FOR INCLUSIVENESS   Joseph Bruchac, who has enriched and deepened our knowledge of Native American heroes and legends, is concerned that contemporary, as well as traditional, events in Native American life be portrayed in an accurate, informative, and readable manner.

Spotlight On
Joseph Bruchac

Native American history holds a deep fascination for author Joseph Bruchac, who was born in 1942 in Saratoga Springs, New York. He is part-Native American and is a member of the Abenaki tribe of New York State. As a child he hesitated to talk about his Indian ancestry because of feelings of shame. But now he is passionate about being a Native American representa-

Michael Greenlar/The Image Works

tive. Carefully using research, he skillfully interweaves American Indian traditions, while acknowledging the wide diversities between tribes.

Bruchac has contributed to children's knowledge of Indian heroes and legends in books such as *A Boy Called Slow: The True Story of Sitting Bull*. Younger children are also fascinated by *Crazy Horse's Vision*, his story of the leader of the Lakota, as well as *Wabi: A Hero's Tale*, where he relates how a horned owl takes the form of a human and becomes enamored of an Abenaki Indian girl.

In *Skeleton Man*, for middle-school children, Bruchac bases his contemporary story on a Mohawk legend about a man with an appetite so voracious that he eats himself down to his bones. Molly, the main character of the story, which is set in modern New York, courageously saves her parents from an evil stranger who claims to be her uncle.

Among his 100-plus published works, readers will discover fiction and nonfiction, books for adults as well as children, and books on Native American traditions and contemporary native American matters. In *Fox Song*, for example, he includes elements of Native American culture in the story of a contemporary child's grief over her great-grandmother's death. For children in middle school, Bruchac has written *Code Talker: A Novel About the Navajo Marines of World War Two*. The narrator is Ned Begay, a Navajo grandfather, who begins his story when he was a young boy in an Anglo boarding school, Bruchac continues to be a powerful advocate for Native American culture.

WABI: A HERO'S TALE
Reproduced by permission of Penguin Group USA, Inc.

ENDURING WISDOM
Reprinted by permission
of Holiday House, Inc.

Paul Goble, although born in England, was adopted by the Sioux and Yakima tribes and is well-known for his stories and illustrations about Iktomi, the trickster character of the Lakota Indians (*Iktomi and the Berries, Iktomi and the Boulder*, and *Iktomi and the Ducks*)—books that are ideal for reading aloud to young children. He also wrote the Caldecott Medal book *The Girl Who Loved Wild Horses*. A Plains Indian legend, it is a transformational story about a youngster so enamored with horses that she becomes one. Illustrated by the author, it is filled with traditional Indian design motifs, as are his Iktomi stories. Children in the early grades find Paul Goble's story of *Buffalo Woman* an exciting love story of a young hunter's bride who returns to her buffalo nation. She is transformed into a buffalo, as are her husband and son. Again, it is beautifully illustrated with full-color Indian motifs.

Other Native American writers include Louise Erdich, whose *Birchbark House* (for ages 4–8) is narrated by a young Ojibwa Indian child, whose ancestral land on a Lake Superior island is taken by white people in 1847. Beatrice O. Harrell's *Longwalker's Journey: A Novel of the Choctaw Trail of Tears* is avidly read by children in grades three through six. Ten-year-old Minko Ushi, a Choctaw, feels more secure when his faithful pony follows him as he and his people undergo unbelievable hardships when forced to march from their Mississippi home to Oklahoma in 1831.

Virginia Driving Hawk Sneve's *Enduring Wisdom* (2003) is a beautifully illustrated selection of quotations from American Indians, dating from the earliest contact with Europeans, to contemporary tribal persons. Not only do these quotations reflect Indian culture, they also inspire children of all cultures. Jay Harjo, Jan Bourdeau Waboose, and Michael Lacopa are other Native American writers whose works are a part of Native American literature.

Given the large number of independent tribes, we can make several generalizations that are true of most, if not all, tribes. For example:

• Native American children are taught to believe that their behavior should be in harmony with nature.

• Considerable emphasis is placed on teaching children the value of patience and the importance of controlling their emotions.

• Many Native American children live in poverty.

• Although the educational achievement rate of Native Americans improved significantly during the past few decades, it still remains significantly below that of the total population.

• In their child rearing practices, the parents of Native American children stress the importance of group welfare, as opposed to the individualism encouraged by the parents of other children.

These generalizations lead to several important guidelines for those working with Native American children, especially teachers and librarians. For example, forms of nonverbal communication differ sharply between Native American and European American children. Gestures, mannerisms, and bodily movements all reflect a particular culture and convey meanings that increases our understanding of a child. For example: most teachers and librarians expect eye contact with children when working with them, but Native American children are taught that eye contact is a form of disrespect!

Understanding the cultural characteristics of Native American children, and those of the other groups we've discussed, helps improve the reading skills of children, furthers their motivation, and contributes substantially to enhanced achievement. Increasing children's cultural awareness aids them in avoiding stereotypes about other groups by presenting realistic and authentic characters and settings. You can see, then, if the ideas presented in this chapter are followed, brain connections increase, cognitive skills advance, and social relationships flourish—all of which constitutes a welcome addition to the efforts of teachers, parents, and librarians who seek to encourage the development of happy, achieving children.

Chapter Checklist

Read the following items carefully. If you have difficulty responding to any of them, return to the chapter and review the material.

After reading this chapter, you can

1. apply the statement *we are a nation of immigrants* to the themes of children's literature.

2. illustrate through your familiarity with children's literature how children who seem different are not deficient.

3. explain the significance of Graham Salisbury's *Island Boyz* in light of the ideas discussed in this chapter.

4. demonstrate how the history of multiculturalism in children's literature testifies to the changes occurring in society.

5. discuss the meaning of the statement that as multiculturalism becomes more widespread in children's literature, the nature of the stories changes.

6. identify those stories you think best demonstrate an author's understanding of culture at a significant level.

7. explain how the attitudes of teachers and librarians help to shape children's reactions to other cultures.

8. specify those features of a particular culture that help others to understand a child's behavior.

9. using specific stories, illustrate how Vygotsky's zone of proximal development helps teachers and librarians to advance a child's level of learning and understanding.

10. analyze how a child's learning style reflects a specific culture and the implications for children's literature.

Children's Bibliography

Ada, Alma Flor. (1993). *My Name is Maria Isabel*. New York: Atheneum.

Ada, Alma Flor, & Campoy, F. Isabel. (2003). *Pio Pee! Traditional Spanish Nursery Rhymes*. New York: HarperCollins.

Alarcon, Francisco X. (1997). *Laughing Tomatoes and Other Spring Poems/Jitomates risuenos y otros poemas de primavera*. San Francisco, Children's Book Press.

Alarcon, Francisco X. (1998). *From the Bellybutton of the Moon and Other Summer Poems/Del ombligo de la luna y otros poemas de verano*. San Francisco: Children's Book Press.

Allington, R., & Cowles, Kathleen. (1980). *Feelings*. Milwaukee: Raintree Children's Books.

Alvarez, Julia. (2001). *How Tia Lola Came to (Visit) Stay*. New York: Alfred Knopf.

Armstrong, William H. (1969). *Sounder*. New York: HarperCollins.

Blatchford, Claire. (1998). *Going with the Flow*. Minneapolis: Carolrhoda Books.

Brownridge, William Roy. (1997). *The Final Game*. New York: Orca.

Bruchac, Joseph. (1995). *A Boy Called Slow: The True Story of Sitting Bull*. New York: Putnam.

Bruchac, Joseph. (2000). *Crazy Horse's Vision*. New York: Lee & Low.

Bruchac, Joseph. (2001). *Skeleton Man*. New York: HarperCollins.

Bruchac, Joseph. (2005). *Code Talker: A Novel about the Navajo Marines of World War Two*. New York: Dial.

Bruchac, Joseph. (2005). *Wabi: A Hero's Tale*. New York: Dial.

Bryan, Ashley. (1980). *Beat the Story Drum, Pum-Pum*, New York: Atheneum.

Byars, Betsy. (1970). *The Summer of the Swans*. New York: Viking.

Choldenko, Gennifer. (2004). *Al Capone Does My Shirts*. New York: Scholastic.

Curtis, Christoper Paul. (1999). *Bud, Not Buddy*. New York: Delacorte.

Danticat, Edwidge. (2002). *Behind the Mountains*. New York: Orchard.

Diakite, Penda. (2006). *I Lost My Tooth in Africa*. New York: Scholastic.

Erdrich, Louise. (1999). *The Birchbark House*. New York: Hyperion.

Feelings, Tom. (1978). *Something On My Mind*. New York: Dial Press.

Flourney, Valerie, illus. Jerry Pinkney (1985). *The Patchwork Quilt*. illus. New York: Dial.

Friedman, Ina. (1984). *How My Parents Learned to Eat*. Boston: Houghton Mifflin.

Fritz, Jean. (1983). *The Double Life of Pocahontas*. New York: Putnam.

Goble, Paul. (1978). *The Girl Who Loved Wild Horses*. New York: Bradbury Press.

Goble, Paul. (1988). *Iktomi and the Boulder*. New York: Orchard Books.

Goble, Paul. (1989). *Iktomi and the Borries*. New York: Orchard Books.

Goble, Paul. (1990). *Iktomi and the Ducks*. New York: Orchard Books.

Greenfield, Eloise. (1972). *Good News*. New York: Coward, McCann & Geoghegan.

Greenfield, Eloise. (1974). *She Come Bringing Me That Little Baby Girl*. New York: Lippincott.

Greenfield, Eloise. (1988). *Nathaniel Talking*. San Francisco: Children's Books.

Greenfield, Eloise. Amos Ferguson, illus. (1988). *Under the Sunday Tree*. New York: HarperCollins.

Greenfield, Eloise. (2003). *Honey, I Love*. New York: HarperCollins.

Hamilton, Virginia. (1967/1978). *Zeely*. New York: Dell.

Hamilton, Virginia. (1968). *House of Dies Drear*. New York: Macmillan.

Hamilton, Virginia. (1971). *Planet of Junior Brown*. New York: Simon & Schuster.

Hamilton, Virginia. (1974). *M. C. Higgins, The Great*. New York: Simon & Schuster.

Hamilton, Virginia. (1985). *The People Could Fly: American Black Folktales*. New York: Knopf.

Harrell, Beatrice O. (1999). *Longwalker's Journey: A Novel of the Choctraw Trail of Tears*. New York: Dial.

Hill, Kirkpatrick. (2002). *The Year of Miss Agnes*. New York: Aladdin.

Holling, Clancy. (1970). *Tree in the Trail*. Boston: Houghton Mifflin.

Houston, Jeanne Wakatsuki, & Houston, James. (1973). *Farewell to Manzanar*. Boston: Houghton Mifflin.

Jordan, June. (1981). *Civil Wars*. Boston: Beacon Press.

Keats, Ezra Jack. (1962). *Snowy Day*. New York: Scholastic.

Keats, Ezra Jack. (1964). *Whistle for Willie*. New York: Viking.

Keats, Ezra Jack. (1969). *Goggles*. New York: Macmillan.

Konigsburg, E. L. (1996). *The View from Saturday*. New York: Atheneum.

Lester, Julius. (1968). *To Be a Slave*. New York: Scholastic.

Lester, Julius. (1970). *Black Folktales*. New York: Grove Press.

Lester, Julius. (1994). *The Last Tales of Uncle Remus*. illus. by Jerry Pinkney. New York: Dial.

Lofting, Hugh. (1920c., 1967). *The Story of Dr. Dolittle*. Philadelphia: Lippincott.

Lord, Bette Bao. (1984). *In the Year of the Boar and Jackie Robinson*. New York: Harper & Row.

Lynch, Chris. (2000). *Gold Dust*. New York: HarperCollins.

Madrigal, Antonio Hernandez. (1999). *Erandi's Braids*. New York: Putnam.

Mathis, Sharon Bell. (1971). *Sidewalk Story*. New York: Viking.

Mathis, Sharon Bell. (1972). *Teacup Full of Roses*. New York: Viking.

Mathis, Sharon Bell. (1975). *The Hundred Penny Box*. New York: Viking.

McGill, Alice. (1999). *Molly Bannaky*. Boston: Houghton Mifflin.

McKissack, Patricia. (1988). Jerry Pinkney, illus. *Mirandy and Brother Wind*. New York: Knopf.

McKissack, Patricia. (2000). *The Honest-To-Goodness Truth*. New York: Atheneum.

McKissack, Patricia C. (2001). *Goin Someplace Special*. New York: Atheneum.

Mochizuki, Ken. (1993). *Baseball Saved Us*. New York: Lee & Low.

Mochizuki, Ken. (1995). *Heroes*. New York: Lee & Low.

Morrison, Toni. (2004). *Remember: The Journey to School Integration*. Boston: Houghton Mifflin.

Myers, Walter Dean. (1979). *The Young Landlords*. New York: Viking.

Myers, Walter Dean. (1981). *Hoops*. New York: Dell.

Myers, Walter Dean. (1988). *Fallen Angels*. New York: Scholastic.

Myers, Walter Dean. (1994). *The Glory Field*. New York: Scholastic.

Myers, Walter Dean. (1999). *Monster*. New York: HarperCollins.

Namioka, Lensey. (2001). *Yang the Eldest and His Odd Jobs*. New York: Little, Brown.

Na, An. (2001). *A Step From Heaven*. New York: Front Street.

Nelson, Marilyn. (2001). *Carver: A Life in Poems*. Asheville, NC: Front Street Books.

Nolen, Jerdine. (1999). *In My Momma's Kitchen*. New York: HarperCollins.

Orgill, Roxane. (2002). *Mahalia*. Cambridge, MA: Candlewick.

Ortiz, S. (1988). *The People Shall Continue*. San Francisco: Children's Book Press.

Park, Linda Sue. (2001). *A Single Shard*. New York: Clarion.

Park, F., & Park, G. (2002). *Good-bye 382 Shin Dang Dong*. New York: National Geographic.

Patterson, Lillie. (1969). *Martin Luther King, Jr.: Man of Peace*. New York: Dell.

Perez, Amada Irma. (2002). *My Diary from Here to There/Mi diario de aqui hasta alla*. San Francisco: Children's Book Press.

Ringgold, Faith. (1991). *Tar Beach*. New York: Crown.

Ringgold, Faith. (1993). *Aunt Harriet's Underground Railroad in the Sky*. New York: Crown.

Rohmer, H. (1988). *How We Came to the Fifth World*. San Francisco: Children's Book Press.

Salisbury, Graham. (2002). *Island Boyz*. New York: Wendy Lamb Books.

Say, Allen. (1993). *Grandfather's Journey*. Boston: Houghton Mifflin.

Say, Allen. (2002). *Home of the Brave*. Boston: Houghton Mifflin.

Senisi, Ellen. (1998). *Just Kids: Visiting a Class for Children with Special Needs*. New York: Dutton.

Smith, Cynthia Leitich. (2000). *Jingle Dancer*. New York: HarperCollins.

Smith, Cynthia Leitich. (2001). *Rain Is Not My Indian Name*. New York: HarperCollins.

Smith, Cynthia Leitich. (2002). *Indian Shoes*. New York: HarperCollins.

Sneve, Virginia Driving Hawk. (2003). *Enduring Wisdom*. New York: Holiday House.

Snyder, Diane. (1988) illus. by Allen Say. *The Boy of the Three-Year Nap*. Boston: Houghton Mifflin.

Soto, Gary. (1991). *Taking Sides*. New York: Harcourt

Soto, Gary. (1992). *Pacific Crossing*. New York: Harcourt.

Soto, Gary. (1992). *Neighborhood Odes: Poems by Gary Soto*. San Diego: Harcourt Brace Jovanovich.

Soto, Gary. (1994). *Jesse*. New York: Harcourt.

Soto, Gary. (2002). *If the Shoe Fits*. New York: Putnam.

Speare, Elizabeth George. (1983). *The Sign of the Beaver*. New York: Dell.

Steptoe, John. (1969). *Stevie*. New York: Harper & Row.

Steptoe, John. (1987). *Mufaro's Beautiful Daughters*. New York: Lothrop & Shepard.

Suarez, Ana Veciana. (2002). *Flight to Freedom*. New York: Orchard.

Taylor, Mildred. (1976). *Roll of Thunder, Hear My Cry*. New York: Dial Books.

Taylor, Mildred. (2001). *The Land*. New York: Fogelman.

Taylor, Theodore. (1990). *The Cay*. Santa Barbara, CA: Cornerstone Books.

Tuyet, T. (1987). *The Little Weaver of Thai-Yen Village*. San Francisco: Children's Book Press.

Wilder, Laura Ingalls. (1932). *Little House in the Big Woods*. New York: HarperCollins.

Wisniewski, David. (1994) *The Wave of the Sea-Wolf*. New York: Clarion.

Woodson, Jacqueline. (2001). *Miracle's Boys*. New York: Scholastic.

Woodson, Jacqueline. (2002). *Hush*. New York: Putnam.

Woodson, Jacqueline. (1990). *Last Summer with Maizon*. New York: Putnam.

Yang, Gene. (2006). *American Born Chinese*. New York: Roaring Brook.

Yoshiko, Uchida. (1949). *Dancing Kettle*. New York: Harcourt Brace.

Yoshiko, Uchida. (1971). *Journey to Topaz*. Berkeley, CA: Creative Arts.

Yoshiko, Uchida. (1978). *Journey Home*. New York: Atheneum.

Yep, Laurence. (1975). *Dragonwings*. New York: Harper & Row.

Professional References

Apseloff, Marilyn. (1983). "A Conversation with Virginia Hamilton." *Children's Literature in Education*, Winter.

Bader, B. (2002). "How the Little House Gave Ground: The Beginnings of Multiculturalism in a New, Black Children's Literature." *The Horn Book*. November/December, 657–673.

Bader, B. (2003a). "Multiculturalism Takes Root." *The Horn Book*. March/April, 143–162.

Bader, B. (2003b). "Multiculturalism in the Mainstream." *The Horn Book*. May/June, 265–291.

Bader, B. (2005). "Echoes of the Old Plantation." *The Horn Book*. March/April, 147–152.

Banks, J. & Banks C. , eds. (1993). *Multicultural Education: Issues and Perspective*. Boston: Allyn & Bacon.

Banks, J. (1995). "Introduction." In J. Banks & C. Banks, eds. *Handbook of Research on Multicultural Education*. New York: Macmillan.

Behr, C. (1995). "Allen Say." In Anita Silvey, ed. *Children's Books and Their Creators*. Boston: Houghton Mifflin.

Berk, L., & Winsler, A. (1995). *Scaffolding Children's Learning*. Washington, DC: National Association for the Education of Young Children.

Bishop, Rudine Sims. (1997). "Selecting literature for a multicultural curriculum." In V. Harris, ed. (1997). *Using Multiethnic Literature in the K-8 Classroom*. Norwood, MA: Christopher-Gordon Publishers.

Bishop, Rudine Sims. (2002). "Remembering Virginia." *The Horn Book*. University Press.

Cai, M. (2002). *Multicultural Literature for Children and Young Adults*. Westport, CT: Greenwood Press.

Cai, M., & Bishop, R.S. (1994). "Multicultural Literature for Children: Towards a Clarification of the Concept." In A. Dyson & C. Genishi, eds. *The Need For Story: Cultural Diversity in Classroom and Community*. Urbana, IL: National Council of Teachers of English.

Casas, J., & Pytluk, S. (1995). "Hispanic Identity Development: Implications for Research and Practice." In J. Ponterotto, J. Casas, L. Suzuki, & C. Alexander, eds. *Handbook of Multicultural Counseling*. Thousand Oaks, CA: Sage.

Chou, N. Y. (2002). Unpublished manuscript.

Cole, M. (1996). *Cultural Psychology*. Cambridge, MA: Harvard University Press.

Cole, M., & Cole, S. (1996). *The Development of Children*. New York: Freeman.

Criticas: An English speaker's guide to the latest Spanish language titles. (2001). New York: Criticas Publishing.

Elliott, S., Kratochwilol, T., Littlefield Cook, J., & Travers, J. (2000). *Educational Psychology: Effective Teaching, Effective Learning*. New York: McGraw-Hill.

Greenfield, P., & Suzuki, L. (1998). "Culture and Human Development: Implications for Parenting, Education, Pediatrics, and Mental Health." In W. Damon (series ed.) & I. Sigel & K. Renninger (vol. eds.), *Handbook of Child Psychology: Volume 4. Child Psychology in Practice*. New York: John Wiley.

Hamilton, Virginia. (1981). *Something About the Author*. Detroit: Gale Research.

Harris, V. ed. (1997). *Using Multiethnic Literature in the K-8 Classroom*. Norwood, MA: Christopher-Gordon Publishers.

Harris, V. (1997). "Children's Literature Depicting Blacks." In V. Harris, ed. (1997). *Using Multiethnic Literature in the K-8 Classroom*. Norwood, MA: Christopher-Gordon Publishers.

Kim, U. (1990). "Indigenous Psychology: Science and Applications." In R. Brislin, ed. *Applied Cross-Cultural Psychology*. Newbury Park, CA: Sage.

Larrick, N. (1965). "The All-White World of Children's Books." *Saturday Review*. 44, 63–65, 84–85.

Manning, M., & Baruth, L. (2004). *Multicultural Education of Children and Adolescents*. Needham Heights, MA: Allyn & Bacon.

Marin, G. (1994). "The Experience of Being a Hispanic in the United States." In W., Lonner, & R., Malpass, eds. *Psychology and Culture*. Boston: Allyn & Bacon.

McAdoo, H. (2002). "African American Parenting." In Marc Bornstein, ed. *Handbook of Parenting. Volume 4: Social Conditions and Applied Parenting*. Mahwah, NJ: Lawrence Erlbaum.

Muse, D., ed. (1997). *Multicultural Resources for Young Readers*. New York: The New Press.

Norton, D. (2001). *Multicultural Children's Literature: Through the Eyes of Many Children*. Upper Saddle River, NJ: Merrill/Prentice Hall.

Odean, Kathleen. (2001). *Book*. September/October.

Park, Linda Sue. (2002). "Newbery Medal Acceptance." *The Horn Book*. July/August, 377–384.

Parke, R., & Buriel, R. (1998). "Socialization in the Family: Ethnic and Ecological Perspectives." In W. Damon (series ed.) & N. Eisenberg (ed.), *Handbook of Child Psychology: Volume 3. Child Psychology in Practice*. New York: John Wiley.

Payne, C. R., & Welsh, B. H. (2000). "The Progressive Development of Multicultural Education Before and After the 1960s: A theoretical Framework." *Teacher Educator*. 36(1), 29–48.

Rogoff, B. (2003). *Cultural Nature of Human Development*. New York: Oxford University Press.

Rogoff, B. (1990). *Apprenticeship in Thinking*. New York: Oxford University Press.

Rosenberg, L. (2003). "The Magic of the Elemental." *Boston Globe*, April 13, E10.

Rudman, M., & Muse, D. (1997). "Cultural Traditions." In D. Muse, ed. *Multicultural Resources for Young Readers*. New York: The New Press.

Savage, J. (2000). *For the Love of Literature*. New York: McGraw-Hill.

Say, Allen. (1995). "Voices of the Creators." In Anita Silvey, ed. *Children's Books and Their Creators*. Boston: Houghton Mifflin.

Seppa, N. (1996). "Rwanda Starts Its Long Healing Process." *The APA Monitor*. August, 1996, 14.

Shweder, R. (1991). *Thinking Through Cultures*. Cambridge, MA: Harvard University Press.

Smith, Cynthia Leitich. (2002). "A Different Drum: Native American Writing." *The Horn Book*. July/August, 409.

Soto, Gary. (1995). *Something About the Author*. Detroit: Gale Research.

Steward, E. (1995). *Beginning Writers in the Zone of Proximal Development*. Hillsdale, N J: Lawrence Erlbaum.

Sue, D., & Sue, D. (1991). *Counseling the Culturally Different*. New York: John Wiley.

Tucker, C., & Herman, K. (2002). "Using Culturally Sensitive Theories and Research to Meet the Academic Needs of Low Income African American Children." *American Psychologist*. 57(10), 762–773.

Valsiner, J. (1998). "The Development of the Concept of Development: Historical and Epistemological Perspectives." In R. M. Lerner, ed. *Handbook of Child Psychology: Volume 1. Theoretical Models of Human Development*. New York: John Wiley.

Vygotsky, L. S. (1962). *Thought and Language*. Cambridge, MA: MIT Press.

Vygotsky, L. S. (1978). *Mind in Society*. Cambridge, MA: Harvard University Press.

Warder, R. (1997). "Milestones in Children's Literature." In D. Muse, ed. *Multicultural Resources for Young Readers*. New York: The New Press.

Wertsch, J., & Tulviste, P. (1992). "L. S. Vygotsky and Contemporary Developmental Psychology." *Developmental Psychology*. 28(4), 548–557.

Yamate, S. (1997). "Asian Pacific American Children's Literature: Expanding Perceptions About Who Americans Are." In V., Harris, ed. (1997). *Using Multiethnic Literature in the K-8 Classroom*. Norwood, MA: Christopher-Gordon Publishers.

Yokota, Junko, Ed. (2001). *Kaleidoscope*. Urbana, IL: National Council of Teachers of English.

Literature for the Early Years (Ages Birth–2)

Recently, when we were examining the infants' books at our local bookstore, we almost tripped over a toddler sitting on the floor with a board book on his lap. When his mother called him, we saw him put the book down and head back to his mother. Halfway down the aisle, he turned around and ran back to the book, picked it up, and whispered "Goodnight, Book," before he put it down again. Perhaps his parents had shown him how the light in the room darkens on each page or he himself had discovered how the mouse appeared in each illustration. Whatever made him return to the green room, he knew he loved it. Everyone does. The book was Margaret Wise Brown's Goodnight, Moon.

In this chapter we explore the literary world of infants and trace their abilities, inclinations, and preferences from birth to 2 years of age. It's an exciting period, much more so than originally thought because of what research is telling us. Physical growth is amazingly rapid, the most accelerated of any period in the human lifespan. The brain research of the past few years suggests techniques for improving cognitive development, which inevitably affects the structure of children's literature.

We have learned a great deal about environmental elements that attract infants' attention and have unmistakable implications for presenting children's stories. Studies have also opened new vistas into the growth and development of infants' temperament and the appearance of attachment behavior. So our task is clearly drawn in this chapter: how can we appeal to children of these years and set them on the road to a lifetime of satisfaction and contentment in the world of books?

GOODNIGHT MOON
*Used with permission
of HarperCollins*

Guidelines for Reading Chapter 7

After you read Chapter Seven, you should be able to answer the following questions.

• What developmental features offer clues to the selection of appropriate books for children of these years?

• What is the appeal of peek-a-boo books for children of this age?

• How should the place of snack brand books in children's literature, given the developmental features of this age group, be evaluated?

• In analyzing books for children of these years, what does it mean that the stories should match the developing cognitive maturity of the children?

• A well-known commentator on children's literature, Joanne Lynn, has noted that nursery rhymes retain a power that is both "emotional and aesthetic." What developmental features of these years explain this statement?

• What is there about fantasy that attracts children? How do the basic elements of fantasy stories for these children match the developmental characteristics that explain their behavior?

• What literary elements are needed in informational books to attract and hold the attention of children of these years?

Characteristics of Children of These Years

Before we begin our analysis of the literature of this period, we should address an intriguing question: do children respond to certain books even *before* they are born? Although our concern in this chapter is with children from birth to 2 years of age, recent developmental research includes the child in the womb in the world of children's literature. Beginning in the 1980s Anthony DeCasper, at the University of North Carolina, began experiments by having mothers read to fetuses in utero. Realizing that fetuses can hear sounds in the last months of pregnancy, DeCasper and Spence (1986) wanted to discover if hearing *The Cat in the Hat* (Dr. Seuss) while in the womb would cause children to prefer this story *after* birth. DeCasper had sixteen pregnant women read selections from *The Cat in the Hat* twice a day for the last six weeks of their pregnancies.

Approximately fifty-two hours after birth, the mothers read their babies the selections from *The Cat in the Hat*, or selections from *The King, the Mice, and the Cheese*, which has a different rhythm and pace. The infants reacted quite differently to the readings from *The Cat in the Hat*. (They sucked on a nipple at a significantly slower rate to produce their mothers' voices reading *The Cat in the Hat*.) What does this tell us about child development? Two clues emerge from this study:

1. THE HUMAN BRAIN IS PROGRAMMED TO LEARN BEFORE BIRTH. If this is true, and research continually supports the finding, then the implications for those of us concerned with children's literature seem obvious. Far from being an exercise in futility, reading to the fetus during the last weeks of pregnancy becomes an exercise in learning. (For an excellent discussion of the consequences of prenatal taste, smell, and hearing see Eliot, 2000.)

2. The second conclusion we can reach concerns *the impact that this early exposure to literature has on memory*. Obviously, the infant remembered the cadence of *The Cat in the Hat* it heard as a fetus, as indicated by how the reading affected its behavior. As incredible as it may seem, at birth the fetus has 100 billion neurons in its brain. Does this imply that we should bathe the fetus in a sea of literature? Of course not, but it does imply a recognition of how connections between and among neurons can be furthered by reading to the fetus during the final weeks of pregnancy.

The Perceptual Development of Infants

Why do infants respond to some things more attentively than others? The answer lies in the manner in which developmental psychologists have tracked infant behavior using *habituation* studies. If infants are interested in something or somebody, they'll continue to attend to it until they become bored, when they *habituate* and turn their attention elsewhere. When their attention is rekindled, they *dishabituate*. In other words, babies are attracted by novelty. Holding a book in front of infants while you read it aloud fascinates them for awhile. Lullabies, like those in Jane Yolen's *The Lullaby Songbook*, are especially appealing to infants who are not going to judge your singing voice, but will absorb the lilting rhymes and rhythm of words when you softly read (or sing) words such as

Bye baby bunting, / Your daddy's gone a hunting

or the Gaelic lullaby that celebrates the small inner room, the "ben," or nursery, where the baby sleeps:

Baloo, baleerie, baloo balee. / Go away, little fairies, go away little fairies, from our small room.

For those small children who are listening to their native language for the first time, *The Baby Chicks Sing* or *Los Pollitos Dicen*, written by Nancy Hall and Jill Syverson-Stork and illustrated by Kay Chorao, is a bilingual collection of short songs and selections that are playful, joyful, and thoughtful. The book ends with the popular *De Colores / Oh, the Colors*, which includes the sounds of the rooster, the hen, the chicks, and the birds—all noises that infants react to instantly.

Why Some Books Remain Popular

Using these tools of the developmental psychologist, we can begin to trace the reasons why some books, such as Margaret Wise Brown's *Goodnight Moon*, remain so popular for children 0–2 years of age.

- **CHILDREN OF THESE YEARS PREFER CERTAIN KINDS OF OBJECTS, COLORS, FORMS, AND SO ON.** It's important to remember that children are born with certain sensory capacities: touch, taste, smell, hearing, and vision. To accommodate these senses, books for infants should appeal not only to their sight, but also to their touch, taste, smell, and hearing. They should be durably made as *board books*, to withstand wear and tear. Helen Oxenbury's *Big Baby Book*, for instance, is a big board book, written and illustrated by the well-known and much loved author that offers a simple sampling of what babies can see, hear, touch, and do.

  The classic *Pat the Bunny* (Kunhardt, 1970), although a novelty when it was first published, now has many imitators. One of these is the totally interactive *Peek-aboo Kisses* by Barney Saltzberg, a soft pastel-colored flap-book in which the child opens each flap to touch (and perhaps kiss) a kitten, a puppy, a sheep, or a duckling. On the final page, the flap opens to reveal an unbreakable mirror so children can play peek-a-boo with themselves.

- **OBJECT PERMANENCE DEVELOPS.** Other peek-a-boo books encourage a child to play, which is a main precursor to reading. For example, a baby who is developing Piaget's *object permanence* thinks an object is gone for good when it disappears and is surprised when it reappears. Janet and Allan Ahlberg's *Peek a boo! book*, the board book edition, is fascinating for children at this developmental stage. The baby peeks through diecut holes to see members of the family (grandmother, daddy, mommy, and sister) performing familiar chores. Jan Ormerod's *Peek-A-Boo!* also plays this game by picturing on each page a baby holding objects (such as mittens) up to its face. When the small child pulls open the flap, the baby appears in full.

- **TOUCH AND FEEL THROUGH STORIES.** *The Touch and Feel Dinosaur* (DK), with its large, colored photographs of dinosaurs, encourages the small child to feel the *bumpy* skin of the giganotosaurus, the *smooth* horns of the triceratops, the *rough* plates on the stegosaurus's back, before asking the question, "Are you brave enough to feel T. Rex's soft sticky tongue?" That's a big decision for a small child to make. Not only may the concepts (bumpy, smooth, etc.) be outside the realm of the child's experience, but the child may also be timid about touching strange animals. If this is so, then we should learn from the child and put this book away for a future time.

Potentially fearful books have their place only when small children are ready to take on their fears and, by so doing, defeat them at the same time

(Tucker, 2002, p. 84)

For example, Sandra Boynton's book *Oh My Oh My Oh Dinosaurs!* is a lighthearted look at these prehistoric animals. Her drawings, cartoon-like and humorous, are more attractive to a child who is fearful of what is large and unknown.

DISTINCTIVE FEATURES OF BOOKS FOR INFANTS   Environmental features such as contrast, movement, and changes in sound and light intensity also attract infants' attention. For example, they are fascinated by the changing landscape of faces because each face is different and changes from moment to moment. Each page of the board book *Baby's Good Night Book* (Chorao, 2002) highlights the smiling face of a young child and introduces the infant to a simple but familiar word, associated with preparing for bed: *towel, shampoo, pajamas, pillow, teddybear,* and especially *goodnight kiss.* By repeating the words on each page and connecting them to objects surrounding the child, the adult not only shares the joy of reading with the child, but facilitates the child's language development. One day, if she continues to be attentive, she will connect objects around her to the illustrations.

The child's sensory capacities, such as hearing and vision, are particularly significant in development. Newborns are sensitive to various sound patterns, especially the sounds of human speech. For example, they'll turn their heads in the direction of a sound and they seem genetically programmed to respond to human language. Eyesight is the least developed sense in newborns; they cannot focus their eyes well. Estimates are that newborns see objects at 20 feet about as well as adults do at 600 (a newborn's vision quickly improves to about 300 feet). Nevertheless, infants constantly scan their surroundings and attempt to track moving objects. Other babies often attract them. In Susan Meyers' *Everywhere Babies*, with its rhyming text and cozy watercolor illustrations, infants see all kinds of babies and, as their perception develops, are able to detect differences among them.

READING COMPLEXITY AND DEVELOPMENT   Let's now put these ideas together and demonstrate how literature and development blend together during these years.

• **HEARING.** Infants, even in their first hours after birth, are particularly sensitive to the sounds of human speech, which they can distinguish from other sounds. During these first days, "baby talk" (high pitch, slow pronunciation) is preferred. The accomplishments of these first days are used as a base for the acquisition and mastery of the child's native language. You can see, then, how the word content of stories for children at this age needs to be carefully controlled for amount, sound patterns, and rhythmic sensitivity (Berk, 2005).

When infants first hear Maurie J. Manning's *The Aunts Go Marching*, they will be immediately mesmerized by the rhythmic sound of the aunts "marching one by one, hurrah! hurrah!" As their senses continue to develop, they react more emphatically, especially when the little girl in the yellow raincoat beats her drum

"Rat-a-tat! Rat a tat-tat! Ba-rump, ba-rump, barump!" Later, as children approach the end of the infancy period, they notice the little dog that follows the parade. As they grow older, they discover how much fun it is to join in the repetitive text in this gem of a book.

- **VISION.** Much of our knowledge of just how well children see can be traced back to the pioneering work of Robert Fantz (1961, 1963), who demonstrated that infants are extremely near-sighted until they're about 7 or 8 months of age. When they begin to crawl, however, their visual acuity is about that of an

Spotlight On
Eric Carle

©AP/Wide World Photos

It's not often that a famous author and illustrator establishes his own museum. In 2002, however, Eric Carle did just that. In Amherst, Massachusetts, the *Eric Carle Museum of Picture Book Art*, the first museum of its kind in the United States, was built in an apple orchard on seventy-five acres—originally part of the campus of Hampshire College. The museum includes three galleries devoted to regular presentations of Carle's works, along with rotating exhibitions of international artists like Maurice Sendak, Nancy Ekholm Burkert, and Mitsumasa Anno. The Museum contains an art studio, a 130-seat auditorium, a library for 3000 books, a café, and a shop that sells books, art supplies, and toys. The museum does not contain interactive, technological displays.

Instead, children and their caregivers are encouraged to share the special experience of reading together in the large picture book section, which is arranged to look like a comfortable living room. Lolly Robinson (2003) noted that Carle and his colleagues expect the museum to do what picture books have always done: create intimate moments between adults and children as they talk with each other about what they see and feel. Carle himself believes that a picture book is interactive. As the museum's curator, H. Nicholas B. Clark, explained (2004), once people are removed from electronic interaction and return to the basics, they come to realize how meaningful the eyes and hands are.

Bright color is a trademark of Carle's tissue paper collages. In an interview with Leonard Marcus, he related that in his studio he has files full of his papers, "hundreds and hundreds of tissue papers, all filed by color" (Marcus, 2002). Children are inspired by his drawings and paintings, which are hung low at their eye level. There is also a large studio where children may practice being artists. In fact, as children (and adults) walk into the grand lobby surrounded by four paintings—each eight feet by six feet, in bright red, green, blue, and yellow, hung against white walls—they can easily imagine themselves walking into one of Carle's seventy books. *The Very Hungry Caterpillar* alone has been translated into twenty-five languages and has sold more than twelve million copies since its publication in 1969.

Carle grew up in a very dark period in history. Although he happily started school in the United States as a German immigrant—an experience in his life that he describes as "a large piece of paper, beautiful"—his family returned to Germany in 1935 and, when he was six years old, his life became bleak. "I had to start school all over again with a teacher who was a disciplinarian. It was small sheets of paper, hard pens, and I think I'm still trying to resolve that period through my books. I asked my mother to write my teacher and explain I was not suited for education" (Thomas, 2002, p. C5). The teacher responded by screaming at Eric, which left him devastated.

Carle was only ten years old when war broke out and his father was drafted into the army and was ultimately imprisoned in Russia. Eric was 15 when the SS came to his home to sign him up for the army, but his mother refused to let him go. Carle and his wife now live in Northampton, Massachusetts, where he remembers his father, who taught him to observe the natural world. His observations of the world's smallest creatures now populate his books. An adult sharing a picture book with a child gives to that child the same kind of attention that Eric Carle shared with his father. Together, they share time with each other: looking, listening, loving, and learning. Website: www. picturebookart.org.

adult. As we have indicated, in spite of their poor vision, infants from birth constantly scan their environments and are attracted to bright colors. Children of these years are also drawn to the "irresistible allure of stripes" (Gopnik, Meltzoff, & Kuhl, 1999), such as those pictured in Eric Carle's *The Very Hungry Caterpillar*. They then use these to structure their environments. As these researchers indicate, a sharp contrast between the brightness and texture of two surfaces usually indicates where objects begin and end.

The Very Hungry Caterpillar is an example of how developmental features come together in an enduring story, which was originally published in 1969. When you examine it, notice how Carle uses the perceptual characteristics we've discussed, such as the use of vividly colored stripes, to make his caterpillar collage and the striped rays of the brightly colored sun. Even adults are intrigued by the glorious colors throughout the book, which culminate with the presentation of the butterfly at the book's end. Carle, however, went beyond appealing to infants' visual abilities, he capitalized on their sense of touch by encouraging them to *feel* the holes the caterpillar makes as he chews his way into various foods. It's no surprise to the child when the caterpillar has a stomach ache before he crawls into his cocoon.

• **PATTERN VISION.** Once again, thanks to Robert Fantz and his "looking chamber," we know that infants are drawn to the most complex patterns they're capable of responding to. Babies placed on their backs in the looking chamber were shown many different forms, and a record was kept of how long they looked at each form. It was discovered that they looked longest at patterned figures such as faces, especially long at faces that moved in front of them. For one or two months after birth, infants scan the border of a face before slowly beginning to explore internal features.

Think about these facts: as children age, their perceptual abilities change rapidly. By 12 months of age infants are sensitive to pictorial cues and have become increasingly wary of heights. They are now able to detect more complex patterns and show an ability to perceive and react to emotional expressions. These are all features recognized and utilized in the pleasing—and lasting—books for infants to age 2. *The Very Hungry Caterpillar* is only one of many examples of how authors recognize and use developmental data to enhance their stories. As you examine and discuss the books arranged by the genres we discussed in Chapter Three, try to discover the growth characteristics of children from birth to 2 years of age that make these books so captivating to them. Among the most important developmental features are those seen in Figure 7.1

BIOPSYCHOSOCIAL CHARACTERISTICS

BIO	PSYCHO	SOCIAL
Rapid physical growth	Object permanence	Social smile
Control of bodily movements	Attention improves	Self-concept appears
Habituation	Memory improves	Struggle for self-control
Organizes world into meaningful patterns	Goal-directed behavior	Emotional expression
	Deferred attention	Stranger anxiety
Sensitive to speech sounds	Vocabulary grows	Separation anxiety
Stands, walks	Acquires grammar	Attachment behavior
Bodily coordination improves	Symbolic activity	Relationships emerge

Figure 7.1

Types of Books for Infants

Although picture storybooks such as *Goodnight, Moon* come immediately to mind as the genre of choice for parents, librarians, and teachers to read to infants, a baby's first book often comes from a subgenre of picture books. *Play (toy) books*, or book toys, come in a bewildering array of shapes and sizes. For new librarians, new teachers, and especially new parents, the choice of books for the newborn can be overwhelming. For example, consider the following:

• There are the soft shaped, floatable books that can be used in the tub during baby's bath time, and the tube-shaped books with a small (sometimes dangerously small) toy hidden in their hollows.

• There are books for babies to cut their teeth on such as Melanie Walsh's *Tiny Teethers*, which have colorful, water-filled acrylic teething rings attached to them.

• There are the snack-brand books such as *Kellogg's Froot Loops! Counting Fun*, which invite toddlers to insert the sugary cereal into cut-out holes in its cardboard pages.

• There is even a book toy, *The Secret of the Three Butterpillars* (designed by Charlotta Janssen, an industrial engineer), that is totally different from anything ever seen. It is called a tumbling book because it tumbles, flips, twists, and bends. It begins at the beginning but never ends (Arnold, 2001).

Some of these books are novelties that disintegrate or disappear after babies use them a few times. Most enduring are the *board books* with nontoxic cardboard pages, which are often waterproof and can be used casually.

What's Your View?

Is Children's Literature Good for Your Appetite?

The first snack-brand children's book was originally suggested in 1994 by a Massachusetts nursery school teacher, Barbara Barbieri McGrath, who discovered that when she used M & M's to teach her students how to count, they were immediately attentive. After trying unsuccessfully to market her idea, she finally persuaded Charlesbridge Publishing Company to publish her book, *The M & M Brand Chocolate Candies Counting Book*, and it became the publisher's best selling title.

Now, after at least eight editions of the M & M's books, five Cheerios editions (including Spanish-language versions), a Kellogg's Froot Loops book, and three Pepperidge Farm Gold Fish books, snack-brand books are being sold in millions of copies by various publishers (Kirkpatrick, 2000). Companies like Harper-Collins, Simon & Schuster, and Scholastic continue to explore the tie-in of books with foods such as candy, cookies, cereal, and snacks, but emphasize that they often turn down some brands. Such a partnership with a publisher is ideal for food manufacturers because snack-brand books go to places not ordinarily open to advertisers and target the appropriate age range.

Since their first success as books for toddlers, snack-brand books are now being offered to elementary school children with titles such as *Reese's Pieces Count by Fives*, the *Hershey's Milk Chocolate Bar Fractions* book, and *Skittles Math Riddles*. As Kirkpatrick notes, "most publishers are blasé about introducing books that look like advertisements into the high chair and the classroom" (Kirkpatrick, 2000, p. C17). But some publishers are not proud of it, seeing these books as nothing more than advertising.

Although some bookstore owners highly recommend snack-brand books, especially for restless toddlers, others have refused to stock many of the titles because children do not have the cognitive ability to realize they are being manipulated (Kirkpatrick, 2000). Many parents appreciate the ability of their child to sit still in a high chair and fill in the diecut holes with Cheerios or Fruit Loops while they're dining out. Other parents and professionals are concerned that snack-brands will be imprinted on their children's minds and could possibly lead to eating problems later in life.

After taking an informal poll of parents in your class who have young children, or by questioning young parents you know, discuss with your fellow students whether snack-brand books are developmentally appropriate for a small child to use. What's your view?

Picture Books

Although in the following chapters we include examples of books from all genres, in this chapter about literature for infants to 2 years of age, we consider only the genre of the picture book. Included in this category are wordless books, alphabet books, counting books, concept books, and picture storybooks. Within the format of the picture book, however, we also discover characteristics of the genres of *traditional literature, fantasy, poetry,* and *informational books* that match an infant's developmental goodness-of-fit. By carefully choosing books written and illustrated by outstanding authors and illustrators, we hope that teachers, librarians, and other caregivers will designate our selections as "keepers," valuable additions to a child's growing literary experience.

Wordless Books

Wordless may seem at first to denote books for babies that are simplistic, devoid of plot, and dull, but actually they are often humorous, challenging, and clever. *Tuesday,* for example, an almost wordless picture book by David Wiesner and a Caldecott Medal selection, is so complex and subtle that infants would find it difficult to comprehend. Other wordless books that offer a better goodness-of-fit are

CHANGES, CHANGES. Pat Hutchins, in 1971, broke literary boundaries by adroitly weaving a story about two wooden figures by merely using brilliant colors, clean lines, and odd-shaped blocks.

YELLOW UMBRELLA. Reminiscent of *The Umbrellas of Cherbourg,* this book by Jae Soo Liu contains paintings of umbrellas as viewed from above, so that when they are gathered together they shelter children going to school. Accompanied by a CD that is cued to the pages, it is a beautiful wordless book.

Alphabet Books

Alphabet books have long been a source of pleasure and information for young book lovers, even before Kate Greenaway's *A Apple Pie* was published in 1886. Her book pictured young boys and girls dressed in a style eagerly copied by designers of the time, actively and alphabetically pursuing the pie (cutting, fighting, jumping) until "six little girls in night caps and night gowns all had a large slice and went off to bed." Even though infants are unable to read the letters when they begin listening to alphabet books, they absorb the rhythm and sequence; as their memory and ability to speak develop, they will one day, much to their caregiver's surprise, recite the alphabet!

ALPHABET UNDER CONSTRUCTION. Denise Fleming has written and illustrated *Alphabet Under Construction,* a book that conveys a sense of fluid movement. In this book, the busy mouse carpenter carves the letter C, glues the G, welds the W, and so on. The colors are brilliant, the mouse is joyful, and the book is rich without unnecessary distractions.

ABC: A CHILD'S FIRST ALPHABET BOOK. Jay Alison has created a new way to highlight ordinary objects. Using what seems to be a crackling glaze, the author/artist places only one image on a page ("a is for apple") and surrounds it with appropriately related objects. She also foreshadows the following letter by including an object beginning with that letter on the previous page.

ABC BY BRUNO MUNARI. Fortunately, this book, originally published in 1960 by the internationally known artist and designer Bruno Munari, has been reissued. Even very young children who can only look and listen will be captivated by the artistically drawn lines that make up the twenty-six letters. (They will also wonder whither goes the fly that jumps off the F page.)

Counting Books

At this age, children are not likely to count. Yet small children hear numbers constantly as they listen to verses that are read to them such as those in Marc Brown's books, *Finger Rhymes*, *Play Rhymes*, and *Hand Rhymes*, as well as the rhymes from *Mother Goose*. (*One, Two, Three, Four / Mary's at the cottage door, / Five, six, seven, eight / Eating cherries off a plate*, etc.). Children are entertained by the repetition, the rhyme, and the frequent acts of appearing and disappearing in Eileen Christelow's humorous series of books about the *Five Little Monkeys* that jump into bed, or bake a birthday cake, or sit in a tree, or play hide-and-seek, or have nothing else to do. Other counting books that are intended more for listening fun than for figuring include the following:

THE BABY GOES BEEP. Rebecca O'Connell has written catchy, cumulative tunes—*The baby goes Beep / The baby goes Beep Beep / the baby goes Beep, Beep, Beep*—to accompany the everyday actions of a baby, e.g., when singing (*la, la, la*), reading (*flip, flip, flip*), or going to bed (*sh, sh, sh*). But the most charming action is the moment when kisses are given (*smooch, smooch, smooch*). Illustrated by Ken Wilson-Max, whose paintings are dark and bold, this book is a great read aloud for story time.

MY NUMBERS/MIS NUMEROS. By using everyday objects familiar to little children, and by painting objects in bright, vivid colors, Rebecca Emberley has written and illustrated a board book that makes counting numbers a pleasant game. With words written in English and Spanish, this book, together with her three other books in the series about learning colors, shapes, and opposites, provides parents, teachers, and librarians with an outstanding resource to share with infants and toddlers.

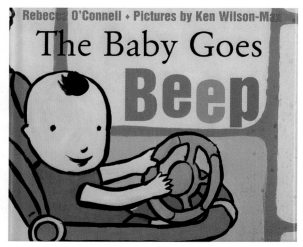

THE BABY GOES BEEP *Copyright 2003 by Ken Wilson-Max. Reprinted by permission of Henry Holt and Company.*

Concept Books

As we noted at the beginning of the chapter, these years are a time of amazing cognitive, physical, and psychosocial growth. Yet the question often arises: are we expecting too much of infants? It's an interesting question when you consider the gains they make during these two years. Brain growth, for instance, is so rapid as to be staggering; cognitive differences between the 6-month-old and the 2-year-old can't be ignored. But as Bjorklund (2005) notes, there is increasing evidence that these obvious behavioral differences are due to smaller changes in underlying competencies than we initially realized. Again, in your book selections we urge you to match the growing complexity of stories with the growing cognitive sophistication of the infant reader.

THE EVERYTHING BOOK. Written and illustrated by Denise Fleming, this book provides small children with everything they could possibly want to know. Games, rhymes, and general knowledge are spread out on vividly colored pages. Young children will be curious about the animals, plants, letters, numbers, and more. As they grow more curious, they will ask many questions. The adult reader who appropriately answers them will add to the child's enjoyment of a book that can be read again and again.

GOOD AS GOLDIE. Children have only to look at the cover of this book by Margie Palatini to see Goldie the toddler, with her hair pulled back in ponytails and grinning from ear to ear, to guess that she thinks she can do anything. She points out immediately that she is "big" and her baby brother is "little." She dresses herself, but he doesn't. She can go very fast on her bike and can swing high in the air, but he can't. The contrasts continue. There is only one thing he does as good as Goldie—he sucks his thumb! Children will relate to the gentle rivalry between brother and sister in this humorous story of opposites.

Picture Storybooks

The most popular subgenre of the *picture book* is the picture storybook, in which words and illustrations are integrated to make a complete story. The following are examples of the picture storybook.

SPOT. Eric Hill's beloved brown and white puppy appears in various sized editions that suit many situations. For reading aloud to a large audience (a library story hour), there is the extra large edition of *Spot's Big Touch and Feel Book*. In this book, children become acquainted not only with Spot, but with other characters like the cat and the squeaky toy mouse. Since it is an interactive book, children can touch the glistening pond, the sail on the boat, and the mouse.

SPOT BLOCK BOOK. For a board book that a very small child can hold, there is the small *Spot Block Book* by Eric Hill. Another book by Hill illustrates *Spot's Favorite Words*, words with which young children are familiar, such as apple, sock, hat, train, and spoon. *Spot's Favorite Colors* illustrates a color, such as orange, on one page and has Spot drinking orange juice on the opposite page. If pink is found on a page, Spot is seen holding a pink birthday cake on the opposite page.

WHERE'S SPOT? In this picture board book, Eric Hill challenges the older child to find Spot since he has disappeared. While Spot's mother looks for him high and low, the child raises a flap on each page. Instead of finding Spot, however, the infant finds something totally unexpected, such as a bear, a snake, a lion, or a crocodile. When

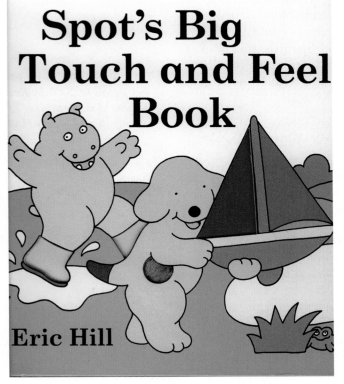

SPOT'S BIG TOUCH
AND FEEL BOOK
*Reproduced by permission
of Penguin Group USA Inc.*

Spot's mother finds him, they are joyfully reunited and the game of hide-and-seek is over. But the child's interest in the book is not over. Children may request *Where's Spot* to be read again and again, since looking for Spot under each flap is fun.

WHERE CAN IT BE? Ann Jonas's book presents a game of hide-and-seek that children closer to 2 years of age find exciting. The little girl who is the narrator tells her audience that she doesn't know where she left IT. She is sure she brought IT home. She knows she must find IT. But where? The hunt is on. She checks her closet—and the young child who is reading helps her by opening the flap in her cupboard to find only toys. She checks her bed—and the reader opens the flap in the bedspread to find only a cat. She checks the kitchen—and again the reader opens a flap to find only pots and pans. As she scours the house, the child reading or listening to the story continues to open one flap after the other. Finally, the mystery is solved to the satisfaction of both narrator and reader.

TIME TO GET DRESSED. Elivia Savadier introduces small children to Solomon, who wants to be in charge of dressing himself. "ME . . . . ME," he cries as the clock ticks and the illustrations reveal how funny he looks!

Traditional Literature

How can infants possibly comprehend traditional literature? The term itself, "traditional literature," is intimidating when we consider that the category contains myths and legends, fables and parables, and folktales and fairy tales whose authors are unknown. Yet we have seen in Chapter Three that since the seventeenth century, children have been fascinated by traditional tales folklorists such as Charles Perrault, the Grimm brothers, and Hans Christian Andersen have collected and retold. In Chapter Three we also mentioned the Opies, the couple who have amassed an enormous collection of Mother Goose Rhymes. Children in the twenty-first century are enthralled by the traditional folklore that many contemporary writers retell in their own unique style, and by nursery rhymes that have been orally transmitted from generation to generation.

One reteller of traditional tales whose books children in later infancy enjoy listening to is Paul Galdone. Galdone has told and illustrated many familiar folktales through the years, such as *The Three Billy Goats Gruff, The Elves and the Shoemaker, The Three Little Pigs, The Little Red Hen, The Gingerbread Boy,* and *The Teeny-Tiny Woman.* Fortunately, many of these enduring stories have been recently reissued and are bringing pleasure to a new generation of children. His characters are easily identifiable and non-threatening. Most have pleasant, smiling faces—even his animals smile—and could easily inhabit any of his books interchangeably. When reading books such as these to children in late infancy, teachers and caregivers provide them with a zone of comfortable security, even when the wolf is destroying the pig's house, or the gingerbread boy is running away from home, or the mean, ugly troll is meeting the Billy Goat Gruff face-to-face.

Nursery Rhymes

Nursery rhymes have survived throughout the centuries and are still giving pleasure to small children. Whether it is their short lines, brief stanzas, or forceful rhythms that amuse, nursery rhymes "are more than mere historical curiosities and more than vehicles for successful illustrators. They retain a power that is both emotional and aesthetic" (Lynn, 1996, p. 118). Often called babies' first poetry, Mother Goose rhymes have a long and interesting history that Peter and Iona Opie, in their *Oxford Dictionary of Nursery Rhymes* (1997), have recorded. This husband and wife team has given us the first publishing dates and subsequent publishing history for over 550 rhymes. They also have collected a wide range of children's books from the eighteenth century to the present and are considered two of children's literature's outstanding authorities.

MOTHER GOOSE   Iona Opie's knowledge of Mother Goose is revealed in her various editions such as *Here Comes Mother Goose* (1996), *My Very First Mother Goose* (1999), and the compilation of both these books into *The Very Best of Mother Goose* (2002), all vividly illustrated by Rosemary Wells. Iona Opie sees the rhymes as pages of music for the very young. She suggests singing *Boys and girls come out to play* to a baby of three months old (Opie, 2001, Preface), urging the singer to notice how the infant responds to the music and magical words of the rhyme. She explains that nursery rhymes are so much in our psyche that we can't remember when we first heard them. Yet, when children fall down, aren't they less fearful when they remember that Jack and Jill fell down too? We know children laugh easily when they hear the story of *Old Mother Hubbard*, or *Diddle, Diddle, My Son John*. As infants grow older, they are quick to repeat *Twinkle, Twinkle Little Star*, and move to the music of *I danced with the girl with a hole in her stocking*. Although many words like cock-horse, hoe-cake, farthings, and pease porridge, are archaic and beyond a small child's experience, the sound and rhythm of the verses continue to live on.

A theory originally suggested by Katherine Elwes Thomas claimed that Mother Goose rhymes were originally written for adults as political treatises or parodies on government. Joanne Lynn partially disputes this claim in her Notes, maintaining that the rhymes, although originally told to adults, have always been directed toward children.

They encode vital concerns of their double (adult and child) audience. The concerns of the nursery are remarkably conservative and unchanging; the limitations imposed on those who care for small children today are much the same as those thus imposed when the rhymes first entered the culture.

(Lynn in Egoff, 1996, p. 120).

Fantasy

Fantasy is not a complicated genre for infants. They need not suspend disbelief when they listen to stories about people who do magical things or animals that talk. From their experience listening to nursery rhymes whose authors are unknown, they assume it is natural for the cow to jump over the moon and the dish to run away with the spoon. They have repeatedly heard that the *elephant jumped so high he reached the sky, / And didn't come back until the Fourth of July*. For them, fantasy written by a known author is indistinguishable from folklore written by an unknown author, and from reality. All they really know is how much they like to listen!

THE VERY BUSY SPIDER. Written and illustrated by Eric Carle, the master of fantasy for very small children, this book is one of several interactive "Very" books. While listening to *The Very Busy Spider*, for example, they can see the colorful pictures of various animals and hear their typical sounds. They can also feel the spider's web as it becomes progressively more complex. Children in later infancy will notice that the fly that appears in each illustration plays an important role in the day of a very busy spider.

THE VERY CLUMSY CLICK BEETLE. The fact that an electronic chip with a built-in battery is included in this book in order to create clicking sounds makes this book by Eric Carle special. Carle explains in the Foreword what a click beetle is and how it maneuvers its body. This beetle is a show-off; he loves to demonstrate to the other creatures how he can click . . . until he rolls over with his legs in the air and is unable to flip right side up. Fortunately, an older, wiser click beetle rescues him.

THE MAGIC HAT. Australian writer Mem Fox has created a joyous, fun-loving story of what happens when a magic hat spins through the air and lands on the heads of various animals. Only the smiling wizard can stop its flight. The ink and watercolor illustrations by Tricia Tusa not only enhance the story, but keep children turning each page, wondering what will happen next.

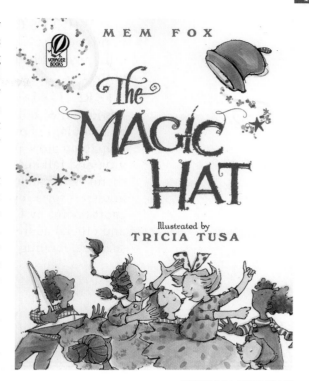

THE MAGIC HAT
Book cover from THE MAGIC HAT by Mem Fox, illustrations copyright 2002 by Tricia Tusa, reproduced by permission of Harcourt, Inc.

Poetry

Contemporary poems and songs, as well as books of interactive games, are important for an infant's linguistic development. As we know, children develop their language skills quickly. The more frequently they hear words, especially those with rhythm and rhyme, the more easily they will read and have fewer learning difficulties later on. In the following books, authors and illustrators introduce small children to music and the music of words.

PLAY RHYMES. Marc Brown has collected and illustrated play rhymes as a good way to introduce children to the feeling of poetry. He has also devised accompanying hand movements that are especially helpful for parents, teachers, and librarians who want to engage youngsters in the active enjoyment of the verses. The classic *I'm a Little Teapot*, for example, is charmingly illustrated with a two-page picture showing a comfortable attic bedroom where three children are playing. Stuffed animals are shown sitting at a table set for tea, while the older brother demonstrates the poem.

CLAP YOUR HANDS. This happy, exuberant book of verses written and illustrated by Lorinda Bryan Cauley is filled with activities for children to imitate. Following pictures of children (and animals dressed like children) in constant motion, the small child can easily follow rhymes like *Reach for the sky* / *Wiggle your toes* / *Stick out your tongue* / *and Touch your nose.*

WHEELS ON THE BUS. Another favorite old song assumes a new look in this pudgy board book. Illustrated by Jerry Smath, the lively words and colorful pictures invite young children to sing the words and imitate the sounds of the bus.

READ ALOUD RHYMES FOR THE VERY YOUNG. Jack Prelutsky has joined with illustrator Marc Brown to provide the youngest children with an anthology of over 200 short poems that satisfy their brief attention span and help them grow. As Jim Trelease writes in the book's Introduction, next to hugging and talking to children, reading aloud is the greatest gift we can give them. We stimulate their imagination, build their vocabularies, and whet their appetites for a love of reading (Prelutsky, 1986). This collection (including short poems by David McCord, Eve Merriam, Edward Lear, Aileen Fisher, and others) addresses infant interests like blowing bubbles, playing hide-and-seek, celebrating a birthday, and other everyday events children experience.

Informational Books

Very small children do not listen to books to gain information. They want the comfort and security of the reader's lap and the personal attention they receive when a book is read just to them. They enjoy listening because they like the sound and rhythm of the voice of the person who reads to them. As they grow older, they are able to notice and match objects in the book with those familiar to them. They also begin to make distinctions and gradually become developmentally ready to absorb simple facts about fascinating subjects. The books suggested below offer them this opportunity.

HERE ARE MY HANDS. Bill Martin Jr. and John Archambault have created the perfect story hour book for adults to read to small children. The rhyming content encourages children to act out the parts of the body as they respond to words like *Here are my hands / for catching and throwing. / Here are my feet for stopping and going. / Here is my head / for thinking and knowing / Here is my nose / for smelling and blowing.* The illustrations are large and uncluttered. The colors are bright and distinctive. And the children in the illustrations come from many cultures. So, children gain knowledge not only about the parts of their body, but also about the universality of their world.

THE BABY'S CATALOGUE. Janet and Allan Ahlberg created this catalogue, which is now a classic of infant literature, to point out to small children how many different kinds of babies there are, who have different mothers and dads, high chairs, and carriages. On each page is a picture from which small children can learn. On the first page the adult and child meet five different babies. On the last page are pictured the same babies, all sleeping but one. The father, exhausted and in his pajamas, is pacing the floor to soothe the baby who cannot sleep. Gentleness and family intimacy are pictured throughout the book, which is a timeless tribute to parents and their loving care of small children.

Emergent Literacy

Teachers, librarians, and caregivers not only provide a warm and caring environment when they spend time reading and playing with children from birth to age 2, but they are also encouraging an emerging literacy. Emergent literacy is the "constellation of skills young children accumulate through hands-on, age-appropriate, playful experiences involving listening, speaking, being read to, handling books, and using writing implements before they are ready for formal reading and writing" (Byrne, 2003, p. 43). Making toys and books, especially interactive books, accessible to small children is important, because play is a child's work and a primary learning activity. It is the means by which emergent literacy is fostered.

Long before emergent literacy was considered an important issue, teachers and librarians conducted story hours for children who were old enough to sit quietly on the floor or in small chairs, and who would listen attentively. Now, college students, using their knowledge of children and their literature, often volunteer to help educational professionals reach even the youngest in small groups for brief but active gatherings.

Jane Yolen has collected favorite songs and poems such as "Patty-Cake, Patty-Cake," "The Eensy Weensy Spider," and "Where Is Thumbkin?" in a book illustrated by Margot Tomes entitled *The Lap-Time Song and Play Book*. For new mothers and other caregivers, this collection is valuable because words are connected to actions and sounds to rhythms. Parts of the body are pointed at and named. Not only is it a source of entertainment for small children; it can also be an adult's loving attempt at teaching.

Indicative of the increasing popularity of the idea of emergent literacy, volunteers in Portland, Oregon have been trained to present story times at child-care centers since 2002 (Arnold & Colburn, 2004). They may begin by having the infants listen to a simple song, hear a brief story, and then play finger games. (If adults participate, the children model their gestures more readily.) Later, while the infants play with toys that are developmentally appropriate, students may go from one infant to another sharing a board book with each of the children. CARE (*Create a Reader Early*) volunteers often bring a toy with them. Hand puppets or finger puppets especially attract the infants' attention.

The *Lapsitter's Story Hour* such as the one being offered at the Edith Fox Library in Arlington, Massachusetts by Page Lindsay, the *New York Times* "Librarian of the Year" (2005), has not only become a weekly event in many public libraries, but is an idea that has been introduced to nursery schools and day-care centers, where it is a strong link to emergent literacy.

Play

Play aids cognitive development and cognitive development aids play (Dacey & Travers, 2009). Through play and interacting with board books—picture books that children this age can handle themselves—small children learn about the objects in their world, what these objects do, and how they work. To use Piaget's terms, children *operate* on these objects and by manipulating them learn behavioral skills that will help them in the future. Creating an effective physical environment by offering young children materials such as toys, books, puzzles, and puppets is an important role that caretakers play in emergent literacy.

Spin Off
The Lap time Story Hour

If you would like to organize (or join) a lap time story hour, remember that its primary purpose is to introduce infants to books in a pleasing way. With young children, you must be adaptable. (Remember that an infant's attention span is unpredictable and you must be ready to adjust your plans accordingly.) To begin your story hour, you might like to start with a familiar song or rhyme. Two of the many books that combine rhyme with dazzling illustrations are

The Farmer in the Dell, illustrated by Ilse Plume. Vividly colored pencil drawings and Pennsylvania Dutch motifs add to the familiar words. Music is also included. (Older siblings will appreciate the instructions on how to play the game.)

Froggy Went A-Courtin by Gillian Tyler is enhanced with a shiny, gold-ink text that is bound to capture infants' attention.

The book you decide to read must captivate the infants' interest quickly (regardless of copyright date; some of the oldest books are their favorites). It must have large, colorful illustrations (preferably pictures of babies, parents, children, and familiar animals), very few words, and lots of action. The following books by David Shannon, Michael Lawrence, Lisa Kopper, and Helen Oxenbury seem to offer a genuine goodness-of-fit.

Good Boy, Fergus! David Shannon's illustrations of Fergus, an irrepressible, well-intentioned, but often naughty puppy, are hilarious. Simple commands such as "sit" cause Fergus to do the opposite. He only eats his supper when it is smothered in whipped cream.

Baby Loves. Michael Lawrence's book, illustrated by Adrian Reynolds, is ideally suited for infants, because the illustrations are full page and represent people and objects the baby knows and loves: mommy, daddy, granny, kitty, hat, drum, and so on. It reassures the infant that Mommy and Daddy love *baby* more than anything in the world.

GOOD BOY, FERGUS
Reprinted by permission of Scholastic, Inc.

Daisy Thinks She's a Baby. Children are delighted to hear about Lisa Kopper's character Daisy, the dog who copies everything the baby does. The two-page spread of Daisy wearing the baby's hat and holding the teething ring even makes adults laugh out loud. But the baby in the story doesn't laugh. When Daisy has a nap, the baby pulls his blanket from him. And when Daisy takes a bath, the real baby doesn't like that, either. Only when Daisy becomes a mother and isn't a baby anymore, is the baby in the story happy.

Good Dog, Daisy! Also by Lisa Kopper. Daisy, as this book shows, is a mother with three puppies. Since small children look forward to reading about characters they have previously met in a series (such as Tom and Pippo), they love reading again about Daisy and Little Daisy, who is the human baby's favorite puppy. Together, Daisy, Little Daisy, Mommy, and the baby teach each other simple commands, such as "Lie down," "Sit," and "Speak," which cause a great deal of humorous confusion.

Tom and Pippo in the Garden. (Helen Oxenbury.) Children everywhere are fascinated when they hear young Tom tell how he takes care of his toy monkey Pippo. He and Pippo have many misadventures. The simplicity of the story and the uncluttered illustrations capture the very young child's attention.

Tom and Pippo Go Shopping. (Helen Oxenbury.) In another book in the series, Tom tells his young audience how he takes Pippo into department stores. Although he promises Pippo a piece of bread, then a plum, and a piece of cheese, he must confess that he has eaten them all himself.

If you think about the conditions we just described—attractive books, a warm and inviting setting, people they love, toys, books, and puzzles that the children can play with—The Lap Time Story Hour is a wonderful way to bring children into the world of literacy.

Spin Off

Infants Interact with Books

The most important thing when you interact with children this age is that they know you're there to love and care for them. Hold them gently when you sing to them. When you read to them, turn each page slowly and give them the time to see and explore. When playing games with them, make sure the games are fun and help develop their physical and cognitive skills. Offer them warmth and security as you introduce them to the world of books.

Singing

• Books like Jane Yolen's *Lullaby Songbook* and Marc Brown's *Play Rhymes* afford you many opportunities to test your singing voice. As infants grow older, let them join in.

• Help them sing old favorites like "Jack and Jill," "Hey Diddle Diddle," "Mistress Mary," "Twinkle, Twinkle Little Star," and other Mother Goose rhymes. As infants become toddlers and attend daycare and nursery school, they enjoy dramatic programs planned around Mother Goose. In settings as simple as *The Old Lady's Shoe* (a work table turned on its side), each child in a simple costume may pantomime the nursery rhyme character he or she represents.

• *The Wheels on the Bus* is perfect for a sing–along, especially when accompanied by a guitar.

Reading

• Books like *Where's Spot?* and *Where Is It?* challenge young children to solve a mystery. Let them open the flaps, touch the pages, and make guesses to seek and find out for themselves what the mystery is.

• Invite at least one of each child's favorite stuffed animal to share the read-aloud session with you. Select stories about pets and serve animal crackers for a treat.

• Select poems from *Read Aloud Rhymes for the Very Young* to read aloud. All of them beg to be acted out spontaneously.

Playing

• Jane Yolen's *The Lap Time Song and Play Book* is filled with suggestions for activities that children and their caregivers can do together.

• Your young charges will be motivated into action just by following the songs and pictures in Lorinda Bryan Cauley's *Clap Your Hands*.

• *The Aunts Go Marching In* is a great jumping-off spot for marshaling a group of 2 year olds in costume (boots and umbrellas) to march around the room or playground to the music of the book, led by a girl (or boy) in a yellow raincoat who is pounding a drum!

Chapter Checklist

Read the following items carefully. If you have difficulty responding to any of them, return to the chapter to review the material.

After reading this chapter, you can

1. Describe how the developmental characteristics of children from birth–2 help shape the nature of stories for infants.

2. Discuss the relationship between reading to preterms or infants and the growth of connections among brain cells.

3. Illustrate (using stories from this chapter) how habituation studies provide clues to the popularity of infant stories.

4. Demonstrate the appeal of stories (again, taken from this chapter) that relate to an infant's sensory capacities.

5. Explain the enduring popularity of peek-a-boo books.

6. Using the books in this chapter, identify the range of picture books for infants.

7. Distinguish among the vast scope of nursery rhymes grouped under the title "Mother Goose."

8. Evaluate the role poetry plays in an infant's language development.

9. Explain why fantasy appeals to infants because of their cognitive immaturity.

10. Link the changing nature of infant stories (particularly informational books) to their cognitive development.

Children's Bibliography

Ahlberg, Janet, & Ahlberg, Allan. (1982). *The Baby's Catalog*. Boston: Little, Brown.

Ahlberg, Janet, & Ahlberg, Allan. (1992). *Baby's Good Night*. New York: Simon & Schuster.

Ahlberg, Janet and Allan. (1997). *Peek-a-boo!* New York: Viking.

Alison, Jay. (2003). *ABC: A Child's First Alphabet*. New York: Dutton.

Baum, L. Frank. Engineered by Robert Sabuda. (2000). *The Wonderful World of Oz*. New York: Simon & Schuster.

Boynton, Sandra. (1993). *Oh My Oh My Oh Dinosaurs!* New York: Workman Publishing.

Brown, Marc. (1980). *Finger Rhymes*. New York: Dutton.

Brown, Marc. (1985). *Hand Rhymes*. New York: Dutton.

Brown, Marc. (1993). *Play Rhymes*. New York: Penguin.

Brown, Margaret Wise. (1947). *Goodnight, Moon*. New York: Harper & Row.

Carle, Eric. (1970). *The Very Hungry Caterpillar* (Board book ed.). New York: World.

Carle, Eric. (1984). *The Very Busy Spider*. New York: Philomel.

Carle, Eric. (1990). *The Very Quiet Cricket*. New York: Philomels.

Carle, Eric. (1999). *The Very Clumsy Click Beetle*. New York: Philomel.

Cauley, Lorinda Bryan. (1992). *Clap Your Hands*. New York: Putnam.

Chorao, Kay, (2002). *Baby's Goodnight Book: Lullabies and Bedtime Stories*. New York: Random House Lap Library.

Christelow, E. (1991). *Five Little Monkeys Sitting in a Tree*. New York: Clarion Books.

Christelow, E. (1992). *Five Little Monkeys Bake a Birthday Cake*. New York: Clarion Books.

Christelow, E. (2000). *Five Little Monkeys Wash the Car*. New York: Clarion Books.

Christelow, E. (2004). *Five Little Monkeys Play Hide-and-Seek*. New York: Clarion Books.

Dorling Kindersley. (2002). *Touch and Feel Dinosaur*. New York: Dorling Kindersley.

Emberley, Rebecca. (2000). *My Numbers, Mis Numeros*. Boston: Little, Brown.

Fleming, Denise. (2000). *The Everything Book*. New York: Holt.

Fleming, Denise. (2002). *Alphabet Under Construction*. New York: Holt.

Fox, Mem. Tricia Tusa, illus. (2002). *The Magic Hat*. CA: Harcourt.

Galdone, Paul. (1975). *The Gingerbread Boy*. New York: Clarion Books.

Galdone, Paul. (1984). *The Elves and the Shoemaker*. New York: Clarion Books.

Galdone, Paul. (1984). *The Teeny-Tiny Woman*. New York: Clarion Books.

Galdone, Paul. (1998). *The Three Little Pigs*. New York: Clarion Books.

Galdone, Paul. (2001). *The Little Red Hen*. New York: Clarion Books.

Galdone, Paul. (2001). *The Three Billy Goats Gruff*. New York: Clarion Books.

Greenaway, Kate. (1975). *A Apple Pie*. New York: Frederick Warne and Co., Ltd.

Hall, Nancy Abraham, & Syverson-Stork, Jill,. (1994). *Los Pollitos Dicen/The Baby Chicks Sing*. Boston: Little, Brown.

Hill, Eric. (1980). *Where's Spot?* New York: Putnam.

Hill, Eric. (1997). *Spot's Favorite Words*. New York: Putnam.

Hill, Eric. (1997). *Spot's Favorite Colors*. New York: Putnam.

Hill, Eric. (2000). *Spot's Big Touch and Feel Book*. New York: Philomel.

Hutchins, Pat. (1971). *Changes, Changes*. New York: Macmillan.

Janssen, Charlotta. (2001). *The Secret of Three Butterpillars*. New York: Workman.

Jonas, Ann. (1986). *Where Can It Be?* New York: Greenwillow.

Kopper, Lisa. (2001). *Good Dog, Daisy!* New York: Dutton.

Kopper, Lisa. (1994). *Daisy Thinks She's A Baby*. New York: Alfred A. Knopf.

Kunhardt, Dorothy. (1970). *Pat the Bunny*. Racine, WS: Golden Press.

Lawrence, Michael. (1999). *Baby Loves*. New York: Dorling Kindersley.

Liu, Jae Soo. Music by Dong Il Sheen. (2002). *Yellow Umbrella*. La Jolla, CA: Kane/Miller Book Publishing.

Manning, Maurie J. (2003). *The Aunts Go Marching*. Honesdale, PA: Boyds Mills.

Martin, Bill Jr., & Archambault, John. (1985). *Here Are My Hands*. New York: Henry Holt.

McGrath, Barbara Barbieri. (1997). *The M & M's Brand Chocolate Candies Counting Book*. Cambridge, MA: Charlesgate.

Meyers, Susan. (2001). *Everywhere Babies*. San Diego: Harcourt.

Munari, Bruno. (2003). *ABC by Bruno Munari*. San Francisco: Chronicle Books.

O'Connell, Rebecca. (2003). *The Baby Goes Beep*. Brookfield, T: Roaring Brook Press.

Omerod, Jan. (1997). *Peek-a-boo!* New York: Dutton.

Opie, Iona. Rosemay Wells, illus. (2002). *The Very Best of Mother Goose*. Cambridge, MA: Candlewick.

Oxenbury, Helen. (1988). *Tom and Pippo in the Garden*. New York: Macmillan.

Oxenbury, Helen. (2003). *Helen Oxenbury's Big Baby Book*. Cambridge, MA: Candlewick.

Oxenbury, Helen. (1988). *Tom and Pippo Go Shopping*. New York: Macmillan.

Palatini, Margie. (2000). *Good as Goldie*. New York: Hyperion.

Plume, Ilse. (2004). *The Farmer in the Dell*. Boston: Godine.

Prelutsky, Jack. (1986). *Read-Aloud Rhymes for the Very Young*. New York: Alfred A. Knopf!

Potter, Beatrice. (1993).*Peter Rabbit and His Friends* (Board book edition). New York: Warne.

Saltzberg, Barney. (2002). *Peekaboo Kisses*. New York: Harcourt.

Savadier, Elivia. (2006). *Time to Get Dressed*. CT: Roaring Brook Press.

Seuss, Dr. (1956). *The Cat in the Hat*. New York: Random House.

Shannon, David. (2006). *Good Boy, Fergus!* New York: Blue Sky Press.

Smath, Jerry. (2002). *Wheels on the Bus* (Board book edition). New York: Grosset & Dunlap.

Tyler, Gillian. (2005), *Froggy Went A-Courtin'*. Cambridge, MA: Candlewick.

Wade, Lee. (1998). *The Cheerios Play Book*. New York: Simon & Schuster.

Walsh, Melanie. (2000). *Tiny Teethers*. Cambridge, MA: Candlewick.

Wiesner, David (1991). *Tuesday*. New York: Clarion Books.

Willis, Jeanne. (2003). *The Boy Who Thought He Was a Teddy Bear*. New York: Peachtree Press.

Yolen, Jane, ed. (1986). *The Lullaby Songbook*. San Diego: Harcourt Brace.

Yolen, Jane, ed. (1989). *The Lap-Time Song and Play Book*. San Diego: Harcourt Brace.

Professional References

Arnold, Matthew. (2001). "Something New To Chew On." *New York Times*. October 18, E3.

Arnold, Renea, & Colburn Nell, (2004). "Into the Mouths of Babes." *School Library Journal*. April, 39.

Berk, L. (2005). *Infants, Children, and Adolescents*. Boston: Allyn & Bacon.

Bjorklund, D. (2005). *Children's Thinking*. Belmont, CA: Wadsworth.

Byrne, Marci, et al. (2003). "Book a Play Date: The Game of Promoting Emergent Literacy." *American Libraries*. September, 42–45.

Clark, H. Nichols. (2004). "Conversation With . . . . "*The Foundation of Children's Books*. Boston: Boston College. January 20.

Cole, M., & Cole, S. (2001). *The Development of Children*. New York: Worth.

Dacey, John S., & Travers, John F. (2009). *Human Development Across the Lifespan*. 7th Ed. Boston: McGraw-Hill.

DeCasper, A., & Spence, M. (1986). "Prenatal Maternal Speech Influences Newborn's Perception of Speech Sounds." *Infant Behavior and Development*. 9, 133–170.

Egoff, Sheila, et al. eds. (1996). *Only Connect*. New York, Oxford University Press.

Eliot, L. (2000). *What's Going on There? How the Brain and Mind Develop in the First Five Years of Life*. New York: Bantam.

Fantz, R. (1961). "The Origin of Form Perception." *Scientific American*. 240, 66–72.

Fantz, R. (1963). "Pattern Vision in Newborn Infants." *Science*. 140, 296–297.

Gopnik, A., Meltzoff, A., & Kuhl, P. (1999). *The Scientist in the Crib*. New York: William Morrow.

Kirkpatrick, David. (2000). "Snack Books Become Stars of Books for Children." *New York Times*. September 22, 17.

Lynn, Joanne L., Sheila Egoff et. al. ed. (1996). "Runes to Ward Off Sorrow: Rhetoric of the English Nursery Rhyme." *Only Connect*. New York: Oxford University Press.

Marcus, Leonard S. (2002). *Ways of Telling*. New York: Dutton's Children's Books.

Opie, P., & Opie, I. (1997). *Oxford Dictionary of Nursery Rhymes*. New York: Oxford University Press.

Robinson, Lolly. (2003). "What Do You See? The Eric Carle Museum of Picture Book Art." *The Horn Book Magazine*, May/June.

Silvey, Anita, ed. (1995). *Children's Books and their Creators*. Boston: Houghton Mifflin.

Thomas, Jack. (2002). "The Very Playful Museum." *Boston Globe*. November 16, C1, C5.

Tucker, Nicholas. (2002). *The Rough Guide to Children's Books*. London: Penguin.

CHAPTER 8

Literature for the Preschool Years (Ages 2–4)

Patricia Polacco introduces us to her brightly colored picture book Babushka's Doll, by explaining that young Natasha, the main character in the story, is not a truly naughty child. She just never understands why she has to wait for things. In those few words, Polacco captures the essence of the preschool child: vibrant, impatient, and adventurous. She is also forewarning us to be prepared for events in the story that will change Natasha's life forever.

Natasha demanded much of her grandmother, whom she called "Babushka." She always wanted her undivided attention. When Natasha asked her grandmother to take the doll from the shelf, Babushka acquiesced because she knew that it was the right time for Natasha to play with her. Babushka herself had played with the doll only once when she was a little girl.

A series of events begins to unfold that cause a painful, but humorous, role reversal. The doll comes alive. She jumps to her feet and does a little dance. She demands that Natasha come out to play. Then, she demands that Natasha keep pushing her on the swing. Her demands continue until Natasha grows tired. She makes lunch for the doll who spills the tea, sloshes the soup, and flings the noodles over her head. Natasha begins to cry and tearfully admits to her Babushka that she is only a little girl. Babushka comforts her by saying that it must have been a bad dream and promises her that she can play with the little doll any time she wants. But Natasha refuses. "No, thank you, Babushka. Once is enough," she says. And Natasha turns out to be quite a nice little girl after all.

In this brief, somewhat exaggerated, description of Natasha's thoughts and moods, Patricia Polacco has captured the frustrating—and charming—twists and turns of 2-, 3-, and 4-, year-olds. With Natasha, she has almost written a case study of children of these years. And yet, should this be a surprise to us? Think of all that's going on in children's lives during these years.

- Physically, their bodies grow rapidly and their movement becomes more coordinated.

- Brain development races ahead as more and more neural connections are formed.

- Cognitive development steadily improves, but egocentrism remains a major force in their thinking.

- The language explosion provides them with more words to engage in conversations—some pleasant, some not so pleasant.

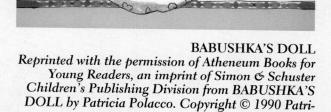

Babushka's Doll

Patricia Polacco

BABUSHKA'S DOLL
Reprinted with the permission of Atheneum Books for Young Readers, an imprint of Simon & Schuster Children's Publishing Division from BABUSHKA'S DOLL by Patricia Polacco. Copyright © 1990 Patricia Polacco.

• Relationships increase quickly and dramatically. New brothers and sisters may be born into the family; other, possibly older, children join the family through parental remarriages. Grandparents are more involved than ever with their grandchildren.

• Preschool brings additional relationships to most children.

• Children's evaluations of themselves are slowly changing as they compete with others; strengths are accepted, weaknesses recognized.

These are only a few of the developmental accomplishments that make these years challenging, tumultuous, and exciting. They also present delightful opportunities for authors to capitalize on the humor, pathos, and happiness of this colorful time.

Guidelines for Reading Chapter 8

After you read Chapter Eight, you should be able to answer the following questions.

• How do the developmental characteristics of children this age influence the themes and illustrations authors weave throughout their stories?

• How significant is it to read aloud to children of this age?

• Why are picture books so attractive to children of these years?

• Given the growing but still limited cognitive ability of these children, what developmental features should authors include in their work?

• Are there legitimate biopsychosocial reasons for combining poetry with acting?

• What cautions should authors of information books for children of these years keep in mind?

Characteristics of Children of These Years

These years—the energy, the restlessness, the challenges—present wonderful opportunities for coordinating growth and development with the richness and depth of children's literature. By the age of 2, typical children walk, talk, and eagerly explore their environment, while steadily acquiring physical, cognitive, and social skills that become the foundation of the years to come. The world is theirs!

The Impact of Brain Development

Physical growth slows slightly as the rounded bodies of infancy give way to the slimmer torsos of early childhood. Muscles begin to firm, bones begin to harden, and continued brain development provides a basis for a world of symbolic promise. During these years, activity in the frontal area of the brain expands, which enables children to detect differences in words and their meanings. As the rapid acquisition of words continues, it's followed a few months later by a corresponding increase in understanding the grammar of the language. When these changes combine with feelings of confidence—"I can do it"—parents and other adults working with children this age face challenges that are overcome only by patience and understanding.

Kurt Fischer, a cognitive psychologist at the Harvard Graduate School of Education, has concluded as a result of his research that brain growth spurts appear at 2 years and 4 years (see particularly Dawson & Fischer, 1994). At 4 years of age, children understand much more about the world around them. They probably experience some type of preschool world, which they enjoy, because they find pleasure interacting with others. They're beginning to decide which of their playmates they like and which they don't; most importantly, they're learning *why* they like some and dislike others. They can run, jump, chase others, and *play!* With their steadily growing cognitive abilities, they imagine all kinds of playmates and engage in fantastic activities.

Children of these years gobble up information from the outside world through their eyes, ears, nose, and hands, and translate it into nerve impulses that travel along neurons (from the axon of one cell to the dendrites of another), thereby making connection with the dendrites of other neurons along its path. In Tana Hoban's *So Many Circles, So Many Squares* (1998), for example, outstanding photographs challenge children to look at and see shapes, from simple to complex. The more children examine the shapes, the more shapes they see! Hoban's book is also a puzzle and game book that humorously engages children's senses. Children who receive this type of visual and verbal stimulation are building a rich network of neural connections. The brain cells that receive this information survive; those that don't, die. It's as simple as that.

The Brain, Books, and Behavior

Cognitively, during the time of Piaget's *preoperational period* the amount of information a child can attend to steadily increases. For Piaget, "preoperational" refers to those children who have begun to use symbols such as language, but can't manipulate words and ideas. The great accomplishment of this period is a growing ability to represent; children see the word "car" and visualize four wheels, a hood, roof, and so on. It's an important time for those working with children because of the steady development of thought during this period.

Piaget's ideas about children of these years are apparent in books written for small children. For example, Kevin Henkes's understanding of the cognitive processes of the preschool child is evident in his picture book *Kitten's First Full Moon*, winner of the Caldecott Medal. Illustrated in black and white, Henkes reveals a kitten's determination to reach the moon, which she thinks is a bowl of milk. Children laugh when the kitten gets a firefly on her tongue as she tries to lick the moon. And they laugh at how soaked her skin is when she tries to drink its reflection. The moon is as real to the kitten as it is to children who believe the moon follows them.

Preoperational youngsters are unable to decenter; they do not notice features that would give balance to their reasoning. You can see how authors and illustrators must take this into consideration. Cartoonist Mo Willems, in his humorous story *The Pigeon Finds a Hot Dog!*, reveals how a daring pigeon (read, preschooler) zeroes in on a discarded hot dog that he wants to keep for himself. A duckling (read, younger sibling) also sees the hot dog and wants it. The question is: should the hot dog be shared or not?

An example of mental imagery can be seen in *The Carrot Seed*. Many books written for children of these years are intended to increase their knowledge and understanding of their environment. Ruth Kraus's book relates the story of a confident little boy faithfully watching a seed he planted and imagining how it will grow. Gradually, it matures into a plant in spite of the doubt of those around him. Kraus's line drawings are simple and uncomplicated, ideal for children ages 2–4. (*The Carrot Seed* is now in a board book edition for even the smallest child to hold.)

Language holds a special fascination for young children as they acquire it, use it, and play with it. The allure of words is particularly obvious in poetry. In *The Frogs Wore Red Suspenders*, Jack Prelutsky charms and pleases children with humorous verse. Twenty-eight animals are represented in his gentle, whimsical poems—all related to cities and towns in the United States. Petra Mathers' watercolor illustrations set off Prelutsky's light-hearted verse. It is a perfect book for reading aloud.

An Overview of the Classic Picture Book

Since Randolph Caldecott created the first modern picture book, the genre has been an essential part of every small child's collection of favorite books. Even before children are developmentally ready to read, they experience the joy of picture books being read to them by parents, teachers, and other adults. As they enter nursery school or day care, move into kindergarten, and continue through their elementary school years, children read and listen to picture story books with absolute joy.

Picture books like Maurice Sendak's *Where The Wild Things Are*, Margaret Wise Brown's *Good Night, Moon*, Ezra Jack Keats' *Snowy Day*, and Virginia Lee Burton's *Mike Mulligan and the Steam Shovel* have withstood the test of time and are considered classics of children's literature. *Where the Wild Things Are* has emerged from the negative criticism it received when it was first published in 1963, to eventually becoming a universal success. But it was not accepted in Great Britain until circa 1967, because it was thought to be too scary for small children! Nicholas Tucker, one of England's leading experts in children's literature, now calls it "One of the most celebrated picture books ever created" (Tucker, 2002, p. 148).

Margaret Wise Brown's *Goodnight, Moon*, on the other hand, published in 1947, was immediately received with total approval both here and abroad. "This is far more than just another book inviting children to use their powers of observation and object recognition. What stays in the memory, above all, is the mood of security and tranquility generated by Brown's simple rhyming text and Clement Hurd's delightful pictures" (Tucker, 2002, p. 129).

The complete works (omnibuses) of Ezra Jack Keats and Virginia Lee Burton have been reissued for another generation of children to enjoy. Although too large for the hands of very small children to hold, these books contain valued stories that adults will read to children for years to come. In *Keats's Neighborhood: An Ezra Jack Keats Treasury* (Viking), children make the acquaintance of Peter, a small black boy with a red coat, who is the main character in *The Snowy Day* (originally written in 1962). Peter was the first black child to be featured in a major American full-color picture book. In *A Letter To Amy*, Keats writes about Peter's (or any young child's) dilemma: whether or not he should invite a girl to his birthday party.

In *Mike Mulligan and More, A Virginia Lee Burton Treasury* reissued by Houghton Mifflin, Virginia Burton tells the story of *Mike Mulligan and His Steam Shovel* and the story of Mary Ann who "could dig as much in a day as a hundred men could dig in a week." Katy is another character who earns great respect for the work she does as a tractor in *Katy and the Big Snow*. While *Maybelle the Cable Car* is less well known, all of Burton's picture books, including *The Little House*, are significant for honoring simple virtues—such as hard work, patience, and perseverance—that even little children can admire.

Other favorite picture books from past years such as the *Cat in the Hat* (Dr. Seuss), *Make Way for Ducklings* (Robert McCloskey), *Lyle, Lyle, Crocodile* (Bernard Waber), *Frederick* (Leo Lionni), *Peter Rabbit* (Beatrix Potter), and *Curious George* (H. A. Rey) continue to entertain small children. They are the kinds of books that are read to children before they go to sleep at night and are packed into the suitcase when families go on vacation.

What's Your View?

Picture Books Reissued

Today, many books adults remember reading as children are being reissued and are reappearing on bookstore and library shelves for another generation to read. Books such as Randall Jarrell's *The Gingerbread Rabbit* (1964) are as innovative today as ever. Richard Egielski's *The Gingerbread Boy* (1997), Crockett Johnson's *Ellen's Lion* (1959)—which is even more imaginative than his well-known *Harry and the Purple Crayon*—and the remarkable William Steig's *Yellow and Pink* (1984), one of the most engaging books ever published, are being reissued as they were originally written (Schmitz, 2003). Like Esther Averill's *Jenny and the Cat Club*, these books are welcome additions to a contemporary child's collection.

Reissues, however, may carry some unwanted problems. When the original book is recolored, rewritten, or redesigned, it does not always mean it has been improved. David McPhail's *Henry Bear's Park* (1976), which we discuss on page 182, for instance, is larger and its original black and white illustrations have been gaudily colored by another artist. *Emmet's Pig* (1959) by Mary Stolz has had several makeovers. Published originally as a *Harper I Can Read* book, it is now a picture book with color illustrations. Terri Schmitz, whose reviews often appear in *The Horn Book*, believes such a change was unnecessary: "The new trim size is not an enhancement and the colorization, no matter how respectfully done, still looks like paint-by-numbers and not an integrated whole" (Schmitz, 2003, p. 581).

If publishers continue to reissue books like these, or add words to a wordless picture book like Emily Arnold McCully's *Picnic* (1984), do you think teachers, librarians, and children may be tempted to agree with Schmitz's observation that being "out of print is not always a bad thing" (Schmitz, 2004, p. 153)?

Since our view of children's development continues to change along with society's changing idea of childhood (as we traced in Chapter Two), do you believe that reissuing a previously published picture book such as Lois Lenski's *The Little Family* (1932), which emphasizes traditional gender roles (the father drives the car, the mother does the dishes, the boy plays ball, the girl plays with her doll) is *always* a good idea, given the changes in today's family life? What's your view?

PERSONALITY IN PICTURE BOOKS: THE WORK OF KEVIN HENKES

During these years, children blossom into distinctive personalities. Although temperamental differences appear at birth, they now flourish until even the most casual observer notices a child's "personality." As we saw in the vignette at the beginning of this chapter, many authors and illustrators capture the preschool child's personality with humor and understanding. Author and illustrator Kevin Henkes is an author/illustrator who shows how children of these years make new friends and how they act and react in the family, in the neighborhood, and in preschool. He has a remarkable talent for getting inside the thoughts and emotions of children and capturing the vicissitudes of their lives, even though his characters are mice.

Imagine Kevin Henkes' characters all being together in preschool. What a remarkable class that would be! Perhaps standing in the doorway, hesitating to enter, would be Wemberly, the main character in *Wemberly Worried*, who is fraught with anguish about everything. Wemberly might then meet Jewel, to whom she can relate, because she also wears stripes and clutches her favorite doll. In front of the class would be Lilly, the main character in *Lilly's Purple Plastic Purse*, who adores her teacher, Mr. Slinger, until the morning she brings her purple plastic purse to school. Lilly pesters Mr. Slinger and her classmates to examine her new acquisition, but Mr. Slinger is not impressed and asks her to bring it to his desk. She then decides she no longer likes Mr. Slinger, even when he writes her the note: "Today was a difficult day, tomorrow will be better." But her anger is short-lived; the following day is better—just as Mr. Slinger promised. In *Lilly's Big Day*, when she discovers Mr. Slinger is planning to marry, Lilly is miffed that she is not in the wedding party. How she makes it into the wedding party provides insight into the complicated mind of a favorite picture book character.

Some young children will recognize Lilly from other books by Kevin Henkes. She is the imaginative, independent, creative, and often lovable new kid on the block in *Chester's Way*. Readers admire her determination to join the two mice, Chester and Wilson, who are inseparable. At first, they ignore her, but Lilly proves difficult to ignore for long. She loves wearing disguises and she saves the day for Chester and Wilson when she scares bullies away from their bikes with her spooky disguise. Where it once was Chester and Wilson, now it is Chester, Wilson, and Lilly.

Writing with humor, Henkes reveals his understanding that children this age are entering a period in which they must learn to reconcile their individuality with the demands of the world around them. He lets the mouse "Chrysanthemum," in the book by the same name, experience her first encounter with children who tease her about her name. "You're named after a flower," they taunt. When she discovers that the first name of her beloved music teacher is "Delphinium," Chrysanthemum's dark world turns to sunshine.

Henkes knows how difficult it is for small children to give up their security blankets. *Owen*, the title character in another of his books, insists on taking *Fuzzy*, his yellow blanket, to preschool, much to the dismay of his parents. Only when he and his mother solve the problem of the "yellow blanky" is Owen happy.

New abilities, new friends, and new ideas come up against parental restrictions, and parents often find themselves searching for the ideal mix of firmness and love. Like

LILLY'S BIG DAY
Used with permission of HarperCollins

Lilly, some youngsters in this age group are faced with adjusting to a new sibling (or siblings), which can be a time of great frustration if not handled carefully. In *Julius, the Baby of the World*, Lilly is very articulate about her feelings for her new baby brother. Looking into his crib, she tells him that she hates him, until she overhears a cousin at a family party make a mean remark about her new brother. She immediately defends him then and becomes his staunch supporter. Family, day care, self-concept, and play are all used by Henkes, and others, as rich sources for stories written for preschool children.

Other aspects of development that will help you to understand children of these years are shown in the following figure.

BIOPSYCHOSOCIAL CHARACTERISTICS

BIO	PSYCHO	SOCIAL
Brain connections increase	Conversation appears	Family relations develop
Growth slows slightly	Representational thinking	Siblings become influential
Walking, running, jumping consistently improve	Problem solving behavior	May experience divorce
Learns to throw and catch ball	Vocabulary growth	Spends time in daycare
Plays with expanding network of friends	Basics of grammar	Emerging self-concept
Coordination steadily improves	Use of questions	Social growth improves with play

Figure 8.1

Building the Language Network

Children who are talked to and read to receive enormous environmental stimulation that furthers cognitive development. The language areas of the brain respond, resulting in superior language skills for a child. Children also need a warm, emotionally supportive environment that produces more connections in those parts of the brain responsible for developing emotions. The result is children who are gifted with feelings of security and emotional well-being, which spread throughout all aspects of their lives. Consequently, we can say that continued brain development during the early childhood years parallels cognitive and language accomplishments, thus providing another example of the continued impact of biopsychosocial forces.

Age 2–4 is a time of stupendous sensitivity to verbal stimulation. But children do more than merely listen to stories; they process information—watching, listening, questioning, rehearsing, and acting on it—until it becomes deeply embedded in their memory. In other words, the more children read and are read to, the more they like what they're reading and listening to. Motivation increases, language improves, and cognitive skills progress. We also know that when children turn the full force of their attention to what they are reading and listening to, the more efficient their memory.

Talking, Talking, Talking

Brain development and the influence of the environment produce the "word spurt"— that outburst of words and ideas that sweep through a child's life from 18 months to 3 years. *And it's a world-wide phenomenon!* The sounds, the words, the two- and three-word sentences, and the growth of the vocabulary are stunning achievements that experts are hard-pressed to explain. Think of it this way: with no formal training—in fact, often exposed to seriously flawed language models—children not only learn words, meanings, and syntax, they also learn how to ask questions in a logical, purposeful manner. Karla Kuskin, an award-winning poet, echoes our amazement:

What separates each one of us / from all the beasts and bugs and birds? / Well they have feathers, / fur and wings / But we have words, / and words, / and words

(Kuskin, 2003)

Spin Off
Dialogic Reading: A Shared Reading Strategy

One way to introduce small children to books long before they can actually read them is to read aloud to them, frequently and enthusiastically. When volunteers participate in a Lap Sitter's Story Hour, infants benefit enormously from listening to stories (see Chapter Seven). For preschoolers, listening to adults read aloud introduces them to vocabulary, grammar, and the literary elements that are important for an appreciation of quality literature. Russ Whitehurst, Director of the Institute of Education Science, reminds us that *how* we read to children is "every bit as important as *how often* we read to them" (Arnold, 2005, p. 30). He advocates that adults practice *dialogic reading*—a strategy that stresses the value of shared reading. In dialogic reading adults ask children open-ended questions and then ask them to expand on their answers (Arnold, 2005, p. 31).

Similar to the strategy used for many years by the outstanding teacher Christine Kelly at the James E. Biggs Early Childhood Education Center in Kentucky, dialogic reading has effectively improved the reading ability of many semi-literate families throughout the country (Richards, 2005, p. 13).

From Bandura's theory (see Chapter One) that imitation is a natural skill for children, it's clear that when an adult reads aloud to a child or a class, she becomes a role model. Much of what children learn is determined by the amount and richness of the language they hear from adults. Early readers are usually those children whose parents frequently read to them when they were young (Papalia, Olds, & Feldman, 2003). Yet reading aloud should be not only a time for instruction, but a time for child and adult to share a love of reading in a comfortable, warm environment.

A Time of Pleasure

As adults who read aloud to children, we should sense whether the book we select to read to them is a genuine goodness-of-fit. Alternate choices should be available so that the child can help us make another choice. (Small children readily listen to a favorite book over and over again because of repetition, familiar themes, and security). Also, it may be wise to skim a book before reading it aloud, to make sure it is consistent with what the child is emotionally ready to hear. For example, will the child become upset upon discovering that the dog in Rosemary Wells's picture book edition of *Lassie Come Home* is lost, or that the cat is injured in Lynne Rae Perkins' *Broken Cat?* Perhaps learning that the little boy in Toro Gomi's *I Lost My Dad* is alone in a large Japanese department store will cause the child to be overly concerned.

To ensure that reading aloud is a happy experience for both adult and small child, the book should be chosen by both. Adults should also be patient when the child wants to intermittently stop and talk about the book.

When we join our children in talks about the characters, in musing over what happens next, or in noticing the craft of the author, it is crucial to remember that these conversations are not detours around reading, but are instead the essence of what it means to be thoughtful readers. To read well is to think well (Calkins, 1997, p. 48).

Young children who are emotionally comfortable with the books that have been read to them will glow with familiarity when they enter preschool. To discover that they recognize many of the books on the classroom or library shelves and have already made the acquaintance of *Curious George, Madeline, Babar,* or *Clifford the Big Red Dog,* is to feel comfortable in their new environment, as they see familiar "book" faces in the crowd.

By the time children are about 4 years of age (the end of the period we're discussing), they've acquired the basics of language, which is an astonishing accomplishment. Lois Bloom (1998), a well-known linguist at Columbia University, states that most children have acquired about fifty words by 18 months, but by the time these same children reach first grade they can recognize about 10,000 words. No one knows how many words children acquire each day during this explosion, but estimates range from about six to twelve. You can see, then, why these years present such an unparalleled opportunity to captivate children with the world of books!

Motivating Reluctant Readers

What happens, however, if small children do not enjoy having books read to them? Being too restless or easily distracted can make listening a struggle. To offset this, teachers, librarians, parents, and other interested adults must select books with special care, and then draw children into the book by asking simple questions or by commenting on particularly attractive illustrations that will motivate reluctant children to listen attentively. Teachers and librarians often skillfully introduce children to books by showing them an item that is featured in the book they are about

Culture and Children's Literature

When English Is Not Spoken

In the last few years, the public schools of New York City have enrolled more than 150,000 immigrant children. Imagine the language problems facing these children, their parents, and grandparents (Dacey & Travers, 2009)! What can be done to help? Through TESOL (Teaching English to Speakers of Other Languages, Wong, 2006), teachers are encouraged to use their students' families and communities as resources. Probably the most effective step is to obtain as much information as possible about the cultures of immigrant children so that they can be understood at the intermediate or significant level. (See Chapter 6 p. 131.) In this way, adults who work with immigrant children can better appreciate their needs, their attitudes, and the values underlying their behaviors. Parents, grandparents, and other interested adults should also be encouraged to share books with these children, even though they may not read or write English.

Wordless books that portray touching themes are excellent bridges for non-English speaking children to share with their families. Books such as those by Pat Hutchins (*Changes, Changes*), Mitsumasa Anno (*Anno's Journey*), Molly Bang (*The Grey Lady and The Strawberry Snatcher*), and Quentin Blake (*Clown*) are very helpful. By taking turns explaining to each other what is happening on each page, adult and child can enjoy a rewarding learning experience together.

Books by such well-known authors and illustrators as William Steig and Tomie dePaola are also available in other languages. Rebecca Emberley's *My Numbers/ Mis Numeros* (see Chapter Seven) uses everyday objects in bright, vivid colors to encourage children to match words in English with those of another language. Teachers, librarians, and interested adults are constantly exploring innovative ways to encourage and motivate *all* children to be readers.

CD's, audio, and videotapes of books for English language learners are available at public libraries. Examples of videotapes that are expertly produced and appeal to small children are *There Was an Old Lady Who Swallowed a Fly* (Simms Taback), *How Do Dinosaurs Say Good Night?* (Jane Yolen), and *Merry Christmas, Space Case* (James Marshall). The American Library Association annually selects videos, recordings, and software for all ages based on the recommendations of librarians and educators from across the country, who consider their originality, creativity, and suitability.

Recordings of books such as *The Frogs Wore Red Suspenders* (Jack Prelutsky), *Good Night Gorilla* (Peggy Rathmann), and *Martin's Big Words* (Doreen Rappaport) are helpful as adults and young children follow the words of the book together. In each recording, the narrator speaks slowly and distinctly so that the listener can follow easily.

to read, such as a small wind-up mouse to introduce Leo Lionni's *Alexander and the Wind-up Mouse,* or a red painted stone for William Steig's *Sylvester and the Magic Pebble.* Before reading Van Allsburg's *The Polar Express,* one educator arranged the chairs like a train and issued tickets to each of the participants as they went "all aboard." Kathleen Odean (*Book,* March, 2003) recommends that adults first try a humorous book to capture the attention of their young readers.

Reading picture books to children that are short, humorous, and fast moving, and that feature characters to whom they can relate, appeals to small children. Picture books by such authors as Bill Peet (*The Whingdingdilly*), Cynthia Rylant (*The Relatives Came*), James Marshall (*George and Martha*), William Steig (*Doctor De Soto*), Patricia Polacco (*Chicken Sunday*), and David Shannon (*No David!*) are an enjoyable experience for adults and children. Children continue to benefit cognitively from being read to, even after they are able to read for themselves.

In this chapter we continue to introduce books by genres that are developmentally suitable for the children about whom we are writing. It is important to reiterate, however, that children should not be confined to reading only the books we recommend. You, the one who understands the child biopsychosocially, should select what you think are the best books for that child. Since the genre of the picture book—wordless, alphabet, counting, concept, and story—continues to be the most relevant category for these years, we will consider the characteristics of other genres that appear in this category, such as *traditional literature, modern fantasy, poetry and drama,* and *informational books.*

Picture Books

Considering children's short attention span at this age, it is not surprising that books for them are usually brief and simple. Some books have no words at all. Barbara Lehman's Caldecott Honor book *The Red Book* is an example. Yet children can relate to the little boy who finds a book in the snow. Using their cognitive skills, they follow the book across the world to where another boy finds it in the sand. Later, they follow it to a little girl who reads it and dreams of a playmate. As the book continues on its journey, readers see how the book helps two boys become friends, and how it is picked up by another boy on his bike, who carries it to another adventure that readers can only imagine.

Picture books frequently depend on humor, repetition, and characters who are usually members of the family, friends, or pets with whom children play. As children grow, they begin turning the pages of the book themselves as the story is read to them. They often identify objects in their favorite books. As they approach 4 years of age they attempt to read (or pretend to read) some of the words themselves. While listening to Jan Brett's *The Mitten,* for example, it is not unusual for preschool children to identify the animals as they proceed into the mitten, and to react with a resounding "BOOM" when the mitten explodes.

Alphabet Books

Small children love listening to the alphabet and gradually, by listening carefully, begin to learn it letter by letter. They enjoy playing with words because the language explosion is at its peak during these years when they are in the process of analyzing their language. During this time, most children are well along in the process of language acquisition (Dacey & Travers, 2009). The following are several alphabet books that children find particularly appealing.

MATTHEW A.B.C. Peter Catalanotto's setting for his alphabet book is both complicated and engaging. He has created a classroom with twenty-six children, all named Matthew. The teacher not only distinguishes them by alphabetizing their names—Matthew A., Matthew B., and so on—but by their activities. Matthew B., for example, covers himself with bandaids, while Matthew X. swallows a xylophone. It is a book that caregivers and small children easily share together. Children continue to appreciate Catalanotto's sense of humor, as do his adult readers!

CHICKA CHICKA BOOM BOOM. Bill Martin has written an attractive alphabet book that John Archambault illustrated in bright, primary colors, and to which geometrical shapes were added by Lois Ehlert. It cleverly demonstrates what happens when all the letters of the alphabet try to climb a coconut tree and simultaneously fall off. They go "chicka chicka boom boom." Children enthusiastically respond to the rhythm and chant as they become engrossed in the story.

THE DINOSAUR ALPHABET BOOK. Jerry Pallotta has written over eighteen alphabet books about birds, flowers, frogs, and icky bugs. In this story about dinosaurs, readers are asked questions such as "If you were a dinosaur, would you have eaten these vegetables?" or "The Nodosaurus had plating on its back that looked like hundreds of little buttons. Should it have been called a Buttonosaurus?" Arrange time for children to develop their problem-solving skills by answering these questions.

ON MARKET STREET. This Caldecott Honor book by Anita and Arnold Lobel is awash with soft pastels. It's a visual feast. On each page, within a store window, a single letter of the alphabet is elaborately presented—a man is dressed in zippers to represent Z, a woman is dressed in toys, to represent T, and so on. A young boy who looks in all the store windows to see what he will buy is fascinated by the letters and decides to spend all his money on presents for a friend.

THE CENTIPEDE'S 100 SHOES
Copyright 2002 by Tony Ross. Reprinted by permission of Henry Holt and Company.

Counting Books

Children enjoy counting and most children, at the beginning of these years, have grasped the notion of *ordinality* (i.e., three is more than two). The use of verbal labels (e.g., little, big) follows next, and they begin to count. At about 4 years of age, children understand the meaning of *cardinality*, that is, the last number in a counting sequence indicates the number in the set—one, two, three, so there are three spoons. (For an excellent summary of these ideas, see Berk, 2005.) The pleasurable feeling they get from realizing they are doing something adults do gives them a sense of confidence, which is reinforced by listening to the rhythm of counting stories and games. Here are some popular counting books.

CENTIPEDE'S 100 SHOES. Tony Ross's story of a centipede who buys shoes to protect his 100 feet is hilarious. When he decides the shoes are a lot of trouble to take off and put on, and a nuisance to tie, he piles them in his wheelbarrow to give to his friends. Five spiders, four beetles, two woodlice, and a grasshopper are the first beneficiaries of this generosity. The final cartoon-like illustration shows two amazed worms with shoes on their heads, trying to stand upright with shoes on their feet.

ONE LEAF RIDES THE WIND. Celeste Davidson Mannis was inspired to write this story about counting after visiting a Japanese garden. The illustrations by Susan Hartung reflect the garden's gentle tranquility. The narrator, a small Asian child, awakens the reader's imagination as she walks through the garden reciting a haiku (a three-line verse) about each of the ten treasures she sees.

QUIET NIGHT. In Marilyn Singer's story, a night in the country is anything but quiet. A number of animals contribute to the cacophony of sound, beginning with one frog, two owls, three geese, and so on. Drawn by John Manders, the animals suddenly become still when ten sleepy campers tumble on the scene.

OVER IN THE MEADOW. Paul Galdone, who illustrated over 300 books (many of which have become classics), has a talent for touching the feelings of children. One of his enduring books is this counting and rhyming book, with its charming, smiling creatures, whether fish, bees, pigs, or crows. Each number, with its corresponding number of animals, receives four full pages of delightful illustrations, in addition to comical sound effects for each animal.

FISH EYES: A BOOK YOU CAN COUNT ON. Lois Ehlert is the author and illustrator of this exciting counting book. In its deep, cobalt-blue pages, unusually colored fish (many brightly striped to catch the infant's attention) swim and dive. As the reader counts, the child listens and is invited to touch the cutout holes and repeat the simple rhyme.

Concept Books

When you think of all that is going on with children in this group, it's no wonder parents, teachers, and librarians want to seize the moment to develop existing potential. Nerve impulses are racing through brain neurons searching for connections. Words chase each other and form ever-lengthening sentences, as the language explosion sprints ahead. Ideas tumble over themselves as children are exposed to the wonders of their environment. (For an excellent description of these accomplishments, see Rutter & Rutter, 1993.)

PUMPKIN PUMPKIN. A book that asks the young child to watch and be patient is *Pumpkin Pumpkin* by Jeanne Titherington. The little boy Jamie plants a pumpkin seed and watches it grow into a pumpkin. Presumably with help, he scoops it out, carves a pumpkin face, and puts it in the window. Jamie demonstrates that he is capable of undertaking a project and following it to completion.

The following books illustrate how children's literature encourages the steady growth and development of biopsychosocial interactions.

OLIVIA'S OPPOSITES. Since Ian Falconer's first book about Olivia became a Caldecott Honor book, this creative, independent pig has become famous. Most recently, she became an entertainer in *Olivia Forms a Band*—much to the consternation of her parents and young sibling.

Previously, she showed off her "seven accessories" in *Olivia Counts*, and in *Olivia's Opposites* she is daring enough to roar back at a lion to demonstrate *loud* versus *quiet*. Readers have come to expect such behavior from Olivia, who could be a typically independent preschooler. Falconer uses charcoal and gouache on paper to

make strikingly black and white illustrations with a touch of red. In *Olivia Saves the Circus*, she tells her class how she (in her imagination) saved the day when all the performers were sick. The reader sees her as the Tatooed Lady, the Lion Tamer, and in the centerfold, on a flying trapeze.

AS BIG AS YOU. Elaine Greenstein's book introduces children to the concept of comparisons. In a unique manner, she compares children to animals ("You were as waddly as a duck"), or to other objects from nature ("Then you grew as high as the tomato plant / your face was as bright as a sunflower / your fingertips as sweet as raspberries."). Although children may not know *all* the objects being compared, they will find the illustrations of animals perfectly understandable and appealing.

BUILD IT UP AND KNOCK IT DOWN. Since repetition is rarely boring to small children, they will be inclined to actively join two friends in Tom Hunter's book when they are "Sitting down and standing up and sitting down again." Participating physically in these activities will further children's understanding of new concepts and provide exercise for their bodies as well.

OLIVIA FORMS A BAND
Reprinted with the permission of Atheneum Books for Young Readers, an imprint of Simon & Schuster Children's Publishing Division from OLIVIA FORMS A BAND by Ian Falconer. Copyright © 2006 by Ian Falconer.

Picture Story Book

Children this age constantly ask that their favorite stories be read aloud, again and again. Sometimes it is the humor of the situation that tickles them; at other times it is the incongruity. They are beginning to match the storyline with the illustrations and anticipate what is going to happen next.

GOSSIE & GERTIE. Olivier Dunrea's sequel to *Gossie* makes both books an exciting duo for preschoolers to read. *Everywhere that Gossie goes, Gertie goes, too*—most of the time. A brief narrative and constant repetition encourage small children to anticipate the action, which is simple but often unpredictable. The use of white space makes readers focus on the goslings Gossie and Gertie, and their blue and red boots. But other small creatures are also begging to be found within the pages of this easy-to-hold book, and that makes for a good game of hide-and-seek.

LIZETTE'S GREEN SOCK. Catharina Valckx's simple narrative and black-line drawings make the small bird Lizette's quest to find her green sock very important to preschoolers. How she uses her memory in encounters with other small creatures helps her to find what she is looking for.

ALBERT'S IMPOSSIBLE TOOTHACHE. Written by Barbara Williams in 1974, this book emphasizes that no one listens to Albert the turtle, especially his sister and brother, when he complains of a toothache. His sister says he's sick because he does not want to eat his black ants; his brother says he doesn't want to fight Dilworth Dunlap. Only when his grandmother visits and asks him *where* he has the toothache is something done that makes Albert feel better.

SKELETON HICCUPS. Margery Cuyler's humorous story is cleverly illustrated by S. D. Schindler. When children listen to the ghost's suggestions of how the skeleton can be cured of his ailment, they find it very amusing, especially when he suggests that the skeleton drink water while standing upside-down and the water pours out. Children enjoy the fun further when they repeat the *hic, hic, hic* of this rhyming escapade.

THE STRAY DOG. Marc Simont's Caldecott Honor book is charming in its simplicity. Set in the park on a "great day for a picnic," a family adopts a stray dog. The young boy takes off his belt so that the dog can have a collar, and the girl provides her hair ribbon as a leash. When the dog catcher questions them, they demonstrate how quickly the dog responds to being called "Willy." Willy thus becomes a member of the family where he truly belongs.

Traditional Literature

Traditional literature is filled with folk tales and fairy tales that children this age are eager to hear. Although collections like Berlie Doherty's *Fairy Tales* are comprehensive and colorful, small children usually prefer a single tale with uncluttered illustrations.

Fairy Tales

It is interesting to note that small children often prefer the comic-like drawings of characters in fairy tales and other stories, in which witches, ghosts, or other ugly creatures may be threatening to them. Nicholas Tucker (2002, p. 115) remarks that characters often drawn in cartoon shape enable small children to identify with them, and at the same time keep their distance should the story in which they appear look as if it might be spinning out of control. James Marshall, an expert artist, sketched his tales (*Little Red Riding Hood* and *Hansel and Gretel*) in a humorous, light-hearted manner that delights children because the wolf is "funny" and the witch is "funny, too."

Folk Tales

THE GINGERBREAD BOY. Richard Egielski makes *The Gingerbread Boy* a city boy who lives in Manhattan. When he runs away, he jumps out the window of a tenement, then onto a bus, disappears down the subway, and finally shows up in Central Park, where he meets his fate in an encounter with the fox.

THIS IS THE HOUSE THAT JACK BUILT. Simms Taback has added his own verse in honor of Randolph Caldecott to the end of this old (1755), cumulative story. Embellished with collage illustrations that are very funny—even the end papers are decorated with building tools—children find this book extremely attractive.

STONE SOUP: AN OLD TALE. Originally written by Marcia Brown in 1947, this book endures today because of the simplicity of its illustrations and the charm of its story. No one in the French village will feed the three hungry soldiers until the stone soup is prepared and a lesson is learned about sharing. An unusual edition of this story, written and illustrated by Jon J. Muth, is set in Japan. Delicate watercolors depict three Japanese monks arriving in a village and gently persuading the villagers to share with others the little they have in order to make stone soup.

THE THREE LITTLE PIGS. Barry Moser's large, humorous illustrations make the story of the fox devouring two little pigs a lighthearted romp. Readers and listeners cheer for the third pig who is pictured wearing new, furry wolf slippers as he sits down to a supper of wolf stew. Children know he will never be troubled by a wolf again!

HANSEL AND GRETEL. This Caldecott Honor book story is retold by Rika Lesser. Paul O. Zelinsky's illustrations are oil paintings done in the style of eighteenth-century European landscape painters. Although the illustrations are exquisite, small children may not fully comprehend their beauty. Interestingly, it has been translated into braille.

RED RIDING HOOD. James Marshall has retold a friendly version of Little Red Riding Hood, a folktale originally found in Grimm that is comfortable for small children. Trina Schart Hyman's beautiful illustrations make her version a Caldecott Honor book. Michael Emberley's *Ruby*, however, a parody of Little Red Riding Head, is the most humorous and clever of all. *Ruby* takes place in Boston, where Ruby the mouse meets a slimey reptile. Rescued by the Cat, a slick, well-dressed stranger, Ruby calls on the street phone to 34 Beacon St. to warn her grandmother.

EACH PEACH PEAR PLUM. Once children become familiar with many of the characters in folk tales and nursery rhymes, they will enjoy this book by Janet and Allan Ahlberg. Small children delight in finding characters such as *The Three Bears*, *Goldilocks*, and *Jack and Jill* half-hidden in the scenery. Written in 1979, it continues to challenge the cognitive skills of small children.

Fantasy

Selma Fraiberg immortalized the pre-school period as *The Magic Years* (1959), when children begin to believe that their thoughts and actions can bring about wonderful events such as when a firefighter saves others. In Peter Sis's book *Fire Truck*, Matt, the young narrator, is not the firefighter, but the firetruck! As children grow, their interests turn away from real-life conditions. Thus, a story needn't be about a real telephone, but can describe a block of wood used as a telephone. By the ages of 2 1/2 to 3 years, make-believe is changing to include more complex, cognitive schemes. By about 4 years of age, children develop a relatively sophisticated understanding of the role fantasy plays in their reading. Children these ages easily relate to book characters and sometimes, in pretend play, assume roles that further such mental abilities as attention, memory, language, and creativity, among other cognitive skills (Berk, 2005).

MAX. Bob Graham, the author and illustrator of this unusual story, revealed that when writing his earlier books such as *Benny* and *Queenie One of the Family*, he tried to make the ordinary extraordinary. But in *Max* his problem was just the opposite—how to make an extraordinary family seem ordinary. And Max's family is extraordinary. Max was born a superbaby—the son of superheroes Captain Lightening and Madam Thunderbolt—yet he had a problem: he couldn't get his feet off the ground. What finally prompted him to become a superhero makes *Max* a good story to read or to hear.

THE ADVENTURES OF SPARROWBOY. Brian Pinkney's fantasy concerns Henry, a young paperboy who collides with a sparrow. Another superhero like Max, Sparrowboy flys through his neighborhood like his hero Falconman, helping people while having exciting adventures that are pictured in paneled, vividly colored illustrations.

HE SAVES THE DAY. Marsha Hayles relates the backyard adventures of a young boy in simple rhyming text. Illustrated in cartoon-like style by Lynne Cravath, the boy's fantasy play includes saving himself from pirates and wild jungle cats, but seeking help from his mother when he meets a terrible dragon.

Animal Fantasy

Children this age especially relate to the escapades of animals. Whether it's the lowly mouse in Kevin Henkes' stories, the ingenious pig in Ian Falconer's books, or the big, lovable bear in Martin Waddell's stories, animals are considered human and children do not question their ability to talk or act like humans.

FAMOUS BEARS & FRIENDS. Janet Wyman Coleman has written an attractive animal-fantasy anthology. She includes poems by such writers as Judith Viorst and Shel Silverstein, Don Freeman's *Corduroy*, excerpts from A. A. Milne's *Winnie the Pooh*, and Michael Bond's *A Bear Called Paddington*, as well as *The Teddy Bear's Picnic* (complete with music).

BLACKBOARD BEAR. Fortunately reissued in 2000, Martha Alexander's book continues to hold the interest of children whose vivid imaginations permit them to have make-believe playmates. Blackboard Bear becomes the best friend of a little boy who longs to play with the older children

YOU AND ME, LITTLE BEAR, LET'S GO HOME, LITTLE BEAR, CAN'T YOU SLEEP, LITTLE BEAR? These tales by Martha Waddell are all endearing and highly recommended as bedtime stories. *Can't You Sleep, Little Bear* has been translated into Vietnamese, Chinese, and Portuguese so that children from many countries throughout the world can listen to this classic, quiet, comforting story.

THE BOY WHO THOUGHT HE WAS A TEDDY BEAR. Jeanne Willis tells a bear story with an unusual twist. It is challenging to preschoolers and must be seriously considered before read aloud. It may be scary for some to listen to because it tells about a baby who was found by fairies in the woods. They take him to the Three Bears, who are having a picnic. The bears offer him their food, put him to sleep in a cupboard, cuddle him, and show him how to sit on a shelf

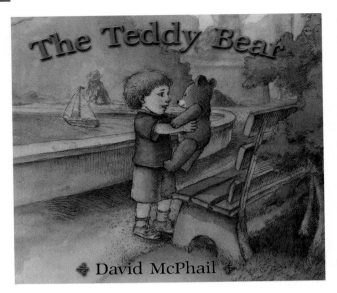

David McPhail

where he unsuccessfully tries to act like a stuffed animal, until he is rescued by his caregiver.

THE TEDDY BEAR. David McPhail's *The Teddy Bear* is a sensitive tale about a child who loses his favorite teddy bear, until he discovers it sitting on a park bench beside an elderly, homeless man who found it in a dumpster. Although delighted to find the bear, he is faced with the dilemma of whether or not to tell the man that the bear belongs to him.

THE TEDDY BEAR
Copyright 2002 by David McPhail. Reprinted by permission of Henry Holt and Company.

Spotlight On

David McPhail (1940–)
Author and Illustrator

Even as a young boy, David McPhail loved to draw. "I always drew. I did it for fun—drawing was always there—waiting in the background." His parents, however, did not consider drawing a worthwhile occupation. Being poor, they thought he should be working. He admits that he wasn't aware of how poor he was. After graduating from high school, he worked in a factory by day and played the guitar in clubs at night. Fortunately, he won a scholarship to Vesper George School of Art, but remained there only a year. He tried other jobs, such as partnering with his brother to make and sell greeting cards, but resuming his art education remained his goal. McPhail always wanted to illustrate books for children (Maurice Sendak was his favorite illustrator). When he was asked what specific traits about children motivated him, he was quick to reply that it was enthusiasm and curiosity (McPhail, 2003).

Enrolling in the School of the Boston Museum of Fine Arts, he selected graphics as his field of concentration, because at that time in Boston, illustration was not considered "art." While he was a senior, he married and had a child, which made it necessary for him to work to support his family. Taking a job in a warehouse delivering books to the Boston Public Library, he rediscovered his love of reading, particularly children's books. Ultimately, he fulfilled his

Rick Friedman/Harcourt, Inc.

longtime ambition: to write and illustrate a trade book.

Since 1971, McPhail has either written *and* illustrated, or just illustrated, hundreds of children's books. Drawing animals, especially bears, is his specialty. In 1975 *The Bear's Bicycle* was selected as *New York Times* Most Outstanding Book and an Honor book, by both the *Horn Book* and the Caldecott award committees. *The Bear's Toothache* is also popular, along with *Henry Bear's Park*. McPhail's original *Henry Bear's Park* (1976), with illustrations in crow-quill pen and ink, has now been redone in bright watercolors (which some would consider a questionable improvement).

McPhail finds animal characters easy to deal with. In fact, friends and critics have commented that his animals look human. They certainly act human. Henry Bear, the main character in *Henry Bear's Park*, takes very good care of the park his father bought before he took off in a balloon. Only when he relinquishes hope that his father will return does he neglect the beautiful park. (An aerial view of it appears on the end papers.) When he meets Alfred Pine, however, this impressive pig explains that Henry's father is where he wants to be and that "he went where he is." Hearing this, Henry Bear becomes hopeful again.

Like Henry's father, David McPhail is also where he wants to be: illustrating children's books.

Poetry and Drama

To combine poetry with acting is fun for children at this age. For example, acting out Nancy Willard's story of The *Mouse, the Cat, and Grandmother's Hat* can be easily done. Children also love to improvise the actions of Jack Prelutsky's imaginative animals. And when they respond to the noise of Old Mac-Donald's Woodshop, story time is guaranteed to be an hour of controlled chaos.

THE MOUSE, THE CAT, AND GRANDMOTHER'S HAT. Nancy Willard has created a humorous and brightly illustrated cumulative story in rhyme that takes place at a birthday party. This is the mouse (originally in Grandmother's Hat) that tickled the young narrator's shoe as she "carried the cake that jiggled and bounced when the hungry cat gave a yowl and pounced"—and so the story continues until its surprising conclusion.

OLD MACDONALD HAD A WOODSHOP. Here is a humorous twist on a familiar song as interpreted by Lisa Shulman and illustrated by Ashley Wolff. Ms. Old MacDonald has a woodshop behind the barn and involves her corps of animal helpers in a woodshop project. The sound of tools resonates in the workshop, as Ms. Old MacDonald, sheepishly wearing a flowered carpenter's apron and rimless granny glasses, takes charge. Illustrations of the various tools referred to in the story are explained on the end pages.

BATS AT THE BEACH. Brian Lies has written and illustrated, in dark grey tones, a picture rhyming book that lights up the activities of what bats do at the beach at night: *sailing to terrific heights / taking turns at being kites / Little bats dig their sand caves deep / As old bats lie in the moon, asleep.* It is a winning combination of moonlight, firelight, and bats.

OUT AND ABOUT. Shirley Hughes is a prolific writer, illustrator, and poet. Well-known for her stories *All About Alfie*, she also has written this "Nursery Collection" of rhymes that takes a little girl and her baby brother through a year, in which they experience simple pleasures like *wind, sunshine at bedtime,* the *seaside,* and *squirting rainbows*. These poems are small pleasures for small children, skillfully illustrated by an author who has received international recognition for her contributions to children's literature.

CENTRAL PARK SERENADE. Laura Godwin and Barry Root have combined their extraordinary talents to create an exquisite picture book of poetry about a small child's day in New York's Central Park. The book opens in the apartment where the little boy lives, and readers immediately see the sail boat he will later take to the Park. As they turn the pages, readers follow his journey and repeat Godwin's couplets:

And the pigeons coo And the big dogs bark
And the noises echo through the park.

The boy skips from the zoo to the ball field and then to the pond; as the sun sets, he returns home, places his boat beside his bedside lamp, and remembers his perfect day.

Informational Books

During these preschool years, children's ability to pay attention changes dramatically; by the end of the period they can focus much more efficiently (Santrock, 2007). At this age they are filled with wonder as they begin to look at the world around them. In the sky they may see a plane; on the ground they discover an ant, or a worm, or a caterpillar. In the tree are birds they may be hearing for the very first time. Being with them challenges caregivers to pay close attention to their questions and to offer appropriate books that help them find simple but accurate answers.

WHAT DO WHEELS DO ALL DAY? April Jones Prince and Giles La Roche have written and illustrated a book that preschoolers, who are fascinated by wheels that move, will be reluctant to put down. Wheel collages of all sizes occupy entire pages. The text, which is written in rhyme, adds to the young child's delight.

IS YOUR MAMA A LLAMA? In a most appealing way, Deborah Guarino, supported by the illustrations of Steven Kellogg, answers the questions a gentle, long-eye-lashed llama asks his friends. Written in rhyme, the llama approaches the bat, the kangaroo, the swan, the cow, and the seal to find out just what kind of animal his mother really is. As he does so, little children who are listening discover the characteristics of these baby animals and what makes them different from each other.

Is your mama a llama?
I asked my friend, Dave.
No, she is not, Is the answer Dave gave.
She hangs by her feet
And she lives in a cave
I do not believe that's
How llamas behave—
Oh, I said. You are
Right about that.
I think that your mother
Sounds more like [and the child excitedly turns the page]
A bat.

I LOVE PLANES! Philemon Sturgis illustrates various planes with uncluttered pictures and simple explanations. Bright, colorful blimps, biplanes, gliders, dive bombers, helicopters and others fill the pages, while on the end pages the author provides brief definitions.

I LOVE GUINEA PIGS. Children who are thinking about having a pet for the first time are bound to be fascinated by Dick King-Smith's conversational tone, as he explains where guinea pigs come from, the sounds they make, and how to care for them. This is a book for children to keep and reread when they are old enough to personally assume an animal's care.

FIRE FIGHTERS. This book, written and illustrated by Norma Simon, tells children everything they would like to know about fire vehicles, equipment, and the procedures used to fight fires. The illustrations are bright and fully colored.

WAITING FOR WINGS. Lois Ehlert's book about the butterfly is deceptively comprehensive. She begins with half pages of leafy illustrations before the butterfly emerges from the greenery. She then identifies different butterflies by their color, such as the Tiger Swallowtail, the Painted Lady, the Buckeye, and the Monarch. It is amazing how much significant information is contained in this short book, such as what the butterfly is, how it begins life, what it eats, and the flowers that contribute to its nourishment. It even discusses how to grow a butterfly garden.

RED LEAF, YELLOW LEAF. Lois Ehlert's autumn-colored illustrations help children understand how a tree grows from a seedling into a shelter for many kinds of birds. As the young narrator explains how his father planted a maple tree so that he could watch what happens to it through the seasons, children become more aware of the changing year.

Spin Off

The Teddy Bear's Picnic—A Party

What better way is there to become acquainted with preschool children than to have a party for them—a special party called *The Teddy Bear's Picnic*. Invited guests could include parents and teddy bears. Entertainment for the party could include the following.

- Children can sing *The Teddy Bear's Picnic*, using the music found in Janet Coleman's book, *Famous Bears & Friends*.

- Stories about bears (e.g. David McPhail's *Henry Bear's Park*) could be read aloud.

- Books could be displayed that children have made individually or in small groups. These will reflect their newly developed talent for drawing and can be filled with colorful impressions of stories you have read to them during previous visits. Before assembling the children's books:

Carefully examine each illustration.

Find out what each one represents (hopefully by holding it right side up!).

Write a descriptive sentence below each illustration.

Staple the pages together and use an original, laminated (if possible), hand-drawn cover for each book. After displaying the books, suggest they be taken home.

- Children may wish to discuss what information they have found out (researched) about bears, such as where they live, what they like to eat, and what hibernation means.

- Children may want to present a short skit or a puppet show based on a favorite bear story, such as *Goldilocks and the Three Bears* or *the Bear's Toothache*.

- For their concluding performance, preschoolers could present the poem about bears by Zhenya Gay called *In The Summer We Eat* (Prelutsky, 1986, p. 58).

In the summer we eat	(children make munching sounds)
In the winter we don't	(children stop)
In the summer we'll play	(children pretend to play)
In the winter we won't	(children stop).
All winter we sleep, each curled in a ball	(children lie quietly on the floor and pretend to sleep)
As soon as the snowflakes start to fall	(paper snowflakes fill the air)
But in spring we each come out of our den	(children awaken, stretch, and crawl on floor)
And start to eat all over again	(munching sounds, again)

- If refreshments are served, children may like to drink juice and eat something simple like teddy bear crackers, from tablecloths spread out on the floor.

Chapter Checklist

Read the following items carefully. If you have difficulty responding to any of them, return to the chapter and review the material.

After reading this chapter, you can

1. Describe the developmental features most frequently reflected in the children's literature of these years.

2. Demonstrate how children's art work carries over to their love of the illustrations in their stories.

3. Explain how the peak years of the language explosion can be enhanced by children's literature.

4. Analyze the ways in which reading aloud benefits children.

5. Specify how the literature of these years contributes to the personality development of children.

6. Evaluate the use of illustrations in light of children's attraction to certain developmentally appropriate features of the art.

7. Identify the features of books and stories for these years that exercise a fascination for children.

8. Discuss the role traditional literature plays in the emotional development of children.

9. Specify how the features of fantasy aid the psychosocial development of children.

10. Explain the appeal of combining poetry with acting for children.

Children's Bibliography

Ahlberg, Allan. (2003). *A Bit More Bert*. New York: Farrar.

Ahlberg, Janet, & Ahlberg, Allan. (1979). *Each Peach Pear Plum*. New York: Viking.

Alexander, Martha. (1969, 2000). *Blackboard Bear*. Cambridge, MA: Candlewick.

Allard, Harry, (1977). *Miss Nelson Is Missing*. Boston: Houghton Mifflin.

Anno, Mitsumasa. (1978). *Anno's Journey*. New York: Philomel.

Averill, Esther. (1973) *Jenny and the Cat Club*. New York: Harper and Row.

Bang, Molly. (1980). *The Grey Lady and the Strawberry Snatcher*. New York: Four Winds.

Baum, L. Frank. (1900). *The Wonderful Wizard of Oz*. New York: Morrow.

Blake, Quentin. (1996). *Clown*. New York: Henry Holt.

Brett, Jan. (1989). *The Mitten*. Scholastic.

Brown, Margaret Wise. (1947). *Goodnight Moon*. New York: HarperCollins.

Brown, Marcia. (1947). *Stone Soup*. New York: Scribner.

Burton, Virginia Lee. (2003). *Mike Mulligan and More: A Virginia Lee Burton Treasury*. Boston: Houghton Mifflin.

Carle, Eric. (1970). *The Very Hungry Caterpillar*. New York: World.

Catalanotto, Peter. (2002). *Matthew A.B.C.* New York: Atheneum.

Coleman, Janet Wyman. (2002). *Famous Bears & Friends*. New York: Dutton's Children's Books.

Cuyler, Margery. (2003). *Skeleton Hiccups*. New York: McElderry.

Doherty, Berlie. (2000). *Fairy Tales*. Cambridge, MA: Candlewick.

Dunrea, Olivier. (2002). *Gossie*. Boston: Houghton Mifflin.

Dunrea, Olivier. (2002). *Gossie & Gertie*. Boston: Houghton Mifflin.

Egielski, Richard. (1997). *The Gingerbread Boy*. New York: HarperCollins.

Ehlert, Lois. (1989). *Color Zoo*. New York: HarperCollins.

Ehlert, Lois. (1990). *Fish Eyes*. San Diego: Harcourt Brace.

Ehlert, Lois. (1991). *Red Leaf, Yellow Leaf*. San Diego: Harcourt Brace.

Ehlert, Lois. (2001). *Waiting for Wings*. San Diego: Harcourt.

Emberley, Rebecca. (2000). *My Numbers/Mis Numeros*. Boston: Little, Brown.

Emberley, Michael. (1990). *Ruby*. Boston: Little, Brown.

Falconer, Ian. (2001). *Olivia Saves the Circus*. New York: Atheneum.

Falconer, Ian. (2002). *Olivia Counts*. New York: Atheneum.

Falconer, Ian. (2002). *Olivia's Opposites*. New York: Atheneum.

Falconer, Ian. (2006). *Olivia Forms a Band*. New York: Simon & Schuster.

Galdone, Paul. (1986). *Over in the Meadow*. New York: Simon & Schuster.

Godwin, Laura. (2002). *Central Park Serenade*. New York: Cotler/HarperCollins.

Gomi, Taro. (2001). *I Lost My Dad*. New York: Kane Miller.

Graham, Bob. (2000). *Max*. Cambridge, MA: Candlewick.

Greenstein, Elaine. (2002). *As Big as You*. New York: Knopf.

Guarino, Deborah. (1997). *Is Your Mama a Llama?* New York: Scholastic.

Hayles, Marsha. (2002). *He Saves the Day*. New York: Putnam.

Henkes, Kevin. (1989). *Chester's Way*. New York: Puffin.

Henkes, Kevin. (1990). *Julius, the Baby of the World*. New York: Greenwillow.

Henkes, Kevin. (1991). *Chrysanthemum*. New York: Greenwillow.

Henkes, Kevin. (1993). *Owen*. New York: Greenwillow.

Henkes, Kevin. (1996). *Lilly's Purple Plastic Purse*. New York: Greenwillow.

Henkes, Kevin. (2000). *Wemberly Worried*. New York: Greenwillow.

Henkes, Kevin. (2004). *Kitten's First Full Moon*. New York: Greenwillow.

Henkes, Kevin. (2006). *Lilly's Big Day*. New York: Greenwillow.

Hoban, Tana, illus. (1998). *So Many Circles, So Many Squares*. New York: Greenwillow.

Hughes, Shirley. (1988). *Out and About*. New York: Lothrop, Lee, & Shepard.

Hunter, Tom. (2002). *Build It Up and Knock It Down*. New York: Harper.

Hutchins, Pat. (1971). *Changes, Changes*. New York: Macmillan.

Jarrell, Randall. (2003). *The Gingerbread Rabbit*. New York: HarperCollins.

Johnson, Crockett. (1996). *The Adventures of Harold and the Purple Crayon*. New York: HarperCollins.

Johnson, Crockett. (2003). *Harry and the Purple Crayon*.

Johnson, Crockett. (2003). *Ellen's Lion*. New York: Knopf.

Keats, Ezra Jack. (2003). *Keat's Neighborhood: An Ezra Jack Keats Treasury*. New York: Viking.

King-Smith, Dick. (2001). *I Love Guinea Pigs*. Cambridge, MA: Candlewick.

Kraus, Ruth. (1989). *The Carrot Seed*. New York: HarperRow.

Kuskin, Karla. (2003). *Moon, Have You Met My Mother?* New York: HarperCollins.

Lehman, Barbara. (2004). *The Red Book*. Boston: Houghton Mifflin.

Lenski. Lois. (2002). *The Little Family*. New York: Random House.

Lesser, Rika. (1989). *Hansel and Gretel*. New York: Putnam.

Lies, Brina. (2006). *Bats at the Beach*. Boston: Houghton Mifflin.

Lionni, Leo. (1967). *Frederick*. New York: Random House.

Lionni, Leo. (1969). *Alexander and the Wind-up Mouse*. New York: Pantheon.

Lobel, Arnold. Anita Lobel, Illus. (1981) *On Market Street*. New York: Scholastic.

Mannis, Celeste Davidson. (2002). *One Leaf Rides the Wind*. New York: Viking.

Marshall, James. (1972). *George and Martha*. Boston: Houghton Mifflin.

Marshall, James. (1987). *Red Riding Hood*. New York: Dial.

Martin, Bill, & Archambault, John. (2000). *Chicka Chicka Boom Boom*. New York: Aladdin.

McCloskey, Robert. (1941). *Make Way for Ducklings*. New York: Viking Press.

McCully, Emily Arnold. (1984). *Picnic*. New York: Harper & Row.

McPhail, David. (1972). *The Bear's Toothache*. Boston: Little, Brown.

McPhail, David. (2002). *The Teddy Bear*. New York: Henry Holt & Co.

McPhail, David. *The Bear's Bicycle*.

McPhail, David. (2003) *Henry Bear's Park*. New York: Atheneum.

Moser, Barry. (2001). *The Three Little Pigs*. Boston: Little, Brown.

Muth, Jon J. (2003). *Stone Soup*. New York: Scholastic.

Pallotta, Jerry. (1991). *The Dinosaur Alphabet Book*. Watertown, MA: Charlesbridge Publishing.

Peet, Bill. (1970). *The Whingdingdilly*. Boston: Houghton Mifflin.

Perkins, Lynne Rae. (2002). *The Broken Cat*. New York: Greenwillow.

Pinkney, Brian. (1997). *The Adventures of Sparrowboy*. New York: Simon & Schuster.

Polacco, Patricia. (1990). *Babushka's Doll*. New York: Simon & Schuster.

Polacco, Patricia. (1992). *Chicken Sunday*. New York: Philomel.

Perkins, Lynne Rae. (2002). *The Broken Cat*. New York: Greenwillow.

Potter, Beatrix. (1902). *The Tale of Peter Rabbit*. New York: Frederick Warne.

Prelutsky, Jack, (1986). *Read-Aloud Rhymes for the Very Young*. New York: Alfred Knopf.

Prelutsky, Jack. (2002). *The Frogs Wore Red Suspenders*. New York: Greenwillow.

Prince, April Jones. Giles LaRoche, illus. (2006). *What Do Wheels Do All Day?* Boston: Houghton Mifflin.

Ross, Tony. (2003). *Centipede's 100 Shoes*. New York: Henry Holt.

Rey, H. A. (1942). *Curious George*. Boston: Houghton Mifflin.

Rylant, Cynthia. (1985). *The Relatives Came*. New York: Bradbury.

Sendak, Maurice. (1963). *Where the Wild Things Are*. New York: HarperCollins.

Seuss, Dr. (1956). *The Cat in the Hat.* New York: Random House.

Shannon, David. (1998). *No David!* New York: Scholastic.

Shulman, Lisa. (2002). *Old MacDonald Had a Woodshop.* New York: Putnam.

Simon, Norma. (1995). *Fire Fighters.* New York: Simon & Schuster.

Simont, Marc. (2001). *The Stray Dog.* New York: HarperCollins.

Singer, Marilyn. (2002). *Quiet Night.* New York: Clarion.

Sis, Peter. (1999). *Fire Truck.* New York: Greenwillow.

Steig, William. (1969). *Sylvester and the Magic Pebble.* New York: Windmill Books.

Steig, William. (1982). *Doctor De Soto.* New York: Farrar, Straus, & Giroux.

Steig, William. (2003). *Yellow and Pink.* New York: Farrar, Straus, & Giroux.

Stolz, Mary. (1959). *Emmet's Pig.* New York: Harper.

Sturgis, Philemon. (2003). *I Love Planes!* New York: HarperCollins.

Taback, Simms. (2002). *This Is the House that Jack Built.* New York: G. P. Putnam and Sons.

Titherington, Jeanne. (1986). *Pumpkin Pumpkin.* New York: Greenwillow.

Valckx, Catharina. (2005). *Lizette's Green Sock.* New York: Clarion.

Van Allsburg, Chris, (1985). *The Polar Express.* Boston: Houghton Mifflin.

Waddell, Martha. (1993). *Can't You Sleep Little Bear?* London: Magi.

Waber, Bernard. (1965). *Lyle, Lyle Crocodile.* Boston: Houghton Mifflin.

Wells, Rosemary. (1995). *Lassie Come-Home.* New York: Henry Holt.

White, E. B. (1952). *Charlotte's Web.* New York: HarperCollins.

Willard, Nancy. (2002). *The Mouse, the Cat, and Grandmother's Hat.* Boston: Little, Brown.

Willems, Mo. (2004). *The Pigeon Finds a Hot Dog!* New York: Hyperion.

Williams, Barbara. (2003). *Albert's Impossible Toothache.* Cambridge, MA: Candlewick.

Willis, Jeanne. (2003). *The Boy Who Thought He Was a Teddy Bear.* New York: Peachtree Press.

Professional References

Arnold, Renea (2005). "Charming the Next Generation." *School Library Journal.* July, 30–32.

Berk, L. (2005). *Infants, Children and Adolescents.* Boston: Allyn & Bacon.

Bloom, I. (1998). "Language Acquisition In Its Developmental Context." In W. Damon (Series ed.) & D. Kuhn & R. Siegler(Volume Eds.) Handbook of Child Psychology, Vol. 2. Cognition, Perception, and Language. New York: John Wiley.

Calkins, Lucy. (1997). *Raising Lifelong Learners.* Reading, MA: Perseus.

Dacey, John & Travers, John. (2009). *Human Development Across the Lifespan.* New York: McGraw-Hill.

Dawson, G., & Fischer, K. (eds.). (1995). *Human Behavior and the Developing Brain.* New York: Guilford.

Eliot, L. (2000). *What Goes On in There? How the Brain and Mind Develop in the First Five Years of Life.* New York: Bantam.

Fraiberg, Selma. (1959). *The Magic Years.* New York: Charles Scribner's Sons.

Hetherington, E.M., & Parke, R. (2003). *Child Psychology: A Contemporary Viewpoint.* New York: McGraw-Hill.

McPhail, David. (2003). *Something about the Author.* Vol. 47, 150–165. Belmont, CA: Gale Publishing.

Odean, Kathleen. (2003). "The Sound Barrier." *Book.* March/April 36.

Papalia, Diane, Olds, Sally, & Feldman, Ruth. (2006). *A Child's World.* New York: McGraw-Hill.

Richards, Patricia (2005). "Kentucky Embraces a Powerful Strategy for Turning Toddlers into Readers." *School Library Journal.* September, 13.

Rose, S. (2005). *The Future of the Brain.* New York: Oxford.

Rosenberg, Liz. (2003). "The Magic of the Elemental." *The Boston Globe.* April 13.

Rutter, M., & Rutter, M. (1993). *Developing Minds.* New York: Basic Books.

Santrock, John. (2007). *Children.* New York: McGraw-Hill.

Schmitz, Terri. (2003). "Guilty Pleasures." *The Horn Book.* September/October, 569–584.

Schmitz, Terri. (2004). "Recommended Reissues: Magic Casements." *The Horn Book,* March/April, 153–164.

Tucker, Nicholas. (2002). *The Rough Guide to Children's Books.* London: Penguin.

Weissbourd, R. (1996). *The Vulnerable Child.* Reading, MA: Addison Wesley.

Wong, Shelley. (2006). *Dialogic Approaches to TESOL: Where the Ginkgo Grows.* Mahwah, NJ: Erlbaum.

Videos and Recordings

Good Night. Gorilla. By Peggy Rathmann. Cassette or CD. Weston Woods.

How Do Dinosaurs Say Good Night? By Jane Yolen. Cassette or CD. Weston Woods.

Martin's Big Words. By Doreen Rappaport. Cassette or CD. Weston Woods.

Merry Christmas, Space Case. By James Marshall. Weston Woods.

So You Want to Be President? By Judith St. George. Weston Woods.

The Frogs Wore Red Suspenders. By Jack Prelutsky. Cassette. HarperChildren's Audio.

There Was an Old Lady Who Swallowed a Fly. By Simms Tarback. Weston Woods.

Literature for the Early Elementary School Years (Ages 5—7)

In the fantasy Selkie, written and gracefully illustrated by Gillian McClure, the young boy Peter is determined to find out for himself what lies beyond the edge of the sea. Despite his granny's warning, he ventures out to Sea Island at low tide, following the line of sticks the oysterman has placed in the sand. Hearing splashing in a nearby pool, he struggles to release a beautiful seal caught in one of the oysterman's nets. When the seal's skin slips off, Peter discovers the seal has turned into a girl—a Selkie. Meanwhile, the tide had risen and Peter is stranded on the island with the beautiful Selkie, who teaches him to "hear the voices of the fish, to see the patterns of the waves and to know the words of the wind."

Hours later the oysterman returns at low tide, recaptures Selkie in his net, grabs her seal skin, and hauls her back to his cottage by the sea. Peter follows and tries to rescue Selkie, but she cannot swim without her sealskin. After a dramatic search (illustrated in three separate panels), Peter climbs to the rafters of the oysterman's cottage and recovers Selkie's seal skin. Remembering the pattern of the oysterman's sticks, Peter replaces them in the sand and he and Selkie return to Sea Island. Selkie, wearing her sealskin, slides down to the water's edge to swim again with the seals, which leaves Peter sad and lonely. But he returns to his home unafraid, knowing that the patterns of the waves, the voices of the fish, and the words of the wind will lead him safely back to shore.

In this fantasy, Peter represents an early elementary school child, filled with curiosity and determination, who enthusiastically looks forward to experiencing whatever lies ahead. An insatiable curiosity propels him into unknown adventures. He is almost the perfect picture of what Erikson meant by a sense of initiative. Peter has been through the language explosion and can express himself clearly and accurately, sometimes astounding readers with an unexpected polysyllabic word. His growing cognitive ability is seen in his more focused attention, his improved memory, and his sharpened problem-solving skills. Peter is a robust representative of the years we'll discuss in this chapter.

SELKIE
Used by permission of Farrar,
Straus and Giroux, LLC.
Jacket design from SELKIE
by Gillian McClure.
Copyright ©1999 by
Gillian McClure.

Guidelines for Reading Chapter 9

After you read Chapter Nine, you should be able to answer the following questions.

• What are the outstanding characteristics of the 5–7-year-old child that underlie children's literature for this period?

• Does the literature for this period match the developmental characteristics of 5–7-year-olds?

• What are several examples of stories that reflect the cognitive abilities of this age group?

• What themes in the stories for this age group encourage a child's sense of initiative?

• Do you approve of the way that today's children's books are marketed?

• Many of the books for children of this age are picture books. Do they offer sufficient challenge for children?

• Does the literature for this period help to improve a child's sense of self-efficacy? Give examples.

• How do the genres discussed in this chapter contribute to a child's biopsychosocial development? Be specific in your answer.

Characteristics of Children of These Years

A 7-year-old came home tearfully one day from school to question her parents about something they had protected her from since birth: her classmates had told her that there was no Santa Claus. When her mother and father admitted that what she heard was true, she stared at them dolefully while reaching a more disheartening conclusion: "This probably means that there's no Easter Bunny or Tooth Fairy either!"

(Sameroff & Haith, 1996, p. 3)

This is as revealing as it is emotional. Think for a moment about what's happening here: a child's loss of an imaginary but treasured figure is logically extended to other, similar creatures. In Mary Olson's book for early elementary children *Nice Try, Tooth Fairy*, Emma writes a series of letters, asking the Tooth Fairy to please return her tooth; she would like to show it to her grandfather. The Tooth Fairy responds by leaving her a tooth from an elephant, a skunk, and other animals, all of which Emma rejects. The humor develops when the Tooth Fairy turns the house upside down while looking for the tooth! This book is a big hit with children from 5 to 7, for whom losing a tooth is a major topic of conversation.

Developmental psychologists refer to this change in thinking as *the 5 to 7 shift*, in which children's thinking after age 7 differs from their thinking before age 5 (Sameroff & Haith, 1996). After all, a first-grader's thinking is *quite* different from a preschooler's, a difference that is reflected in the types of stories they enjoy. Children's attitudes, interests, attention span, and cognitive abilities all combine to produce multiple benefits from the stories you carefully select for them. Imagine how excited children of these years are when they realize they have the ability to *read* an alphabet book that they previously had only been able to listen to. What developmental changes explain these behaviors?

Changes in Thinking, Changes in Reading

According to Piaget's theory, children ages 5–7 are at the upper level of their preoperational period. During the years 2 to 4, which Piaget called the *symbolic function substage*, children can mentally represent an object not present. During the years 5 to 7, they move to the *intuitive thought stage*, in which they exhibit basic reasoning and seek answers to all sorts of questions. It's a marvelous time to capitalize on this tendency and to help them with their thinking skills by encouraging them to ask themselves questions about the stories they are reading. For example:

- What is theme of this story?
- What does this material remind me of?
- How can I put this into my own words?
- What is a good example of this that I'm familiar with?
- How does this apply to me?

Questions such as these go a long way toward helping children build meaning and further their brain development.

When children were preschoolers, they intently listened to simple, rhythmical books such as *Chicka Chicka Boom Boom* (Martin, 1989). Since writing in English is based on the alphabetical principle, it is important that they now try to sound out each letter and match them to the word. Being able to identify and sound out letters, they are now ready for books like the *Alphaboat*, written and illustrated by Michael Chesworth. This rhythmic tale challenges them to envision the entire alphabet through outrageous visual and verbal puns as the crew—The Alpha-crew—crosses the sea in search of hidden treasure.

To the deck comes Captain C,
And at his side old Admiral T.
The Alpha-crew has come to B.
And where is the remaining crew?
Ah, here they come now—right on Q.
But first, before we sail to sea,
We have to raise our N R G.

Children also begin to think about cause-and-effect when they read books such as *Tomorrow's Alphabet* by George Shannon. A child is first drawn to the picture on the left page, in order to find out what tomorrow's object will be on the right page. For example, on the left-hand page may appear a large watercolor of "A is for seed," while on the right-hand page is "tomorrow's Apple." The positioning of the pictures suggests to the child that it might be fun to play a guessing game, by placing his hand over the right-hand page as he reads the words on the opposite page.

Challenging Emotional and Social Issues

The 5- to 7-year span is a remarkable period. Not only are children experiencing the cognitive changes just mentioned, they are also facing challenging social issues. For example, relationships in the home may involve a divorce and the upset of familial arrangements, at the very time children are beginning their formal education, which can introduce considerable stress into their lives. Michael Willhoite's controversial *Daddy's Roommate*, a gay-themed picture book, and Leslea Newman's *Heather Has Two Mommies*, although sometimes criticized by school and public officials, provide a sense of security for children who identify with these situations. Paula Danziger's *Amber Brown Is Not a Crayon* details the personal life of an irrepressible third-grader whose parents have recently divorced. Many children experience traumatic, stressful events that can have a serious impact on their lives. And as we (teachers, librarians, psychologists) have come to realize, emotional development is closely tied to social competence (Saarni et al., 2006).

CHILDREN: THEIR FEARS AND ANXIETIES, AND STORIES THAT HELP   Children growing up in a modern society learn to fear many things—from a fear of strangers as an infant (*stranger anxiety*), to a fear associated with school (*school phobia*), to a fear of failed achievement as an adolescent. Children travel an emotional path littered with increasingly sophisticated fears. When they realize that other children share many of their anxieties, through the reassurance of trusted adults and characters they come to identify with in the stories they love, they learn to cope with the nightmares that can affect their relationships, haunt their nights, and threaten their emotional security. School entrance is a good example of children's fears and anxieties.

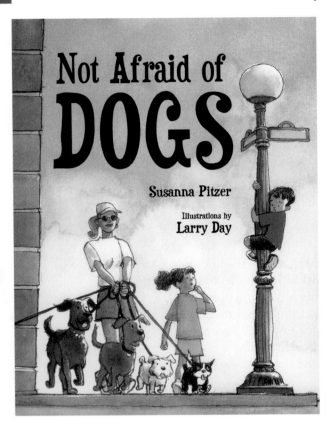

NOT AFRAID OF DOGS
Reprinted by permission of Walker & Co.

ENTERING SCHOOL When children enter school and measure their sense of self against others, they may be challenged by something as simple as being able to tie their shoes. An example of an author who understands a situation like this is Alison McGhee, who wrote *Count Down to Kindergarten*. Another cause for alarm in children is the surprise appearance of a substitute teacher. Harry Allard covers this theme when he introduces the horrible Miss Viola Swamp to first-graders in *Miss Nelson Is Missing*— amusingly reinforced by the comical drawings of James Marshall. Fear and misconceptions can grip a child entering a new school. In *First Day in Grapes* (L. King Perez), Chico, a third-grader, begins his first day in a new school in California with much trepidation. He has moved there with his parents for the grape-picking season. But he manages to stand up against two fourth-grade bullies and make a friend.

Selecting books that help ease a child's worries requires a knowledge of children and an understanding of their concerns. A good beginning is to remember that psychologists typically distinguish fear from reality. Fear refers to a frightening feeling toward a real threat or danger, while anxiety refers to a frightening feeling toward something unknown (Dacey & Fiore, 2000). These emotional reactions may have a specific target (e.g., the bully in school) or may be relatively unfocused, as in free-floating anxiety (Ohman, 2000).

Developmental psychologist Jerome Kagan (1994, 2005), using children's reactions to unfamiliar objects, events, and people, identifies two types of children: the *inhibited* and the *uninhibited*. Children who are shy or timid when confronted with the unknown are the inhibited; children who remain undaunted under the same circumstances are the uninhibited. These distinctions should help you to select stories that will appeal to each type of child. (See Table 9.1.)

Not all children, of course, react in the same manner to challenging stimuli. But it is the rare child who escapes all frightening encounters during these early years.

DEATH: FRIGHTENING FACTS, SOOTHING STORIES Many children during the years 5–7 come in contact with death: the death of parents, grandparents, a pet, or someone close to them. In Judith Viorst's *The Tenth Good Thing about Barney*, for example, the young narrator mourns the death of his cat, Barney. When his mother asks him to remember ten good things about Barney, he recalls only nine—until the day when he plants some seeds with his dad, who explains that now that Barney has been placed in the ground, he will help the seeds to grow. "A pretty nice job for a cat," he comments to his son, who now knows a tenth good thing about Barney.

Books like *The Tenth Good Thing about Barney* that discuss death in a developmentally appropriate manner help children of these years deal with their concerns. As with all aspects of their cognitive development, however, children only gradually develop the concept of what death means. In *Each Little Bird that Sings*, Deborah Wiles writes about 10-year-old Comfort Snowberger, who

Table 9.1 EXAMPLES FROM

AGE	FEAR/ANXIETY	CHILDREN'S LITERATURE
9 months	Stranger anxiety	Milord, *Love That Baby!*
15 months	Separation anxiety	Jolley, *I'll See You in the Morning*
3 years	The unknown	Bogan, *Goodnight, Lulu*
4 years	Distorted human figures (TV, movies)	Willems, *Leonardo, the Terrible Monster* Mayer, *There Are Monsters Everywhere*
5 years	School phobia, darkness	Davis, *Kindergarten Rocks* Ormerod, *When an Elephant Comes to School*
6 years	Threats, anticipation of harm, rejection	Gorbachev, *When Someone Is Afraid.* Pitzer, *Not Afraid of Dogs*
7 years	Realistic reactions (war stories, shootings, violence)	Woodson, *Show Way*

(Table based on data from Kagan, 1994, 2005; Dacey & Fiore, 2000; Ohman, 2000; Berk, 2005; Saarni et al., 2006.)

is surrounded by death (since her family owns a funeral home) and has attended 247 funerals.

As children develop, they face death in different ways. In *Michael Rosen's Sad Book*, for example, the author, in response to the death of his teenage son, offers adolescents simple but effective ways to deal with death. He encourages them to find joy in memories and to look forward to the good times that lie ahead. Katherine Paterson, in her classic, award-winning *Bridge to Terabithia*, treats the deepening friendship of Jesse the farm boy with the city-wise girl Leslie, and then deals with Leslie's sudden death in tragic detail. Nikki Grimes, in *What Is Goodbye?*, poetically expresses the grief of two children whose brother is terminally ill. Reynolds and others, in the essay "Anticipatory Grief and Bereavement" in the *Handbook of Pediatric Psychology*, state that to fully grasp the meaning of death, children must grasp the essence of the following components of the death concept (1995, p. 143).

1. IRREVERSIBILITY, which conveys the conclusion that death is final and irrevocable

2. UNIVERSALITY, which means that all living things die, whether human, animal, or plant

3. NONFUNCTIONALITY, which testifies to the realization that all living functions—thinking, feeling, and sensing—cease

4. CAUSALITY, which refers to the comprehension of the actual causes of death: disease, accidents, and so on

These interrelated elements develop in individual children depending on their cognitive development and level of maturity. In their early years, probably by the age of 3, children have some familiarity with the meaning of death, even if it entails the idea of "going away" or a "long sleep." Between the ages of 5 and 7, children typically acquire a truer but still limited meaning of these concepts.

Teachers and librarians, while recognizing the cognitive limitations in the development of the death concept, should not hesitate to educate children about death by reading or suggesting books that are developmentally appropriate for them. It is easy to understand the caution that guides authors and illustrators of stories for children of this age. Although cognitive abilities are steadily improving, limitations such as egocentrism are still active and could cause children to think that they are the cause.

INITIATIVE   These are the years of Erikson's stages of initiative versus guilt and of industry versus inferiority. If children are encouraged to *develop* as well as *control* their newfound abilities, they acquire feelings of competence and independence that further development. As Erikson noted, parental control during these years must be firmly reassuring in order to protect children from shame and doubt. Teachers and librarians can also offer support for these needs.

When David Shannon's incorrigible David, in the book *No, David!*, finds it easy to do the wrong thing just to satisfy his curiosity, his mother and teacher continuously say, "No, David." Yet they reassure him that they still love him. In *David Gets in Trouble*, David is a little older and finds more ways to express his individuality. But at the end of the day, after receiving much chastisement, his mother reassures him that she loves him and his teacher forgives him. Love and forgiveness enable children like David to move on and use their growing sense of initiative in a manner that frees them from excessive guilt.

Although we have mentioned a few of the developmental milestones that are natural sources of stories for these children, other aspects of their development include the following:

BIOPSYCHOSOCIAL CHARACTERISTICS

BIO	PSYCHO	SOCIAL
Children become thinner	Memory steadily improves	Adjusts to rules
Bodily strength and coordination increase	Attention improves	Gender role apparent
First permanent teeth	Formal education begins	More sophisticated self-concept
Motor skills improve	Reading is a major concern	Television becomes a major force
Brain lateralization becomes more obvious	Brain connections multiply	Relationships influence development
	Improved symbolic activity	
	The 5 to 7 shift	
	Egocentrism still an issue	
	Basics of language in place	

This is the time when teachers and librarians marvel at the children in their care, with their heads deep into books, reading independently for the first time and completely oblivious to the world around them. Although they want to read to *you*, they still enjoy it when you read aloud to them.

Spotlight On
Dr. Seuss

Children of these years enjoy Dr. Seuss's stories for beginners. With the publication of *The Cat in the Hat*, Dr. Seuss (Theodore "Ted" Geisel) realized his goal of identifying appealing subjects that would cause young readers to avidly turn the pages (Cohen, 2004). These were the first beginning-to-read books, which revolutionized the reading world of children. Children became more confident in their reading ability and delighted at the humor and exaggerated situations of the Dr. Seuss books. While reading books such as *One Fish, Two Fish, Red Fish, Blue Fish*, they are happily

AP Photo

drawn into answering the many questions the author poses to them in the text: "Did you ever fly a kite in bed? Did you ever walk with ten cats on your head?" In *The Cat in the Hat*, when the mother asks the children what they have been doing while she was gone, young readers, perched on the horns of a dilemma, ask themselves:

Should we tell her about it?

Now, what SHOULD we do?

Well. . .

What would YOU do

If your mother asked YOU?

It's a question that often leads to a discussion of right and wrong.

Even preschoolers are enthusiastic about the message in Dr. Seuss's *Great Day for Up*. The buoyancy of Quentin Blake's illustrations excites everyone in the world to be *up*.

Except for me.

Please go away.

No UP.

I'm sleeping in today.

College students may still remember trying to get their tongues around the twisters in *Fox in Socks*.

Who sews crow's clothes? / Sue sews crow's clothes.

Slow Joe Crow / sews whose clothes? / Sue's clothes.

In his beginning-to-read books, Dr. Seuss treats children as thinking individuals. He challenges their imagination and their growing cognitive abilities. It's no surprise, then, that Dr. Seuss seriously discussed issues in his story books that often advanced his opinions. In *The Butter Battle Book*, for example, he has been criticized for over-simplifying the issue of warfare. And the *Lorax* has been controversial because of its emphasis on saving the environment at the expense of the loggers.

Although books such as these may contain a particular message, or critics may say that the writing is didactic, who can criticize Horton in *Horton Hatches the Egg*, for sitting on a bird's nest for an AWOL mother, since he is an elephant who is "one hundred per cent" faithful. *Thidwick the Big-Hearted Moose, And to Think That I Saw It on Mulberry Street*, and the more than forty other books (including *How the Grinch Stole Christmas*) that Dr. Seuss wrote during his lifetime are sheer fantasy, read by children throughout the world. When Dr. Seuss died in 1991, he was considered a national treasure and is still perhaps the most popular children's author in the United States. After his death, the citizens of Springfield, Massachusetts, his birthplace, honored him in a unique way. They filled a park in the center of the city with sculptures of his famous characters, so that all who come to visit can reminisce about Dr. Seuss and what his books have meant to them.

A year after his death, Dr. Seuss's widow brought the unpublished manuscript *My Many Colored Days* (1996) to the attention of his editor. Steve Johnson and Lou Fancher, a prize-winning pair of artists, seized upon the idea of illustrating it as an unusual opportunity to "create something that is at once both childlike and sophisticated." As a result, they created illustrations that perfectly complemented the text and revealed much about Dr. Seuss himself. "On yellow days, he is a busy, buzzy bee; on brown days, he feels slow and low, and some days are so mixed up he doesn't know who or what he is. *But it all turns out all right, you see, And I go back to being me*," readers throughout the world are grateful (Cohen, 2004).

Reading Aloud

As children develop their listening skills, reading aloud becomes even more satisfying since they are now able to recall details of the story from one read-aloud session to the next. Without such understanding, stories would be little more than strings of unrelated words and pictures, passing through a child's head while he or she is thinking about something else (Tucker, 2002, p. 29). As you continue reading aloud books such as Beverly Cleary's *Ramona's World*, Judy Blume's humorous story of Fudge in *Tales of a Fourth Grade Nothing* (and its sequels), and classics like *Mr. Popper's Penguins* (Atwater & Atwater, 1994) note how the complexity of the story matches the developing cognitive maturity of the children.

Adults may choose to vary the types of books they read aloud so that children become acquainted with various genres. If a child, for example, is interested in shells, fish, or rocks, the adult and child should seek out information about these subjects and discuss what they learn. (Jim Arnosky's books such as *Crinkleroot's Nature Almanac* are an excellent resource.) A genre should not be neglected merely because the adult doesn't like it. A short joke, a newspaper clipping, a pertinent magazine article, a journal entry, or a humorous poem can all contribute to the variety of read-aloud materials that interest children of this age.

For reading aloud, Shel Silverstein's poems about Runny Babbit, from the book by the same name, are particularly challenging. *Runny Babbit* was published six years after his death.

Runny Shearns to Lare

Runny got the picken chox
And had to bay in sted.

With sped rots on his belly
And sped rots on his head.
His friends all gave him sticken choup,
Bumgalls and bicorice lends.
And guess what little Runny Babbit
Fave to all his griends!

Alfred Knopf books include the following suggestion on the jackets of their children's literature: "Read to a child. The most important 20 minutes of your day." We agree.

Literature for Beginning Readers

For children, especially those who have been read to consistently since their earliest years, reading independently is an exciting adventure, and an *easy reader* can be their first step into the world of reading. Publishers such as Random House (*Beginner Books*), HarperCollins (*I Can Read Books*), Bantam Doubleday Dell (*Bank Street Ready-to-Read*), and Dial (*Easy-to-Read*) have been successfully publishing hard-cover and soft-cover books for beginning readers for many years. These easy reader books are written with short words and controlled vocabularies. They are carefully written with humorous situations, simple plots, and memorable characters. Many easy readers such as Dr. Seuss's *The Cat in the Hat*, P. D. Eastman's *Are*

You My Mother?, Arnold Lobel's *Frog and Toad Are Friends*, James Marshall's *George and Martha*, and Else Minarik's *A Kiss for Little Bear* are now considered classics.

Easy Readers

As noted above, the authors of easy readers must tell their stories using carefully controlled vocabularies and appropriate sentence structure. Children of these years have acquired the basics of their language and are now using these linguistic tools in their reading. They have learned that certain sounds make words that have meaning, which they can use to form sentences. These are tremendous accomplishments that open up the world of enjoyment and information. Table 9.2 provides examples of the types and meaning of these language accomplishments.

EASY READERS AND THE GENRES   Easy readers introduce children to many of the genres we discussed in Chapter Four. *Traditional literature*, for example, is well represented in this format. One of the most popular books and a perennial favorite is *Bony-Legs* by Joanna Cole (who is also author of *The Magic School Bus* series). Based on the Russian tale of Baba Yaga, it tells the suspenseful story of how young Sasha escapes from a horrible witch who threatens to eat her for supper. Using a magical mirror and comb given to her by the witch's cat and dog, she is able to thwart the witch and send her stamping her feet, pulling her hair, and pinching her nose all the way back to her hut.

Although *animal fantasy* is included in many easy readers, *Little Rat Sets Sail*, written by Monika Bang Campbell and illustrated by Molly Bang, offers the beginning reader more than just a good story. As the little rat prepares for his sea voyage, he is beset with fears that children this age readily understand. An animal fantasy such as *Inspector Hopper* by Doug Cushman relates the adventures of a grasshopper, Inspector Hopper, and his continually hungry assistant McBugg, who solve cases involving the missing lady bug, the disappearing boat, and the new detective. For beginning readers, *mystery stories* are appealing because they, too, are solving the mystery of how to read.

Poetry is a genre children like to read. An entire book may be written in rhyme such as Barbara Brenner's touching and ethereal *Moon Boy*. The easy reader may be a collection of individual poems such as Charlotte Zolotow's

Table 9.2   CHILDREN'S LANGUAGE ACCOMPLISHMENT

ACCOMPLISHMENT	MEANING	EXAMPLE
Phonological development	Putting sounds together to form words	*Bears on Wheels* (Stan and Jan Berenstain)
Syntactic development	Combining words to form sentences	*Are You My Mother?* (P. D. Eastman)
Semantic development	Interpreting the meaning of words	*Oliver Pig and the Best Fort Ever* (Jean Van Leeuwen)
Pragmatic development	Learning how to take part in a conversation	*Henry and Mudge and the Careful Cousin* (Cynthia Rylant)

Seasons: A Book of Poems, which includes poems about childhood experiences that are reflected in the seasons of the year. On the other hand, the rhymes may be as simple as those found in the very easiest of the easy readers, such as Joanna Cole and Stephanie Calmenson's *Bug in a Rug: Reading Fun for Just Beginners* and Dr. Seuss's *Fox in Socks*.

Contemporary fiction plays a significant role in easy readers. The books of author-illustrator Crosby Bonsall have been long time favorites. His *And I Mean It, Stanley* could be analyzed by professionals, but children this age understand that it is the story of a little girl who is determined not to let Stanley (whoever Stanley may be) see what is being made, while continuing to dare Stanley to try. *Take the Lead, George Washington*, by Judith St. George, gives beginning readers who are learning the sequence of time, a small window into American history. Although easy readers contain more fiction than fact, *informational books* such as *Arctic Tundra* by Allan Fowler are included in the extensive *Rookie-Read about Science* Books.

EASY READERS IN SERIES   Fortunately for the beginning reader, easy-to-read books continue to be written and are often serialized by popular, well-known authors such as Cynthia Rylant (the *Mr. Putter* series and the *Henry and Mudge* series), Betsy Byars (*The Golly Sisters Go West* and sequels), and Karla Kuskin (*Something Sleeping in the Hall*). The many *I Can Read Books* written by Peggy Parish, some of them published as early as 1972, are being reissued for a new generation. *Play Ball, Amelia Bedelia* concerns the lovable, literal-minded Amelia Bedelia, who substitutes for the Grizzlies in a sandlot baseball game. How to run home, tag a runner, and take a player out puzzles her, but her biggest problem is how to steal the bases! Such recent easy readers as Megan McDonald's *Beezy and Funnybone* and Ann Dodd Doyle's *Where's Pup?* add to the young child's beginning-to-read adventures.

Transitional Books

Besides offering their beginning readers picture books and easy readers, teachers and librarians often introduce them to transitional books. Kate DiCamillo's *Mercy Watson to the Rescue*, the third in a series that tells the humorous story of a lovable but selfish pig who is obsessed with toast. It is aptly characterized as transitional because it helps children make the transition from reading easy books to reading "chapter" books. Transitional books have fewer illustrations, are longer than beginning readers, have a larger vocabulary, and are more difficult to comprehend. They are not full-length novels, but neither are they picture books. Laura McGee Kvasnosky has created Zelda and Ivy, two fox sisters who travel together. In *Zelda and Ivy: The Runaways*, Ivy mixes a "creative juice" to cure Zelda's writer's block! Megan McDonald's books about Judy Moody and her brother Stink rarely stay long on library shelves. Judy gets famous, saves the world, and even predicts the future, much to her readers' delight; Stink reconciles himself to being the shortest kid in his class.

Transitional books may be between 50 and 100 pages in length. Patrick Jennings, for example, writes transitional books (sixty-four pages or less) about Ike, the big brother, and Mem, the younger sister, in *The Tornado Watches* and *The Weeping Willow*. Children learn about Ike's concern for Mem and the little arguments they have with their best friends. Well-known author Marc Brown has entered the transitional book field with a series of chapter books about *Arthur*, which was adapted by Stephen Krensky from teleplays for the PBS series. Ordinarily, books from television get lost in the transition, but Arthur, his sister D. W., and their friends retain their liveliness and appeal.

TRANSITIONAL BOOKS FOR MORE ADVANCED READERS Many transitional book series, such as Stephanie Greene's *Owen Foote*, make children aware of the contemporary fiction genre. The exploits of other characters in short, illustrated series such as *Cam Jansen* (David Adler), *Encyclopedia Brown* (Donald Sobol), *Rosy Cole* (Sheila Greenwald), *Ronald Morgan* (Patricia Reilly Giff), and *Amber Brown* (Paula Danziger) are addictive, and children look forward to their latest exploits. Series books are comforting because readers become familiar with the characters, the plots are formulaic, and the vocabulary is consistent throughout the series.

Patricia Reilly Giff makes a particularly significant contribution to multicultural understanding with her *Friends and Amigos* series. While learning to be bilingual, the young characters Sarah and Benjamin enjoy humorous stories such as *Adios, Anna* with the help of their friend Anna Ortiz, whose mother is from Ecuador. Children's enjoyment is enhanced by the pronunciations of the Spanish words included in the stories. Easy readers and transitional books play an important part in motivating early elementary children to love reading.

Then and Now

Publishing Yesterday and Today

When Congress passed the National Defense Act in 1958, more money became available for the purchase of books than ever before. Books meant to advance children's knowledge, especially in science and mathematics, were selected by professional librarians as the nation reacted to the success of the Russian Sputnik satellite (Epstein, 1995). Independent bookstores proliferated. Children and adults could browse their neighborhood bookstores, where booksellers often knew their readers personally and could hand-sell them a book in stock. Thousands of small bookstore owners had the power to order books matching their customers' preferences and expected the publishers to honor their requests. Publishers kept their warehouses stocked with backlists for long periods of time. Bookstores specifically designed for children began to flourish and by 1985 were sufficiently numerous for owners to form their own professional organization, the *Association of Booksellers for Children*.

Children went to the neighborhood public library for their books; those fortunate enough to have a school library could borrow books there. To increase sales, publishers promoted book clubs and even stocked books in grocery stores. In 1942, *Golden Books* made their debut. Priced at twenty-five cents each, Golden Books Publishers sold 39 million copies in five years (Epstein, 1995). Often, encyclopedias and editions of classic stories were sold as store premiums or by salespeople who went door-to-door, encouraging families to buy the books on the installment plan.

Today, however, publishing in the United States is a vastly different endeavor. Eight global corporations control children's publishing, with small, independent bookstores in sharp decline (Hade, 2002). A wider variety of children's books are available, but are more likely to be purchased from a large bookstore chain. At present, we're in a golden age for children's books. "The range of selection for children has never been better. The quality has improved as the market has become more competitive" (Richter, 1997).

Modern publishers often search for stories that transcend the medium of the book to become a recognizable brand. Marketing and publicity are the key words. Publishers must make sure the book is *synergized* by being *vertically integrated* and *licensed*. "*Synergy* is the word for this sort of a cross-promoting of merchandise. Primarily, the corporation achieves synergy in one of two ways. The first is by vertically integrating the brand throughout the entire company. The second way to create synergy is to sell licenses of the brand to other companies to make games, toys, clothing, and other products that will display the brand" (Hade, 2002, p. 514).

Publishers are also creating exciting ways to introduce teachers to new books. Through their websites they offer posters, biographies of authors and illustrators, sample chapters, and extensive study guides to use in the classroom. Students are encouraged to join a fan club of their favorite author. *Scholastic* has been talking to the National Basketball Association to work out something that will appeal to children who play basketball. Barbara Marcus, Scholastic's vice president noted, "There are tens of thousands of kids who love basketball and are not readers" (Marcus, 1997). By successfully selling more children's books, publishers are making the future bright for young readers.

Picture Story Books

Although we have discussed how many children ages 5 to 7 are cognitively ready for easy readers and transitional books, and very good readers are ready to read full-length novels (that is "chapter books"), the picture book genre remains the format within which other genres such as traditional literature, poetry, contemporary realistic fiction, historical fiction, fantasy, and informational books find expression.

Traditional Literature

In Chapter Three we learned how the tales and legends of traditional literature enhance children's cognitive abilities and aid in their understanding of other cultures. Their competence in the use of basic cognitive skills such as the mastery and use of concepts, an expanding language base, and a rich imagination combine to produce a reader eager to enter into the world of heroes, warriors, and villains. The following stories (many in picture book format) are examples of traditional tales that enchant young readers as they capture their attention, expand their world of words and ideas, and broaden their knowledge of others.

PECOS BILL. Steven Kellogg has retold and illustrated the *tall-tale* adventures of Pecos Bill so dramatically that children will be lassoed into reading every page of his outrageous life as a Texas cowboy. From the time he tangles with a huge reptile until he captures the horse Lightning and rescues Slewfoot Sue, the wildest woman in the West, young readers are enthralled by his exploits. Kellogg is also the author and illustrator of *Paul Bunyan*, another rip-roaring adventure for beginning readers.

ANANSI THE SPIDER. Gerald McDermott's Caldecott Honor book is an African folktale from the Ashanti tribe in Ghana. Anansi is a clever folk hero with six sons: See Trouble, Road Builder, River Drinker, Game Skinner, Stone Thrower, and Cushion. How they come to his aid when he is in distress creates a fascinating story with distinctive illustrations that children find challenging.

THE LEGEND OF THE INDIAN PAINTBRUSH. Talented illustrator Tomie dePaola retells the Native American legend about Little Gopher, who has a dream-vision in which his grandfather promises him that he will paint pictures of deeds of warriors, and a maiden offers him a white buckskin to find the colors of the sunset. DePaola admits that he, too, relates to this legend when he is searching for the appropriate colors for his artistic creations.

MIRANDY AND BROTHER WIND. Patricia McKissack's folktale describes Mirandy's determination to do the cake walk with Brother Wind. She is encouraged by Miss Poinsetta, the *conjure* woman, who gives her two see-through scarves to help her. In the introduction, McKissack recalls how her Papa believed that her Mama had "captured the wind" when they did the cake walk together, a dance introduced in America by slaves in 1906.

LON PO PO: A RED RIDING HOOD STORY FROM CHINA. Ed Young, author and illustrator of this slightly menacing version of a universally favorite fairy tale, won the Caldecott Medal for his fine illustrations that cleverly foreshadow the dangers lying ahead for the three sisters. Vertical panels of pastels and watercolors simulate ancient Chinese art and tell the story of the wolf and the frightened children who mistake him for their grandmother ("Po, Po"). Fortunately, they are able to trick him and live happily ever after, but not without several scary scenes.

SEVEN BLIND MICE. Ed Young retells and illustrates an old Indian folktale about the seven little mice, each depicted in a different color collage. They try to guess what the creature is (an elephant) that is standing near a pond. Children will enjoy discussing the reasons why each mouse made his decision.

THE DAY JIMMY'S BOA ATE THE WASH. Trinka Hakes Noble's boisterous tall tale begins with a simple question a mother asks her primary school daughter: how was your class trip to the farm? As the child relates one disastrous incident after another, each illustrated by Steven Kellogg's hilarious drawings, the mother wonders what could possibly happen next. She is totally unprepared for the events that lead up to Jimmy's boa constrictor eating the family's wash.

AND THE DISH RAN AWAY WITH THE SPOON. Janet Stevens and Susan Stevens Crummel have created a novel nursery rhyme. They have spun a postmodern dream tale of a familiar story where the dish and spoon disappear one night, and the Cat, Dog, and Cow try to locate the lost pair. In their journey, they encounter other nursery rhyme characters like Little Boy Blue, the Big Bad Wolf, and Miss Muffet's Spider. Children who are thoroughly familiar with Mother Goose will find this story fascinating, and will eagerly compare it to David Weisner's *The Three Pigs*, another postmodern tale filled with irony and imagination.

BABUSHKA'S MOTHER GOOSE. Patricia Polacco has written her version of the Mother Goose rhymes that she recalls hearing from her own Babushka (grandmother). Children will delight in the brightly colored illustrations of over twenty short poems and stories that Polacco has reshaped from tales of Aesop, Mother Goose, and Moldavia.

AND THE DISH RAN
AWAY WITH THE
SPOON
Book cover from AND THE DISH RAN AWAY WITH THE SPOON by Janet Stevens and Susan Stevens Crummel, illustrations copyright © 2001 by Janet Stevens, reprinted by permission of Harcourt, Inc.

Spin Off

Children Interact with Traditional Literature

• Using *And to Think that I Saw It on Mulberry Street* and *The Day Jimmy's Boa Ate the Wash* as examples, ask your young students the question: what happened to you on the way home from school yesterday? The children can then tell a tall tale about what they *imagined* happened to them on the way home from school. This could develop into a class project, with one child beginning the story, and by each child in turn adding to the story, illustrating it, and eventually making it into a picture book.

• After examining Polacco's *Babushka's Nursery Rhymes*, children select those that remind them of other nursery rhymes they have read. For example, ask

the children to compare *The Old Lady Who Lived in a Shoe* with Polacco's *Babushka's Boot*, which begins, "There once was a Babush / who lived in a boot. / She had too many children / who cried with a hoot." Children may want to try writing their own rhymes.

• While one child is the narrator and reads *The Dish Ran Away with the Spoon*, other children in the class can assume the characters and pantomime the action.

• Anansi's sons' names suggest various actions such as throwing stones, building roads, and drinking water. Each child can select a name and weave a story around the action mentioned.

Fantasy

Children of these years have entered the world of reading, and it's a world that teachers, librarians, and parents should make so enticing that young readers come to realize that enjoyment and information are only words away. It's a wonderful period for children that will contribute substantially to their self-confidence. As Sameroff and Haith (1996) noted, during the first 5 to 7 years, most children's basic reading skills and phoneme awareness develop rapidly. This tremendous milestone—learning to read—coupled with imaginative scenes, plots, and characters can only further a child's cognitive and emotional development.

When we discuss stimulation for cognitive and emotional development, we enter the fascinating field of children's *theory of mind*, which pertains to children's growing understanding of how the human mind works (Siegler & Alibali, 2005). One aspect of this process involves fantasy, that is, ways of reasoning about the physical world that violate known physical principles (Woolley, 1997). In the works of fantasy that we describe here, children come face to face with "beliefs in magic, imaginary companions, and in fantasy figures such as witches, fairies, and Santa Claus" (Siegler & Alibali, 2005, p. 325). Often, however, it is difficult for children of these years to distinguish reality from imagination.

ZATHURA. Chris Van Allsburg's sequel to *Jumanji*, while not quite as satisfying to read, continues the board game that his characters Danny and Walter Budwing began over twenty years ago. When Danny and Walter again open the *Jumanji* box, they find a second game board with "flying saucers, rockets, and planets in outer space, with a path of colored squares leading from Earth to a purple planet called Zathura and back to Earth." Although the boys are still in their house, they are thrust into the heavens when they throw the dice to begin the new game.

FLAT STANLEY. Similar to *The Shrinking of Treehorn*, which captured children's imagination a generation ago, Jeff Brown's *Flat Stanley* is the story of an average boy who wakes up to discover he is only half an inch thick! At first, he takes this change in his stride, casually slipping under doors and retrieving his mother's ring by lowering himself through a grating. He even helps foil a robbery and is pleased to be a hero, until his peers begin to laugh at him. Then he wants to return to his normal size. How he does this captures and holds the fascination of readers.

HORACE AND MORRIS JOIN THE CHORUS (BUT WHAT ABOUT DOLORES?) James Howe's series about Bunnicula, the Dracula-like rabbit, has captured the interest of early elementary school children for many years. In *Horace and Morris but Mostly Dolores* he introduces them to three mice of considerable individuality. In the sequel, *Horace and Morris Join the Chorus (But What about Dolores?)*, Dolores turns out to be a star, even though she was originally cut from the school chorus because she could not sing. Thanks to her ingenuity and determination, she persuades the chorus master, Moustro Provolone, to give her private singing lessons. Amy Walrod's illustrations contribute greatly to the hilarity and uniqueness of each mouse in the chorus, as well as those in the audience.

TRACTION MAN IS HERE! Welch author and illustrator Mini Grey makes *Traction Man*, a young child's

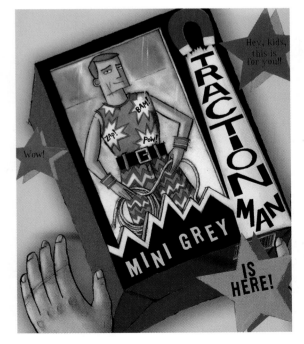

TRACTION MAN IS HERE
Used by permission of Alfred A. Knopf, a division of Random House, Inc.

Spin Off

Children Interact with Fantasy

- Calling themselves *Sylvester's Star Act*, each child memorizes a simple magic trick (found in books such as *Magic Tricks* by Cynthia Klingel and Robert B. Noyed) and performs it for the class.

- Wesley's success in creating Weslandia can inspire children to discuss what kind of civilization they would like to create. What would they eat? How would they dress? What games would they play?

- As a group or individually, children who have read *Zathura* may be encouraged to invent their own simple board game, similar to *Candyland*. The theme of their game, is "Out of This World." Cardboard space vehicles could be the markers. Things to consider might include: How many spaces would they advance to reach the planets? What would be the penalties for polluting the environment? What must they do when they land? How would they return to Earth? Their game could be a stepping-off place for them into the science curriculum.

- Using food as a theme, children write a simple fantasy about their favorite food—pizza, chicken fingers, donuts, and so on—coming to life. Illustrate it and read it to the class. Begin with a topic sentence such as "when fish could fly and food could talk." Or write a poem similar to those found in *Hot Potato: Mealtime Rhymes*.

Christmas gift, come to life. He is the perfect superhero in his combat boots, battle pants, and warfare shirt—that is, until granny knits him a green romper suit and a bonnet to match.

FOOD FIGHT. Carol Diggory Shield's *Food Fight* is a rhyming story of refrigerator foods that come alive late one night and join together in a pun-filled party. The cat is the only observer to this fanciful scene, which is reminiscent of Dr. Seuss's *The Cat in the Hat*.

SYLVESTER AND THE MAGIC PEBBLE. It is difficult to select just one of William Steig's books when so many are perfect for this age group. Even adults are devoted readers of Steig's *Abel Island*, *Brave Irene*, *Morris and Boris*, to name only a few. But *Sylvester and the Magic Pebble* is particularly appealing because it is about the magic within one small, insignificant stone that turns Sylvester the donkey into a rock, leading to endless confusion.

WESLANDIA. Paul Fleischman's book concerns Wesley, a young boy who knows he is an outcast from the civilization around him because he dislikes pizza and soda, finds football stupid, and refuses to shave half his head (the hairstyle worn by the other boys). So what does he do? He creates an alternate world—his own civilization, Weslandia.

Poetry

When you examine words such as those used by Dr. Seuss in *Fox in Socks* (such as "tweetle beetle" and "noodle poodle bottled paddled, muddled, duddled, fuddled wuddled fox in sox"), you can readily understand why children love playing with words. It's important to note that the kind of language children are exposed to influences the extent and success of their fluency. Poetry is a natural for this task. Its richness, diversity, and linguistic playfulness should occupy a central role in the classroom. In this way, poetry becomes a vehicle for the expression and interpretation of ideas, in that the contents of children's minds can be shared in a manner calculated to appeal to all ages (Bloom,

1998). These are the years when children are most susceptible to developing a love of poetry; language acquisition is flourishing; reading is becoming a cherished, adult-like activity; and cognitive development is leading to an appreciation of word usage.

IT'S RAINING PIGS AND NOODLES. Here is another of Jack Prelutsky's poetry books filled with short, witty poems that are just right for children this age to sing or recite. James Stevenson's illustrations contribute greatly to the content of the poems.

HOT POTATO: MEALTIME RHYMES. These brief poems by such well-known poets as Mary Ann Hoberman, John Ciadi, and Arnold Adoff, selected by Neil Philip, charm early elementary school children. Douglas Florian's *Cake Mistake*, for example, in which "Mother made a birthday cake / For icing she used glue. / The children sit so quiet now, / And chewandchewandchew" is one of the many poems that offer a perfect goodness-of-fit.

PEACOCK AND OTHER POEMS. Although Valerie Worth's poems (twenty-six of them) are short, they have a large impact on children. She sees beauty in the ordinary and expresses her feelings in exquisite imagery. Natalie Babbitt's line drawings convey the simplicity of the poems.

MAMA LIKES TO MAMBO. Helaine Becker has written mostly short (but some very long) poems that are fun for children to read. The large, bright illustrations by John Beder contribute greatly to the imagery of the poetry.

A GRAND CELEBRATION: GRANDPARENTS IN POETRY. This collection of poems selected by Carol G. and Daniel R. Hittleman is written by such well-known poets as Arnold Adoff, Lucille Clifton, Donald Graves, and Jack Prelutsky. The diversity of the parents represented here makes it easy for children to identify their own grandparents, whatever their culture or occupation.

THE ANIMALS AND THE ARK. In happy, rollicking verse, Karla Kuskin gaily describes the animals who "came from the plains / They came from the hills. / The elephants came with the whippoorwills" into the Ark. But as they all are squished together, they became bored and "the small animals seemed to be tearful," until the magic moment when the sun came out. "And that of course, is the end of the poem. / They all got up and they all went home." Michael Grejniec's bright watercolor illustrations add immeasurably to the vitality of the story.

Spin Off
Children Interact with Poetry

• Children take pictures (or shoot video) of their grandparents and then organize their photography. Beneath each picture they can choose suitable lines from *A Grand Celebration*, or create their own captions.

• *The Animals and the Ark* is perfect for children to read and use to create free-standing illustrations for a Noah's Ark class project. Making cardboard figures, clay figures, or miniatures, their Noah's Ark could be a large panorama or a small shoebox diorama.

• Poetry—especially the rhymes children read from Dr. Seuss' books and Jack Prelutsky's *It's Raining Pigs and Noodles*—lend themselves to organizing a "class poetry slam," where each child memorizes a poem and recites it to the class. Since children readily memorize jump rope songs, the poems suggested here should be fun for them to memorize as well.

Contemporary Realistic Fiction

In the genre of contemporary realistic fiction, we see a new dimension for children: the opportunity to gain a greater understanding of other cultures and be immersed in a story whose plot, setting, and conflicts mirror the reality they see around them every day. In other words, what they are reading presents events that could happen to them or to children from other cultures.

ANGELO. Surprisingly different from other books by David Macauley, which often include intricate drawings detailing the making of a cathedral, or the pyramids, or a skyscraper, *Angelo* is the touching story of an old plasterer working in Rome who befriends an injured pigeon. (It may also be a gentle way to comfort children on the death or illness of a beloved grandparent.) Children notice the gentleness he shows the pigeon, "Sylvia," and how carefully he nurses her back to health. She later returns to keep him company and amuse him. Most remarkable of all are Macauley's pen and ink and watercolor illustrations of the Eternal City, to which they both are as attached as they are to each other.

THE BROKEN CAT. At first glance, Lynne Rae Perkins' picture story book about Frank, Andy's cat, who is at the veterinarian's, seems confusing. Yet when Andy's mother, grandmother, and aunt Cookie recall conflicting versions of what happened to Andy's mother a long time ago, it all begins to connect for Andy. When Andy hears how his mother broke her arm and recovered, he becomes convinced that Frank's head will also mend. So he begins a story all his own. Illustrations and narrative seamlessly interact to provide the early elementary school child with a heartwarming, comforting story.

THE BROKEN CAT
*Used by permission of
HarperCollins Publishers*

Spin Off

Children Interact with Contemporary Realistic Fiction

• After children read *The Broken Cat*, encourage them to find out from a parent or caregiver if they were ever injured. Then have the children write their own story of what happened, how it happened, and how they recovered.

• *If the Shoe Fits* and *Indian Shoes* are written about children from two different cultures. Ask your students how they think the characters are similar. Children may also research different kinds of shoes that represent other cultures, climates, and occupations (e.g., moccasins, wooden shoes, sandals, snow boots). When they are finished, they can draw pairs of shoes, paint them, cut them out, and hang them on shoetrees throughout the classroom where they can serve as a springboard for a discussion of diversity.

• Pets are very special to children. In this selection, they read about Barney the cat, and Angelo's pigeon. They may want to talk about their own pets and relate a story about them to the class.

• In the books selected, children develop strong friendships with other persons. Discuss how a child becomes a friend, whether it is with his father (*Bippity Bop Barbershop*), grandfather (*Indian Shoes*), uncle (*If the Shoe Fits*), or playmate (*Sam, Bangs and Moonshine*).

• Ask your students: how could Samantha (*Sam, Bangs, and Moonshine*) have been a better friend? This may also be a teaching moment for you to relate Samantha's distortion of reality to Kohlberg's moral reasoning (Chapter One).

OWL MOON. Jane Yolen's book has always been intriguing for beginning readers, but since the remarkable popularity of J. K. Rowling's *Harry Potter* series, owls have become an even more interesting species for children to explore. This remarkable walk in the woods, shared by a father and daughter to find and respond to the call of an owl, is further enhanced by the Caldecott medal illustrations of John Schoenherr. He has the ability not only to draw the obvious, but—to the readers' delight—also to draw half-hidden objects, such as the fox behind an old stone wall, and a mouse hiding in a log, which add more excitement to the walk in the woods.

BIPPITY BOP BARBERSHOP. Natashia Anastasia Tarpley's picture book is a warm, loving story about how a young African American responds (timidly) to his first haircut. The process involves other members of his urban neighborhood, whose traditional meeting place is the barbershop. His close relationship with his father, however, leads him to get a haircut just like his dad's.

INDIAN SHOES. Realistic black and white illustrations reflect Cynthia Lietich Smith's short, interconnected stories about a young Seminole-Cherokee boy's adventures in contemporary Chicago. It is a touching story of a boy's strong relationship with his grandfather.

IF THE SHOE FITS. In this Gary Soto story, Rigo, a young Mexican American boy, receives a pair of loafers, which he puts aside because he is teased by a bully. When he gives them to his uncle, the giver and the receiver are both delighted.

SAM, BANGS & MOONSHINE. This Caldecott Medal book by Evaline Ness describes the consequences of Sam's (or Samantha's) constant elaboration of the truth. Her habit almost leads to disaster when her friend Thomas believes her, and becomes stranded on a narrow stretch of sand during high tide.

Historical Fiction

Later in this developmental period, to prepare students for their formal introduction to social studies, teachers and librarians may choose to offer them examples from the historical fiction genre. These stories have been selected because they are developmentally appropriate; that is, their language; themes, plot, and conflicts are presented in a framework that matches the biopsychosocial development of children.

STAGE FRIGHT ON A SUMMER NIGHT. Although any of the twenty-five books Mary Pope Osborne has written in her Magic Treehouse series would be suitable for children in this developmental range, her twenty-fifth adventure is the most challenging. In this short book with a fast-moving plot, Jack and Annie travel back to Shakespeare's time and perform in *A Midsummer Night's Dream*. The author briefly explains about Shakespeare and Queen Elizabeth in a manner children can understand.

SLEDS ON BOSTON COMMON: A STORY FROM THE AMERICAN REVOLUTION. Since the author, Louise Borden, in an appendix attributes the story to "local folklore," we can assume that 9-year-old Henry Price's experience trying out his sled on Boston Common is fiction. Yet his narration about the tension between the colonists and King George in 1774 is a fact. The encampment of British soldiers on the Common is also true. The political situation *almost* prevents Henry from using the Common to try his sled "with the slick beef bones for runners."

Spin Off
Children Interact with Historical Fiction

- Brightly colored sleds could be drawn by the children, each one with a word you would like emphasized from the story *Sleds on Boston Common*. These could be displayed throughout the room. Smaller drawings could be used as flash cards.

- Children will find it fun to draw stick figures to tell a story Ug would tell. The story could be drawn on large brown wrapping paper used to replicate a cave.

UG, BOY GENIUS OF THE STONE AGE AND HIS SEARCH FOR SOFT TROUSERS. Although little is known about how families survived in prehistoric times, Raymond Briggs skillfully and humorously, using cartoon-like illustrations, introduces his readers to Ug, a boy ahead of his time. Ug finds his world of hard, cold, dark, and damp to be unacceptable, and believes that warm, cozy, and comfy would be more to his liking. He pleads with his dad to make him a pair of trousers, to no avail. "One day, perhaps, in the future things will get better . . . won't they?," is his final plea.

Biography and Autobiography

As children become more and more immersed in the symbolic world, they begin to use language and reading skills to learn more about themselves and their environment. Who are the trailblazers in various fields that shaped history? How did they manage their accomplishments? Was their work accepted and recognized? Reading biographies such as those suggested below not only acts to enchant and inform children, it also provides examples of character, loyalty, and achievement. In other words, children learn about models who can shape their lives.

Modeling and Self-efficacy

Perhaps the leading exponent of modeling and observational learning is Albert Bandura (1997). In his powerful theory, he discusses the sources of self-efficacy (a belief in one's personal capability), one of which is modeling. Children of this age are uncertain about their capabilities and for the first time are beginning to match their talents and abilities against those of others. To read about the exploits of others, to understand the obstacles they managed to overcome, including their own self-doubt, is to further every aspect of their development. The following stories reflect Bandura's explanation of modeling and self-efficacy.

TO FLY: THE STORY OF THE WRIGHT BROTHERS. Wendie Old commemorates the historic flight of the Wright Brothers in 1903 in a picture book biography that uses a simple format: a flight timeline, with suggestions for further reading and notes. Her introduction, the poem *Crazy Boys*, written by Beverly McLoughland, synthesizes the story:

Watching buzzards / Flying kites. / Lazy boys / The Wrights. They / Tried to fly / Just like a bird / Foolish dreamers / Strange. Absurd. / We scoffed and scorned / Their dreams of flight / But we were wrong / And they were Wright.

Spin Off

Children Interact with Biography and Autobiography

• With the celebration of the Wright brothers' flight centennial (2003), children's interest in planes and flying has been rekindled. For those who would like to read more about Bessie Coleman, we recommend Nicki Grimes' *Talkin' about Bessie*, as well as Louise Borden and Mary Kay Kroeger's *Fly High!*

• We have included two books about the roles Martin Luther King and Ruby Bridges played in the civil rights movement that lend themselves to a Grand Conversation (see Chapter Four). You may like to point out to your students the difference between biography and autobiography.

NOBODY OWNS THE SKY. Reeve Lindbergh tells the daring story in verse about Bessie Coleman, who in 1921 became the first licensed African American aviator in the world. Reeve, the daughter of Charles Lindbergh, wrote this exciting story because "Bessie was an incredibly brave person who was hardly noticed. I saw the crazy imbalance (between the unknown Bessie and Charles Lindbergh) and wanted to set things right."

MARTIN'S BIG WORDS: THE LIFE OF DR. MARTIN LUTHER KING JR. In a format that early elementary school children will find challenging, Doreen Rappaport introduces them to Dr. Martin Luther King by using quotations from his speeches that reflect crucial events in his life, such as the March on Washington. Attractive collages, a Foreword, a chronology, further readings, and websites add to the authenticity of this biography.

THROUGH MY EYES. Ruby Bridges' autobiography will impress children this age, either as they read the story themselves or while they listen to how she integrated her New Orleans elementary school when she was a first-grader in 1960. They will be inspired by the photographs, newspaper clippings, and other materials that are included in the retelling of a remarkable experience by a brave little girl.

Informational Books

Children now find themselves immersed in the realm of words, books, and facts on a daily basis. And as our discussion of their cognitive abilities indicates, they are ready and willing to meet the challenges that lie on the horizon. But this is not to say that the informational books they use should be dry and uninteresting. Authors of informational books should possess a minimum level of expertise and present their subject matter in a carefully organized, well-written, and appropriately illustrated fashion. We believe the following selections meet these criteria.

TODAY I FEEL SILLY & OTHER MOODS THAT MAKE MY DAY. Colorful watercolor illustrations contribute to the appeal of this book by actress Jamie Lee Curtis. To add to its appeal, the book contains a mood wheel for children to identify their own mood swings. Tending toward bibliotherapy, it is one of the more informative of the celebrity-written books.

I LIVE IN TOKYO. Mari Takabayashi introduces children to contemporary Japan by including many detailed illustrations in this deceptively simple book. The narrator, 7-year-old Mimiko, invites her readers to tour Japan with her, as she de-

What's Your View?

Celebrity-Written Books

Roger Sutton (2001) notes that children's books by movie stars and other celebrities were published with numbing regularity throughout the last decade. Although he cites Jamie Lee Curtis's adoption story, *Tell Me Again about the Night I Was Born* as "a fresh breeze in 1996," many of the books by celebrity authors that are filling the shelves in malls and bookstores are causing aspiring authors to complain that a prominent name can get just about anything published.

Tracey Mayor, in her article *A Star-Studded Kid-Lit Scam* (*Boston Globe*, February 23, 2003), rightly points out that books by celebrities are not winners of respected awards like the Caldecott, the Newbery, or the American Library Association's List of Notable Books. As one reader of her article commented, "For those of us who treasure children's books and the time spent reading them, this new crop of fast-food literature is just another byproduct of our cultural mentality. Celebrity children's books are a sweet, calorie filled fix with no healthy literary benefit" (Letters to the Editor, *Boston Globe*, March 2, 2003).

A preschool teacher and mother who reads the same good books over and over to her children points out that you know you're reading a good book when there is a pause between the prose, the imagery never becomes tiresome, and you experience a contented feeling that makes you think, "Yes, this *is* a good book." Mayor finds that reading aloud books written by celebrities frequently requires her to stumble over words that don't flow, flip back pages to figure out missing details, and skip over obvious aphorisms that would benumb a 3-year-old brain (Mayor, 2003).

When Jerry Seinfeld's *Halloween* was published, it received mixed reviews. *The Horn Book* reviewer, who characterized it as an "over-the-top sarcastic scenario," wrote that it "would draw readers of all ages, but its sardonic reveries will probably have adults laughing hardest of all" (*The Horn Book*, September/October, 2002). But in a lengthy letter to the editor (*The Horn Book*, January/February 2003), Glenna Sloan, professor of Children's Literature at Queens College, City University of New York, calls Seinfeld's book a "production," since it is a book with little literary value. She suspects that candy companies subsidized its publication, since brand-name candies are pictured throughout, and that the book *perpetuates ageist ideas* and demonstrates rudeness and ingratitude.

After reading *Halloween*, and other celebrity-written books, and Daniel Hades' article *Storyselling: Are Publishers Changing the Way Children Read?* (*The Horn Book*, September/October 2002), discuss with your peers the literary value of celebrity-written books and the changes you have noticed in children's book publishing.

---

scribes events that take place during each month of the year. Children will be engrossed by her travelogue and narration and will be tempted to assess how their lives are similar to and different from hers.

THE DARING ESCAPE OF ELLEN CRAFT. As part of the *On My Own History* series, Cathy Moore provides an easy-to-read account of William and Ellen Craft's escape from slavery. With Ellen disguised as a white man and William pretending to be her slave, they travel from Georgia to Philadelphia and freedom.

STEPHEN BIESTY'S INCREDIBLE CROSS-SECTIONS. Unbelievable drawings of what is inside a castle, or an ocean liner, or a submarine capture the interest of children this age and beyond. A classic of its kind, Richard Platt's book will be used not only for entertainment, but also for information and reference.

ABOUT REPTILES: A GUIDE FOR CHILDREN. Cathryn Sills' opening lines—"Reptiles have dry, scaly skin / Some reptiles have a hard, bony plate. / Reptiles have short legs . . . / Or no legs at all"—introduce children to an informational book they will find fascinating. Each page presents the young reader with one fact. Then the opposite page supports that fact with a carefully detailed illustration of a reptile and its habitat. The Afterword includes black and white plates and additional information about each reptile. Children wanting to learn about reptiles are fortunate to have access to this book.

Spin Off

Children Interact with Informational Books

- Children will be fascinated by Lucy Micklethwait's *Child's Book of Art*. To add to their knowledge of great painters, we suggest that you also introduce them to Paul O. Zelinsky's Caldecott Medal–winning illustrations in *Rapunzel* and Trina Schart Hyman's illustrations of *Snow White* (Heins, 1974) so that they can compare and contrast them with the illustrations in *Child's Book of Art*.

- *Zin! Zin! Zin! A Violin* (Moss, 1995) is a pleasantly simple way to introduce your students to orchestral instruments. To further their interest, Elizabeth Patridge's *This Land Was Made for You and Me* and *The Song and Dance Man* by Karen Ackerman will certainly further enrich their musical knowledge.

- Show your students where Tokyo is located on a world map when discussing *I Live in Tokyo* (Takabayashi, 2001). Have your students research Asian customs, festivals, and clothing and discuss their discoveries with the class.

- Taking young students on a nature walk is always an exciting adventure. By pointing out animal tracks you will be satisfying their curiosity. They may not hear the call of Yolen's owl, but their knowledge of nature will certainly be enriched.

- To encourage their scientific curiosity, plan a class trip to a museum of natural history or a science museum in order to learn more about reptiles.

CHILD'S BOOK OF ART: DISCOVER GREAT PAINTINGS. Author Lucy Micklethwait not only includes thirteen paintings from all artistic periods, but details each one with notations and biographical information about the artist. She also includes an investigation section that is relevant for children who may be researching famous artistic works for the first time. Using a technique similar to that of the New York Museum of Modern Art's *Visual Thinking Strategies*, the author draws readers into a painting by asking them pertinent questions about what they see and how they feel. Children learn to look at art and art museums in a non-intimidating way.

ZIN! ZIN! ZIN! A VIOLIN. In this fabulous introduction in rhyme, written by Lloyd Moss, children learn about orchestral instruments in a unique way. The exuberant illustrations depict cats and dogs surrounding musicians with their instruments, as they group together in combinations ranging from duets to nonets.

||| Chapter Checklist

Read the following items carefully. If you have difficulty responding to any of them, return to the chapter to review the material.

After reading this chapter, you can

1. Explain the meaning of the 5-to 7-year-old shift.

2. Describe how children's cognitive abilities enable them to understand the essentials of a story.

3. Discuss the appeal of the Dr. Seuss books for children of these years.

4. Analyze the function of easy-reader and transitional books.

5. Identify several of the personal issues children of these years may experience and the literature that can help them.

6. Describe the changes that have occurred in publishing over the years.

7. Demonstrate how the various genres of this period lend themselves to modeling techniques.

8. Evaluate how the role of particular genres and specific books contribute to a child's sense of self-efficacy.

9. List the features of informational books that are needed to attract, inform, and stimulate readers of this age.

10. Give examples of how the traumatic events that some children of these years experience are eased by the stories they read.

Children's Bibliography

Adler, David. (2003). *Cam Jansen and the School Play Mystery*. New York: Puffin.

Ackerman, Karen. (1988). *The Song and Dance Man*. New York: Knopf.

Alexander, Sue. (1985). *Witch, Goblin, and Ghost Are Back*. New York: Pantheon.

Allard, Harry. (1977). *Miss Nelson Is Missing*. Boston: Houghton Mifflin.

Arnosky, Jim. (1999). *Crinkleroot's Nature Almanac*. New York: Simon & Schuster.

Atwater, Richard, & Atwater, Florence. (1994). *Mr. Popper's Penguins*. New York: Scholastic.

Barrett, Judi. (1982). *Cloudy With a Chance of Meatballs*. New York: Aladdin.

Becker, Nelaine. (2002). *Mama Likes to Mambo*. Canada: Stoddard Books LTD.

Benchley, Nathaniel. (1977). *George the Drummer Boy*. New York: Harper & Row.

Berenstain, Stan, & Bernstain, Jan. (1969). *Bears on Wheels*. New York: Random House.

Blume. Judy. (2002). *Fudge a Mania*. New York: Dutton.

Bogan, Paulette. (2005). *Goodnight, Lulu*. New York: Bloomsbury Children's Books.

Bonsall, Crosby. (1984). *And I Mean It, Stanley*. New York: HarperCollins.

Borden, Louise. (2000). *Sleds on Boston Common: A Story from the American Revolution*. NewYork: McElderry.

Borden, Louise, and Kroeger, Mary Kay. (2001). *Fly High! The Story of Bessie Coleman*. New York: Simon & Schuster.

Brenner, Barbara. (1999). *Moon Boy*. Milwaukee, WI: Gareth Stevens.

Bridges, Ruby. (1999). *Through My Eyes*. New York: Scholastic.

Briggs, Raymond. (2002). *Ug: Boy Genius of the Stone Age and His Search for Soft Trousers*. New York: Knopf.

Brett, Jan. (1949). *The Mitten*. New York: Putnam Sons.

Brown, Jeff. (1996). *Flat Stanley*. New York: Harper.

Brown, Marc. (1998). *Arthur and the Lost Diary*. Boston: Little, Brown.

Byars, Betsy, (1994). *The Golly Sisters Ride Again*. New York: HarperCollins.

Campbell, Monika Bang. (2002). *Little Rat Sets Sail*. San Diego: Harcourt.

Chesworth, Michael. (2002). *Alphaboat*. New York: Farrar, Straus, & Giroux.

Cleary, Beverly. (1999). *Ramona's World*. New York: Morrow.

Cole, Joanna. (1983). *Bony-Legs*. New York: Four Winds Press.

Cole, Joanna, & Calmenson, Stephanie. (1996). *Bug in a Rug*. New York: Morrow Junior Books.

Curtis, Jamie Lee. (1996). *Tell Me Again about the Night I Was Born*. New York: HarperCollins.

Curtis, Jamie Lee. (1998). *Today I Feel Silly & Other Moods That Make My Day*. New York: Harper.

Cushman, Doug. (2000). *Inspector Hopper*. New York: HarperCollins.

Davis, Katie. (2005). *Kindergarten Rocks*. New York: Harcourt.

Danziger, Paula. (2003). *Amber Brown Is Green with Envy*. New York: Putnam.

dePaola, Tomie. (1988). *The Legend of the Indian Paintbrush*. New York: Putnam.

dePaola, Tomie. (2002). *What a Year*. New York: Putnam.

DiCamillo, Kate. (2005). *Mercy Watson to the Rescue*. Cambridge, MA: Candlewick.

Doyle, Ann Dodd. (2003). *Where's Pup?* New York: Putnam.

Eastman, P. D. (1960). *Are You My Mother?* New York: Random House.

Fleischman, Paul. (1999). *Weslandia*. Cambridge, MA.: Candlewick.

Fowler, Allan. (1996). *Arctic Tundra: Land with No Trees*. New York: Children's Press.

Giff, Patricia Reilly. (1988). *Ronald Morgan Goes to Bat*. New York: Viking Kostrel.

Giff, Patricia Reilly. (1998). *Adios, Anna*. New York: Gareth Publishing.

Gorbachev, Valeri. (2005). *When Someone Is Afraid*. New York: Star Bright.

Greene, Stephanie. (2001). *Owen Foote, Super Spy*. New York: Clarion.

Greenwald, Sheila. (1997). *Rosy Cole: She Grows and Graduates*. New York: Orchard Books.

Grey, Mini. (2005). *Traction Man Is Here!* New York: Knopf.

Grimes, Nikki. (2002). *Talkin' about Bessie (The Story of Aviator Elizabeth Coleman)*. New York: Scholastic.

Grimes, Nikki. (2004). *What Is Goodbye?* New York: Hyperion.

Heins, Paul. Tina Schart Hyman, illus. (1974). *Snow White*. Boston: Little, Brown.

Hittleman, Carol G., & Hittleman, Daniel R. (2002). *A Grand Celebration: Grandparents in Poetry*. Honesdale, PA: Boyds/Wordsong.

Howe, James.(2002). *Horace and Morris Join the Chorus. (But What about Dolores?)*. New York: Atheneum.

Jennings, Patrick. (2002). *The Tornado Watches (An Ike and Mem Story)*. New York: Holiday.

Jennings, Patrick. (2002). *The Weeping Willow (An Ike and Mem Story)*. New York: Holiday.

Jolley, Mike. (2005). *I'll See You in the Morning*. San Francisco: Chronicle.

Kellogg, Steven. (1986). *Pecos Bill*. New York: Wm. Morrow and Co.

Klingel, Cynthia, & Noyed, Robert. (2002). *Magic Tricks*. Minneapolis: Carolrhoda Books.

Kuskin, Karla. (1985). *Something Sleeping in the Hall*. New York: Harper & Row.

Kuskin, Karla. (2002). *The Animals and the Ark*. New York: Atheneum.

Kvasnosky, Laura McGee. (2006). *Zelda and Ivy: The Runaways*. Cambridge, MA: Candlewick.

Lindbergh, Reeve. (1996). *Nobody Owns the Sky*. Cambridge, MA: Candlewick.

Lobel, Arnold. (1970). *Frog and Toad Are Friends*. New York: Harper.

Macauley, David. (2000). *Angelo*. Boston: Houghton Mifflin.

Marshall, James. (1972). *George and Martha*. Boston: Houghton Mifflin.

Martin, Bill. (1989). *Chicka Chicka Boom Boom*. New York: Scholastic.

Mayer, Mercer. (2005). *There Are Monsters Everywhere*. New York: Dial.

McClure, Gillian. (1999). *Selkie*. New York: Farrar, Straus, & Giroux.

McDermott, Gerald. (1986). *Anansi the Spider: a Tale from the Ashanti*. New York: Holt.

McDonald, Megan. (2000). *Judy Moody*. Cambridge, MA. Candlewick.

McDonald, Megan. (2000). *Beezy and Funnybone*. New York: Orchard Books.

McDonald, Megan. (2003). *Judy Moody Predicts the Future*. Cambridge, MA: Candlewick.

McDonald, Megan. (2006). *Stink: The Incredible Shrinking Kid*. Cambridge, MA: Candlewick.

McGhee, Alison. (2002). *Count Down to Kindergarten*. San Diego: Harcourt.

McKissack, Patricia. (1988). *Mirandy and Brother Wind*. New York: Knopf.

Micklethwait, Lucy. (1999). *Child's Book of Art: Discover Great Paintings*. New York: Dorling Kindersley.

Minarik, Else. (1968). *A Kiss for Little Bear*. New York: HarperCollins.

Moore, Cathy. (2002). *The Daring Escape of Ellen Craft*. Minneapolis, MN. Carolrhoda Books.

Moss, Lloyd. (1995). *Zin! Zin! Zin! A Violin*. New York: Simon & Schuster.

Ness, Evaline. (1966). *Sam, Bangs & Moonshine*. New York: Holt, Rinehart, & Winston.

Newman, Leslea. (2000). *Heather Has Two Mommies*. Los Angeles: Alyson Wonderland.

Noble, Trinka Hakes. (1980). *The Day Jimmy's Boa Ate the Wash*. New York: Dial.

Old, Wendie. (2002). *To Fly: The Story of the Wright Brothers*. New York: Clarion.

Olson, Mary. (2000). *Nice Try, Tooth Fairy*. New York: Simon & Schuster.

Ormerod, Jan. (2005). *When an Elephant Comes to School*. New York: Scholastic/Orchard.

Osborne, Mary Pope. (2002). *Stage Fright on a Summer Night*. New York: Random House.

Parish, Peggy. (1972). *Play Ball, Amelia Bedelia*. New York: Harper & Row.

Paterson, Katherine. (1977). *Bridge to Terabithia*. New York: Crowell.

Patridge, Elizabeth (2002). *This Land Was Made for You and Me: The Life and Songs of Woody Guthrie*. New York: Viking.

Perez, L. King. (2002). *First Day in Grapes*. New York: Lee & Low.

Perkins, Lynne Rae. (2002). *The Broken Cat*. New York: Greenwillow.

Philip, Neil (2004). *Hot Potato: Mealtime Rhymes*. New York: Clarion Books.

Pitzer, Susanna. (2006). *Not Afraid of Dogs*. New York: Walker.

Platt, Richard. (1992). *Stephen Biesty's Incredible Cross-Sections*. New York: Knopf.

Polacco, Patricia. (1995). *Babushka's Mother Goose*. New York: Philomel.

Prelutsky, Jack. (2000). *It's Raining Pigs and Noodles*. New York: Greenwillow.

Rappaport, Doreen. (2001). *Martin's Big Words*. New York: Hyperion.

Rosen, Michael. (2005). *Michael Rosen's Sad Book*. Cambridge, MA: Candlewick.

Rylant, Cynthia. (1998). *Henry and Mudge and the Sneaky Crackers*. New York: Simon.

Rylant, Cynthia. (1998). *Mr. Putter & Tabby Toot the Horn*. Prince Frederick, MD: Harcourt.

St. George, Judith. (2005). *Take the Lead, George Washington*. New York: Philomel.

Seinfeld, Jerry. (2002). *Halloween*. Boston: Little, Brown.

Seuss, Dr. (1957). *The Cat in the Hat*. Boston: Houghton Mifflin.

Seuss, Dr. (1964). *And To Think That I Saw It on Mulberry Street*. New York: Random House.

Seuss, Dr. (1965). *Fox in Socks*. New York: Random House.

Seuss, Dr. (1968). *Horton Hatches the Egg*. New York: Random House.

Seuss, Dr. (1971). *The Lorax*. New York: Random House.

Seuss, Dr. (1974). *Great Day for Up*. New York: Random House.

Seuss, Dr. (1996). *My Many Colored Days*. New York: Random House.

Seuss, Dr. (1988). *One Fish, Two Fish, Red Fish, Blue Fish*. New York: Random House.

Seuss, Dr. (1984). *The Butter Battle Book*. New York: Random House.

Seuss, Dr. (1948). *Thiawick The Big-Hearted Mouse*. New York: Random House.

Shannon, David. (2002). *David Gets in Trouble*. New York: Scholastic.

Shannon, George. (1996). *Tomorrow's Alphabet*. New York: Greenwillow.

Shields, Carol Diggory. (2002). *Food Fight HC*. New York: Handprint.

Sill, Cathryn. (1999). *About Reptiles: A Guide for Children*. Atlanta: Peachtree.

Silverstein, Shel. (2005). *Runny Babbit*. New York: HarperCollins.

Smith, Cynthia Lietich. (2002). *Indian Shoes*. New York: HarperCollins.

Sobol, Donald. (2003). *Encyclopedia Brown and the Case of the Jumping Frogs*. New York: Random House.

Soto, Gary, (2002). *If the Shoe Fits*. New York: Putnam.

Steig, William. (1969). *Sylvester and the Magic Pebble*. New York: Simon & Schuster.

Stevens, Janet, & Crummel, Susan Stevens. (2001). *And the Dish Ran Away with the Spoon*. San Diego: Harcourt.

Takabayashi, Mari. (2001). *I Live in Tokyo*. Boston: Houghton Mifflin.

Tarpley, Natasha Anastasia. (2002). *Bippity Bop Barbershop*. Boston: Little, Brown.

Van Allsburg, Chris. (2002). *Zathura: A Space Adventure*. Boston: Houghton Mifflin.

Van Leeuwen, Jean. (2006). *Oliver Pig and the Best Fort Ever*. New York: Dial Books.

Viorst, Judith. (1971). *The Tenth Good Thing about Barney*. New York: Atheneum.

Wiesner, David. (2001). *The Three Pigs*. New York: Clarion.

Willhoite, Michael. (1990) *Daddy's Roommate*. Boston: Alyson Wonderland.

Wiles, Deborah. (2005). *Each Little Bird that Sings*. Orlando: Harcourt.

Willems, Mo. (2005). *Leonardo the Terrible Monster*. New York: Hyperion.

Woodson, Jacqueline. (2005). *Show Way*. New York: G. P. Putnam's Sons.

Worth, Valerie. (2002). *Peacock and Other Poems*. New York: Farrar.

Yolen, Jane. (1987). *Owl Moon*. New York: Philomel.

Young, Ed. (1989). *Lon Po Po*. New York: Philomel.

Young, Ed. (1992). *Seven Blind Mice*. New York: Philomel.

Zelinsky, Paul O. (1997). *Rapunzel*. New York: Dutton Children's Books.

Zolotow, Charlotte. (2002). *Seasons: A Book of Poems*. New York: HarperCollins.

Professional References

Bandura, A. (1997). *Self-Efficacy: The Exercise of Control*. New York: Freeman.

Berk, L. (2005). *Infants, Children, and Adolescents*. Boston: Allyn and Bacon.

Bloom, L. (1998). "Language Acquisition in its Developmental Context." In W. Damon (Series ed.) & D. Kuhn & R. Siegler (Volume eds.). *Handbook of Child Psychology: Volume 2. Cognition, Perception, and Language*. New York: John Wiley.

Bjorklund, D. (2005). *Children's Thinking*. Belmont, CA: Wadsworth.

Cohen, Charles. (2004). *The Seuss, the Whole Seuss, and Nothing But the Seuss*. New York: Random House.

Dacey, John & Fiore, Lisa. (2000). *Your Anxious Child*. San Francisco: Jossey-Bass.

Dacey, J., & Travers, J. (2009). *Human Development Across the Lifespan*. New York: McGraw-Hill.

Epstein, C. (1995). "Publishing Children's Books." In Anita Silvey (ed.). *Children's Books and their Creators*. Boston: Houghton Mifflin.

Erikson, E. (1963). *Childhood and Society*. New York: Norton.

Hade, Daniel. (2002). "Storyselling: Are Publishers Changing the Way Children Read?" *The Horn Book*. September/October, 509–517.

Kagan, Jerome. (1994). *Galen's Prophecy*. New York: Basic Books.

Kagan, Jerome, & Herschkowitz, Norbert. (2005). *A Young Mind in a Growing Brain*. Mahwah, NJ: Lawrence Erlbaum.

Marcus, Barbara. In Nina McCain. (1997). "Strong Sales Make for 'Golden Age.'" *Boston Globe*. February 23, 1997.

Mayor, Tracy. (2003). "A Star-Studded Kid-Lit Scam." *Boston Globe Magazine*. February 23, 25–27.

Richter, Rick. In Nina McCain. "Strong Sales Make for 'Golden Age.'" *Boston Globe*. February 23, 1997.

Ohman, Arne. (2000). "Fear and Anxiety: Evolutionary, Cognitive, and Clinical Perspectives." In Michael Lewis and Jeannette Haviland-Jones (eds.). *Handbook of Emotions*. New York: Guilford Press.

Reynolds, Lynn. (1995). "Anticipatory Grief and Bereavement." In *Handbook of Pediatric Psychology*. New York: Guilford Press.

Sameroff, A., & Haith, M. (eds). (1996). *The Five to Seven Year Shift: The Age of Reason and Responsibility*. Chicago: University of Chicago Press.

Santrock, J. (2000). *Children*. New York: McGraw-Hill.

Saarni, Carolyn, Campos, Joseph, Camras, Linda, & Witherington, David. (2006). "Emotional Development: Action, Communication, and Understanding." In W. Damon and Richard Lerner (eds.-in-chief) and Nancy Eisenberg (Volume ed.), *Handbook of Child Psychology: Volume 3, Social, Emotional, and Personality Development*. New York: John Wiley.

Siegler, R., & Alibali, M. (2005). *Children's Thinking*. Upper Saddle River, NJ: Prentice Hall.

Sieruta, Peter D. *Halloween*. *The Horn Book*. September/October, 2002.

Sutton, Roger. (2001). "Looking Beyond the Winner's Circle." In *American Library Association. The Newbery and Caldecott Medal Books, 1986–2000*.

Tucker, Nicholas. (2002). *The Rough Guide to Children's Books. 0–5 yrs*. New York: Penguin

Valsiner, J. (1998). "The Development of the Concept of Development: Historical and Epistemological Perspectives." In R. M. Lerner (ed.), *Handbook of Child Psychology: Volume 1, Theoretical Models of Human Development*. New York: John Wiley.

Woolley, J. (1997). "Thinking About Fantasy: Are Children Fundamentally Different Thinkers and Believers from Adults?" *Child Development*. 68, 991–1011.

Literature for the Intermediate School Years (Ages 8–10)

In Canadian author Kit Pearson's award-winning book Awake and Dreaming, *Theo, the 9-year-old main character, wishes she belonged to a family like the one in Sidney Taylor's book* All-of-a-Kind Family. *What a wonderful family. They were poor like her, but they didn't seem poor, for they were rich with love and laughter. What would it be like to belong to such a family? She thought about this story as she huddled freezing in her bed, clutching a thin gray blanket around her shoulders.*

What saved Theo from being overcome by poverty was her love for books. In second grade, after she had learned to read, she had picked up E. B. White's Charlotte's Web *in her classroom. She began to read it in her free time, holding it secretly on her lap behind her desk, and finished it after sneaking it home. (She and her mother, Rae, were living at a shelter.) Theo devoured picture books about James Marshall's George and Martha, chapter books like* Freckle Juice *by Judy Blume, and humorous books like* How to Eat Fried Worms *by Thomas Rockwell. Sometimes, facts about building igloos and faraway countries like India were as fascinating to her as fiction.*

In this chapter we enter the world of the intermediate grades, the world in which Theo moves. Children of these years grow at a slower and steadier rate than previously. Their thinking becomes more logical; they love the rules that bring order to their world! They're beginning to evaluate the reactions of others, particularly those whom they respect. As they compare themselves to their peers, their self-concept is either enhanced or challenged. Consequently, they often search for insight and support in the world of books.

AWAKE AND DREAMING
Reproduced by permission of
Penguin Group USA Inc.

Guidelines for Reading Chapter 10

After you read Chapter Ten, you should be able to answer the following questions.

• How do themes from the fantasies presented in this chapter demonstrate how the make-believe dimension stimulates both cognitive and emotional development?

• How does the language of the poems discussed in this chapter help children understand the range and power of their rapidly expanding vocabulary?

• What are the plots of the various stories in the fiction section and how do they interact with the interpersonal needs of the intermediate school child?

• How do the points of view of the informational books discussed in this chapter help readers learn about themselves and their world?

Characteristics of Children of These Years

This chapter demonstrates how the biopsychosocial characteristics of children in grades 3 through 5 relate to the books they find most suitable. Much is happening to students in these grades that eludes initial detection. As developmental psychologists are the first to admit, these years seem less dramatic than other times of development, such as infancy or adolescence. Yet these years are marked by subtle changes that leave their mark on development—changes that astute authors incorporate into their stories.

Children are forming new friendships, feeling increased competition, engaging in more school activities, and meeting new demands that challenge their self-concepts and affect their emotional development. Their cognitive competence continues to expand, even as they are challenged by the tasks they face. Their network of relationships grows, and with it comes inevitable comparisons with others, which typically results in a reevaluation of the self and mounting stress.

These years continue Erikson's *industry* versus *inferiority* period, during which children acquire needed information and the skills required by their culture. Informational books, such as those we have selected below, help provide them with this information. These books, which match the cognitive skills manifested by children during these years, are based on Howard Gardner's theory of multiple intelligences. You can understand the impact on children's sense of self as they acquire feelings of satisfaction and accomplishment when they master information that interests them. You can also understand how they can slip into a sense of frustrating inferiority when they cannot find the information they seek. The stories, legends, and biographies in this chapter are designed to enhance a child's appreciation of the value of industry.

Families

Although Theo (mentioned in the introductory vignette) is a fictional character whose home conditions are extreme, developmentally she reflects a typical intermediate school child in her needs, interests, and attitudes. She has a desire for family and a need for love and belonging, security, and safety. (See Chapter Thirteen.) Books like *All-of-a-Kind Family* are her haven and safety net. Yet the family in Sydney Taylor's book—an intact Jewish family with five charming daughters living happily in a tenement on New York's East Side—was more conventional in 1951 than is the case today. A modern family may have both parents working. It may be a single-parent family. It may consist of unrelated people living together. Or it may be a blended family (divorce and remarriage). Families are in a greater state of flux and redefinition today than perhaps ever before (Bornstein, 2002).

THE CHILDREN OF POVERTY   As developmental concerns in our society encompass an ever-growing network of problems, psychologists have focused on such environmental issues as poverty and homelessness, similar to what Theo and her mother experienced in our opening vignette. In *Awake and Dreaming*, Pearson describes how Theo is fighting to preserve her sense of self in the face of wrenching poverty and homelessness during her intermediate school years.

Sadly, estimates are that at least 30 percent of American children experience poverty at some time in their lives (Dacey & Travers, 2009). Among the problems associated with poverty are the following:

- More poor children die in the neonatal and infancy periods.
- Children of poverty experience more health problems due to a lack of medical care.
- More disadvantaged children die from accidents.
- Children of poverty are subject to greater and longer periods of stress.
- Children of poverty are more frequently the targets of violence (assault, rape, shootings).
- Children of poverty inevitably live their lives with feelings of powerlessness.

Although serious attempts to help impoverished children began in the 1960s with the advent of Head Start and smaller, private programs, the struggle has been difficult and promises to be long-lasting (McLoyd, Aikens & Burton, 2006).

Teachers and librarians should realize *that the poor are not all alike*. The child living in an urban ghetto faces a different set of problems than a chronically malnourished and sick child in Appalachia. The goodness-of-fit concept that we have stressed throughout this text is particularly relevant as caring adults search for stories, themes, and suggestions that could help these children.

FAMILY ADJUSTMENTS   Given all these changes, parents are less certain of their roles at a time when their relationships with their children are slowly but inevitably changing. Following the intense *under the roof* culture that most children have previously experienced, parents now spend less time with their children, who begin moving into the wider world. Others (teachers, counselors, coaches) offer support and guidance in activities outside the home. Children must learn how to cooperate in this new social network and behave without constant adult supervision. While this is happening, peers are slowly assuming a more important role in their lives.

In the Newbery Award book *The Higher Power of Lucky* by Susan Patron, for example, we are given a unique look into an unusual family situation that challenges Lucky, the 10-year-old protagonist. When Lucky's mother is electrocuted in a severe storm, her father brings his ex-wife, Brigitte, from France to care for her. Two years later, Lucky realizes that to survive she must find her higher power and gain control of her life. Families develop a unique style or climate for adapting to change while simultaneously attempting to maintain their integrity. Stories that show the diverse roles families play include *The Penderwicks*, which is Jeanne Birdsall's National Book Award winner about four sisters with two rabbits who spend an exciting summer vacation with their father. The amusing story of Miguel Guzman in *How Tia Lola Came to ~~Visit~~ Stay*, by Julia Alvarez, describes his difficulty accepting his aunt Tia Lola into his family. Marilyn Sachs' *The Bears' House* illustrates the too-common theme of how a child often assumes the role of parent in a troubled family.

The style that emerges has developmental consequences for both parents and their children because *parents*

THE PENDERWICKS
Used by permission of Alfred A. Knopf, a division of Random House, Inc.

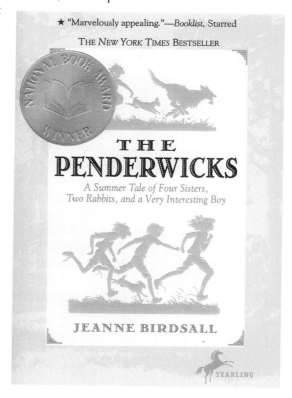
★ "Marvelously appealing."—*Booklist*, Starred
THE *NEW YORK TIMES* BESTSELLER
NATIONAL BOOK AWARD WINNER
THE PENDERWICKS
A Summer Tale of Four Sisters, Two Rabbits, and a Very Interesting Boy
JEANNE BIRDSALL
YEARLING

and children are in it together, for better or worse. In the stories you read about in this chapter and the chapters that follow, you will discover that the definition of what is "right" usually equates to what "works" for families in their culture. Children of different ages, with different problems, and from different cultures require different types of parenting. We're quite sure that parents and children actually *construct* their relationships; no one model fits all families.

THE PROBLEM OF OBESITY   As parents and children work out their relationships, questions concerning nutritional issues often arise. Parents worry that their children aren't eating enough, but given the slower growth rate of these years, less food is needed. More important than quantity is the quality of the food that is eaten. Junk food with excessive fats and sugars should be avoided. Although the need for protein, vitamins, and minerals remains high, children may begin to accumulate empty calories from high-sugar and high-fat foods that can lead to obesity.

The theme of childhood obesity, with its social, psychological, and medical consequences, is evident in books such as Barthe DeClementis' *Nothing's Fair in Fifth Grade*. Elsie, the newcomer in fifth grade, is shunned because of her appearance. In *When Zachary Beaver, Came to Town*, by Kimberly Willis, Zachary, the circus boy, is headlined as "The Fattest Boy in the World." A National Book Award winner, it reveals much about a community's attitude towards obesity. In the prize-winning *Fat Kid Rules the World* (Going, 2003) for older students, Troy Billings contemplates suicide because he is overweight and friendless.

Obesity is becoming a national concern. Former President Clinton and the Robert Wood Johnson Foundation have selected 285 schools in thirteen states to initiate an $8 million program to improve the nutritional value of food served in the schools, to increase students' physical activity, and to provide lessons in health and wellness (*Boston Globe*, 2006). Angela Royston has written in the *Stay Healthy* series how important it is for children to make healthy choices and strike a balance in their lives by being active and eating nutritious foods.

The topic of food, regardless of its potential for contributing to a child's obesity, has frequently been a positive rather than a negative in children's literature. Adults remember the little badger wanting nothing more all day than to eat bread and jam in Russell Hoban's *Bread and Jam for Frances*. Children reading Laura Jaffe Numeroff's *If You Give a Mouse a Cookie* never dreamed the mouse could be on the road to obesity when he demands a glass of milk from a harried young boy who is eager to please. Judi Barrett's imaginary village Chewandswallow, in her entertaining fantasy *Cloudy with a Chance of Meatballs*, is filled with foods coming from the sky, until a downpour causes the residents to run and hide from such largesse. Tomie dePaola entertained a past generation of children with his story (reissued in 1994) of a grandmother who unwittingly made her grandchild jealous when she handed his friend the feet of a chicken in *Watch Out for the Chicken Feet in Your Soup*. More recently, Nancy Castaldo's *Pizza for the Queen* relates the story of Raffaele Esposito, a patriot who owns the best pizzeria in Naples in 1899. He has the honor of creating a pizza for the Queen and surprises her with *three* pizzas whose ingredients represent the colors of the Italian flag.

Continuing Cognitive Changes

The cognitive changes described thus far continue unabated. This is the time of Piaget's concrete operational period, when children give mounting evidence of their growing symbolic ability. Their thinking displays greater flexibility and they become more secure in reversing their mental reasoning; they can retrace their thoughts, which is the foundation for successful problem solving. Collins and his colleagues (2002) have identified three characteristic changes that appear during the intermediate school years.

1. Growing symbolic ability enables children to reason more effectively about increasingly complex problems.

2. Children can organize tasks more maturely and independently, and their classification skills improve.

3. Greater opportunities are available to children to widen their body of knowledge and use that knowledge in reasoning and problem solving.

Children of these years understand others more accurately. In Virginia Hamilton's book *Bluish*, Natalie, a fifth-grader in a wheelchair, is initially shunned. Yet her classmates, who are at first apprehensive and timid about approaching her, learn to understand that she is like them, only different. Her classmates are cognitively ready to make comparisons between themselves and Natalie. They also begin to evaluate their own competence.

As we have seen in our discussion of cognition, a tight link exists between realistic self-esteem and the attainment of competence. During these years, children's developing sense of self helps to shape their personal goals; any discrepancy between what they think about themselves and their real selves can be a strong cognitive force. Cognitive complexities, subtle reasoning, the beginnings of intense relationships, and the use of humor characterize these intermediate years.

CHILDREN AND THEIR HUMOR   Humor has long intrigued individuals from a broad spectrum of academic disciplines and activities: philosophy, psychology, medicine, history, literature, and so on. When you think of humor, names such as Sigmund Freud (*Jokes and Their Relation to the Unconscious*), Henri Bergson (*Laughter*), Mark Twain (*The Notorious Jumping Frog of Calaveras County*), James Thurber (*Writings and Drawings*), Nathaniel Benchley (*The Benchley Roundup*), and Dave Barry (*Dave Barry Talks Back*) come to mind. Both humor and attempts to analyze it have been with us almost as long as the printed word.

How do children acquire a sense of humor that gradually becomes more sophisticated? What is it that makes them enjoy the wit, the sarcasm, and the slapstick of jokes and fun-filled events? How does this appreciation develop?

Why did Daddy tiptoe past the medicine cabinet?
Because he didn't want to wake the sleeping pill.

Probably the most productive way of determining how children develop humor is to follow its connection to cognitive development. In tracing children's appreciation of humor in the books they read, it becomes obvious that they can't appreciate a joke or a comic situation unless they understand the words and the circumstances, which takes us into the world of cognition.

Paul McGhee (1971, 1979, 2003), a longtime student of humor, believes that cognitive processes offer the most promising explanation of how humor develops. For McGhee, the key element in comprehending humor is *incongruity*, and he traces its development through the following four stages. To match his theory about the development of humor from Stage 1 (books for small children) to Stage 4 (books appealing to children 7 years and older), we have selected four authors and illustrators who have mastered the art of writing humorous stories for children: James Marshall, David Shannon, Mini Grey, and Roald Dahl.

- **STAGE 1: INCONGRUOUS ACTIONS TOWARD OBJECTS.** Stage 1 usually occurs sometime during the second year, when children play with objects. They are able to form internal images of the object and thus start to "make believe." Mini Grey's graphic picture book *The Adventures of the Dish and the Spoon* is beyond the comprehension of a 2-year-old, but her cartoon illustrations of a spoon and a dish with eyes and legs running and rolling down a hill appeal to their sense of incongruity.

- **STAGE 2: INCONGRUOUS LABELING OF OBJECTS AND EVENTS.** Stage 2 humor is more verbal, which distinguishes it from Stage 1. Children in this stage delight in calling a dog a cat, or a foot a hand, and then start laughing. When they read *The Stupids* by James Marshall, they identify with his humor. The Stupids call their dog "Kitty," they sleep upside down in their bed, they put their jam jar in the bathroom, and they label a picture of a flat field "Mount Stupid." Perfect examples of Stage 2 humor continue throughout the entire series: *The Stupids Die, The Stupids Have a Ball, The Stupids Step Out.*

- **STAGE 3: CONCEPTUAL INCONGRUITY.** Around age 3, most children begin to play with ideas, which reflects their growing cognitive ability. For example, Stage 3 children laugh when looking at a drawing of a cat with two heads. When children as young as 3 see the vivid, full-page illustrations of David Shannon's *Good Boy Fergus*, they are captivated by the antics of the irrepressible wire-haired terrier, and laugh when Fergus eats his dinner only if it is sprayed with whipped cream.

- **STAGE 4: MULTIPLE MEANINGS.** Once children begin to play with the ambiguity of words, their humor approaches the adult level.

"Hey, did you take a bath?"

"No. Why, is one missing?"

Children at Stage 4 (usually around age 7) understand the different meanings of "take" in both instances and see the humor in the ambiguity. Roald Dahl's books, such as *The Twits* and *Charlie and the Chocolate Factory*, are still in demand because they offer children a quirky way of looking at their world. Children who read even one of his books are eager to read more. Authors like Dahl seem to write humorous books naturally. But, writers who write humor succeed only when they write dialogue the way children actually talk, without talking down to them.

We previously commented on the shift in children's thinking from ages 5 to 7 that allows them greater access to the symbolic world. As children move into the years we're now discussing (8 to 10), their increasing logical reasoning, more systematic thinking, and maturing cognitive ability permit them to appreciate the incongruity of jokes and riddles, and lets them imagine themselves getting into the situations they read about. For example:

- Beverly Cleary, in new editions of her *Beezus and Ramona, Ramona Quimby Age 8*, and *Ramona the Pest*, continues to demonstrate her skill as master of the art of humor to a new generation who, like their parents, smile knowingly at the familiar mishaps of the Quimbys.

- Barbara Seuling's *Robert and the Practical Jokes* uses Robert's big brother Charlie to effectively, but good-naturedly, play jokes on 9-year-old Robert at his birthday party, while he does his homework assignment, and during other everyday experiences.

- Phyllis Reynolds Naylor's transitional chapter book *Roxie and the Hooligans* involves 9-year-old Roxie's entanglement with the bullying Hooligans (whom he is trying to avoid), as they all get caught in a load of garbage heading out to sea!

By offering humorous books to children, you not only bring laughter into their world, but you help stimulate new learning and creative thinking, instill an interest in literature, facilitate social development, and enhance their emotional development.

A Changing Sense of Self

A child's feeling about self is powerfully affected by school, which provides constant feedback with its network of social contacts and its emphasis on achievement. The media, especially television with its stereotypical models, furnishes children with artificial, often self-destructive goals of what the self should be. Stress, stemming from their widening social world, school, and personal problems, becomes a factor that children must learn to cope with (Travers et al., 1993).

These are compelling reasons why teachers and librarians should turn to children's literature for insights into the issues and concerns children inevitably face. Theo's search for stability and security, for example, led her to stories of families that portrayed these characteristics. To select the right book for a child this age, teachers and librarians should consider the following developmental characteristics.

BIOPSYCHOSOCIAL CHARACTERISTICS

BIO	PSYCHO	SOCIAL
Bodily agility	Logical thinking	Self-concept
Steady weight and height gains	Improved memory	Self-esteem
Nutritional concerns	Intellectual skills	Impulse control
Prevention of disease and injury	Problem-solving ability	Peer relationships
	Language achievements	School achievement
	Moral dilemmas	Coping with stress
	Appreciates humor	Changing parental relationships

Picture Books

In Chapter Three, we introduced the term *genre* and discussed the characteristics of the genres of picture book, traditional literature, fantasy, poetry and drama, contemporary fiction, historical fiction, biography and autobiography, and informational books. We also demonstrated in later chapters how the books children select from these genres satisfy their biopsychosocial characteristics. The picture book, however, may incorporate many genres because it is unique. Leonard Marcus in his *Ways of Telling* describes it "as a dialogue between two worlds: the world of images and the world of words" (Marcus, 2002, p. 3). Designed originally for small children, the picture book is now a treasure of literature, art, cultural traditions, and trends for all ages.

With these ideas in mind, let's turn to the picture book for children in the intermediate school years and trace the goodness-of-fit that leads to the right book for the right child. It's not the size or the number of pages that conveys a book's excitement and appeal, but what it says and how it reaches out to children's level of development and personal interests.

Picture Books Across the Curriculum

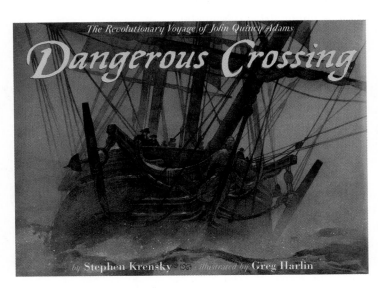

DANGEROUS CROSSING
Reproduced by permission of Penguin Group

The Picture Book Biography series, including David Adler's *Picture Book of Harriet Beecher Stowe*, is a short but entirely factual series that analyzes various individuals' character traits, family members, and major events in their lives, without overwhelming the reader with excessive information. Adler's series leads into discussions of the civil rights era and other outstanding periods in American history. Pam Munoz Ryan's biography of Marian Anderson, entitled *When Marian Sang,* and her retelling of historical incidents in the lives of Amelia Earhart and Eleanor Roosevelt in *Amelia and Eleanor Go for a Ride,* provide intermediate-age children with an attractive segue into their social studies and history curricula. *Mercedes and the Chocolate Pilot,* written by Margot Theis Raven and based on a true story during the Berlin airlift when candy was dropped from the sky by American pilots, is told in a picture book format, and is another excellent introduction to intermediate social studies.

Young readers will obtain an informative and enjoyable glimpse of the world of mathematics by reading Don Brown's picture book biography of young Albert Einstein, *Odd Boy Out,* and Marfe Delano's *Genius: A Photobiography of Albert Einstein.* Einstein's story will help many young readers understand the importance of mathematics.

Stephen Krensky's *Dangerous Crossing: The Revolutionary Voyage of John Quincy Adams* is an exciting account of young Johnny's first voyage across the Atlantic Ocean with his father. It is considered historical fiction, but it is based on facts from John Quincy's diary. Young readers will be drawn into learning more about the Revolutionary War, while exploring how a strong relationship developed between a famous father and his equally famous son.

Teachers accustomed to assigning informational books with a minimum page requirement may doubt the value of students reading a picture book without chapters, and may question its value compared with a chapter book on the same subject. Yet they realize that these books may provide an excellent lead into nonfiction because they are authentically written and attractively illustrated. James Cross Giblin believes that picture books are gaining acceptance from older children because "young people today, accustomed to getting so much of their information from television and the Internet, want the same sort of emphasis on the visual in their books" (Giblin, 2000, p. 422).

Traditional Literature

Traditional literature delights children of the intermediate school years because of its variety. Its fables, ballads, folksongs, epics, tall tales, myths and legends, folktales, and fairy tales provide them with a vast array of books about topics from around the world. Traditional literature provides the information children are seeking while heightening their imagination.

Virginia Hamilton's *In the Beginning: Creation Stories* is an outstanding collection of African legends; Native American tales as told by Joseph Bruchac in *Between Earth and Sky* are beautifully illustrated. The following myths, legends, and folktales are further examples and range in levels of complexity that encourage intermediate school children to explore this genre independently.

Myths and Legends

ODYSSEUS IN THE SERPENT MAZE. In this retelling by Jane Yolen and Robert Harris, 13-year-old Odysseus dreams of being a hero. But he fears his chance to accomplish heroic deeds has passed him by. Fortunately (at least for him), he and his friends are kidnapped by pirates. In the future he fights in the Trojan War and then endures the dangerous voyage of the *Odyssey*, thus becoming one of the most renowned heroes of ancient Greece.

BEOWULF. James Rumford has provided intermediate school children with a version of the legend of Beowulf that is especially written for them. In it, he relates the strength and courage of the small, near sighted Beowulf, who is that rare kind of person who turns his weaknesses into strengths. Hrothgar, the Danish leader, welcomes Beowulf, who comes to the aid of his people by slaying the evil monster Grendel. Beowulf is treated as a hero as he continues to work for the justice of all.

THE WOLF OF GUBBIO. Canadian author Michael Bedard retells the ancient legend of St. Francis through the eyes of a young boy who marvels at the heroism and gentleness of this hero. When a wolf terrorizes the people of Gubbio, St. Francis confronts the wolf and quiets him. He promises the townspeople that the hungry wolf will never frighten them again as long as they feed him and are kind to him. Although *The Wolf of Gubbio* is a legend, the author writes in the Afterword that in 1873, when a chapel dedicated to St. Francis was renovated, the skull of a large wolf was found under the flagstones.

Folklore

Children listened to stories that begin "Once upon a time in a land far away" long before these tales were ever in print. They discover through their ability to compare and contrast that although these traditional tales come from every part of the world, they are often similar in characters, plot, theme, and setting. Dragons have traditionally played a fascinating role in fantasy and folklore. Now they are included with wizards and pirates in a group of large, hard-cover books called *Ologies* (Candlewick) that purport to be true stories of magic, myths, and monsters. The books themselves (e.g., *Dragonology* by Dugald A. Steer) are presented as if they were written when such phantasms as dragons ruled the world.

THE GOLDEN MARE, THE FIREBIRD, AND THE MAGIC RING. In this story, Ruth Sanderson combines elements from many Russian fairy tales. Alexi, the young hero of the story, is a huntsman who is helped by a golden mare to perform daring deeds for the Czar. Reluctantly, he captures the Firebird, which the Czar immediately locks in a cage. When the Czar asks him to find Yelena, the beautiful princess, and bring her to him, Alexi is faced with a dilemma: He himself wishes to marry Yelena. How can he solve his dilemma? With the help of the magic ring, Alexi arrives at a surprising solution, which offers a good example in problem solving for readers of these years.

THE SERPENT SLAYER AND OTHER STORIES OF STRONG WOMEN. A daughter, Katrin Tchana, and mother, Trina Schart Hyman, collaborate to retell thirteen fairy tales from around the world in which strong women are the heroines with strong self-concepts. Their exploits exhibit courage, strength, ingenuity, and intelligence, and their stories are written to be read aloud by mothers to their daughters and by sisters to their sisters. This book is large and beautifully illustrated, and the content is ideal for the intermediate school child.

THE BLACK BULL OF NORROWAY. Charlotte Huck retells this charming Scottish tale that appeared in 1842 in the *Popular Rhymes* of Scotland. Two of three sisters who leave the wise woman's house to seek their fortunes drive away in horse-driven coaches. But Peggy Ann, the youngest, leaves on the back of the Black Bull of Norroway.

BEAUTY AND THE BEAST. Originally published in England, Geraldine McCaughrean's *Beauty and the Beast* re-creates Beauty as a heroine who is exquisitely beautiful, and unusually kind and good. She gallantly agrees to live with the Beast, fulfilling her father's promise to the Beast because "a promise given must be a promise kept." Yet she is overcome with loneliness and longs to see her family again. The illustrations of *Beauty and the Beast* are the work of English artist Gary Blythe, winner of England's Kate Greenaway Medal. Entirely contemporary, the pictures will appeal to intermediate school children who dream of happy endings.

Spin Off

Children Interact with Traditional Literature

• *Who Am I?* Using *Heroes and Heroines* as a literary theme, children read a story (or stories) about courageous men and women, such as the *legend* of King Arthur, the *myth* of Odysseus, or the heroines depicted in *The Serpent Slayer and Other Stories of Strong Women*, and summarize what they read on cards. On one side they draw or copy a picture of their hero or heroine, and on the reverse side they write a short description. Each student in turn selects one of the cards, reads the description out loud, and asks the group to guess "Who Am I?"

• *Fractured Fairy Tales.* The fairy tale is a genre that lends itself to various interpretations. Jon Scieszka, for example, has written *The True Story of the 3 Little Pigs*, a hilarious account of what really happened as told by A. Wolf. Ask your students to write their version of what really happened in *Beauty and the Beast* from the viewpoint of A. Beast. By extending their reading to include other versions of favorite fairy tales, such as Cinderella and Little Red Riding Hood, they can write their own fractured versions of "what really happened" and then read them to the class.

• *Make a Graphic Novel.* Suggest that your students draw cartoons based on their reading of *Beowulf*. Each child cuts a letter-sized piece of paper into two-inch-wide strips and then divides each strip into three sections. Students illustrate one event in each section—for example, Grendel attacking the village, Beowulf meeting Hrothgar, Beowulf wrestling with Grendel, and so on. Using balloons to contain the imagined conversations of each of the characters, they staple the pages together to make a book similar to a graphic novel.

Fantasy

Fantasy as a genre gained many young followers with the publication of J. K. Rowling's *Harry Potter* series. Children who have been reluctant to explore the wonders of this genre are now drawn to it by their intense desire to seek information and their voracious desire to read each Harry Potter book as soon as it is published. Many have expanded this interest and are reading classical fantasies such as C. S. Lewis's *The Chronicles of Narnia* series, L. Frank Baum's *Oz* series, Mary Norton's *The Borrowers*, and Kenneth Grahame's *The Wind in the Willows*. Books like these are an excellent resource for teachers to read aloud in their classrooms.

Fantasy to Read Aloud

Due to their growing cognitive maturity, children of these years make rapid strides on the path to distinguishing fantasy from reality. The fantasy world remains attractive and can be a spur to healthy development. In fact, Vygotsky (1978) argued that the make-believe dimension creates a special *zone of proximal development* that encourages children to behave beyond their years. When teachers and librarians select books to read aloud, such as *Tom's Midnight Garden* (Pearce, 1959), they are motivating their students to read widely and broaden their interests, as well as enhancing cognitive and emotional aspects of their development (Berk, 2000).

Modern Fantasy

HARRY POTTER AND THE SORCERER'S STONE. Around the world children (and many adults) are enjoying J. K. Rowling's stories. Beginning with *The Sorcerer's Stone*, Harry Potter accepts an invitation delivered by Hadwig, the owl messenger, to leave his miserable existence with his Muggle relatives, the Dursleys, and join the witches in Hogwarts School of Wizardy and Witchcraft. There he learns to play quiditch; makes friends with Ron Weasley, Hermione, and the headmaster, Albus Dumbledore; and discovers that Lord Voldemort caused his parents' deaths.

ROWAN OF RIN. When it was first published in Australia, *Rowan of Rin* won its country's Children's Book Council Award for Book of the Year for Younger Readers. Its author, Emily Rodda, has won this award five times. In *Rowan of Rin*, she skillfully develops the main character, Rowan. In the beginning, he is too timid to investigate for himself why the stream of water so important to the village has stopped flowing from the mountain. The villagers are convinced that a dragon living at the top of the mountain is the cause. Rowan becomes a hero when he courageously faces the dragon. Since this book was written, others have followed. In the fifth book, *Rowan and the Ice Creepers*, Rowan and his friends face the ice creepers—snakelike monsters—as events from the previous books are interwoven into the plot.

AFTERNOON OF THE ELVES. Janet Taylor Lisle's Newbery Honor book is the story of 9-year-old Hillary and her friendship with Sara-Kate, an 11-year-old whom everyone warns Hillary to stay away from. But the inquisitive Hillary can't resist the miniature village in Sara-Kate's backyard, which was supposedly built by elves, and she becomes increasingly interested in what Sara-Kate is really like.

• *Dominic* needs a map to carry in his bandana to guide him in his picaresque journey. Suggest that your students collaborate in making a large map, illustrating it with the people and places Dominic meets along the way.

• In *Afternoon of the Elves*, Sara-Kate meets elves—but does she realize how many different kinds of little people exist in fantasies throughout the world? Little people belong to every culture: the leprechauns of Ireland, the goblins of France, the brownies of Scotland, and the dwarfs of Scandinavia, to mention only a few. Your students may like to research this topic and then categorize their findings into:

Name   Place of Origin   Qualities   Place in Literature

• A discussion with children about the importance of eating well may lead to an analysis of the popular *If You Give a Mouse a Cookie* (Numeroff, 1985). It offers you the opportunity to suggest that each student or pair of students (one designated as writer and the other as illustrator) write a book using Numeroff's as a model. Imagine what the results might be if they chose a title such as *If You Give a Mouse a Trip to Disney World*, or a chance to play professional football or become a movie star!

Animal Fantasy

STUART LITTLE. The idea of Stuart came to E. B. White in a dream. He is not your usual mouse, but is the offspring of the Littles, a New York family. Stuart has many friends, such as Margalo the bird and Snowball the cat, and skills such as driving a car and maneuvering a boat. He is a unique mouse who is much loved and is a worthy literary partner for Wilbur, White's well-known pig.

DOMINIC. William Steig is a master of fantasy. His picture books (*Amos and Boris*, *Doctor DeSoto*, and *The Amazing Bone*) are classics of this genre. Many of his books have also been translated into Spanish. *Dominic* is a fantasy that appeals to intermediate school children because of its altruism. Dominic is brave, kind, and generous. A dog who wears many hats, Dominic begins a journey and confronts the evil Doomsday Gang on many occasions. Using his wit and ingenuity, he overcomes them, becomes well known throughout the land, and makes many friends.

Poetry

Children of the intermediate school years are bathed in a world of words. Their vocabulary continues to exhibit swift growth, they have mastered the basic grammatical elements of their language, and they are constantly devising ways to use new words. Writing in their journals is exciting for them as their cognitive development stimulates their language expression (Dacey & Travers, 2009). Children's language acquisition is one of the most amazing features of their development.

Knowing this, you can understand the appeal of poetry to children of these years. The words, the sequence, and the rhythm can draw them from the here-and-now into another world where they can vividly explore new ideas. As Konner (1991) notes, poetry acts on all ages, even adults, in a similar manner. The words become a vehicle for children to evoke their own emotions about the world around them. For them, poetry expresses humor and sadness, love and loss, courage and strength. The power of poetry can be demonstrated in the selections by which teachers and librarians introduce this genre to their readers.

Poets who specialize in writing light verse for children include Shel Silverstein (*Where the Sidewalk Ends, A Light in the Attic*, etc.) and Children's Poet Laureate Jack Prelutsky (*The Beauty of the Beast, A Pizza the Size of the Sun*, and others). They have succeeded in amassing a huge audience of intermediate school children. Often children are seen reading their books and giggling as they share poems like *Spaghetti* (*Where the Sidewalk Ends*, p. 100) with their friends:

Spaghetti, spaghetti all over the place.

Up to my elbows—up to my face.

Over the carpet and under the chairs.

Into the hammock and wound round the stairs.

Filling the bathtub and covering the desk,

Making the sofa a mad mushy mess.

The party is ruined. I'm terribly worried,

The guests have all left (unless they're all buried)

I told them, "Bring presents." I said, "Throw confetti."

I guess they heard wrong

'Cause they all threw spaghetti.

Unfortunately, although children gravitate toward his work, Shel Silverstein never received an award from the National Teachers of English as an outstanding poet for children.

Poetry for Reading Aloud

As teachers, librarians, and parents, you can help children appreciate the works of poets like John Ciardi (*You Read to Me, I'll Read to You*), Arnold Lobel (*The Book of Pigericks: Pig Limericks*), David McCord (*All Day Long: Fifty Rhymes of the Never Was and Always Is*), and A. A. Milne (*When We Were Very Young*) by reading selections aloud. As you share your enthusiasm for poetry and relate it to their experiences, you will develop in your listeners a love of poetry. Below are examples of poems and attractive anthologies that appeal to a child's imagination, humor, and love of nonsense. These poems are also more fun when they are shared.

Anthologies

SING A SONG OF POPCORN. Illustrated by nine Caldecott Medal artists and selected by Beatrice Schenk de Regniers, Eva Moore, Mary Michaels White, and Jan Carr, *Sing a Song of Popcorn* contains over 125 poems about the weather, spooks, animals, people, nonsense, feeling, seeing, and thinking. Some are short, such as Langston Hughes' *Winter Moon*, defined in metaphor and simile. He conveys in verse how children may imagine the moon on a bitter, cold night.

Others are narrative poems, like Edward Lear's classic *The Jumblies* and Ogden Nash's *The Adventures of Isabel*, both cleverly illustrated by Maurice Sendak. Christina G. Rossetti's *The Caterpillar* and *Who Has Seen the Wind* are both included in this beautiful anthology, as well as poems by Eve Merriam, Lillian Moore, Carl Sandburg, and many others.

THE OXFORD ILLUSTRATED BOOK OF AMERICAN CHILDREN'S POEMS. Edited by Donald Hall, this collection begins with anonymous Native American verses and spans two centuries of children's poetry. It includes many classic poems by well-known poets such as Robert Frost, Emily Dickinson, and T. S. Eliot, and contemporary poetry written by Karla Kuskin, Shel Silverstein, Nancy Willard, Mary Ann Hoberman, and others. The selections reflect America's diversity, and range from a humorous African American selection to poems by Sonia Sanchez and Francisco X. Alarcon. It is brightly illustrated and contains poems that were once popular, but would now be difficult to find in other recent anthologies.

THE BEAUTY OF THE BEAST. Jack Prelutsky, the Children's Poet Laureate, has selected two hundred poems illustrated by Meilo So for this anthology about the animal kingdom. The poems range from long, humorous poems such as Michael Flanders' *Crocodile* to Prelutsky's three-line stanza *Jubilant We Swim* narrated by a fish and filled with alliterative words.

Individual Poets

LIFE DOESN'T FRIGHTEN ME. Maya Angelou's poem has special significance for intermediate school children, who may sometimes suffer from Erikson's sense of inferiority. She herself experienced trauma as a child, but has survived to become a well-known author, actress, and lecturer. In her poem she describes all the things that could frighten her: shadows on the wall, unexpected noises and dogs that bark too loud. They do not because she has a "magic charm" that gives her power over her fears.

The illustrations of Jean-Michel Basquiat, and his contemporary images from movies, television, jazz, and sports, reflect the feelings expressed in Maya Angelou's *Life Doesn't Frighten Me*.

PAUL. Award-winning Karla Kuskin interweaves her poetry throughout *Paul*, along with Milton Avery's contemporary illustrations. Paul is searching for someone to listen to him, much like other children in this developmental period. When his parents are too busy to listen to him, he seeks his magic grandmother through a series of adventures with a flying pig, a blue-eyed caterpillar, a fish that turns into a wand, and a singing cat, among other elusive characters. Paul sings a song for each character he encounters.

Contemporary Realistic Fiction

As you may remember, Theo, the young girl in our opening vignette missed being part of a real family. She was not happy in school, because her moving from place to place precluded her from being involved in school activities. Many children of intermediate school age are concerned about these issues and are eager to read about different kinds of families and other children's experiences at school. They also have an innate curiosity about the world around them, have a quirky sense of humor, and love to solve mysteries. The following books, examples of contemporary realistic fiction, will increase children's enjoyment of stories about family, school, sports, and mysteries.

Family

SIMEON'S FIRE. Cathryn Clinton's story about the young Amish boy Simeon reveals many realistic details about how children live in contemporary Amish society. Although 10-year-old Simeon is destined to be a farmer like his forebears, he enjoys caring for animals so much so that he wonders if he should become a veterinarian.

THE QUIGLEYS IN A SPIN. The fourth book in a series by Simon Mason reveals hilarious new hijinks of a very "ordinary" family. Each member—Dad, Mum, Will, and Lucy—have a story to tell. Even the family cat's rescue becomes a noodleheaded adventure.

CADDY EVER AFTER. In her fourth book about the Casson family, Hilary McKay continues to reveal the trials and tribulations of a regular, down-to-earth, engaging family. Although the book is nominally about the oldest daughter, Caddy, the plot involves other members of the family and their relationships with each other.

HAPPY KID! In Gail Gauthier's novel, an insecure young boy, impressed by what he has read in a self-help book, startles his friends and family with his change of personality. His troubles begin, however, when he starts to believe that the book is sending him messages!

School

ENCORE, GRACE. In Mary Hoffman's first book about Grace (*Boundless Grace*), the main character thinks she is not a member of a real family because she and her father live apart. Not until she and her nanna visit him and his new family in Africa does she discover that even though she and her father are separated, they can still love each other. In this sequel, popular, happy, and talented Grace shares adventures with her school friends. When the new girl, Chrishell, almost drowns as the chums are playing hookie from school, Grace and her schoolmates are faced with many questions they must answer.

ME, TARZAN. Popular author Betsy Byar's *Me, Tarzan* relates a humorous, lighthearted event in the school life of Dorothy, the girl who wins the part of Tarzan in the school play. Every time she practices her Tarzan yell, strange things happen: dogs, cats, and horses appear from miles around. When the circus comes to town, a puma escapes and is found in a tree in Dorothy's yard. What happens the night of the school play when Dorothy gives the yell of her life delights readers of this age, and they too may be heard yelling out loud.

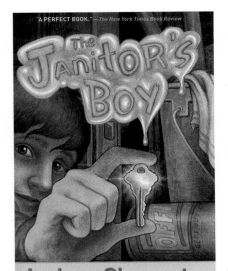

THE JANITOR'S BOY. Andrew Clements has written another school story that touches children of intermediate school age. Jack, embarrassed because his father is the school janitor, plans his revenge: he plants huge gobs of gum under one of the desks in the classroom. The assistant principal punishes him by assigning him to work with his dad and clean every desk and chair in the school. Gradually, by talking with his dad, he begins to understand why his dad chose to be a janitor. He also discovers the significance of the two keys he removes from his father's office and how they relate to his father's past experiences.

JANITOR'S BOY
© 2000 *Brian Selznick. Used with permission. All rights reserved.*

Spotlight On
Patricia Reilly Giff

© Tim Keating for Random House Children's Books

Patricia Reilly Giff was born April 26, 1935, in New York. She was educated at Marymount College and St. John's University, and received a diploma in reading from Hofstra University in 1975. Being an elementary school teacher from 1964 to 1971 offered her many opportunities to interact with children. Her work as a reading specialist from 1971 to 1984 contributed to her understanding of the reading difficulties young children experience. "I had worked with so many children who had terrible problems, that I wanted to say things that could make them laugh. . . . I did not begin writing about these incidents until the 70's" (Giff, 2001, p. 89). She confesses that she wishes she had started sooner telling children they were special (*Something about the Author*).

Her books are attuned to young children's sense of humor. *The Kids of the Polk Street School* series began in 1985 and was followed by *The New Kids at the Polk Street School* in 1988. In the meantime, she had written the *Polka Dot, Private Eye* series in 1987. She continues to write for this age group. Giff has an unerring sense of what appeals to children and explores situations with which they are familiar, such as putting on a class play or having a pet. Although she has written many books, getting started was not easy for her. She admits that at first writing was slow and painful, but now it is as important to her as breathing.

Patricia Reilly Giff—although a popular author of choice for beginning independent readers for many years and an author that teachers and librarians constantly recommend to their students—only recently attracted the attention of critics when her novel *Lily's Crossing* was selected as a Newbery Honor book, a Boston Globe–Horn Book Honor Book, and an ALA Notable Book for Children. She was also the winner of a Parenting Reading Magic Award. *Lily's Crossing* is one of her first books of historical fiction. In 2000, she wrote a dramatic story for intermediate and middle school students, *Nory Ryan's Song*, which describes the suffering and starvation of the Ryan family in Ireland during the famine of the mid-nineteenth century. A story far different from the lighthearted series she began writing years ago, it is a serious study of survival that she wanted to write so that her children, grandchildren, and others could understand how brave and courageous their ancestors were. She has added a sequel to this story, *Maggie's Door* (2003), about another journey Sean and Nory make as they begin a new life in America.

Patricia Giff writes about the quiet sorrows and simple pleasures of ordinary children. She understands the developmental needs of the intermediate school child and continues to address the growing maturity of the older, middle school student. She is an author who is devoted to fulfilling the goodness-of-fit concept.

DEAR WHISKERS. Ann Whitehead Nagda has created a generous, enthusiastic character in Jenny, the fourth-grader who is assigned a younger child to be her pen pal. Since Jenny's pen pal cannot speak or write English, Jenny at first wonders why she has to work with Sameera, who has just immigrated from Saudi Arabia. She tries reading mouse books to her, but not even *If You Give a Mouse a Cookie* (Numeroff, 1985) elicits a response from Sameera. Determined to help her, Jenny bakes her "mouse cookies." Through her English as a Second Language classes and Jenny's attention, Sameera gradually becomes a real pen pal, and Jenny discovers as much about Sameera's Middle Eastern culture as she does about the power of her home-baked cookies.

THE YEAR OF MISS AGNES. In this short but sensitive story, written by Kirkpatrick Hill, 10-year-old Fred (short for Frederika) welcomes her new teacher Miss Agnes to the one-room schoolhouse in her small Athabascan village on the Koyukuk River in Alaska. Although she and her classmates know little about Sylvia Ashton-Warner's teaching techniques, they know that Miss Agnes treats each of them as an individual, encourages them to succeed, and considers even the most difficult child to be teachable.

Sports

Children this age are ready—physically, mentally, and socially—to play sports (though some children may prefer other activities). The following book by Avi will be especially interesting to the latter group.

S.O.R. LOSERS. In this book, Avi writes about a group of players who are drafted for a special soccer team, even though none of them wants to play and none of them wants to win. Their captain actually tapes the word "LOSERS" on their shirts so all the fans will know how contrarian they are, how independent they are, and how unimportant the game is for them. Each excels in other subjects, like writing, mathematics, and science, but refuses to take sports seriously.

For sports-oriented children, the following books serve their goodness-of-fit.

THE FOX STEALS HOME. Matt Christopher's book *The Fox Steals Home* deals not only with Bobby's perseverance in baseball, but also with the resolution of his feelings about his parents' impending divorce. Christopher has written over fifty other books about school sports that also help children to face non–sports-related problems, whether biological, psychological, or social.

PLAY-BY-PLAY. Mel Glenn's first book concerns a group of fourth-graders who are encouraged by their new gym teacher to play soccer, regardless of gender. Girls and boys learn to get along, while discovering a great deal about themselves and their teammates. Lloyd, for example, is extremely competitive and mean to Jeremy, who is his friend off the playing field. Jeremy wants to feel good about himself, but wonders what he is made of. He'd certainly like to be made of the same stuff as his comic book heroes, because they never let anyone down. Through games and practices, however, the players grow together into a cohesive team.

A NEGRO LEAGUE SCRAPBOOK. Carole Weatherford has provided sports enthusiasts with a scrapbook to browse through and discover baseball artifacts, such as short biographies of sports figures like Jackie Robinson and Roberto Clemente, and authentic archival photos of a bygone era.

Mysteries

Mystery stories filled with action are a staple of the intermediate school child's reading diet. Mysteries capture their imagination and increase the speed of their silent reading as they seek to discover the fates of their favorite characters. Students this age are challenged to use their mental ability to seek solutions to problems, and are pleased when they discover the clues that lead to a satisfying conclusion.

WHO IS STEALING THE 12 DAYS OF CHRISTMAS? Martha Freeman tells the story of Alex, his best friend Yasmeen, and his ace detective cat Luau, who are determined to discover who has taken the Twelve Days of Christmas display from their street. Especially challenging for first-time mystery readers, the plot, frequently humorous, develops quickly and almost tragically, before concluding satisfactorily for young readers.

THE MEANEST DOLL IN THE WORLD. Written by Ann M. Martin and Laura Godwin, this book is cleverly illustrated by Brian Selznick, who knows dolls: action dolls, dollhouse dolls, baby dolls, trolls, and paper dolls. The dolls are running from the meanest doll in the world, Princess Mimi doll. When the dolls finally take a stand to defend themselves against this evil one, their secret lives are about to be revealed.

THE BAD BEGINNING. Lemony Snicket (Daniel Handler's pseudonym) captures the imagination and interest of children with a *Series of Unfortunate Events*, which opens with a warning that there are no happy endings in these books. The thirteen-book series relates the hair-raising and often humorous adventures of the three Baudelaire orphans. In each book, the orphans attempt to outwit adults such as Count Olaf, who is scheming to trick the children out of their inheritance. In addition, the author offers offhand advice to his readers and explains words (e.g., *denouement*) to help them understand what is happening.

The following stories, with their engaging themes, carefully controlled vocabularies, and appropriate level of difficulty, are particularly attractive to reluctant readers.

THE CASE OF THE CHOCOLATE SNATCHER. Written under the pseudonym M. Masters, *The Case of the Chocolate Snatcher* relates the adventures of Hawkeye Collins and Amy Adams, two of the most popular sleuths for intermediate school children. In nine short stories they solve each mystery they encounter by using Hawkeye's ability to sketch important clues. Like Sobol's *Encyclopedia Brown* series, readers are asked to solve the mysteries themselves, and solutions are given at the end of the book. Unlike Sobol, however, M. Masters uses mirror writing for the solutions, which make them a little more challenging for the reader.

THE MYSTERY OF THE STOLEN CORN POPPER. In this David Adler mystery, Cam Jansen and her sidekick, Eric, use her photographic memory to track down a thief during a department store sale. Short chapters, a limited vocabulary, and a realistic plot appeal to children who are beginning to read independently.

THE GIGANTIC ANT AND OTHER CASES. This book by Seymour Simon is a revision of *Einstein Anderson Makes Up for Lost Time*. Einstein Anderson is now called the "Science Detective," who uses his scientific knowledge to solve a variety of puzzles, including a snake that chases people and a machine that can stop hurricanes. It is geared to the child who likes riddles and jokes and is beginning to develop a knowledge of science.

SEBASTIAN AND THE EGYPTIAN CONNECTION. Mary Blount Christian involves the dog Sebastian, a "four-on-the-floor" detective, in helping his master solve the mystery of a shipment of Egyptian artifacts that have disappeared. Although the thoughts of Sebastian are carefully recorded, giving the book a touch of fantasy, children like it for its realistic humor and its element of mystery. Other books in the series are *Sebastian (Super Sleuth) and the Stars in His Eyes Mystery*, and *Sebastian (Super Sleuth) and the Purloined Sirloin*.

Spin Off

Children Interact with Contemporary Realistic Fiction

The following are suggestions for activities to motivate your students to read a wide variety of contemporary literature.

An informal discussion. By informally discussing the value of reading books in a series (*The Bad Beginning*, for example), your students may discover how much they like reading about characters they have already met, or, conversely, how bored they become reading about the same characters repeatedly.

Planning a board game. Students in a group designing a mystery board game based on a story like *Encyclopedia Brown* not only recall the setting, characters, and plot, but also share the fun of working together.

Adopting a pen pal. Each student recommends a book to her/his pen pal that they both will enjoying reading. Before long, an email book club may develop.

Favorite sports books. Two "sports talk hosts" (with microphones), after preparing questions, walk up and down the classroom asking their "audience" about their favorite sports books to demonstrate that reading books is "cool." Be sure to include the girls.

Historical Fiction

Historical fiction encompasses so much that is true and so much that is imaginary, it is amazing that writers have been able to skillfully blend both into an appealing genre for the intermediate school child. Talented authors, by capitalizing on the cognitive and moral levels of development of this age group, address the interest children in this group have in the past and in how the past influences the present. Authors of historical fiction for intermediate school children subtly pose questions of right and wrong (See Chapter One discussion of Kohlberg) that force readers to detect and solve moral dilemmas. In this way, they help children face real issues and sharpen their critical thinking skills (Santrock, 2007).

Culture and Children's Literature

Understanding Each Other

When the fictitious heroine Theo, in our opening vignette, mentions the *All-of-a-Kind Family* and how much she would like to be part of one, she is thinking about one immigrant Jewish family and its remarkable adjustment to living in New York City at the beginning of the twentieth century. But children's literature is filled with stories of families from all nations who experience happiness and heartbreak as they struggle to retain their culture while adapting to life in their adopted country. For many, the English language is difficult to learn.

In Carol Flynn Harris's touching historical novel for intermediate school children *A Place for Joey*, Joey Calabro is a young boy who has been living in the North End of Boston since arriving with his family from Italy in the early 1900s. Although he struggles with speaking and writing English, he patiently teaches his mother how to speak English. He enjoys living in the North End, where family and friends live close together and work together in the neighboring stores and restaurants. He attends school with his best friend Dominic and is devastated when his mother informs him that they're moving to a farm in the country. "I gotta get a job. I gotta stay in the North End with Dominic," he mutters to himself. But jobs are scarce, especially for a young immigrant with little education like Joey.

One day when he skips school to look for work, he is trapped in the "molasses flood." (It is a historical fact that a massive tank of molasses exploded on the waterfront and covered the streets in that part of Boston with five feet of molasses. Twenty-one people lost their lives and many more were injured.) When Joey unselfishly saves the life of an Irish policeman who had previously been mean to him, he becomes a hero. He also fulfills his promise to the Saints in Heaven that he will go with his family to Watertown, but will return to his beloved North End when he is older and will become the first Italian policeman in Boston.

Through this engaging book, Flynn Harris captures the difficulty of families adjusting to a different culture. She also reveals animosity between the Irish and the Italians until they come to understand their reciprocal values. Simultaneously, she sympathetically reveals the struggle of immigrants making a home for themselves in a strange land.

Historical Fiction and Curriculum Connections

Authors of historical fiction write about events from many historical periods that make contemporary children think they are actually there. Historical fiction such as the following offers students a natural segue into their social studies curriculum.

- **ALMOST TO FREEDOM.** Vaunda Nelson's *Almost to Freedom* is the story of a brave young slave girl's escape, told through the words of her rag doll. It increases children's awareness of the bitter days of slavery.

- **LILY'S CROSSING.** The main character in Patricia Reilly Giff's book is Lily, whose family spends summer every year at the beach in Rockaway, New York, until the summer of 1944. That's the summer her father enlists and goes overseas to fight in France. Her best friend Margaret moves away, and Lily lives in the cottage with her demanding grandmother. Not until Albert, a shy and lonely young Hungarian refugee, arrives to stay with a neighbor does Lily have a friend.

- **THE WATSONS GO TO BIRMINGHAM—1963.** Christopher Paul Curtis's Newbery Honor book is the journey of the Watson family: Byron the "juvenile delinquent," Kenny the 10-year-old narrator their little sister Joetta, and Momma and Dad. When they leave their home in Flint, Michigan to head south to visit Grandma, they are in a jovial mood. Both Dad's sense of humor and his new car, the "Ultra Glide," take them merrily on their long journey without stopping. But when they arrive in Alabama they experience the bombing of the Sixteenth Street Baptist Church in Birmingham, where four young worshipers are killed.

HISTORICAL FICTION IN A SERIES   Historical events related in a well-written fiction series captivate children who are beginning to study the social sciences. Yet it is important that they distinguish fiction (not true, but based on truth) from nonfiction (which is true and thoroughly documented). Two carefully researched series are the *Dear Mr. President* series, written by Jennifer Armstrong (one entry of which is *Thomas Jefferson: Letters from a Philadelphia Bookworm*) and the *Dear America* series written by various outstanding authors such as Mary Pope Osborne, who wrote *After The Rain* (about Washington, DC, in 1864); Jim Murphy, who wrote *My Face to the Wind* (about Broken Bow, Nebraska, 1881); and Kathryn Lasky who wrote *A Time for Courage: The Suffragette Diary of Kathleen Bowen*. Each series is a group of letters or journals *supposedly* written by a young person about a specific historic event. Children often consider these series biographical since the events and some of the characters are real, but these journals and letters are works of historical fiction.

Biography and Autobiography

Often when children this age select biographies, they select them because "they have to." Unfamiliar with the qualities of good biographies, they gravitate to those that puff up their favorite movie icon or television hero. Only when teachers and librarians offer them the opportunity to read biographies of outstanding men and women of various cultures will intermediate school children have the pleasure of reading about a person—*a role model*—who may give them courage or inspiration. (See the discussion of Bandura in Chapter Nine.)

Biographies and Autobiographies of Musicians, Writers, Artists, and Inventors

Students in the intermediate years who are eager to learn more about a subject like music and the arts, history and adventure, or sports and hobbies can be gently guided to biographies of literary merit such as the following.

FRIDA. Jonah Winter's biography about the Mexican artist Frida Kahlo is filled with Ana Juan's imaginative illustrations based on traditional Mexican folk art. The author attributes Frida's remarkable artistic ability to the time that she was bed-ridden at age 7 with polio, and when she was critically injured in a bus accident at 18. Even though she was lonely at times, instead of crying, she paints pictures of herself crying.

E. B. WHITE. In *To The Point: A Story about E. B. White*, David Collins makes reference to the essays White wrote for *The New Yorker*, *Harper's Bazaar*, and other magazines, but emphasizes that the books he wrote for children are his legacy. White's first book was about the mouse Stuart Little, and Collins movingly describes how Stuart's amazing adventures gained him many fans—50,000 of them purchased copies of *Stuart Little* in one month. White's second book, *Charlotte's Web*, appeared in 1952 and became an instant best-seller, as did *Trumpet of the Swan*, his third and last book written for children.

Then and Now

Biographies

Although biography has always been an appealing genre of children's literature, discussion has generally focused on the following questions: Should biography include fictionalized scenes and dialogue in order to interest young readers? Should children be protected from negative factors in the subject's life, or should children read about both the negative and positive aspects of the person the author portrays? Can biography for children be just as engaging if it is based entirely on facts?

Then

In 1959, when Jean Latham won the Newbery Award for her biography *Carry On, Mr. Bowditch,* she readily admitted that her book was a "fictionalized biography." Such an acknowledgment was not unusual. Many critics believed that fictionalized biography was the best style of biography for young people, especially since it was difficult for authors to combine readability with original research in a way suitable for young readers.

As early as 1932 a series of biographies called The Bobbs-Merrill Childhood Books followed the fictionalized approach. They were very popular and continue to be read by young students. Typically, these biographies used inventive dialogue. Called "the orange biographies," they were identified by the color of their covers. These books concentrated entirely on the youth of famous people so that children were required to use additional sources to learn about their adult years.

For many years, biographies about minorities or women were not readily available for children. The first biography of a non-Western individual to be recognized as worthy of a Newbery Honor was Jeanette Eaton's *Gandhi, Fighter without a Sword* (1951). Only since the 1960s, when the civil rights movement intensified, did the courageous stories of men and women like Martin Luther King, Rosa Parks, and Harriet Tubman become the subjects of biographies for children.

Biographers at this time unintentionally immortalized their subjects by not discussing their death. In 1940 the D'Aulaires won the Caldecott Medal for *Abraham Lincoln,* even though they made no mention of Lincoln's assassination. Apparently, biographers were protecting youngsters from the harsh realities of life. The D'Aulaires also had a unique way of impressing their young readers, writing that "George Washington learned to be good and honest and never tell a lie," or pontificating that after Ben Franklin spent too much for a whistle, "it was the last time [he] ever spent a penny unwisely," without cautioning youngsters not to take these admonitions too seriously.

Now

Today's biographers do not avoid the sadness and unhappy incidents in a person's life. Louise Borden and Mary Kay Kroeger in their biography *Fly High!* (2000) describe the unfortunate circumstances of the death of Bessie Coleman, the first black person to receive a pilot's license. Jean Fritz, the author of very readable biographies for children such as *Where Do You Think You're Going, Christopher Columbus?,* has commented that she gathers as much evidence as she can to make her biographies accurate and authentic, and includes the positive aspects of her subjects' characters and their foibles as well.

In *Martin's Big Words: The Life of Martin Luther King Jr.,* written by Doreen Rappaport for early and intermediate elementary school children, Dr. King's life is described using appropriate quotations from his speeches that reflect crucial events in his life, including the March on Washington. Attractive collages, a Foreword, a chronology, further readings, and websites add to the authenticity of this biography.

Contemporary biographers emphasize thorough research, the use of actual letters, diaries, and conversations, as well as extensive bibliographies, maps, and actual photographs. Marc Aronson, author of *Sir Walter Ralegh and the Quest for El Dorado,* a biography for older children, raises the bar of excellence in biographies for children when he emphasizes the intelligence of children who read biographies and asks us not to underestimate their abilities. He urges authors of nonfiction for young readers to experiment, take risks, and try all sorts of narrative forms (Aronson, 2001).

The writing of biographies for children continues to evolve. It is one of the most exciting genres in children's literature, where children are encouraged to model the outstanding characteristics of another's life.

White died at the age of 83, and as Wilbur the pig said at the death of his spider friend Charlotte in *Charlotte's Web*, "It is not often that someone comes along who is a true friend and a good writer." White's millions of friends could say the same about him.

MARVELOUS MATTIE: HOW MARGARET E. KNIGHT BECAME AN INVENTOR. Emily Arnold McCully has written and illustrated with humor and gentleness the unusual story of a young girl who was an inventor even as a child. Using tools in the box she inherited from her father, she made whirligigs, kites, and a foot warmer for her mother. Very methodically, she drew her innovative designs in a notebook she called *My Inventions*. Later, when she worked in the New England mills, she invented many life-saving devices; the patent of one was almost stolen from her.

PHILIPPE PETIT. On one level, Mordicai Gerstein's story *The Man Who Walked Between the Towers* relates a breath-taking incident in the life of Philippe Petit, the French high-wire walker who could not resist the urge to dance between New York City's twin towers. That was in 1974. After the police arrested him, he was sentenced to perform in Central Park. On an entirely different level, Gerstein recalls for his readers the memory laden incident of September 11, 2001, when New York's twin towers were destroyed. His remarkable illustrations create a bond in the reader's mind between the daring exploits of a French street performer and the tragedy of the World Trade Center.

AUTOBIOGRAPHICAL JOURNALS   Many children this age are required to write personal diaries and journals as a class assignment. The *I Was There* series by Connie and Peter Roop provide them with excellent examples, such as *The Diary of David R. Leeper, Rushing for Gold*. These models provide a blueprint of how a biography or autobiography should be written.

Biographies about Adventurers

Intermediate school children will discover models to emulate when they read about the bravery of the following adventurers and historical figures.

MARY KINGSLEY. Don Brown has written and illustrated *Uncommon Traveler: Mary Kingsley in Africa*, the biography of a young woman who endured a dreary childhood in Victorian England while caring for her sick mother. After her parents' death, she explored places and rivers in Africa where no one else had ever been. She managed to defend herself against crocodiles, hippos, and other wild animals, and she once "clipped an eight foot crocodile on the mouth with a paddle" because it "had not learned manners."

ROY CHAPMAN ANDREWS. Ann Bausum's photobiography *Dragon Bones and Dinosaur Eggs* about the famous explorer Roy Chapman Andrews, will satisfy the most scientifically curious intermediate school child. Chapman is credited with finding the bones of a new species of dinosaur named *Protoceratops andrewsi* in his honor. He also led five scientific expeditions into Mongolia's Gobi Desert, where he had many hair-raising, death-defying adventures.

DANIEL HALL. Diane Stanley based her amazing adventure (*The True Adventure of Daniel Hall*) on the personal journal of Daniel Hall, who was only 14 when he set sail in 1856 from New Bedford, Massachusetts, on the *Condor*, a whaling ship heading for the Arctic. Although his life had been dangerously spent hunting whales and enduring horrible weather, he had no idea how terrible it would be when he ended up in the penal colony of Oudskoi in Siberia, in the most desolate and coldest part of Russia.

Biographies about Historical Figures

Historical biographies for children far outnumber biographies that target other age groups. Not all biographies, however, are of equal literary merit. Jean Fritz, a favorite biographer of intermediate school age children, uses catchy titles such as *Where Do You Think You're Going, Christopher Columbus?* to sustain the curiosity of children to the point where they want to read "everything she has written." When Fritz writes biographies, she makes certain her subjects are accurately portrayed, warts and all.

ANDREW JACKSON. The title of Robert Quackenbush's *Who Let Muddy Boots into the White House?* makes children this age smile. How often have they heard their parents warn them not to come inside with muddy shoes? The title refers to the description of the common people who came dancing, singing, and roaring to Jackson's inaugural celebration, where they soiled carpets with their heavy, dirty boots. Other biographies in this series are *What Has Wild Tom Done Now?*, about Thomas Edison, and *Don't You Dare Shoot That Bear!*, about Theodore Roosevelt.

MARTIN LUTHER KING, JR. Diane Patrick traces the life of this Baptist minister from his early days and education to his leadership in the civil rights movement. King was the youngest man to receive the Nobel Peace Prize. He was always at the forefront of advocating equal rights for blacks and was instrumental in the passage of the Voting Rights Act of 1963. He led thousands of blacks and whites in the March on Washington in August 1963.

SOJOURNER TRUTH. In *Only Passing Through*, Ann Rockwell relates how Isabella was sold as a slave when she was 9 years old. By the time she was 16, she was six feet tall and had been given in marriage to another slave. Through the kindness of a Quaker family she was set free. Deciding then that her old name belonged to her old life, she adopted the name Sojourner Truth. She traveled throughout New York and New England to let people know the terrible truth about slavery. More than a hundred years after her death in 1883, the United States launched a small vehicle to explore Mars that was named Sojourner, in honor of the slave who had looked to the stars.

ONLY PASSING THROUGH: SOJOURNER TRUTH
Used by permission of Alfred A. Knopf, an imprint of Random House Children's Books, a division of Random House, Inc.

Biographies about Sports Figures

Although many biographies have been written for children about outstanding men and women from all cultures and walks of life, some children prefer to read about contemporary sports figures. Books about athletes often are written in a series. Teachers and librarians realize that sports books can lead children into other areas of literature. Outstanding publishers know that stories about sports stars that are authentic, unbiased, and carefully researched will be popular with children, teachers, librarians, and parents.

SPORTS BIOGRAPHIES IN A SERIES

SCOTT HAMILTON. In *Scott Hamilton, Fireworks on Ice* by Linda Shaughnessy, we discover that by the time Scott was 9 years old—a time when other intermediate school children are growing rapidly—he had grown little since age 2. At that time, specialists in Boston told his adoptive parents he would only live another year at most. But Hamilton proved the specialists wrong. As he grew he was told that he was too small to make it to the Olympics and that male figure skaters were not popular with audiences. By overcoming the obstacles confronting him, he has given encouragement to children so that they too can succeed.

MIA HAMM. The Chelsea House Publishers series *Great Female Athletes, Women Who Win,* written by Robert Schnakenberg, is a needed addition to the biography genre, since its emphasis is on women and women sports figures in particular. It encourages girls in the intermediate school years to think about sports as an acceptable extracurricular activity (and possibly as a career), and it includes many pictures of Mia Hamm. An honest appraisal of the sports scene appears in the Foreword by Hannah Storm.

WAYNE GRETZKY. Chelsea House has a popular series called *Ice Hockey Legends.* Biographies of Brett Hull, Jaromir Jagr, Mario Lemieux, Eric Lindros, Mark Messier, and Wayne Gretzky focus on the careers of these well-known hockey players. These books are especially appealing to boys in the intermediate school years who are actively engaged in sports. Josh Wilker, for example, describes Gretzky's life in exciting terms and includes a chronology and suggestions for further reading. The cardinal rule in the Gretzky household was that you always finish what you start. By the time the 1983–84 hockey season began, Wayne knew that to complete some unfinished business, he had to help his team, the Edmonton Oilers, defeat the New York Islanders, who were the reigning champions.

A COLLECTION OF SPORTS BIOGRAPHIES

LATINOS IN BEISBOL. James Cockcroft has arranged the short biographies of fourteen famous baseball players into an attractive format. Each page is a replica of a baseball card, complete with a player's picture and statistics. Many of the players, including Roberto Clemente, were born outside the United States and offer readers, especially recent immigrants, models they can relate to and emulate as they adjust to living in new surroundings.

Spin Off

Children Interact with Biography and Autobiography

Now that your students have become acquainted with a well-known artist like Frida Kahlo, they may like to learn more about her art and try to imitate Ana Juan's wonderful illustrations.

• Plan a "Meet a Famous Person day." Match students who would like to be sports stars, scientists, writers, or other celebrated figures to other students who will compile a list of questions they can use to interview these "celebrities." The interviewer and the student to be interviewed should have read the same biography so that they are familiar with the facts of the famous person's life. These interviews could be reported in the school newspaper or be a part of a radio or television program.

• "Will the real person (musician, writer, sports hero, scientist) please stand up" is based on a former television show. A moderator introduces the show and the panel members, who have been se-lected previously. The remaining members of the class are the interviewers. Although only one panel member is the real person (and has read the biography), the other panel members also pretend that they are that person. The interviewers keep a record of the panel's answers and decide individually who the "real person" is. After everyone has guessed, the moderator asks the "real person" to stand up. (Just for fun, the other panel members make up names and occupations).

• Photobiographies, such as the biography *Roy Chapman Andrews* and the Newbery Medal--winning *Lincoln: A Photobiography* by Russell Freedman, are very popular. Your students may like to search their photograph albums for pictures of themselves and their families in order to write their own photoautobiographies, which they may later transfer to a videotape.

Informational Books

Children in the intermediate school years find informational or nonfiction books an invaluable part of their school lives, not only for use in research projects, but also to satisfy their own native "intelligences." The plural "intelligences" is consistent with the ideas of Howard Gardner (1983, 1997) who theorized that children may have at least eight intelligences: *a linguistic intelligence, a musical intelligence, a logical-mathematical intelligence, a spatial intelligence, a bodily-kinesthetic intelligence, an interpersonal intelligence, an intrapersonal intelligence, and a naturalistic intelligence.* (Gardner defines an intelligence as the ability to solve problems or fashion products of consequence in a particular culture or community.) You, as a teacher or librarian, should not be "trapped" into seeing a student as "mathematical" or "musical" and so forth. Students need to see themselves as having a combination of *all* these intelligences. And they need to be offered books that encourage them to develop in all these areas. See Table 10.1 for the meaning of the various intelligences.

These intelligences appear as themes in many informational books, as well as in other genres. Using Gardner's categories of intelligence, we believe the following informational books are suitable for intermediate school children just beginning to discover their personal preferences. We also believe these books will motivate them to seek further information as they continue to develop biologically, psychologically, and socially.

Table 10.1 GARDNER'S MULTIPLE INTELLIGENCES

TYPES OF INTELLIGENCE	MEANING
Linguistic	Organizing thoughts for verbal tasks
Musical	Recognizing the themes in musical works; distinguishing melodies and responsiveness to music
Logical-mathematical	Understanding the components of thinking and problem solving
Spatial	Forming mental representations to aid thinking and remembering
Bodily-kinesthetic	Smooth development of bodily movements and adaptations
Interpersonal	Ability to work with others and to understand them
Intrapersonal	Ability to be aware of inner feelings, intentions, and goals
Naturalistic	Ability to be aware of the environment and to protect it

Linguistic Intelligence

CDB! William Steig uses letters and numbers to create the sounds of words and simple sentences "4 u 2" figure out with the aid of illustrations. Originally created in 1968 with black and white illustrations, this book was reissued by popular demand in 2000 with colorful illustrations, without which the letters would be meaningless.

GIFTS OF WRITING. Susan and Stephen Judy offer children suggestions on how to express themselves in writing activities. They learn how to design their own stationery and to make posters, greeting cards, and a family tree. Included are directions for making and writing their own books, and detailed writing projects for major holidays. Each project is meticulously illustrated and many suggestions are offered.

Musical Intelligence

I WANT TO BE A DANCER. This book, written by Stephanie Maze with Catherine O'Neill, is one of an attractive series that includes wanting to be an astronaut, an engineer, and a veterinarian. It is beautifully illustrated with full-color photographs, and it discusses topics such as high-tech dance, ballroom dancing, dancing around the world, dance-related careers, onstage experience, types and training for dance, and other, related information. Children who display a musical intelligence may wish to consider a career as a dancer.

MAKING MUSICAL THINGS. Ann Wiseman illustrates how musical sounds can be created by enthusiastic children with a musical intelligence. She offers them directions, for example, on how to create a bushman's bow, a lyre, a tincan harp, a milk carton guitar, and a plucking fiddle. She encourages them not to be disappointed if they find it hard to tune the wooden bars of the xylophone they are making—instead, they should just invent their own new sounds.

Spin Off

Children Interact with Informational Books

- Present *CDB!* to the class and ask fellow students to translate the letters into simple sentences.

- Create one of the musical instruments mentioned in *Making Musical Things* and demonstrate it to the class.

- Design a structure (from paper, cardboard, etc.) that Frank O. Gehry might have designed as an intermediate school student from the ideas spelled out in *frank o. gehry: outside in*.

Logical/Mathematical Intelligence

WHODUNIT MATH PUZZLES. For the intermediate school child who enjoys solving mysteries and mathematical problems, this book provides the opportunity to do both. Bill Wise has designated each problem a "case" to solve, and there are over twenty cases, such as "The Case of the Fishy Alibi," "The Case of the Green Pepper and Onion Pizza Decisions," and "The Case of the Worried Lottery Winner".

ROCKET! This book—an introduction to the physics of space flight—is written by the award-winning scientific writer Richard Maurer and is a must-read for children who are fascinated by logical or mathematical challenges. It is illustrated throughout with photographs, diagrams, experiments, and rocket activities that readers can try safely at home. It is a book that parents, teachers, and librarians will like to peruse and discuss with their children.

Spatial-Visual Intelligence

frank o. gehry: outside in. Jan Greenberg and Sandra Jordan have combined to give intermediate school and middle school children a glimpse into the mind and talent of Frank O. Gehry, one of the world's foremost architects. His buildings "surge with energy and movement, revealing forms never before seen in architecture," such as the Guggenheim Museum, which he designed in Bilbao, Spain, and the Disney Concert Hall in California.

Bodily-Kinesthetic Intelligence

BEGINNING GYMNASTICS. This book by Julie Jensen covers the history, equipment, and basic techniques of gymnastics, as well as competitions and performances. It is extensively illustrated with multi-colored action photographs and includes three pages of "Gymnastics Talk."

THE GREATEST SPORTS STORIES NEVER TOLD. Bruce Nash and Allan Zullo have filled this book with thirty-two chapters, each two or three pages in length, about incredible events that have never been written about the lives of athletes. These incidents reveal amazing feats, outstanding courage, and unusual sportsmanship that will fascinate children. Stories include "The Girl Who Managed the Dodgers," "The Day the Batboy Played," "The Night Danny Heater Lit Up the Scoreboard," and "The Bench-Warmer Who Won the Rose Bowl!" Children will enjoy reading these short chapters and may be inspired to further their own athletic endeavors.

Interpersonal Intelligence

CHILDREN JUST LIKE ME. In association with the United Nations Children's Fund, Barnabas and Anabel Kindersley interviewed children from over thirty countries and questioned them about families, homes, hobbies, and schools. Children concerned about others will be fascinated by the similarities and differences in the lives of children their own age from all over the world and will develop an understanding and respect for them. The illustrations are upbeat and happy, in spite of the conditions in which many of these children live.

COMING TO AMERICA: THE STORY OF IMMIGRATION. Children are constantly seeking ways to enhance their knowledge of other people. Betsy Maestro's lively story of the history of immigration to the United States—from the first settlers to refugees from all parts of the world that still seek asylum—will deepen their understanding of the diversity and richness of the people that make up the United States, now and in the past.

Intrapersonal Intelligence

BEING YOUR BEST. Barbara A. Lewis encourages children to be the best they can be by briefly discussing ten important character traits: safety, responsibility, respect, relationships, honesty, forgiveness, fairness, cooperation, citizenship, and caring. There are also short, true stories and activities that will help children develop these traits. Resources such as books and websites for learning more about character development are included.

FRIENDS! This is a short, lively discussion by Elaine Scott about the difficulties and satisfactions of making friends: how to deal with a bully, how to join a group, the difference between tattling and talking constructively about what is bothering you, and how to handle the "betrayal" of a friend. Although the book is appealing to children to read by themselves because of its attractive illustrations, it easily lends itself to discussion when children and caring adults read it together.

Naturalistic Intelligence

I WANT TO BE AN ENVIRONMENTALIST. Stephanie Maze's book (with Catherine O'Neill) is one in a series on career choices and describes all facets of environmentalism: the types of environmentalists, the eco-issues, the education needed, the history of environmentalism, and the environmental vocabulary. It illustrates endangered species, offers alternative solutions for generating energy, and encourages environmentally friendly lifestyles. The phrase "You Can Make a Difference" is reiterated throughout the book, which provides positive reading for children who want to make a difference in their environment.

VANISHING OZONE. Laurence Pringle, an award-winning author, has written an informative book for intermediate school (and older children) to help them better understand what is happening to the ozone layer. It answers the question: is there really an ozone crisis? It begins with an explanation of the ozone molecule and the structure of the atmosphere, then traces "the fascinating trail of evidence uncovered by scientists all over the world to show that the ozone layer is indeed thinning."

OIL SPILL! Melvin Berger has written several *Let's-Read-and-Find Out!* science books for HarperCollins. Each book is checked for accuracy by an expert in the field. In this book, readers find out why many oil spills occur and how experts clean them up. More important, children who read this book can inform the rest of us about what we can do to help prevent oil spills from happening.

Spin Off

Children Interact with Informational Books

- Invent a new gymnastic technique after reading *I Want to Be a Dancer* and explain it step by step to the class.

- Develop a way to teach the words *hate* and *love* and compose a song of friendship as described in *Friends!*

- Evaluate alternative solutions to generate sources of energy based on criteria you learned from *I Want to Be an Environmentalist.*

Chapter Checklist

Read the following items carefully. If you have difficulty responding to any of them, return to the chapter to review the material.

After reading this chapter, you can

1. Describe how changes in children's thinking during these years influence their book selections. Use picture books as a model.

2. Discuss the reasons why children's self-concepts are often crucial to the types of stories they prefer (e.g., Theo in *Awake and Dreaming*).

3. List several features of traditional literature that appeal to children of these grades.

4. Analyze how stories of fantasy help children make important distinctions between fantasy and reality, using any of the *Harry Potter* books as an example.

5. Demonstrate, perhaps with a poem of your own, how the subtle play of words furthers an appreciation of language.

6. Illustrate how themes in the stories of contemporary realistic fiction hold an attraction for children of these years (*Boundless Grace* is a good example).

7. Explain the appeal of series to children, using mysteries as an example.

8. Evaluate the role historical fiction, such as *Lily's Crossing*, plays in the lives of children from the perspective of both literature and factual data.

9. Discuss the pros and cons of fictionalized biography.

10. Defend the point of view that nonfiction should be more than a compilation of facts.

Children's Bibliography

Adler, David. (1986). *Cam Jansen and the Mystery of the Stolen Corn Popper*. New York: Viking.

Adler, David. (2003). *Picture Book of Harriet Beecher Stowe*. New York: Holiday House.

Alvarez, Julia. (2001). *How Tia Lola Came to Visit Stay*. New York: Knopf.

Angelou, Maya. Jean-Michel Basquiat illus. (1993). *Life Doesn't Frighten Me*. New York: Stewart, Tabori, & Chang.

Armstrong, Jennifer. (2000). *Thomas Jefferson: Letters from a Philadelphia Bookworm*. Delray Beach, FL: Winslow Press.

Aronson, Marc. (2000). *Sir Walter Ralegh and the Quest for El Dorado*. New York: Clarion.

Avi. (1984). *S.O.R. Losers*. New York: Bradbury Press.

Barrett, Judi. (1978). *Cloudy with a Chance of Meatballs*. New York: Simon & Schuster.

Baum, L. Frank. (2000). *The Wonderful Wizard of Oz*. New York: Harper Trophy.

Bausum, Ann. (2000). *Dragon Bones and Dinosaur Eggs*. Washington, DC: National Geographic Society.

Bedard, Michael. (Murray Kimber illus.). (2001). *Wolf of Gubbio*. Toronto, ON: Stoddard Publishing Co.

Berger, Melvin. (1994). *Oil Spill!* New York: HarperCollins.

Birdsall, Jeanne. (2005). *The Penderwicks*. New York: Knopf.

Blume, Judy. (1971). *Freckle Juice*. New York: Simon & Schuster.

Borden, Louise, Kroeger, Mary Kay. (2001). *Fly High! The Story of Bessie Coleman*. New York: Simon & Schuster.

Brown, Don. (2000). *Uncommon Traveler: Mary Kingsley in Africa*. Boston: Houghton Mifflin.

Brown, Don. (2004). *Odd Boy Out: Young Einstein*. Boston: Houghton Mifflin.

Bruchac, Joseph. (1996). *Between Earth and Sky*. New York: Harcourt.

Byars, Betsy. (2000). *Me, Tarzan*. New York: HarperCollins.

Castaldo, Nancy. (2005). *Pizza for the Queen*. New York: Holiday House.

Christian, Mary Blount. (1988). *Sebastian (Super Sleuth) and the Egyptian Connection*. New York: MacMillan Publishing Co.

Christopher, Matt. (1978). *The Fox Steals Home*. Boston: Little, Brown.

Ciardi, John. (1987). *You Read to Me, I'll Read to You*. New York: HarperCollins.

Cleary, Beverly. (1990). *Beezus and Ramona*. New York: Morrow.

Cleary, Beverly. (1992). *Ramona the Pest*. New York: Morrow.

Cleary, Beverly. (1992). *Ramona Quimby, Age 8*. New York: Morrow.

Cleary, Beverly. (1999). *Ramona's World*. New York: Morrow.

Clements, Andrew. (2000). *The Janitor's Boy*. New York: Simon & Schuster.

Clinton, Cathryn. (2005). *Simeon's Fire*. Cambridge, MA: Candlewick.

Cockcroft, James. (2001). *Latinos in Beisbol*. New York: Ingram Book Co.

Collins, David. (1989). *To The Point: A Story about E. B. White*. Minneapolis: Carolrhoda.

Curtis, Christopher Paul. (1989). *The Watsons Go to Birmingham–1963*. New York: Delacorte Press.

Dahl, Roald. (1964). *Charlie and The Chocolate Factory*. New York: Viking Penguin.

Dahl, Roald. (1980). *The Twits*. New York: Knopf.

D'Aulaire, Edgar. (1987). *Abraham Lincoln*. New York: Dell.

D'Aulaire, Edgar. (1996). *George Washington*. Sandwich, MA: Beautiful Feet.

DeClementis Barthe, (1990). *Nothing's Fair in Fifth Grade*. New York: Puffin.

dePaola, Tomie. (1994). *Watch Out for the Chicken Feet in Your Soup*. New York: Scholastic.

Delano, Marfe Ferguson. (2006). *Genius: A Photobiography of Albert Einstein*. Washington, DC: National Geographic Society.

De Regniers, Breatrice. (1998). *Sing a Song of Popcorn*. New York: Scholastic.

Eaton, Jeanette. (1950). *Gandhi*. New York: Morrow.

Erikson, Eric. (1963). *Childhood and Society*. New York: Norton.

Freedman, Russell. (1987). *Lincoln: A Photobiography*. New York: Clarion Books.

Freedman, Russell. (2003). *Confucius*. New York: Scholastic.

Freeman, Martha. (2003). *Who Is Stealing the Twelve Days of Christmas?* New York: Holiday.

Fritz, Jean. (1980). *Where Do You Think You're Going, Christopher Columbus?* New York: Putnam.

Gauthier, Gail. (2006). *Happy Kid!* New York: Putnam.

Gerstein, Mordicai. (2003). *The Man Who Walked Between the Towers*. Brookfield, CT: Roaring Brook.

Giff, Patricia Reilly. (1988). *The Polk Street School Series*. New York: Turtleback, Demco.

Giff, Patricia Reilly. (1997). *Lily's Crossing*. New York: Random House.

Giff, Patricia Reilly. (2000). *Nory Ryan's Song*. New York: Delacorte Press.

Giff, Patricia Reilly. (2003). *Maggie's Door*. New York: Random.

Glenn, Mel. (1986). *Play-by-Play*. Boston: Houghton Mifflin.

Going, K. L. (2003). *Fat Kid Rules the World*. New York: Putnam.

Grahame, Kenneth. (1994). *The Wind in the Willows*. New York: Baronet.

Grey, Mini. (2006). *The Adventures of the Dish and the Spoon*. New York: Knopf.

Greenberg, Jan., & Jordan, Sandra. (2000). *frank o. gehry outside in*. New York: Dorling Kindersley.

Hall, Donald (ed.). (1999). *The Oxford Illustrated Book of American Children's Poems*. New York: Oxford University Press.

Hamilton, Virginia. (1988). *In the Beginning: Creation Stories from Around the World*. New York: Harcourt.

Hamilton, Virginia. (1999). *Bluish*. New York: Blue Sky Press.

Harris, Carol Flynn. (2001). *A Place for Joey*. Honesdale, PA: Boyds Mill Press.

Hill, Kirkpatrick. (2000). *The Year of Miss Agnes*. New York: McElderry.

Hoban, Russell. (1993). *Bread and Jam for Frances*. New York: HarperCollins.

Hoffman, Mary. (1995). *Boundless Grace*. New York: Penguin.

Hoffman, Mary. (2003). *Encore, Grace*. New York: Dial.

Huck, Charlotte. (2001). *The Black Bull of Norroway*. illus. Anita Lobel. New York: HarperCollins.

Jensen, Julie. (1957). *Beginning Gymnastics*. New York: Lerner Publications.

Judy, Susan, & Judy, Stephen. (1980). *Gifts of Writing*. New York: Charles Scribner's Sons.

Kindersley, Barnabas, & Kindersley, Anabel. (1995). *Children Just Like Me*. New York: Dorling Kindersley.

Krensky, Stephen. (2005). *Dangerous Crossing: The Revolutionary Voyage of John Quincy Adams*. New York: Dutton.

Kuskin, Karla. (1994). Milton Avery illus. *Paul*. New York: HarperCollins.

Lasky, Kathryn. (2000). *A Time for Courage: The Suffragette Diary of Kathleen Bowen*. (2000). New York: Scholastic.

Latham, Jean. (1955). *Carry On, Mr. Bowditch*. Boston: Houghton Mifflin.

Lewis, Barbara A. (2000). *Being Your Best*. Minneapolis: Free Spirit Press.

Lewis, C. S. (1998). *Complete Chronicles of Narnia*. New York: Harper.

Lisle, Janet Taylor. (1989). *Afternoon of the Elves*. New York: Franklin Watts.

Lobel, Arnold. (1984). *The Book of Pigericks: Pig Limericks*. New York: Ballantine Publishing Group.

Maestro, Betsy. (1996). *Coming to America: The Story of Immigration*. New York: Scholastic.

Marshall, James. (1981). *The Stupids Die*. Boston: Houghton Mifflin.

Marshall James. (1972). *George and Martha*. New York: Scholastic.

Martin, Ann M., & Godwin, Laura. (2003). *The Meanest Doll in the World*. New York: Hyperion.

Mason, Simon. (2006). *The Quigleys in a Spin*. New York: Random House.

Masters, M. (1984). *The Case of the Chocolate Snatcher and Other Mysteries*. New York: Simon & Schuster.

Maurer, Richard. (1995). *Rocket!* New York: Crown Publishers.

Maze, Stephanie, with Catherine O'Neill. (1997). *I Want to Be a Dancer*. San Diego: Harcourt Brace.

Maze, Stephanie, with Catherine O'Neill. (2000). I *Want to Be an Environmentalist*. San Diego: Harcourt Brace.

McCaughrean, Geraldine. (2000). *Beauty and the Beast*. Minneapolis: Carolrhoda.

McCord, David. (1992). *All Day Long: Fifty Rhymes of the Never Was and Always Is*. Boston: Little, Brown.

McCully, Emily Arnold. (2006). *Marvelous Mattie*. New York: Farrar, Straus, & Giroux.

McKay, Hilary. (2006). *Caddy Ever After*. New York: McElderry Books.

Milne, A. A. (1992). *When We Were Very Young*. New York: Penguin.

Murphy, Jim. (2001). My *Face to the Wind*. New York: Scholastic.

Nagda, Ann Whitehead. (2000). *Dear Whiskers*. New York: Holiday House.

Nash, Bruce, & Zulio, Allan. (1993). *The Greatest Sports Stories Never Told*. New York: Simon & Schuster.

Naylor, Phyllis Reynolds. (2006). *Roxie and the Hooligans*. New York: Atheneum.

Nelson, Vaunda. (2003). *Almost to Freedom*. Minneapolis: Carolrhoda.

Norton, Mary. (1997). *The Complete Borrowers*. New York: Harcourt.

Numeroff, Laura Jaffe. (1985). *If You Give a Mouse a Cookie*. New York: Harper & Row.

Osborne, Mary Pope. (2002). *After the Rain*. New York: Scholastic.

Patrick, Diane. (1990). *Martin Luther King, Jr.* New York: Franklin Watts.

Patron, Susan. (2006). *The Higher Power of Lucky*. New York: Atheneum.

Pearce, Philippa. (1959). *Tom's Midnight Garden*. Philadelphia: Lippincott.

Pearson, Kit. (1998). *Awake and Dreaming*. Toronto, ON: Puffin.

Prelutsky, Jack. (1996). *A Pizza the Size of the Sun*. New York: Greenwillow.

Pretlutsky, Jack. (1997). *The Beauty of the Beast*. New York: Knopf.

Pretlutsky, Jack. (1999). *The 20th Century Children's Poetry Treasury*. New York: Knopf.

Pringle, Laurence. (1995). *Vanishing Ozone*. New York: Morrow Junior Books.

Quackenbush, Robert. (1986). *Who Let Muddy Boots into the White House?* New York: Simon & Schuster.

Raven, Margot. (2002). *Mercedes and the Chocolate Pilot: A True Story of the Berlin Airlift*. Chelsea, MI: Sleeping Bear Press.

Rockwell, Anne. (2000). *Only Passing Through: The Story of Sojourner Truth*. New York: Knopf.

Rockwell, Thomas. (2000). *How to Eat Fried Worms*. New York: Random House.

Rodda, Emily. (2001). *Rowan of Rin*. New York: Harpers.

Rodda, Emily. (2003). *Rowan and the Ice Creepers*. New York: Greenwillow.

Roop, Connie, & Roop, Peter. (2001). *The Diary of David R. Leeper, Rushing for Gold*. New York: Benchmark Books.

Rowling, J. K. (1998). *Harry Potter and the Sorcerer's Stone*. New York: Scholastic.

Royston, Angela. (2005). *Why Do We Need to Drink Water?* MA: Heinemann.

Rosyton, Angela. (2005). *Why Do We Need to Eat?*. MA: Heinemann.

Rumford, James. (2007). *Beowulf*. Boston: Houghton Mifflin.

Ryan, Pam Munoz. (2000). *Amelia and Eleanor Go for a Ride*. New York: Scholastic.

Ryan, Pam Munoz. (2002). *When Marian Sang*. New York: Scholastic.

Sachs, Marilyn. (1987). *The Bears' House*. New York: E. P. Dutton.

Sachs, Marilyn. (1987). *Fran Ellen's House*. New York: E. P. Dutton.

Sanderson, Ruth. (2001). *The Golden Mare, the Firebird, and the Magic Ring*. Boston: Little, Brown.

Schnakenberg, Robert. (2001). *Mia Hamm*. Philadelphia: Chelsea House Publishers.

Scieszka, Jon. (1999). *The True Story of the 3 Little Pigs by A. Wolf*. New York: Viking.

Scott, Elaine. (2000). *Friends!* New York: Atheneum.

Seuling, Barbara. (2006). *Robert and the Practical Jokes*. New York: Cricket.

Shannon, David. (2006). *Good Boy Fergus*. Parsippany, New York: Blue Sky Press.

Shaughnessy, Linda. (1998). *Scott Hamilton. Fireworks on Ice*. NJ: Crestwood House.

Silverstein, Shel. (1974). *Where the Sidewalk Ends*. New.York: Harper.

Silverstein, Shel. (1996). *Fall Up*. New York: Harper.

Silverstein, Shel. (1981). *A Light in the Attic*. New York: Harper.

Simon, Seymour. (1997). *The Gigantic Ant and Other Cases*. New York: Wm. Morrow.

Snicket, Lemony. (1999). *The Bad Beginning*. New York: HarperCollins.

Sobol, Donald. (1995). *Encyclopedia Brown, Boy Detective*. New York: Bantam.

Stanley, Diane. (1995). *The True Adventure of Daniel Hall*. New York: Dial.

Steer, Dugald. A. (2003). *Dragonology*. Cambridge, MA: Candlewick.

Steig, William. (1983). *The Amazing Bone*. New York: Farrar, Straus, & Giroux.

Steig, William. (1972). *Dominic*. New York: Farrar, Straus, & Giroux.

Steig, William. (1990). *Doctor De Soto*. New York: Farrar, Straus, & Giroux.

Steig, William. (1999). *Amos and Boris*. New York: Farrar, Straus, & Giroux.

Steig, William. (2000). *CDB!* New York: Simon & Schuster.

Taylor, Sydney. (1984). *All-of-a-Kind Family*. New York: Bantam.

Tchana, Katrin. (2000). *The Serpent Slayer and Other Stories of Strong Women*. Trina Schart, illus., Boston: Little, Brown.

Wells, Rosemary. (1999). *Tallchief*. New York: Penguin, Putnam.

Weatherford, Carole. (2005). *A Negro League Scrapbook*. Honesdale. PA: Boyds Mill.

White, E. B. (1945, 1974). *Stuart Little*. New York: Harper.

White, E. B. (1974). *Charlotte's Web*. New York: Harper.

White, E.B. (1974). *Trumpet of the Swan*. New York: Harper.

Wilder, Laura Ingalls. (1953). *Little House Books* (9 vols.) New York: Harper.

Wilker, Josh. (1998). *Wayne Gretzky*. Philadelphia. Chelsea House.

Willis, Kimberly. (1999). *When Zachary Beaver Came to Town*. New York: Holt.

Winter, Jonah. (2002). *Frida*. New York: Scholastic.

Wise, Bill. (2001). *Whodunit Math Puzzles*. New York: Sterling Publishing.

Wiseman, Ann. (1979). *Making Musical Things*. New York: Charles Scribner.

Yolen, Jane, & Harris, Robert J. (2001). *Odysseus in the Serpent Maze*. New York: HarperCollins.

Professional References

Aronson, Marc. (2001). "Fanfare. The Horn Book Honor List." Boston: *The Horn Book*. January/February, 2001. 49–50.

Berk, L. (2000). *Awakening Children's Minds*. New York: Oxford Press.

Bornstein, M. (2002). *Handbook of Parenting*. Mahwah, NJ: Erlbaum.

Collins, W., Madsen, S. & Susman-Stillman, A. (2002). "Parenting in Middle Childhood." In M. Borstein (ed.), *Handbook of Parenting*. Mahwah, NJ: Erlbaum.

Dacey, John & Travers, John. (2009). *Human Development Across the Life Span*. New York: McGraw Hill.

Erikson, E. (1963). *Childhood and Society*. New York: Norton.

Freud, Sigmund. (1905). Jokes and Their Relation to the Unconscious. *Standard Edition of the Complete Psychological Works of Sigmund Freud*. (Vol. 8). New York: Hogarth Press.

Garbarino, J. & Bedard, M. (2001). *Parents Under Siege*. New York: The Free Press.

Gardner, Howard. (1983). *Frames of Mind*. New York: Basic Books.

Gardner, Howard. (1997). *Extraordinary Minds*. New York: Basic Books.

Gardner, Howard. (1999). *Intelligence Reframed*. New York: Basic Books.

Giblin. James Cross. (2000). "More Than Just Facts." *The Horn Book*, July/August. 413–424.

Giff, Patricia. (2001). *Something about the Author*. Vol. 121. Belmont, CA: Gale Publishing, 87–91.

Konner, M. (1991). *Childhood*. Boston: Little, Brown

Marcus, Leonard. (2002). *Ways of Telling*. New York: Dutton Children's Books.

McGhee, Paul. (1971). "Cognitive Development and Children's Comprehension of Humor." *Child Development*. 42, 123–138.

McGhee, Paul. (1979). *Humor: Its Origin and Development*. San Francisco: Freeman.

McGhee, Paul. (2003). *Small Medium at Large: How to Develop a Powerful Verbal Sense of Humor*. New York: Authorhouse.

MacLeod, Anne Scott. (1994). *American Childhood*. Athens & London: University of Georgia Press.

McLoyd, V., Aikens, N., & Burton, L. (2006). "Childhood Poverty, Policy, and Practice." In William Damon & Irving Sigel (Series eds.) & K.A. Renninger & Irving Sigel (Volume eds.), *Handbook of Child Psychology: Volume 4, Child Psychology in Practice*. New York: John Wiley.

Piaget, J. (1981). *Intelligence and Affectivity*. Palo Alto, CA: Annual Reviews.

Restak, Richard. (2003). *The New Brain*. New York: Rodale/St. Martin's Press.

Santrock, John. (2007). *Children*. New York: McGraw-Hill.

Sulloway, Frank. (1992). *Freud, Biologist of the Mind*. Cambridge, MA: Harvard University Press.

Travers, Barbara. (1985). *Myths and Magical Monsters*. New York: Macmillan Co.

Travers, John, Elliott, Stephen, & Kratochwill, Thomas R. (1993). *Educational Psychology*. Madison, WS: Brown & Benchmark.

Vygotsky, L. (1978). *Mind in Society*. Cambridge, MA: Harvard University Press.

CHAPTER 11

Literature for the Middle School Years (Ages 11–14)

In Olive's Ocean, Kevin Henkes invites middle school readers to enter into the thoughts and emotions of 12-year-old Martha Boyle. After reading a note from Olive, a classmate who dies accidentally, Martha regrets that they were not better friends. As she spends a few summer weeks with her grandmother, Godbee, on Cape Cod, she continues to think of Olive and of how much love she has for her grandmother. Struggling to find her own identity, Martha is delighted when Jimmy, the boy next door, takes her hand and says he needs her. In her mind she is no longer just her little sister's babysitter or the daughter who washes the dishes or runs errands. Now she sees a whole new world opening up for her. These coming-of-age feelings, so typical of this age group, are repeated themes in many of the stories designed for middle school readers.

The middle school years see the beginnings of changes that foreshadow the rapid and dramatic development of *puberty*. The initial signs of "coming of age" may appear as early as 9 or 10 years of age and continue until 16 or 17 years. Explosive changes in the biopsychosocial forces acting on youths have often caused parents and teachers to comment on the difficulties of these years. More recent research (Dacey & Travers, 2009; Santrock, 2007) testifies to a fairly smooth transition from childhood. But we cannot dismiss the turbulent nature of the broader society into which children in this age group are moving with their emerging skills.

Their abilities may become obvious, often to the point where they experience considerable adult pressure: baseball coaches competing for an outstanding Little League pitcher; drama coaches wanting the child with the beautiful voice to appear in too many shows; parents, realizing they have intelligent children who may be capable of winning scholarships, placing excessive pressure on them to excel. Whether the expertise is athletic, artistic, mathematical, scientific, or musical, teachers, librarians, and parents should be sensitive not only to these exciting developments, but also to the developmental needs and limitations of their readers.

OLIVE'S OCEAN
Used with permission of
HarperCollins

KEVIN HENKES

Olive's Ocean

Guidelines for Reading Chapter 11

After you read Chapter Eleven, you should be able to answer the following questions.

• How does traditional literature examined in this chapter describe the settings and situations that produce stress, while portraying resilient young people who cope and overcome adversity?

• What are the themes in the fantasies presented in this chapter that capture, hold, and maintain the reader's attention while simultaneously suspending the tug of reality?

• Children of the middle school years begin to use language in a different manner; they are no longer dependent on a narrow, literal interpretation of a word. How do the points of view in the poems analyzed in this chapter appeal to the reader's appreciation of word usage and the expression of ideas?

• Children of the middle school years have become quite sophisticated in their thinking. How do the plots in the historical and contemporary fiction challenge the cognitive abilities of children of these years?

• The search for identity begins to intensify during these years as children struggle to define their self-concepts. Which of the biographical characters whose personality characteristics are discussed in this chapter most help readers in their search for self?

Characteristics of Children of These Years

Similar to Martha, who is intent on writing a book, children of the middle school years begin to demonstrate the abilities they have previously been nurturing. These strengths in physical, cognitive, and psychosocial areas of development apply to boys and girls.

Gender

Gender has always played a part in children's literature. As far back as the eighteenth and nineteenth centuries, authors wrote books specifically for boys or girls. Mark Twain, for instance, affirmed that *"The Adventures of Tom Sawyer* was a boy's book." In Chapter Two, where we discussed the history of children's literature, we saw that boys' books, such as those written by Jack London and Mark Twain, addressed the needs and interests of boys (hunting, fishing, nature, and wildlife), while other books were written for girls from a feminine perspective, such as those by Louisa May Alcott and Laura Ingalls Wilder. Magazines were also characterized as being directed at boys or girls.

It is difficult, however, to divide all children's literature into books for boys and books for girls. Most noteworthy books are, and always have been, avidly read by both groups. As the authors of *Children's Literature: A Developmental Perspective*, we believe the content of a well-written children's book should be gender free. Whatever genre is represented, children's literature can be a goodness-of-fit for both girls and boys. We understand, however, that culture and environment play a major role in what boys and girls choose to read; therefore, throughout this text we will include titles suitable for both sexes.

BOYS' READING   Whether or not boys read less than girls, and what boys prefer to read, are topics constantly being discussed. Reluctant readers, especially boys, are inclined to show an interest in informational books because they connect them with their everyday lives (Smith & Wilhelm, 2002). Michael Sullivan, author of *Connecting Boys with Books*, suggests that boys act out the stories and "create their own versions of a tale—writing themselves into "it" (Sullivan, 2004, p. 39). Books for boys, especially those reluctant to read, must have a clear purpose and offer immediate feedback, because students want to use what they read not only to talk about it but to do something with it (Smith & Wilhelm, 2002, p. 18).

At the Haverford School for Boys in Philadelphia, boys selected F. Scott Fitzgerald's *The Great Gatsby* as their favorite novel because it is short, the action is fast, and the style is vivid and alive. This classic novel also asks them questions about the meaning and value of life—the same questions they face in their own lives (McCauley, 2005). On the other hand, Roger Sutton, editor in chief of *The Horn Book*, makes the thoughtful comment that boys may be reading more than we think. They must be able to read, for example, to use the Internet to check out Jon Scieszka's www.guysread.com. When boys' attention does not measure up to our satisfaction, Sutton suggests that perhaps those of us who select the books are at fault, rather than the boys themselves (Sutton, 2004).

Initially, genes direct the formation and distribution of the neurons, but then nurture steps in and completes the wiring process, which leads to the production of new neural connections. Unless these connections are repeatedly fired, nature has deter-

What's Your View?

Books, Brains, and Behavior

Boys and girls are different, and this difference extends to what they read, how they read, and how much they read. Given the amount of research and theorizing about this issue, it's no surprise that many investigators have turned to brain differences for an explanation. Thanks to recent research (see Rose, 2005; Bear, Connors & Paradiso, 2007), we are only now beginning to realize how subtle the brain differences are. The safest conclusion we can draw is that brain differences are few and minor (Rose, 2005).

But the question remains. And in the final analysis, variations between the sexes translate into different types of behavior, including interests, attitudes, and even the kinds of books they like to read. What causes these differences? One answer researchers are exploring is the manner in which girls' and boys' brains are wired and what this means for development and behavior. For better or worse, the brain is tightly bound to all aspects of children's lives. Brain wiring involves an intricate dance between nature and nurture. The neuroscientist Lise Eliot (2000) summarized this reality when she noted that while the genes may pass on the genetic program that forms the nervous system, and the brain may direct children's behavior, *experience ultimately determines the extent of children's brain development.* What's your view?

mined that they will perish—hence the truth of that old cliché, *use it or lose it.* Consequently, given the relative lack of knowledge concerning structural brain differences between the sexes, we are probably most comfortable in stating that any significant differences between the brains of males and females are undoubtedly due to the richness or paucity of environmental stimulation. The inescapable conclusion, then, is that in the early years parents should expose their toddlers to the rhythm and beauty of children's books and, as their children grow and mature, continue to supply them with those books that motivate, inform, and excite them, whether boys or girls.

Family Ties

The world of middle school children is changing as rapidly as they are. They may encounter circumstances, ideas, and individuals for whom they are not prepared. Yet their family ties continue to be strong in spite of emotional conflicts with individual family members. In *Olive's Ocean*, for example, Martha's relationship with her older brother remains steadfast although he is sometimes nasty and insensitive toward her. Her feelings for her mother, however, "bounce between love and hate quickly and without warning, as if her feelings were illogical, willful and completely out of Martha's control" (Henkes, 2003, p. 23).

Middle School Students and the Elderly

Frequently, novels and poetry written for middle school students reflect the deep regard they have for their grandparents and older caregivers. Often characters fear their beloved older family members may lose their memory, require hospital care, or are close to death. In Alison McGhee's *Snap*, for example, the main character, Edwina (Eddie), is concerned about the ill health of Sally's (her best friend's) grandmother. She can't believe that Sally is in denial and is unable to accept the fact that her grandmother is dying. In *Olive's Ocean*, Godbee's well-being was so heavy on Martha's mind that when she says goodbye,

Martha thought she'd break Godbee if she hugged her back as hard as she wanted to, but she was filled with such love and longing and happiness and sorrow (not bravery, definitely not bravery) that she grabbed her grandmother's shoulders and squeezed with all her might.

(Henkes, 2003, p. 192)

Becoming Joe DiMaggio, Maria Testa's free verse novel, is a simply written testament to a young boy's deep relationship with his grandfather. During the World War II years, Joe DiMaggio's name was on everyone's lips. Testa uses the baseball player's determination, patriotism, and devotion to his father as a model for the main character's life with his grandfather. "We stand there / On the hill / My grandfather and I / knowing who we are / who we have become" (Testa, 2000, p. 51).

These engaging themes are found in many stories written for this age group. In *Pictures of Hollis Woods*, Patricia Reilly Giff portrays Hollis as a foster child who becomes increasingly aware of and concerned about the lapses of memory she notices in Josie, the retired art teacher with whom she lives. British writer Peter Dickinson has written the touching story *Inside Granddad* about a boy's devotion to his grandfather and his determination to help him recover from a stroke.

The characters in the books we have selected for middle school children reveal not only their compassion and emotional involvement, but also the cognitive maturity that enables them to engage in truly abstract thinking. Young readers may also find that the problems some of these characters face within and outside their school day would be a challenge for them also.

Bullying

Although peer opinion at these ages is important to a young person's developing sense of self and is a powerful motivator of behavior (Harter, 1999), children in the early elementary years are also aware of the impact of peer opinion. Nine-year-old Roxie in Phyllis Reynolds Naylor's *Roxie and the Hooligans*, for example, cringes when his classmates bully him because of his big ears. Stink, Judy Moody's little brother in Megan McDonald's series, abhors the fact that he is ridiculed for being the smallest second-grader in his school, and tries to convince himself that "you're only as short as you feel."

Maybe you, too, had difficulties in school involving a "monster" who loved to tease, humiliate, threaten, and fight. Too often bullies see this behavior as a way of becoming popular and competent (Rodkin & Farmer, 2000). Today, most middle school principals list bullying among their major worries.

One survey of about 16,000 students, grades 6 through 10, estimated that more than one in three children was either a bully or a victim (Nansel, 2001). In this study, bullying was defined as verbal or physical behavior intended to harm another. Boys and younger students were usually the participants. The most frequent type of bullying was belittling others about their looks or speech. Those who were bullied reported a low level of self-esteem.

The range of bullying behavior seems to be growing. For example, the most common forms of bullying have been physical, verbal, and emotional. Today, however, new types of bullying have appeared. *Racial* bullying targets children because of their race or color. In Anjali Banerjee's *Maya Running*, Maya, an Indian girl who lives in Canada, is constantly taunted because of her race. Undaunted, she continues to find ways to adjust to both cultures.

An even more recent kind of intimidation has emerged from the technological world: the *cyberbully*. Similar to traditional forms of bullying, the goal of the cyberbully is to abuse another by using the Internet. Email, chat rooms, cell phones, and so on become tools for cyberbullies to use to harass their victims night and day, seven days a week. As Willard (2006, p. 55) states, "these devastating effects include low self-esteem, poor academic performance, depression, and, in some cases, violence, even suicide."

Who is the bully? Olweus (1993, 1995) identified bullies as those who are overly aggressive and possess considerable physical strength. Peer victimization, on the other hand, describes those children who are anxious, insecure, cautious, and sensitive, with low self-esteem (Coie & Dodge, 1999). Among the causes of bullying are the following:

- *Indifference* (usually by the mother), in itself a form of silent violence
- Parents who are *permissive* with an aggressive child
- Parents who typically resort to *physical punishment*
- A *temperamentally aggressive* child

Jerry Spinelli, the popular author of the award-winning *Maniac Magee*, introduces his readers to Crash Coogan in his novel *Crash*. Crash Coogan is intimidating because he is a seventh-grade football star—big, powerful, and a bully who can't resist taunting the weak and defenseless. Penn Webb, a peaceful Quaker, a cheerleader, and the new kid in school, is easy for him to torment. Even more annoying to Crash is the fact that the prettiest girl in the class prefers Penn to him. How Crash finally reveals his hidden generosity of spirit in a heroic gesture has all the ingredients of a good story: action, conflict, and a plot that is realistic for middle school students. Nancy Garden's hard-hitting book for young adults, *Endgame*, is a startling story that opens with 15-year-old Gray's murder trial and concludes with his sentencing. Gray endured such physical abuse and bullying that he tried to solve his problems by using a gun when no adult tried to help straighten him out.

CONTEMPORARY PROBLEMS   The plots and themes of literature for these years often make children more aware of the turmoil in the world around them. Novels such as Deborah Ellis's trilogy—*The Breadwinner, Paravana's Journey*, and *Mud City*—about Shauzia's daring escape from Kabul, Afghanistan, to a refugee camp in Pakistan and her frustrated goal to reach France, brings the War on Terror closer to home. Wilborn Hampton's sensitive narrative *September 11, 2001*, about the destruction of the Twin Towers told through his interviews with people directly involved, also makes a lasting impression on children's minds. The major developmental features of these years are seen in the following diagram.

BIOPSYCHOSOCIAL CHARACTERISTICS

BIO	PSYCHO	SOCIAL
Brain size similar to adults	Abstract thinking continues to improve	Search for self intensifies
Physical skills improve noticeably: running, etc.	Attention becomes more selective	Appearance and peer reaction critical
Skill performances progress	Memory strategies sharpen	Peer relations important
Care needed with nutritional needs	More advanced problem-solving strategies evolve	Obesity could be a problem
Health usually good	Language usage becomes more sophisticated	Stress is met more frequently
Gender		

Themes Across the Curriculum

Frequently, teachers and librarians develop a theme such as immigration and develop it across the middle school curriculum by using many genres of children's literature. Required reading involves books that offer various perspectives on the theme. One example would be the informational book *Coming to America: The Story of Immigration* by Betsy Maestro. Students are encouraged to discuss the myriad problems that concern immigrants who come into the United States legally and illegally. Since all immigrant experiences are not alike, the teacher or school librarian may also assign the historical novel *Esperanza Rising* by Pam Munoz Ryan, and the graphic novel and Printz Award winner *American Born Chinese* by Gene Luen Yang, so that students can compare and contrast the experiences revealed in these books and many others.

Although *Miss Bridie Chose a Shovel* by Leslie Connor is a picture book, it also tells the journey of a hardworking, determined Irish immigrant, whose shovel is a metaphor for her life in the United States. Lenore Look's picture books about Ruby Lu (*Ruby Lu, Brave and True* and *Ruby Lu, Empress of Everything*) add a humorous dimension to serious life-changing transitions when Ruby's cousin, Flying Duck, arrives from China. The biography *Say It with Music* by Nancy Furstinger tells the story of songwriter Irving Berlin and provides additional resources to extend students' study of immigrants who became famous.

Although *We Rode the Orphan Trains* by Andrea Warren is not strictly about immigration, it nevertheless tells the heartbreaking story of migration—the migration of "homeless" American children, mostly from New York (about 200,000 in all), who traveled by train to every state in the union, hoping some family would adopt them and give them a home. Books like these (even picture books) all make significant connections to the curriculum, sharpen students' thinking skills, and develop their critical literacy.

THE PICTURE BOOK IN THE LANGUAGE ARTS CURRICULUM

The picture book is finding its niche as an essential strategy in the middle school language arts program. Selected picture books are often used to teach *the six traits of creative writing*: inspiring ideas, expanding word choice, sparkling voice, developing sentence fluency, shaping organization, and strengthening connections. Picture book biographies such as *Michaelangelo* and *Saladin, Noble Prince of Islam*, written by Diane Stanley, are so informative, accurate, and authentically illustrated that they provide essential information for use in the history of art and current events curricula. For her story of *Michaelangelo*, for example, Stanley received permission from the Vatican Museums to reproduce the illustrations that cover each page. To write and illustrate *Saladin, Noble Prince of Islam*, she placed Saladin in the context of later world events and included outstanding bibliographic research that is beneficial to students in other areas of study. Jennifer Armstrong's well-documented *Photo by Brady: A Picture of the Civil War* combines a biography of the famous photographer with a visual document of the Civil War, making it a natural segue into the study of American history.

Traditional Literature

The appeal of traditional literature to middle school students lies in its ability to encourage readers to let their imaginations soar. Bound by rules in math, science, and language, these stories provide a sense of emotional relief.

Myths and Legends

Two comprehensive sets of encyclopedias of *myths and legends* that have been published in London and New York provide formidable, but very readable, sources of research for middle school students seeking accurate information about traditional literature. In *Myths and Legends* Oxford scholars O. B. Duane and N. Hutchison have retold tales form Scottish, Celtic, Greek, Chinese, African, Indian, Viking, and Native American legends. These books include additional readings, a glossary, an index, and notes on the illustrations.

The *World Mythology* series (Duane, O. B. ed.) includes topics about angels, prophets, rabbis, and kings in *Stories of the Jewish People*; gods and heroes in *Viking Mythology*; gods, men, and monsters in *Greek Myths*; heroes, gods, and emperors in *Roman Mythology*; and warriors, gods, and spirits in *Central and South American Mythology*.

THE LOST YEARS OF MERLIN
Reproduced by permission of Penguin Group USA, Inc.

ARAB MYTHS AND LEGENDS   This volume, selected from the *World Mythology* series and retold by Khairat Al Saleh, includes subjects such as fabled cities, princes, and jinn. Students will be fascinated by stories about the gods of the ancient Arabs, as well as stories about their priests, soothsayers, and wise men, along with tales of generosity, honor, and loyalty. A section devoted to the new world of Muslim Arabs includes a description of the Koran and elaborates on the Muslim Arab belief in celestial and terrestrial worlds.

THE WINGS OF MERLIN   T. A. Barron has completed his final book in *The Lost Years of Merlin* (2000) epic. Young people who have read *The Seven Songs of Merlin*, *The Fires of Merlin*, and *The Mirror of Merlin* will enjoy continuing this fascinating journey to its conclusion. Merlin has taken the reader through the legendary Isle of Fincayra, and now the old man is faced with a staggering challenge. He must unite all the peoples, including dwarfs, eagles, walking trees, and the living stones of Fincayra against the invasion of evil.

ODYSSEUS   Geraldine McCaughrean offers middle and high school students a brilliant retelling of the epic adventures of Odysseus, Homer's famous hero.

Spin Off

Children Interact with Myths and Legends

Contemporary legends such as the Loch Ness Monster, the Abominable Snowman, and Bigfoot, are fascinating for middle school students to investigate. They could present an "eyewitness account" or debate about whether such a creature really exists. These legends lend themselves naturally to media presentations. A humorous retelling of the legend of *Bigfoot* was videotaped in a neighborhood park by a group of middle school students, with much success.

ARTHUR AT THE CROSSING PLACES　Kevin Crossley-Holland's *Arthur at the Crossing Places*, the second of a proposed trilogy, assumes its rightful place as a must-read legend for middle school students. It is divided into 100 short chapters and narrated by Arthur, who traces his life in exciting incidents from later childhood to young adulthood.

GRAPHIC NOVEL OF GREEK MYTHS　Marcia Williams has created a book of graphic drawings and brief stories, *Greek Myths for Young Children*, about famous mythical creatures—such as Pandora, Orpheus and Eurydice, Daedalus, and Icarus—for students who prefer a lighthearted look at mythology. The pictures are watercolors and pen and ink drawings done in bright colors. The pages are attractively bordered. Reluctant readers will be captivated and amused.

Literary Fairy Tales

Middle school students who are turning away from traditional fairy tales still enjoy books that contain many of the elements of a fairy tale but are written by authors who give them a special twist. Although traditional tales have no known authors, contemporary writers like Gail Carson Levine and Margaret Peterson Haddix have enlivened the traditional tale of Cinderella in the following literary folk tales.

ELLA ENCHANTED. Gail Carson Levine has created the character of Ella of Frell, a strong, spirited, and capable "Cinderella." But she is handicapped by a foolish fairy's spell and consequently must obey any order given to her. Her wicked stepsisters, the Step-Evils, take advantage of this weakness. She originally bows to their wishes, until faced with the possibility of marrying Char. Then she manages to be independent and to realistically consider what her possibilities are for living happily ever after.

FAIREST. In this retelling, Gail Carson Levine's Cinderella is Aza, a clumsy and unattractive young woman with an exquisite singing voice. In a kingdom where singers are valued, her voice is highly sought after. The conflict arises for Aza when it is discovered that the beautiful queen is tone deaf.

JUST ELLA. Margaret Peterson Haddix's story depicts another independent and beautiful Cinderella, who is imprisoned in the castle because she refuses to marry the prince. Treated inhumanely by the selfish prince and his cohorts, she manages to escape to a refugee camp, where she meets her old friend Jed Reston. Unlike the fairy tale, she takes her fate into her own hands, and what happens is her own decision.

Spin Off

Children Interact with Literary Fairy Tales

Suggest that your students find as many stories about Cinderella as they can (movies and television shows excluded). They may be surprised to discover a Caribbean Cinderella (*Cendrillon* by Robert D. San Souci), a Middle Eastern Cinderella (*The Golden Sandal* by Rebecca Hickox), a Native American Cin- derella (*The Rough-Face Girl* by Rafe Martin), an African Cinderella (*Mufaro's Beautiful Daughters* by John Steptoe), and many more. By comparing and contrasting the literary elements and dramatizing their favorite scenes, they will enjoy enhancing their knowl- edge of traditional literature.

Fantasy

The elements of fantasy hold great appeal to middle school readers because, in a very real sense, they touch many developmental features of the middle school years. Cognitively, these young people understand the parallel universes that are the settings of many fantasies. Emotionally, they are often captivated by the des- perate struggle between good and evil. Psychosocially, they can picture themselves in the relationships that evolve and, amazingly, they are not discouraged by fan- tasies that contain a great number of pages! Cornelia Funke's *Inkheart*, for exam- ple, a German translation and a *New York Times* bestseller, as well as an ALA Notable Book, is 548 pages long. Skillful writers of fantasy draw imaginative stu- dents into other worlds and make these worlds as real to them as the world in which they live. Lewis Carroll (*Alice's Adventures in Wonderland*, 1865), L. Frank Baum (*The Wonderful Wizard of Oz*, 1900), J. R. Tolkien (*The Hobbit*, 1938), and C. S. Lewis (*The Chronicles of Narnia*, 1950) accomplished this feat many years ago. Now, talented writers, many drawing from their knowledge of myths and leg- ends, continue to enchant their readers.

THE DARK IS RISING. In her *The Dark Is Rising* series, Susan Cooper transports her readers from the present to the age of King Arthur.

CHRONICLES OF PRYDAIN. Lloyd Alexander, whose extensive knowl- edge of Wales and its legends has enlightened the pages of the *Chronicles of Pry- dain*, relates the trials and tribulations of a group of characters beset by magic as they journey to warn the High King that evil troops are about to attack.

HARRY POTTER. J. K. Rowling has captured the attention of both chil- dren and adults throughout the world with her books about the young wizard Harry Potter. A publishing phenomenon, Harry's adventures in Hogwarts, the school of wizardry, are spellbinding.

TEHANU: THE LAST BOOK OF EARTHSEA. In the last book of her Earthsea series, Ursula K. LeGuin describes a gentle, older Goha to the reader. Goha rescues a reticent young child, Therru, from a burning fire and brings her to an ordinary farmhouse to nourish her with loving kindness. Then the author cat- apults unsuspecting readers into the fantasy that fascinated them in the four pre- vious books about Earthsea. Readers discover that Goha is really Tenar, Therru is Tehanu, and Ged is Sparrow Hawk. Readers are introduced or reintroduced to the witches, wizards, archmags, and dragons that have long inhabited the Island of Gont in a very readable fantasy.

CIRCLE OF MAGIC: SANDRY'S BOOK. Tamara Pierce has written a less serious but popular fantasy for middle school readers. Sandry, Daja, Briar, and Trisana are four young people of diverse backgrounds whose lives intersect at the Winding Circle Temple in Emalan—the center for learning and magic. Under the aegis of Niklaren Goldeye, they learn "uvumi" (patience), "Trader Talk," and how to use their powers of magic for the good of all. In the final book *The Will of the Empress* (2005), the mages, now 16 years old, are reunited, continue to develop their powers, and plan their future.

Animal Fantasy

REDWALL. Brian Jacques has captured the imagination of middle school students with his endearing but daring series (over fifteen books) of fantastic adventures about a band of field mice living in Redwall Abbey in Mosstown, England. Although they are content to live the life of ordinary mice, they band together with their friends to stand firmly against Cluny the Scourge, an ugly rat, and his five hundred rat thugs. Jacques has created heroes like Matthias (who recovers the lost sword), Martin the Warrior, Mariel, Salamandaston, and many others. Young people excitedly read each book as it becomes available.

PERLOO THE BOLD. Avi has created a series of lighthearted, often humorous books of fantasy that middle school readers who like animals will find enjoyable. Perloo is a peace-loving, intelligent "Montmer" who looks very much like a rabbit "three hops high and twelve years new." His favorite activity has been to read in his burrow about mythology and the history of the Montmers. This all changes, however, when Lucabara, a fellow Montmer, urges him to come with her (in the greatest snowstorm since the Frog Year) to the Great Hall, where he meets Jolaine. The elderly, dying Jolaine selects Perloo to take her place as Granter, much to the chagrin of her evil son Berwig, who declares himself the new Granter.

THE TALE OF DESPEREAUX. In an unusual format similar to a Victorian novel, Kate DiCamillo combines four "books" in this Newbery Medal winner about the romance of Despereaux Tilling, a large-eared, small mouse, and the beautiful human Princess Pea. When Despereaux uses a needle and spool of thread to save Princess Pea from the knife of the vengeful rat Roscuro, he becomes the hero. Throughout the book the interplay of light and shadow is accented by Timothy Ering's black and white illustrations.

Science Fiction

Science fiction has become a fascinating part of fantasy and continues to be avidly read by middle school students, who are challenged to think deeply about what could be. When Paul Churchland, a well-known philosophy professor at the University of California, was a middle school student he was enthralled by Robert Heinlein's books. He still remembers from his science fiction reading that "however certain he may be about something, however airtight an argument appears, or however fundamental an intuition, there is always a chance that both are completely wrong, and that reality lies in some other place that he hasn't looked because he doesn't know it's there" (McFarquhar, 2007, p. 62).

A WRINKLE IN TIME. Ever since Madeline L'Engle's A *Wrinkle in Time* received the Newbery Medal (1963), it has been the exemplar of how authors can combine science and fantasy to make this genre particularly popular with middle school students and young adults. In her dramatic tale of Dr. Murry's rescue from the planet Camatoze, L'Engle coined the word *tesseract* to denote the ability of humans to go from one planet to another. Students remain absorbed in her themes of individuality, family, self-esteem, intelligence, and the responsible use of science and technology.

ROCKET SHIP GALILEO. Robert Heinlein has long been a science fiction writer of books primarily for adults. Fortunately, however, his first science book written for children, *Rocket Ship Galileo* (1947), has been reissued as science fiction and is experiencing a rebirth among young people, who often wait in long lines to attend science fiction conventions. There they meet others like themselves who are seeking stories that challenge their ideas about time, space, and gravity.

MRS. FRISBY AND THE RATS OF NIMH. A Newbery Medal book by Robert O'Brien may have increased in popularity among children and adolescents since it became a movie, but it has always been widely read. The novel deals with talking rats, escapees from the NIMH, who have the ability to read and a scientific plan to prolong life. Although the author was always shy and shunned publicity, "O'Brien gained his devoted following solely by writing one of the great science-fiction stories of the modern age" (Silvey, 2004, p. 116).

THE GIVER. Lois Lowry's multi–award-winning book takes place in a controlled, colorless, and futuristic society. In this place, no one makes choices until the young protagonist, Jonas, is selected to follow in the footsteps of the Giver and discovers what he and other members of the community have been missing. Other books in the trilogy are *Gathering Blue,* concerning yet another futuristic society dominated by the artistic talents of Kira, the weaver, Thomas the carver, and Jo the singer of the future. *The Messenger* includes characters from the two preceding books, who are now active in another community. Lois Lowry has created a trilogy that lends itself to spirited discussion.

THE TIME HACKERS. Gary Paulsen, noted for his survival stories, has successfully jumped into a swiftly paced time travel experience. His story of spinning through colliding timelines to save time from destruction is popular science fiction for middle school students.

THE TIME HACKERS
Used by permission of Dell Publishing, a division of Random House, Inc.

Poetry

Teachers who encourage their students to turn to poetry to gain insight into themselves and their personal feelings will be pleased to introduce their students to the following.

BEHIND THE WHEEL. Janet Wong's collection of poems for teenagers reflects their growing psychosocial maturity and their entrance into the "almost adult" world.

LOCOMOTION. Jacqueline Woodson's powerful poems can incite students to read and possibly write poetry, in spite of their reluctance to do either. Her book (with lots of white space) relates a story in free verse that inspires and motivates middle school students not only to enjoy poetry, but to experiment with writing in poetic form.

Spin Off

Children Interact with Poetry

- Once your students have read Gary Soto's *Neighborhood Odes*, they may like to try to write an ode of praise to one of their favorite objects, such as a pizza, a soccer ball, a baseball cap, or a locket. Have them examine the object carefully and consider what words they should choose to describe their feelings about it, and then have them write about it in poetic form.

- Have your students reread Paul Janeczko's book *How to Write Poetry* (in the Informational Books section) and then, following his suggestions, write their own poetry in their literary journal.

- Ask your students to talk about some event in their life that they will never forget. Suggest that they write their feelings about it (as they remember it) in their journals. Later, they may want to write a poem about it using some of the words they have already written.

FRENCHTOWN SUMMER. In this slight book of poems that is a thinly disguised memoir from Robert Cormier's childhood, young people gradually understand more about this popular novelist and as a consequence, come to learn more about themselves and their relationships. As Cormier admits, "I knew my name / but did not know who I was."

THE AMERICAN SPORTS POEMS COLLECTION. Edited by R. R. Knudson and May Swenson, this collection contains doggerel and serious verse written by such well-known poets as Carl Sandburg, Robert Frost, John Updike, and Ogden Nash. Students can relate to a poem such as Michael S. Harper's "Makin' Jump Shots," which includes the lines.

A sniff in the fallen air / he stuffs it through the chains / riding high: "traveling" someone calls / and he laughs, stepping / to a silent beat, gliding / as he sinks two into the chains.

It creates a vivid picture of a tense basketball game, a topic that is popular with many students in middle school.

NEIGHBORHOOD ODES. Many young people are familiar with the author Gary Soto. His stories about the inner city are filled with the joys and heartbreak of Hispanic youth. Soto the poet, however, takes a lighthearted look at the neighborhood where he grew up. He writes of celebrations. He recalls his happiness when going to the small library, picnicking with his family, running under the sprinkler, and buying snowcones from the ice cream truck.

Drama

Drama is an integral part of the poetry genre, especially for young people in middle school. Not only does the current interest in Shakespeare fascinate them, but many students who choose drama as an elective, an after-school activity, or a weekend class discover that as they join others in performing plays, they are developing their personal, social, and academic skills.

DAY OF TEARS. The poignancy of Julius Lester's Newbery Honor book is punctuated with grief when it is read aloud in a classroom setting. Readers Theatre (see Chapter Four) permits many voices to speak about the 1859 tragedy in Georgia involving the biggest slave auction in American history.

MAKING THEATER. Students (and teachers) may be motivated when they read Herbert Kohl's book *Making Theater* to develop plays with young people. His book explores improvisation, reading and acting with scripts, and adapting plays for young actors.

SEEK. Paul Fleischman continues to write multi voice novels and poetry for ensembles. His book *Joyful Noise: Poems for Two Voices* won a Newbery Medal. In *Seek*, the main character, Rob Radkovitz, listens to many voices, but the one he is seeking is his father's. Although he has only one tape recording of his father's voice, he is determined to find him. When he does, he has his chance to "blast him, to tell how I've tracked him through the airwaves, how I'd done all my school reports in his honor. . . but the words weren't waiting on my tongue, as they'd once been." The script for this story challenges middle school readers and is also an integral part of the plot.

Then and Now

Shakespeare in the Twenty-first Century

Then

If children in sixth, seventh, or eighth grade in past years were assigned the reading of a play by William Shakespeare, they would have balked at the thought. Reading Elizabethan plays was not a part of their curriculum. Shakespeare was assigned reading in the high school English program (and was usually required reading only for the college bound). In college, English majors could select Shakespeare for a complete semester. The language of Shakespeare, however, was presumably too difficult for middle school students to understand.

Consequently in past years, students attending grammar school would have found few plays or books in their school libraries about the Elizabethan world. Charles and Mary Lamb's *Tales of Shakespeare* may have been the only summary of Shakespeare's plays to which students had access. Totally devoid of illustrations and written in a stilted manner, often with only one paragraph to an entire page, the Lambs' book has been frequently reissued here and abroad since it was first published in the 1800s.

Fortunately, in 1951, Marchette Chute made Shakespeare come alive in her *Introduction to Shakespeare*. She describes how Shakespeare's plays were written and where they were performed. She was the first to open a small window allowing later elementary school children to understand a little of Shakespeare's amazing talent.

Now

Today, many middle school children are reading Shakespeare, performing Shakespearean plays, and examining his life and times, and they are not as intimidated as such children have been in the past. Yet the language of the plays has not changed. What has happened between **Then** and **Now**? Books such as *The Shakespeare Stealer* (1998) and its sequel, *Shakespeare's Scribe* (2000), two mystery novels written by Gary Blackwood, are educating middle school students about life in Shakespeare's time — the theatre, the actors, the playgoers — in a way that is entertaining and absorbing.

Well-known author Susan Cooper succeeds in making Will Shakespeare a young boy's friend and companion in *King of the Shadows*. It was Shakespeare whom the main character Ned Fields meets in his feverish dreams, when he becomes ill on a trip to London. Together, Will (who sees his deceased son in Ned) and he explore the Globe Theater of the seventeenth century and rehearse *Midsummer's Night's Dream* for Queen Elizabeth. When Ned finally awakens and realizes he is in the present and at an English hospital where his friends and fellow actors visit him, he is surprised to discover he already knows one of Shakespeare's sonnets because the playwright himself gave it to him.

Julius Lester creatively introduces middle school students to Shakespeare by taking Shakespeare's play

Othello and developing it into a novel. His purpose is to make students more confident about reading the original play themselves.

Bruce Coville, noted for humorous novels such as *My Teacher Is an Alien*, retells Shakespearean plays such as *Hamlet* in a picture book format. Readers experiencing Shakespeare for the first time will find *Hamlet* filled with full-page, dream-like illustrations that provide a goodness-of-fit, especially for reluctant students.

Even graphic novels are being used as a source of information. The cartoon book *Tales from Shakespeare* by Marcia Williams is intended to make the Bard more accessible to reluctant middle school readers. Seven of Shakespeare's most famous plays make up the content. Williams divides each performance into three parts: the words Shakespeare actually wrote are spoken by the actors; the story, or plot of the play, is told below the pictures; and the spectators—who are famously rude and noisy—can be seen shouting around the stage.

Performances, legitimate theatre presentations, and outstanding movies about Shakespeare that star popular teenagers challenge middle schoolers to read Shakespeare's original plays. In fact, children this age are attending performances and demonstrating such respect and understanding of the plays that adults wonder why Shakespeare was not part of the middle school curriculum in the past.

Contemporary Realistic Fiction

Fiction for middle school is often a reflection of who the students are or who they want to be. As you read the stories suggested in this section, be aware that impulse control is a key aspect of their personality and extremely significant for healthy psychosocial development (Jack Gantos treats this subject sensitively in his stories about Joey Pigza). Young people this age are also concerned with the relationships they have with members of their family and how friends' family relationships measure up to theirs. They know from their own experiences and from what they read that all families are not alike. Longtime favorite authors like Katherine Paterson (*The Bridge to Terabithia*), Paula Fox (*Monkey Island*), Virginia Hamilton (*Plain City*), and Ruth White (*Belle Prater's Boy*), who write with understanding about these relationships, have consistently been popular with readers. Yet some subjects that today's middle school students take for granted have not always been accepted topics.

Controversial Subjects

Only during the social upheaval of the 1960s did the subject matter of middle school novels begin breaking long-standing taboos (Burns, 1995). Adolescents read about young Dave and his belligerent feelings toward his father in Emily Neville's *It's Like This, Cat* (1963). Adolescents also examined the gamut of emotions of 11-year-old Harriet in Louise Fitzhugh's *Harriet the Spy* (1964c). They likewise eagerly absorbed discussions of such previously forbidden subjects as menstruation in Fitzhugh's sequel, *The Long Secret* (1965). Vera and Bill Cleaver, whose forte was the realistic novel, introduced their readers to a strong, unusually independent heroine in *Where the Lilies Bloom* (1969) and continued to write into the next decade about contemporary concerns with their customary candor.

Even a book like Astrid Lindgren's *Pippi Longstocking* (1950), whose heroine was extraordinarily independent and impudent, was criticized as being something unpleasant that scratches the soul. The topics in Judy Blume's *Are You There, God? It's Me,*

Margaret, published in 1970a, and *Then Again, Maybe I Won't*, written in 1971, and Betsy Byars' Newbery Medal book the *Summer of the Swans* (1970) were not widely accepted in those years as appropriate reading for middle school students. Critics argued that the trend toward the "realistic inclusion of adolescent concerns and societal ills in books of fiction for middle-level readers has gone so far in its quest for truth that it has drained children of their hopes and dreams" (Burns, 1995, p. 460). Contemporary fiction, however, empowers young readers to realize that whatever happens can be overcome provided the reader has courage and assumes responsibility for what lies ahead.

School and Family

JOEY PIGZA SWALLOWED THE KEY. Jack Gantos has created an unusual character in his series about Joey Pigza. Joey often loses his self-control because he is wired, especially when his meds aren't working. Despite sympathetic teachers, Joey's behavior does not improve until he is sent to the Special Ed center downtown. Readers root for Joey and hope that the patch he must wear will be his entrance into the real world of the middle school. Another story about Joey (*Joey Pigza Loses Control*) reveals that Joey is still struggling for emotional control and for better relations with his father.

THE OUTCASTS OF 19 SCHUYLER PLACE. E. L. Konigsburg wrote her first novel, *Jennifer, Hecate, Macbeth, William McKinley and Me, Elizabeth*, in 1967 and it won a Newbery Honor. In 1968, when her second novel, *From the Mixed-Up Files of Mrs. Basil E. Frankweiler*, won a Newbery Medal, Konigsburg was again recognized as an outstanding storyteller whose characters are especially well drawn. Now, over thirty years later, she still merits that reputation for writing *The Outcasts of 19 Schuyler Place*. Her protagonist, the precocious Margaret Rose Kane, is not afraid to ask the big questions: What is the meaning of art? What is the value of nonconformity? What is the power of the community? Nor is she afraid to actively work toward finding the answers. Konigburg's secondary characters are also cutting-edge.

BELLE TEAL. Ann Martin's story of Belle Teal, an independent-thinking fifth-grader, is a metaphor for many of the developmental issues that trouble young students: schoolmates who are bullies, a grandmother who is losing her memory, and a mother who must work and cannot give her the attention she wants. Most distressing to Belle, however, is the cruelty some of her classmates show toward the new student Darryl because he is black. Especially appealing to reluctant readers because the plot moves quickly, it will appeal to all students with its warmth and honesty.

EVERYTHING ON A WAFFLE. Polly Horvath has created an unforgettable character in preteen Primrose, who lives in a small fishing village in British Columbia. As narrator she explains that she is convinced that although her parents were lost at sea, they will soon return. Meanwhile her Uncle Jack, a developer and entrepreneur, cares for her, along with well-meaning interference from a cast of characters that includes Miss Perfidy (whose memories "float around") and Miss Honeycut (a descendent of English royalty). It is Miss Bowzer, the owner/cook of The Girl in the Red Swing, however, who offers Primrose the most delicious recipes and the wisest advice.

KIRA-KIRA. Using Katie Takeshima's first-person voice in this Newbery Medal book, author Cynthia Kadohata sensitively describes the day-to-day life of a financially strapped Japanese American family in the 1950s who must move from Iowa to Georgia to find work. The most difficult experience in Katie's life, however, is the death of her beloved sister.

Sports

For girls, the passage of Title IX increased their participation and recognition in sports and has led to the exciting possibility that they may be eligible to play on a college team. Karen Blumenthal's book *Let Me Play: The Story of Title IX, the Law that Changed the Future of Girls in America* is a must-read for middle school and high school girl athletes. Other books about sports for boys and girls are:

MAD CAT. Kathy Mackel addresses fast-pitch softball and how the rivalries between some players and the poor sportsmanship of others influence the game. The main protagonist is Madcat Campione, whose relationship with her best friends suffers when her team competes nationally.

HEAT. Mike Lupica's fast-paced book about high school baseball includes a young Spanish immigrant among a diverse group of athletes. He is in danger of not playing because his birth certificate is missing, until the daughter of the coach comes to his rescue.

TRAVEL TEAM. Mike Lupica's *New York Times* best-selling book captures what is happening with the team generally and individually, and how family and school problems affect the way individual players play the game.

Adventure and Survival

ON MY HONOR. Although Marion Dane Bauer's book was published in the late 1980s, its theme about the difference between right and wrong remains timeless. Bauer has written a thought-provoking book that middle school children will seriously consider for a long time. The dilemma that Joel experiences when his best friend drowns easily provokes a discussion of Kohlerg's theory of moral development (see Chapter One).

BRIAN'S RETURN. Gary Paulsen is a skillful and knowledgeable writer about the outdoors whose books reflect the adventurous spirit of young people. Students who have read other books about Brian Robeson (*Hatchet, The River,* and *Brian's Winter*) know that he is a genuine hero and a survivor. Now, having returned home to complete his schooling, he faces another conflict: physical confrontations with his classmates. He longs to return to the wilderness and eventually takes off in a small plane to put into practice all the survival skills he has learned.

HOLES. Louis Sachar's Newbery Medal book is well worth reading and discussing in the classroom. It is built on the premise of a generations-old curse in the Yelnats family that involves Stanley's no-good, rotten, pig-stealing grandfather. When Stanley is unjustly sent to a boys' detention center in Texas called Camp Green Lake (which is parched due to lack of water) for stealing a famous basketball player's sneakers, he learns to live and work with a varied group of misfits like Hector, Zero, Zigzag, Armpits, and X-Ray. The boys are forced to dig holes five feet by five feet every day in the brutal sun, sometimes with nothing to quench their thirst. The rationale is that this will build character in the boys, but the female warden-in-charge has a totally different purpose.

Mystery

THE HOUSE OF DIES DREAR. Virginia Hamilton uncovers the mystery of two murdered slaves who had been hiding in the House of Dies Drear. The house, now the home of the Smalls, a contemporary black family, was originally a stop on the Underground Railroad. A sequel, *The Mystery of Drear House*, uncovers a hidden treasure that reveals the Small family's skill as detectives.

SAMMY KEYES AND THE SKELETON MAN. Edgar Allan Poe Award winner Wendelin Van Draanen has created Sammy Keyes, a contemporary Nancy Drew with a sense of humor, a way with words, and an uncommon talent for solving mysteries. Even her *Grams*, with whom she lives, wants to know "How do you get yourself into these things?" This story begins on Halloween night, when Sammy, dressed as a green monster, her best friend Marissa, dressed as a mummy, and her new friend Dot, who is dressed as a bumblebee, bump into Skeleton man running from the Bush house. When they open the door they find a man tied to a chair, unable to talk, with a bruise on his head and a Frankenstein mask on his face.

THE GHOST OF FOSSIL GLEN. Cynthia DeFelice, award-winning author of *The Apprenticeship of Lucas Whitaker*, has written an engaging story for the reluctant reader about the ghost of Lucy Stiles, who saves Allie's life when she loses her footing on Fossil Glen. While Allie, a sixth-grader, is writing in her journal, she discovers a red diary in the desk her mother bought from the Stiles house (which is scheduled to be torn down). In the diary many revelations lead ultimately to what really happened to Lucy. It's a fast-moving story with believable characters and an exciting plot.

Culture and Children's Literature

Migrant Workers

Pam Munoz Ryan's *Esperanza Rising* offers hope for Mexican immigrant Esperanza Ortega. Initially, the author informs readers about Esperanza's struggle to overcome the loss of her father, the illness of her mother, and her own struggle to survive the hardships of settling in a camp for Mexican migrant workers during the Great Depression of the 1930s.

Esperanza was a wealthy 13-year-old who lived with her parents and servants in El Rancho de los Rosas, Aguascalientes, Mexico. She can't imagine not wearing beautiful dresses, going to festivals, or being surrounded by people who love her. It was a stunning blow when her father was ambushed and killed by bandits and her home burned. She and her mother, without money or belongings, were forced to leave Mexico and travel by train in the middle of the night to California. There, they worked in the fields harvesting fruit. Esperanza at first was despondent. "She fell to her knees and sank into a dark hole of despair and disbelief." Only through the support of friends like Miguel, his parents, and others she met was she able to survive.

When her mother was taken ill, Esperanza found a way to rise above her circumstances to learn skills to help her mother return to their camp. She also saved her meager earnings to pay for her grandmother to come from Mexico to live with them. Her grandmother was always hopeful. "Right now you are in the bottom of the valley and your problems loom big around you. But soon, you will be at the top of a mountain again," she often said to Esperanza as she crocheted her blanket with the zigzag stitches.

By reading the novel, middle school students gain a greater understanding of the struggle of migrant workers, especially during the 1930s. The conditions under which they lived were terrible, yet many were reluctant to join a union to better their conditions lest they lose their only means of livelihood. They also knew there were other workers ready to step in and replace them. "They focused only on survival and put their hopes and dreams into their children's and grandchildren's futures." That's what Ryan's grandmother did—whose life parallels that of Esperanza. "All of her children learned English and so did she. Her children became successful and our accomplishments were her accomplishments. She wished the best for all of us and rarely looked back on the difficulties of her own life" (Ryan, 2000, p. 262).

Historical Fiction

The work of Robert Selman (1980), called *social perspective taking*, suggests that middle school students gradually acquire the ability to think critically. They can "step into another's shoes" and more fully appreciate how others think. In the historical fiction recommended in this section, middle school students step into the character's shoes and decide if they would act the same way. While reading historical fiction about the Holocaust and other genocides throughout the world, it is hoped that they will ask themselves the question: *what would I have done?* Hazel Rochman, author of the award-winning *Against Borders: Promoting Books for a Multicultural World*, feels it is important for students to make the connection between the atrocities of racism in the past and its more recent forms involving the American Indian, slavery, apartheid, and ethnic cleansing. "Extreme as the Nazi genocide was, it was not a thing apart; it was human experience" (Rochman, 2006, p. 550). Every period in history is a source of historical fiction, from ancient times through the twentieth century. Examples from major historical periods include:

Historical Fiction about Medieval Times

CATHERINE, CALLED BIRDY. Medieval England is the setting for three of Karen Cushman's award-winning historical novels. *Catherine, Called Birdy* details in a diary the adventures of Birdy, the daughter of a member of English royalty in 1290, and her conflict with her parents about her impending marriage. Readers witness a social and religious setting that Cushman describes in such authentic style that they are transported to another era where they *become* Birdy: curious, generous, independent, and a feminist living before her time.

THE MIDWIFE'S APPRENTICE. In *The Midwife's Apprentice* Karen Cushman again chooses the setting of medieval England and an independent character who is curious, generous, and a quick learner. Unlike Birdy, however, "Beetle" is a homeless young girl who is picked up off the road by midwife Jane Sharpe. Jane makes her an apprentice so that she can clean the cottage and accompany her when a woman is in labor. Beetle's conflict is with herself. When she is given a comb, she discovers she has beautiful hair; when she assumes the name Alyce, she begins to develop the self-confidence she is lacking. When she delivers a baby herself, however, she presents herself to the demanding Jane Sharpe as a genuine apprentice who knows "how to try and risk and fail and try again and not give up."

MATILDA BONE. In *Matilda Bone* Karen Cushman explores the theme of how the practice of medieval medicine is totally unrecognizable in today's world. In medieval Europe, physicians were not the doctors we know but "philosophers, astrologers, numerologists and dream interpreters. . . they believed in charms, incantations, relics, devils, fairies, gnomes, flying witches and the power of the unicorn's horn" (Cushman, 2000, p. 161). Matilda, another strong female character, serves Red Peg the Bonesetter, in Blood and Bone Alley, in a variety of tasks unrelated to "medicine." She at first yearns to devote her life to prayer and study, but she eventually discovers that healing requires more than belief in superstitions.

Historical Fiction about the American Experience

WATER STREET. Patricia Reilly Giff's novel offers middle school students the opportunity to walk in the steps of Nory Ryan during the year 1875. From where she lives, she can see the Brooklyn Bridge being built, and it becomes her symbol of strength as she struggles to create a happy and successful life in America for her family—especially for her daughter, Bird, who, at 13, wonders if she will ever be the healer she dreams of becoming.

BREAD AND ROSES, TOO. Another well-known writer, Katherine Paterson, winner of many awards, returns to a New England setting (which is also the setting for *Lyddie*, a novel she wrote in 1991) to recount the adventures of two young people, Jake and Rosa, totally different in all aspects of their development, who are unwittingly involved in the Bread and Roses Strike of 1912.

BUD, NOT BUDDY. Christopher Paul Curtis's Newberry Medal winner is set in 1936 in Flint, Michigan, where a young boy, Bud, is determined to find his father at any cost. Homeless and motherless, he has only a few possessions in his battered suitcase, but they contain clues to his past, along with flyers about the famous Herman E. Calloway, who he thinks is his father. As he drifts from place to place he encounters kindness from an unlikely assortment of people, spends time and shares soup with the homeless in Hooverville, jumps a train, and finally arrives at the Log Cabin in Grand Rapids, Michigan, where Calloway is performing.

Spotlight On
Christopher Paul Curtis

James Keyser/ Getty Images

When Christopher Curtis gave his acceptance speech at the Annual Conference of the American Library Association in Chicago, Illinois, on July 9, 2000, the entire audience was moved by what he said. With his extended family present, he thanked them for his achievement: a Newbery Medal for *Bud, Not Buddy*. He was especially grateful for his wife, Kay, who encouraged his writing and deserved credit for the award he received. He also feared that when his wife encouraged him to take a year off to write, it might be wasted. Many of his listeners were writers themselves and could relate to his apprehension that by taking a year off, he was openly admitting that he was going to try to make a career as a writer. As a writer whose work is respected and loved by adults as well as children, Curtis proved that he had nothing to fear.

His first book, the Newbery Honor book, *The Watsons Go To Birmingham—1963*, is already a classic. It is filled with humor, honesty, and sensitivity about a family traveling from Flint, Michigan, to Alabama during the civil rights movement. When Wendy Lamb, an editor at Delacorte, accepted the manuscript, she was amazed by the wonderful details, especially the incident when Kenny looks inside his sister Joetta's shoe as she sleeps on the drive south and sees Buster Brown's face printed on the heel. "After the bombing, Kenny looks inside the shoe he finds at the church and sees Buster Brown. I stopped reading. Not Joetta! I turned the page face down. I thought, 'Wow. Look what he did with a shoe. Who is this guy?'"(Lamb, 2000, p. 397).

"This guy" was born in Flint, Michigan, in 1953 and had many jobs before he began to write. He worked in an automobile factory for thirteen years, hauled garbage, mowed lawns, unloaded trucks, and did other menial jobs while his wife urged him to write. After receiving the Avery and Jules Hopwood Award at the University of Michigan, where he was a part-time student, he decided to become a writer. He spent many days writing in the children's room of the public library and is grateful for the support and assistance librarians have always given him. In Chapter Seven of *Bud, Not Buddy*, Bud describes the feel and smell of libraries. After closing the library door, he comments that "since it had closed the next one was about to open." Young people who read his books are looking forward to that next open door being another book written by Christopher Paul Curtis.

Historical Fiction about the Great Depression

A LONG WAY FROM CHICAGO. Richard Peck, a Newbery Medal author, describes the main character, Grandma Dowdel, with great insight and humor in the setting of a small town outside Chicago during the Great Depression. Joey, her grandson, describes various incidents that reflect his grandmother's uniqueness during those summers that he and his younger sister Mary Alice spent with her. The book captures the authentic details of an era that was remarkable in its contradictions: Prohibition, crime, and poverty versus generosity, honesty, and richness of spirit. Readers will appreciate Peck's humor and the excitement generated by the exploits of Grandma Dowdel.

Historical Fiction about War

UNDER THE BLOOD-RED SUN. From the point of view of a young Japanese boy, Graham Salisbury describes how the events following the Japanese bombing of Pearl Harbor on December 7, 1941, changed his life forever. No longer can he enjoy carefree fishing expeditions with his father or long conversations with his grandfather, or play baseball with the "Rats," his school chums. Now Tamikazu and his family are under suspicion as spies. With the assistance of his "haole" friends, who remain loyal to him, he is determined that he and his family will survive these difficult days.

A BOY AT WAR. Harry Mazer relates events following the Japanese bombing of Pearl Harbor from the point of view of Adam, a young American boy from a military family. He and his Japanese friend Davi are fishing when they witness the bombing. Adam is immediately pressed into action to help the wounded and protect a busload of people. When his father, a Navy lieutenant on the warship *Arizona*, is declared missing in action, he must assume the task of being head of the family for his mother and little sister. Harry Mazer creates a setting of turmoil and terror that is unforgettable.

AND ONE FOR ALL. Theresa Nelson has deftly crafted a novel that presents the pros and cons of the Vietnam War while introducing readers to the characters and family relationships that made taking a stand at that time such a difficult choice. Geraldine, Wing's sister and Sam's friend, is the main character and cherishes her relationship with each. Her loyalty, however, is torn apart when Wing decides to sign up for the military shortly before he graduates from high school, while Sam chooses college and actively participates in antiwar marches. How Geraldine recaptures the trust she had pledged years earlier makes for a sensitive, emotional story for middle school readers.

PARK'S QUEST. Skilled storyteller Katherine Paterson describes the feelings and questions that trouble Parkington Waddell Broughton the Fifth ("just call me Park") as he seeks information about his father, who died in Vietnam. Considering his search similar to the search for the Holy Grail, Park receives little information from his mother and so decides to visit the Virginia home of his dad. There he finds a situation that troubles him: his father's brother, his grandfather, and a nasty, irksome Vietnamese girl. Gradually, the story of what happened to his father in Vietnam is revealed to him.

Historical Fiction about the Holocaust

THE LILY CUPBOARD. Although *The Lily Cupboard* is a picture book written by Shulamith Oppenheim and illustrated by Ronald Himler, it recalls Lois Lowry's *Number the Stars* in that it also reveals that some people are conscience-stricken and make sacrifices for others in the darkest of times. The story revolves around a young Jewish child in Holland in 1940 who had to leave her parents to live with a Gentile family on their farm. The simplicity of her life in these peaceful surroundings contrasts vividly with the lives of her parents from whom she is separated.

EMIL AND KARL. Written by Yankev Glatshteyn and translated from Yiddish, it relates the experiences of two boys—Emil, who is Jewish and Karl who is not—and their lives during the Nazi occupation. They encounter kindness and depravity and are hounded by the question: *what makes them do it?*

THE BOOK THIEF. This is an unusual book. Written by Markus Zusak as an adult novel set in Austria, it is narrated by Death, and is especially recommended for the informed middle school or high school student. Deeply compassionate, Death observes every detail in the life of 9-year-old Liesel. From the first book she steals from a graveyard, to books she recovers from the Nazi book burnings, to books from her foster parents, to the book that reveals her own story, Liesel develops into a brave, caring young person who lives, works, and suffers in the small town of Molching during the Nazi occupation.

The #1 *New York Times* Bestseller

THE BOOK THIEF
Used by permission of Alfred A. Knopf, an imprint of Random House Children's Books, a division of Random House, Inc.

Spin Off

Children Interact with Historical Fiction

As a teacher or librarian, you may like to select one book in this genre to read to the class as a whole, not only to find out how students personally respond, but also to find out if they can analyze and understand why they responded the way they did.

• First, they should understand the historical background, which may require more research (perhaps from the informational books we have reviewed).

• They should be aware of the descriptive language used in the book. Metaphors and other expressions that are not familiar to them should be written down in their journals and discussed.

• They should list the characteristics and physical appearance of the characters and the problems they face.

• Finally, students should consider what they would do in the same situation. How would they react to the demeaning or hurtful situations the characters experience?

Perhaps your students could role-play and pretend to counsel these characters. Selecting a scene from the book, they could create a short play, a radio or television interview with the character, or even a letter to a columnist like Ann Landers. From reading *Stress* (included in informational books), they may even find solutions to the characters' problems! The purpose of this *Spinoff* is for you as a teacher or librarian to find out how your students act and react to the situations in the books they read, and then to have them share their thoughts with their fellow students.

Historical Fiction—Post-war America

THE LOUD SILENCE OF FRANCINE GREEN. Karen Cushman has recently written *The Loud Silence of Francine Green* (2006), which takes place in Los Angeles during the anti-communist hysteria in 1949–1950. The main character, Francine Green, is remarkably similar to the characters Cushman has placed in medieval times. A quiet 13-year-old she becomes friends with Sophie Bowman, finds her voice, and is determined to speak the truth and take a stand.

Biography

Children of these years are becoming progressively more realistic about their skills, abilities, and expectations. Their reactions, which result from comparing themselves to others, feed back into their self-concepts. The biographies summarized here give you a wonderful opportunity to guide young people to the characteristics of outstanding individuals which, in turn, could improve their feelings of self-efficacy—their belief that they can exercise control over their lives.

Bandura's work (1997) on self-efficacy (see Chapter One), which is solidly rooted in social cognitive theory, testifies to the power that verbal persuasion (reading, discussion) can exercise in furthering a child's sense of self. A feeling of mastery and competence, based on successful performance, is a powerful, constantly recurring motivational device for children that improves their performance and makes them more willing to face riskier challenges. Biographies are a wonderful vehicle for accomplishing important goals in children's lives.

Biographies and Autobiographies about Writers

GARY PAULSEN. *Guts*, Gary Paulsen's memoir, is appealing to young people who have read his fiction because of the adventures he experienced. His stories of facing a wild bear and of being involved in a plane crash parallel those of his character Brian Robeson in *Hatchet, The River, Brian's Winter*, and *Brian's Return*. At one point, when he goes face to face with a violent moose, Paulsen writes, "I had become Brian Robeson."

SID FLEISCHMAN. In *The Abracadabra Kid*, Sid Fleischman admits that he "had backed into the field of children's books and I liked the scenery." Since elementary school, he liked to perform. First he practiced being a magician, "a trade he learned from library books." Later he did vaudeville in a midnight ghost and goblin show. During World War II, after enlisting in the Navy, he began writing adult books. Later on, he became a Hollywood screenwriter. When he finally decided that he wanted to write children's books, he knew that it was not something that could be done in his spare time.

ROALD DAHL. Dahl's award-winning autobiography *Boy* is another book that middle school readers find interesting because most of them have read his funny, and sometimes fantastic, stories *James and the Giant Peach, Charlie and the Chocolate Factory, Charlie and the Great Glass Elevator*, and *The BFG and the Witches*, to name only a few. He himself has had many adventures. In one incident at the age of 8, he recalls putting a dead mouse in a jar of candies at the sweet-shop. When the owner of the shop failed to show up for work the following day, he really thought he was a murderer.

Biographies and Autobiographies about Adventurers

PAM FLOWERS. *Alone Across the Arctic*, Pam Flowers' autobiography, tells the story of her epic journey that began on Valentine's Day 1993 across the top of the world with her dog team. Independent and undaunted, she sold all that she owned, gave up her job as a respiratory therapist in the States, and moved to Alaska. There, she learned the skills and strategies needed to command her own team of eight huskies coast to coast across the North American arctic.

SIR WALTER RALEGH AND THE QUEST FOR EL DORADO. When Marc Aronson wrote this Newbery Medal biography, he set high standards for those who write biographies for young people. Scrupulously researched and authenticated, it is a fascinating read. Aronson delves into the history of Elizabethan England and categorizes the era based on famous families and their spheres of influence. Aronson points out that Ralegh's entire life was a drama, and he presents it to his readers act by act until Ralegh (original spelling) is executed on October 29, 1618.

Biographies about Presidents

LINCOLN: A PHOTOBIOGRAPHY. In this biography by Russell Freedman, Abraham Lincoln comes alive for readers, who relive his struggle to become president, and then to carry out his promise that the Union would withstand the Civil War. Knowing that the war cost the country 600,000 lives, we can understand why Lincoln suffered so much grief. The scene of his death at Ford's Theatre is etched in the reader's mind, especially since the author reveals that Lincoln had just mentioned that he had "never felt so happy" in his life. Besides the many photographs that illustrate the book (hence the term photobiography), Freedman includes an index, an annotated bibliography, a list of historic places entitled "In Lincoln's Footsteps," and direct quotations from his speeches in a section called "A Lincoln Sampler."

FRANKLIN DELANO ROOSEVELT. This biography by Russell Freedman is as meticulously written as his *Abraham Lincoln* and others. Middle school students who have read historical fiction about the Depression and World War II will be particularly interested in reading this story about the president who served an unprecedented four terms during the "most momentous era in American History." Although he seemed to be a simple man, the author points out that there were many mysteries and contradictions in Roosevelt's personality.

Biographies about Sports Figures

WILLIAM GATES AND ARTHUR AGEE. *Hoop Dreams* by Ben Joravsky traces the successes and failures of two boys—William Gates and Arthur Agee—as they travel from the basketball courts of Chicago's playgrounds to university campuses. Originally planned as a thirty-minute documentary, their story evolved into six years and 250 hours of unedited footage and a full-length book. Gifted basketball players, William and Arthur each compiled a brilliant record in their high school careers while struggling to maintain passing grades. Intensely recruited as they neared graduation, both athletes embarked on the next phase of their lifelong dream of an NBA career—William at Marquette and Arthur at Arkansas State. How these years played out, with all of their twists and turns, is told in an uncompromising manner and makes this biography appealing for middle school readers.

WILMA RUDOLPH. Victoria Sherrow describes how Wilma, born June 23, 1940, weighed only four and a half pounds at birth in a time when anyone born under five pounds was in serious trouble. Sickly at birth, she contracted polio, and doctors feared the damage would be permanent and she would have to use a heavy metal brace. But encouraged by a loving family, she struggled to get back on her feet. By age 10, Wilma was able to walk short distances without her brace. Eight years after she stopped wearing a leg brace, she was called "the fastest woman in history." Overcoming polio, poverty, and racial segregation, Rudolph went on to become the first American woman to win three Olympic gold medals.

JIM THORPE, ORIGINAL ALL-AMERICAN. Joseph Bruchac's touching biography of Native American Jim Thorpe, an outstanding football player at the turn of the twentieth century, concentrates on his early athletic experiences at the Carlisle Indian School. It also reveals his ability to overcome the racism he encountered during his athletic career.

Informational Books

We now see the cognitive skills of middle school students developing rapidly, but the demands they encounter likewise grow in complexity. Memory improves as maturing neural pathways become fixed, and thinking and problem-solving skills continue to sharpen. To capitalize on these changes, the informational books presented here help to provide knowledge that demands the focused use of cognitive skills. Robert Sternberg (1996) noted that critical thinking comprises the mental processes, strategies, and representations people use to solve problems, make decisions, and learn new concepts.

As mentioned in Chapter Ten, Howard Gardner, developmental psychologist at Harvard University, questioned traditional explanations of intelligence and proposed a theory of multiple intelligences in his widely acclaimed book *Frames of Mind* (1983).

We'll again follow his guidelines as we did in Chapter Ten by selecting informational books for middle school students that reflect their interests and encourage exploration of the various intelligences.

Linguistic Intelligence

HOW TO WRITE POETRY. In his poetry anthologies, Paul Janeczco introduces middle school students to other poets. In this book, however, he introduces his own ideas for writing poetry. He is emphatic about keeping a journal (and protecting it from prying eyes) and admits that "writing poetry gives you the chance to fall in love with language again and again." By giving many examples (from his poetry and the poetry of others) and tips (in his "try this" boxes throughout the breezy, lighthearted text) he encourages a would-be poet to sit down and write.

Table 11.2 GARDNER'S MULTIPLE INTELLIGENCES

TYPES OF INTELLIGENCE	MEANING
Linguistic	Organizing your thoughts for verbal tasks
Musical	Recognizing the themes in musical works; distinguishing melodies and responsiveness to music
Logical-mathematical	Understanding the components of thinking and problem solving
Spatial	Forming mental representations to aid thinking and remembering
Bodily-kinesthetic	Smooth development of bodily movements and adaptations
Interpersonal	Ability to work with others and understand them
Intrapersonal	Ability to be aware of inner feelings, intentions, and goals
Naturalistic	Ability to be aware of the environment and to protect it

SEQUOYAH: THE CHEROKEE MAN WHO GAVE HIS PEOPLE WRITING. James Rumford points out that Sequoyah was an ordinary man who gave his people, the Cherokee, the extraordinary gift of a writing system so that they could write and read in their own language. The Cherokee learned the system so quickly that they were able to publish newspapers and books that ensured their words would never fade away.

Musical Intelligence

THIS LAND WAS MADE FOR YOU AND ME: THE LIFE AND SONGS OF WOODY GUTHRIE. Elizabeth Partridge recounts the story of Woody Guthrie, complex antihero, beloved singer, and songwriter. He was as comfortable writing silly songs for his family as he was writing serious songs to uplift the downtrodden. He wrote his most famous song, *This Land Is Your Land*, in reaction to *God Bless America*, which he thought was too sentimental. The book is personalized by Guthrie's own sketches and snapshots of his family and friends. It also includes detailed source notes, a bibliography, and an index.

AIDA. This picture book, by Leontyne Price and beautifully illustrated by Leo and Diane Dillon, is the simple retelling of Verdi's popular opera. Tragically, the enslaved Ethiopian princess Aida and the Egyptian general Radames die in each other's arms. Aida provides inspiration for the middle school reader who is seeking musical knowledge, and offers insights into the life and work of Leontyne Price.

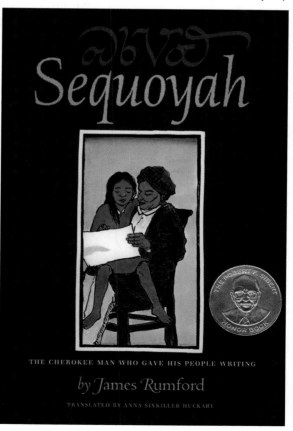

SEQUOYAH: THE CHEROKEE MAN WHO GAVE HIS PEOPLE WRITING
Reprinted by permission of Houghton Mifflin Company

Logical/Mathematical Intelligence

MATH IN SCIENCE AND NATURE. Authors Robert Gardner and Edward Shore answer questions such as: how does the deflection of a curve ball change with the amount of spin on the ball? How many stars are visible in the sky? They even discuss everyday issues such as how to choose the "best buy" light bulb by finding out the amount of light energy delivered by each bulb over its lifetime. Middle school students who are scientifically oriented will find this book both challenging and fascinating.

MATH PROJECTS IN THE COMPUTER AGE. David Thomas presents readers with the challenges of mathematical problems and puzzles and urges his readers to treat them as "candy for the mind." He also suggests that readers play with the ideas and not expect to find solutions immediately. This book encourages students to explore the mathematical and scientific implications that are introduced.

Spatial Intelligence

BROOKLYN BRIDGE. The attractive format of Lynn Curlee's book *Brooklyn Bridge*, combined with the vision of the bridgebuilder, John Augustus Roebling, will delight students. Roebling died soon after work on the bridge began, and Washington Roebling stepped into his father's shoes and continued his work, which took fourteen years to complete. Curlee's illustrations of cross-sections of the bridge in progress heighten the reader's excitement about building what was called the "Eighth Wonder of the World."

MOSQUE. David Macaulay, the author of *Mosque*, creates works of art on paper that illustrate his spatial intelligence. These include popular titles such as *Cathedral, Unbuilding, Castle, Pyramid, City,* and *Rome Antics*. As he does so vividly in all his books, he describes how the mosque was built, by whom, and why. He has a remarkable ability to simplify complex processes and explain not only to adults, but to eager middle school students, how buildings are made and what impact they have on the people who build, as well as on those who live in, work in, or pray in them.

Bodily-Kinesthetic Intelligence

ENDURANCE. Albert Gross discusses sports that involve endurance more than skill or practice, such as swimming, running, or racewalking. In other sports,

Spin Off
Children Interact with Informational Books

- Demonstrate the knowledge you gained from submitting a poem you wrote to your school or local newspaper for publication.
- Using *Aida* as retold by Leontyne Price as your model, retell in your own words another opera you have researched.

- From reading *Math in Science and Nature*, outline the steps scientists take to find mathematical patterns in nature.
- Construct a model of a bridge from the information presented in *Brooklyn Bridge*.

endurance athletes depend on equipment like bicycles, cross-country skis, rowing shells, kayaks, and other human-powered craft. The men and women involved in endurance competitions are amateur and professional, young and old, rich and poor, female and male, and come from all over the world.

Interpersonal Intelligence

CHILDREN OF THE DUST BOWL. When reading books like Karen Hesse's *Out of the Dust* or Pam Munoz Ryan's *Esperanza Rising*, middle school children may want to learn more about the true story of this sad era in America's history. Jerry Stanley's *Children of the Dust Bowl* will provide students with a better understanding of what people endured during this desperate time. California was the promised land. But when travelers arrived there, thousands were turned away daily—there were too many workers and not enough jobs.

THERE COMES A TIME. This incisive examination of the civil rights movement by Milton Meltzer is informative, authentic, and a must-read for middle school students interested in enhancing their intrapersonal intelligence. The author traces the plight of African Americans from their arrival in the United States on slave ships, through the Supreme Court decision of 1954 in *Brown v. Board of Education of Topeka*, to the present day, when, despite the many advances in civil rights, much more needs to be done to bring about equality.

AN AMERICAN PLAGUE. Jim Murphy has again won the Robert Sibert Medal (awarded to the author of the most distinguished information book of the preceding year), this time for *An American Plague: The True and Terrifying Story of the Yellow Fever Epidemic of 1793*. He continues to demonstrate his talent for thoroughly researching a topic and then relating it in a readable manner. Most remarkable is the author's reference in the text to *The Narrative*, the very first document published in the United States that recounts the outstanding work that Philadelphia's free black community did for the sick and dying.

Spotlight On
Jim Murphy

When Jim Murphy was growing up in New Jersey, he was more interested in becoming a nationally ranked track athlete than an author of nonfiction for children. Only after graduating from Rutgers University, when he worked as an editor at Seabury Press, did he decide to become a writer. Fortunately for his readers, Murphy has given them many books of outstanding nonfiction, from *The Boy's War: Confederate and Union Soldiers Talk about the Civil War* (1992), to *American Plague: The True and Terrifying Story of the Yellow Fever Epidemic of 1793* (2003). His nonfiction has earned him many accolades, including two Golden Kite Awards, two Orbis Pictus Awards, a Newbery Honor, a Robert F. Sibert Medal, and inclusion in the YALSA List of Best Books for Young Adults.

What Murphy offers to children is an intense experience that results form his deep love for research and his determination to have his readers see and feel a disaster such as a war, a plague, a blizzard, or a fire that envelops a city. He spends considerable time on his projects before they are published, refining his research and polishing his writing (Zarnowski, 2001). He refuses to cut details because he often finds something so bizarre that readers will love it. He writes that his nonfiction journey has been one of "little steps—stumbling on interesting subjects and fresh voices, doing detective work, learning from other writers, listening to my editors, playing with ideas and words, worrying, and bringing out story lines and themes" (Murphy, 2001, p. 98). Murphy looks forward to continuing his writing journey into the new century.

Spin Off

Children Interact with Informational Books

- Put together the gear needed for a vicarious trip to the top of Mount Everest. Explain why each item is necessary.

- Compare and contrast the physical conditions mentioned in *Esperanza Rising* with those described in *Children of the Dust Bowl*.

- Discuss a stressful experience you have had and how you would handle it now that you have read *Stress*.

- Utilize the information you gained from *The Amateur Naturalist* to make a waterscope.

Intrapersonal Intelligence

UNDERSTANDING STRESS. Robert S. Feldman, Professor of Psychology at the University of Massachusetts, provides middle school readers with knowledge about what stress is, what causes it, and how they can deal with it in their lives. Informally written, logically organized, filled with pertinent problems and realistic solutions, middle school readers will appreciate the author's approach.

POPULARITY HAS ITS UPS AND DOWNS. This small paperback by Meg Schneider (with consulting editor Dennis Meade) deals with topics that are uppermost in the minds of many young readers. Topics include "Who Wants to Be Popular?," "The Great Popularity Myths," "Friendships—The Only Popularity that Really Counts" and an especially pertinent topic, "The Shyness Factor." Schneider offers young people commonsense solutions and self-help questionnaires in a pocket-size book they can tuck into their backpacks.

Naturalistic Intelligence

THE AMATEUR NATURALIST. Charles E. Roth, an environmental educator, asks young people in this book, one entry in the *Amateur Science* series, to examine carefully the world around them. He demonstrates how to make charts, label specimens, make a waterscope, and various other activities that will increase young people's understanding of living things and their habitats. Middle school students will appreciate Roth's willingness to share his knowledge with them so that they can enhance their naturalistic intelligence.

WILDFIRE. Writer and illustrator Taylor Morrison has combined her remarkable talents to provide young people with detailed drawings, diagrams, landscapes, and paintings to emphasize the environmental catastrophe that occurs when a forest catches fire.

Chapter Checklist

Read the following items carefully. If you have difficulty responding to any of them, return to the chapter to review the material.

After reading this chapter, you can

1. Describe how changes in children's thinking during these years changes their book selections.

2. Discuss how middle school children use language and why that helps to explain the appeal of poetry.

3. Illustrate with stories why the plots of novels appeal to the greater cognitive complexity of these children.

4. Analyze the role of myths and legends in children's reading by linking these stories to native folklore.

5. Explain the ways that fantasy touches many of the developmental characteristics of these children.

6. Analyze why middle school children, at the end of these years, begin to lose their creative tendencies, such as writing poetry.

7. Identify the developmental characteristics that cause middle school children to select stories such as *Everything on a Waffle*, which sharpen their awareness of who they are and who they want to become.

8. Discuss the appeal of such stories as *Bud, Not Buddy*, which entice children to step into the main character's shoes.

9. Evaluate the role of self-efficacy in *Guts* and demonstrate its possible impact on readers.

10. List the ways in which nonfiction can improve a reader's critical thinking skills.

Children's Bibliography

Al Saleh, Khairat. (1995). *Fabled Cities, Princes & Jinn from Arab Myths and Legends*. New York: Peter Bedrick Books.

Alexander, Lloyd. (1973). *Chronicles of Prydain*. New York: Guild America Press.

Armstrong, Jennifer. (2006). *Photo by Brady: A Picture of the Civil War*. New York: Simon & Schuster.

Aronson, Marc. (2000). *Sir Walter Ralegh and the Quest for El Dorado*. New York: Clarion Books.

Avi. (1998). *Perloo the Bold*. New York: Scholastic.

Banerjee, Anjali. (2005). *Maya Running*. New York: Random House.

Barron, T. A. (2000). *The Wings of Merlin*. New York: Philomel.

Bauer, Marion. (1987). *On My Honor*. New York: Dell.

Baum, L. Frank. (2003). *The Wonderful Wizard of Oz*. Ann Arbor, MI: Ann Arbor Media Group.

Blackwood, Gary. (1998). *The Shakespeare Stealer*. New York: Dutton.

Blackwood, Gary. (2000). *Shakespeare's Scribe*. New York: Dutton.

Blume, Judy. (1971). *Then Again, Maybe I Won't*. New York: Dell.

Blume, Judy. (1970c). *Are You There God? It's Me, Margaret*. New York: Bradbury Press.

Blumenthal, Karen. (2005). *Let Me Play: The Story of Title IX, the Law That Changed the Future of Girls in America*. New York: Simon & Schuster.

Bruchac, Joseph. (2006). *Jim Thorpe, Original All-American*. New York: Dial Books.

Byars, Betsy. (1981). *Summer of the Swans*. New York: Puffin.

Carroll, Lewis. (1969). *Alice's Adventures in Wonderland*. Belmont, CA: Wadsworth.

Chute, Marchette. (1951). *An Introduction to Shakespeare*. New York: Dutton.

Cleaver, Vera and Owen, Bill. (1969) *Where the Lillies Bloom*. New York: HarperCollins.

Connor, Leslie. (2004). *Miss Bridie Chose a Shovel*. Boston: Houghton Mifflin.

Cooper, Susan. (1999). *King of the Shadows*. New York: Margaret McElderry Books.

Cooper, Susan. (1975). *Dark Is Rising*. New York: Doubleday.

Cormier, Robert. (1999). *Frenchtown Summer*. New York: Delacorte.

Coville, Bruce. (2004). *William Shakespeare's Hamlet*. New York: Penguin.

Creech, Sharon. (2001). *Love that Dog*. New York: HarperCollins.

Crossley-Holland, Kevin. (2002). *Arthur at The Crossing Places*. New York: Arthur Levine.

Curlee, Lynn. (2001). *Brooklyn Bridge*. New York: Atheneum Press.

Curtis, Christopher Paul. (1989). *The Watsons Go to Birmingham—1963*. New York: Delacorte.

Curtis, Christopher Paul. (1999). *Bud, Not Buddy*. New York: Delacorte.

Cushman, Karen. (1994). *Catherine, Called Birdie*. New York: Clarion.

Cushman, Karen. (1995). *The Midwife's Apprentice*. New York: Clarion.

Cushman, Karen. (2000). *Matilda Bone*. New York: Clarion.

Cushman, Karen. (2006). *The Loud Silence of Francine Green*. New York: Clarion.

Dahl, Roald. (1999). *Boy: Tales of Childhood*. New York: Puffin.

DeFelice, Cynthia. (1998). *The Ghost of Fossil Glen*. New York: Avon.

DiCamillo, Kate. (2003). *The Tale of Despereaux*. Cambridge, MA: Candlewick.

Dickinson, Peter. (2004). *Inside Granddad*. New York: Random House.

Duane, O. B. (ed.). (1998). *Myths and Legends*. London: Brockhampton Press.

Ellis, Deborah. (2003). *Mud City*. Toronto: Douglas & McIntyre.

Feldman, Robert. (1992). *Understanding Stress*. New York: Franklin Watts.

Fitzhugh, Louise. (1964). *Harriet the Spy*. New York: Harper & Row.

Fitzhugh, Louise. (1965). *The Long Secret*. New York: Harper & Row.

Fleischman, Paul. (2001). *Seek*. Chicago: Cricket Books.

Fleischman, Sid. (1996). *The Abracadabra Kid*. New York: Greenwillow.

Flowers, Pam (with Ann Dixon). (2001). *Alone Across the Arctic*. Portland, Oregon: Alaska Northwest Books.

Fox, Paula. (1991). *Monkey Island*. New York: Orchard Books.

Freedman, Russell. (1987). *Lincoln: A Photobiography*. New York: Clarion.

Freedman, Russell. (1990). *Franklin Delano Roosevelt*. New York: Clarion.

Funke, Cornelia (2006). *Inkheart*. Waterville, Me. Thorndike Press.

Furstinger, Nancy. (2003). *Say It with Music: The Story of Irving Berlin*. New York: Morgan.

Gallo, Donald. (1990). *Center Stage*. New York: HarperCollins.

Gantos, Jack. (1998). *Joey Pigza Swallowed the Key*. New York: Farrar, Straus, & Giroux.

Gantos, Jack (2000). *Joey Pigza Loses Control*. New York: Farrar, Straus, & Giroux.

Garden, Nancy. (2006). *Endgame*. Orlando, Florida: Harcourt.

Gardner, Robert, & Shore, Edward A. (1995). *Math in Science and Nature*. New York: Franklin Watts.

Giblin, James Cross. (2003). *The Life and Death of Adolf Hitler*. New York: Clarion.

Giff, Patricia Reilly. (2002). *Pictures of Hollis Woods*. New York: Random House.

Giff, Patricia Reilly. (2006). *Water Street*. New York: Random House.

Glatshteyn, Yankev. (2006). *Emil and Karl*. CT: Roaring Brook.

Gross, Albert. (1986). *Endurance*. New York: Dodd.

Haddix, Margaret Peterson. (1999). *Just Ella*. New York: Simon & Schuster.

Hamilton, Virginia. (1968). *The House of Dies Drear*. New York: Collier.

Hamilton, Virginia. (1987). *The Mystery of Drear House*. New York: Greenwillow.

Hamilton, Virginia. (1993). *Plain City*. New York: Scholastic.

Hampton, Wilborn. (2003). *September 11, 2001*. Cambridge, MA: Candlewick.

Heinlein, Robert. (1947). *Rocket Ship Galileo*. New York: Scribner.

Henkes, Kevin. (2003). *Olive's Ocean*. New York: HarperCollins.

Hickox, Rebecca. (1998). *The Golden Sandal: A Middle Eastern Cinderella Story*. New York: Holiday House.

Horvath, Polly. (2001). *Everything on a Waffle*. Toronto: Douglas & McIntyre, Ltd.

Jacques, Brian. (2000). *Redwall*. New York: Penguin.

Janeczko, Paul B. (1999). *How to Write Poetry*. New York: Scholastic.

Jenkins, Steve. (1999). *The Top of the World*. Boston: Houghton Mifflin.

Joravsky, Ben. (1996). *Hoop Dreams*. New York: HarperCollins.

Kadohata, Cynthia. (2004). *Kira-Kira*. New York: Atheneum.

Knudson, R. R. & Swenson, May (eds.). (1988). *American Sports Poems*. New York: Orchard Books.

Kohl, Herbert. (1988). *Making Theater*. New York: Teachers and Writers Collaborative.

Konigsburg, E. L. (1967). *From the Mixed-Up Files of Mrs. Basil E. Frankweiler* New York: Atheneum.

Konigsburg, E. L. (2004). *The Outcasts of 19 Schuyler Place*. New York: Atheneum.

Konigsburg, E. L. (2007). *Jennifer, Hecate, Macbeth, William McKinley and Me, Elizabeth*. (2007). New York: Aladdin.

Lamb, Charles & Lamb, Mary. (1994). *Lamb's Tales from Shakespeare*. London: Bloomsbury.

L'Engle, Madeleine. (1983). A *Wrinkle in Time*. New York: Dell.

LeGuin, Ursula K. (1990). *Tehanu, The Last Book of Earthsea*. New York: Atheneum.

Lester, Julius. (1995). *Othello, a Novel*. New York: Scholastic.

Lester, Julius, (2005). *Day of Tears*. New York: Hyperion.

Levine, Gail Carson. (1997). *Ella Enchanted*. New York: Harper.

Levine, Gail Carson. (2006). *Fairest*. New York: HarperCollins.

Lindgrens, Astrid. (1950). *Pippi Longstocking*. Oxford, Eng: Clio Press Ltd.

Look, Lenore. (2004). *Ruby Lu, Brave and True*. New York: Atheneum.

Look, Lenore. (2006). *Ruby Lu, Empress of Everything*. New York: Atheneum.

Lowry, Lois. (1999). *The Giver*. New York: Bantam.

Lupica, Mike. (2004). *Travel Team*. New York: Philomel Books.

Lupica, Mike. (2006). *Heat*. New York: Philomel Books.

Macaulay, David. (2003). *Mosque*. Boston: Houghton Mifflin.

Mackel, Kathy. (2005). *Mad Cat*. New York: HarperCollins.

Maestro, Betsy. (1996). *Coming to America: The Story of Immigration*. New York: Scholastic.

Martin, Rafe. (1992). *The Rough-Face Girl*. New York: Putnam.

Martin, Ann M. (2001). *Belle Teal*. New York: Scholastic.

Mazer, Harry. (2001). *A Boy at War: A Novel of Pearl Harbor*. New York: Scholastic.

McGaughrean, Geraldine. (2004). *Odysseus*. New York: Cricket.

McGhee, Alison. (2004). *Snap*. Cambridge, MA: Candlewick.

Meltzer, Milton. (2001). *There Comes a Time*. New York: Random House.

Morrison, Taylor. (2006). *Wildfire*. Boston: Houghton Mifflin.

Murphy, Jim. (2003). *An American Plague. The True and Terrifying Story of the Yellow Fever Epidemic of 1793*. New York: Clarion.

Myers, Walter Dean. (1992). *Somewhere in the Darkness*. New York: Scholastic.

Naylor, Phyllis Reynolds. (2006). *Roxie and the Hooligans*. New York: Atheneum.

Nelson, Theresa. (1989). *And One for All*. New York: Bantam.

Neville, Emily. (1963). *It's Like This, Cat*. New York: Harper & Row.

O'Brien, Robert. (1971). *Mrs Frisby and the Rats of NIMH*. New York: Scholastic.

Oppenheim. Shulamith. (1992). *The Lily Cupboard*. New York: HarperCollins.

Partridge, Elizabeth. (2002). *This Land Was Made for You and Me: The Life and Songs of Woody Guthrie*. New York: Viking.

Paterson, Katherine. (1988). *Park's Quest*. New York: Dutton.

Paterson, Katherine. (2006). *Bread and Roses, Too*. New York: Clarion.

Paulsen, Gary. (1999). *Brian's Return*. New York: Delacorte.

Paulsen, Gary. (2001). *Guts*. New York: Delacorte.

Paulsen, Gary. (2005). *The Time Hackers*. New York: Random House.

Peck, Richard. (1998). *A Long Way from Chicago*. New York: Dial Books.

Pierce, Tamara. (1997). *Sandry's Book*. New York: Scholastic.

Pierce, Tamara. (2005). *The Will of the Empress*. New York: Scholastic.

Price, Leontyne. (1990). *Aida*. New York: Harcourt, Brace, & Jovanovich.

Roth, Charles. (1993). *The Amateur Naturalist: Explorations and Investigations*. New York: Franklin Watts.

Rumford, James. (2004). *Sequoyah: The Cherokee Man Who Gave His People Writing*. Boston: Houghton Mifflin.

Ryan, Pam Munoz. (2000). *Esperanza Rising*. New York: Scholastic.

Sachar, Louis. (1998). *Holes*. New York: Farrar, Straus, & Giroux.

Salisbury. Graham. (1995). *Under the Blood-Red Sun*. New York: Delacorte.

San Souci, Robert D. (1998). *Cendrillon: A Caribbean Cinderella*. New York: Simon & Schuster.

Schneider, Meg F. (1991). *Popularity Has Its Ups and Downs*. Englewood Cliffs, N.J.: Simon & Schuster Inc.

Sherrow, Victoria. (2000). *Wilma Rudolph*. Minneapolis: Carolrhoda.

Soto, Gary. (1992). *Neighborhood Odes*. New York: Scholastic.

Spinelli, Jerry. (1996). *Crash*. New York: Alfred Knopf.

Stanley, Diane. (2000). *Michelangelo*. New York: HarperCollins.

Stanley, Diane. (2002). *Saladin*. New York: HarperCollins.

Stanley, Jerry. (1992). *Children of the Dust Bowl*. New York: Crown.

Steptoe, John. (1987). *Mufaro's Beautiful Daughters*. New York: Scholastic.

Stevens, Carla. (1993). *A Book of Your Own*. New York: Clarion.

Testa, Maria. (2001). *Becoming Joe DiMaggio*. Cambridge, MA: Candlewick.

Thomas, David. (1995). *Math Projects in the Computer Age*. New York: F. Watts.

Tolkien, J. R. R. (1990). *The Hobbit*. New York: Ballantine.

Van Draanen, Wendelin. (1998). *Sammy Keyes and the Skeleton Man*. New York: Alfred Knopf.

Warren, Andrea. (2001). *We Rode the Orphan Trains*. Boston: Houghton Mifflin.

White, Ruth. (1996). *Belle Prater's Boy*. New York: Farrar, Straus, & Giroux.

Wiilliams, Marcia. (1997). *Greek Myths for Young Children*. Cambridge, MA: Candlewick.

Williams, Marcia. (1998). *Tales from Shakespeare*. Cambridge, MA: Candlewick.

Woodson, Jacqueline. (2003). *Locomotion*. New York: G.P. Putnam's Sons.

Wong, Janet. (1999). *Behind the Wheel*. New York: Margaret McElderry.

Yang, Gene Luen. (2006). *American Born Chinese*. New York: First Second.

Zusak, Markus. (2006). *The Book Thief*. New York: Knopf.

Professional References

Bandura, A. (1997). *Self-Efficacy*. New York: Freeman.

Bear, M., Connors, B., & Paradiso, M. (2007). *Neuroscience: Exploring the Brain*. NY: Lippincott, Williams, & Wilkins.

Burns, Constance. (1995). "Middle Grade Fiction." In Anita Silvey (ed.). *Children's Books and Their Creators*. Boston: Houghton Mifflin.

Coie, J, & Dodge, K. (1999). "Aggression and Antisocial Behavior." In W. Damon (Series ed.) & N. Eisenberg (Volume ed.), *Handbook of Child Psychology: Volume 3. Child Psychology in Practice*. New York: John Wiley.

Dacey, John, and Travers, John. (2009). *Human Development Across the Lifespan*. New York: McGraw Hill.

Eliot, L. (2000). *What's Going on in There?* New York: Bantam.

Gardner, Howard. (1983). *Frames of Mind*. New York: Basic.

Gardner, Howard. (1997). *Extraordinary Minds*. New York: Basic.

Gardner, Howard. (1999). *Intelligence Reframed*. New York: Basic Books.

Guzzetti, Barbara, ed. (2002). *Literacy in America*. Santa Barbara, CA: / ABC-CLIO.

Harter, Susan. (1999). *The Construction of the Self*. New York: Guilford.

Lamb, Wendy. (2000). "Christopher Paul Curtis," In Roger Sutton, ed. *The Horn Book*. July/August, 397–401.

McCauley, Mary Beth. (2005). "Matching Boys with Books." *Christian Science Monitor, May 25, 11*.

McFarquhar, Larissa. (2007). "Two Heads." *The New Yorker*. February. 12, 58–69.

Murphy, Jim. "Serendipity, Detective Work, and Worry. One Nonfiction Writer's Journey Through the 1990s." In Mura Zarnowski (ed.), *The Best In Children's Nonfiction*. Urbana, IL: National Council of Teachers of English.

Nansel, T., Overpeck, M., Pilla, R., Ruan, W., Simons-Morton, B., & Scheidt, P. "Bullying Behaviors among U.S. Youth." *Journal of the American Medical Association*. 285, 2094–2100.

Olweus, D. (1993). *Bullying at School: What We Know and What We Can Do*. Cambridge, England: Oxford.

Olweus, D. (1995). "Bullying or Peer Abuse at School: Facts and Interventions." *Current Directions in Psychological Science*. 4(6), 196–200.

Rochman, Hazel. (2006). "Beyond Oral History." *The Horn Book*. October, 547–551.

Rochman, Hazel. (1993) "*Against Borders. Promoting Books for a Multicultural World*." American Library Association.

Rodkin, R., & Farmer, T. (2000). "Heterogeneity of Popular Boys: Antisocial and Prosocial Configurations." *Developmental Psychology*. 36(1), 14–24.

Rose, S. (2005). *The Future of the Brain*. New York: Oxford.

Santrock, John. (2007). *Children*. New York: McGraw Hill.

Selman, Robert. (1980). *The Growth of Interpersonal Understanding*. New York: Academic.

Silvey, Anita. (2004). *100 Best Books for Children*. Boston: Houghton Mifflin.

Smith, Michael & Wilhelm, Jeff. (2002). *Reading Don't Fix No Chevys: Literacy in the Lives of Young Men*. New York: Heinemann.

Sternberg, Robert. (1996). *Successful Intelligence*. New York: Simon & Schuster.

Sullivan, Michael. (2004). "Why Johnny Won't Read." *School Library Journal*, August, 36–39.

Sullivan, Michael. (2003) *Connecting Boys with Books*. Chicago: American Library Association.

Sutton, Roger. (2004). *Where the Boys Aren't. The Horn Book*, November/December, p. 628.

Willard, N. (2006). "Flame Retardant." *School Library Journal*, 52(4), 55–57.

Zarnowski, Mura (ed.). (2001). *The Best in Children's Nonfiction*. Urbana, IL: National Council of Teachers of English.

CHAPTER 12

Literature for the High School Years (Ages 14–18)

In British writer David Almond's novel Kit's Wilderness, *winner of the Michael Printz Award, we meet Kit Watson, who has moved with his parents to Stoneygate, England, to be near his grandfather, who is alone. Alison Keenan, his classmate and new friend, calls Kit "Mr. New Boy," "Mr. Perfectly Behaved," "Mr. Perfect," and "Mr. Butter Wouldn't Melt." She immediately warns Kit to stay away from John Askew, "that brute, hunking and lurching like a caveman."*

Kit, however, is drawn to John, who is his age, an artist, and a member, like Kit, of the old families of Stoneygate that have worked in the coal mines for generations. Memories of lost pit children, darkness, and tragedy surround the caves that ring the wilderness. When John asks Kit to join the gang in the game of Death, Kit at first refuses. Later, he agrees to participate—a decision that changes his life forever.

This gripping narrative is a compelling introduction into the mind of the young adult. With themes that center around the challenges young adults face—problem solving, moral decisions, physical courage, the powerful pull of peers, and mercurial family relationships—it draws the reader into the world of these years. John Askew's relationship with his abusive father, for example, is the most upsetting aspect of his life, one that may be familiar to some young adults. Consequently, the literature that we discuss in this chapter reflects the uncertainties and the joys, the problems and the triumphs, and yes, the turbulence and the worries that concern young adults.

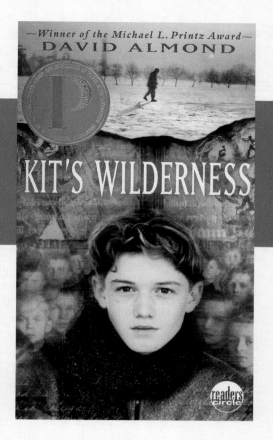

KIT'S WILDERNESS
*Used by permission of Random House
Children's Books, a division of Random
House, Inc.*

‖ Guidelines for Reading Chapter 12

After you read Chapter Twelve, you should be able to answer the following questions.

• What developmental features highlight the changes that occur between infancy and adolescence?

• What does the revealing Judy Blume quote tell you about parent-child relationships during these years?

• How should Robert Cormier's defense of the themes he introduced in *The Chocolate War* be evaluated?

• Do you agree with the "storm and stress" interpretation of the young adult years? Does it appear in any of the stories you read?

• Why does the saying that adolescence begins in biology and ends in culture have relevance for adolescent reading? Are there examples of this saying in the literature introduced in this chapter?

• What sources of crises are there for the high school years other than those discussed in this chapter?

• What are some examples of Erikson's analysis of identity versus identity confusion during these years that appear in the novels discussed in this chapter?

• Are the issues discussed in this chapter similar to the themes in the young adult literature?

Characteristics of the High School Years

What are we to make of the changes and attitudes of students in the high school years? Should we agree with G. Stanley Hall when, in his two-volume *Adolescence* (1904), he referred to these years as a time of "storm and stress?" Or do we nod in agreement with Albert Bandura (1997) when he notes that by adolescence most children have accepted the values and standards of their parents and that friction between the generations is only slightly higher than during childhood?

Perhaps the best way of thinking about adolescence is to realize that it begins in biology and ends in culture (Petersen, 1988). In other words, students' physical maturation initiates the process, but their experiences with different types of relationships, their understanding of sexuality, and their constant search for identity strongly shape the nature and direction of their behavior.

Grotevant (1998), for example, views the young adult years as richly textured, that is, a time of diverse and changing events that designate the road to adulthood. He argues that cross-cultural research clearly demonstrates that the lines separating the various phases of adolescence—including the period's beginning and ending—are not precise. This position is supported by recent interpretations of human development that stress interactions among the different systems, such as physical, psychological, and social. (See Chapter 1).

Lerner and Galambos (1998, p. 414) nicely summarize the nuances of adolescence when they state that adolescence is that time when a person's biological, psychological, and social (biopsychosocial) characteristics change from what is considered childlike to what is considered adultlike. Several of the developmental features of this period are illustrated in the following diagram.

BIOPSYCHOSOCIAL CHARACTERISTICS

BIO	PSYCHO	SOCIAL
Active pubertal changes	Abstract thinking progresses	Identity/identity confusion
Growth spurt occurs	Adolescent egocentrism is apparent	Sexual behavior commences
Health may be an issue	Problem-solving skills improve	Relationships (peers, family) change
Sex becomes a key part of their lives	Imaginary audiences exist	Mood changes frequent
Emotional problems can accompany physical changes	Cognitive demands intensify	Antisocial behavior apparent
	Academic pressures increase	School performance intensifies

Young Adult Relationships

Young adults' relationships with their parents are undergoing transformations that range from normal, occasionally prickly interchanges to those that sadly contain no affection, and perhaps even mutual dislike. When Ken's mother in *Razzle* (Ellen Wittlinger) tells him the family is leaving Cape Cod for Vermont, Ken is enraged. "You can forget about me getting used to the idea [of moving] because I never will," he yells. "I hate you for this. I really hate you." When his mother reaffirms her belief that the move is appropriate since it will get Ken away from the friends he has made on the Cape, he explodes: "But these are the people I feel comfortable around. And I just found them . . . Gay people, low-class people, strange people—you can't tolerate anybody who's the least bit different from you" (Wittlinger, 2001, p. 238).

In J. D. Salinger's *The Catcher in the Rye*, a book that continues to be discussed and is still a must-read on many high school reading lists, Holden Caulfield offers the classic description of the evolving, warm, frustrating, parent-adolescent relationship.

If you really want to hear about it, the first thing you'll probably want to know is where I was born, and what my lousy childhood was like, and how my parents were occupied and all before they had me, and all that David Copperfield kind of crap, but I don't feel like going into it, if you want to know the truth. In the first place, that stuff bores me, and in the second place, my parents would have about two hemorrhages apiece if I told anything personal about them. They're quite touchy about anything like that, especially my father. They're nice and all—I'm not saying that—but they're also touchy as hell.

(Salinger, 1945, p. 1)

In a similar manner, Judy Blume has raised some interesting issues about communication, both in her fiction and in her interviews with others. Since her understanding of these years and the uncertainty of the times come through sharply and unmistakably in her novels, it would be natural to assume that when her children were teenagers they confided their innermost thoughts to her. Not so. When she heard an interviewer say how lucky her children must have been because they could discuss their problems with her, she (as quoted in Konner, 1991, p. 352) responded:

Wrong. I hoped they would feel they could. But when the going got tough, my daughter went to someone else. . . At sixteen, my sweet daughter became angry, sullen, judgmental, emotionally closed to me. In other words, a typical adolescent.

My son, Larry, who is two years younger, swore he would never act so stupid. Ha! Two years later, it was his turn, and he made Randy's rebellion seem tame. I felt alone and frightened.

We know that Robert Cormier, author of many controversial young adult novels, including *The Chocolate War*, understands young people—but what was his relationship with his father when he was young? From reading *Frenchtown Summer* we discover that his father was an enigma to him. "My mother continued to make tents and my father squinted at the newsprint while I sat there wondering if I would ever solve the mystery of my father" (Cormier, 1999, p. 1).

Challenges Facing Young Adults Are Found in Young Adult Books

The internal and external changes young adults face in these years have led some theorists to identify a cluster of adolescent risk behaviors—certainly not the storm and stress of earlier interpretations of adolescence, but more in the nature of modern challenges facing young adults (Lerner & Galambos, 1998). Many of the books teenagers read describe how their peers deal with these challenges. These include:

- **SUBSTANCE ABUSE.** There is little doubt that adolescents drink (some heavily) and engage in widespread drug abuse. Miles Halter, the main character in John Green's Printz Award–winning novel *Looking for Alaska*, encounters not only outstanding classes in his high school, but a hard-drinking roommate as well. He falls madly in love with Alaska, another classmate, in a "drunken make-out session," only to find her killed in a car accident hours later.

It is not unusual for young adult novels to discuss parents' alcoholism as it affects their teenagers. Joan Bauer's novel *Best Foot Forward*, a sequel to her *Rules of the Road*, continues the story of Jenna, who has gained great self-respect, only to become emotionally distressed by her father's alcoholism. The National Institute on Drug Abuse (2004) reported that although the overall use of drugs declined slightly in 2003, the use of cocaine increased significantly and the number of heroin users remained stable.

In Barbara Haworth-Attard's novel *Theories of Relativity*, Dylan, a 16-year-old, leaves his mother for a life of panhandling on the street. He encounters Brendan, who uses drugs and forces young people like Dylan to beg and work the streets. Fortunately, Dylan discovers that with brains and a good self-concept he can escape this damaging environment. Although most young adults believe that substance usage is a matter of personal judgment, several protective factors act to keep adolescents like Dylan from abusive behavior (Lerner & Galambos, 1998, p. 422). These include *personal controls*, such as a good self-concept and religious beliefs, and *social controls*, such as good parenting and strong social support.

• **SEXUAL BEHAVIOR.** Today, more and younger adolescents are involved in sexual behavior. According to the National Center for Health Statistics (2004), by the age of 18, 25–30 percent of females in the United States have been pregnant at least once. The realistic novel *Doormat*, by teen author Kelly McWilliams, relates how shy Jaime, a 14-year-old, plans to protect her best friend who is pregnant. Not preachy, the novel presents some of the difficulties her best friend must overcome. The popular novel *Prom* by Laurie Halse Anderson describes how Ashley Hannigan is more determined to find an apartment with her boyfriend, T. J., than she is to attend the senior prom. Events ensue, however, that make Ashley look forward to the life she will lead after the prom and after graduation.

• **SCHOOL UNDERACHIEVEMENT, FAILURE, AND DROPOUT.** About 25 percent of all elementary and secondary school students in the United States are at risk for school failure. A total of 700,000 students drop out of school each year. About 25 percent of all 18- and 19-year-olds have not graduated from high school, and the dropout rate is roughly equal for males and females. The cost to society of such large numbers is great, having enormous impact on future economic prospects.

• **DELINQUENCY, CRIME, AND VIOLENCE.** Youth gangs, youth unrest, and youth violence are all terms with which the public is too familiar. There are at least 25,000 youth gangs in the United States that include almost 800,000 young adults. These gangs are responsible for considerable violence, and their numbers continue to increase (NYVPRC, 2004). Walter Dean Myers, an outstanding author of young adult novels, writes empathetically in such novels as *Monster* and *Shooter* about the rebellious teenager who becomes entangled with police.

In spite of these risk factors, most young adults accept the challenges of their environment, adjust to the demands made on them, and, supported by adult patience and understanding, achieve their goals.

Another contemporary theme, which has rarely been scrutinized statistically, yet concerns many young people and deserves discussion, is the theme of homosexuality and lesbianism.

Young Adult Concerns about Sexuality

Nancy Garden, the 2003 recipient of the Margaret A. Edwards Award for her lifetime contribution to young people's literature, broke new ground when she published her first novel *Annie on My Mind* (1982), about a same-sex romance between high school seniors Liza Winthrop and Annie Kenyon. Although now listed as one of the One Hundred Books that Shaped the Century by the *School Library Journal*, it has been one of the most frequently challenged books according to ALA's Office for Intellectual Freedom (Jenkins, 2003). It has been banned, and burned, and it was embroiled in a 1994 federal court case until a U.S. district judge in Kansas ordered the book returned to school library shelves (Jenkins, 2003). Garden (2004) has stated that she personally was concerned about her sexuality during her high school years.

Before Garden's book was published, gay and lesbian literature for young adults was rare. Through the 1970s there was on average a single young-adult title per year dealing with gay issues. In 2000, for example, only one story about gay or lesbian characters or themes was published, Jean Ferris's rodeo novel *Eight Seconds*, and one short story in *What's in a Name* (Campbell, 2000). Today, however, the total number of gay novels for young adults has grown to more than 140 titles (Jenkins, 2003).

M. E. Kerr, another winner of the Margaret A. Edwards Award and a prolific writer for young adults, tries to prepare adolescents for experiences they may have now or in the future, and often presents complex moral issues to her readers for their consideration. In *Deliver Us from Evie* (1994) she questions the notion of what is normal and uses the tragedy of a flooding river to make her readers aware of people who think they can get away with hurting others. In *Night Kites* (1986) she introduces Pete, the protagonist's brother, who has AIDS. Comparing him to a night kite, she quotes him as saying, "I go up in the dark, alone, on my own and I'm not afraid to be different."

Kerr's novel *Hello, I Lied* (1997) spans three months in the lives of three young people. The protagonist, 17-year-old Lang Penner, has a 19-year-old lover, Alex. Although Lang has decided to tell his friends that he is gay, he struggles with his infatuation with the pretty French girl, Huguette. The book concludes without a resolution about Lang's sexual preference, leaving young adults to ponder the consequences of his decision.

TALKING IT OUT   The themes of well-written stories that detail the social complexities we've mentioned attract young adults, some of whom may be reluctant to reveal their concerns to their parents or caregivers. Openly discussing the problems in a young adult novel in a group led by a teacher, librarian, or other adult—often called the Great Conversation—may be beneficial to young adults (see Chapter Four). They may feel free to raise and discuss personal questions in a general way during such a discussion. A teacher or librarian may also find that booktalking (presenting a brief oral review of a novel or nonfiction, including audio versions or books they can download) may lead young adults to discuss books with each other. When young adults are given the opportunity to booktalk, argue, and present their own views, they develop psychosocial maturity and become more adult.

The Young Adult Search for Identity

"Boy!" I said. I also say "Boy!" quite a lot. Partly because I have a lousy vocabulary and partly because I act quite young for my age sometimes. I was sixteen then and I'm seventeen now, and sometimes I act like I'm about thirteen. It's really ironical, because I'm six feet two and a half and I have gray hair. I really do. The one side of my head—the right side—is full of millions of gray hairs. I've had them ever since I was a kid. And yet I still act sometimes like I was only about twelve. Everybody says that, especially my father. It's partly true, too, but it isn't all true.

(Salinger, 1945, p. 7)

Here, in this return to *The Catcher in the Rye*, Holden Caulfield provides a taste of middle adolescent thought. Storm and stress? Yes, some. Turbulence and uncertainty? Yes, some. But he also offers a thoughtful analysis of his own behavior. It is this sense of confusion that draws the psycholgist Erik Erikson to the young adult years as he attempts to unravel the complexities of *identity versus identity confusion.*

Erikson and Identity

By the end of the young adult years, those who have resolved their personal crises have achieved a *sense of identity*. They know who they are. Those who remain locked in doubt and insecurity experience what Erik Erikson calls *identity confusion*. (See Chapter One.) Erikson's views on identity have generated considerable speculation, theorizing, and research. Helping young adult readers integrate the biopsychosocial changes of adolescence and focus on clearly defined goals is a crucial task, one whose successful attainment leads to healthy feelings of identity.

Erikson's fifth stage (from ages 12 to 18 years) deals with the end of childhood and the beginning of adulthood. Young people become more concerned with what others think of them, and peer opinion plays a large part in how they think of themselves. If uncertainty at this time results in identity confusion, a bewildered youth may withdraw, run away, or turn to drugs. When faced with the question "Who am I?" young people may be unable to answer. It is the same question that Ron Koertge in his novel *The Boy in the Moon* (1990) assigns to his students as an essay, and it is the underlying theme of most young adult novels.

Jacqueline Woodson, the Edwards Award winner for 2006, poignantly describes in her novel *Hush* how Towsiah Thomas and her entire family find it difficult to answer the question of who they are. Before her father, a policeman, witnessed members of the police force shoot a young boy, Towsiah was a happy-go-lucky girl with lots of friends and a beloved grandmother who lived near her. When her father "did the right thing" by revealing who committed the crime, Towsiah's family was placed in the federal protection program. They lost their identity, moved to another state, assumed new names, and attempted to find a new life. It was not easy. The challenges were new, the tasks were difficult, and the alternatives were bewildering.

Without the support of her mother, who turns away from her family and moves toward religion, or her father, who sits helplessly in front of the window day after day, Evie (Towsiah) confides in her older sister Anna, who is also struggling with her identity. Anna, however, resolves her confusion when she secretly enrolls in college and leaves home. Sometimes Evie feels like she is Toswiah Green, while at other times she is Evie Thomas. "And some days I like and love either and both of me." She begins to resolve her confusion when she makes new friends and becomes a successful member of the track team.

According to Erikson, the young in our society are searching for something or someone to be true to. They yearn for stability in an age of change, and their search may lead to extremes. But the search is a time for testing both self and the world. In *Razzle* by Ellen Wittlinger, Kenyon Baker, during the summer before his junior year in high school, helps his parents open a group of tourist cabins at Cape Cod. He also opens himself to new friends, many of whom his mother does not approve. Razzle, the young, high-spirited girl who works at the swap shop, bewitches him. Consequently, he chooses her as the subject for many of his photographs. Yet in his confusion about his feelings for the boy-crazy Harley, he hurts Razzle. The summer he spends at Cape Cod helps him discover who he really is and whom he can trust.

Adolescence is the period with which Erikson is most often associated, mainly because of his speculations about the adolescent *identity crisis*. Faced with a combination of physical, sexual, and cognitive changes joined with heightened adult expectations and peer pressure, adolescents understandably feel insecure about themselves—who they are and where they're going. Sometimes this insecurity leads to deeper emotional and physical problems. In their search for identity, they often find that reading about these issues in their literature helps them realize they are not alone in the problems they face. On the other hand, the adolescent who has turned away from reading needs special attention and understanding during these years, not only to cope with the academic demands of the high school curricula, but to attain what Erikson calls "identity." Here are several examples of the interaction between the individual needs of the reluctant adolescent reader and the themes of teenage literature from the various genres.

Reluctant Adolescent Readers

Books that are biologically and psychologically appropriate will help the reluctant adolescent reader. If you, as a teacher or librarian, have a young person who has difficulty reading at the secondary level, select reading material that is interesting but not too difficult (high in interest, low in vocabulary). "Good reading materials are the greatest factor in students' motivation" (Broaddus & and Ivey, 2002, p. 7). Having students read biographies in which the characters work out personal problems may help them find out about themselves by exploring the world of others who are similarly engaged in the search for identity. Gary Paulsen's *Guts*, for example, in only 148 pages relates his own daring, true adventures. Jack Gantos, author of the Joey Pigza books, has written *Hole in My Life*, the autobiography of his sadly twisted young adult years. Walter Dean Myers describes his childhood in an illiterate family in *Bad Boy: A Memoir*.

Reading must be taught as a developmental process, and instruction should be based on what teachers learn from individual students. Broaddus and Ivey (2002) stress the need for teachers and librarians to pay more attention to students' personal interests since *each struggling reader is complex*. Students (especially reluctant readers) at designated times could choose their reading not only from the narrower selection of award-winning novels (most frequently required), but from a wider selection that could include out-of-school reading, picture books, information books, short stories, and graphic novels.

Spin Off

Interacting with Books for Reluctant Readers

The ideal situation for readers who want immediate feedback is to select and read books about topics in which they are interested. They may find the following books (many more are listed in the annual YASLA Quick Pics for Reluctant Young Adult Readers) to be suitable: Each provides some form of self-help for the adolescent.

Daldry, Jeremy. *The Teenage Guy's Survival Guide.*

Erlbach, Arlene. *Worth the Risk: True Stories about Risk Takers Plus How You Can Be One, Too.*

Covey, Sean. *The 7 Habits of Highly Effective Teens: The Ultimate Teenage Success Guide.*

Jacobs, Thomas A. *What Are My Rights? 95 Questions and Answers about Teens and the Law.*

By using their technological skills and working together, students may develop a book, such as those mentioned above, into a PowerPoint presentation, a video documentary, a comic strip, or even a website so that they can share their learning with their classmates.

If the young adult is interested in music, for example, a picture book for older readers such as *Shake, Rattle & Roll: The Founders of Rock and Roll* by Holly George-Warren may be the goodness-of-fit that the teacher or librarian is seeking for that individual student. Another student may be interested in World War II and find *Attack on Pearl Harbor* by Shelley Tanaka suitable, not only because of its length (sixty-four pages), but because of its outstanding photography and action-packed content. A larger but still riveting book is *Out of War: True Stories from the Front Lines* (Sara Cameron, editor), which is about teenagers seeking their ultimate goal of world peace. A fascinating book for the undersea adventurer would be *Swimming with Hammerhead Sharks* by Kenneth Mallory.

Since it is difficult for teachers and librarians to analyze each student's skills, the researchers (Broaddus & Ivey, 2002) suggest that they use the "running alongside the reader" technique as the class reads together. This affords the teacher an excuse to stop and informally question individual students about their preferences, and thereby discover their strengths and weaknesses.

Traditional Literature

BETWEEN HEAVEN AND EARTH: BIRD TALES FROM AROUND THE WORLD. Howard Norman's book, beautifully illustrated by Leo and Diane Dillon, is *living* folklore—living because the tales are the result of a workshop conducted by the author for immigrants in 1989 and 1990. One story relates the Australian aboriginal tale in which a pelican reveals the ancient secret of how to make fishing nets. Another tells the Norwegian tale of the troll with a scarf full of live birds who attempts to prevent a trio of ice skaters from winning a race. Other stories include the tale of the much-loved quail who is dying from thirst, and the elusive bird who sings like a warthog. For centuries, birds, because of their ability to fly, have inspired tales of mystery, magic, and mischief.

SECRETS OF THE SPHINX. Author James Cross Giblin undertakes the task of interweaving legends surrounding Egypt's famous Sphinx. His description of the legend of King Thutmose's first restoration of the Sphinx (circa 1401 BCE) is particularly fascinating.

Fantasy

Although fantasy is a popular genre for most young people in each developmental level, some young adults may be reluctant to read something that does not deal directly with their real world. These students may find Patricia Elliot's *Murkmere*, however, whose characters are strangely connected to an ancient race of half-bird, half-human creatures ("avia"), to be a good introduction to this genre. High school students who have been captivated by the first two books in Jonathan Stroud's Bartimaeus trilogy (*The Golem's Eye* and *Amulet of Samarkand*) will be pleased to discover that the third book, *Ptolemy's Gate*, is now available and is an outstanding story.

Fantasies written by young adults for young adults are rare, but often successful. Amelia Atwater-Rhodes, for example, published her novel *Falcondance* when she was 19 years old. She has been writing fantasies since 1999, when she wrote her first young adult novel, *In the Forests of the Night*. Another popular fantasy writer, Christopher Paolini, wrote *Eragon* when he, too, was a teenager.

THE GOLDEN COMPASS. Philip Pullman's first book of *His Dark Materials* trilogy, introduces readers to memorable characters who will captivate readers throughout the three books. Always beside Lyra Belacqua is her daemon, Pantalaimon. Together they ride on the white bear's back into Arctic country to settle an epic struggle between the Gobblers, stolen children, witch clans, and armored bears. As the author explains "This first volume is set in a universe like ours but different in many ways. The second volume, *The Subtle Knife*, is set in the universe we know. The third volume, *The Amber Spyglass*, moves between the universes." Pullman's work is high fantasy at its best.

SILVERWING. Canadian author Kenneth Oppel relates the life of Shade, a runt silverwing bat whose one desire is to see the sun. Challenged by the big, boasting bat Chinook, he dares to try but is disciplined by his mother Ariel and the elders. Then he learns the story of the Winged Spirit Nocturna, and how that millions of years ago owls and other animals of the forest prevented bats from seeing the sun. Now Shade wants to be the bat who fulfills the Promise of Nocturna to end the bats' banishment.

FIREBIRDS. For the high school student who has little time for recreational reading, Sharyn November has edited a group of short fantasies and science fiction stories (plus two realistic stories), each of which is entirely unrelated to the others. Besides satisfying high school students' literary craving, the stories offer a wide variety of topics, plots, and situations. Although some can be disregarded (e.g., *Hope Chest* as gratuitously bloody) others can be perused with satisfaction (e.g., *Cotillion* and *Crown Duel*, true beauty and true love).

THE *NEW YORK TIMES* BEST SELLER
THE BARTIMAEUS TRILOGY
BOOK THREE

Ptolemy's Gate

JONATHAN STROUD

PTOLEMY'S GATE
Reprinted with permission of Hyperion Books for Children

Spotlight On

Christopher Paolini

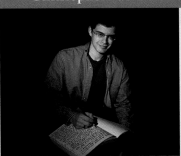

William Campbell/©Corbis

When he was 15 years old Christopher Paolini began writing *Eragon*, a 500-page fantasy novel that is the first volume of his proposed trilogy *Inheritance*. In 2005 he published, *Eldest*, the second book in his trilogy, and even his publisher Random House, is amazed that with a first printing of 1.3 million, more than 425,000 copies were sold in the first week. It was the publisher's largest-ever one-week sale for a children's book title (Mehegan, 2003).

Paolini was home-schooled and graduated from high school at 15. He attributes his early graduation to not having had any vacation time. Too young to go to college, he spent his time reading fantasy: *Beowulf*, as well as Norse and Icelandic mythology. At the time, he had no idea of becoming a writer; in fact, he could not even type. But when he shared his story with his

parents, they loved it and encouraged him to publish it himself. To sell *Eragon*, he undertook a promotional tour and gave talks at schools and libraries throughout the country. As fate would have it, Carl Hiaasen's stepson bought the book. Hiaasen, the well-known writer and author of *Hoot*, read it, was impressed, and showed it to his publisher, Random House, who republished the book.

Paolini "was completely blown away" by the success of *Eragon* and never expected that his books would be read by so many people. His goal now is to finish the trilogy. He is also enjoying the movie version, which stars John Malkovich and Jeremy Irons.

Note: To learn more about *Eragon* and its author, Paolini, and to download a book talk and a reader's guide with dozens of discussion questions, visit Librarians@Random at www.randomhouse.com.

Poetry

In many classrooms throughout elementary, middle, and high school, poetry continues to be the stepchild of the genres we discuss. Sylvia Vardell, a professor at Texas Women's University, in an anecdotal poll of twelve elementary schools across Texas, is concerned that despite such exceptions as Shel Silverstein and Jack Prelutsky, outstanding poets such as Barbara Esbensen, Karla Kuskin, David McCord, and Valerie Worth, along with other poets of diverse cultures are not properly represented on school library shelves (Vardell, 2006, pp. 40–41). Such neglect, she feels, hurts a school's curriculum. "Poetry taps the essence of a subject and is accessible to a wide range of reading abilities" (Vardell, 2006, p. 41). Below are poets whose works are appealing to young adults.

PREPOSTEROUS. Paul Janeczko has collected many poems that deal with adolescence. His *Brickyard Summer* (1989) and *The Music of What Happens* (1988) have been well received by teachers, librarians, and especially young people who share similar experiences. In this collection of 108 poems written by 82 poets, young adults can relate to many of the humorous, poignant, or embarrassing incidents they read about (Janeczko, 1991).

BRONX MASQUERADE. Nikki Grimes, a prolific author and poet, skillfully juggles the thoughts, feelings, and questions of eighteen Bronx high school students in *Bronx Masquerade* (2002) as they read aloud their poems at an Open Mike Night. One that many young adults will remember is Diondra Jordan's poem to her father, in which she reiterates a familiar theme: "It's time, Dad / Time you stop telling me / who to be / how to live. This is my portrait. / You chose your canvas. / Let me choose mine."

RUNNING BACK TO LUDIE. Angela Johnson has written a series of free verse vignettes about a teenager seeking her mother, Ludie, whom she hasn't seen in many years. Although she has many friends and a good relationship with her dad and Aunt Lucille, she cannot shake the feeling that she was abandoned.

GOD WENT TO BEAUTY SCHOOL. Cynthia Rylant's understanding, humor, of and sympathy, for simple folk come through in this group of twenty-three poems. Even God is treated as a homespun character—not above climbing a mountain or going to beauty school, but still all-knowing and god-like enough to demonstrate through his own life's suffering that pain can produce a reverence for life.

A MAZE ME. Naomi Shihab Nye was only 12 years old when she began to fill notebooks with her poetry. In her latest book of seventy-five free verse poems, she captures the thoughts and feelings of the adolescent girl and her struggle to find her own identity.

Drama

MONSTER. Walter Dean Myers has turned his novel *Monster*, winner of the Printz Prize for Outstanding Young Adult Literature, into a drama. Narrator Steve Harmon is a 16-year-old in prison for being a lookout for a drugstore robbery in which the proprietor, Mr. Nesbitt, was shot. Steve, who had been studying moviemaking in school, feels that to fully understand what is happening, he should make a movie. And that's what he does. The entire book becomes a movie script of the trial, presumably written by Steve, the main character of the novel.

CENTER STAGE. Donald Gallo's book about plays is as enjoyable for young people to read as it is for them to perform. Students are offered ten original, sophisticated, one-act plays. Some are serious and others are humorously written by authors such as Susan Beth Pfeffer, Ouida Sebestyen, and Walter Dean Myers. Gallo introduces the collection by noting that it contains plays written by famous authors who had little experience writing plays! He also notes that they have more than proven that novelists can write successful plays for teenagers. He hopes this collection is part of a trend that will provide more opportunities for novelists to try something new.

Spin Off
Interacting with Drama

Young people will find *Monster* engrossing to read, but will respond at a deeper level when they assume the parts of the witnesses and the lawyers. Not only will they experience the play itself, but they will understand more keenly what it is like to be in prison, awaiting sentencing, knowing that your parents are present and your life hangs in the balance.

Contemporary Realistic Fiction

The theme of most young adult books is about becoming an adult, and finding an answer to the questions "Who am I"? and "What am I going to do about it?" (Campbell, 2000). Yet it is sometimes difficult for librarians and teachers to distinguish whether a novel is primarily aimed at middle school readers or at young adults. Even though authors such as the late Robert Cormier wrote primarily for young adults, he also wrote *Other Bells for Us to Ring* and *Tunes for Bears to Dance To*, both perfectly acceptable for younger readers.

Publishers like Elizabeth Law from Viking are aware that young adult literature is selling well in bookstores throughout the country. "Fifteen years ago," Law admits, "I was attending symposiums on whether the young-adult novel was dead" (Mehegan, 2003). At that time, young adult books were shelved at the end of the children's books section. When high school teachers assigned books for summer reading, they inevitably required classics like *Pride and Prejudice*, *To Kill a Mockingbird*, and even *Lorna Doone*. Now, young adult books command a large section in nationwide bookstore chains and have rooms of their own in public libraries.

Wide Range of Books for Young Adults

A high school student's choice of literature should not be restricted to young adult books, but should include literature from the middle school years through adult literature. When choosing books for young adults to read and *enjoy*, teachers and librarians may wish to take the advice of Tim Wynne-Jones.

The world of the passionate reader is one of serendipitous connections, of leaps across genres, across age groups. It's worth looking, sometimes, a little farther afield. . . . After all, the whole idea is to find the right book for the right reader.

(Wynne-Jones, 2001, p. 275)

Today's young adult novels, directly impact a teenager's experience, and young adults can see themselves reflected in their reading. Although there are few figures industry-wide that distinguish young adult literature from the $1.8 billion juvenile publishing segment, according to the nation's largest booksellers young adult hardcover books are experiencing tremendous growth, contrary to previous assumptions.

Free Verse Poetic Novels

In Kutiper and Wilson's well-known and often quoted article in *The Reading Teacher* (1993), the authors compiled several of the best-known studies about children's poetry preferences and summarized them, noting that free verse was one of children's least favorite forms of poetry. Yet today's adolescents from middle school through high school seem to have rethought their negative opinion of free verse and are being drawn to poetry written by some of their favorite novelists.

TRUE BELIEVER. Virginia Euwer Wolff's Printz Honor book *True Believer*, and a sequel to *Make Lemonade*, contains all the literary elements that comprise a good novel. She makes the protagonist, LaVaughn, come alive through her personal poetic expressions about the problems and joys in her day-to-day life as a high school student, which makes it even more appealing. LaVaughn is a sympathetic character. Readers understand her as outgoing, helpful to the tenants in her building, loyal to her friends, diligent at the lab, and smitten by a boy she has known since she was very young. Readers are affected when LaVaughn discovers that because of the boy's sexual orientation, he cannot return her sentiments, but they admire her when she finally accepts the situation without resentment.

SHAKESPEARE BATS CLEANUP. Ron Koertge is the author of several young adult novels, including *The Brimstone Journals* and *Stoner and Spaz*, a sensitively written story of a 16-year-old boy with cerebral palsy who teams up with a drugged-out young girl. His *Shakespeare Bats Cleanup*, however, is a touching novel written in free verse. In it, Kevin Boland, a 14-year-old baseball player confined to his bed because of mono, decides to "fool around a little" and "see what's what poetry-wise." With humor and sadness, he reveals his thoughts about his parents, the death of his mother, his romances, and his dreams of being a baseball great.

HARD HIT. Ann Turner's poetic novel is written in the first person. As a young man grieves over the impending death of his father, the writer takes her readers through the stages of grief and recovery.

OUT OF THE DUST. It is a work that is considered a novel and is a winner of the Newbery Medal. Karen Hesse writes in free verse about Billie Joe and her family, who live in the Dust Bowl of the 1930s. In poignant lines, she reveals the courage and determination of a young girl who must overcome her mother's death, her father's alienation, and her own burnt and scarred hands and how they affect her ability to play the piano. She finally comes to the realization that:

I know now that all the time I was trying to get / Out of the dust / The fact is, / What I am, / I am because of the dust. / And what I am is good enough / Even for me.

Trends in Young Adult Books

An interesting trend in publishing today is the success that writers, primarily associated with adult books, are experiencing when they write young adult and middle school novels. Joyce Carol Oates, for example, has written *Big Mouth & Ugly Girl*, about a high school junior who allegedly threatens to bomb the school. The "ugly girl" is Ursula, who defends him. A reader has only to read a book like this to know that it is definitely more complex than the customary plot of a middle school novel. Carl Hiassen, on the other hand, a popular writer of adult mysteries, has written two novels for middle school students: his *Horn Book–Boston Globe* honor book *Hoot* and, more recently, *Flush*.

What distinguishes *Hoot* from *Big Mouth & Ugly Girl*? While the action in a young adult novel is "essentially internal," the action in a book for middle school students is more external. As Campbell (2000) notes, boy-girl relationships are more innocent in the middle school novel, whereas sexuality is one of the definitive subjects of young adult books. What makes it particularly confusing, however, to distinguish a middle school novel from a young adult novel (without reading it) is the publisher's decision to label a book as "a teenage novel" or a book "for readers 12 years and older." Although professionals may assume that the middle school novel is more innocent and the protagonist younger, they may not always be correct in their judgment. Again, the issue of "developmentally appropriate" becomes increasingly significant.

CHICK LIT   Another group of young adult novels that has its genesis in adult book fare is what is commonly (and sometimes scornfully) called *Chick Lit*, also referred to as "bad girls" books. Since Helen Fielding successfully authored *Bridget Jones's Diary*, young adult writers such as Louise Rennison (*Angus, Thongs and Full-Frontal Snogging*) and Ann Brashares (*The Sisterhood of the Traveling Pants*) have captured a large segment of the young adult market with their series of books about independent young people. Their books, in turn, have produced paperbacks such as *Clique, Gossip Girls,* and *A List* that are currently being reviewed by such well-known critics as Naomi Wolf of the *New York Times,* who writes, "Unfortunately for girls, these novels reproduce that dilemma they experience all the time: they are expected to compete with pornography, but can still be labeled sluts" (Wolf, March 12, 2006, p. 22). She continues by saying that teenagers are being hoodwinked by a values system that is based on "meanness rules, parents check out, conformity is everything and stressed-out adult values," all of which are presumed to be meaningful for teenagers.

Ironically, chick lit like *Clique, Gossip Girls,* and *A List* (created by media packager 17th Street Productions) sell millions of copies to teenagers who may be seeking risky narratives that would not meet with the approval of their adult guardians. Other chick lit books, such as those by the writing team Laura Mosher and Lauren Mechling, are also popular but entirely different. Their first book, *The Rise and Fall of a 10th-Grade Social Climber,* has been so successful that they have written another, *All Q, No A,* and are planning a third to complete the trilogy, set in a quirky private school in New York.

These young writers, who met as freshmen at Amherst College, had opposite experiences in high school. Mosher attended St. John's in Texas, a traditional school, while Mechling attended an alternative school in Brooklyn. They agreed, however, to develop their main character Mimi into a high school student who thinks for herself. In an interview with Kate Bolick in *The Boston Globe,* the team admits that Mimi "is very much a kid. She's sexually inexperienced . . . but she's not an outcast. Feeling alienated from the world is a big thing in adolescent literature. But Mimi has a good time. Part of the first book was that she wanted to fit in, wasn't sure she could, and ultimately does" (Bolick, 2006, p. E3). Teenagers relate to their books at the same time they escape into them.

THE CROSSOVER   To add to our description of the kinds of teenage novels, we should consider the *crossover,* that is, the adult novel that *becomes* a young adult novel, or the young adult novel that becomes an adult novel. *The Catcher in the Rye* (Salinger), for example, was published as an adult novel. Yet the protagonist, Holden Caulfield is a teen and the story is told through his limited point of view. On the other hand, *A Step from Heaven* (An Na) and *Postcards from No Man's Land* (Aidan Chambers) "seem to be adult novels masquerading under the publisher's YA label" (Campbell, 2004, p. 361). In *A Step from Heaven* the reader is subjected to long passages written from the perspective of a child. In *Postcards from No Man's*

Land, large sections concern adults, while the main teenage character's actions are often hidden from the view of the reader.

To conclude this discussion, teachers, librarians, and other professionals may like to consider what Patty Campbell (2004), a longtime young adult librarian and critic, defines as a young adult novel. She believes the young adult novel has five distinct elements:

- A protagonist who must be a teenager
- No extended introspective passages from an adult or a child's point of view
- A plot driven with a minimum of description
- Priority to immediacy and brevity
- A point of view having the limitations of an adolescent perspective

An outstanding young adult novel is also identified by its underlying clues and layers of meanings. A teenager who rereads Cormier's *I Am the Cheese,* for example, discovers a structure, a theme, and a shift in voice that are more readily apparent when the young adult reads it a second time. Cormier was one of the first young adult novelists to experiment with forms unlike the traditional linear narrative (beginning, middle, and end). Other young adult novelists, such as those mentioned below, also experiment with literary devices.

Spotlight On
Literary Devices of Young Adult Novelists

Aidan Chambers. British author Aidan Chambers, winner of the United Kingdom's Carnegie Medal, the Hans Christian Andersen Author Award (2002), and the Printz Award (2003), constantly uses various forms and structures in his young adult books. In his *Postcards from No Man's Land* he alternates narratives from different time periods. He is totally absorbed in how a story should be told and comments frequently about his interest in form and structure.

David Klass. This well-known author in his novel *You Don't Know Me* narrates in second-person present tense. When readers open *You Don't Know Me,* they may be puzzled about the second person being addressed by John, the protagonist. "You don't know where I'll end up. The good news is that you may have created my past and screwed up my present but you have no control of my future. You don't know me at all" (Klass, 2002, p. 7). Later, readers discover it is his mother, whom he accuses of placing him in the middle of his personal hurricane. As he talks to himself, he asks her rhetorically: "Do you really think I will come down to breakfast tomorrow and call the man who is not my father, sir?"

Chris Lynch. In *Freewill* Chris Lynch creates the double voice of Will, the protagonist, who is constantly asking and answering his own questions, cryptically, throughout the book. "Why are you in woodshop? You are meant to be a pilot. How does wood-shop get you any closer to being a pilot? But here you are. You don't know why you are here but you know you are, and you are meant to be doing something, so you might as well" (Lynch, 2000, p. 2).

The pithy questions, the clipped answers, and the unfortunate situations become more complex as the story develops and the bodies of young suicides (with a sculpture of Will beside them) are discovered throughout the town. Faith, hope, and charity divide the sections of the book, but the greatest of these is the charity of his Pop and Gran, who sustain the confused Will throughout the narrative.

Nancy Werlin. Author of *Locked Inside,* Nancy Werlin totally engages her readers when she experiments with an over-the-top format. She entangles her 16-year-old character Marnie in the Internet game Paliopolis, where she seeks safety and is befriended by Elf. In actuality, she is kidnapped and locked inside an empty basement cell. Her two worlds collide when she is rescued by Frank from cyberspace.

HOW I LIVE NOW. A first novel by Meg Rosoff, *How I Live Now* (winner of the 2005 Printz Award) is capturing wide attention both here and abroad. The main character, 15-year-old Daisy, leaves New York to live with her English cousins on their farm. From the spoiled, narcissistic girl who was furious when her father married a woman she couldn't stand, she matures into a warm, witty girl who loves beauty. During the invasion of England by an unnamed power—similar to today's terrorism—Daisy and her friends react with courage—the kind of courage the novelist herself has demonstrated in her fight against cancer (Mehegan, 2004).

THE GOATS. Brock Cole's first novel, *The Goats*, opens with a startling scene. Two adolescents, "the boy" and "the girl," are stripped of their clothes and left stranded on an island beach by a group of peers from the summer camp where they have been staying. They are the goats. Together, they are determined to survive rather than give up in defeat. They go on a rampage of law-breaking: stealing clothes from a resort dressing area, picking up change from the front seat of a truck, using a stranger's key to get into a motel room, and even tangling with the police. Meanwhile, they come to know and understand each other, resolve to restore whatever they've taken, and become sufficiently secure and mature so that when they finally get in touch with the girl's mother to come to their rescue, they are more than prepared to meet whatever awaits them.

WHALE TALK. In Chris Crutcher's *Whale Talk* the protagonist T. J., a multicultural, adopted teenager, recruits a swimming team at Cutter High School (which has no swimming pool) that includes some of the school's less popular students, including the retarded classmate, Chris. Through his encouragement and determination he develops his recruits into the winning Cutter All Night Mermen. His adoptive parents, who challenge themselves in a parallel plot to save a family of three small children from an abusive father, are his constant role models. Through them, he learns how to be understanding, considerate, and respectful of the rights of others.

SOMEWHERE IN THE DARKNESS. Walter Dean Myers, well known for his award-winning novels, introduces his readers to Jimmy, a 14-year-old. Jimmy's father, Crab, has just escaped from prison, where he had spent many years falsely accused of murder. Together, they travel cross-country and become reacquainted. In the course of their travels, Jimmy discovers many things about his father, who uses stolen money and false credit cards to rent the cars they are traveling in. His father, however, wants Jimmy to learn only one thing about him: he never killed a man. At the end of the journey, they come to Crab's childhood home, where Crab meets The Conjure Man and confronts the man who falsely accused him.

HEAVEN. Angela Johnson writes about Marley, a 14year-old who thinks she really lives in a heaven on earth. She has a loving mother and father, a younger brother whom she can tolerate, and an Uncle Jack, whom she does not remember ever meeting, but with whom she corresponds. Only when she is told her Momma and Pops are not her real parents do her emotions go into a tailspin. Marley no longer trusts them and questions why they did not let her know sooner. Filled with anger and misgivings, she tries unsuccessfully to confide in her friends, although she finds some answers talking with Bobby, a single father whose child she babysits. It is only when she reads a love letter that her real mother, Christine, wrote to her father, whom she knows as Uncle Jack, that she is gradually reconciled to the truth.

THE FIRST PART LAST. Angela Johnson's Printz Award–winning book is a prequel to *Heaven*. In it, she reveals the difficulties that Bobby, the 16-year-old father, experiences when he must assume full care of the infant Feather. The reader did not meet the young mother, Nia, in the previous book, and only later in this book discovers that she is in an irreversible coma because of pregnancy-related eclampsia. It is the strength and sacrifice Bobby displays that readers will remember, as well as Johnson's skillful juxtaposition of the then- and-now to trace Bobby's developing maturity.

THE BOY IN THE BURNING HOUSE. In this engrossing story, Canadian writer Tim Wynne-Jones, author of *Lord of the Fries*, expands one of his short stories to describe how Jim Hawkins' father was murdered. Jim is devastated but determined to find out how and why this tragedy occurred. Fully developed characters like Ruth Rose, the stepdaughter of his father's friend who accuses her minister stepfather of the crime, and Father Fisher add to the suspenseful plot. Wynne-Jones concludes each chapter with a cliffhanger that makes the reader want to continue reading until the last page.

What's Your View?

Young Adult Literature Awards

Two awards by the American Library Association confirm the viability of young adult novels:

- The Michael L. Printz Award is for the young adult book that best exemplifies literary excellence. The Printz Award is named for a school librarian in Topeka, Kansas, who was an active member of the Young Adult Library Services Association.

- The Margaret A. Edwards Award, named for an outstanding young adult librarian, is given to an author for exemplary work in young adult literature.

The Michael Printz Award is often in the eye of the literary storm. This award, comparable to the Newbery Medal for children's literature, honored *Monster* (Walter Dean Myers) as its first recipient in 2000. This was followed by *Kit's Wilderness* (David Almond) in 2001, *A Step from Heaven* (An Na) in 2002, *Postcards from No Man's Land* (Aidan Chambers) in 2003, *The First Part Last* (Angela Johnson) in 2004, *How I Live Now* (Meg Rosoff) in 2005, and *Looking for Alaska* (John Green) in 2006. Yet these books were not selected without the age-old discussion of what comes first, quality or popularity? (See Chapter Four for additional information about book award selections.) Should a book's popularity be a factor in considering it for a Printz Award, and if so, how much weight should it be given? Did the members of the Printz Award committee retain the balance between popularity and quality when they selected *American Born Chinese*, Gene Luen Yang's graphic novel and National Book Award finalist, as the winner of the Printz Award for 2007?

Some professionals believe the Printz Award winner should not only have outstanding literary standards, but also be readable and be appealing to teens, since teen choices give young adult literature its authenticity. The ALA website, on the other hand, where the rules governing the Printz Award selection appear, states that the ALA hopes the award will have a wide audience among readers 12 to 18 years old. Yet that popularity is not *the* criterion for the award. Literary standards are the criteria, and they include:

- Interesting and fully developed characters
- Believable and absorbing plot
- Content that has something worthwhile to say

Professionals who criticized the selection of Aidan Chambers' *Postcards from No Man's Land* for the 2003 Printz Award admit it is a book of excellent literary quality, but believe it may have a limited young adult readership. Its proponents, however, defend it on the basis of its contribution to outstanding literature (Campbell, 2002). What's your view?

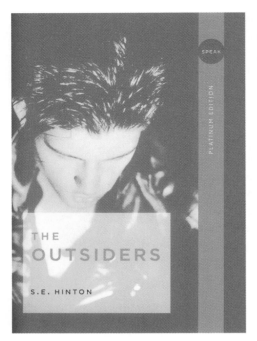

THE OUTSIDERS
Reproduced by permission of Penguin Group USA, Inc.

THE "NEW REALISM" IN YOUNG ADULT NOVELS

When *The Outsiders* (S. E. Hinton) was written in 1967, the author was a teenager, but the book immediately established itself as the first important contemporary young adult novel. Young adults discovered that even though they may not have actually experienced its events, they could vicariously experience what was then called "the new realism."

Patrick Jones writes that it is difficult to imagine a better young adult novel than *The Outsiders*. In it all the literary elements of a novel are intact: characters, plot, theme, and good writing (Jones, 1995). Hinton writes sensitively about the common fear shared by teenagers everywhere, of being an outsider. To be accepted, the protagonist Ponyboy, tries to establish his identity as a member of the Socs, a dangerous gang whose goal is terrorizing the "greasers."

Spotlight On
S. E. Hinton

Born in Tulsa, Oklahoma, in 1950, Susan Eloise Hinton was only 15 years old when she began writing *The Outsiders*, which was published two years later, in 1967. It sold over 4 million copies in the United States and became a popular movie. Since then, she has received the first annual Margaret A. Edwards Award (1988) for a lifetime of work with young people and for being an authentic voice that continues "to illuminate their experiences and emotions, giving insight into their lives." She has also written *That Was Then, This Is Now* (1971, 1985); *Rumble Fish* (1975); *Tex* (1979); *and Taming the Star Runner* (1988).

Around the time she wrote *The Outsiders*, Hinton became acutely aware of the unruly and often violent behavior of her peers after she witnessed the cold-blooded beating of a friend. It was natural for her to write her novels from a boy's viewpoint because her best friends were boys. As a novelist, she used the initials S. E., rather than Susan Eloise, because she felt that no one would believe that a girl could—or would—write such a realistic story as *The Outsiders*.

When she wrote *That Was Then, This Is Now*, she found that her writing was slower and more deliberate compared with *The Outsiders*, but she considers *That Was*

Ed Lallo/Getty Images

Then, This Is Now a better-written book. "I'm a character writer," she admitted in an interview with *Seventeen* magazine, and all her characters are a part of herself. Although they are fictional, she gets her ideas from real people. She is concerned primarily with relationships and perceives any relationship to be complicated, even for simple people.

Today, over forty years since *The Outsiders* was published, high school teachers who may have difficulty motivating students to read still ask them to read the first few pages of *The Outsiders*. Doing this invariably pulls them into the story. They discover for themselves that Hinton understands teenagers and really likes them. Although the problems of young adults may be different now than they were when she began writing, Hinton believes their feelings are the same (Hinton, 2000).

Adam Langer of *Book* magazine interviewed Hinton in 2003. While discussing her body of work, she stated emphatically that for her writing to be any good, she has to be emotionally committed to it and "for a long time, I was just emotionally committed to being a mother. I didn't have anything left over" (Langer, 2003, p. 36). Now, however, she is ready to publish an adult novel, *Hawkes Harbor*, and her readers look forward to it.

Graphic Novels

A wide range of genres are available to high school students, including the *graphic novel*, a comic book that is more extensive in format and often contains a complete story. It has a more durable cover than a comic book, more carefully detailed artwork, and its own ISBN, which makes it easier for libraries and bookstores to order. Graphic novel sales in bookstores have grown by almost 200 percent in the last few years. Most of this growth is due to increased sales of *manga* (Japanese comic books). But do graphic novels belong in the high school library?

Teachers and librarians who realize that some students have a shorter attention span, are more visual, or may not be attracted to a longer novel, a classic, or even a magazine may see the graphic novel as a vehicle to keep students reading. Some adults who know little about comic books may wonder how they became mainstream. What is the literary value of a graphic novel? How does a young adult librarian like Mike Pawuk, who was featured in the *School Library Journal* and has 1,000 comic book titles in his collection at the Cuyahoga County Library in Ohio, make his selections? (Answer: *Diamond Comics' Previews* and other reviews.) These and other questions deeply concern high school teachers and librarians.

Categories of Graphic Novels

Philip Crawford, who writes *Thought Bubbles*, a column that explores and evaluates the world of graphic novels for *Knowledge Quest* (an *ALA* publication), divides graphic novels into three categories: all ages, mainstream, and mature. Those for all ages, which are suitable for children in elementary school but still appeal to older readers, would include *The Batman Adventures*, *Bone*, and *The Simpsons*. Mainstream graphic novels include stories about superheroes, such as *Superman*, *The X-Men*, *Wonder Woman*, and *Spiderman*. Graphic novels for mature readers, such as *Ghost World*, *From Hell*, and the *Sandman* series (Neil Gaiman), are aimed at high school students and may include nudity, sexual situations, adult language, graphic violence, and recreational drug use (Crawford, 2004, p. 35).

Julia Michaels, writing in *The Horn Book*, cites Gaiman's *Sandman* as the "ultimate epic comic-book story." It was originally conceived as a reimagining of an old DC superhero who fought crime by sprinkling dust on his quarry. Gaiman completely re-envisioned the Sandman as a deity rather than a superhero, who is the literal avatar of dreams. "In ten stunning graphic novels, Gaiman created an unprecedented fantasy epic, with a vast host of moral and immoral characters" (Michaels, 2004, p. 304).

MANGA. *Manga* has been popular in Japan for decades. Japanese school children have avidly consumed all manner of *shonen* (boys' manga) and *shoujo* (girls' manga) in their native land. Now it is one of the driving forces behind the mainstreaming of comics in the Western world. Manga enjoys a wide and varied market in the United States, aimed at high school students and adults, and includes a great deal of violent and sexually explicit content "that can sometimes shock unprepared Western readers who are primarily familiar with kiddie fare" (Michaels, 2004, p. 300).

LITERARY QUALITY OF GRAPHIC NOVELS Although graphic novels have only recently become acceptable as "literature" in the United States, there is already a pilot program active in seven states where two series of graphic novels from

CrossGeneration comics are being used in a supplemental reading-comprehension program called *Bridges* (Weiner, 2003). One series, *The Meridian*, is targeted at middle school students, while *Ruse* is suitable for high school students. Both come with books, teacher's guides, and CD-ROMs with skill activities. The publishers assure the buyers that they have been edited for language and occasional sexual innuendo. Michelle Tregoning, a literary coach who coordinates *Bridges* as an extracurricular reading program in Los Angeles, believes comics are an ideal solution that really engages students. Dan Tandarich, an English teacher in Brooklyn, is convinced that "comics are the perfect tool. With comics, if your reading skills aren't up to speed, you've got the visual cues, the pictures to help you fill in the blanks" (George, 2003, p. 202).

So what can we conclude from this discussion? Graphic novels are making inroads into our consciousness at a rapid pace and serve as an *alternative* to the conventional novel. But do they have literary value? Scott McCloud, author of *Understanding Comics*, offers a positive interpretation of their place in his writing on the history and nature of comics (George, 2003, p. 202). Art Spiegelman, moved comics "from the basement of the contemporary literary establishment to the living room" when he won a special Pulitzer Prize in 1992 for *MAUS: A Survivor's Tale*—his graphic novel that recounts his parents' persecution by and escape from the Nazis. He has always defended comics for their beauty and innovation, but may not have envisioned such a swift acceptance of comics. As recently as 2001, he called them "the hunchback dwarf of the art" (Wasserman 2001).

Historical Fiction

THE INNOCENT SOLDIER. Michael Hofmann's translation of Josef Holub's novel tells the story of a teenage farm boy who is betrayed into fighting in the Napoleonic Wars not as himself but as the farmer's own son.

BLOODY JACK: BEING AN ACCOUNT OF THE CURIOUS ADVENTURES OF MARY "JACKIE" FABER SHIP'S BOY. L. A. Meyer writes a swashbuckling adventure story of a girl who transforms herself to join the crew of a British warship. Mary Fabert, after her family dies of pestilence (the scourge of the eighteenth century), dresses as a boy, enlists in the English Royal Navy, and finds herself involved in many intriguing adventures.

DON'T YOU KNOW THERE'S A WAR ON? Avi, a Newbery Medal recipient for *Crispin*, cleverly uses the title as the theme of his book about World War II. In it he incorporates many of the sacrifices—such as food rationing, air raid warnings, blackouts, and mothers working overtime in factories—that were the everyday experiences of the homefront. At the same time, he develops the larger theme involving a young student's concern about his teacher being fired because she was pregnant. Howie, the young narrator, is 16 years old, and the war is over when he relates what happened in his Brooklyn, New York, classroom during a week in March 1943. This is an excellent book for a reluctant reader.

EXTRA INNINGS. Robert Newton Peck, who wrote *A Day No Pigs Would Die*, offers inspiration to Tate, a young man who loses his family in a plane crash. Tate loses his leg and with it the dream he had of being a major league baseball player. No one can cheer him and help him cope with his loss as well as his great-aunt Vidalia. With good humor and a remarkable memory, she traces for Tate her own ups-and-downs during the Great Depression as a member of "Ethiopia's Clowns," a "rollicking" good baseball team.

TROY. Adele Geras has re-created Homer's *Iliad* so that it comes alive for the young adult reader. Told from the point of view of the women of Troy, it details the last weeks of the Trojan War, when the women are weary of taking care of the wounded, the men are exhausted from fighting, and the frustrated gods and goddesses are seeking ways to end it. *Booklist* calls it "a sexy, sweeping tale, filled with drama, sassy humor, and vividly imagined domestic details" (Geras, Intro.). It is also the perfect companion for today's high school student studying Greek and Roman history and classical languages.

Biography, Autobiography, and Memoir

KING OF THE MILD FRONTIER. Chris Crutcher's autobiography, which he subtitles *An Ill-Advised Autobiography*, is a collection of autobiographical episodic essays in which he details events in his life with humor and insight. He uses a thematic, rather than chronological, approach that appeals to young adults (as if he were talking to them spontaneously, heart to heart). He reveals how anger, heroism, religion, and cruelty play a role in his life and how these themes are reflected in his writing.

LOOKING BACK. Children have always asked writers where they get their ideas. Lois Lowry tells her readers in her memoir *Looking Back* that she gets ideas from the many places she has lived and the remembrances she has of her family. In a book filled with photographs, much like a family album, she recalls incidents and characters in her life that she has included in much of her fiction. Her most heartbreaking memory is the death of her adult son in a plane crash.

HOLE IN MY LIFE. Jack Gantos, author of the Joey Pigza series, wrote this uninhibited memoir about a segment of his life when, as a teenager, he was imprisoned for smuggling drugs. It is a frank, honest self-examination of a period in his life when he thought he had no future.

Informational Books

Below are informational books that reflect Howard Gardner's *Multiple Intelligences: The Theory and Practice* (1993) explained in Chapters Nine and Ten. We suggest that when you offer these books to an individual student, consider that the student is not only mathematically or musically or scientifically inclined, but is endowed with a combination of all of the eight intelligences that Gardner believes are, to a greater or lesser degree, present in all of us.

Linguistic Intelligence

HOW I CAME TO BE A WRITER. Phyllis Reynolds Naylor's book, although written in 1978, has gone through many editions not only because it is succinct and to the point, but because it is a model for young adults who want to write.

Many students have been fans of her fifteen-book series about Alice, from the time she was 8 through her teenage years. Naylor, who began writing in the 1960s, is still enthusiastic about her craft. "I am happy and excited, restless and driven, all at the same time. But I go on writing because an idea in the head is like a rock in my shoe; I just can't wait to get it out" (Naylor, p. 121).

STAND UP, MR. DICKENS. This book, by Edward Blishen, is recommended to young adults who are wrestling with assignments to read Dickens' novels (eg., *Pickwick Papers*, *Great Expectations*, *Dombey and Son*, *Oliver Twist*). In just eighty-seven pages, with Jill Bennett's black and white and multi-colored illustrations, Blishen brings Dickens to life and dramatizes selections from his novels to demonstrate how he captivated his audiences.

Musical Intelligence

CLARA SCHUMANN: PIANO VIRTUOSO. Susanna Reich sets the stage by introducing Clara Schumann as the nineteenth century's most talented female pianist. In 1844 she took Moscow by storm. Yet her husband, Robert Schumann, and friend Johannes Brahms are more recognizable today. A woman far ahead of her time, who as a child was controlled by a demanding father, she worked tirelessly, even after she was widowed with seven children, seemingly from a craving for an audience's applause.

MAHALIA: A LIFE IN GOSPEL MUSIC. Roxane Orgill has written a tribute to the powerfully voiced, strong-willed Mahalia Jackson and her indelible influence on gospel music. Born poor in New Orleans in 1911, Mahalia came to record bestselling records. Apollo sold fifty thousand copies of her *Move on Up a Little Higher* in Chicago in 1948 in four weeks, and could not press enough records to keep up with the demand (Orgill, 2003, p. 46). On August 28, 1963, she joined the March on Washington comprising 100,000 blacks and 60,000 whites who marched down Constitution Avenue, Washington, DC, with Martin Luther King, Jr., to encourage passage of the Civil Rights Act. Her rendition of *Stand by Me* became a symbol of the civil rights movement. Mahalia went to bed that night with her Bible beside her, still unable to imagine "all those people wanting freedom for her people. And not a single rock thrown" (Orgill, 2003, p. 101).

Logical/Mathematical Intelligence

THE CODE BOOK. Simon Singh's book, originally written for adults, is a challenging crossover for young adults who value their mathematical intelligence. It explains not only code making but code breaking, and highlights the skills of famous cryptographers. It also includes decoded messages that proved decisive historically.

THE LONGITUDE PRIZE. Joan Dash explains how the British Board of Longitude eventually offered the Longitude Prize in 1714 to the crotchety John Harrison, a maker of clocks, who spent forty years working on a timepiece that would be so accurate that it could determine one's longitude at sea. Today,

THE CODE BOOK
Used by permission of Doubleday, a division of Random House, Inc.

although watches have become cheap and longitude has lost its mystery, readers will not forget that it was John Harrison, a country inventor, whose logical-mathematical intelligence and passion for perfection helped him create the first timepiece that kept ships from being destroyed for lack of accurate "reckoning."

Spatial Intelligence

BUILDING THE BOOK CATHEDRAL. David Macaulay has a talent few authors-illustrators possess. Not only can he present a reader with the completed project (whether it is a pyramid, mosque, or cathedral), but he can demonstrate the step-by-step *process* of how the project is developed. In this book, the reader looks over Macaulay's shoulder as he reviews in large drawings and small, detailed sketches how his book, *Cathedral*, was conceived and implemented.

EUREKA! The men and women whose inventions Richard Platt honors in this stunning book certainly expressed their spatial intelligence in a unique way. As Sir Paul Nurse, a Nobel Prize winner, writes in the Introduction, "they were able to see what everybody else had seen but think what nobody else had thought. Their discoveries highlight where a curious and inquiring mind can lead and illustrate why science is so important today" (Platt, 2003). Each invention is explained in a full-page article complete with diagrams, colored photographs, and the "Eureka Moment" of discovery.

Bodily-Kinesthetic Intelligence

BABE DIDRIKSON ZAHARIAS: THE MAKING OF A CHAMPION. Readers who have enjoyed Russell Freedman's biographies about historical figures may wonder why he chose to write about an outstanding figure in women's sports. Yet he brings to this biography the same skills, including an ability to seek out memorable quotations and true-to-life anecdotes. The text is filled with clear black and white photographs of Babe's career. The reader discovers that Babe, a tomboy when she was young, was considered the greatest athlete of the twentieth century. She is a great role model for today's young athletes and for those who aspire to greatness in any field.

BLACK HOOPS. Frederick McKissack, Jr., a sportswriter, has thoroughly researched the history of African Americans in basketball and presents it to young adults in a conversational, breezy style. He devotes chapters to the Harlem Globetrotters, Dr. J, Magic Jordan, and Shaq, and discusses the increasing popularity of black women in basketball. Interspersed throughout with black and white photographs, it also includes a glossary and bibliography.

Interpersonal Intelligence

TALKING PEACE. President Jimmy Carter explains that young people, for whom he wrote the book, will soon find out that they have inherited a planet in less than perfect shape. He wants them to know that many people are working diligently to make the world a better place in which to live, and he asks them to become aware of the many conflict resolutions that are helping the peoples of the world survive in a more humane universe.

ONE WORLD, MANY RELIGIONS: THE WAYS WE WORSHIP. Mary Pope Osborne, in an entirely objective and respectful manner, approaches each section of this Orbis Pictus Award book like the storyteller she is. Without getting into philosophy or dogma, she provides basic information about Christianity, Judaism, Islam, Hinduism, Buddhism, Confucianism, and Taoism. The narrative contributes a great deal to the high school reader's understanding of these religions.

Intrapersonal Intelligence

KENNEDY ASSASSINATED! THE WORLD MOURNS: A REPORTER'S STORY. Wilborn Hampton was a rookie reporter just out of college when he covered the story of Kennedy's assassination. His book will inspire high school students with the thoroughness, sincerity, and quality of his investigation. The black and white photographs add another dimension to the terrible tragedy.

WITCH-HUNT: MYSTERIES OF THE SALEM WITCH TRIALS. For serious readers who may have wondered what *really* happened at the Salem witch trials, Marc Aronson refutes the popular accounts and explores possible motives and causes for the trials. He examines the intentions of the participants and the consequences of the community's judgment. Its in-depth analysis offers great possibilities for students making the link to a play such as Arthur Miller's *The Crucible*.

Naturalistic Intelligence

FOSSIL FISH FOUND ALIVE: DISCOVERING THE COELACANTH. Sally Walker is adept at dramatizing the search for additional specimens that has ensued since a coelacanth was found in 1938. She shows that scientists can be successful by being at the right place at the right time and, conversely, they can be frustrated by international conflicts that may be taking place.

THE SNAKE SCIENTIST. For students interested in science, Sy Montgomery's detailed description of how Bob Matson, an Oregon State University zoologist, has tracked the red-sided garter snake for fifteen years is fascinating to read. Through controlled experiments and observations, Matson reveals how the snake uses trails of pheromones (chemicals given off by an animal) to migrate to feeding grounds and to find a possible mate. He emphasizes the importance of scientific fieldwork and credits Mason with unraveling reptilian mysteries of the natural world (Zarnowski, 2001).

Chapter Checklist

Read the following items carefully. If you have difficulty responding to any of them, return to the chapter and review the material.

After reading this chapter, you can

1. Explain how developmental changes affect the book selections of young adult readers.

2. Describe how summer reading lists should match the varied developmental levels of young adult readers.

3. Illustrate how the authors of young adult books must be sensitive to the developmental changes of these years.

4. Analyze the stories reflecting the relationships between young adults and their parents, and how they are treated in the literature.

5. Discuss the reasons for the growing number of books with gay and lesbian themes.

6. Identify themes from stories such as *The Catcher in the Rye* that reflect Erikson's ideas concerning identity.

7. Evaluate the place of graphic novels in reading programs for young adult readers.

8. Assess the influence of the writers of adult novels on young adult fiction.

9. Identify the importance of Gardner's multiple intelligences in young adult readers.

10. List several suggestions for helping reluctant young adult readers.

Young Adult Bibliography

Almond, David. (2000). *Kit's Wilderness*. New York: Delacorte.

Anderson, Laurie Halse. (2005). *Prom*. New York: Viking.

An Na. (2001). *A Step From Heaven*. Asheville, NC: Front St. Press.

Aronson, Marc. (2003). *Witch-Hunt: Mysteries of the Salem Witch Trials*. New York: Atheneum.

Atwater-Rhodes, Amelia. (1999). *In the Forests of the Night*. New York: Laurel Leaf.

Atwater-Rhodes, Amelia. (2005). *Falcondance*. New York: Delacorte.

Atwater-Rhodes, Amelia. (2006). *Snake Charm*. New York: Laurel Leaf.

Avi. (2001). *Don't You Know There's a War On?* New York: Scholastic.

Bauer, Joan. (2005). *Best Foot Forward*. New York: Putnam.

Blishen, Edward. (1995). *Stand Up, Mr. Dickens*. Boston: Houghton Mifflin.

Brashares, Ann. (2005). *The Sisterhood of the Traveling Pants*. New York: Laurel Leaf.

Cameron, Sara (Ed). (2001). *Out of War: True Stories from the Front Lines*. New York: Scholastic.

Carter, Jimmy. (1996). *Talking Peace: A Vision for the Next Generation*. New York: Penguin.

Chambers, Aidan. (2002). *Postcards from No Man's Land*. New York: Random House.

Cole, Brock. (1987). *The Goats*. New York: Farrar, Straus, & Giroux.

Cormier, Robert. (1974). *The Chocolate War*. New York: Dell.

Cormier, Robert. (1977). *I Am the Cheese*. New York: Random House.

Cormier, Robert. (1983). *Tunes for Bears to Dance To*. Pittsburg: University of Pittsburg Press.

Cormier, Robert. (1990). *Other Bells for Us to Ring*. New York: Delacorte.

Cormier, Robert. (1991). *We All Fall Down*. New York: Delacorte.

Cormier, Robert. (1999). *Frenchtown Summer*. New York: Delacorte.

Covey, Sean. (1998). *The 7 Habits of Highly Effective Teens: the Ultimate Teenage Success Guide*. New York: Simon & Schuster.

Crutcher, Chris. (2001). *Whale Talk*. New York: Greenwillow.

Crutcher, Chris. (2003). *King of the Mild Frontier: An Ill-Advised Autobiography*. New York: Greenwillow.

Daldry, Jeremy. (1999). *The Teenage Guy's Survival Guide*. New York: Little, Brown.

Elliot, Patricia. (2006). *Murkmere*. Boston: Little, Brown.

Erlbach, Arlene. (1999). *Worth the Risk: True Stories About Risk Takers Plus How You Can Be One, Too*. New York: Free Spirit.

Ferris, Jean. (2000). *Eight Seconds*. San Francisco: Harcourt.

Fielding. Helen. (1998). *Bridget Jones' Diary*. New York: Viking.

Freedman, Russell. (1999). *Babe Didrikson Zaharias: The Making of a Champion*. New York: Clarion.

Gaiman, Neil. (1990). *The Sandman*. New York: DC Comics.

Gallo, Donald. (1990). *Center Stage*. New York: HarperCollins.

Gantos, Jack. (2002). *Hole in My Life*. New York: Farrar, Straus, & Giroux.

Garden, Nancy. (1982). *Annie on My Mind*. New York: Farrar, Straus, & Giroux.

George-Warren, Holly. (2001). *Shake, Rattle & Roll: The Founders of Rock and Roll*. Boston: Houghton Mifflin.

Geras, Adele. (2000). *Troy*. San Diego. Harcourt.

Giblin, James Cross. (2004). *Secrets of the Sphinx*. New York: Scholastic.

Green, John. (2005). *Looking for Alaska*. New York: Dutton.

Grimes, Nikki. (2002). *Bronx Masquerade*. New York: Dial Books.

Hampton, Wilborn. (1997). *Kennedy Assassinated! The World Mourns: A Reporter's Story*. Cambridge, MA: Candlewick.

Haworth-Attard, Barbara. (2005). *Theories of Relativity*. New York: Holt.

Hesse, Karen. (1997). *Out of the Dust.* New York: Scholastic.

Hiaasen, Carl, (2005). *Flush.* New York: Knopf.

Hiaasen, Carl, (2002). *Hoot.* New York: Knopf.

Hinton, S. E. (1967). *The Outsiders.* New York: The Viking Press.

Hinton, S. E. (1975). *Rumble Fish.* New York: Delacorte.

Hinton, S.E. (1980). *That Was Then, This Is Now.* New York: Dell.

Hinton, S. E. (1988). *Taming the Star Runner.* New York: Dell.

Holub, Josef. (2005). *An Innocent Soldier.* New York: Arthur Levine Books.

Jacobs, Thomas A. (1997). *What Are My Rights?: 95 Questions and Answers about Teens and the Law.* New York: Free Spirit.

Janeczko, Paul. (1989). *Brickyard Summer.* New York: Orchard Books.

Janeczko, Paul. (1988). *The Music of What Happens.* New York: Orchard Books.

Janecczko, Paul. (1991). *Preposterous.* New York: Orchard Books.

Johnson, Angela. (2001). *Running Back to Ludie.* New York: Orchard Books.

Johnson, Angela. (1998). *Heaven.* New York: Simon & Schuster Books for Young Readers.

Johnson, Angela. (2003). *The First Part Last.* New York: Simon & Schuster.

Kerr, M.E. (1986). *Night Kites.* New York: Harper & Row.

Kerr, M. E. (1994). *Deliver Us from Evie.* New York: HarperCollins.

Kerr, M. E. (1997). *Hello, I Lied.* New York: HarperCollins.

Klass, David. (2002). *You Don't Know Me.* New York: Avon.

Koertge, Ron. (1990). *The Boy in the Moon.* Boston: Joy Street Books.

Koertge, Ron. (2002). *Stoner & Spaz.* Cambridge, MA: Candlewick.

Koertge, Ron. (2003). *Shakespeare Bats Cleanup.* Cambridge, MA: Candlewick.

Lowry, Lois. (1998). *Looking Back.* New York: Houghton Mifflin.

Lynch, Chris. (2001). *Freewill.* New York: HarperCollins.

Macaulay, David. (1999). *Building the Book Cathedral.* Boston: Houghton Mifflin.

Mallory, Kenneth. (2001). *Swimming with Hammerhead Sharks.* Boston: Houghton Mifflin.

McKissack, Frederick Jr. (1999). *Black Hoops.* New York: Scholastic.

McWilliams, Kelly. (2004). *Doormat.* New York: Delacorte.

Meyer, L. A. (2002). *Bloody Jack: Being an Account of the Curious Adventures of Mary "Jackie" Faber, Ship's Boy.* San Diego: Harcourt.

Montgomery, Sy. (1999). *The Snake Scientist.* Boston: Houghton Mifflin.

Myers, Walter Dean. (1987). *Crystal.* New York: Viking Penguin.

Myers, Walter Dean. (1992). *Somewhere in the Darkness.* New York: Scholastic.

Myers, Walter Dean. (1999). *Monster.* New York: HarperCollins.

Myers, Walter Dean. (2001). *Bad Boy: A Memoir.* New York: HarperCollins.

Myers, Walter Dean. (2004). *Shooter.* New York: Harper.

Naylor, Phyllis Reynolds. (1987). *How I Came to Be a Writer.* New York: Aladdin.

Norman, Howard. (2004). *Between Heaven and Earth: Bird Tales from Around the World.* Orlando, Florida: Harcourt Brace.

November, Sharyn. (2003). *Firebirds: An Anthology of Original Fantasy and Science Fiction.* New York: Penguin.

Nye, Naomi Shihab. (2005). *A Maze Me: Poems for Girls.* New York: Greenwillow.

Oates, Joyce Carol. (2002). *Big Mouth & Ugly Girl.* New York: Harper Tempest.

Oppel, Kenneth. (1997). *Silverwing.* New York: Harper-Collins.

Oppel, Kenneth. (1999). *Sunwing.* New York: HarperCollins.

Orgill, Roxanne. (2002). *Mahalia: A Life in Gospel Music.* Cambridge, MA: Candlewick.

Osborne, Mary Pope. (1996). *One World, Many Religions: The Ways We Worship.* New York: Knopf.

Paolini, Christopher. (2002). *Eragon.* Livingston, MT: Polini International.

Paolini, Christopher. (2005). *Eldest.* N.Y.: Knopf.

Paulsen, Gary. (2001). *Guts.* New York: Laurel Leaf.

Peck, Robert Newton. (2001). *Extra Innings.* New York: HarperCollins.

Platt, Richard. (2003). *Eureka! Great Inventions and How They Happened.* Boston: Houghton Mifflin.

Pullman, Philip. (2003). *The Amber Spyglass.* New York: Laurel Leaf.

Reich, Susanna. (1999). *Clara Schumann.* New York: Clarion.

Rennison, Louise. (2003). *Angus, Thongs and Full-Frontal Snogging.* New York: Avon.

Rosoff, Meg. (2004). *How I Live Now.* New York: Random House.

Rowling, J. K. (2000). *Harry Potter and the Chamber of Secrets.* New York: Scholastic.

Rowling, J. K. (2003). *Harry Potter and the Prisoner of Azkaban.* New York: Scholastic.

Rylant, Cynthia. (2003). *God Went to Beauty School.* New York: Harper Tempest.

Salinger, J. D. (1945). *The Catcher in the Rye.* Boston: Little, Brown.

Singh, Simon. (2002). *The Code Book: How to Make It, Break It, Hack It, Crack It.* New York: Delacorte.

Spiegelman, Art. (1991). *Maus: A Survivor's Tale.* New York: Pantheon.

Stanley, Diane. (2002). *Saladin: Noble Prince of Islam.* New York: HarperCollins.

Stroud, Johnathan. (2006). *Ptolemy's Gate.* New York: Hyperion.

Tanaka, Shelley. (2001). *Attack on Pearl Harbor.* New York: Hyperion.

Walker, Sally M. (2002). *Fossil Fish Found Alive: Discovering the Coelacanth.* Minneapolis: Carolrhoda

Warren-George, Holly. (2001). *Shake, Rattle & Roll: The Founders of Rock & Roll.* Boston: Houghton Mifflin. Carolrhoda.

Werlin, Nancy. (2000). *Locked Inside.* New York: Delacorte.

Wittlinger, Ellen. (2001). *Razzle.* New York: Simon & Schuster.

Wolff, Virginia Euwer. (2001). *True Believer.* New York: Atheneum.

Woodson, Jacqueline. (2002). *Hush*. New York: G. P. Putnam.

Woodson, Jacqueline. (1998). *If You Come Softly*. New York: G. P. Putnam.

Wynne-Jones, Tim. (2001). *The Boy in the Burning House*. New York: Farrar, Straus, & Giroux.

Yang, Gene Luen. (2006). *American Born Chinese*. New York: First Second.

Professional References

Bandura, A. (1997). *Self-Efficacy: The Exercise of Control*. New York: Freeman.

Bogenschneider, K., Wu, M., Raffelli, M., & Tsay, J. (1998). "Other Teens Drink, But Not My Kid": Does Parental Awareness of Adolescent Alcohol Use Protect Adolescents from Risky Consequences? *Journal of Marriage and Family*. 60, 356–373.

Bolick, Kate. (2006). "Laura Moser and Lauren Mechling." *Boston Sunday Globe*. June 11, E3.

Broaddus, Karen, & Ivey, Gay. (2002). "Taking Away the Struggle to Read in the Middle Grades." *Middle School Journal*. November, 5–10. New York: Atheneum.

Campbell, Patty. (2000). "Middle Muddle." *The Horn Book*. July/August, 483–475.

Campbell, Patty. (2002). "Blood on the Table: Looking at Best Booking." *The Horn Book*. May/June, 275–280.

Campbell, Patty. (2004). "Our Side of the Fence." *The Horn Book*. May/June, 359–362.

Centers for Disease Control. (2005). *The Tool of Teenage Drinking*. Atlantic: CDC.

Crawford, Philip. (2002). "Thought Bubbles." *Knowledge Quest*. November–December.

Dacey, J., & Travers, J. (2009). *Human Development Across the Lifespan*. NewYork: McGraw-Hill.

Gardner, Howard. (1983). *Frames of Mind*. New York: Basic.

Gardner, Howard. (1993). *Multiple Intelligences: The Theory and Practice*. New York: Basic.

Gardner, Howard. (1997). *Extraordinary Minds*. New York: Basic.

Gardner, Howard. (1999). *Intelligence Reframed*. New York: Basic.

George, Stephen. (2003). "Comics with Class." *Better Homes and Gardens*. June, 202–206.

Grotevant, H. (1998). "Adolescent Development in Family Contexts." In W. Damon (Series ed.) & N. Eisenberg (Volume ed.), *Handbook of Child Psychology: Volume 3. Social, Emotional, and Personality Development*. New York: John Wiley.

Hall, G. Stanley. (1904). *Adolescence*. New York: Appleton-Century-Crofts.

Jenkins, Christine A. (June, 2003). "Annie On Her Mind." *School Library Journal*. 48–50.

Jones, Jami. (2003). "Saving Kids from Despair." *School Library Journal*. August, 46–49.

Jones, Patrick. (1995). Hinton, S. E. In Anita Silvey, *Children's Books and Their Creators*. Boston: Houghton Mifflin.

Konner, M. (1990). *Childhood*. Boston: Little, Brown.

Kutiper, Karen, & Wilson, Patricia. (1993). "Updating Poetry Preferences: A Look at the Poetry Children Really Like." *The Reading Teacher*. 47, September, 28–35.

Langer, Adam. (2003). "Where Are They Now?" *Book*. July/August, 34–40.

Lerner, R. (1998). "Theories of Human Development: Contemporary Perspectives." In W. Damon (Series ed.) & R. Lerner (Volume ed.), *Handbook of Child Psychology: Volume 1. Theoretical Models of Human Development*. New York: John Wiley.

Lerner, R. (2002). *Concepts and Theories of Human Development*. Mahwah, NJ: Lawrence Erlbaum.

Lerner, R., & Galambos, N. (1998). "Adolescent Development: Challenges and Opportunities for Research, Programs, and Policies." In Janet Spence, John Darley, Donald Foss (Ed.), *Annual Review of Psychology*. Palo Alto, CA: Annual Reviews.

Lerner, Jacqueline, and Learner Richard (ed). (2001). *Adolescence in America*, Vol. 2. Santa Barbara, CA: ABC LIO.

Long, T., & Davis, W. (2002). "'Chocolate and 'Cheese': Author Gave Voice to Adolescent Angst." *The Boston Globe*. November 3.

McCloud, Scott. (1993). "Understanding Comics." New York: DC Comics.

Mechling, Lauren & Moser, Laura. (2005). *The Rise and Fall of a 10th-Grade Social Climber*. Boston: Houghton Mifflin.

Mechling, Lauren & Moser, Laura. (2006). *All Q, No A: More Tales of a 10th-Grade Social Climber*. Boston: Houghton Mifflin.

Mehegan, David. (2003). "Young Adults Are Reading One of their Own." *The Boston Globe*. September 16, A1–A65.

Mehegan, David. (2004). "Seeing Life's Fragility, She Seizes the Day." *The Boston Globe*. October 23, F1, F6.

Michaels, Julia. (2004). "Pulp Fiction." *The Horn Book*. May/June, 299–306.

National Institute on Drug Abuse. (2004). "NIDA Info Facts: High School and Youth Trends." Washington, DC.: US HHS.

National Youth Violence Prevention Resource Centers (2004). *Youth Gangs*.

Petersen, A. (1988). "Adolescent Development." *Annual Review of Psychology*. 3.

Spiegelman, Art. (1991). *Maus: A Survivor's Tale*. New York: Raw Books & Graphics.

Vardell, Sylvia M. (2006). "Don't Stop with Mother Goose." *School Library Journal*. April, pp 40–41.

Wasserman, Dan. (2001). Comic Book Hero. *The Boston Globe*. December 13.

Weiner, Steve. (2003). "Graphic Novel Roundup." *School Library Journal*.

Wolf, Naomi. (2006). "Wild Things." *New York Times Book Review*, March 12, pp. 22–23.

Zarnowski, M. (Ed.). (2001). *The Best in Children's Nonfiction*. Urbana IL: National Council of Teachers of English.

Science Literature through the Grades: A Curricular Model

The Eagle Has Landed!

On Sunday, July 20, 1969, these magical words were flashed to earth from the moon. The Apollo 11 flight had successfully landed on the moon's surface. Michael Collins, the command module pilot, had been faced with the twin responsibilities he always kept in mind: He must get his crewmates back to Earth safely and he couldn't make any mistakes that would jeopardize the mission.

He could not tell whether his crewmates felt anxiety, for they seemed entirely relaxed. Of the three of them, he was least comfortable with the risks they were undertaking, most conscious of the fallibility of complex machines. He had come to see the flight as a long and fragile daisy chain of events, and was only too aware that at any time the chain could break. Now he felt something like an anxious parent with two children about to go away on a long trip. (Chaikin, 1994, p. 189)

In recent remarks (personal interview), Collins, author of the children's book *Flying to the Moon*, noted that he was motivated to become a test pilot—the kind of pilot NASA was looking for. Consequently, he applied for admission to the astronaut training program as soon as he was eligible. During this interview, and without being asked, Collins emphasized how important reading and science were to him.

Stories about space (such as biographies of Collins and other astronauts) and books like *If You Decide to Go to the Moon* (Faith McNulty) and *Team Moon: How 400,000 People Landed Apollo 11 on The Moon* (Catherine Thimmesh) effectively attract the attention and interest of young readers. In this chapter we'll take into consideration national frameworks and offer suggestions about exciting and informative stories, themes, plots, conflicts, and information that can weave their way into a student's intellect and imagination. The significant, even critical, functions of teachers and librarians in this process will also be considered.

Teachers and librarians, as experienced communicators, are aware that children's literature serves as a *search engine* for making interdisciplinary connections across the curriculum. In preparing their lesson plans, they frequently seize upon a genre of children's literature, such as a contemporary novel, a historical novel, a book of poetry, or traditional literature, to integrate into their

IF YOU DECIDE TO GO TO THE MOON
Reprinted by permission of Scholastic Inc.

language arts, social studies, math, science music, and art studies. In the *Spin-offs*, which appear throughout this book, we often demonstrate how individual works of literature may be effectively used across the curriculum.

In this chapter, we'll focus on the role that children's literature plays in the *science* curriculum in the early elementary, intermediate, middle, and high school years. We have selected science as our exemplar because of its appeal to young readers. With its exciting discoveries and practical applications, science acts as a dynamic, motivating force that encourages creativity. We also believe science is a superb model to demonstrate how other subjects can be employed in an interactive and inspiring manner. In this way, children's literature enriches the subjects students are taking, broadens their vision of a discipline, and introduces a personal and often emotional tone to their learning. We want to commend the National Council of Teachers of English (NCTE) for establishing the Orbis Pictus Award in 1989, to be given annually to the writer of an informational book that meets its criteria for outstanding accuracy, organization, design, and style (Zarnowski, 2001).

Not only do we select, analyze, and review up-to-date and appropriate informational books (many of which have been designated as Orbis Pictus Award books) that support the science curriculum from early elementary through high school, but we also include other genres that may not be strictly scientific but can be used as springboards for the study of science. We have chosen genres such as picture books, traditional literature, biography, poetry, and science fiction to stimulate discussion and to enhance students' formal study. These books provide a goodness-of-fit between the students and the scientific subjects they are studying, such as the environment, space exploration, the brain, and the human genome.

First, we will turn our attention to the key issues of motivation and creativity since they play an important role in scientific discovery and in students' academic achievement. Without positive motivation and the opportunity for creative thinking, students cannot produce their best work.

311

Guidelines for Reading Chapter 13

After you finish reading Chapter Thirteen, you should be able to answer the following questions.

• What are some techniques teachers and librarians use to encourage the habit of reading?

• How can teachers and librarians use visualization techniques to encourage children's love of reading?

• Why is science an excellent example to illustrate the importance of children's literature across the curriculum?

• Why is science such an appealing subject for children of the primary grades?

• What are the stages involved in setting up a science literacy center?

• How do stories about individuals such as Michael Collins motivate children to read more about space?

• What are some books that would motivate middle school readers to learn more about brain development?

• How can stories and facts about our genetic makeup help readers understand and appreciate our biological future?

Motivating Children to Read

Children's literature should reach across the curriculum to enrich, enthrall, and entertain young readers in their insatiable search for information. Although competition for the attention of our young people today is greater than ever, as technology provides colorful and provocative alternatives, good literature and the information it conveys are still in demand. Consequently, teachers and librarians have a major responsibility: how do they bring children into the world of reading and build on that interest over the years with reading material that is appropriate, compelling, and enlightening? To help you make meaningful connections with potential readers, we would like you to think about ways to *motivate* children by interacting with them in a creative and meaningful manner while using appropriate literature. Let's begin by examining several key ideas relating to motivation.

Maslow's Hierarchy of Needs

Building on the idea that children function more effectively and happily when their needs are satisfied, astute psychologist Abraham Maslow (whom we mentioned in Chapter One) proposed a meaningful, helpful, and practical model for providing appropriate experiences for children. The books you select for young readers, especially those that illustrate how others overcome their challenges and frustrations and satisfy their needs, fit Maslow's model perfectly. His ideas were built around a hierarchy of five needs: physiological, safety, love and belongingness, esteem, and self-actualization.

CHILDREN'S LITERATURE AND MASLOW'S HIER-ARCHY OF NEEDS   As we look at each of these needs we recall Katherine Paterson's novel *The Same Stuff as Stars*. As we see in the lives of 11-year-old Angel and her little brother Bernie the significance of stars and the night sky, we also hear their cry for help.

THE SAME STUFF AS STARS
Reprinted by permission of Clarion Books, an imprint of Houghton Mifflin Company.

   1. PHYSIOLOGICAL NEEDS. When physiological needs, such as hunger and sleep, are unsatisfied they dominate children's lives. And until they are satisfied, everything else recedes. Children who do not eat breakfast or who suffer from poor nutrition, or adolescents who are extremely sensitive about their weight and who diet endlessly, experience a sharp drop in their energy levels and are less likely to be motivated. In the *Same Stuff as Stars*, when Bernie and Angel live with their mother, they are always hungry. Bernie cries "I didn't have no lunch," to which his mother, Verna, replies, "I never thought of it."

   2. SAFETY NEEDS. Children need to be free from fear and anxiety to perform and achieve their potential. Children who are subject to regular abuse—whether neglect, a home atmosphere marked by the uncertainties of drug or alcohol abuse, physical trauma, or psychological sarcasm and ridicule—are constantly anxious. At first, safety, security, and freedom from fear and anxiety were not options for Bernie and Angel, since their father was in jail and their mother had abandoned them. And when Angel goes to middle school and is called "pond scum" because of her father's misdeeds, she continues to be insecure. Only when she goes to live with her great-grandmother and makes friends with the librarian and the man who knows the stars does she gradually become comfortable and free from fear.

   3. LOVE AND BELONGINGNESS NEEDS. Feelings of being alone, of not being part of the group, and not having any sense of belongingness pose genuine threats to a child's self-esteem. Children need to feel wanted and accepted. If these needs remain unsatisfied, they may go to great lengths to be accepted. Angel tries to justify her mother's cruelty when Bernie cries, "I hate her. She's mean." She knows she should stick up for her mother but she doesn't know what to say. When her mother later kidnaps Bernie from school, however, Angel is desolate. "Why just Bernie? Why did she take Bernie and leave me behind? Doesn't she love me too? Oh, Momma, I need you, too."

   4. ESTEEM NEEDS. The opinions of others and a child's own self-judgment combine to produce a sense of self-esteem, which, if positive, leads to a continuous desire to excel. Deserved reinforcement (praise, rewards, etc.) goes a long way to stimulate and maintain motivation. If children lack self-esteem, their motivation is also lacking. In the beginning, Angel's self-esteem is zero. Her mother constantly calls her "Miss Know-It-All" and complains, "I don't know what I'm going to do with you kids." As the story progresses, and Angel and Bernie find a home with their great-grandma and make new friends, Angel's self-esteem improves.

5. NEED FOR SELF-ACTUALIZATION. As Maslow states (1987, p. 22), even if all needs are satisfied there is a tendency to feel restless unless we are doing what we think we are capable of doing. Angel is moving toward self-actualization; her basic needs are gradually being satisfied. "If it hadn't been for the stars she might have given up trying" is not only the theme of the book, but it also describes Angel's determination and thoughtfulness. Angel is an unforgettable character.

As children move toward self-actualization they satisfy their basic needs and continue to progress toward a state of physical and psychological health. If you convince children, by encouragement and the examples of appropriate literature, that they should—and can—fulfill their promise, they will have started on the path to self-actualization.

Creativity

To encourage children to embrace the notion that problems demand creative solutions, teachers and librarians have only to seek out books readily available to them in their classroom, school, and public libraries. For example, the following poem by Jack Prelutsky, *I'm Making a Pizza the Size of the Sun*, is an excellent model for children's creative writing, which is a natural response to their reading.

I'm making a pizza the size of the sun / a pizza that's sure to weigh more than a ton/ a pizza too massive to pick up and toss / a pizza resplendent with oceans of sauce.

I'm topping my pizza with mountains of cheese, with acres of peppers, pimentos, and peas with mushrooms, tomatoes, and sausage galore / with every last olive they had in the store.

My pizza is sure to be one of a kind / my pizza will leave all other pizzas behind / my pizza will be a delectable treat / that all who love pizza are welcome to eat.

The oven is hot, I believe it will take / a year and a half for my pizza to bake/I hardly can wait till my pizza is done / my wonderful pizza the size of the sun.

Jack Prelutsky's poem is particularly appropriate as a model in this chapter about science. And it is interesting to know how the poem came to the author. Flying high above the clouds, watching the sunlight bouncing off the plane's wings, Prelutsky's imagination took flight as lunch was served. Looking at the lasagna on his plate, he thought of pizza, which he loved. Seeing the sun and thinking of pizza caused him to visualize a giant pizza flying through the air like a Frisbee. Other elements of the environment—such as the sky, oceans, and mountains—were interwoven throughout the poem.

Elements of Creativity: Knowledge and Visualization

As we conclude this brief section on creative thinking, we would like you to consider two aspects of creativity that underlie your attempts to blend children's literature into the curriculum: knowledge and visualization.

KNOWLEDGE AND CREATIVITY In Chapter One we described how developmental psychologists struggle to understand the workings of the human brain. Developmental theorists have long insisted that as children assimilate information they translate it in a fashion that is consistent with their developmental level.

Spin Off

Poetry's Link to Science

You can challenge children to write their own poetry about science. Many primary and intermediate school children will be inspired by the humorous poems in the well-known writer Jon Scieszka's book *Science Verse* (2004). Searching for the poetry of science, the boy in the book begins to find the mysteries and beauty of science everywhere. George Ladd, professor of science at Boston College, has been successful in encouraging elementary school children throughout Massachusetts to submit their science poetry in a Science Poetry Contest, which he directs annually. Coincidentally, two of the poems that have been submitted concern topics we discuss in this chapter: *The Environment, and Space,* (excerpts follow). Third-graders Kathleen, Suzanne, and Melissa submitted a poem about the rainforest that reflects their knowledge of the environment and resonates with primary school children.

"The Rainforest"

Do you ever wonder why the rainforest might die?
Because nobody really gives a care,
About the animals that live in there.
From the animals that live in the trees.
To the ones that are as small as bees.
All the rainforests that are around,
Soon will be falling down!

From the toucan with the big colorful beak,
To the little birds that go tweet tweet.
From the heavy rains that fall from the sky
To the rainforests that may soon die!

So snuggle in your bed tonight,
And think of all the things you might do
To help the animals that depend on you!

The astronaut Sally Ride and her experiences at NASA are the subjects of a poem written by Andrew, a fifth-grader.

"Sally Ride"

Sports nut by the age of five,
In tennis, she learns to strive.
She could be a star tennis player,
Or even may be, just maybe, a big city mayor.

Instead she goes to college,
And there she learns a lot of knowledge.
In English and Physics, she gets a degree,
Also in Physics, she gets her Ph.D.

Later, Sally worked at Stanford and now at UCSD
Teaching women to be scientists and engineers,
And maybe if they're lucky
To go out into space and see the things that she sees.

When working with students, suggest that they carefully examine their environment. What are its outstanding features? Urge them to select a theme and write a first draft of a short poem, similar to Prelutsky's. Without pressure, let them use what naturally comes to mind. Suggest ideas they can think about while looking at the sky, or playing with their dog, or watching snow fall.

For example, a teacher tells an 8-year-old child how scientists increased the flow of the Colorado River through the Grand Canyon by opening the water gates from a man-made lake. As she describes the scene, the child shakes her head and exclaims, "Oh, just like the water coming out of the faucet into the sink." The child changed the idea to fit what she knows, but at the same time learned something new. When you think about this, it's hard to avoid the conclusion that nature has programmed children to be creative and look for change. Your awareness of where a young reader is developmentally will inevitably help you to make a connection among the child, literature, and the curriculum.

Molly Cone, in *Come Back Salmon, How a Group of Dedicated Kids Adopted Pigeon Creek and Brought It Back to Life* (1992), an Orbis Pictus Honor Book for outstanding nonfiction, relates a similar story. She describes how a group of elementary school children, once they understood the importance of an unpolluted environment, cleaned a stream in Everett, Washington, seeded it with tiny salmon, and preserved it so the salmon could return to spawn a few years later. The book is a fascinating documentary of how young children approached a scientific endeavor with motivation and creativity.

VISUALIZATION AND CREATIVITY   Sometimes you just have to see it, which brings us to the second aspect of creativity we wish to discuss: visualization. For example, during the hearings on the *Challenger* disaster, Nobel Prize winner and scientist Richard Feynman displayed creativity at a basic level. Believing that the O-rings designed to prevent gas from escaping became brittle at low temperatures, Feynman could visualize what would happen to them. At the next meeting, Feynman dropped a piece of an O-ring into a glass of ice water, waited a few minutes, removed it, and then simply snapped it. It broke immediately, indicating that the failure of the O-rings was inevitable, given the temperatures to which they were exposed (Gleick, 1992).

It's not always easy for teachers and librarians to attempt different things, explore different options with their students, and develop their ability to search for different patterns, because it demands sensitivity, persistence, and understanding. Yet it's possible, and important when introducing children to the study of science, to emphasize discovery and problem solving.

For example, the following experience of what happened when a second-grade teacher read aloud the story *One Hundred Hungry Ants* (Pinczes, 1997) is a lesson in seizing the teachable moment. The story concerns hungry ants heading for a picnic and one ant's frustration (obviously a leader) at their slow pace. When the ants arrive too late and the food is all gone, the children are then asked: what happened?

Their answers are a lesson in creativity. "They had to go around thousands of nasty Ninja turtles." "Bugs from another planet ate the food." "They were on a diet and really didn't want the food." Are these ideas novel? Absolutely. Are they appropriate? They're close enough. But these children demonstrated that *creativity is the application of whatever talent they have in the search for solutions.* The roots of creativity are deeply embedded in children, which should encourage teachers and librarians to search for novel and exciting ways to transfer children's knowledge of literature to their study of science.

The teacher who read this book to her class was so delighted with her students' responses that she decided to read another ant story: *The Life and Times of the Ant* by Charles Micucci (2003). An informational book appropriate for K–3 that details the history, behavior, and attributes of ants, Micucci's book was the ideal follow-up. Written in clear, simple language, it contains a flowchart about life inside an anthill and includes a timeline of an ant's earthly existence. By reading this book aloud and having her students carefully examine the illustrations, she brought her class into *the language of science.*

The students responded in many ways to what they were reading, hearing, and visualizing as they continued to examine other informational books about ants. Two

THE LIFE AND TIMES OF THE ANT
Reprinted by permission of Houghton Mifflin Company

Spotlight On
Thomas Edison

As soon as he could talk he began to ask his parents and everyone else interminable questions. There were so many "whys" and "wheres" and "whats" that Sam Edison, the father of the future scientist and inventor, said that he was often reduced to exhaustion. Tom's mother, however, was more patient.

"Why does the goose squat on the eggs, Mother?" he would ask.

"To keep them warm," she replied.

"Why does she keep them warm?"

"To hatch them, my dear."

Hulton Archive/Getty Images

"What is hatching?"

"That means letting the little geese come out of the shell; they are born that way."

"And does keeping the eggs warm make the little geese come out?" he went on breathlessly.

"Yes."

That afternoon he disappeared for hours. At length his father found him in their neighbor's barn, "curled up in a nest he had made in the barn, filled with goose eggs and chicken eggs. He was actually sitting on the eggs and trying to hatch them" (Baldwin, 1995, p. 18).

We have seen how motivation is essential for children to succeed, yet creativity is equally valuable. How can we encourage creativity along with the motivation that Thomas Edison experienced? First, we need to agree on what is meant by creativity: generating novel and appropriate ideas, a process of which we're all capable. Since psychologists believe creativity is an essential element in human nature, let's explore several methods for encouraging it in young readers.

children discovered the easy-reader *Ants Are Fun (Science I Can Read Books)* by Mildred Myrick in their classroom library. Don, the new kid on the block, introduces Jimmy and Jack to his ant nest, which is mysteriously destroyed a few days later. In the process of building a new one, the three boys learn a great deal about science—habitats, social relations, and food preferences—and decide that ants are fun.

The class begins to think differently—scientifically—about ants. They are not only reading about ants, but are writing stories and poems about ants. Two of the children bring their ant farms from home to explain the ants' habitat to their classmates. They are gaining motivation, exercising creativity, and demonstrating to their teacher that they are ready to become scientists.

Science Literature about the Environment: Early Elementary Grades

Even as early as kindergarten through grade 3, students learn about science through discovery. Children who attend the Davis Elementary School in Bedford, Massachusetts, for example, are introduced to simple techniques for searching, analyzing, and synthesizing information by using a basin near their school as a "fabulous learning laboratory." Although originally built to collect and filter storm-water runoff from the parking lot, Cattail Corner (as the basin is known) is now the place where primary school children learn about wetlands and the creatures that live in them (McDonald, 2005). The Science Literary Center is another place where teachers and school librarians collaborate to provide visuals, computers, internet sites, and appropriate books. Books written by knowledgeable scientists, such as those mentioned below, inspire children's creativity and help them develop a positive attitude toward science from their earliest years.

Well-Known Science Writers

MILLICENT SELSAM. One of the early writers of science for children, Selsam wrote her first book *Egg to Chick* in 1946 about the development of a chicken, familiar to most children. Educated as a botanist and biologist, she captivated children's natural curiosity and used the technique of suggested activities to challenge children, who she believed should learn by doing. She also acquainted children with the scientific method—how to organize and analyze data so that others could duplicate their methods. Later, as a science editor at Walker and Company, she developed the science series *First Look*, which became a mainstay in many elementary science programs (Epstein, 1995).

SEYMOUR SIMON. An award-winning science author of over 150 informational books, Simon knows what appeals to children and how to make new concepts understandable. The manner in which he relates his narrative teaches readers how to frame problems and search for answers on their own. His books *Whales* (1989) and *Oceans* (1990) contain full-page illustrations and detailed descriptions, which characterize all the books he has written (Flynn, 1995).

VICKI COBB. A "hands-on" scientist who encourages an attitude of adventure and risk taking, Cobb encourages children to experiment with things around them. Her book *I Get Wet* (2002) is simple enough for preschoolers to experiment with, while her book *I See Myself* (2002) encourages small children to use a mirror and flashlight to discover the properties of light. She has a knack for simplifying the most difficult concepts (Cooney, 1995).

JOANNA COLE. Joanna Cole turns science into an excursion by taking children on a magical school bus with the strange teacher Miss Frizzle. As drops of rain, the children on this bus examine a city's water supply in *The Magic School Bus at the Waterworks* (1986). As red blood cells, they learn how blood circulates through the body in *The Magic School Bus Inside the Human Body* (1989). Along with her illustrator, Bruce Degen, Cole changed the course of science for children from a serious, somber study to an engaging "trip," complete with word balloons and an uninhibited main character. Fortunately for children, writers like Cole, Selsam, Simon, and Cobb continue to draw young readers to science.

We recommend the following books for further study of these topics. They have been carefully selected from various reading levels, for children to read independently or with help. Research for beginners may be

THE MAGIC SCHOOL BUS LOST IN THE SOLAR SYSTEM
Reprinted by permission of Scholastic Inc.

simple, but scientific information for students throughout the school years should be presented authentically, be attractively illustrated to hold their attention, and be written to motivate them to learn salient scientific facts. In addition to informational books, we also select books from other genres such as picture storybooks, traditional (*pourquoi* tales), science fiction, poetry, and biography that make connections to the science topics they are studying.

Informational Books about Endangered Species

- **WHALES.** One of the *All Aboard Reading* books by Graham Faiella is a brief but informative discussion of various whales, including the endangered blue whale.
- **BIRDS.** Written by Bev Harvey, *Birds* is one of the science books for kindergarten through grade 3 in the *Animal Kingdom* series. In a simple text with clear color photographs, it introduces small children to bird classifications, including wild, domestic, and endangered species such as the whooping crane.
- **MANATEES: PEACEFUL PLANT-EATERS.** This book, written by Adele Richardson, is part of the *Wild World of Animals* series, written for beginning scientists. Only twenty-four pages, it offers information about habitat, enemies, and offspring, as well as sidebars containing additional information.
- **WHALES: STRANGE AND WONDERFUL.** This picture book written by Lawrence Pringle captivates children in kindergarten through third grade with its large illustrations and straightforward content. Pringle is the 1998 Orbis Pictus Award–winning author for *An Extraordinary Life: The Story of a Monarch Butterfly* and many other informational books for children.

Spin Off
The Science Literacy Center (K-3)

In developing a unit on the environment, teachers can collaborate with the school librarian to make certain enough science-oriented books at various reading levels are available in the classroom library. Children are encouraged to read and reread (either independently, with partners, or in small groups) about their subject during the school day. The teacher should prepare a simple science literacy center. It may be a corner of the classroom, a group of tables arranged together, or any space available where small groups of children can go at specific times to work on their observational logs. They then use these to follow the growth of plants or animals, to take notes, or to make charts or diagrams.

Gail Tompkins in *Literacy for the 21st Century* offers the example of a group of second graders

walking in the woods with old socks covering their shoes to collect seeds, in much the same way that animals pick up seeds on their fur coats and transport

them. To simulate winter, the teacher placed the students' socks in the freezer for several weeks. Then they planted one student's sock in the class terrarium and observed it each day as they waited for the seeds to sprout. Students kept science logs with daily entries that were brief, but telling, with unique illustrations.

(Tompkins, 2003, p. 438)

When children in kindergarten through grade 3 are researching a topic such as the environment, they are often asked to brainstorm about what it means to them. Working together, they may develop an *environment web*. After briefly discussing each topic and considering the developmental stage of their students, their familiarity with each concept, and of course, the requirements of the science curriculum for their grade level, their teachers should ask which topics they would like to pursue in depth. Groups of students may then select three of the topics—such as endangered species, pollution, and recycling.

- **TO THE TOP OF THE WORLD. ADVENTURES WITH ARCTIC WOLVES.** Jim Brandenburg is the author of this Orbus Pictus Honor Award book that dispels the myth that wolves are extremely dangerous, as it demonstrates the efforts of dedicated scientists to prevent the extinction of the much-maligned wolf.
- **WILL WE MISS THEM?** Alexandra Wright, an 11-year-old writer, describes each endangered species—its habitat and its enemies—in two pages with full-color illustrations. She answers her title question on the last two pages with a firm YES, giving her reasons why we should protect them.

Informational Books about Pollution

- **MORE NATURE IN YOUR BACKYARD.** This book, written by Susan Lang, is recommended for the teacher's use and for third-graders who read well. It provides simple, scientific, hands-on activities for children. Organized into five categories—insects, birds, snow, soil, and plants—it offers suggestions such as how to preserve a spider web and how to use soil to clean water. It makes use of common materials and provides clear directions, a bibliography, and index.
- **KEEPING THE AIR CLEAN.** Written by John Baines for the highly motivated child, the entire *Protecting Our Planet* series demonstrates how to keep the air and water clean, and discusses waste, recycling, and reuse. Younger children can benefit from the detailed information the books provide, if the teacher reads aloud and explains small segments of pertinent topics.

Informational Books about Recycling

- **RECYCLE EVERY DAY!** Here is a book written by Nancy Wallace that is filled with information about ways to recycle: donating clothing, composting, using cloth bags instead of paper bags for groceries, and using products from recycled material. It is also the picture storybook of Minna the Bunny and her efforts to create a prizeworthy environmental poster.
- **WE NEED GARBAGE COLLECTORS.** In this book from the *Helpers in Our Community* series, Lisa Trumbauer describes the invaluable contributions made by people who keep neighborhoods clean and safe. Each page of this small, square book contains a full-page color photo that faces a simple sentence in large type.

Picture StoryBooks about the Environment (Endangered Species, Pollution, Recycling)

- **I STINK!** Kate McMullan's popular picture book, illustrated by Jim McMullan, is narrated by a tough, loud-talking garbage truck that explains to its young readers how it takes care of all the bags of trash it collects while the neighborhood sleeps. It even alphabetically lists what it picks up—arousing not only the readers' senses of sight (through cartoon-like illustrations) and hearing, but taste and smell as well.
- **WHAT DO YOU DO WITH A TAIL LIKE THIS?** In this Caldecott Honor book, Steve and Robin Jenkins offer riddles that challenge small children to match the parts of the animals partially depicted on the pages. It also includes fascinating facts of nature.
- **JOSEPH HAD A LITTLE OVERCOAT.** In this story Joseph's overcoat is recycled into many other pieces of clothing, down to the last button. Here is a

charming retelling by Simms Taback of a Yiddish folktale, complete with words, music, and outstanding Caldecott Medal illustrations.

- **BIG MOMMA MAKES THE WORLD.** Phyllis Root wrote this *Boston Globe–Horn Book* Honor book, illustrated in pastel tones by Helen Oxenbury. The story places a mother with her infant on a soft cloud in the center of the universe, where she gently pleads with her readers to "take care of the earth."

- **THE POLAR BEARS ARE HUNGRY.** Carol Carrick, through her beautiful illustrations, points out how global warming has affected the polar bears' environment.

Biographies of Environmentalists

- **RACHEL CARSON: AUTHOR AND ENVIRONMENTALIST.** Charan Simon tells the story of Rachel Carson, author of *The Silent Spring*, who began the environmental movement in the 1950s. It also highlights the events of her life for young children.

- **JOHN MUIR, AMERICA'S NATURALIST.** The emphasis in this book is on Muir's efforts to preserve nature as opposed to being a comprehensive look at his life. Through Thomas Locker's exquisite illustrations, this book conveys the vastness and magnificence of Yosemite National Park, which intrigued Muir and motivated him to found the Sierra Club. The book is beautifully illustrated in blue, green, and gold tones. Full-page scenes of forests and mountains motivate children to take care of the natural world.

Spin Off

Interacting with Books about the Environment

Readers' Theater

Patrick Dias, writing in *Making Meaning in the Response-Based Classroom* (2002), suggests that children who enact a play from a book improve their self-confidence, develop a spirit of cooperation, and extend their reading experience. Often called Readers' Theater, the play must include parts for all students and contain peppy dialogue. (The audience seems to respond more actively to a play that is light-hearted and frequently humorous.)

Children find it exciting to help their teacher write and perform in a play such as one based on *Joseph Had a Little Overcoat*. With the encouragement of their teacher, one group of third-grade students could turn the narrative into dialogue and perform simple actions in front of the class, without diverging from the developing plot and characters as they understand them. Another group could be a chorus and sing the song "I Had a Little Overcoat" (words and music are at the back of the book).

Posters, Stickers, and Badges

Kindergarten and first-grade children can imitate Minna the Rabbit in *Recycle Every Day!* by Nancy Wallace by making colorful posters, stickers, and even badges. These activities are an effective way for them to spread the word about protecting the environment. Other projects could include writing original slogans or rephrasing old ones such as "Save the World: Protect the Animals, Keep the Water Clean, Stop Pollution." These could then be displayed in their classroom and throughout the school.

Recycled Inventions

Second- and third-graders display their creativity by making their own inventions using trash or recycled materials. One third-grade class worked in small groups to assemble pieces of rubbish (tin cans, twigs, boxes, etc.) into heaps, then arranged them in a darkened room in front of a screen and shone a spotlight on them. Amazing figures appeared!

Poetry about the Environment
(Early Elementary Grades)

- **SPLISH SPLASH.** Joan Bransfield Graham encourages children to think about water as they read these twenty-one concrete poems about the various forms of water: ponds, oceans, icicles, and steam. The poems are also springboards for a scientific discussion of the environment.
- **DEAR WORLD.** *Dear World* by Takayo Noda is a book of short poems written for small children in the voice of a small child. Trees, flowers, stars, and other natural objects are illustrated with colorful cut-paper and watercolor collages that make each scene come alive.
- **TALKING LIKE THE RAIN.** These read-to-me poems edited by X. J. and Dorothy M. Kennedy captivate children by their fresh expressions. One section about birds, bugs, and beasts is particularly pertinent to the study of endangered animals.

Science Literature about Space
Exploration: The Intermediate Grades

Although President John F. Kennedy made a pledge early in 1961 that America would send a man to the moon, it wasn't until the last part of that decade that three astronauts—Neil Armstrong, Edwin Aldrin, and Michael Collins—were launched on Apollo 11 to travel 25,000 miles an hour to the moon. On July 20, 1969, Armstrong and Aldrin emerged from the landing craft Eagle and walked on that part of the moon called the Sea of Tranquility. Collins remained in the command module. It was a dramatic moment when Armstrong and Aldrin later reentered the module, thanks to Collins' ability to rendezvous with the Eagle, and then head for home.

Since America and the world watched the landing of the Spirit rover on Mars on January 4, 2004, interest in space has been reignited. As we enter the twenty-first century, another president (Bush) has predicted that America will put a man on "Mars within a decade." Children who are currently learning about science are now looking forward to someday watching (or being) the first American to land on Mars! But first, it is important that they have a knowledge of the history, background, successes, and failures of space exploration.

THE VALUE OF PROBLEM SOLVING   Besides briefly reviewing the history of flight, teachers in grades 4 and up should consider how many science books with *recent copyright dates* are on the shelves of their classroom library. How much technological information is available from the school and local public libraries? What hands-on materials should be included in a science literacy center, where individual students and small groups can conduct research independently, and what approach should students use to write their scientific research?

Then and Now

Pioneers in the Sky

For centuries the study of space has intrigued philosophers, astronomers, and mathematicians. As long ago as the second century BC, Hipparchus, a Greek astronomer, tried to discover how far the sun was from Earth. Hundreds of years later, authors and illustrators continue to draw children's attention to men like Copernicus (1473), who dared suggest that the sun was the center of the solar system and that the Earth and other planets revolved around it. Peter Sis, in 1996, adapted the title of Galileo's book *The Starry Messenger* to describe and illustrate the life of this sixteenth-century genius who invented a telescope to further his observations of space.

THE STARRY MESSENGER
Used by permission of Farrar, Straus, & Giroux, LLC.
Jacket design from THE STARRY MESSENGER by
Peter Sis. Copyright © 1996 by Peter Sis.

Laurence Anholt (2000) weaves a fictitious tale about another Renaissance man, Leonardo da Vinci (*Leonardo and the Flying Boy*), which revolves around da Vinci's two apprentices and their discovery of da Vinci's revolutionary design for a flying machine, the precursor of all aviation crafts.

It was not until the twentieth century, however, in Dayton, Ohio, that the Wright brothers invented a controlled, heavier-than-air flying machine that worked. It made its first flight at Kitty Hawk, North Carolina, on December 17, 1903. Since then a plethora of writers, including Russell Freedman (*The Wright Brothers: How They Invented the Airplane*, grades 5–9), Stephen Krensky (*Taking Flight: The Story of the Wright Brothers*, grades 2 and up), and Wendie Old (*To Fly: The Story of the Wright Brothers*, grades 3–5), have celebrated this historic scientific accomplishment that occurred over 100 years ago.

As described in Bo Zaunders' *Feathers, Flaps, and Flops: Fabulous Early Fliers* (grades 3–6), many attempts have been made to conquer the sky: from the hot-air balloonists of the 1700s, to Wrong-Way Corrigan in 1938, to the first black female pilot, Bessie Coleman. At the time that Bessie (*Bessie Coleman: Daring to Fly* by Sally Walker) was quietly making aviation history, Charles Lindbergh stunned the world by flying the *Spirit of St. Louis* solo from New York to Paris nonstop in 1927. Orbis Pictus Award winner Robert Burleigh chronicles this historic mission in *Flight: The Journey of Charles Lindbergh*, a first-person narrative that keeps young readers in suspense for the 3,600-mile, thirty-hour trip across the Atlantic (Zarnowski, 2001). James Cross Giblin offers the older reader (10 and up) another view of Lindbergh in his *Charles Lindbergh: A Human Hero*, in which he personalizes the pilot and points out his flaws (e.g., his Nazi sympathies) as well as his remarkable successes.

Teachers and librarians owe a debt of gratitude to the Smithsonian National Air and Space Museum for its contribution to the history of flight. Without the use of the thousands of photographs and memorabilia including stamps, patches, and posters from the museum, books such as *Flight: 100 Years of Aviation*, written by R. C. Grant for young adults, and Judith Rinard's *The Story of Flight: The Smithsonian National Air and Space Museum* would not be so riveting. Rinard's book, detailing the history of flight from hot-air balloons to spacecraft headed for Mars, is a concise and informative overview for students who are studying pioneers in the sky.

Currently, the Big6 model, an information problem solving strategy devised by Mike Eisenberg and Bob Berkowitz, is being successfully used throughout the United States to teach students problem solving and decision making techniques. Based on Vygotsky's idea of scaffolding, students are taught to approach a problem by using the following six stages:

1. Task definition
2. Information-seeking strategies
3. Location and access
4. Use of information
5. Synthesis
6. Evaluation

In addition, two substages are included in each main category (which are often called the Little 12). *www.big6.com/kids*

By selecting such topics as women in space, the planets, and the language of space, students in the intermediate grades ready themselves for the countdown–all systems are GO for further investigation into space exploration.

Informational Books about Women in Space

- **EXPLORING OUR SOLAR SYSTEM.** This book, co-authored by astronaut Sally Ride with Tam O'Shaughnessy, along with *Voyager: An Adventure to the Edge of the Solar System* and *The Third Planet: Exploring the Earth from Space*, are scholarly and scientific, but simplify complex concepts so that intermediate and middle school level students achieve a goodness-of-fit.

- **ALMOST HEAVEN: THE STORY OF WOMEN IN SPACE.** This book written for adults by Bettyann Holtzmann Kevles, emphasizes the struggle women have experienced penetrating a profession that was originally closed to them. Students in grades 4 and 5 would be interested in a read-aloud of selected sections. The story of how women overcame the competition and legal restrictions to become the pilots, scientists, engineers, and physicians that NASA needs is inspiring.

- **THE SKY'S THE LIMIT: STORIES OF DISCOVERY BY WOMEN AND GIRLS.** Catherine Thimmesh offers students brief insights into the contributions made to science by women such as astronomer Vera Rubin, whose "dark matter" theory revolutionized how scientists view the cosmos.

- **WOMEN OF SPACE.** Laura Woodmansee has conducted over one hundred personal interviews with women in NASA and provides the reader with many personal anecdotes explaining why these women chose space as a career. Subjects range from Claudia Alexander, who is a project manager and research scientist, to Clarice Lolkich, a space educator and solar system ambassador. Clarice is also a member of a religious order of nuns, and she bungee-jumped when she was 75 years old and celebrated her 80th birthday by skydiving!

Informational Books about the Planets

- **SEEING EARTH FROM SPACE.** NASA photographs complement this Orbis Pictus Honor book by Patricia Lauber that provides a unique perspective of the earth as "one planet, small and fragile, wondrous and lovely" (Lauber, 1990,

p. 75). It introduces children to space terms such as *remote sensing*, *atoll*, and *spectral signature*, along with amazing images that can be accessed through advanced space technology.

- **THE MAGIC SCHOOL BUS LOST IN THE SOLAR SYSTEM.** In this book Joanna Cole introduces children to Miss Frizzle and her students as they float in space and examine the planets they encounter. Her students, dressed in space suits, prepare science reports by answering familiar questions—What is gravity? Why is it so hot on Venus? Readers are offered a planet chart and a mobile of the solar system to help them on their vicarious trip through the solar system.

- **HOME ON THE MOON: LIVING ON A SPACE FRONTIER.** Author Marianne Dyson was a NASA flight activities officer in Mission Control when she began writing children's books about space. When *Home on the Moon* won a Golden Kite award, she felt that she was truly helping "children reach for the stars."

- **LOOKING FOR LIFE IN THE UNIVERSE: THE SEARCH FOR EXTRATERRESTRIAL INTELLIGENCE.** Here is Ellen Jackson's fascinating look at the work of the Search for Extraterrestrial Intelligence (SETI) program, which analyzes radio signals from space for signs of intelligent life.

- **OUR SOLAR SYSTEM.** In this book and *The Long View into Space*, Seymour Simon gives students an overview of the solar system and specific space missions, and explains how space is measured.

Informational Books about the Language of Space

- **THE NATIONAL AIR AND SPACE MUSEUM ABCs.** Florence Cassen Mayers has written this book to help children understand and identify numerous space terms. It defines not only words like *telescope*, but describes the kinds of observatories that relate to telescopes, the early discoveries of telescopes, and information that helps children to expand their knowledge of space terms.

- **1000 FACTS OF SPACE.** Children will appreciate the concise information, full-color illustrations, and "fascinating facts" contained in this encyclopedic compilation written by John Farndon. Six units cover the earth, sun and moon, the planets, the stars, the universe, and astronomy and space travel. A fourteen-page index is also included.

Science Fiction

- **NORBY AND THE INVADERS.** This is one of six books in a series written by Isaac and Janet Asimov that also includes *Norby, the Mixed-Up Robot*, *Norby and the Lost Princess*, and *Norby Finds a Villain*. All are lighthearted, fantastic tales of Norby, the barrel-shaped robot, and his friend Jeff, who become entangled in far-out escapades on other planets and thereby involve children in reading about space. Asimov, a leader in science fiction, wrote over 350 books about every aspect of science.

- **ALIENS ATE MY HOMEWORK.** Intermediate school students will read with delight Bruce Coville's popular *My Teacher* series. When Rod Allbright tells his teacher Miss Maloney that aliens ate his homework, his teacher is mystified. In other books in the series, Rod also claims that *My Teacher Is an Alien*, *My Teacher Fried My Brains*, and *My Teacher Glows in the Dark*.

SCIENCE FICTION FOR THE HIGHLY MOTIVATED READER   Recently reissued books by Robert Heinlein (*Rocket Ship Galileo, Beyond this Horizon, The Red Planet,* and *Orphans of the Sky*) and John Christopher (*The White Mountains, The City of Gold and Lead,* and *The Pool of Fire*) are challenging and interesting.

SCIENCE FICTION FOR THE RELUCTANT READER

- **SOMETHING QUEER IN OUTER SPACE.** Humorously written by Elizabeth Levy, this story about the first dog in outer space is especially appealing to the reluctant reader.
- **TAKE ME TO THE MOON!** This fun-to-read book by Sal Murdocca is an amusing, easy-reading, out-of-this world adventure with the Queen, the Carpenter, the Astrologer, and, most prominently, Theresa the Dragon.
- **COMMANDER TOAD AND THE INTERGALACTIC SPY.** This humorous and engaging introduction into the genre of science fiction by Jane Yolen introduces young children to the irrepressible Commander Toad, the captain of Star Warts, who sends "Tip Toad through the tulips" to find out who among the monsters is the real Tip Toad.

Traditional Literature: Pourquoi Tales

These tales are told throughout the world to explain natural phenomena by answering the question *why?* in a decidedly non-scientific manner—a feature that teachers and librarians can use to segue into a discussion of scientific versus non-scientific explanations of natural phenomena.

- **THE SUN, THE MOON, AND THE SILVER BABOON.** An amusing story about the influence of the sun and the moon on the colorful coat of the baboon has been retold by Susan Field.
- **MUSICIANS OF THE SUN.** An Aztec myth retold and strikingly illustrated by award-winning artist Gerald McDermott, *Musicians of the Sun* tells the *pourquoi* story of how color and sound came to the earth when the Lord of Night granted freedom to four musicians who were being held hostage by the sun.
- **TALES FROM THE RAIN FOREST: MYTHS AND LEGENDS FROM THE AMAZONIAN INDIANS OF BRAZIL.** Ten simply told *pourquoi* tales, retold by Mercedes Dorson and Jeanne Wilmot, cover the origins of humans and animals, night and the stars, and thunder and lightning. Such stories often motivate children to create their own *pourquoi* tales.

Science Literature about the Brain: The Middle School

We recently asked Maddie, an 11-year-old soccer player, to describe for us what she thought as she was racing down the field. Maddie is quite patient with the curious questions of adults, and after looking at us quizzically, she said that first she would have to decide whether to pass or shoot. "I'd pass if I had to go through the defense; Lauren would pass back and I'd score. Or she would shoot and I'd be there for the rebound if she missed. But if there were no defense, I'd take the shot. If our goalie made a good save and a good drop kick out to me, I'd do a scissors to get by the defense and shoot. But if someone got behind the defense, I'd pass.

What does this have to do with the brain of a middle school child? We can answer with one word: everything! Imagine the thoughts of these two players as they make split-second decisions on what to do for their team. *Memory* has to enter into their decision as they rapidly recall what happened in previous, similar situations. This means that the hippocampus area of the brain, which is crucial for memory, is activated. Clearly, *problem solving* is necessary, which requires involvement of the frontal area of the cerebral cortex. Were the young girls' *emotions* aroused? Of course—goes without saying. Consequently, the brain area known as the amygdala swings into action.

It's estimated that children of these years have *100 billion neurons* active in their brains! With this kind of brain power at their disposal, we can safely state that teachers and librarians must motivate these young readers to read at whatever level is suitable for them to fulfill their potential. Middle school students usually enjoy investigating one of the following topics: memory, emotions, and problem solving.

Informational Books about Memory

- **PHINEAS GAGE: A GRUESOME BUT TRUE STORY ABOUT BRAIN SCIENCE.** This mysterious case study by John Fleischman is about a railroad worker who had an iron rod blast through his head in 1848, but lived to tell about

Spin Off
Interacting with Books about Space

Space Cards from A to Z

After reading Mayers' *The National Air and Space Museum ABCs* and Farndon's *1000 Facts of Space*, children may like to make their own space cards about space themes. Examples could be a series on heroes in space, space vehicles, the planets, and so on. Cards would be the size of baseball cards with an illustration on one side and statistics on the other. They could be traded, used as playing cards, or included in games such as What's my name? Who am I? What is my job in space?

Interview with a Pioneer in the Sky

Using whatever technology is available, along with carefully detailed planning and research, children can conduct interviews with persons pretending to be space pioneers. Interviews could be conducted using a video camera. Background music could be added to the tape. This project requires time and help from a teacher who understands that careful preparation should be done before using the technology.

Space Newspaper

A newspaper is fun to create, provided that children know beforehand what their jobs will be. Have them submit preliminary copies of their articles to a senior editor for editing, and then to the teacher, before "going to press." Besides the senior editor, children may enjoy being a news editor, food editor, travel editor, opinion editor, advertising editor, and so on. Let their imaginations be their guide! The topic is space, but the newspaper could have as many articles on the various aspects of space as their creativity allows. Children especially enjoy drawing comics and writing and illustrating the real estate section (which describes a house for sale on Mars, for example). It is an effective way to integrate their skills, energize their motivation, and stimulate their creativity. It could also be created by using the newsletter template in Claris Works or Microsoft Word.

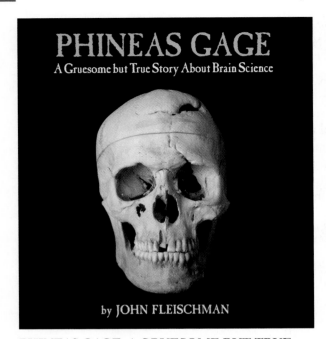

PHINEAS GAGE
A Gruesome but True Story About Brain Science

by JOHN FLEISCHMAN

PHINEAS GAGE: A GRUESOME BUT TRUE STORY ABOUT BRAIN SCIENCE
Reprinted by permission of Houghton Mifflin Company

it. A medical debate lasted long after his death in 1860, and questions still linger: How did his brain endure such abuse? What do we know about the brain now that we did not know then? Photographs, computer-generated reconstructions, and a horrific cover photograph add to the story's authenticity.

- **HOW THE BRAIN LEARNS.** David Sousa not only includes basic brain facts, but explains how the brain processes information. He devotes considerable space to memory, retention, and learning. This is an excellent resource for teachers and students.

Informational Books about Emotions

- **IT'S PERFECTLY NORMAL: A BOOK ABOUT CHANGING BODIES, GROWING UP, SEX, AND SEXUAL HEALTH.** In chapters such as "Back and Forth, Up and Down," Robie Harris discusses the changing emotions of boys and girls from age 9 to 15, along with many frank sex discussions and detailed illustrations about teens' changing bodies.

- **RECOGNIZING YOUR EMOTIONS.** Emotions are only one of the many topics relevant to middle school students that are discussed in the five-volume *Managing Your Teenage Life* from *World Book Encyclopedia*.

Informational Books about Problem Solving

- **BRAIN: INNER WORKINGS OF THE GRAY MATTER.** Richard Walker has managed to present an uncomplicated examination of the evolution of the brain that includes a brief history of neurological theory, senses in humans and animals, and brain teasers that are especially appealing to middle school students.

- **YOU'RE SMARTER THAN YOU THINK: A KID'S GUIDE TO MULTIPLE INTELLIGENCES.** Young readers will enjoy reading this interesting, informative, and appropriate discussion by Thomas Armstrong about Howard Gardner's theory of multiple intelligences, which is done in an exceptionally creative format.

Contemporary Realistic Fiction

- **THE LAST TREASURE.** *The Last Treasure* by Janet Anderson is a fascinating read for children who are problem solvers. Two young teens who are cousins seek a treasure left behind by the family patriarch. The clues and miscues they find on the map, and their growing understanding of each other and the older members of their family, make this a worthwhile challenge.

- **POINT BLANK: AN ALEX RIDER ADVENTURE.** Readers familiar with other books in this series by Anthony Horowitz will look forward to this new adventure of Alex Rider, a 14-year-old member of Great Britain's intelligence organization. He has been asked to find out what happened to the boys in a boarding school in the French Alps, whose brains have been mysteriously altered.

Science Fiction

- **DR. FRANKLIN'S ISLAND.** Ann Halam is the author of this science fiction novel involving three teenagers who land on an island thought to be deserted, only to discover a band of humans living there. They are aghast to learn that the brains of these people have been genetically altered by the scientist Dr. Franklin, who plans to genetically reengineer their brains as well.
- **EVA.** The title character in this novel by the English writer Peter Dickinson is horror-stricken when, as a result of a serious accident, she awakens in a hospital room to discover that her brain has been transplanted into a chimpanzee's body. What follows is a well-written adventure with a subtle message about the problems of over-population, endangered species, and the ethical limits of science.
- **A WRINKLE IN TIME.** Madeleine L'Engle's (1962) Newbery Medal book emphasizes the power of the brain and how it affects the Murry's children's search for their scientist father, who has "tesseracted" to another planet.

Science Literature about the Human Genome Project: High School

At first glance, James Watson and Francis Crick looked like any other young instructors at England's Cambridge University. But there was soon to be something quite different about them. On a winter's day in 1953, they shocked the biological world and took the first step toward their future Nobel Prizes when they burst into a pub near their laboratory and announced to their astonished colleagues that "they had discovered the secret of life." Just hours before, they had finally determined the exact model of DNA. After years of theory building, testing, failure, and theory revision, Watson and Crick persevered and triumphed. The significance of their discovery can't be overlooked. As Watson noted in a speech delivered at Cold Spring Harbor Laboratory in 1989:

When finally interpreted, the genetic messages encoded within our DNA molecule will provide the ultimate answers to the chemical underpinnings of human existence.

These strong words reflected the magnitude of the work that signaled a new era in biology (Dacey & Travers, 2009). On June 26, 2000, Dr. Francis Collins (director of the National Human Genome Research Institute) and Dr. J. Craig Venter (president of Celera Genomics) announced at a White House ceremony that they had completed a rough draft of the human genome (the total number and arrangement of human genes). Young adult readers, with their growing knowledge of the tremendous biological advances of the past years, will enjoy reading about the lives of those involved and the challenges they faced.

Informational Books about the Human Genome Project

- **THE HUMAN GENOME PROJECT: WHAT DOES DECODING DNA MEAN FOR US?** In the young adult *Issues in Focus* series, Kevin Alexander Boon offers helpful information about genetics and the genome project, as well as a discussion of the ethical and legal problems surrounding the decoding.

- **DNA.** In the young adult *Science Concepts* series, Alvin Silverstein clearly explains the meaning, reproduction, and disorders of the smallest units of life. Profusely illustrated with diagrams, color photographs, and photomicrographs, it also includes sidebars, additional facts, bibliography, glossary, and index.

- **GENETICS.** Four volumes in the Macmillan Science Library series contain over 250 articles edited by Richard Robinson, which gives information on everything high school students need to know about genetics. Color photographs, detailed diagrams, and tables add to the usefulness of these reference books. Concise definitions and important terms are printed in boldface and explained in the margin.

- **MEDICINE'S BRAVE NEW WORLD: BIOENGINEERING AND THE NEW GENETICS.** This is a young adult book written by Margaret O. Hyde and John F. Setaro that introduces readers to recent medical advancements such as cloning, gene therapy, and stem cell treatments. Using understandable scientific language, it balances the discussion of its topics with rational explanations of their ethical ramifications.

Science Fiction

- **THE HOUSE OF THE SCORPION.** Nancy Farmer, a well-known science fiction writer, delves into futuristic themes, cloning, and drugs in this exciting tale.

- **THE GIVER.** It would be a serious omission if Lois Lowry's *The Giver* were not mentioned as a significant book of science fiction that demonstrates how mind control affects behavior.

Biography

- **BARBARA MCCLINTOCK: GENETICIST.** In this book from the *Women in Science* series, J. Heather Cullen briefly tells the story of Nobel Prize winner Barbara McClin-

THE HOUSE OF THE SCORPION
Reprinted with the permission of Atheneum Books for Young Readers , an imprint of Simon & Schuster Children's Publishing Division from THE HOUSE OF SCORPION. Jacket illustration copyright © 2002 Russell Gordon.

tok, who discovered mobile genetic elements. This biography includes sidebars, photographs, a bibliography, and an index.

• **FRANCIS CRICK AND JAMES WATSON: PIONEERS IN DNA RESEARCH.** In the *Unlocking the Secrets of Science* series, John Bankston provides the high school reader with basic information about the contributions of two famous geneticists. The information is well presented, but the black and white photographs and lack of diagrams somewhat hinder the value of this book.

Poetry

• **IMAGINATION'S OTHER PLACE: POEMS OF SCIENCE AND MATHEMATICS.** The thoughtful young adult reader will appreciate Helen Plotz's compilation of science poetry that includes works by T. S. Eliot, Ogden Nash, Dylan Thomas, and others.

Contemporary Realistic Fiction

• **DOUBLE HELIX.** Although the title is formidable and the cover unattractive, the content of Nancy Werlin's young adult novel is exciting for mature high school students who are acquainted with the awesome power of the human gene. The narrator, Eli Samuels, has discovered that his mother is insane due to a genetic problem called Huntington's disease. Eli declines being tested to find out whether or not he has the dangerous gene, and goes to work in a research laboratory, where he is befriended by a Nobel Prize winning scientist. There he discovers a secret sub-basement that holds many biological secrets. Questions about the pros and cons of genetic engineering are interwoven in the plot.

Spin Off
Interacting with Books about the Genome Project

Conversations and shared reading. Louise Rosenblatt would describe shared reading as a *transaction between teacher, text, and students* that draws students into a clearer understanding of a topic that is read aloud and then discussed. A guest expert, who may be a practicing psychologist, a university professor, or a research scientist, could be invited to join students in a *conversation about the genome project.* Students' questions and concerns could be the focus of discussion.

High school science teachers are fortunate when they can draw on resources from science and technology centers to motivate their students' interest in science. The Massachusetts Institute of Technology, for example, offers summer programs to teachers at their Haystack Observatory, where they work with staff scientists developing new science projects that teachers can use in their schools.

Debate. A spirited debate arouses interest among high school students when it is carefully and thoughtfully presented. Students can listen to both sides of a question, whether it concerns the ethics of human cloning or the unrestricted use of stem cell experimentation.

Science fair material. Students are often at a loss about how to prepare an assignment, such as one on *the Human Genome Project,* for the inevitable science fair. Bill Haduch's *Science Fair Success Secrets: How to Win Prizes, Have Fun, and Think Like a Scientist* tells students everything they would like to know about how to activate their natural curiosity, and, most importantly, how to conduct a good scientific inquiry.

Chapter Checklist

Read the following items carefully. If you have difficulty responding to any of them, return to the chapter to review the material.

After reading this chapter, you can

1. Evaluate the power of motivation in a children's literature program.

2. Explain how a theory such as Maslow's aids teachers and librarians in their efforts to satisfy children's needs through reading.

3. Describe how teachers and librarians can encourage students to seek creative solutions to their problems based on what they have read.

4. Demonstrate how an informational book such as Molly Cone's *Come Back Salmon* presents an attractive model of creative thinking for young readers.

5. Illustrate the techniques you would use in designing a Science Literacy Center.

6. Identify several books that help children learn about their environment in an interesting and stimulating manner.

7. Specify how the theory of readers' responses can guide children's selections of pertinent science books.

8. Evaluate the importance of narratives such as those in *Pioneers in the Sky* in the science curriculum.

9. Identify stories about the human brain that can help middle schoolers appreciate the significance of a stimulating environment for brain development.

10. Describe how colorful and exciting stories about our genetic heritage encourage young adult readers to view science as a key element in our lives.

Children's Bibliography

Anderson, Janet. (2003). *The Last Treasure*. New York: Dutton.

Anderson, M. T. (2002). *Feed*. Cambridge, MA: Candlewick.

Anholt, Laurence. (2000). *Leonardo and the Flying Boy*. New York: Barron's.

Apfel Necia H. (1991). *Voyager to the Planets*. New York: Clarion.

Armstrong, Thomas. (2002). *You're Smarter Than You Think: A Kid's Guide to Multiple Intelligences*. Minneapolis, MN: Free Spirit.

Asimov, Janet, & Asimov, Isaac. (1985). *Norby and the Invaders*. New York: Walker.

Asimov, Janet, & Asmov, Isaac. (1987). *Norby Finds a Villain*. New York: Walker.

Baines, John. (1998). *Keeping the Air Clean*. New York: Raintree.

Bankston, John. (2002). *Francis Crick and James Watson: Pioneers in DNA Research*. New York: Mitchell.

Boon, Kevin Alexander (2002). *The Human Genome Project: What Does Decoding DNA Mean for Us?* Berkeley Heights, NJ: Enslow.

Brandenburg, Jim. (1993). *To the Top of the World: Adventures with Arctic Wolves*. New York: Walker.

Burleigh, Robert. (1991). *Flight: The Journey of Charles Lindbergh*. New York: Philomel.

Carrick, Carol. (2002). *The Polar Bears Are Hungry*. New York: Clarion.

Christopher, John. (2003). *The City of Gold and Lead*. New York: Simon.

Christopher, John. (2003). *The Pool of Fire*. New York: Simon.

Christopher, John. (2003). *The White Mountains*. New York: Simon.

Cobb, Vickie. (2002). *I See Myself*. New York: HarperCollins.

Cobb, Vickie. (2002). *I Get Wet*. New York: HarperCollins.

Cole, Joanna. (1986). *The Magic School Bus at the Waterworks*. New York: Scholastic.

Cole, Joanna. (1989). *The Magic School Bus Inside the Human Body*. New York: Scholastic.

Cole, Joanna. (1990). *The Magic School Bus Lost in the Solar System*. New York: Scholastic.

Collins, Michael. (1994). *Flying to the Moon: An Astronaut's Story*. New York: Farrar, Straus, & Giroux.

Cone, Molly. (1992). *Come Back Salmon, How a Group of Dedicated Kids Adopted Pigeon Creek and Brought It Back to Life*. San Francisco: Sierra Club.

Coville, Bruce. (1993). *Aliens Ate My Homework*. New York: Pocket Books.

Cullen, J. Heather. (2003). *Barbara McClintock: Geneticist*. Philadelphia: Chelsea. House.

Dewey, Jennifer Owings. (1994). *Wildlife Rescue: The Work of Dr. Kathleen Ramsay*. Honesdale, PA: Boyds Mills.

Dickinson, Peter. (1990). *Eva*. New York: Dell.

Dorson, M., & Wilmot, J. (1997). *Tales from the Rain Forest: Myths and Legends from the Amazonian Indians of Brazil*. Hopewell, NJ: Ecco Press.

Dyson, Marianne. (2003). *Home on the Moon: Living on a Space Frontier*. Washington, DC: National Geographic.

Faiella, Graham. (2002). *Whales*. New York: Grosset.

Farmer, Nancy. (2002). *The House of the Scorpion*. New York: Atheneum.

Farndon, John. (2001). *1000 Facts of Space*. New York: Barnes and Noble.

Field. Susan. (1993). *The Sun, the Moon, and the Silver Baboon*. New York: HarperCollins.

Fleischman, John. (2002). *Phineas Gage: A Gruesome but True Story about Brain Science*. Boston: Houghton Mifflin.

Frank, E. R. (2002). *America*. New York: Atheneum.

Freedman, Russell. (1991). *The Wright Brothers: How They Invented the Airplane*. New York: Holiday House.

Giblin, James Cross. (1997). *Charles Lindbergh: A Human Hero*. New York: Clarion Books.

Graham, Joan Bransfield. (1994). *Splish Splash*. New York: Ticknor & Fields.

Grant, R. C. (2002). *Flight: 100 Years of Aviation*. New York: DK Publishers.

Halam, Ann. (2002). *Dr. Franklin's Island*. New York: Dell.

Haduch, Bill. (2002). *Science Fair Success Secrets: How to Win Prizes, Have Fun, and Think Like a Scientist*. New York: Dutton.

Harris, Robie H. (1994). *It's Perfectly Normal: A Book about Changing Bodies, Growing Up, Sex, and Sexual Health*. Cambridge, MA: Candlewick.

Harvey, Bev. (2002). *Birds*. New York: Chelsea Clubhouse.

Heinlein, Robert. (1947). *Rocket Ship Galileo*. New York: Scribner.

Heinlein, Robert. (1947). *The Red Planet*. New York: Ballantine.

Heinlein, Robert. (1948). *Beyond This Horizon*. New York: Grossett & Dunlap.

Heinlein, Robert. (1987). *Orphans of the Sky*. New York: Ace Books.

Horowitz, Anthony. (2002). *Point Blank: An Alex Rider Adventure*. New York: Philomel.

Hyde, Margaret O., & Setaro, John F. (2001). *Medicine's Brave New World: Bioengineering and the New Genetics*. Brookfield, CT: Twenty-first Century.

Jackson, Ellen. (2000). *Looking for Life in the Universe: The Search for Extraterrestrial Intelligence*. Boston: Houghton Mifflin.

Jenkins, Steve, & Jenkins, Robin. (2003). *What Do You Do with a Tail Like This?* Boston: Houghton Mifflin.

Kennedy, X. J. & Kennedy, Dorothy. (1992). *Talking Like the Rain*. Boston: Little, Brown.

Kevles, Bettyann Holtzmann. (2003). *Almost Heaven: The History of Women in Space*. New York: Basic Books.

Krensky, Stephen. (2000). *Taking Flight: The Story of the Wright Brothers*. New York: Simon & Schuster.

Lang, Susan. (1998). *More Nature in Your Backyard*. New York: Milbrook.

Lauber, Patricia. (1990). *Seeing Earth from Space*. (1990). New York: Orchard.

L'Engle, Madeleine. (1962). *A Wrinkle in Time*. New York: Farrar, Straus, & Giroux.

Levy, Elizabeth. (1993). *Something Queer in Outer Space*. New York: Hyperion.

Locker, Thomas. (2003). *John Muir, America's Naturalist.* Golden, CO: Fulcrum.

Lowry, Lois. (1993). *The Giver.* Boston: Houghton Mifflin.

Mayers, Florence Cassen. (1987). *The National Air and Space Museum ABCs.* New York: Harry N. Abrams, Inc.

McDermott, Gerald. (1997). *Musicians of the Sun.* New York: Simon & Schuster.

McMullan, Kate. (2002). *I Stink!* New York: HarperCollins.

McNulty, Faith. (2005). *If You Decide to Go to the Moon.* New York: Scholastic.

Micucci, Charles. (2003). *The Life and Times of the Ant.* Boston: Houghton Mifflin.

Moser, Barry. (1993). *Fly! A Brief History of Flight Illustrated.* New York: HarperCollins.

Murdocca, Sal. (1976). *Take Me to the Moon!* New York: Lothrop, Lee, & Shephard.

Myrick, Mildred. (1968). *Ants Are Fun.* New York: Harper.

Neve, Eve. (2002). *Water.* New York: Grosset & Dunlap.

Nicholls, Judith. (2003). *The Sun in Me: Books about the Planet.* New York: Barefoot Press.

Noda, Takayo. (2003). *Dear World.* New York: Dial.

Old, Wendie. (2002). *To Fly: The Story of the Wright Brothers.* New York: Clarion.

Paterson, Katherine. (2002). *The Same Stuff as Stars.* New York: Clarion Books.

Pinczes, Elinor. (1993). *One Hundred Hungry Ants.* Boston: Houghton Mifflin.

Plotz, Helen. (1955). *Imagination's Other Place: Poems of Science and Mathematics.* New York: Crowell.

Prelutsky, Jack. (1996). *A Pizza the Size of the Sun.* New York: Greenwillow.

Pringle, Lawrence. (1997). *An Extraordinary Life: The Story of a Monarch Butterfly.* New York: Orchard Books.

Pringle, Lawrence. (2003). *Whales: Strange and Wonderful.* Honesdale, PA: Boyds Mills.

Richardson, Adele D. (2002). *Manatees: Peaceful Plant Eaters.* Mankato, MN: Bridgestone.

Ride, Sally. (1994). *Voyager: An Adventure to the Edge of the Solar System.* New York: Crown Publisher.

Ride, Sally. (1994). *The Third Planet: Exploring the Earth from Space.* New York: Crown Publishers.

Ride, Sally. (2003). *Exploring Our Solar System.* New York: Crown.

Rinard, Judith. (2002). *The Story of Flight: The Smithsonian National Air and Space Museum.* New York: Firefly.

Robinson, Richard, ed. *Genetics.* New York: Macmillan.

Root, Phyllis. Helen Oxenbury illus. (2003). *Big Momma Makes the World.* Cambridge, MA: Candlewick.

Rustad, Martha. (2006). *Sea Snakes.* Mankato, MN: Pebble.

Scieszka, Jon. (2004). *Science Verse.* New York: Viking.

Selsam, Millicent. (1980). *All about Eggs.* Reading, MA: Addison-Wesley.

Shusterman, Neal. (2003). *Full Tilt.* New York: Simon & Schuster.

Silverstein, Alvin. (2002). *DNA.* Brookfield, CT: Twenty-first Century.

Simon, Charan (2004). *Rachel Carson: Author and Environmentalist.* Chanhassen, MN: Child's World.

Simon, Seymour. (1979). *The Long View into Space.* New York: Crown.

Simon, Seymour. (1989). *Whales.* New York: Crowell.

Simon, Seymour (1990). *Oceans.* New York: Morrow Junior Books.

Simon, Seymour (1992). *Our Solar System.* New York: Morrow Junior Books.

Simon, Sheridan. (1991). *Stephen Hawking: Unlocking the Universe.* Minneapolis: Dillon Press.

Sis, Peter. (1996) *The Starry Messenger.* New York: Farrar, Straus, & Giroux.

Sousa, David A. (1995). *How the Brain Learns.* Reston, VA: National Association of Secondary School Principals.

Swanson, Diane. (2003). *Eagles.* Milwaukee: Gareth.

Taback, Simms. (1999). *Joseph Had a Little Overcoat.* New York: Viking.

Thimmesh, Catherine. (2002). *The Sky's the Limit: Stories of Discovery by Women and Girls.* Boston: Houghton Mifflin.

Thimmesh, Catherine. (2006). *Team Moon: How 400,000 People Landed Apollo 11 on the Moon.* Boston: Houghton Mifflin.

Tremblay, E. (2003). *Rachel Carson.* Philadelphia: Chelsea House.

Trumbauer, Lisa. (2003) *We Need Garbage Collectors.* Mankato, MN: Pebble.

Walker, Richard. (2002). *Brain: Inner Workings of the Gray Matter.* New York: DK.

Walker, Sally. (2003). *Bessie Coleman: Daring to Fly.* New York: Carolrhoda.

Wallace, Nancy. (2003). *Recycle Every Day!* New York: Cavendish.

Werlin, Nancy. (2004). *Double Helix.* New York: Dial.

Wilkinson, Philip. (1998). *Spacebusters: The Race to the Moon.* New York: DK.

Woodmansee, Laura S. (2003). *Women of Space.* Burlington, ON: Apogee Books.

World Book. (2002). "Recognizing Your Emotions." In *Managing Your Teenage Life.* New York: World Book Publishing Co.

Wright, Alexandra. (1992). *Will We Miss Them?* Watertown, MA: Charlesbridge.

Yolen, Jane. (1986). *Commander Toad and the Intergalactic Spy.* New York: Coward-McCann.

Zaunders, B. (2001). *Feathers, Flaps, and Flops: Fabulous Early Fliers.* New York: Dutton.

Professional References

Baldwin, N. (1995). *Edison: Inventing the Century*. New York: Hyperion.

Boyer, E. (1990). "Giving Dignity to the Teaching Profession." In D. Dill, ed., *What Teachers Need to Know*. San Francisco: Jossey-Bass.

Chaikin, A. (1994). *A Man on the Moon*. New York: Penguin.

Cooney, Barbara. (1995). "Vicki Cobb." In Anita Silvey, ed., *Children's Books and Their Creators*. Boston: Houghton Mifflin.

Dacey, John, & Fiore, Lisa. (2000). *Your Anxious Child*. San Francisco: Jossey-Bass.

Dacey, John, & Travers, John. (2009). *Human Development Across the Lifespan*. New York: McGraw-Hill.

Dias, Patrick. (2002). "Reading as Rewriting." In Margaret Hunsberger and George Labercane, eds., *Making Meaning in the Response-Based Classroom*. Boston: Allyn & Bacon.

Epstein, Connie C. (1995). "Millicent E. Selsam." In Anita Silvey, ed., *Children's Books and Their Creators*. Boston: Houghton Mifflin.

Flynn, Catherine. (1995). "Seymour Simon." In Anita Silvey, ed. *Children's Books and Their Creators*. Boston: Houghton Mifflin.

Flynn, Catherine. (1995). "Joanna Cole." In Anita Silvey, ed., *Children's Books and Their Creators*. Boston: Houghton Mifflin.

Gleick, J. (1992). *Genius*. New York: Pantheon.

Hefner, Christine Roots, & Lewis, Kathryn Roots. (1995). *Literature-based Science*. Phoenix: Oryx Press.

Maslow, A. (1987). *Motivation and Personality*. New York: Harper & Row.

McDonald, Matt. (2005). "At Cattail Corner, Students Study the Catch of the Day." *Boston Sunday Globe*. May 8, 2005.

Rasinski, Timothy, et al. (2000). *Motivating Recreational Reading and Promoting Home-School Connections*. Newark, DE: International Reading Association.

Sumara, Dennis. (2002). "Challenging the "I" That We Are." In Margaret Hunsberger and George Labercane, eds. *Making Meaning in the Response-Based Classroom*. Boston: Allyn & Bacon.

Tompkins, Gail. (2003). *Literacy for the 21st Century*. Upper Saddle River, NJ: Merrill Prentice Hall.

Zarnowski, Myra, et al. (2001). *The Best in Children's Nonfiction*. Urbana, IL: National Council of Teachers of English.

Issues for Teachers and Librarians

In Maurice Sendak's Where the Wild Things Are, *Max makes mischief of one kind or another. When his mother calls him "wild thing" he retorts, "I'll eat you up." His mother then sends him to bed "without eating anything." That night his room becomes full of vines that close out the world where he was naughty, and a new world opens up for Max when a private boat takes him to "where the wild things are." There he regains his self-confidence, tames the wild things, and is crowned the king of all wild things. Yet he becomes bored with the rumpus and longs to be "where someone loved him best of all." Sailing back "into the night of his very own room," he finds his supper waiting for him. Surprisingly, it is still hot!*

Since it was published in the United States in 1963, *Where the Wild Things Are* has been a source of considerable controversy. Author and illustrator Maurice Sendak acknowledged in an interview with Leonard Marcus (2002) that when *Where the Wild Things Are* was originally published, "people said it was too frightening, too ugly, and that it wasn't a children's book" (Marcus, 2002, p. 167). In Great Britain, publishers were reluctant to print *Where the Wild Things Are* because of the outcry that it was too scary for little children. Consequently, publication there was delayed for four years. Brian Alderson, a well-known English author and critic, questioned why England had been deprived of "such glories" for so long. He described the "collective terror" that captured the British publishing industry when *Wild Things* was published in New York. Alderson regretted that "Not a Wild Thing was allowed to enter (children's) imaginations" and that "adult queasiness on a pathological scale held up publication" (Alderson, 2003, p. 721).

Unfounded fears can prevent an outstanding picture book like *Where the Wild Things Are* from being published, or, when it is published, cause it to be re-called and taken off the shelves in school and public libraries because a person, group, or even a community does not want it there. Censorship occurs when a controversy about a book written for children leads to its removal, not necessarily because of a lack of literary merit, but because an adult decides it's not suitable for children.

In this chapter we will focus our attention on three issues that are important to teachers and librarians.:

1. *Censorship*—the controversy that surrounds many children's books

2. *Technology*—its value and relationship to children's literature

3. *Literacy*—which, in the twenty-first century, often depends on the collabo-ration between the classroom teacher and the librarian

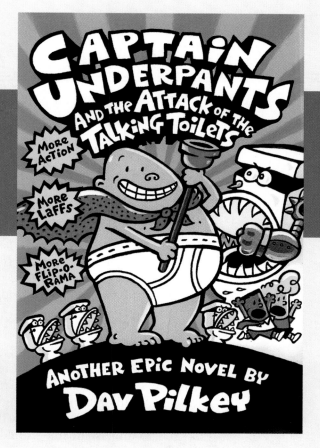

CAPTAIN UNDERPANTS AND THE
ATTACK OF THE TALKING TOILETS
*by Dav Pilkey. Copyright © 2005 by Dav
Pilkey. Reprinted permission of Scholastic
Inc.*

Guidelines for Reading Chapter 14

After you read Chapter Fourteen, you should be able to answer the following questions.

• Should reading be described as an act of privacy?

• How could any of the *Harry Potter* books become the object of censorship?

• What is the relationship between censorship and the context of a series such as *Captain Underpants*?

• What defense can be made for using issues such as sexuality and violence as themes for children's books? How does the answer to this question link to the developmental level of children?

• In what ways does children's use of the Internet improve their achievement?

• What is your position on the Children's Internet Protection Act?

• What is the worth of an Internet resource?

• Are there specific principles to follow in teaching children the proper use of Internet resources?

• How should a student's question about the value of information literacy in a modern society be answered?

Children's Literature and the Issue of Censorship

Censorship is associated with the right to privacy, and since reading is such a private endeavor, it is understandable that teachers and librarians are concerned when a child's right to privacy is invaded. At the White House Conference on School Libraries in the spring of 2002, Dr. Vartan Gregorian of the Carnegie Institute impressed his audience with his description of the innate relationship between the book and the reader. When a person is reading, he explained, that person is experiencing pleasure, discretion, silence, and creative solitude. Gregorian emphasized the aspect of privacy that is inherent in reading a book.

A person reading is a person suspended between the immediate and the timeless. Being able to transcend the limitations of time and space oneself is one of the primary pleasures of the act of reading. For it allows not only the renewal of one's imagination but also the development of one's mind.

(Gregorian, 2002, p. 9).

Since reading is such a private endeavor, the denial of children's right to read is a denial of the First Amendment of the United States Constitution, which guarantees to all the right to freedom of speech and of the press. How long would young children, preteens, and teenagers continue to seek information from a teacher or librarian if they knew their requests were not being kept confidential? It would be understandable if children decided not to seek information if they risked being discovered by others.

On June 19, 2002, the American Library Association reasserted its Library Bill of Rights, which affirms patrons' right to privacy concerning what they read. Stating that privacy is essential to the exercise of free speech, free thought, and free association, the ALA also declared its opposition to the use of profiling as a basis for any breach of privacy rights. For example, patrons have the right to use a library without any abridgement of privacy that may result from equating the subject of their inquiry with behavior. What is especially important for students to remember is that teachers and librarians have a long-standing commitment to the ethic of *facilitating*, not monitoring, access to information.

Protecting Children's Privacy

Helen R. Adams, past president of the ALA's American Association of School Librarians and a high school media specialist, interviewed library media specialists throughout the country about the status of privacy in school and public libraries. She learned that librarians and teachers receive many requests for books and materials on subjects such as suicide, having a parent in jail, living with a disabled sibling, overeating, sibling rivalry, loss of a job, and a death in the family. Although requests such as these may place adults in a difficult position, they must protect the confidential nature of the requests while providing the desired information (Adams, 2002, p. 42). Violating the privacy of a student is not acceptable for teachers and librarians. These professionals agree that protecting a minor's privacy is essential but, unfortunately, throughout the United States attacks on this right to privacy continue with repeated attempts to remove books from library shelves that some believe children should not be reading.

What's Your View?

The Law and Children's Privacy

In Massachusetts, a state that has always protected the confidentiality of its library records, a group of bi-partisan state lawmakers worked to pass a bill that would allow librarians to use the computer to disclose to parents the titles their children borrow from the state's public libraries. The sponsors of the bill cited their desire to keep "parents involved in their child's reading and education."

Coincidentally, the impetus for such a law arose when librarians became aware of the demand for the book *The Perks of Being a Wallflower* (Stephen Chbosky, 1999), the story of a disturbed high school freshman who has been molested by a family member. The book not only concerns the everyday problems of being an adolescent, but also touches on subjects such as sex, drugs, and alcohol.

A *Boston Globe* editorial responding to the lawmakers' action urged that the privacy and confidentiality of library patrons, including minors, be preserved; the duty of librarians is to encourage children to read, not to discourage them by trampling on their right to privacy (*Boston Globe*, 2003).

This controversial issue has generated considerable and contentious debate throughout the country. What is the role of parents? Should children have unrestricted freedom in their reading choices and Internet usage? What is the place of teachers and librarians in this dispute? What's your view?

Defining Censorship

Censorship is difficult to define since its meaning varies based on who is defining it. For example, Peter Hunt, historian and author of a well-known history of children's literature, maintains that censorship of children's books is an "expression of a power-relationship mediated through adults and unprotected by any supposed literary status" (Hunt, 2001, p. 255). He also states, "The history of children's literature world-wide is characterized by the struggle to control it: from criticism of folk and fairy tales in the eighteenth and nineteenth centuries, to debates about the dumbing-down effects of the tellytubbies in the 1990's" (Hunt, 2001, p. 257).

Mother Goose rhymes and other traditional folktales have often been considered violent. For example, *The Three Blind Mice* is considered violent because the mice chase after the farmer's wife, who cuts off their tails with a butcher knife. Yet the question is: how much violence is too much? The answer lies in the developmental level of the child who is reading or listening to the nursery rhyme. Critics point out that what children see, what they hear, and what they read will affect their behavior, for better or worse, and they offer Bandura's observational learning or modeling as an example. As we have seen in previous chapters, Bandura and his colleagues used adult models displaying aggression toward an inflated doll before a group of children. Later, in a play setting, these children exhibited significantly more aggression than children who had been in a control group. (For a detailed examination of Bandura's early experiments, see Bandura, Ross & Ross, 1963.)

THE HISTORICAL CONTEXT SURROUNDING CENSORSHIP   Often the historical context surrounding a book affects the type and timing of the disapproval it receives. The context could involve religion, morality, sexuality, offensive language, portrayal of women, stereotypes, racism, or violence that adults find offensive in children's literature. In the opinion of some adults, a children's book containing any of these characteristics is unacceptable and should not be kept in the library or offered as part of a class assignment. For example, in the 1960s,

What's Your View?

Folktales and Censorship

As successors of the oral tradition, folktales have withstood the critical test of time and are considered favorite books for many children. But they too have undergone the scalpel of censorship. Supporters of folktales believe they are stories with uncomplicated conflicts, direct characterizations, and satisfying resolutions. Further, they allow children access to that which is meaningful at their stage of development. Folk and fairy tales stimulate children's imagination, develop their intellects, clarify their emotions, and reflect their anxieties and aspirations—while at the same time suggesting solutions (Bettleheim, 1976).

Yet parents, caregivers, teachers, and librarians remain concerned about how violence in books impacts small children. They must use good judgment when selecting books that portray stepmothers who plot their stepchildren's demise, ugly sisters' toes that are crushed when they try on the silver slipper, and little children whose parents abandon them in the woods. Whether books such as these are a goodness-of-fit and developmentally appropriate for young children continues to be debated.

After reading examples of traditional literature and drawing on your knowledge of child development, discuss with your peers whether traditional literature is too violent for small children. What's your view?

William Steig's picture book *Sylvester and the Magic Pebble* (1969) was criticized by politically minded groups who believed Steig's portrayal of police as pigs (even though they were appealing and friendly) amounted to a derogatory epithet about policemen. Today, similar to the affection that is expressed for *Where the Wild Things Are*, *Sylvester and the Magic Pebble* is treasured by adults and children alike as a warm, loving story.

Although Helen Bannerman's *Little Black Sambo* was written in 1899, it was not until the 1960s that critics came to view the word *Sambo* as a racial slur and the book's

Culture and Children's Literature

Censorship Here and Abroad

In Moscow, Russian school children were almost banned from reading *Harry Potter* until the Moscow City Prosecutor's Office declined to bring criminal hate-crime charges against Rosman Publishing for making available a Russian language version of *Harry Potter and the Chamber of Secrets*. An unidentified Moscow-area woman had filed charges that the book "instilled religious extremism and prompted students to join religious organizations of Satanist followers." A Russian online publication theorized that the charges were reminiscent of Soviet times when works of art that happened to displease authorities were confiscated and banned from bookstores and library circulation at the "request of outraged working people" (*American Libraries*, 2005).

In Canada, a kindergarten teacher was exonerated after a five-year battle over the appropriateness of gay-positive books in a Surrey, British Columbia, school system. The Chief Justice ruled that learning is impossible unless children are exposed to a wide range of material. In England, Hugh Lofting's *Dr. Dolittle* was on library shelves for years before it was considered racist. Roald Dahl's *Charlie and the Chocolate Factory* (1964) was rewritten when its original characters, the black pygmy slaves, were considered unacceptable.

In Australia, an aboriginal community in the Northern Territory expressed its determination to ban a children's book about a teddy bear that visits Uluru, the great monolith formerly known as Ayers Rock. The Anangu people claim that *Bromley Climbs Uluru* is offensive and denigrates traditional culture. National park officials, acting on behalf of the Anangu, who reclaimed ownership of the site in 1985, have threatened authors Alan and Patricia Campbell with a fine unless they destroy the book or write a more culturally sensitive version (*School Library Journal*, May 2003).

drawings of the characters as racist. Many libraries discontinued stocking the book, although it had always been popular with children. In the 1990s, Julius Lester (*Sam and the Tigers*) purposefully omitted reference to the word *Sambo*, and his retelling became more widely accepted. But now, *Little Black Sambo* is again the subject of controversy. The story appealed so much to Christopher Bing (2003), illustrator of the Caldecott Honor book *Casey At the Bat*, that he published another version of it. The question remains, however, whether the cultural context has changed to the point where people can now admit they like the story, without being called a racist (Kennedy, 2003).

Similar controversy erupts with the publication of each new Harry Potter book. Some adults are convinced J. K. Rowling is promoting occultism, witchcraft, mysticism, and sorcery, and that "moral relativism" is rampant at Hogwarts, the school of wizardry Harry attends (Beam, 2001). For four consecutive years (2000–2003) the *Harry Potter* series has topped the list of challenged books according to the American Library Association's Office for Intellectual Freedom (*American Libraries*, March 2003), which underscores the importance of context in any evaluation of children's literature. (The seventh and last Harry Potter, *Harry Potter and the Deathly Hallows*, appeared in July, 2007.)

CENSORSHIP: A CONSTANT ISSUE   Hunt (2001, p. 257) noted that "it is hard to find a 'classic' of a hundred years ago which is not blatantly sexist or racist although such texts have been protected, until very recently, by their status." As mentioned previously, Dr. Seuss's *Lorax* (1971) was criticized for favoring environmentalists over timber workers in rural California. Another court case involved *Annie on My Mind* by Nancy Garden, a Margaret Edwards Award author, because it stressed a homosexual romance between two high school girls.

Books such as *Heather Has Two Mommies* (1991) by Leslea Newman, *Daddy's Roommate* (1991) by Michaela Willhoite, and other works about lesbians and gay couples frequently face challenges because they portray different values and lifestyles (Salvadore, 1995).

It is unusual, however, that a contemporary book such as *So Far from the Bamboo Grove* by Yoko Watkins, which has been read avidly by middle school children from Massachusetts to Hawaii since it was written in 1986, should be the subject of controversy in 2007. In this fictionalized autobiography, Yoko, an 11-year-old Japanese girl, along with her mother and older sister escape from Korea to Japan at the end of World War II. The author, an activist for peace, has always acknowledged the suffering caused by the Japanese government during World War II when she talks in schools throughout the country. She is now being asked to defend her controversial memoir before groups of Koreans and Korean Americans who claim that her book distorts history (Kocian, 2007, p. 22).

Parents and Significant Adults as Censors

It is natural for parents to be interested in what their children, especially their young children, are reading. Unless parents are interested in their children's reading and read to them often, their children will not become lifelong readers. Controversy arises, however, when their interest in the content of what their children are reading extends to what children other than their own are reading. Such concern can deteriorate into censorship and affect a child's personal right to freedom when it is used to deny a child access to books that others consider objectionable.

Teachers and librarians who are questioned about the value of having a particular book on their shelves should accept the challenge graciously, understanding that parents have the right to question what their child is reading. They should know whether the book is being used in a classroom or library as part of the required curriculum or as a supplemental title, and at what grade. They should know the length of time it has been in the school or library. They must explain courteously to the person complaining what the library's policy is and what procedures must be followed before a book is removed from the shelf. Most communities have a materials selection policy that is rooted in and supportive of the U.S. Constitution, the Students Right to Read, and the intellectual freedom documents of the American Library Association.

Parents of adolescents are among the most vocal about what their children should or should not read. Teachers and librarians also are often torn over concern that for particular children a children's book that is a "good read" might not be a "good-for-them read." Patty Campbell, an experienced young adult librarian and critic, defines this duality between a "good read" and a "good-for-them read" as

the pull between reading pleasure and the didactic value of a book, especially for adolescents. All of us who judge and select books for teens teeter back and forth on these perplexes constantly and the only way not to fall off is to balance in the middle.

(Campbell, 2003, p. 504)

The three topics parents are most concerned about in the books their adolescents read are sex and sexuality, obscene language, and violence.

THE HIGHER POWER OF LUCKY
Reprinted with the permission of Atheneum Books for Young Readers, an imprint of Simon & Schuster Children's Publishing Division from **THE HIGHER POWER OF LUCKY** *by Susan Patron, illustrated by Matt Phelan. Jacket illustration copyright © 2006 Matt Phelan.*

SEX AND SEXUALITY   Judy Blume's books, many of which were written in the 1970s and 1980s, continue to be major targets of parents because of their discussion of sexuality. Her work has been criticized and censored from her first book, *Are You There God? It's Me, Margaret* (1970), which is about preteen concerns such as menstruation and developing breasts, to her controversial novel *Forever* (1975), which concerns teenage sex.

Others, however, praise Blume for advocating sexual responsibility and her recognition of a child's developmental and physical needs. As Zena Sutherland noted, "few authors have equaled Judy Blume's popularity, whether one judges by the sales of her books, all of which seem to stay in print ad infinitum, or by the number of awards chosen by children, primarily in statewide contests" (Sutherland, 1995, p. 66).

Parents of adolescents who are seriously concerned with their young adults' well-being (defined as "parental monitors" by Raymond Montemayor in Jacqueline and Richard Lerner's *Adolescence*, 1999) make a sincere effort to keep open the channels of communication with their children. Parental monitoring is not an isolated activity but part of the parent-adolescent relationship. Yet adolescents must be willing to share their experiences with their parents and be honest about those experiences. Parents who have established a good rapport with their teenagers trust them and the choice of books to read. If parents are confident that nothing criminal or illegal is upsetting their children's lives, they should respect their privacy.

From your reading of Chapters Eleven and Twelve in this text, you are aware that many of today's books for older children and young adults pose a challenge to concerned teachers, librarians, and parents. Ironically, however, the objections being voiced by teachers, librarians, and parents about the word *scrotum* on the first page of the 2007 Newbery Medal winner, *The Higher Power of Lucky*, are unusual. Author Susan Patron defends the use of the word in the *New York Times* (Bosman, 2007) as "just so delicious. The sound of the word to Lucky (the 10-year- old protagonist) is so evocative. It's one of those words that's so interesting because of the sound of the word." But many adults disagree. They maintain that explaining this word to a child would be difficult and that the word has no place in children's literature. So, the debate about censorship continues.

OFFENSIVE LANGUAGE   Advocates of children's literature (teachers, librarians, authors, editors, and parents) try to shield children and teenagers from some of life's realities for their own good. They want to protect them from literature that may be seriously harmful. Yet they frown at the efforts of censors to protect older teens and young adults from mild expletives and sexual references (Campbell, 2003).

The main character in Katherine Paterson's novel *The Great Gilly Hopkins*, for example, caused controversy when Gilly used offensive language to express her frustration about being moved from one foster home to another. She was lonely and unhappy, and her occasional use of a "dirty word" captures the essence of her feelings. In Lois Lowry's fun-loving series about Anastasia Krupnik, the presence of some offensive words caused teachers and librarians to remove it from their shelves. The language of Lowry's Anastasia, as well as Paterson's Gilly, "is appropriate within the context of the book's character, plot and theme; only when seen in isolation does it become controversial" (Salvadore, 1995, p. 164).

In March 2005 the Limestone County, Alabama, school district turned down the recommendation of the district superintendent that Chris Crutcher's novel *Whale Talk* be kept on high school library shelves, because the message the book contains "is more important than the language used." In an open letter to the adults of the county the author responded, "By showing our fear of issues and language that are everyday to our children, we take ourselves off that short list of people to turn to in a real crisis" (*American Libraries*, 2005, p. 15).

VIOLENCE   Today, violence extends from neighborhood gang fights to international mass killings. In light of this widespread cultural change, the search for understanding, causation, and intervention has become more frenzied than ever, leading some to blame movies, television, family dysfunction, religion, and society in general for what is happening. The content of some books, particularly for young adults, is becoming increasingly violent. Many parents believe that controlled exposure helps young people acquire the knowledge and skill that

WHALE TALK
Used by permission of
HarperCollins Publishers

Spin Off

Banned Books

Libraries and bookstores across the country often set aside one week (usually in the fall) to "Open Your Mind to a Banned Book." To celebrate "banned books week," the organizers include exhibits and readings that celebrate the freedom to read. Judith Krug, director of the American Library Association's Office for Intellectual Freedom, hopes that festivities such as these will remind Americans of the importance of the freedom to read (*School Library Journal*, Sept. 2003).

School librarians and teachers are also concerned about their students' loss of freedom to read. In one school (Downers Grove Illinois' South High School, a large diverse suburban high school near Chicago), English teachers and school librarians worked together to create a curriculum on the issues surrounding book censorship and book banning (Krepps, Null & Pakowski, 2003). "Teachers scheduled library

classes in which students learned about intellectual freedom, pornography, obscenity, and community standards. Students then read passages from banned books, and assumed the role of parent, teacher, librarian, administrator, board member, or high school student. "Each group voted on whether to remove the book from our library. At our workshop, we shared the voting results, some of which were surprising" (Krepps, et al., 2003, p. 44).

Students continued their examination of banned books and searched for the reasons the books had been banned, why they disturbed some members of the community, as well as the literary merits they possessed. They analyzed why they reached their conclusions about accepting or rejecting a book for their library (Krepps, et al., 2003). For further information on banned books visit www.ala.org/bbooks.

will help them to adjust to the mayhem and brutality inherent in today's world. Other parents, as well as teachers and librarians, believe that merely growing up in a modern society is violent enough, and that additional exposure is excessive.

Kathleen T. Isaacs, who is familiar with countless young adult books as a committee member who helps select the Best Books for Young Adults for the American Library Association, writes, "I can't help but notice this troubling trend [the amount of violence in books for teens] even in the best of the literature" (Isaacs, 2003, p. 50). Isaacs remarks that child abuse is now accepted unabashedly in such books as E. R. Frank's *America*, Teresa Toten's *The Game*, and Jeanne Willis's *The Truth or Something: A Novel*. She asks if teenagers need to learn how a killer is made in John Halliday's *Shooting Monarchs*, or witness the amputation of a character's leg in Melvin Burgess's *Bloodtide*. The answer undoubtedly lies somewhere between the opposing views of violence. Helpful clues can also be found in our understanding of the developmental level of the students who read books like those mentioned. For example, what is known about their cognitive and emotional maturity? Does the book in question reflect reality or does it venture too deeply into the realm of the unreal? Parents, teachers, and librarians must consider a book from many points of view before they select or reject it.

Ten Most Frequently Challenged Books (2005)

According to the Office of Intellectual Freedom (OIF) of the American Library Association, the Ten Most Challenged Books of 2005 were:

1. IT'S PERFECTLY NORMAL by Robie Harris, for homosexuality, nudity, sex education, religious viewpoint, abortion, and unsuitability for age group

2. FOREVER by Judy Blume, for sexual content and offensive language

3. THE CATCHER IN THE RYE by J. D. Salinger for sexual content, offensive language, and unsuitability for age group

4. **THE CHOCOLATE WAR** by Robert Cormier, for sexual content and offensive language

5. **WHALE TALK** by Chris Crutcher, for racism and offensive language

6. **DETOUR FOR EMMY** by Marilyn Reynolds, for sexual content

7. **WHAT MY GIRLFRIEND DOESN'T KNOW** by Sonya Sones, for sexual content and unsuitability for age group

8. **CAPTAIN UNDERPANTS** series by Dav Pilkey, for anti-family content, unsuitability for age group, and violence

9. **CRAZY LADY!** by Jane Conly, for offensive language

10. **IT'S SO AMAZING! A BOOK ABOUT EGGS, SPERM, BIRTH, BABIES AND FAMILIES** by Robie Harris, for sex education and sexual content

Books, however, are not the only source of controversy in the world of children's literature; how children use technology is also a serious issue for professional librarians and teachers, who must combine their knowledge about children's literature with their knowledge of computers and the Internet, as they deal with the day-to-day activities of children in their schools and libraries in the twenty-first century.

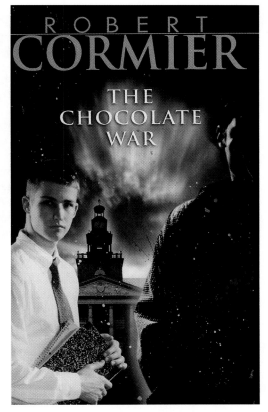

THE CHOCOLATE WAR
Used by permission of Random House Children's Books, a division of Random House, Inc.

Children's Literature and the Issue of Technology

Teachers and librarians carefully maintain children's confidentiality when they are using electronic resources. Sometimes it is a delicate balancing act for teachers and librarians to provide enough supervision of the terminals to aid patrons in need while simultaneously offering privacy to proficient users. Children who do not properly log off their computers provide the next user an opportunity to track their sites, which is an infringement of their privacy. As individual states wrestle with the degree and kind of privacy teachers and librarians should offer the children in their care, Congress has enacted into law the Children's Internet Protection Bill, whose provisions are being explored and tested in libraries across the country. Public libraries are deciding whether the need for federal funds is worth denying young people unblocked access to the Internet.

Children's Internet Protection Act

On June 23, 2003, the Supreme Court upheld the constitutionality of the Children's Internet Protection Act (CIPA), an important decision involving children's right to privacy. Public libraries and schools that receive federal funds for Internet connectivity are required to filter every online workstation, including staff-only machines. It does not, however, appropriate additional funds for purchasing locking

What's Your View?

Children and the Internet

Can children function in a virtual world while simultaneously existing in their "real worlds"? In attempting to answer this question, Greenfield and Yan (2006) argue that the Internet provides a social environment that includes both restricted (for example, instant messaging) and wide-ranging (for example, national and global) experiences. Continuing a theme developed throughout this book, the Internet presents a new challenge to cognitive development. As such, it can be a welcome tool in furthering children's understanding of their world. At this stage, research into children's comprehension of Internet technology and current usage is scarce (Greenfield & Yan, 2006), which raises challenges for teachers and librarians in selecting books for children that match their developmental, technological, and personal needs.

Consequently, children are faced with questions of developmental importance involving technical and social complexity. Studying children 5 – 8 years, 9 – 10 years, 11 – 12 years, and adults, Yan (2005) discovered that age is a more powerful force in comprehension than online experience. There was a significant differ-

ence between the 9 – 10 group and the 11 – 12 group. The same pattern held for social complexity. Yan (2005) concluded that technical understanding of the Internet appears earlier than social understanding.

Following up on these results, Yan (2006) again found age to be the most influential force in explaining Internet understanding. By grades 5 and 6 children have reached the adult level of grasping technical complexity, but it's not until grades 7 and 8 that they attain the adult level of comprehending the social complexity of the Internet (Yan, 2006, p. 426). These findings have serious implications in light of the Children's Internet Protection Act. Since age is critical in children's use and understanding of the Internet, teachers, librarians, parents, and other responsible adults should take age differences seriously (Yan, 2006, p. 427). For example, the use of filtering systems and careful scrutiny of websites are urged. To conclude this section, we'll return to the question with which we opened our discussion: can children function in a virtual world while simultaneously existing in their real worlds?
What's your view?

software. Libraries that do not receive "e-rate" monies (funds from the federal government to purchase discounted Internet and telecommunications materials) are not legally bound to comply with the law (*American Libraries*, August 2003, p. 12).

The 6-3 Supreme Court ruling held that CIPA does not violate the First Amendment, because public libraries do not offer Internet access "to create a public forum for Web publishers but to facilitate research, learning, and recreational pursuits by furnishing materials of requisite and appropriate quality." As for the tendency of filters to block constitutionally protected speech, the late Chief Justice William H. Rehnquist wrote that "because CIPA allows librarians to disable a filter without significant delay on an adult user's request" the goal of "protecting young library users from material inappropriate for minors outweighs any temporary inconvenience to adults" (*American Libraries*, August, 2003, p. 12).

RESPONSES TO THE CIPA   The passage of the CIPA into law has provoked an outcry from many public and school librarians, as well as from teachers and parents. Karen G. Schneider, Director of the Librarians' Index to the Internet, immediately responded by writing in *American Libraries* that librarians will have few problems with small children not having open access to the Internet because librarians would not permit them unsupervised open access even without CIPA. She does, however, advocate that librarians "emancipate Internet access for teens who are now held hostage by CIPA guidelines which deny adolescents any unfiltered access in libraries that receive the e-rate" (Schneider, 2003, pp. 15, 16).

On the other hand, Ron McCabe, director of the McMillan Memorial Library, Wisconsin Rapids, Wisconsin, in his article *The CIPA Ruling as Reality Ther-*

apy (2003), suggests that adults should consider quality standards and community needs when they cry that intellectual freedom is being compromised. He believes that the Supreme Court has extended the protection of public library selection practices to the Internet and affirmed that "libraries are educational institutions and that we are not always wiser than the citizens we serve" (McCabe, 2003, p. 16).

DELETING ONLINE PREDATORS ACT   On July 26, 2006, DOPA, the Deleting Online Predators Act (DOPA) passed the U.S. House of Representatives by a vote of 410 to 15. DOPA is now in the Senate Commerce Committee in search of a sponsor. If passed into law, it will "require schools and libraries receiving e-rate funding to block access to social network sites like MySpace and Friendster, chat rooms, and perhaps blogs" (Olec, 2006, pp. 16, 19). Professionals and parents agree that online predators must be stopped, but question whether this bill is "overbroad, vague, and ineffective" (Olec, 2006, p. 16).

POSITIVE ASPECTS OF USING THE INTERNET   In spite of the restrictions that children using the Web may experience, a positive preliminary report of a three-year study about its advantages has been released. Linda Jackson, a Michigan State University psychology professor, reports that students who are frequent Web users had better school performance than less frequent users (Jackson, 2003). Jackson studied ninety families with annual incomes of about $15,000 and no regular access to the Internet. As part of the study, their children received home computers, Internet connections, operating instructions, and technical support. After sixteen months of Internet access, the children's grade point averages and standardized test scores improved. Internet use also appears to have no negative effect on children's social abilities or mental health (Jackson, 2003, p. 32).

Obviously, the Internet has increased student access to a knowledge base that was unavailable a generation ago. Most professors would agree that students' research papers are more sophisticated and more visually appealing. Students who have the ability to build Web pages, design graphics, and use PowerPoint are sharpening their technology skills to successfully compete in the workplace, which has become increasingly competitive because of globalization.

Suggestions for Using the Internet for Research

(This section was written by Brendan Rapple, Collection Development Librarian, Boston College.)

Developing the skills necessary to successfully deal with such an evanescent tool as the Internet is the first step for you as students conducting research into children's literature. Constant growth keeps the Internet in flux. Greater variability in the quality of information on the Internet differentiates it from traditional library resources. In addition, vast quantities of what can be easily accessed electronically is useless, so researchers must carefully evaluate any document on the Net.

EVALUATING THE WORTH OF AN INTERNET RESOURCE   Most books have been vetted by editors and others prior to publication. Librarians generally conduct a sound winnowing process as well as rigorously check peer review academic journals. Consequently, when using an electronic index to periodicals (e.g., *MLA Bibliography* or *Psychological Abstracts*), one may be confident that the selected journals indexed meet standards of academic quality.

However, the vast majority of material on the Web has not been subjected to referees, editorial boards, and/or peer review to ensure quality. With respect to Web material, always ask: "Can I trust it?" While much Web information is excellent, much is useless. It is important to ask yourself: "Why exactly am I using the Web? Is it just because it's easy and convenient, on my home computer, and I don't want to go to the library?" Going to the library and consulting traditional print resources may be more productive and may, in the long run, be easier.

Teachers and librarians know they can't believe everything they read. They must carefully examine the diverse treatments of their subject, properly interpret research material, and address the frequency with which resources contradict each other. In short, they evaluate their sources and evidence. It is essential to be especially on guard and skeptical when dealing with material found on the Internet. The worth of any material posted on the Internet varies greatly. Remember the old saying "Don't believe everything you read in print." Today, it's "Don't believe everything you read on the Web." Anyone can post anything. There is no filtering or refereeing process. Consequently, all that wonderful, highly valuable research material is often mixed with a plethora of nonsense.

However, the following websites suggest certain strategies one might use when evaluating Web resources:

- **THINKING CRITICALLY ABOUT WORLD WIDE WEB RESOURCES** <http://www.library.ucla.edu/libraries/college/help/critical/index.htm>
- **EVALUATING WEB SITES: CRITERIA AND TOOLS** <http://www.library.cornell.edu/ okuref/research/webeval.html>
- **EVALUATING WEB-BASED RESOURCES: A PRACTICAL PERSPECTIVE** <http://www.thelearningsite.net/cyberlibrarian/elibraries/eval.html>

INTERNET SUBJECT DIRECTORIES   There is nothing intrinsically wrong with surfing or browsing the 'Net when researching an author or a topic concerned with children's literature. Researchers may uncover useful websites and information serendipitously. However, to target your research, it is often useful to limit searching to Web sites that already have been categorized and/or evaluated. It is important to seek out sites where content has been selected according to sound criteria. This reduces the chance that your "hits" will be useless. The following are several respected and authoritative Web subject directories, each of which points to a number of quality children's literature sites.

- **INFOMINE** <http://infomine.ucr.edu> INFOMINE contains over 100,000 links (26,000 librarian-created links and 75,000-plus robot/crawler-created links). The resources, carefully selected by librarians, include databases, e-journals, e-books, bulletin boards, mailing lists, online library catalogs, articles, directories of researchers, and many other types of information.
- **SCOUT REPORT ARCHIVES** <http://scout.cs.wisc.edu/archives/> Scout Report Archives contains thousands of critical annotations of websites, many literature related. Each annotation seeks to provide an overall analysis of a site, including general content, attribution (authors, etc.), currency, availability, accessibility, and presentation. Most of the items reviewed are accessible at no charge.
- **BUBL LINK** <http://bubl.ac.uk/link/index.html> This is a UK-based catalog of selected Internet resources covering numerous academic subject areas. All items are evaluated, and the maintainers of the site declare that each resource is checked and fixed each month. Though BUBL LINK points to a relatively small

number of resources (over 11,000), it is a useful database for locating quality websites across all disciplines, including children's literature.

• **LIBRARIAN'S INDEX TO THE INTERNET** <http://lii.org/search/file/literature> The mission of Librarians' Index to the Internet is to provide a well-organized point of access for reliable, trustworthy, librarian-selected Internet resources. The site is well categorized and points to numerous quality children's literature–related sites.

USING INTERNET SEARCH ENGINES   Individuals researching children's literature on the Internet should realize that there are literally hundreds of different search engines, with different features and capabilities. Every search engine requires the researcher to learn specific searching protocols since every search engine searches a different database—a different grouping of web pages. Researchers get different results depending on the search engine used. The results may vary widely, while at other times the results point to identical sites. Learn the various search techniques and the range of specific databases to better target research efforts. See the website *Search Engine Resources* <http:// www.refdesk.com/news-rch.html> for a comprehensive listing of search engines.

For another excellent overview of Internet search engines, see *Searching Web Resources* <http://www.bc.edu/libraries/research/guides/s-searchengine>, a research guide prepared by Karen McNulty, a librarian at Boston College. This is an annotated guide intended "to help clarify the different kinds of search engines and directories on the web and how they may be most effectively used." The guide discusses and provides examples of multimedia search engines, news search engines, and international search engines.

An excellent general introduction for searching the Internet is UC–Berkeley Library's *Finding Information on the Internet: A Tutorial* <http://www.lib. berkeley.edu/TeachingLib/Guides/Internet/FindInfo.html>. Other tutorials and advice regarding searching the Web include:

• **THE PANDIA GOALGETTER: A SHORT AND EASY SEARCH ENGINE TUTORIAL** <http://www.pandia.com/goalgetter/>
• **GUIDE TO EFFECTIVE SEARCHING OF THE INTERNET** <http://www.brightplanet.com/deepcontent/tutorials/Search/index.asp>
• **SEARCH GUIDE: SEARCH ENGINES & TUTORIALS**
• **THE SPIDER'S APPRENTICE: A HELPFUL GUIDE TO WEB SEARCH ENGINES** <http://www.monash.com/spidap.html>

There are scores of other useful guides/tutorials to searching the Web efficiently and effectively.

INTERNET SEARCHING STRATEGIES   When researching a particular subject in children's literature on the Internet, it is important to break the topic down into discrete, manageable concepts. Suppose you wish to explore the representation of eating disorders among teenagers in children's fiction. You could start by listing the primary concepts of your topic:

Eating Disorders / Teenagers / Children's Fiction

How do you present these in an Internet search? First, you must identify key words or terms pertaining to the concepts. For example, an analysis of "eating disorders" may produce the key words *anorexia, bulimia,* and *eating disorders*; "teenagers" may produce *adolescents, youth, young adults,* and *teenagers*; "children's fiction" may produce

What's Your View?

Plagiarism

The Internet is a wonderful resource for anyone conducting research into diverse aspects of children's literature. However, one problem with the Net for some students writing their research papers is their failure to appropriately attribute the works and references they have utilized on the Web. The problem, of course, is one of possible plagiarism. Plagiarism is taking another's work and passing it off as your own. We all do it each day when we take ideas from others without acknowledging the original source. However, more often than not, we don't even know the original source. And even if we did, we generally do not make a point of attributing the routine quotes of others. When we talk about the decline and fall of the Roman Empire or say, "To be or not to be, that is the question" in normal conversation, we rarely give credit to Gibbon or Shakespeare. Plagiarism in research is quite different. True plagiarism is stealing, and it is increasingly common among those who use the Web in their research.

It is true that plagiarism often stems from sloppy research and subsequent rewriting rather than the deliberate desire to cheat. Nevertheless, even an unintentional failure to cite sources correctly and honestly constitutes plagiarism. Many students take poor notes during the research process. They write someone else's text verbatim on a card or copy it to their computer and forget to add quotation marks. When they write their paper and refer to their notes, they have forgotten that the text on the card or computer is another's and not their own. Any reader who recognizes the original text will assume that the student has cheated. This can lead to tough penalties. Remember the golden rule: take excellent notes, utilize them effectively, write the entire paper yourself, and document sources well and honestly. Do you agree with these conclusions? What's your view?

children's novels, children's books, children's literature, children's fiction. There are undoubtedly other possibilities, and there are no absolutely correct key words to use. You must try different combinations in different search engines and subject directories, and then gauge which ones provide the most useful and pertinent results.

The Internet is so vast that it is important to focus your search. Try narrowing your search to *anorexia*, but without bulimia. To omit hits dealing with eating disorders among teenage boys, use the word *girls* to represent teenage females. Select a search engine to establish the relationship between the chosen terms and perform the search. If you are not satisfied with the results, try other key words and a different search engine.

DIFFERENT TYPES OF PLAGIARISM

- **COPIED TEXT.** Sometimes a person copies the text word for word from an Internet site and pretends to be the author. This constitutes a deliberate aim to deceive.

- **QUOTATION.** A direct quotation from an author must be placed in quotation marks and then referenced in the bibliography or works cited. Forgetting to add quotation marks could result in accusations of plagiarism.

- **PARAPHRASE.** Paraphrasing another's passage, but doing a poor job of it by keeping very close to the original text, is not genuine paraphrasing. Also, paraphrasing a passage or presenting someone else's ideas in their own words, but failing to give the proper references or citations to the original author, is cheating.

WEB PAPERS   Companies sell term papers on the Web. Submitting a paper that is not your own is dishonest and an act of plagiarism.

A useful site with much information about plagiarism is: *Plagiarism: What It Is and How to Avoid It.* <http://www.indiana.edu/~wts/pamphlets/plagiarism.shtml>

PREPARING THE WORKS CITED/BIBLIOGRAPHY   Documenting papers well and knowing the format for citing electronic resources demands attention. It is important that students check with their teacher or instructor for the preferred bibliographical style. It is likely that the requisite style will be that of the American Psychological Association <http://www.apastyle.org/elecref.html>, or the Modern Language Association (MLA)<http://www.mla.org/style>, or the humanities version of *The Chicago Manual of Style*: <http://www.press.uchicago.edu/ Misc/Chicago/cmosfaq/ cmosfaq.html>.

Whichever style you use, it's important to be consistent; there should be no changes from one documentation system to another within a paper. Online guides for documenting papers include the following (although there are numerous others):

- Style Guides (University of Florida) <http://www.uflib.ufl.edu/hss/ref/ style.html>
- Columbia University Press Guide to Online Style <http://www.columbia.edu/ cu/cup/cgos/idx_basic.html>
- The University of Wisconsin–Madison Writing Center <http://www. wisc.edu/writing/Handbook/Documentation.html>
- Bedford/St. Martin's Citation Styles http://www.bedfordstmartins.com/ online/citex.html

Children's Literature and the Issue of Literacy

Teachers and librarians have always been aware that children must learn specific skills in order to solve problems, write fluently, and read with comprehension, as well as be technically knowledgeable when they enter the information-oriented marketplace. Now, however, teachers and librarians are *collaborating*—working more closely together to ensure that all students are literate in all areas. Ironically, it is only now, in the twenty-first century, that literacy skills are being enumerated and defined, and collaboration between teachers and librarians is being emphasized.

Collaboration: The New Buzz Word

Collaboration is not a new concept. Successful teachers and librarians have always coordinated their programs, but currently they are specifically being recognized as partners in student learning. According to *Information Power: Building Partnerships for Learning* (ALA, 2001), school librarians are being encouraged to connect with the larger learning community through shared planning, teaching, collection development, and management strategies.

To make collaboration possible, however, the culture of the individual school has to be such that it welcomes teaching partnerships and team planning. The administration of the school must provide support and accept flexible scheduling in the elementary and middle schools; and teachers and librarians must demonstrate a willingness to compromise so they can acquire common planning time (Abilock, 2002).

Different Forms of Literacy

Many literacies are examined thoroughly in books such as *Literacy for the 21st Century* (Tomkins, 2003). Also, The Department of Education (DOE) is working closely with Apple, Dell, Cisco Systems, and Microsoft to develop a list of technological literacies. DOE hopes to include the public (teachers, librarians, superintendents, and the American Association of School Librarians) in formulating this new plan, The DOE's Office of Educational Technology promises that it will contain "new budgeting models to make laptops more affordable for schools, ways to integrate technology into the curriculum, and the importance of virtual schools, distance learning," and making a plan that focuses on "taking advantage of Internet access and start linking it to real challenges teachers are facing and real opportunities that can best serve students" (Whalen, 2003, p. 20). Time will tell if this plan becomes a reality.

The following literacies, organized by the nonprofit research group North Central Regional Educational Laboratory (NCREL) and the Metiri Group, an educational consulting firm, have been effectively summarized in *The School Library Journal*, May 2003, p. 41, and are being practiced in schools throughout the country.

KINDS OF LITERACY
- Basic literacy (reading, writing, listening, and speaking)
- Scientific literacy (knowledge of science, scientific thinking, and mathematics)
- Technological literacy (the ability to understand and work with computers, networks, and software)
- Visual literacy (the ability to decipher, interpret, and express ideas using images, charts, graphs, and video)
- Information literacy (the ability to find, evaluate, and use information effectively)
- Cultural literacy (knowledge and appreciation of the diversity of peoples and cultures)
- Global awareness (understanding and recognizing the interrelationships of nations, corporations, and politics around the world)

Although each literacy is invaluable and contributes a great deal to a child's education, information literacy is provoking much timely discussion in professional periodicals.

INFORMATION LITERACY   Not only is information literacy relevant, it is a life skill. *The School Library Journal* (Whalen, 2003), in its first comprehensive survey of 783 school librarians nationwide, determined the extent to which information literacy is being taught in K–12 schools. Although the survey discovered that 88 percent of the respondents have information literacy standards in place, only 30 percent of teachers and 14 percent of students actually know what those skills are. This may be due to the confusion of how information literacy differs from information access.

OBSTACLES TO INFORMATION LITERACY   Teachers and librarians must understand the obstacles that separate them and attempt to overcome them so they can collaborate to incorporate information literacy into the school curriculum. Following are several of the obstacles teachers and librarians encounter.

1. THE PREOCCUPATION OF THE ELEMENTARY SCHOOL TEACHER. She is deeply involved in teaching her young students to read and too busy to take her class to the library. Would her students' reading skills improve if she took advantage of the librarian's professional techniques for demonstrating research skills, book talking, and individual selection of appropriate books?

2. THE PRESSURE OF TIME. Teachers in upper grades are concentrating solely on preparing their students to pass state and national tests. Should they remember that the school librarian is trained to teach the skills children need to pass these tests?

3. LACK OF SUPPORT FROM THE PRINCIPAL. Could the classroom teacher and the school librarian confer with the principal and request more time to work together for the benefit of their students?

4. RELUCTANCE OF THE LIBRARIAN TO FORMALLY EVALUATE THE ENTIRE STUDENT BODY. Could an informal evaluation be worked out where the teacher creates the rubrics for evaluating the students and the librarian collaborates on a lesson?

5. LIBRARIANS LACK FORMAL BENCHMARKS TO ESTABLISH THAT STUDENTS HAVE MASTERED INFORMATION LITERACY SKILLS. Could state-mandated benchmarks and programs or a central office for library services be established to support librarians?

OTHER LITERACIES   Other forms of literacy are of interest to teachers and librarians. Among these are emergent literacy (discussed in Chapter Six) and family literacy.

EMERGENT LITERACY. Emergent literacy is important for teachers and librarians to foster, and it occurs in preschool classrooms, kindergartens, school libraries, and in many children's rooms in public libraries across the country that are equipped with the appropriate materials to develop early literacy skills.

Libraries that include science stations, a picture book area, a toy area (perhaps with a puppet theatre), and a spacious area for infants just beginning to crawl offer parents an unparalleled opportunity to share educational games and various programs with their small children so that they can learn science, math, art, and early literary skills through play (Byrne, Derr & Kropp, 2003),

FAMILY LITERACY. Family literacy is significant because immigrants from all over the world are meeting together in schools and libraries throughout the country. Not only do the participants help each other learn English, but they also have access to the resources of the public library, where they can read books with their children and learn about the special programs for families that the library offers. Public library programs such as those we just described have been evaluated by the ALA's Preschool Literacy Initiative and have been found successful in preparing children for preschool, especially by informing parents of the importance of phonological awareness (Arnold, 2003).

Literacy and the Future

This discussion of technology, censorship, and literacy reinforces the mission of teachers and librarians to be strong collaborators in the biopsychosocial education of the whole child in the twenty-first century. *Collaboration* is the key word; it is the essence of the professional relationship between teacher and librarian that empowers students to be successful. Together, teachers and librarians must share their expertise for the benefit of students, who will need these competencies in their future careers.

The classroom teacher and librarian as technology partners is an exciting concept, but it does not mean that reading, book talking, or promoting good books will become irrelevant. The combination of these will keep children reading—as long as books that are a goodness-of-fit and suitable for their biopsychosocial development continue to be published.

Spin Off
Organizing a Literacy Center

Literacy Centers

Effective literacy centers can be organized in various places so that children have access to worthwhile and challenging activities that relate to a specific literacy.

In each classroom, for example, literacy centers could be arranged not only in the lower grades, where they offer teachers valuable time to instruct small groups or individual students, but also in the middle school. These centers make materials available that are geared to a wide range of student interests and reading levels. They provide valuable practice time and furnish teachers in the upper classes with the time needed to work directly with groups of students or individual children. The centers could be tables or special corners in the room (every piece of space should be utilized). As children complete their activities in one center, they move to another at the discretion of the adult in charge.

The school library is another literacy center. With careful planning and thoughtful purchasing of materials, it could be considered the "complete" literacy center serving all classrooms. By collaborating closely with classroom teachers, understanding the needs of the curriculum, and preparing and collecting materials beforehand, the librarian makes space, knowledge, book, and technological resources available for special classroom projects.

The public library has already demonstrated in many parts of the country that it is an active and successful literacy center. Children's rooms are being transformed into literacy centers that contain not only books, but puppet theaters, toys, and storytelling areas that help children learn by listening, observing, and interacting with a variety of educational materials (Byrne, Derr & Kropp, 2003).

Chapter Checklist

Read the following items carefully. If you have difficulty responding to any of them, return to the chapter to review the material.

After reading this chapter, you can

1. Describe what you think are the most controversial issues in children's literature.

2. Explain what is meant by the expression "reading is a private act."

3. Discuss what the "context of censorship" refers to.

4. Identify the most controversial issues that have emerged in modern children's literature.

5. Analyze the impact of the decision of the United States Supreme Court to uphold the constitutionality of The Children's Internet Protection Act.

6. Demonstrate the advantages of student expertise in use of the Internet.

7. Evaluate the value and significance of Internet resources.

8. Illustrate the benefits of Internet searching strategies.

9. Explain the dangers of plagiarism that result from careless or deliberate misappropriation of sources.

10. Explain the growing recognition of children's need for the various forms of literacy.

Children's Bibliography

Angelou, Maya. (1971). *I Know Why the Caged Bird Sings*. New York: Bantam.

Bannerman, Helen. (1955). *Little Black Sambo*. New York: Platt & Munk.

Bing, Christopher. (2003). *Little Black Sambo*. Brooklyn: Handprint Books.

Blume, Judy. (1970, 1990). *Are You There God? It's Me, Margaret*. New York: Bradbury Press.

Blume, Judy. (1975). *Forever*. New York: Simon & Schuster.

Burgess, Melvin. (2001). *Bloodtide*. New York: Penguin Books.

Campbell, Alan, & Campbell, Patricia. (1993). *Bromley Climbs Uluru*. Sydney: Lansdowne.

Chbosky, Steven. (1999). *The Perks of Being a Wallflower*. New York: Pocket Books.

Cormier, Robert. (1974). *The Chocolate War*. New York: Pantheon.

Crutcher, Chris. (2001). *Whale Talk*. New York: Greenwillow.

Dahl, Roald. (1964, 1988). *Charlie and the Chocolate Factory*. New York: Viking Penguin.

Frank, E. R. (2002). *America*. New York: Atheneum.

Garden, Nancy. (1982). *Annie on My Mind*. New York: Farrar, Straus, & Giroux.

George, Julie Craighead. (1972). *Julie of the Wolves*. New York: Harper & Row.

Halliday, John. (2003). *Shooting Monarchs*. New York: McElderry.

Harris, Joel Chandler. (1909). *Uncle Remus and His Sayings*. New York: Appleton.

Lester, Julius. (1996). *Sam and the Tigers: A New Retelling of Little Black Sambo*. New York: Dial.

Lofting, Hugh. (1967). *Doctor Dolittle*. Philadelphia: Lippincott.

Lowry, Lois. (1987). *Anastasia at Your Service*. Boston: Houghton Mifflin.

Naylor, Phyllis Reynolds. (2001). *Alice Alone*. New York: Atheneum.

Newman, Leslea. (1991). *Heather Has Two Mommies*. Boston: Alyson Wonderland.

Paterson, Katherine. (1977, 1987). *Bridge to Terabithia*. New York: Harper & Row.

Paterson, Katherine. (1978, 1987). *The Great Gilly Hopkins.* New York: Harper Trophy.

Patron, Susan. (2006). *The Higher Power of Lucky.* New York: Atheneum.

Pilkey, David. (2005) . *Captain Underpants and the Attack of the Talking Toilets.* New York: Blue Sky Press.

Rowling, J. K. (1999). *Harry Potter and the Chamber of Secrets.* New York: Scholastic.

Rowling J. K. (2007) *Harry Potter and the Deathly Hallows.* New York: Scholastic.

Sendak, Maurice. (1963). *Where the Wild Things Are.* New York: HarperCollins.

Seuss, Dr. (1971). *Lorax.* New York: Random House.

Steig, William. (1969). *Sylvester and the Magic Pebble.* New York: Prentice Hall.

Taylor, Mildred. (1976). *Roll of Thunder, Hear My Cry.* New York: Dial Press.

Toten, Teresa. (2001). *The Game:* Calgary: Red Deer.

Twain, Mark. (1953, 1988). *Huckleberry Finn.* New York: Puffin.

Watkins, Yoko Kawashima. (1986). *So Far from the Bamboo Grove.* New York: Puffin Books.

Willhoite, Michaela. (1991). *Daddy's Roommate.* Boston: Alyson Wonderland.

Willis, Jeanne. (2002). *The Truth or Something: A Novel.* New York: Holt.

Yep, Laurence. (1975, 1977). *Dragonwings.* New York: Harper.

Professional References

Abilock, Debbie. (2002). "Collaborative Leaders, Powerful Partnerships." *Knowledge Quest.*

Adamich, T. (2003). "The Big Three: Instructional Design, Information Literacy, and Information Power." *Knowledge Quest.* September/October, 26.

Adams, Helen R. (2002). "Privacy & Confidentiality: Now More than Ever, Youngsters Need to Keep Their Library Use Under Wraps." *American Libraries.* November 2002, 44–45.

Alderson, Brian. (2003). "Sendak in England." *The Horn Book.* November/December 2003.

American Association of School Librarians and the Association for Educational Communication and Technology. (1998). *Information Power: Building Partnerships for Learning.* Chicago: American Library Association.

American Libraries (2005). *Whale Talk Beached for Bad Words.* May, 15.

American Library Assocation. (2002). *Privacy, An Interpretation of the Library Bill of Rights. Adopted June 19, 2002.* Chicago: American Library Council.

Arnold, Renea. (2003). "Public Libraries and Early Literacy: Raising a Reader." *American Libraries.* September 2003, 52.

Bailey, John. (2003). *The School Library Journal.* September 2003, 20.

Beam, Alex. (2001). "Christians Aren't So Wild about Harry." *Boston Globe.* September 20, 2001, D1–2.

Bettleheim, Bruno. (1976). *The Uses of Enchantment.* New York: Alfred Knopf.

Bosman, Julie. (2007). "With One Word, Children's Book Sets Off Uproar." *New York Times,* February 18.

Boston Globe. (2003). "Editorial: A Young Reader's Right." *Boston Globe.* October 10, 2003.

Byrne, Marci, Derr, Kathleen, & Kropp, Lisa G. (2003). "Book a Play Date: The Game of Promoting Emergent Literacy." *American Libraries.* September 2003, 41–44.

Campbell, Patty. (2003). "Prizes and Paradoxes." *The Horn Book,* July/August 2003, 501–505.

Goldberg, Beverly. (2003). "Supreme Court Upholds CIPA." *American Libraries.* August 2003, 12–13.

Goldberg, Beverly. (2003). "Russians Decide Harry Potter Isn't Satanic." *American Libraries.* February 2003.

Gregorian, Vartan. (2002). Keynote Address, White House Conference on School Libraries Proceedings, Washington, DC, June 4, 2002.

Greenfield, P., & Yan, Z. (2006). "Children, Adolescents, and the Internet: A New Field of Inquiry in Developmental Psychology." *Developmental Psychology.* 42, 391–394.

Hunt, Peter. (2001). *Children's Literature.* Oxford, England: Blackwell Publishers.

Isaacs, Kathleen. (2003). "Reality Check. A Look at the Disturbing Growth of Violence in Books for Teens." *School Library Journal.* October, 50–51.

Jackson, Linda. (2003). "Online Access Improves Academics." *School Library Journal.* September 2003, 32.

Kennedy, Louise. (2003). *New Storybook, Reopens Old Wounds, Boston Sunday Globe,* December 14, 2003, A1, A29.

Kocian, Lisa. (2007). "Author Defends Memoir on Korea, Apologizes for Furor." *The Boston Globe,* February 16. p. 22.

Krepps, Kathy, Null, Mindy, & Pakowski, Kim (2003). "Teen Reading Matters." *Knowledge Quest.* 32, Number 1, September/October 2003.

Lansky, Bruce. (1993). *The New Adventures of Mother Goose: Gentle Rhymes for Happy Times.* New York: Meadowbrook Press.

Lerner, R., & Lerner, J. (ed.). (1999). *Adolescence: Theoretical Foundations and Biological Bases of Development.* New York: Garland Publishing.

Marcus, Leonard S. (2002).*Ways of Telling.* New York: Dutton.

McCabe, Ron. (2003). "The CIPA Ruling as Reality Therapy." *American Libraries*. August 2003, 16.

McCabe, Ron. (2001). *Civic Librarianship: Renewing the Social Mission of the Public Library*. New York: Scarecrow Press.

McCarthy, Brendan. (2003). "Disclosure of Library Choices Sought." *The Boston Globe*. October 4, 2003, B1, B3.

Montemayor, Raymond. (2001). "Parental Monitoring. In Jacqueline V. Lerner and Richard M. Lerner (ed.). *Adolescence in America*. Santa Barbara, CA: ABC-CLIO.

Olec Joan. (2006). "Anti-DOPA Campagn Gears Up." *School Library Journal*. September, 16, 19.

Salvadore, Maria B. (1995). "Controversial Books for Children." In Anita Silvey, ed. *Children's Books and Their Creators*. Boston: Houghton Mifflin.

Schneider, Karen G. (2003). "Let's Begin the Discussion: What Now?" *American Libraries*. August 2003, 14–16.

Stoll, Clifford. (2000). *High Tech Heretic: Why Computers Don't Belong in the Classroom and other Reflections by a Computer Contrarian*. New York: Doubleday.

Sutherland, Zena. (1995). "Judy Blume." In Anita Silvey, ed. *Children's Books and Their Creators*. Boston: Houghton Mifflin.

Tompkins, Gail. (2003). *Literacy for the 21st Century*. Upper Saddle River, NJ: Prentice Hall.

Whalen, Debra Lau. (2003). "Public Helps with Ed Tech Plan." *School Library Journal* September 2003, 20.

Whalen, Debra Lau. (2003). "Why Isn't Information Literacy Catching On?" *School Library Journal*. September 2003, 50–53.

Yan, Z. (2005). "Age Differences in Children's Understanding of Complexity of the Internet." *Journal of Applied Developmental Psychology*. 26, 385–396.

Yan, Z. (2006). "What Influences Children's and Adolscent's Understanding of the Complexity of the Internet?" *Developmental Psychology*. 42, 418–428.

APPENDIX A

From Books to Plays

Part One: Introduction

Throughout *Children's Literature: A Developmental Perspective* we have offered you, as teachers and librarians, many suggestions for responding to the books that we have discussed: engaging in Grand Conversations, journal writing, illustrating, assembling a magazine and a newspaper, and composing original picture books and graphic novels. In this Appendix, however, we plan to introduce you to a unique instructional technique—converting children's literature to plays—using problem-solving strategies that will provide you with extensive, exciting, and effective strategies for a Drama Response.

Adapting a book, such as any one of the many we have discussed, to a play, skit, or musical is an exercise in problem solving, involving crucial ideas from children's literature, developmental psychology, and instructional techniques. An exercise that is productive for teachers, enriching for students, and fun for all, acting out a story's plot, developing its characters, describing the setting, following the themes, and analyzing the author's point of view brings an added dimension of zest and life to the curriculum. (If you decide to use this technique, determine if permission is needed from the publisher.) In Part One of this appendix, we want to discuss the various techniques teachers can use to transform any of the outstanding literature mentioned in this text, and then in Part Two, we'll illustrate how to apply these principles using a popular folktale.

How to Begin

When teachers read a book that is appropriate for their students and wonder if they can turn it into a play, they are engaged in activities that entail the application of several concepts that are central to problem solving. Although several methods have appeared in the problem-solving literature, ranging from the Socratic method to more current systems such as the IDEAL method of John Bransford and Barry Stein, we urge you to consider a technique devised by one of the authors of this text (Travers, Elliott, & Kratochwill, 1993; Elliott, Kratochwill, Littlefield-Cook, & Travers, 2000). The basic premise of this model is that we should never overlook the possibility of recognizing and overcoming the challenges that face us. In this case, teachers should recognize the opportunity they have to make children's literature come even more alive for their students and to do it in a way that makes them more eager to participate in the "wonderful world of books," which reflects Louise Rosenblatt's response theory. First, let's begin our analysis by examining the potential for play construction in **My Brother Sam Is Dead**.

My Brother Sam Is Dead

*James and Christopher Collier are well-known for their children's books on American history, which students enjoy, and which dramatically illustrate how children develop and use problem-solving strategies. In **My Brother Sam Is Dead**, the Colliers turn to the Revolutionary War as their setting. Tim Meeker recounts the tension-filled days in his family when his older brother Sam joined the rebel forces while the rest of the family remained neutral in a Tory town.*

Many exciting incidents in the book reveal young Tim's thoughtful problem-solving strategies. For example, once in the middle of winter, he and his father were driving their oxen and wagon home with goods to replenish their store. Worried that a wild group of rebels reported to be in the area might think they were selling the food to the British, the father had Tim drive the wagon while he scouted ahead. As they rode through the cold, wintry night, Tim discovered his father was no longer up ahead and his concern grew.

He began to follow the tracks of his father's horse. Suddenly he saw dozens of hoof-prints in the clear snow. There were more hoofprints in the hemlock grove, and, going on up the road, Tim saw the tracks of three or four horses. The cowboys had lain in ambush in the hemlock groves, jumped his father, and taken him away someplace.

He stood there in the snow trying to puzzle out what to do next, but his thinking had screeched to a halt. Slowly his mind began to work again. What would Sam (his big brother) do? He'd do the right thing because he was smart and brave. And, of course, Sam wouldn't go running home. He'd do something daring. The most daring thing to do would be to track down Father, and rescue him.

Then he realized that even though rescuing Father might be the daring thing to do, it wasn't the smartest. So he asked himself another question: What would Father do? And the answer that came pretty quickly was that he'd get the oxen and the wagon and the load of goods back home if he could, so they would have something to run the store and the tavern through the winter. The more Tim thought about it, the more he could see that it was the right answer. His father might get away; the rebels might even let him go after awhile. One way or another his father would be counting on Tim to get the wagon home—that was for certain.

On he went, urging the oxen forward when the slippery going made them slow down. Becoming drowsy, he began to dream how nice it would be to have hot food to eat. As he turned a corner he was abruptly jolted out of his reverie—the rebels on their horses were spread out across the road, waiting for him. He almost panicked as terrifying thoughts chased themselves across his mind. Gaining control of himself, he came up with a possible solution. He slapped the oxen as if he hadn't any worries about who was standing in the middle of the road.

He cleared his voice. "Are you the escort? Am I ever glad to see you."

One of the men pulled the cover off a lantern he had been holding. A circle of hazy light spilled out into the night, showing bits of horses and faces and guns and the trampled snow.

"Pull up the oxen," the man with the lantern shouted.

Tim continued, as if he didn't hear him. "Father said that the escort would be along soon, but when you didn't come, I was worried that the rebels would get to me first."

The rebels shifted uneasily and showed signs of nervousness when Tim added, "I thought there'd be more of you, though. Father said there'd be a least a half dozen men in the escort. He said just fall flat when the shooting started."

At this the rebels began to mutter to themselves. "It sounds like an ambush," one of them said. When they heard a dog bark in the distance, they were convinced that they were about to be attacked and decided to take no chances. They wheeled their horses around and disappeared down the road.

This moving story ends sadly. Tim later discovered that his father had died and, during the course of the war, his brother Sam had mistakenly been hanged as a horse thief. But the Colliers's skillful integration of problem-solving strategies in a young boy's life makes My Brother Sam is Dead a particularly pertinent story to illustrate these techniques.

From a teacher's perspective, the dramatization of this story would seem to demand symbolic representation (words, sentences, etc.) in an external manner. Consequently, as the teacher's understanding of the book's plot and themes and its transformation into drama deepens, certain strategies become apparent.

Problem-solving strategies are usually designated as *general strategies* or *strong strategies*. One of the key elements in both strategies is the matter of focused attention. Given our discussion of problem solving in these pages, you are undoubtedly attending more carefully to detail, a simple suggestion but one that can be enormously helpful. As an example, try this problem.

What day follows the day before yesterday
if three days from now it will be Monday?

Good problem solvers analyze details with considerable care and usually break a problem into sections. They might proceed as follows.

- If three days from now it will be Monday, today must be Friday.
- If today is Friday, yesterday was Thursday
- Then the day before yesterday was Wednesday.
- The following day is Thursday.

Although superficially simple, attending to detail is a powerful tool in problem solving. It makes no difference if the strategy is general or strong; *your students'* attention *must be the initial step* that gives shape to strategies. A good example of this is seen in *My Brother Sam Is Dead* when Tim analyzed the dilemma in which he found himself. He attended to all the details and decided that he had to save the goods so his family and store could survive. With these ideas in mind, let's now turn our attention to the teacher deciding to adapt a book to a play.

USING THE STRATEGIES. *General strategies* consist of principles or guidelines that apply to almost any problem. Here are some examples that teachers can use.

- The facts required for solution need to be identified. In this case, the teacher must know, in detail, the book students will be using. *Knowledge is critical for success.*
- The teacher needs to apply certain general and appropriate strategies for solution. These include tactics such as *working backwards*, which can be helpful if the goal and givens (the facts) are stated clearly. In the task facing you, as a teacher, the goal is obvious: translating the givens (themes, characters, plot) to a different form. Consequently, applying the techniques we have been discussing, teachers can analyze such issues as where the play should be presented (the setting), how long the presentation should be, and how many characters will be needed. Continuing to work backwards, teachers must decide who will be best suited for the different characters, how much time will be allotted for rehearsal, and where the rehearsals will take place. Finally, who should do the writing (teacher or students), how much dialogue is necessary, etc.?
- Another powerful general strategy that aids solution when the goal is established is to apply a *means–end analysis*. For example, assume that your house needs painting and you decide to do it yourself. The goal is clear but the means to achieve it require additional planning. If the old paint is peeling, then it first must be scraped and roughed up with a wire brush. You must then decide if these spots need priming. Is there hardware you should remove? What kind of paint is best suited to the weather conditions in your area: latex or oil? While these steps seem simple, if you omit one — such as scraping — the solution is faulty. But no strategy is more critical than the way students store and retrieve their memories.

The *strong strategies* (those that are directed at the core elements of a subject) available to teachers illustrate the great values for students that are inherent in this process: improving their cognitive skills in a way that they enjoy. Literacy, oral presentations, logical thinking, memory skills, their personal problem-solving ability, and the encouragement of creativity are among many other desirable features that are all enhanced. For example, think of how Tim in our story quickly devised a logical series of steps designed to solve a terrifying problem and how this could be transformed into an exciting moment in the children's play.

Let's examine how these strategies apply to another popular story.

The Hundred Dresses

In Eleanor Estes' classic story, **The Hundred Dresses,** *the girls in Room 13 make Wanda Petronski an object of ridicule. She doesn't have a name like the other children; she comes from Boggins Heights, the worst part of town, and she wears the same faded dress to school every day. Peggy, one of the "in" group, started the game of the dresses suddenly one day when Wanda said, "I have a hundred dresses at home—all lined up in my closet." After that the girls thought it was funny to stop Wanda on the way to school and ask, "How many dresses did you say you have?" "A hundred," she would answer. Then every one laughed and Wanda's lips would tighten as she walked off with one shoulder hunched up in a way none of the girls understood.*

Note how, in the first part of this story, Estes immediately forces the reader to focus on one essential element: the hundred dresses. By her careful use of words and sentences, she at once focuses attention on several significant features: the mention of the "poor part of town," the apparent conflict of ideas, and Wanda's different-sounding name. So Estes, without delay, instantly captures the reader's attention by the skillful use of setting and the introduction of conflict—an excellent way for teachers and students to create an interesting Act One.

Just before the annual art contest, Wanda didn't come to school. Maddie, Peggy's friend, was concerned that the girls had hurt Wanda's feelings by teasing her about the dresses. She wanted to send Peggy a letter about her feelings but she tore it up instead. She tried to prepare her lessons but she couldn't put her mind on her work. True, she had not enjoyed listening to Peggy ask Wanda how many dresses she had in her closet but she had said nothing. She had stood by silently and that was just as bad as what Peggy had done. Worse. She was a coward.

Supposing she was the one being made fun of, she tried to put herself in Wanda's shoes and realized she had helped to make someone so unhappy that she couldn't come to school. Wanda didn't even know that she had won the girls' art contest for drawing the most attractive dresses—one hundred of them, with dazzling colors and brilliant lavish designs, all drawn on great sheets of wrapping paper.

Then the teacher read a letter from Wanda's father.
"Dear Teacher:
My Wanda will not come to your school any more. Now we move away to big city. No more holler Polack. No more ask why funny name. Plenty of funny names in the big city.
Yours truly, Jan Petronski."

The teacher then looked directly at the class. "I'm sure none of my boys and girls in Room 13 would deliberately hurt anyone's feelings because her name happened to be a long unfamiliar one. I prefer to think that what was said was said in thoughtlessness. I know that all of you feel the way I do, that this is a very unfortunate thing to have happened. Unfortunate and sad, both. And I want you all to think about it."

Estes, in what would be an ideal Act Two, continues to provide her readers with needed knowledge. We learn about Wanda's absence from school and begin to understand Maddie's feelings. For someone who is supposed to be Wanda's friend, she has nothing but feelings of guilt about not defending Wanda. Even Peggy, one of the "in" group, begins to regret her behavior. The manner in which Estes explores the characters, setting, and conflict contains all the ingredients of a perfect Act Two: get your characters in as much difficulty as seems reasonable.

Maddie wondered if there were anything she could do. If only she could tell Wanda she hadn't meant to hurt her feelings. She and Peggy decided to climb Boggins Heights so that they could tell Wanda she had won the contest, and that they thought she was smart and the hundred dresses were beautiful. But no one was at Wanda's.

The following day, Peggy and Maddie wrote a friendly letter to Wanda and took it to Boggins Heights with instructions to the Post Office to "Please forward." Weeks later, Wanda sent a letter to the class wishing them a Merry Christmas and offering Peggy and Maddie and the girls the drawings she had made for the contest, because "in my new house I have a hundred new ones all lined up in my closet."

As the book begins to come to a conclusion, Estes continues to present conflicting ideas, but in a less intense manner. That is, Maddie and Peggy want to make amends to Wanda—but Wanda is gone! Now what to do? Next comes the resolution of the problem when the girls try to contact Wanda through the post office. Their efforts are rewarded when Wanda answers their letter and sends them her drawings of the hundred dresses. A perfect Act Three!

With these basic ideas (general strategies) in mind, we can appreciate how the principles of problem solving can help teachers to adapt popular books to plays.

A Four-Stage Model

The four stages of this model are as follows.

1. DETERMINING THAT A PROBLEM EXISTS

Some teachers may not realize the potential that children's books offer for dramatic presentations. Either they overlook the connection between book and play or the task may seem too time consuming. But teachers possess all the characteristics of good problem solvers:

- *They have a positive attitude* toward their teaching ability and believe that they can help improve their students' achievement.
- *They are concerned with accuracy*, that is, they realize they must understand the facts and relationships that the daily problems of the classroom present.
- *They are active seekers of solutions* and search many possibilities to discover what works and what doesn't.
- *They are good at breaking problems into parts*, which is an ideal approach to adapting a book into classroom theater.

All of these positive features contribute to an ability to engage students in a meaningful, enjoyable task of creating ideas, planning scenes, assigning parts, and developing plots. Think of the pleasure that both teachers and students have when they create a drama from a story such as **War Comes to Willy Freeman**.

War Comes to Willy Freeman

*In **War Comes to Willy Freeman**, the Colliers introduce us to Willy (short for Wilhemina), an uneducated but intelligent African-American girl whose adventures during the Revolutionary War make her one of the most remarkable heroines in any of the Colliers' historical novels. Her actions in this story are also a perfect example of problem solving in action.*

In one bloody afternoon, Willy's life changes forever. Through horrified eyes, she sees British soldiers shoot and kill her father, a freed slave. Grief stricken, she returns to her home in Groton, Connecticut, where, to her consternation, she found her mother had disappeared. She raced around the house and discovered that her mother's bonnet and cloak were hanging on the hook by the door where they always were. She went back outside and walked around the cabin, calling for her. It was then Willy realized her mother must have been taken by the British.

All that really mattered to Willy now was that Pa was dead and Ma was gone. She knew she couldn't go on crying forever; she had to do something . Her mind racing, she asked herself a series of questions. How was I going to live? Who was there for me? What relatives did I have? Would they take me in? Even if they did, how would I get there? It was fifty miles to Stratford. I could walk it in three days proba- bly. But there was Pa's boat, which was moored at the cove. The British might have found it or somebody might have come along and just plain stole it, but Willy saw it as her only chance.

Before Willy left the top of the hill, she decided she needed a plan, so she sat down for a few minutes and thought. Then she rose to her feet and carefully left the hill, walked swiftly to the shore, and crept along the beach where, to her delight, she found her fa- ther's boat hidden under the branches of a willow tree. The British ships were raising their sails and getting ready to sail back to New York and she knew how dangerous it would be to sail among the British ships. Still she had to take advantage of the daylight, so she decided to sail as close as she could to the shore, avoiding detection and letting her stay near land in case something went wrong.

Finally, after sailing all day, Willy beached the boat close to a wharf that she fig- ured was where her relatives lived. After tying up the boat, she stopped short. "Suppose they don't want me. Suppose they didn't need no extra mouths to feed. Suppose Aunt Betsy didn't love Ma so much as Ma thought. Besides she never met me and didn't know me from a goat, but I do look like my mother."

With her heart pounding, Willy opened the door and timidly stepped into a warm, inviting room. After the first shock, her aunt recognized her and welcomed her kin with open arms. She had made the right decision. As relieved as she was, however, Willy knew she couldn't stay long with her relatives; she had to find some way of getting to New York and begin the search for her mother.

It almost seems as if the Colliers had a problem-solving model in mind when they wrote their moving story of Willy. For example, she had no trouble determining the nature of the problem—where and how to find the means to get immediate help. She clearly understood what she was up against—where to obtain food and shelter, how to get to her relatives, how to get to New York. Her plan was carefully formu- lated—first, discover if the British had left, then decide the best way to travel to her relatives, and, finally, do it without being caught. She objectively evaluated her plan— was walking the best way? No, then she would use the boat. Could she avoid capture? Yes, if she stayed close to the shore.

Visualize the delight that children would experience playing the various roles in the story, as well as the deeper appreciation of reading they would derive from this experience. As the Colliers weave their seductive stories of children's adven- tures, they shine the spotlight of their literary talent on the enduring themes of childhood—getting along with others, thinking clearly, problem solving—themes deeply embodied in Children's Literature: A Developmental Perspective.

Now that you as a teacher recognize that a problem exists—creating a drama from a book your students like—we can turn our attention to the second stage of our model: understanding the nature of the problem, or to put it more simply, just what's involved here?

2. UNDERSTANDING THE NATURE OF THE PROBLEM

In the second stage of the problem-solving model, teachers must do more than real- ize a problem exists; they must also comprehend the essence of the problem if their plan for a solution—writing the play—is to be both accurate and successful. In other words, they must both define and represent the problem; that is, they must have *knowledge* about several key elements of the process, which they can acquire by:

• *recognizing* the strengths and weaknesses of individual students. Who doesn't like to be the center of attention? Which class members have the memory skills needed for presentation? (Here we see the educational value of this technique since students must exercise and continue to develop those cognitive skills that are vital for success in all subjects of the curriculum—language, social studies, science, even math.) (See Schiro,

1997, for an excellent discussion of integrating children's literature and mathematics in the classroom.)

• *knowing and appreciating* the book they're about to adapt. For example, who are the key characters? What members of the class are best suited for a particular role? How long should the play run? What themes should be stressed? How can the setting be presented? Knowledge is a potent force in encouraging problem-solving behavior.

• *representing* the problem for themselves and their students. As teachers wrestle with the problem of adaptation, they should visualize the best means of capturing the critical elements of the process both for their students and for themselves. For example, do children of a particular age learn better when their work is diagrammed or pictured in some way (a process called *diagrammatic representation*) or would it be better to use letters, words, or numbers (a process called *symbolic representation*)?

These forms of representation may be either *internal or external*, depending upon an individual's learning style. That is, some individuals (both teachers and students), when presented with a problem, immediately begin to write down solutions while the first impulse of others is to visualize the problem by drawing a picture of it. Others (again both teachers and students) sit and mentally visualize the elements in the problem. Neither process is better than the other; what's "best" is what works for an individual.

The above suggestions apply to knowledge of the students. But teachers must also have knowledge of how to transform the ideas, characters, plot, and setting of the book into a form that attracts and holds the attention of students. In a classic description of play creation, Lawrence Langner (1960) noted that one of the main differences between writing a novel and writing a play is embodied in the word *construction*.

By construction, Langner referred to the arrangement of individual scenes, one after the other, so that the play builds in suspense until the story reaches its climax (1960, p. 115). These indeed are words of wisdom because teachers desirous of turning a novel into a play should remember that the construction of the play may be modified or dispensed with altogether if the demands of the situation or the abilities of the participants, (the students) require it.

The generally accepted belief (thanks to Aristotle) that a play should have a beginning, a middle, and an end leads to a three-act play, which immediately gives our teacher an initial sense of direction. This formula then leads to a possible structure for the play, which is thought to have originated in France (Langner, 1960) and is as follows.

1. In Act One, get your characters up a tree.
2. In Act Two, throw stones at them.
3. In Act Three, get them down again.

Since the stories teachers and students will be working with are typically well-defined, these ideas should help teachers to decide where to break the original story into acts. Once this is accomplished, they can then begin to fill in the missing pieces. For example, in Act One, they can describe the setting and position the characters so the observers know something about them and understand the problem that engages the characters. (In a sense, the characters are now "up the tree.") In Act Two (as stones are thrown at them), their position is seen to be perilous, dangerous, or dramatically intense. Finally, in Act Three, the characters are saved but not too easily or too quickly.

Since many of these issues have already been established in the book, teachers must decide if any subtle changes are needed or desired.

How do these ideas apply to making an appealing children's book into a play? First, read the following summary of **Homer Price**, a longtime favorite.

Homer Price

*In his classic tale, **Homer Price**, Robert McCloskey has placed his hero in a situation that required intelligent planning and thoughtful resolution, in other words, the* *key elements of problem solving. At his Uncle Ulysses' store, the automatic donut machine had run amuck, spewing out donuts like a robot with a machine gun. Even though Homer, a young boy who loved to tinker with radios, replaced two parts, "the rings of batter kept right on dropping into the hot fat, and the automatic gadget kept right on turning them over and the other automatic gadget kept right on giving them a little push, and the doughnuts kept right on rolling down the little chute just as regular as a clock can tick—they just kept on a-comin' an a-comin' an' a-comin'."*

Here the author, Robert McCloskey, has described a situation that, for Homer, has all the characteristics of a problem. But McCloskey, good author that he is, isn't satisfied with what appears to be a fairly simple problem. He also informs his readers that Homer seems to be a mechanically clever boy. This seems to possess all the needed elements for a good first act because Homer is clearly "up a tree."

Homer was pondering the problem when his anxiety soared dramatically: A wealthy customer told him that she lost her diamond bracelet in the batter! At this point, Homer stepped back and surveyed the situation. How could he sell the hundreds of donuts that were being cranked out of the machine and reclaim the precious bracelet for the lady who was offering a reward? Reflecting on the donut monster, the bracelet, and the anxious woman, Homer hit on a solution: Make a sign saying:

Fresh Doughnuts - 2 for 5 cents
Get Them While They Last
Special Bonus!!!!!!!!
$100 Prize For Finding
A BRACELET
Inside A Doughnut
P.S. You have to give the bracelet back.

Now that McCloskey has Homer up in the tree, he appears to be taking great delight in "throwing stones at him." The author shrewdly tells us about Homer's dilemma by throwing small stones at him—the machine is malfunctioning—but as what will be Act Two continues, McCloskey suddenly begins to throw larger and larger stones at Homer with ever increasing velocity. Given the time in which the story is set—doughnuts 2 for 5 cents!!!—losing a diamond bracelet unexpectedly magnifies the seriousness of the problem. But Homer remained undaunted, thereby exhibiting all the characteristics of the good problem solver: He maintained a positive attitude; he actively searched for a solution; he broke the problem into parts—selling the doughnuts and finding the diamond bracelet.

Customers flocked in. Everybody wanted to buy doughnuts, dozens of them. And there was more good news—the customers bought gallons of coffee to dunk their doughnuts in. When all but the last couple of hundred doughnuts had been sold, Rupert Black, a customer, shouted, "I GAWT IT," and sure enough there was the diamond bracelet right in the middle of his doughnut!

Rupert went home with a hundred dollars, the citizens of Centerburg went home full of doughnuts, the lady and her chauffeur drove off with the diamond bracelet, and Homer went home with his mother when she stopped by with Aunt Aggy. As Homer, covered with batter, staggered out of the door he heard Mr. Gabby say, "Neatest trick of merchandising I ever seen."

As McCloskey completes what will be Act Three of our classroom play, and as Homer wearily wends his way home, we can only admire the tightness of the story and of the play adaptation. Students love performing this story—it's funny, its star is a young person, and teachers also enjoy working with Homer Price because they can combine writing instruction (actually writing the play), language instruction (vocabulary development, sentence construction, paragraph formation, oral language, etc.), and the chance to bring important aspects of the curriculum into a different and enjoyable format. Problem-solving behavior in action!

3. PLANNING THE SOLUTION

Our third stage of the problem-solving model refers to one of the most powerful strategies in solving problems and planning the means to accomplish it: the efficient use of memory, both for teachers and students. As students grow and mature, particularly during the years from seven to eleven, they devise memory strategies to categorize and store needed information, a process that teachers can encourage in adapting books to plays. But there is more to memory strategies than meets the eye. All memory strategies are not equally as effective. A particular strategy is appropriate or not depending on the material and the conditions under which the information must be recalled. Let's see how these ideas apply to Lois Lowry's popular children's story ***Number the Stars.***

Number the Stars

*Lois Lowry, well-known for her contemporary stories about determined, inquisitive, and adventure-seeking young girls, has written an especially poignant drama, **Number the Stars,** about Annemarie Johansen and her best friend Ellen Rosen. As the German troops in Denmark began their campaign to "relocate" Danish Jews, the Johansens vowed to protect Ellen from the horrors of displacement. But Ellen and Annemarie must think quickly when three Nazi officers arrive late one night and order Annemarie and Ellen out of bed.*

Annemarie tugged the Star of David necklace off Ellen's neck and held it tightly in her hand. Since the oldest Johansen daughter, Lisl, had died, Annemarie's father, thinking quickly, identified Ellen as one of his three daughters. "Why isn't she blond like her sisters?" demands one of the officers as he roughly grasped Ellen's hair. The father quickly walked to a table and picked up a photograph album. Annemarie remembered that of all the photographs in the album her father could have shown the soldiers, he chose the photograph of her sister Lisl as an infant with wispy curls that were dark. Without a word, the German officer tore the picture in half and the three of them left the apartment.

Later the Rosens and other Jewish families were forced to flee their homes and hide in a fishing trawler in the harbor while they waited to be spirited out of the country to Sweden. Annemarie found a packet outside on the steps after Ellen left her uncle's house. It had been dropped in their hurry to escape. Her uncle, the captain of the trawler, needed the packet before he transported his hidden passengers to Sweden. As Annemarie ran through the woods toward the harbor, carrying a basket of bread with the packet at the bottom, she was again stopped by German soldiers accompanied by two large dogs, straining at taut leashes, eyes glittering, lips curled. Annemarie's mind raced. She remembered what her mother had said, "If anyone stops you, pretend to be nothing more than a silly little girl."

Terrified, Annemarie kept her wits and recalled another incident when soldiers stopped her, Ellen, and her younger sister, Kirsti, on the way home from school. Annemarie had been frightened but her sister acted like a silly little girl that day. Kirsti was mad because one of the soldiers had touched her hair. She reached up and pushed the soldier's hand away. "Don't," she said loudly. The soldiers began to laugh and let the three girls continue on their way.

All of these thoughts raced through Annemarie's mind and she knew she had to force herself to behave as Kirsti had done. When one of them asked what she was doing there in the woods, Annemarie held out her basket, with the thick loaf of bread visible. "My Uncle Henrik forgot his lunch, and I'm taking it to him. He's a fisherman." One of the dogs growled and both dogs were looking at the lunch basket.

"You came out before daybreak just to bring a lunch? Why doesn't your uncle eat fish?"

What would Kirsti reply? Annemarie tried to giggle the way her sister might. "Uncle Henrik doesn't like fish," she said laughing. "He says he sees too much of it, and smells too much of it." Keep chattering, she told herself, as Kirsti would. Just a silly little girl.

The soldier reached forward and grabbed the crisp loaf of bread from the basket and broke it in half. Annemarie knew that would enrage Kirsti. "Don't," she cried angrily. "That's Uncle Henrik's bread. My mother baked it."

That didn't stop the soldiers who continued to search and found the cheese and the packet so valuable to Annemarie's uncle. They opened the packet to discover only a small white piece of cloth.

"Stop crying, you idiot girl. Your stupid mother has sent your uncle a handkerchief. Go on. Go on to your uncle and tell him the German dogs enjoyed his bread."

Annemarie learned later that the handkerchief contained a special drug invented by Swedish scientists that ruined the sense of smell of the searching dogs. When the boat captain pulled out the handkerchief from his pocket, the Germans assumed he had a bad cold. The dogs, however, picked up the odor, which then left them helpless in detecting any human scents.

How would teachers go about planning the adaptation of Lois Lowry's book?

- *First*, after reading the book and discussing it with students, both teacher and students have acquired the basic knowledge of the book they need so that they can attack the problem of turning it into a play. Now teachers must also use their knowledge of individual students to assign roles that match the individual abilities of students. Who has had leading roles previously? Who should be in the chorus? Who can play the gruff German soldiers?

- *Second*, working backwards comes into play here. If Annemarie is to be played as a quick-witted, brave girl when she meets the soldiers, she should have exhibited these qualities earlier in the play. If the packet is to be successfully transported, how could it be prepared and hidden?

- *Third*, a means–end analysis would help teachers to identify and prepare for the various challenges that need to be presented. Where is the best place to hide the packet? What should it look like? How could it be protected from the searching dogs?

- *Fourth*, having determined these preliminary steps in the plan, our teacher now prepares to write the text. Among the matters to be considered is the issue of authorship. Should the teacher do it alone? Or could more educational value come from having the students share in the writing? Next is the decision about the different acts in the play: how many, how long, how many participants, etc.?

- *Fifth*, once teachers have formulated their plans, it's time to think of the students' participation. A major concern is the ability of the students to remember their lines and the type of characters they are supposed to portray, which introduces what psychologists call *storing and retrieving*. For example, how many times have you had something in your mind (you have stored it) but you cannot get at it (you can't *retrieve* it)— "it's on the tip of my tongue." There are several techniques that teachers can use to help students with their memory. Among the most effective retrieval aids are the following.

Using Retrieval Aids

- *Rehearsal*. Rehearsal refers to the manner in which most of us attempt to memorize something: We repeat it and repeat it again until we feel secure that we have successfully stored it in our memories. Our teacher undoubtedly is considering two types of rehearsal for the students:

  1. *Rehearse (repeat) each line* until they are sure they had memorized it.

     or

  2. *Rehearse several lines together.*

- *Cues*. The most effective cues for students (and for all of us) are those that they generate themselves. We almost always believe that we know more than we can remember at the moment; we simply "cannot get at" the material. The beauty of aiding students by teaching them to use these techniques is that they will improve not only their problem-solving skills for their work in literature but also their memory in all subjects. By helping them to devise tangible cues you ultimately could help them in creating their own cues and use them to pick up the cues from the previous lines.

For example, to help remember the names of the girls involved, perhaps some students could arrange their names as follows:

Annemarie
Ellen
as
Ann-E

The important point is to urge the students to use those cues that *they* decide on.

Teachers can also assist students in devising a sentence or phrase with words whose first letter is the retrieval cue. Most of us who are non-musicians relied on an acrostic to recall the lines of a G cleff.

e very
g ood
b oy
d oes
f ine

Remember that an acrostic is an effective strategy as long as the material is not too complicated or unique. The strategy a teacher adopts should never be more difficult than the task, because students need to use the various memory strategies smoothly and efficiently.

- *Imagery*. Some children—as well as adults—tend to visualize objects or events; they'll tell you "they can see it." If any students seem to prefer memorizing things this way, teachers could encourage them to form a picture relating the items that are to be remembered. For example, if they must remember that John Adams was the second president of the United States, ask them to picture Adams standing for a portrait and holding a large card with the number 2 on it.

  In *Number the Stars*, to help students remember that the packet was a vital part of the story, they could be urged to imagine it as a special piece of bread. Those children who prefer visualizing things, and even those who are more verbal, can improve their use of imagery, and they will find it a dynamic and effective aid to retention and recall.

- *The Method of Loci*. If students do not have appropriate cues available to them as they act in the play, their teachers could explain to them that they can devise personal cues to help pull needed information from their memories. The method of loci has them place memorized items in familiar locations, such as the rooms in their house. Tell them to close their eyes and form a picture of the object that they must recall. Now have them place it on a piece of furniture somewhere in one of the rooms. For example, they may decide to have the German soldiers sit on a sofa in the living room of their home. Or they may place the German dogs in the backyard of their home.

Regardless of the memory strategy students use, the point is to have them find the strategy that works best for them; remember that your children also have their own preferences. *Help them find their preferred strategy and practice it until it becomes automatic.*

Finally, encourage them to *elaborate*, that is, to add information to what they are trying to learn, thus making the material more personally meaningful and easier to remember. Prior knowledge, experiences, attitudes, beliefs, and values all contribute to elaboration. Children can create analogies, paraphrase, summarize in their own words, transform information into another form such as a chart or diagram, use comparison and contrast methods, or try to teach what they are learning to someone else, their brothers and sisters or parents.

Teachers can help their students develop fluent and flexible elaboration tactics by encouraging them to ask themselves questions about the material they are learning, such as:

- What is the main idea of this story?
- What does this material remind me of?
- How can I put this into my own words?
- What is a good example of this that I'm familiar with?
- How does this apply to me?

When teachers think of problem solving as intelligent behavior and consider the various strategies that they can use and the benefits their students acquire, they can appreciate how these techniques improve their students' literacy and cognitive skills. Consequently, they should accept that these procedures are long-term, ongoing, productive processes that consume much of their time, effort, and energy, but are well worth their efforts.

4. EVALUATING THE SOLUTION

In his engaging autobiography, **Act One**, Moss Hart (1959, p. 367) talks about the use of an outline in writing a play and how the play itself, as it develops, changes all the preconceived ideas of the author.

What I failed to take into account was that an outline or scenario is an imprecise instrument at best. It cannot be followed slavishly, for as the outline is translated into dialogue, it shifts mercurially under one's fingers, and the emphasis of a scene or sometimes a whole act will twist out of control, taking with it large parts of the carefully plotted scenario that follows after.

These words of Moss Hart are probably the best possible introduction to the final stage of our problem-solving model: **Evaluating the Solution**. Here teachers, as busy as they are and as simple as adapting a classroom book appears to be, stop and examine what they have done. Are the right students cast in appropriate roles? Is there a smooth match between story and play? Does the writing of the play convey the major themes of the book? The answers to these and similar questions all point directly to the importance of evaluation in our model: Does the play work?

Moss Hart gives a perfect example of how even the best playwrights encounter challenging obstacles and the frustrations that he describes in **Act One**. After describing his early years and a growing fascination with the stage, Hart tells of writing his first play in collaboration with the famous and irascible George Kaufman. Called **Once In A Lifetime,** Hart takes us through the agony of spending an incredible number of hours of writing, changing scenes, and rewriting until finally the play is ready for its pre-Broadway tryout. For the first two acts everything goes smoothly—people are laughing in the right places and enjoying their night out. But suddenly, toward the end of second act, they stop laughing. Something terrible has happened! Hart and Kaufman tried every trick of rewriting they could think of. Nothing seemed to help and their Broadway opening was only two weeks away. And then fate struck. Having dinner with a friend, Hart was bemoaning the failure of the third act, when his friend said rather casually, "I wish, kid," he sighed, "that this weren't such a noisy play." It was if a light had gone on in a dark room. Hart realized that just too much was happening in the third act; he and Kaufman rewrote it; the play was a dazzling success, and Hart had taken the first step on what was to become a brilliant career. *Hart and Kaufman were forced to stop and evaluate their plan.*

The fourth and final stage of our problem solving model includes two phases of analysis:

- evaluating the plan
- evaluating the solution

Evaluating the plan requires that teachers stop here and decide if the play includes all of the key features that made the book successful. Are all of its prominent parts incorporated into the play? Are all of these essentials presented in a way that is calculated to reach a solution? Has the translation of book to play resulted in the loss of any of its basic components? If your answers to these and similar question are affirmative, then the first phase of the evaluation process is complete and you should put your plan into action.

After our teacher has examined the plan for the play, the second phase of evaluation must be addressed. Here a decision has to be made about the solution: Is the play satisfactory? Does it involve all of the class members? Does the solution (writing the play) meet the objective of transferring the book to play in a way that retains the integrity of the story?

Finally, teachers would do well to remember that the books they are using for dramatization are undoubtedly those that children love, because the stories touch on their needs and interests. Langner (1960, p. 36) summarizes these criteria nicely when he notes:

In my opinion, the kind of subject for which the play form is best suited is one in which there is a major situation or situations involving conflict between characters or groups of characters, or between characters and their destiny, which build in conflict, interest, or intensity throughout the play to some sort of conclusion.

As you look back at the thousands of narratives discussed in this text, we hope, and feel certain, that they are of the quality and interest that will tempt you to commence your own adaptations. To help you in your selection and translation, Part Two of this discussion will demonstrate how you can enter into this enjoyable and valuable exercise with your students.

Part Two: The Play's the Thing

We have decided to use a simple folktale from the *Panchatantra* to illustrate the suggestions we have made concerning techniques for turning children's literature into enjoyable and productive plays for students. This folktale for early elementary students, which has appeared in varied forms throughout the world, like all folktales, reflects the culture of its origin rather than that of any individual. By reading folktales, children acquire knowledge about many and different types of cultures that contribute to the cultural diversity so necessary for today's students living in an age of globalization.

Many folktales can be traced back to the fifth and sixth century AD, when they were already considered ancient, and attempts to provide a coherent theoretical explanation of their origins remain elusive. Modern explanations can often be traced to psychoanalysis: Freud and his belief that folktales emerged from the unconscious or Jung's search for the "collective unconscious" that contained the common experiences of the human race. Other interpretations may be rooted in religion, nature, or myth, while still others may be found in the Indo-European Myth Theory, which holds that all folktales originated in Indo-European myths.

Moira the Musical Mouse has its source in the *Panchatantra*, which most experts agree is one of India's most valuable contributions to world literature. This collection of 87 folktales, most of which were composed between the third and fifth centuries, were eventually carried to Europe by oral tradition. Barbara E. Travers, who has adapted this tale for elementary classroom use, has received a *Horace Mann Award* from the Massachusetts Department of Education for her creativity in teaching children's literature. She has also received two cable television awards for writing and directing plays that she has adapted from classic children's stories.

MOIRA THE MUSICAL MOUSE

Adapted by Barbara E. Travers from an ancient folktale

Setting: (An Elementary Classroom)
Macroom. A small town in ancient Ireland.
The setting for ACT ONE is sparse: two chairs and a table.
The scenery for the following acts could be made more elaborate with illustrations of the moon, sun, cloud, wind, and wall as backdrops.
Otherwise, students could just carry or wear placards identifying themselves as the moon, sun, cloud, wind, or the wall.

Characters:

MOIRA MOUSE—beautiful and talented
PATRICK MOUSE, Moira's friend
MRS. MOUSE
MR. MOUSE
THE MOON
THE SUN
THE CLOUD
THE WIND
THE WALL
THE CHORUS: group of students
NARRATOR ONE
NARRATOR TWO

Selection of Characters: Determined by the teacher who knows the capabilities of the class: their ability to read, their skill at memorizing, their ability to project their voices, and, most important, their talent for working together. The number of characters will depend on the size of the class. The teacher may add more students or narrators if necessary. In this way, each student has a part. Some students may prefer to work behind the scenes (working the curtain, staging, moving props, or coaching).

Costumes:

MOIRA MOUSE: headband with ears, a tails, and a pretty dress
PATRICK MOUSE: ears, a tails, a shirt, and trousers
MRS. MOUSE: ears, a tails, a dress, an apron, and a funny hat
MR. MOUSE: ears, a tails, trousers, shirt, and vest
THE CHORUS: ears, tails, and school clothes

INTRODUCTION
(in front of curtain; curtain, however, is not necessary.)

NARRATOR ONE

Once upon a time in the land of Macroom, large families of field mice lived inside the craggy rock crevices of Macroom Castle that had been left in ruins by invading armies. The mice were busy and happy as they worked and played.

NARRATOR TWO

One mouse, Moira by name, was very pretty. Her eyes sparkled, her ears were pointed sharply, and her skin was soft and shiny. Her favorite pastime was playing the harp. (shows audience a cardboard harp.)

Her favorite playmate was Patrick, a handsome mouse, funny and carefree. Together they danced and sang.

(Enter Patrick and Moira, hand in hand. They dance a jig together. A miniature harp is on stage.)

Often, Patrick *(sitting down)* listens to Moira play her harp. *(Background music "When Irish Eyes Are Smiling" comes from a hidden cassette player while Moira pretends to play.)* (music fades)

CURTAIN OPENS.

ACT ONE, SCENE ONE: MR. AND MRS. MOUSE
(on stage sitting at a table)

Father: Our little daughter Moira is growing up to be quite a young lady, don't you think?

Mother: She is, indeed. Not only does she look beautiful with her glistening eyes and smooth skin but she is talented as well. She plays the harp like an angel.

Father: Now, I'm thinking 'tis time for her to look ahead to her future. Whom should she marry? Who would make her happy?

Mother: She should begin to think of her future, 'tis true. But she must not marry just *any lad.* She is so beautiful and talented that she must marry the most powerful of all.

Father: I've heard it said that the MOON is the most powerful of all.

Mother: *(standing up)* Then I shall take her to meet the MOON.

BOTH EXIT. CURTAIN CLOSES.

CHORUS
(in front of curtain)
Shine on, Shine on
Glorious moon
Will you be Moira's true love
Soon?

ACT ONE, SCENE TWO: MOIRA AND HER MOTHER
(in front of the curtain)

Moira: *(playing her harp quietly)* (background music)

But, Mother, I don't wan't to go to the MOON. I want to stay here with my friends and play my harp.

Mother: Listen, Moira, dear. You are beautiful and you are talented and you must marry someone who is powerful to make you happy. Come, come now with me to meet the MOON.

Moira: Oh, all right. Just this once. (*She puts down her harp and exits offstage with her mother.*)

CURTAIN RISES.

ACT TWO: MOIRA, HER MOTHER, AND THE MOON

MOON: To what do I owe this charming visit?

Mother: Moon, my husband and I would like you to marry our daughter, Moira. She is not only beautiful but she is very talented and plays the harp like an angel. You are so powerful, you must be the most powerful being in creation.

MOON: I must admit that I am powerful. I am a light in the darkness and I do guide the way of every creature in the universe. But there is someone more powerful than I.

Mother: Who might that be?

MOON: Why, the SUN, of course. When the SUN shines, I disappear from view. No one can see me when the SUN is in the sky. The SUN is more powerful than I.

MOON: Alas, I think many times how grand it would be to listen to music. When I'm just a sliver of myself, the music must be soft from the strings of a violin. When I become one-half a MOON, I need a full orchestra. And when I'm a full MOON, the music must be a blast from a big brass band. I can't be satisfied with music from the strings of a harp.

Moira: Mother, I do not want to marry the Moon. He may be powerful, 'tis true, but he would never be content with the music I play.

Mother: Then, we will go to the SUN, daughter dear. We have no time to lose.

EXIT MOTHER AND MOIRA.

CURTAIN CLOSES.

CHORUS
(in front of curtain)
Or will the SUN shine
On her pretty face
And make Moira feel
That the SUN's her place?

ACT THREE: MOTHER, MOIRA, AND THE SUN

SUN: Why have you both come to me? 'Tis such a great distance.

Mother: SUN, my husband and I would like you to marry our daughter, Moira. She is not only beautiful but she is very talented. She plays the harp like an angel. And you are so powerful. You must be the most powerful being in creation.

SUN (*clearing his throat*)
    I do have great power, 'tis true. But I have no time to listen to music. Besides, there is another being more powerful than I.

Mother: How can there be someone more powerful than you?

SUN: When a CLOUD passes by, it covers me entirely. I am powerless against the CLOUD. You must go to the CLOUD and ask him to marry your daughter.

Mother: Come, Moira. We must travel to the CLOUD.

Moira: The MOON does not please me. He wants nothing to do with my music. The SUN is too busy to lend an ear. So, why should I think that the CLOUD, as powerful as he is, will be any different?

Mother: Let's find out, Moira. We shall go right now to visit the CLOUD (*This time, she grabs Moira's hand, and together they exit the stage*).

CURTAIN CLOSES.

CHORUS
(*in front of curtain*)
Perhaps she'll wait til the cloud drifts by
To find if her true love lives in the sky

ACT FOUR: MOIRA, THE MOTHER, AND THE CLOUD

Mother: CLOUD, my husband and I would like you to marry our daughter, Moira. She is not only beautiful but she is very talented. She plays the harp like an angel and, you are so powerful. You must be the most powerful being in creation.

CLOUD: I am powerful, 'tis true but I am not the most powerful. I DO have the power to cover the SUN, but I am powerless against the WIND. When the WIND blows, he drives me this way and that way, and sometimes he even shreds me up into little pieces. I cannot withstand the WIND.

　　I move so quickly and go to so many places around the world that I cannot stay in one place long enough to listen to music.

Mother: Then Moira and I shall visit the WIND.

Moira: But, Mother, I do not want to visit the WIND. If the CLOUD cannot stay still long enough to listen to my music, how can I expect the WIND to do so?

Mother: No matter. The WIND must be the most powerful of all. And Moira, only the most powerful being in creation will make you happy. We must continue our journey to the WIND. (*This time, the Mother practically drags her daughter off the stage.*)

CURTAIN CLOSES.

CHORUS
(*in front of curtain*)
Who has seen the WIND
Ever stop awhile?
Will Moira see the WIND
And like his noisy style?

ACT FIVE: MOTHER, MOIRA, AND THE WIND

Mother: WIND, my husband and I would like you to marry our daughter, Moira. She is not only beautiful but she is very talented and plays the harp like an angel. You are so powerful; you must be the most powerful being in creation.

WIND: I am not the most powerful being in creation. The WALL is far more powerful than I. Even though I am strong, the WALL stands firmly against me. I cannot budge the WALL.

　　I, too, cannot stay still long enough to listen to Moira's music. Perhaps the WALL is more suitable for your beautiful daughter.

Moira: I do not like the WIND, Mother. He could not hear my music even if he wanted to stand still because he is so noisy.

Mother: Then, come, Moira. We will go to the WALL. Surely, the WALL will be the most powerful and the most eager to listen to your music. (*She drags Moira offstage.*)

CURTAIN CLOSES.

CHORUS
(*in front of curtain*)
Who could possibly pierce the WALL.
Whoever it is ????????
Is the most powerful of all.

ACT SIX: MOTHER, MOIRA, AND THE WALL

Mother: WALL, my husband and I would like you to marry our daughter, Moira. She is not only beautiful but she is very talented. She plays the harp like an angel and you are so powerful, the most powerful being in creation.

WALL: Even though I can withstand the WIND, I am not the most powerful being in creation.

Mother: Then, in the name of goodness, please tell us who IS the most powerful in creation.
    We have gone to the MOON and he said the SUN.
    We went to the SUN and he said the CLOUD.
    We went to the CLOUD and he said the WIND.
    Now the WIND says that you, the WALL are the most powerful.
    If you aren't the most powerful, pray tell us WHO is?

WALL: Why, MICE are the most powerful.

Mother and Moira together: MICE? MICE!

WALL: Yes, MICE. They can bore holes right through me! And there is nothing that I can do to stop them. I am powerless against mice. Why not have your daughter marry a mouse?

Moira: O, Mother. That is just what I will do. I will marry Patrick. He is the most powerful and funny and loving, and he likes to listen to my music. I want to marry Patrick. I hope he wants to marry me!

    (*Exit Mother and a jubilant Moira.*)

CURTAIN CLOSES.

EPILOGUE

Patrick: (*sitting dejectedly with his face on his arms*)

Moira: (*running breathless on to the stage*)
    Oh, Patrick, Oh, Patrick. Will you marry me? There is no one like you—not the MOON, not the SUN, not the CLOUD, not the WIND, not even the WALL. You are my one and only.

Patrick: And you are my one and only. You alone know how to make me happy.

Together: Let's plan our wedding right away. We will sing and dance to beautiful music.

Patrick: And you will play your beloved harp. It makes us both happy.
    (EXIT Patrick and Moira, hand-in-hand.)

CURTAIN CLOSES.

Narrator One: (in front of curtain)
    And sure, 'tis just what Moira does. She marries Patrick and they live happily ever after.

THE END

APPENDIX B
Children and Young Adult Book Awards
National, International, and Multicultural

THE JOHN NEWBERY MEDAL AND HONOR BOOKS

The Newbery Medal, established in 1922 by the Children's Service Division of the American Library Association, is named in honor of the British bookseller John Newbery. The longest active children's literature award in the United States, it is given annually to the author of the most distinguished children's book published in the United States the previous year.

2007
The Higher Power of Lucky by Susan Patron (Simon & Schuster/Richard Jackson)

HONOR BOOKS
Penny from Heaven by Jennifer L. Holm (Random House)
Hattie Big Sky by Kirby Larson (Delacorte Press)
Rules by Cynthia Lord (Scholastic)

2006
Criss Cross by Lynne Rae Perkins (Greenwillow/ HarperCollins)

HONOR BOOKS
Whittington by Alan Armstrong (Random House)
Hitler Youth: Growing Up in Hitler's Shadow by Susan Campbell Bartoletti (Scholastic)
Princess Academy by Shannon Hale (Bloomsbury Children's Books)
Show Way by Jacqueline Woodson (G. P. Putnam's Sons)

2005
Kira-Kira by Cynnthia Kadohata (Atheneum/Simon & Schuster)

HONOR BOOKS
Al Capone Does My Shirts by Gennifer Choldenko (G. P. Putnam's Sons)
The Voice that Challenged a Nation: Marian Anderson and the Struggle for Equal Rights by Russell Freedman (Clarion/Houghton Mifflin)
Lizzie Bright and the Buckminster Boy by Gary D. Schmidt (Clarion/Houghton Mifflin)

2004
The Tale of Despereaux: Being the Story of a Mouse, a Princess, Some Soup, and a Spool of Thread by Kate DiCamillo (Candlewick Press)

HONOR BOOKS
Olive's Ocean by Kevin Henkes (Greenwillow Books)

An American Plague: The True and Terrifying Story of the Yellow Fever Epidemic of 1793 by Jim Murphy (Clarion Books)

2003
Crispin: The Cross of Lead by Avi (Hyperion)

HONOR BOOKS
The House of the Scorpion by Nancy Farmer (Atheneum)
Pictures of Hollis Woods by Patricia Reilly Giff (Random House/Wendy Lamb Books)
Hoot by Carl Hiaasen (Knopf)
A Corner of the Universe by Ann M. Martin (Scholastic)
Surviving the Applewhites by Stephanie S. Tolan (HarperCollins)

2002
A Single Shard by Linda Sue Park (Clarion/Houghton Mifflin)

HONOR BOOKS
Everything on a Waffle by Polly Horvath (Farrar, Straus, & Giroux)
Carver: A Life in Poems by Marilyn Nelson (Front Street)
Hope Was Here by Joan Bauer (G. P. Putnam's Sons)
Because of Winn-Dixie by Kate DiCamillo (Candlewick Press)
Joey Pigza Loses Control by Jack Gantos (Farrar, Straus, & Giroux)
The Wanderer by Sharon Creech (Joanne Cotler Books/HarperCollins)

2001
A Year Down Yonder by Richard Peck (Dial)

2000
Bud, Not Buddy by Christopher Paul Curtis (Delacorte)

HONOR BOOKS
Getting Near to Baby by Audrey Couloumbis (Putnam)
Our Only May Amelia by Jennifer L. Holm (HarperCollins)
26 Fairmount Avenue by Tomie dePaola (Putnam)

1999
Holes by Louis Sachar (Frances Foster)

HONOR BOOK
A Long Way from Chicago by Richard Peck (Dial)

1998
Out of the Dust by Karen Hesse (Scholastic)

HONOR BOOKS

Ella Enchanted by Gail Carson Levine (HarperCollins)
Lily's Crossing by Patricia Reilly Giff (Delacorte)
Wringer by Jerry Spinelli (HarperCollins)

1997

The View from Saturday by E. L. Konigsburg (Jean Karl/Atheneum)

HONOR BOOKS

A Girl Named Disaster by Nancy Farmer (Richard Jackson/Orchard Books)
Moorchild by Eloise McGraw (Margaret K. McElderry/Simon & Schuster)
The Thief by Megan Whalen Turner (Greenwillow/Morrow)
Belle Prater's Boy by Ruth White (Farrar, Straus, & Giroux)

1996

The Midwife's Apprentice by Karen Cushman (Clarion Books)

HONOR BOOKS

What Jamie Saw by Carolyn Coman (Front Street)
The Watsons Go to Birmingham: 1963 by Christopher Paul Curtis (Delacorte)
Yolonda's Genius by Carol Fenner (Margaret K. McElderry/Simon & Schuster)
The Great Fire by Jim Murphy (Scholastic)

1995

Walk Two Moons by Sharon Creech (HarperCollins)

HONOR BOOKS

Catherine, Called Birdy by Karen Cushman (Clarion)
The Ear, the Eye and the Arm by Nancy Farmer (Jackson/Orchard)

1994

The Giver by Lois Lowry (Houghton Mifflin)

HONOR BOOKS

Crazy Lady by Jane Leslie Conly (HarperCollins)
Dragon's Gate by Laurence Yep (HarperCollins)
Eleanor Roosevelt: A Life of Discovery by Russell Freedman (Clarion Books)

1993

Missing May by Cynthia Rylant (Jackson/Orchard)

HONOR BOOKS

What Hearts by Bruce Brooks (Laura Geringer/HarperCollins)
The Dark-thirty: Southern Tales of the Supernatural by Patricia McKissack (Knopf)
Somewhere in the Darkness by Walter Dean Myers (Scholastic)

1992

Shiloh by Phyllis Reynolds Naylor (Atheneum)

HONOR BOOKS

Nothing But the Truth: A Documentary Novel by Avi (Jackson/Orchard)
The Wright Brothers: How They Invented the Airplane by Russell Freedman (Holiday House)

1991

Maniac Magee by Jerry Spinelli (Little, Brown)

HONOR BOOKS

The True Confessions of Charlotte Doyle by Avi (Jackson/Orchard)

1990

Number the Stars by Lois Lowry (Houghton Mifflin)

HONOR BOOKS

Afternoon of the Elves by Janet Taylor Lisle (Jackson/Orchard)
Shabanu, Daughter of the Wind by Suzanne Fisher Staples (Knopf)
The Winter Room by Gary Paulsen (Jackson/Orchard)

1989

Joyful Noise: Poems for Two Voices by Paul Fleischman (Harper)

HONOR BOOKS

In the Beginning: Creation Stories from Around the World by Virginia Hamilton (Harcourt)
Scorpions by Walter Dean Myers (Harper)

1988

Lincoln; A Photobiography by Russell Freedman (Clarion)

HONOR BOOKS

After the Rain by Norma Fox Mazer (Morrow)
Hatchet by Gary Paulsen (Bradbury)

1987

The Whipping Boy by Sid Fleischman (Greenwillow)

HONOR BOOKS

A Fine White Dust by Cynthia Rylant (Bradbury)
On My Honor by Marion Dane Bauer (Clarion)
Volcano: The Eruption and Healing of Mount St. Helens by Patricia Lauber (Bradbury)

1986

Sarah, Plain and Tall by Patricia MacLachlan (Harper)

HONOR BOOKS

Commodore Perry In the Land of the Shogun by Rhoda Blumberg (Lothrop)
Dogsong by Gary Paulsen (Bradbury)

1985

The Hero and the Crown by Robin McKinley (Greenwillow)

HONOR BOOKS

Like Jake and Me by Mavis Jukes (Knopf)
The Moves Make the Man by Bruce Brooks (Harper)
One-Eyed Cat by Paula Fox (Bradbury)

1984

Dear Mr. Henshaw by Beverly Cleary (Morrow)

HONOR BOOKS

The Sign of the Beaver by Elizabeth George Speare (Houghton Mifflin)
A Solitary Blue by Cynthia Voigt (Atheneum)
Sugaring Time by Kathryn Lasky (Macmillan)
The Wish Giver: Three Tales of Coven Tree by Bill Brittain (Harper)

1983

Dicey's Song by Cynthia Voigt (Atheneum)

HONOR BOOKS

The Blue Sword by Robin McKinley (Greenwillow)
Doctor DeSoto by William Steig (Farrar)
Graven Images by Paul Fleischman (Harper)
Homesick: My Own Story by Jean Fritz (Putnam)
Sweet Whispers, Brother Rush by Viriginia Hamilton (Philomel)

1982

A Visit to William Blake's Inn: Poems for Innocent and Experienced Travelers by Nancy Willard (Harcourt)

HONOR BOOKS

Ramona Quimby, Age 8 by Beverly Cleary (Morrow)
Upon the Head of the Goat: A Childhood in Hungary 1939–1944 by Aranka Siegal (Farrar)

1981

Jacob Have I Loved by Katherine Paterson (Crowell)

HONOR BOOKS

The Fledgling by Jane Langton (Harper)
A Ring of Endless Light by Madeleine L'Engle (Farrar)

1980

A Gathering of Days: A New England Girl's Journal, 1830–1832 by Joan W. Blos (Scribner)

HONOR BOOK

The Road from Home: The Story of an Armenian Girl by David Kherdian (Greenwillow)

1979

The Westing Game by Ellen Raskin (Dutton)

HONOR BOOK

The Great Gilly Hopkins by Katherine Paterson (Crowell)

1978

Bridge to Terabithia by Katherine Paterson (Crowell)

HONOR BOOKS

Ramona and Her Father by Beverly Cleary (Morrow)
Anpao: An American Indian Odyssey by Jamake Highwater (Lippincott)

1977

Roll of Thunder, Hear My Cry by Mildred D. Taylor (Dial)

HONOR BOOKS

Abel's Island by William Steig (Farrar)
A String in the Harp by Nancy Bond (Atheneum)

1976

The Grey King by Susan Cooper (McElderry/Atheneum)

HONOR BOOKS

The Hundred Penny Box by Sharon Bell Mathis (Viking)
Dragonwings by Laurence Yep (Harper)

1975

M. C. Higgins, the Great by Virginia Hamilton (Macmillan)

HONOR BOOKS

Figgs & Phantoms by Ellen Raskin (Dutton)
My Brother Sam Is Dead by James Lincoln Collier & Christopher Collier (FourWinds)
The Perilous Guard by Elizabeth Marie Pope (Houghton)
Philip Hall Likes Me, I Reckon Maybe by Bette Greene (Dial)

1974

The Slave Dancer by Paula Fox (Bradbury)

HONOR BOOK

The Dark Is Rising by Susan Cooper (McElderry/Atheneum)

1973

Julie of the Wolves by Jean Craighead George (Harper)

HONOR BOOKS

Frog and Toad Together by Arnold Lobel (Harper)
The Upstairs Room by Johanna Reiss (Crowell)
The Witches of Worm by Zilpha Keatley Snyder (Atheneum)

1972

Mrs. Frisby and the Rats of NIMH by Robert C. O'Brien (Atheneum)

HONOR BOOKS

Incident at Hawka's Hill by Allan W. Eckert (Little, Brown)
The Planet of Junior Brown by Virginia Hamilton (Macmillan)
The Tombs of Atuan by Ursula K. LeGuin (Atheneum)
Annie and the Old One by Miska Miles (Little, Brown)
The Headless Cupid by Zilpha Keatley Snyder (Atheneum)

1971

Summer of the Swans by Betsy Byars (Viking)

HONOR BOOKS

Knee Knock Rise by Natalie Babbit (Farrar)
Enchantress From the Stars by Sylvia Louise Engdahl (Atheneum)
Sing Down the Moon by Scott O'Dell (Houghton)

1970

Sounder by William H. Armstrong (Harper)

HONOR BOOKS

Our Eddie by Sulamith Ish-Kishor (Pantheon)
The Many Ways of Seeing: An Introduction to the Pleasures of Art by Janet Gaylord Moore (World)
Journey Outside by Mary Q. Steele (Viking)

1969
The High King by Lloyd Alexander (Holt)
HONOR BOOKS
To Be a Slave by Julius Lester (Dial)
When Shlemiel Went to Warsaw and Other Stories by Isaac Bashevis Singer (Farrar)

1968
From the Mixed-Up Files of Mrs. Basil E. Frankweiler by E. L. Konigsburg (Atheneum)
HONOR BOOKS
Jennifer, Hecate, MacBeth, William McKinley, and Me, Elizabeth by E. L. Konigsburg (Atheneum)
The Black Pearl by Scott O'Dell (Houghton)
The Fearsome Inn by Isaac Bashevis Singer (Scribner)
The Egypt Game by Zilpha Keatley Snyder (Atheneum)

1967
Up a Road Slowly by Irene Hunt (Follett)
HONOR BOOKS
The King's Fifth by Scott O'Dell (Houghton)
Zlateh the Goat and Other Stories by Isaac Bashevis Singer (Harper)
The Jazz Man by Mary Hays Weik (Atheneum)

1966
I, Juan de Pareja by Elizabeth Borton de Trevino (Farrar)
HONOR BOOKS
The Black Cauldron by Lloyd Alexander (Holt)
The Animal Family by Randall Jarrell (Pantheon)
The Noonday Friends by Mary Stolz (Harper)

1965
Shadow of a Bull by Maia Wojciechowska (Atheneum)
HONOR BOOK
Across Five Aprils by Irene Hunt (Follett)

1964
It's Like This, Cat by Emily Neville (Harper)
HONOR BOOKS
Rascal: A Memoir of a Better Era by Sterling North (Dutton)
The Loner by Ester Wier (McKay)

1963
A Wrinkle in Time by Madeleine L'Engle (Farrar)
HONOR BOOKS
Thistle and Thyme: Tales and Legends from Scotland by Sorche Nic Leodhas, pseud. (Leclaire Alger) (Holt)
Men of Athens by Olivia Coolidge (Houghton)

1962
The Bronze Bow by Elizabeth George Speare (Houghton)
HONOR BOOKS
Frontier Living by Edwin Tunis (World)
The Golden Goblet by Eloise Jarvis McGraw (Coward)
Belling the Tiger by Mary Stolz (Harper)

1961
Island of the Blue Dolphins by Scott O'Dell (Houghton)
HONOR BOOKS
America Moves Forward : A History for Peter by Gerald W. Johnson (Morrow)
Old Ramon by Jack Schaefer (Houghton)
The Cricket In Times Square by George Selden, pseud. (George Thompson) (Farrar)

1960
Onion John by Joseph Krumgold (Crowell)
HONOR BOOKS
My Side of the Mountain by Jean Craighead George (Dutton)
America Is Born: A History for Peter by Gerald W. Johnson (Morrow)
The Gammage Cup by Carol Kendall (Harcourt)

1959
The Witch of Blackbird Pond by Elizabeth George Speare (Houghton)
HONOR BOOKS
The Family Under the Bridge by Natalie Savage Carlson (Harper)
Along Came a Dog by Meindert DeJong (Harper)
Chucaro: Wild Pony of the Pampa by Francis Kalnay (Harcourt)
The Perilous Road by William O. Steele (Harcourt)

1958
Rifles for Watie by Harold Keith (Crowell)
HONOR BOOKS
The Horsecatcher by Mari Sandoz (Westminster)
Gone-Away Lake by Elizabeth Enright (Harcourt)
The Great Wheel by Robert Lawson (Viking)
Tom Paine, Freedom's Apostle by Leo Gurko (Crowell)

1957
Miracles on Maple Hill by Virginia Sorensen (Harcourt)
HONOR BOOKS
Old Yeller by Fred Gipson (Harper)
The House of Sixty Fathers by Meindert DeJong (Harper)
Mr. Justice Holmes by Clara Ingram Judson (Follett)
The Corn Grows Ripe by Dorothy Rhoads (Viking)
Black Fox of Lorne by Marguerite de Angeli (Doubleday)

1956
Carry On, Mr. Bowditch by Jean Lee Latham (Houghton)
HONOR BOOKS
The Secret River by Marjorie Kinnan Rawlings (Scribner)
The Golden Name Day by Jennie Lindquist (Harper)
Men. Microscopes, and Living Things by Katherine Shippen (Viking)

1955

The Wheel on the School by Meindert DeJong (Harper)

HONOR BOOKS

Courage of Sarah Noble by Alice Dalgliesch (Scribner)

Banner in the Sky by James Ullman (Lippincott)

1954

. . . And Now Miguel by Joseph Krumgold (Crowell)

HONOR BOOKS

All Alone by Claire Huchet Bishop (Viking)

Shadrach by Meindert DeJong (Harper)

Hurry Home, Candy by Meindert DeJong (Harper)

Theodore Roosevelt, Fighting Patriot by Clara Ingram Judson (Follett)

Magic Maize by Mary and Conrad Buff (Houghton)

1953

Secret of the Andes by Ann Nolan Clark (Viking)

HONOR BOOKS

Charlotte's Web by E. B. White (Harper)

Moccasin Trail by Eloise Jarvis McGraw (Coward)

Red Sails to Capri by Ann Weil (Viking)

The Bears on Hemlock Mountain by Alice Dalgliesch (Scribner)

Birthdays of Freedom, Vol. 1 by Genevieve Foster (Scribner)

1952

Ginger Pye by Eleanor Estes (Harcourt)

HONOR BOOKS

Americans Before Columbus by Elizabeth Baity (Viking)

Minn of the Mississippi by Holling C. Holling (Houghton)

The Defender by Nicholas Kalashnikoff (Scribner)

The Light at Tern Rock by Julia Sauer (Viking)

The Apple and the Arrow by Mary and Conrad Buff (Houghton and Mifflin)

1951

Amos Fortune, Free Man by Elizabeth Yates (Dutton)

HONOR BOOKS

Better Known as Johnny Appleseed by Mabel Leigh Hunt (Lippincott)

Gandhi, Fighter Without a Sword by Jeanette Eaton (Morrow)

Abraham Lincoln, Friend of the People by Clara Ingram Judson (Follett)

The Story of Appleby Capple by Anne Parrish (Harper)

1950

The Door in the Wall by Marguerite de Angeli (Doubleday)

HONOR BOOKS

Tree of Freedom by Rebecca Caudill (Viking)

The Blue Cat of Castle Town by Catherine Coblentz (Longmans)

Kildee House by Rutherford Montgomery (Doubleday)

George Washington by Genevieve Foster (Scribner)

Song of the Pines: A Story of Norwegian Lumbering in Wisconsin by Walter and Marion Havighurst (Winston)

1949

King of the Wind by Marguerite Henry (Rand McNally)

HONOR BOOKS

Seabird by Holling C. Holling (Houghton)

Daughter of the Mountains by Louise Rankin (Viking)

My Father's Dragon by Ruth S. Gannett (Random House)

Story of the Negro by Arna Bontemps (Knopf)

1948

The Twenty-One Balloons by Wiliiam Pene DuBois (Viking)

HONOR BOOKS

Pancakes-Paris by Claire Huchet Bishop (Viking)

Li Lun, Lad of Courage by Carolyn Treffinger (Abingdon)

The Quaint and Curious Quest of Johnny Longfoot by Catherine Besterman (Bobbs-Merrill)

The Cow-Tail Switch, and Other West African Stories by Harold Courlander (Holt)

Misty of Chincoteague by Marguerite Henry (Rand McNally)

1947

Miss Hickory by Carolyn Sherwin Bailey (Viking)

HONOR BOOKS

Wonderful Year by Nancy Barnes (Messner)

Big Tree by Mary and Conrad Buff (Viking)

The Heavenly Tenants by William Maxwell (Harper)

The Avion My Uncle Flew by Cyrus Fisher, pseud. (Darwin L. Teilhet) (Appleton)

The Hidden Treasure of Glaston by Eleanor Jewett (Viking)

1946

Strawberry Girl by Lois Lenski (Lippincott)

HONOR BOOKS

Justin Morgan Had a Horse by Marguerite Henry (Rand McNally)

The Moved-Outers by Florence Crannell Means (Houghton)

Bhimsa, the Dancing Bear by Christine Weston (Scribner)

New Found World by Katherine Shippen (Viking)

1945

Rabbit Hill by Robert Lawson (Viking)

HONOR BOOKS

The Hundred Dresses by Eleanor Estes (Harcourt)

The Silver Pencil by Alice Dalgliesch (Scribner)

Abraham Lincoln's World by Genevieve Foster (Scribner)

Lone Journey: The Life of Roger Williams by Jeanette Eaton (Harcourt)

1944
Johnny Tremain by Esther Forbes (Houghton)

HONOR BOOKS
These Happy Golden Years by Laura Ingalls Wilder (Harper)
Fog Magic by Julia Sauer (Viking)
Rufus M. by Eleanor Estes (Harcourt)
Mountain Born by Elizabeth Yates (Coward)

1943
Adam of the Road by Elizabeth Janet Gray (Viking)

HONOR BOOKS
The Middle Moffat by Eleanor Estes (Harcourt)
Have You Seen Tom Thumb? by Mabel Leigh Hunt (Lippincott)

1942
The Matchlock Gun by Walter Edmonds (Dodd)

HONOR BOOKS
Little Town on the Prairie by Laura Ingalls Wilder (Harper)
George Washington's World by Genevieve Foster (Scribner)
Indian Captive: The Story of Mary Jemison by Lois Lenski (Lippincott)
Down Ryton Water by Eva Roe Gaggin (Viking)

1941
Call It Courage by Armstrong Sperry (Macmillan)

HONOR BOOKS
Blue Willow by Doris Gates (Viking)
Young Mac of Fort Vancouver by Mary Jane Carr (Crowell)
The Long Winter by Laura Ingalls Wilder (Harper)
Nansen by Anna Gertrude Hall (Viking)

1940
Daniel Boone by James Daugherty (Viking)

HONOR BOOKS
The Singing Tree by Kate Seredy (Viking)
Runner of the Mountain Tops: The Life of Louis Agassiz by Mabel Robinson (Random House)
By the Shores of Silver Lake by Laura Ingalls Wilder (Harper)
Boy with a Pack by Stephen W. Meader (Harcourt)

1939
Thimble Summer by Elizabeth Enright (Rinehart)

HONOR BOOKS
Nino by Vallentin Angelo (Viking)
Mr. Popper's Penguins by Richard and Florence Atwater (Little, Brown)
Hello the Boat! by Phyllis Crawford (Holt)
Leader by Destiny: George Washington, Man and Patriot by Jeanette Eaton (Harcourt)
Penn by Elizabeth Janet Gray (Viking)

1938
The White Stag by Kate Seredy (Viking)

HONOR BOOKS
Pecos Bill by James Cloyd Bowman (Little Brown)
Bright Island by Mabel Robinson (Random House)
On the Banks of Plum Creek by Laura Ingalls Wilder (Harper)

1937
Roller Skates by Ruth Sawyer (Viking)

HONOR BOOKS
Phebe Fairchild: Her Book by Lois Lenski (Stokes)
Whistler's Van by Idwal Jones (Viking)
The Golden Basket by Ludwig Bemelmans (Viking)
Winterbound by Margery Bianco (Viking)
The Codfish Musket by Agnes Hewes (Doubleday)
Audubon by Constance Rourke (Harcourt)

1936
Caddie Woodlawn by Carol Ryrie Brink (Macmillan)

HONOR BOOKS
Honk, the Moose by Phil Stong (Dodd)
The Good Master by Kate Seredy (Viking)
Young Walter Scott by Elizabeth Janet Gray (Viking)
All Sail Set: A Romance of the Flying Cloud by Armstrong Sperry (Winston)

1935
Dobry by Monica Shannon (Viking)

HONOR BOOKS
Pageant of Chinese History by Elizabeth Seeger (Longmans)
Davy Crockett by Constance Rourke (Harcourt)
Day On Skates: The Story of a Dutch Picnic by Hilda Von Stockum (Harper)

1934
Invincible Louisa: The Story of the Author of Little Women by Cornelia Meigs (Little, Brown)

HONOR BOOKS
The Forgotten Daughter by Caroline Snedeker (Doubleday)
ABC Bunny by Wanda Gág (Coward)
Swords of Steel by Elsie Singmaster (Houghton)
Winged Girl of Knossos by Erik Berry, pseud. (Allena Best) (Appleton)
New Land by Sarah Schmidt (McBride)
Big Tree of Bunlahy: Stories of My Own Countryside by Padraic Colum (Macmillan)
Glory of the Seas by Agnes Hewes (Knopf)
Apprentice of Florence by Ann Kyle (Houghton))

1933
Young Fu of the Upper Yangtze by Elizabeth Lewis (Winston)

HONOR BOOKS
Swift Rivers by Cornelia Meigs (Little, Brown)

The Railroad to Freedom: A Story of the Civil War by Hildegarde Swift (Harcourt)
Children of the Soil: A Story of Scandinavia by Nora Burglon (Doubleday)

1932

Waterless Mountain by Laura Adams Aramer (Longmans)

HONOR BOOKS
The Fairy Circus by Dorothy P. Lathrop (Macmillan)
Calico Bush by Rachel Field (Macmillan)
Boy of the South Seas by Eunice Tietjens (Coward-McCann)
Out of the Flame by Eloise Lownsbery (Longmans)
Jane's Island by Marjorie Allee (Houghton)
Truce of the Wolf and Other Tales of Old Italy by Mary Gould Davis (Harcourt)

1931

The Cat Who Went to Heaven by Elizabeth Coatsworth (Macmillan)

HONOR BOOKS
Floating Island by Anne Parrish (Harper)
The Dark Star of Itza: The Story of a Pagan Princess by Alida Malkus (Harcourt)
Queer Person by Ralph Hubbard (Doubleday)
Mountains Are Free by Julie Davis Adams (Dutton)
Spice and the Devil's Cave by Agnes Hewes (Knopf)
Meggy MacIntosh by Elizabeth Janet Gray (Doubleday)
Garram the Hunter: A Boy of the Hill Tribes by Herbert Best (Doubleday)
Ood-Le-Uk the Wanderer by Alice Lide & Margaret Johansen (Little, Brown)

1930

Hitty, Her First Hundred Years by Rachel Field (Macmillan)

HONOR BOOKS
A Daughter of the Seine: The Life of Madame Roland by Jeanette Eaton (Harper)
Pran of Albania by Elizabeth Miller (Doubleday)
Jumping-Off Place by Marion Hurd McNeely (Longmans)
The Tangle-Coated Horse and Other Tales by Ella Young (Longmans)
Vaino by Julia Davis Adams (Dutton)
Little Blacknose by Hildegarde Swift (Harcourt)

1929

The Trumpeter of Krakow by Eric P. Kelly (Macmillan)

HONOR BOOKS
Pigtail of Ah Lee Ben Loo by John Bennett (Longmans)
Millions of Cats by Wanda Gág (Coward)
The Boy Who Was by Grace Hallock (Dutton)
Clearing Weather by Cornelia Meigs (Little, Brown)
Runaway Papoose by Grace Moon (Doubleday)
Tod of the Fens by Elinor Whitney (Macmillan)

1928

Gay Neck, the Story of a Pigeon by Dhan Gopal Mukerki (Dutton)

HONOR BOOKS
The Wonder Smith and His Son by Ella Young (Longmans)
Downright Dencey by Caroline Snedeker (Doubleday)

1927

Smoky, the Cowhorse by Will James (Scribner)

HONOR BOOKS
(None recorded)

1926

Shen of the Sea by Arthur Bowie Chrisman (Dutton)

HONOR BOOKS
The Voyagers: Being Legends and Romances of Atlantic Discovery by Padraic Colum (Macmillan)

1925

Tales From Silver Lands by Charles Finger (Doubleday)

HONOR BOOKS
Nicholas: A Manhattan Christmas Story by Ann Carroll Moore (Putnam)
The Dream Coach by Anne Parrish (Macmillan)

1924

The Dark Frigate by Charles Hawes (Little, Brown)

HONOR BOOKS
(None recorded)

1923

The Voyages of Doctor Dolittle by Hugh Lofting (Stokes)

HONOR BOOKS
(None recorded)

1922

The Story of Mankind by Hendrik Willem van Loon (Liveright)

HONOR BOOKS
The Great Quest by Charles Hawes (Little, Brown)
Cedric the Forester by Bernard Marshall (Appleton)
The Old Tobacco Shop: A True Account of What Befell a Little Boy in Search of Adventure by William Bowen (Macmillan)
The Golden Fleece and the Heroes Who Lived before Achilles by Padraic Colum (Macmillan)
The Windy Hill by Cornelia Meigs (Macmillan)

THE RANDOLPH CALDECOTT MEDAL AND HONOR BOOKS

The Caldecott Medal, established in 1938 by the Children's Service Division of the American Library Association, is named in honor of the British illustrator Randolph Caldecott. It is given annually to the illustrator of the most distinguished picture book published in the United States the previous year.

2007

Flotsam by David Wiesner (Clarion)

HONOR BOOKS

Gone Wild: An Endangered Animal Alphabet by David McLimans (Walker)

Moses: When Harriet Tubman Led Her People to Freedom illustrated by Kadir Nelson, written by Carole Boston Weatherford (Hyperion/Jump at the Sun)

2006

The Hello, Goodbye Window illustrated by Chris Raschka, written by Norton Juster (Michael di Capua/Hyperion)

HONOR BOOKS

Rosa illustrated by Bryan Collier and written by Nikki Giovanni (Holt)

Zen Shorts by Jon J. Muth (Scholastic)

Hot Air: The (Mostly) True Story of the First Hot-Air Balloon Ride by Marjorie Priceman (Anne Schwartz/Atheneum)

Song of the Water Boatman and Other Pond Poems illustrated by Beckie Prange, written by Joyce Sidman (Houghton Mifflin)

2005

Kitten's First Full Moon by Kevin Henkes (Greenwillow)

HONOR BOOKS

The Red Book by Barbara Lehman (Houghton Mifflin)

Coming On Home Soon illustrated by E. B. Lewis, written by Jacqueline Woodson (Penguin)

Knuffle Bunny: A Cautionary Tale by Mo Willems (Hyperion Books)

2004

The Man Who Walked Between the Towers by Mordicai Gerstein (Roaring Brook Press)

HONOR BOOKS

Ella Sarah Gets Dressed by Margaret Chodos-Irvine (Harcourt)

What Do You Do with a Tail Like This? by Steve Jenkins and Robin Page (Houghton Mifflin)

Don't Let the Pigeon Drive the Bus by Mo Willems (Hyperion)

2003

My Friend Rabbit by Eric Rohmann (Roaring Brook Press)

HONOR BOOKS

The Spider and the Fly illustrated by Tony DiTerlizzi, written by Mary Howit (Simon & Schuster)

Hondo & Fabian by Peter McCarty (Holt)

Noah's Ark by Jerry Pinkney (SeaStar Books, North-South Books)

2002

The Three Pigs by David Wiesner (Clarion/Houghton Mifflin)

HONOR BOOKS

The Dinosaurs of Waterhouse Hawkins illustrated by Brian Selznick, written by Barbara Kerley (Scholastic)

Martin's Big Words: The Life of Dr. Martin Luther King, Jr. illustrated by Bryan Collier, written by Doreen Rappaport (Jump at the Sun/Hyperion)

The Stray Dog by Marc Simont (HarperCollins)

2001

So You Want to be President? illustrated by David Small, written by Judith St. George (Philomel)

HONOR BOOKS

Casey at the Bat illustrated by Christopher Bing, written by Ernest Thayer (Handprint)

Click, Clack, Moo: Cows that Type illustrated by Betsy Lewin, written by Doreen Cronin (Simon & Schuster)

Olivia by Ian Falconer (Atheneum)

2000

Joseph Had a Little Overcoat by Simms Taback (Viking)

HONOR BOOKS

A Child's Calendar illustrated by Trina Schart Hyman, text by John Updike (Holiday House)

Sector 7 by David Wiesner (Clarion Books)

When Sophie Gets Angry-Really, Really Angry by Molly Bang (Scholastic)

The Ugly Duckling illustrated by Jerry Pinkney, text by Hans Christian Andersen (Morrow).

1999

Snowflake Bentley illustrated by Mary Azarian, written by Jacqueline Briggs Martin (Houghton Mifflin)

HONOR BOOKS

Duke Ellington: The Piano Prince and the Orchestra illustrated by Brian Pinkney, text by Andrea Davis Pinkney (Hyperion)

No, David! by David Shannon (Scholastic)

Snow by Uri Shulevitz (Farrar)

Tibet Through the Red Box by Peter Sis (Frances Foster)

1998

Rapunzel by Paul Zelinsky (Dutton)

HONOR BOOKS

The Gardener illustrated by David Small, text by Sarah Stewart (Farrar)

Harlem illustrated by Christopher Myers, text by Walter Dean Myers (Scholastic)

There Was an Old Lady Who Swallowed a Fly by Simms Taback (Viking)

1997

Golem by David Wisniewski (Clarion)

HONOR BOOKS

Hush! A Thai Lullaby illustrated by Holly Meade, text by Minfong Ho (Melanie Krouoa/Orchard Books

The Graphic Alphabet by David Pelletier (Orchard Books)

The Paperboy by Dav Pilkey (Richard Jackson/Orchard Books)

Starry Messenger by Peter Sis (Frances Foster Books/Farrar, Straus, & Giroux)

1996

Officer Buckle and Gloria by Peggy Rathmann (Putnam)

HONOR BOOKS

Alphabet City by Stephen T. Johnson (Viking)

Zin! Zin! Zin! a Violin illustrated by Marjorie Priceman, text by Lloyd Moss (Simon & Schuster)

Tops & Bottoms adapted and illustrated by Janet Stevens (Harcourt)

1995

Smoky Night illustrated by David Diaz, written by Eve Bunting (Harcourt)

HONOR BOOKS

John Henry illustrated by Jerry Pinkney, written by Julius Lester (Dial)

Swamp Angel illustrated by Paul Zelinsky, written by Anne Isacs (Dutton)

Time Flies by Eric Rohmann (Crown)

1994

Grandfather's Journey by Allen Say, text edited by Walter Lorraine (Houghton Mifflin)

HONOR BOOKS

Peppe the Lamplighter illustrated by Ted Lewin, written by Elisa Bartone (Lothrop)

In the Small, Small Pond by Denise Fleming (Holt)

Raven: A Trickster Tale from the Pacific Northwest by Gerald McDermott (Harcourt)

Owen by Kevin Henkes (Greenwillow)

Yo! Yes? illustrated by Chris Raschka, edited by Richard Jackson (Orchard)

1993

Mirette on the High Wire by Emily Arnold McCully (Putnam)

HONOR BOOKS

The Stinky Cheese Man and Other Fairly Stupid Tales illustrated by Lane Smith, written by Jon Scieszka (Viking)

Seven Blind Mice by Ed Young (Philomel)

Working Cotton illustrated by Carole Byard, written by Sherley Anne Williams (Harcourt)

1992

Tuesday by David Wiesner (Clarion)

HONOR BOOKS

Tar Beach by Faith Ringgold (Crown Publishers)

1991

Black and White by David Macaulay (Houghton)

HONOR BOOKS

Puss in Boots illustrated by Fred Marcellino, written by Charles Perrault, translated by Malcom Arthur (DiCapua/Farrar)

"More More More," Said the Baby: Three Love Stories by Vera B. Williams (Greenwillow)

1990

Lon Po Po: A Red-Riding Hood Story from China by Ed Young (Philomel)

HONOR BOOKS

Bill Peet: An Autobiography by Bill Peet (Houghton Mifflin)

Color Zoo by Lois Ehlert (Lippincott)

The Talking Eggs: A Folktale from the American South illustrated by Jerry Pinkney, written by Robert D. San Souci (Dial)

Hershel and the Hanukkah Goblins illustrated by Trina Schart Hyman, written by Eric Kimmel (Holiday House)

1989

Song and Dance Man illustrated by Stephen Gammell, written by Karen Ackerman (Knopf)

HONOR BOOKS

The Boy of the Three-Year Nap illustrated by Allen Say, written by Diane Snyder (Houghton Mifflin)

Free Fall by David Wiesner (Lothrop)

Goldilocks and the Three Bears by James Marshall (Dial)

Mirandy and Brother Wind illustrated by Jerry Pinkney, written by Patricia C. McKissack (Knopf)

1988

Owl Moon illustrated by John Schoenherr, written by Jane Yolen (Philomel)

HONOR BOOKS

Mufaro's Beautiful Daughters: An African Tale by John Steptoe (Lothrop)

1987

Hey, Al illustrated by Richard Egielski, written by Arthur Yorinks (Farrar)

HONOR BOOKS

The Village of Round and Square Houses by Ann Grifalconi (Little, Brown)

Alphabatics by Suse MacDonald (Bradbury)

Rumpelstiltskin by Paul Zelinsky (Dutton)

1986

The Polar Express by Chris van Allsburg (Houghton)

HONOR BOOKS

The Relatives Came illustrated by Stephen Gammell, written by Cynthia Rylant (Bradbury)

King Bidgood's in the Bathtub illustrated by Don Wood, written by Audrey Wood (Harcourt)

1985

Saint George and the Dragon illustrated by Trina Schart Hyman, retold by Margaret Hodges (Little, Brown)

HONOR BOOKS

Hansel and Gretel illustrated by Paul Zelinsky, retold by Rika Lesser (Dodd)

Have You Seen My Duckling? by Nancy Tafuri (Greenwillow)

The Story of Jumping Mouse: A Native American Legend by John Steptoe (Lothrop)

1984

The Glorious Flight: Across the Channel with Louis Bleriot by Alice & Martin Provensen (Viking)

HONOR BOOKS

Little Red Riding Hood by Trina Schart Hyman (Holliday)

Ten, Nine, Eight by Molly Bang (Greenwillow)

1983

Shadow illustrated by Marcia Brown, original text by Blaise Cendrars (Scribner)

HONOR BOOKS

A Chair for My Mother by Vera B. Williams (Greenwillow)

When I Was Young in the Mountains illustrated by Diane Goode, written by Cynthia Rylant (Dutton)

1982

Jumanjii by Chris Van Allsburg (Houghton)

HONOR BOOKS

Where the Buffaloes Begin illustrated by Stephen Gammell, written by Olaf Baker (Walker)

On Market Street illustrated by Anita Lobel, written by Arnold Lobel (Greenwillow)

Outside Over There by Maurice Sendak (Harper)

A Visit to William Blake's Inn: Poems for Innocent and Experienced Travelers illustrated by Alice & Martin Provensen, written by Nancy Willard (Harcourt)

1981

Fables by Arnold Lobel (Harper)

HONOR BOOKS

The Bremen-Town Musicians illustrated and retold by Ilse Plume (Doubleday)

The Grey Lady and the Strawberry Snatcher by Molly Bang (Four Winds)

Mice Twice by Joseph Low (McElderry/Atheneum)

Truck by Donald Crews (Greenwillow)

1980

Ox-Cart Man illustrated by Barbara Cooney, written by Donald Hall (Viking)

HONOR BOOKS

Ben's Trumpet by Rachel Isadora (Greenwillow)

The Garden of Abdul Gasazi by Chris Van Allsburg (Houghton)

The Treasure by Uri Shulevitz (Farrar)

1979

The Girl Who Loved Wild Horses by Paul Goble (Bradbury)

HONOR BOOKS

Freight Train by Donald Crews (Greenwillow)

The Way to Start a Day illustrated by Peter Parnall, written by Byrd Baylor (Scribner)

1978

Noah's Ark by Peter Spier (Doubleday)

HONOR BOOKS

Castle by David Macaulay (Houghton)

It Could Always Be Worse illustrated and retold by Margot Zemach (Farrar)

1977

Ashanti to Zulu: African Traditions illustrated by Leo & Diane Dillon, written by Margaret Musgrove (Dial)

HONOR BOOKS

The Amazing Bone by William Steig (Farrar)

The Contest illustrated and retold by Nonny Hogrogian (Greenwillow)

Fish for Supper by M. B. Goffstein (Dial)

The Golem: A Jewish Legend by Beverly Brodsky McDermott (Lippincott)

Hawk, I'm Your Brother illustrated by Peter Parnall, written by Byrd Baylor (Scribner)

1976

Why Mosquitos Buzz in People's Ears illustrated by Leo & Diane Dillon, retold by Verna Aardema (Dial)

HONOR BOOKS

The Desert Is Theirs illustrated by Peter Parnall, written by Byrd Baylor (Scribner)

Stregna Nona by Tomie de Paola (Prentice-Hall)

1975

Arrow to the Sun by Gerald McDermott (Viking)

HONOR BOOKS

Jambo Means Hello: A Swahili Alphabet Book illustrated by Tom Feelings, written by Muriel Feelings (Dial)

1974

Duffy and the Devil illustrated by Margot Zemach, retold by Harve Zemach (Farrar)

HONOR BOOKS

Three Jovial Huntsmen by Susan Jeffers (Bradbury)

Cathedral by David Macaulay (Houghton)

1973

The Funny Little Woman illustrated by Blair Lent, written by Arlene Mosel (Dutton)

HONOR BOOKS

Anansi the Spider: A Tale from the Ashanti illustrated and adapted by Gerald McDermott (Holt)

Hosie's Alphabet illustrated by Leonard Baskin, written by Hosea, Tobias & Lisa Baskin (Viking)

Snow-White and the Seven Dwarfs illustrated by Nancy Ekholm Burkert, written and translated by Randall Jarrell, retold from the Brothers Grimm (Farrar)

When Clay Sings illustrated by Tom Bahti, written by Byrd Baylor (Scribner)

1972

One Fine Day illustrated and retold by Nonny Hogrogian (Macmillan)

HONOR BOOKS

Hildilid's Night illustrated by Arnold Lobel, written by Cheli Duran Ryan (Macmillan)

If All the Seas Were One Sea by Janina Domanska (Macmillan)

Moja Means One: Swahili Counting Book illustrated by Tom Feelings, written by Muriel Feelings (Dial)

1971

A Story A Story illustrated and retold by Gail E. Haley (Atheneum)

HONOR BOOKS

The Angry Moon illustrated by Blair Lent, retold by William Sleator (Atlantic)

Frog and Toad Are Friends by Arnold Lobel (Harper)

In the Night Kitchen by Maurice Sendak (Harper)

1970

Sylvester and the Magic Pebble by William Steig (Windmill Books)

HONOR BOOKS

Goggles! byEzra Jack Keats (Macmillan)

Alexander and the Wind-Up Mouse by Leo Lionni (Pantheon)

Pop Corn & Ma Goodness illustrated by Robert Andrew Parker, written by Edna Mitchell Preston (Viking)

Thy Friend, Obadiah by Brinton Turkle (Viking)

The Judge: An Untrue Tale illustrated by Margot Zemach, written by Harve Zemach (Farrar)

1969

The Fool of the World and the Flying Ship illustrated by Uri Shulevitz, retold by Arthur Ransome (Farrar)

HONOR BOOK

Why the Sun and the Moon Live in the Sky illustrated by Blair Lent, written by Elphinstone Dayrell (Houghton)

1968

Drummer Hoff illustrated by Ed Emberley, adapted by Barbara Emberley (Prentice-Hall)

HONOR BOOKS

Frederick by Leo Lionni (Pantheon)

Seashore Story by Taro Yashima (Viking)

The Emperor and the Kite illustrated by Ed Young, written by Jane Yolen (World)

1967

Sam, Bangs & Moonshine by Evaline Ness (Holt)

HONOR BOOKS

One Wide River to Cross illustrated by Ed Emberley, adapted by Barbara Emberley (Prentice)

1966

Always Room for One More illustrated by Nonny Hogrogian, written by Sorche Nic Leodhas, pseud. (Leclair Alger) (Holt)

HONOR BOOKS

Hide and Seek Fog illustrated by Roger Duvoisin, written by Alvin Tresselt (Lothrop)

Just Me by Marie Hall Ets (Viking)

Tom Tit Tot illustrated and retold by Evaline Ness (Scribner)

1965

May I Bring a Friend? illustrated by Beni Montresor, written by Beatrice Schenk de Regniers (Atheneum)

HONOR BOOKS

Rain Makes Applesauce illustrated by Marvin Bileck, written by Julian Scheer (Holiday)

The Wave illustrated by Blair Lent, written by Margaret Hodges (Houghton)

A Pocketful of Cricket illustrated by Evaline Ness, written by Rebecca Caudill (Holt)

1964

Where the Wild Things Are by Maurice Sendak (Harper)

HONOR BOOKS

Swimmy by Leo Lionni (Pantheon)

All in the Morning Early illustrated by Evaline Ness, written by Soche Nic Leodhas, pseud. (Leclaire Alger) (Holt)

Mother Goose and Nursery Rhymes illustrated by Philip Reed (Atheneum)

1963

The Snowy Day by Ezra Jack Keats (Viking)

HONOR BOOKS

The Sun Is a Golden Earring illustrated by Bernarda Bryson, written by Natalia M. Belting (Holt)

Mr. Rabbit and the Lovely Present illustrated by Maurice Sendak, written by Charlotte Zolotow (Harper)

1962

Once a Mouse illustrated and retold by Marcia Brown (Scribner)

HONOR BOOKS

Fox Went Out on a Chilly Night: An Old Song by Peter Spier (Doubleday)

Little Bear's Visit illustrated by Maurice Sendak, written by Else H. Minarik (Harper)

The Day We Saw the Sun Come Up illustrated by Adrienne Adams, written by Alice E. Goudey (Scribner)

1961

Baboushka and the Three Kings illustrated by Nicolas Sidjakov, written by Ruth Robbins (Parnassus)

> HONOR BOOK
>
> *Inch by Inch* by Leo Lionni (Obolensky)

1960

Nine Days to Christmas illustrated by Marie Hall Ets, written by Marie Hall Ets and Aurora Labastida (Viking)

> HONOR BOOKS
>
> *Houses from the Sea* illustrated by Adrienne Adams, written by Alice E. Goudey (Scribner)
>
> *The Moon Jumpers* illustrated by Maurice Sendak, written by Janice May Udry (Harper)

1959

Chanticleer and the Fox illustrated and adapted from Chaucer's Canterbury Tales by Barbara Cooney (Crowell)

> HONOR BOOKS
>
> *The House That Jack Built: La Maison Que Jacques A Batie* by Antonio Frasconi (Harcourt)
>
> *What Do You Say, Dear?* illustrated by Maurice Sendak, written by Sesyle Joslin (W. R. Scott)
>
> *Umbrella* by Taro Yashima (Viking)

1958

Time of Wonder by Robert McCloskey (Viking)

> HONOR BOOKS
>
> *Fly High, Fly Low* by Don Freeman (Viking)
>
> *Anatole and the Cat* illustrated by Paul Galdone, written by Eve Titus (McGraw- Hill)

1957

A Tree Is Nice illustrated by Marc Simont, written by Janice Udry (Harper)

> HONOR BOOKS
>
> *Mr. Penny's Race Horse* by Marie Hall Ets (Viking)
>
> *1 Is One* by Tasha Tudor (Walck)
>
> *Anatole* illustrated by Paul Galdone, written by Eve Titus (McGraw-Hill)
>
> *Gillespie and the Guards* illustrated by James Daugherty, written by Benjamin Elkin (Viking)
>
> *Lion* by William Pene du Bois (Viking)

1956

Frog Went A-Courtin' illustrated by Feodor Rojankovsky, retold by John Langstaff (Harcourt)

> HONOR BOOKS
>
> *Play With Me* by Marie Hall Ets (Viking)
>
> *Crow Boy* by Taro Yashima (Viking)

1955

Cinderella, or the Little Glass Slipper illustrated by Marcia Brown, translated from Charles Perrault by Marcia Brown (Scribner)

> HONOR BOOKS
>
> *Book of Nursery and Mother Goose Rhymes* illustrated by Marguerite de Angeli (Doubleday)
>
> *Wheel on the Chimney* illustrated by Tibor Gergely, written by Margaret Wise Brown (Lippincott)
>
> *The Thanksgiving Story* illustrated by Helen Sewell, written by Alice Dalgliesch (Scribner)

1954

Madeline's Rescue by Ludwig Bemelmans (Viking)

> HONOR BOOKS
>
> *Journey Cake, Ho!* illustrated by Robert McCloskey, written by Ruth Sawyer (Viking)
>
> *When Will the World Be Mine?* illustrated by Jean Charlot, written by Miriam Schlein (W. R. Scott)
>
> *The Steadfast Tin Soldier* illustrated by Marcia Wise Brown, written by Hans Christian Andersen, trans. by M. R. James (Scribner)
>
> *A Very Special House* illustrated by Maurice Sendak, written by Ruth Krauss (Harper)
>
> *Green Eyes* by A. Birnbaum (Capitol)

1953

The Biggest Bear by Lynd Ward (Houghton)

> HONOR BOOKS
>
> *Puss in Boots* illustrated and translated from Charles Perrault by Marcia Brown (Scribner)
>
> *One Morning in Maine* by Robert McCloskey (Viking)
>
> *Ape in a Cape: An Alphabet of Odd Animals* by Fritz Eichenberg (Harcourt)
>
> *The Storm Book* illustrated by Margaret Bloy Graham, written by Charlotte Zolotow (Harper)
>
> *Five Little Monkeys* by Juliet Kepes (Houghton)

1952

Finders Keepers illustrated by Nicolas, pseud. (Nicholas Mordvinoff), written by Will, pseud. (William Lipkind) (Lippincott)

> HONOR BOOKS
>
> *Mr. T.W. Anthony Woo* by Marie Hall Ets (Viking)
>
> *Skipper John's Cook* by Marcia Brown (Scribner)
>
> *All Falling Down* illustrated by Margaret Bloy Graham, written by Gene Zion (Harper)
>
> *Bear Party* by William Pene du Bois (Viking)
>
> *Feather Mountain* by Elizabeth Olds (Houghton)

1951

The Egg Tree by Katherine Milhous (Scribner)

> HONOR BOOKS
>
> *Dick Whittington and His Cat* by Marcia Brown (Scribner)

The Two Reds illustrated by Nicolas, pseud. (Nicholas Mordvinoff), written by Will, pseud. (William Lipkind) (Harcourt)

If I Ran the Zoo by Dr. Seuss, pseud. (Theodor Seuss Geisel) (Random House)

The Most Wonderful Doll in the World illustrated by Helen Stone, written by Phyllis McGinley (Lippincott)

T-Bone, the Baby Sitter by Clare Turlay Newberry (Harper)

1950

Song of the Swallows by Leo Politi (Scribner)

HONOR BOOKS

America's Ethan Allen illustrated by Lynd Ward, written by Stewart Holbrook (Houghton)

The Wild Birthday Cake illustrated by Hildegard Woodward, written by Lavinia R. Davis (Doubleday)

The Happy Day illustrated by Marc Simont, written by Ruth Krauss (Harper)

Bartholomew and the Oobleck by Dr. Seuss, pseud. (Theodor Seuss Geisel) (Random House)

Henry Fisherman by Marcia Brown (Scribner)

1949

The Big Snow by Berta and Elmer Hader (Macmillan)

HONOR BOOKS

Blueberries for Sal by Robert McCloskey (Viking)

All Around the Town illustrated by Helen Stone, written by Phyllis McGinley (Lippincott)

Juanita by Leo Politi (Scribner)

Fish in the Air by Kurt Wiese (Viking)

1948

White Snow, Bright Snow illustrated by Roger Duvoisin, written by Alvin Tresselt (Lothrop)

HONOR BOOKS

Stone Soup by Marcia Brown (Scribner)

McElligot's Pool by Dr. Seuss, pseud. (Theodore Seuss Geisel) (Random House)

Bambino the Clown by Georges Schreiber (Viking)

Roger and the Fox illustrated by Hildegard Woodward, written by Lavinia R. Davis (Doubleday)

Song of Robin Hood illustrated by Virginia Lee Burton, written and edited by Anne Malcolmson (Houghton)

1947

The Litte Island illustrated by Leonard Weisgard, written by Golden MacDonald, pseud. (Margaret Wise Brown) (Doubleday)

HONOR BOOKS

Rain Drop Splash illustrated by Leonard Weisgard, written by Alvin Tresselt (Lothrop)

Boats on the River illustrated by Jay Hyde Barnum, written by Marjorie Flack (Viking)

Timothy Turtle illustrated by Tony Palazzo, written by Al Graham (Welch)

Pedro, the Angel of Olvera Street by Leo Politi (Scribner)

Sing in Praise: A Collection of the Best Loved Hymns illustrated by Marjorie Torrey, text selected by Opal Wheeler (Dutton)

1946

The Rooster Crows by Maud and Miska Petersham (Macmillan)

HONOR BOOKS

Little Lost Lamb illustrated by Leonard Weisgard, written by Golden MacDonald, pseud. (Margaret Brown) (Doubleday)

Sing Mother Goose illustrated by Marjorie Torrey, music: Opal Wheeler (Dutton)

My Mother Is the Most Beautiful Woman in the World illustrated by Ruth Gannett, written by Becky Reyher (Lothrop)

You Can Write Chinese by Kurt Wiese (Viking)

1945

Prayer for a Child illustrated by Elizabeth Orton Jones, written by Rachel Field (Macmillan)

HONOR BOOKS

Mother Goose illustrated by Tasha Tudor (Oxford University Press)

In the Forest by Marie Hall Ets (Viking)

Yonie Wondernose by Marguerite de Angeli (Doubleday)

The Christmas Anna Angel illustrated by Kate Seredy, written by Ruth Sawyer (Viking)

1944

Many Moons illustrated by Louis Slobodkin, written by James Thurber (Harcourt)

HONOR BOOKS

Small Rain: Verses from the Bible illustrated by Elizabeth Orton Jones, selected by Jessie Orton Jones (Viking)

Pierre Pidgeon illustrated by Arnold E. Bare, written by Lee Kingman (Houghton)

The Mighty Hunter by Berta & Elmer Hader (Macmillan)

A Child's Good Night Book illustrated by Jean Charlot, written by Margaret Wise Brown (W. R. Scott)

Good Luck Horse illustrated by Plato Chan, written by Chih-yi Chan

1943

The Little House by Virginia Lee Burton (Houghton)

HONOR BOOKS

Dash and Dart by Mary & Conrd Buff (Viking)

Marshmallow by Clare Turlay Newberry (Harper)

1942

Make Way For Ducklings by Robert McCloskey (Viking)

HONOR BOOKS

An American ABC by Maud & Miska Petersham (Macmillan)

In My Mother's House illustrated by Velino Herrera, written by Ann Nolan Clark (Viking)

Paddle-to-the-Sea by Holling C. Holling (Houghton)
Nothing at All by Wanda Gág (Coward)

1941

They Were Strong and Good by Robert Lawson (Viking)

HONOR BOOK

April's Kittens by Clare Turlay Newberry (Harper)

1940

Abraham Lincoln by Ingri and Edgar Parin d'Aulaire (Doubleday)

HONOR BOOKS

Cock-a-Doodle Doo by Berta & Elmer Hader (Macmillan)
Madeline by Ludwig Bemelmans (Viking)
The Ageless Story by Lauren Ford (Dodd)

1939

Mei Li by Thomas Handforth (Doubleday)

HONOR BOOKS

Andy and the Lion by James Daugherty (Viking)
Barkis by Clare Turlay Newberry (Harper)
The Forest Pool by Laura Adams Armer (Longmans)
Snow White and the Seven Dwarfs by Wanda Gág (Coward)
Wee Gillis illustrated by Robert Lawson, written by Munro Leaf (Viking)

1938

Animals of the Bible, A Picture Book illustrated by Dorothy P. Lathrop, selected by Helen Dean Fish (Lippincott)

HONOR BOOKS

Four and Twenty Blackbirds illustrated by Robert Lawson, compiled by Helen Dean Fish (Stokes)
Seven Simeons: A Russian Tale illustrated and retold by Boris Artzybasheff (Viking)

THE BOSTON GLOBE–HORN BOOKS AWARDS

The Boston Globe–Horn Book Awards were first presented in 1967. Since then they have appeared annually and are considered to be among the most distinguished awards for children's and young adult literature. Awards are given in three categories: Fiction and Poetry, Picture Book, and Nonfiction. Honor books are usually selected for each category. Periodically a book receives an award (Special Citation) for its impressive quality. Books must be published in the United States but they may be written and/or illustrated by citizens of any country. The selections are made by a panel of three independent judges.

2007

FICTION AND POETRY

The Astonishing Life of Octavian Nothing, Traitor to the Nation, Volume I: The Pox Party by M. T. Anderson (Candlewick)

FICTION AND POETRY HONOR BOOKS

Clementine by Sara Pennypacker illustrated by Maria Frazee (Hyperion)
Rex Zero and the End of the World by Tim Wynne-Jones (Kroupa/Farrar)

PICTURE BOOK

Dog and Bear: Two Friends, Three Stories written and illustrated by Laura Vaccaro Seeger (Porter/Roaring Brook)

PICTURE BOOK HONOR BOOKS

365 *Penguins* by Jean-Luc Fromental, illustrated by Joelle Jolivet (Abrams),
Wolves written and illustrated by Emily Gravett (Simon)

NONFICTION

The Strongest Man in the World: Louis Cyr written and illustrated by Nicolas Debon (Groundwood)

NONFICTION HONOR BOOKS

Tracking Trash: Flotsam, Jetsam, and the Science of Ocean Motion by Loree Griffin Burns (Houghton)
Escape! by Sid Fleischman (Greenwillow)

2006

FICTION AND POETRY

The Miraculous Journey of Edward Tulane by Kate DiCamillo, illustrated by Bagram Ibatouline (Candlewick)

FICTION AND POETRY HONOR BOOKS

Yellow Elephant: A Bright Beastiary by Julie larios, illustrated by Julie Paschkis (Harcourt)
Yellow Star by Jennifer Roy (Marshall Cavendish)

PICTURE BOOK:

Leaf Man by Louis Ehlert (Harcourt)

PICTURE BOOK HONOR BOOKS

Mama: A True Story in Which a Baby Hippo Loses His Mama During a Tsunami, but Finds a New Home and a New Mama by Jeanette Winter (Harcourt)
Sky Boys: How They Built the Empire State Building by Deborah Hopkinson, illustrated by James Ransome (Schwartz and Wade/Random)

NONFICTION

If You Decide to Go to the Moon by Faith McNulty, illustrated by Steven Kellogg (Scholastic)

NONFICTION HONOR BOOKS

A Mother's Journey by Sandra Markle, illustrated by Alan Marks (Charlesbridge)
Wildfire by Taylor Morrison (Lorraine/Houghton)

2005

FICTION AND POETRY

The Schwa Was Here by Neal Schusterman (Dutton)

FICTION AND POETRY HONOR BOOKS

Kalpana 's Dream by Judith Clarke (Front Street)
A Wreath for Emmett Till by Marilyn Nelson (Houghton)

PICTURE BOOK
Traction Man Is Here! by Mini Grey (Knopf)

PICTURE BOOK HONOR BOOKS
That New Animal by Emily Jenkins, illustrated by Pierre Pratt (Foster/Farrar)
The Hello, Goodbye Window by Norton Juster, illustrated by Chris Raschka (Capital/Hyperion)

NONFICTION
The Race to Save the Lord God Bird by Phillip Hoose (Kroupa/Farrar)

2004

FICTION AND POETRY
The Fire Eaters by David Almond (Delacorte)

FICTION AND POETRY HONOR BOOKS
God Went to Beauty School by Cynthia Rylant (Harper/Tempest)
The Amulet of Samarkand: The Bartimaeus Trilogy, Book One by Jonathan Stroud (Hyperion)

PICTURE BOOK
The Man Who Walked Between the Towers by Mordecai Gerstein (Roaring Brook)

PICTURE BOOK HONOR BOOKS
The Shape Game by Anthony Browne (Farrar)
Snow Music by Lynne Ray Perkins (Greenwillow)

NONFICTION
An American Plague: The True and Terrifying Story of the Yellow Fever Epidemic of 1703 by Jim Murphy (Clarion)

NONFICTION HONOR BOOKS
Surprising Sharks by Nicola Davies, illustrated by James Croft (Candlewick)
The Man Who Went to the Far Side of the Moon: The Story of Apollo 11 Astronaut Michael Collins by Bea Uusma Schyffert (Chronicle)

2003

FICTION AND POETRY
The Jamie and Angus Stories by Anne Fine, illustrated by Penny Dale (Candlewick)

FICTION AND POETRY HONOR BOOKS
Feed by M. T. Anderson (Candlewick)
Locomotion by Jacqueline Woodson (Putnam)

PICTURE BOOK
Big Momma Makes the World by Phyllis Root, illustrated by Helen Oxenbury (Candlewick)

PICTURE BOOK HONOR BOOKS
Dahlia by Barbara McClintock (Foster/Farrar)
Blues Journey by Walter Dean Myers, illustrated by Christopher Myers (Holiday)

NONFICTION
Fireboat: The Heroic Adventures of the John J. Harvey by Maira Kalman (Putnam)

NONFICTION HONOR BOOKS
To Fly: The Story of the Wright Brothers by Wendie C. Old, illustrated by Robert Andrew Parker (Clarion)
Revenge of the Whale: The True Story of the Whaleship Essex by Nathaniel Philbrick (Putnam)

2002

FICTION AND POETRY
Lord of the Deep by Graham Salisbury (Delacorte)

FICTION AND POETRY HONOR BOOKS
Saffey 's Angel by Hilary McKay (McElderry)
Amber Was Brave, Essie Was Smart by Vera Williams (Greenwillow)

PICTURE BOOK
"Let's Get a Pup!" Said Kate by Bob Graham (Candlewick)

PICTURE HONOR BOOKS
I Stink by Kate McMullan, illustrated by Jim McMullan (Cotier/Harper)
Little Rat Sets Sail by Monika Bang-Campbell, illustrated by Molly Bang (Harcourt)

NONFICTION BOOK
This Land Was Made for You and Me: The Life and Songs of Woody Guthrie by Elizabeth Partridge (Viking)

NONFICTION HONOR BOOKS
Handel Who Knew What He Liked by M. T. Anderson, illustrated by Kevin Hawkes (Candlewick)
Woody Guthrie: Poet of the People by Bonnie Christensen (Knopf)

2001

FICTION AND POETRY
Carver: A Life in Poems by Marilyn Nelson (Front Street)

FICTION AND POETRY HONOR BOOKS
Everything On a Waffle by Polly Horvath (Farrar)
Troy by Adele Geras (Harcourt)

PICTURE BOOK
Cold Feet by Cynthia DeFelice, illustrated by Robert Andrew Parker (DK Publishing)

PICTURE BOOK HONOR BOOKS
Five Creatures by Emily Jenkins, illustrated by Tomek Bohgacki (Foster/Farrar)
The Stray Dog by Marc Simont (HarperCollins)

NONFICTION
The Longitude Prize by Joan Dash, illustrated by Dusan Petricic (Foster/Farrar)

NONFICTION HONOR BOOKS
Rocks in His Head by Carol Otis Hurst, illustrated by James Stevenson (Greenwillow)
Uncommon Traveler: Mary Kingsley in Africa by Don Brown (Houghton Mifflin)

2000

FICTION

The Folk Keeper by Franny Billingsley (Atheneum)

FICTION AND POETRY HONOR BOOKS

King of Shadows by Susan Cooper (McElderry)
145th Street: Short Stories by Walter Dean Myers (Delacorte)

PICTURE BOOK

Henry Hikes to Fitchburg by D. B. Johnson (Houghton)

PICTURE BOOK HONOR BOOKS

Buttons by Brock Cole (Farrar)
A Day, A Dog by Gabrielle Vincent (Front Street)

NONFICTION

Sir Walter Ralegh and the Quest for El Dorado by Marc Aronson (Clarion)

NONFICTION HONOR BOOKS

Osceola: Memories of a Sharecropper's Daughter collected and edited by Alan Govenar, illustrated by Shane Evans (Jump at the Sun/Hyperion)
Sitting Bull and His World by Albert Martin (Dutton)

1999

FICTION

Holes by Louis Sachar (Foster/Farrar)

FICTION HONOR BOOKS

The Trolls by Polly Horvath (Farrar)
Monster by Walter Dean Myers, illustrated by Christopher Myers (HarperCollins)

PICTURE BOOK

Red-Eyed Tree Frog by Joy Cowley, illustrated with photographs by Nic Bishop (Scholastic)

PICTURE BOOK HONOR BOOKS

Dance by Bill Jones and Susan Kukli illustrated with photographs by Susan Kukli, (Hyperion)
The Owl and the Pussycat by Edward Lear, illustrated by James Marshall (diCapua/HarperCollins)

NONFICTION

The Top of the World: Climbing Mt. Everest by Steve Jenkins (Houghton)

NONFICTION HONOR BOOKS

Shipwreck at the Bottom of the World: The Extraordinary True Story of Shackelton and the Endurance by Jennifer Armstrong (Crown)
William Shakespeare and the Globe by Aliki (HarperCollins)

SPECIAL CITATION

Tibet: Through the Red Box by Peter Sis (Foster/Farrar)

1998

FICTION AND POETRY

The Circuit: Stories From the Life of a Migrant Child by Franciso Jimenez (University of New Mexico Press)

FICTION HONOR BOOKS

While No One Was Watching by Jane Leslie Conly (Holt)
My Louisiana Sky by Kimberley Willis Holt (Holt)

PICTURE BOOK

And If the Moon Could Talk by Kate Banks, illustrated by Georg Hallensleben (Foster/Farrar)

PICTURE BOOK HONOR BOOKS

Seven Brave Women by Betsy Hearne, illustrated by Bethanne Andersen (Greenwillow)
Popcorn: Poems by James Stevenson (Greenwillow)

NONFICTION

Leon's Story by Leon Walter Tillage, illustrated with collage art by Susan Roth (Farrar)

NONFICTION HONOR BOOKS

Martha Graham: A Dancer's Life by Russell Freedman (Clarion)
Chuck Close Up Close by Jan Greenberg and Sandra Jordan (DK)

1997

FICTION AND POETRY

The Friends by Kazumi Yumonto (Farrar)

FICTION AND POETRY HONOR BOOKS

Lily's Crossing by Patricia Reilly Giff (Delacorte)
Harlem by Walter Dean Myers, illustrated by Christopher Myers (Scholastic)

NONFICTION

A Drop of Water: A Book of Science and Wonder by Walter Wick (Scholastic)

NONFICTION HONOR BOOKS

Lou Gehrig: The Luckiest Man by David Adler, illustrated by Terry Widener (Gulliver/Harcourt)
Leonardo da Vinci by Diane Stanley (Morrow)

PICTURE' BOOK

The Adventures of Sparrowboy by Brian Pinkney (Simon)

PICTURE BOOK HONOR BOOKS

Home on the Bayou: A Cowboy's Story by G. Brian Karas (Simon)
Potato: A Tale from the Great Depression by Katie Lied, illustrated by Lisa Campbell Ernst (National Geographic Society)

1996

FICTION

Poppy by Avi, illustrated by Brian Floca (Jackson/Orchard)

FICTION HONOR BOOKS

The Moorchild by Eloise McGraw (McElderry)
Belle Prater's Boy by Ruth White (Farrar)

NONFICTION

Orphan Train Rider: One Boy's True Story by Andrea Warren (Houghton)

NONFICTION HONOR BOOKS

The Boy Who Lived with the Bears: And Other Iroquois Stories by Joseph Bruchac, ill. by Murv Jacob (Harper-Collins)

Haystack by Bonnie and Arthur Geisert, illustrated by Arthur Geisert (Lorraine/Houghton)

PICTURE BOOK

In the Rain with Baby Duck by Amy Hest, illustrated by Jill Barton (Candlewick)

PICTURE BOOK HONOR BOOKS

Fanny's Dream by Caralyn Buehner, illustrated by Mark Buehner (Dial)

Home Lovely by Lynne Rae Perkins (Greenwillow)

1995

FICTION

Some of the Kinder Planets by Tim Wynne–Jones (Kroupa/Orchard)

FICTION HONOR BOOKS

Jericho by Janet Hickman (Greenwillow)

Earthshine by Theresa Nelson (Jackson/Orchard)

NONFICTION

Abigail Adams: Witness to a Revolution by Natalie S. Bober (Atheneum)

NONFICTION HONOR BOOKS

It's Perfectly Normal: A Book about Changing Bodies, Growing Up, Sex, and Sexual Health by Robie H. Harris, illustrated by Michael Emberley (Candlewick)

The Great Fire by Jim Murphy (Scholastic)

PICTURE BOOK

John Henry retold by Julius Lester, illustrated by Jerry Pinkney (Dial)

PICTURE BOOK HONOR BOOK

Swamp Angel by Anne Isaacs, illustrated by Paul O. Zelinsky

1994

FICTION

Scooter by Vera Williams (Greenwillow)

FICTION HONOR BOOKS

Flour Babies by Anne Fine (Little)

Western Wind by Paula Fox (Orchard)

NONFICTION

Eleanor Roosevelt: A Life of Discovery by Russell Freedman (Clarion)

NONFICTION HONOR BOOKS

Unconditional Surrender: U. S. Grant and the Civil War by Albert Murrin (Atheneum)

A Tree Place and Other Poems by Constance Levy, illustrated by Robert Sabuda (McElderry)

PICTURE BOOKS

Grandfather's Journey by Allen Say (Houghton)

PICTURE BOOK HONOR BOOKS

A Small Tall Tale from the Far Far North by Peter Sis (Knopf)

Owen by Kevin Henkes (Greenwillow)

1993

FICTION

Ajeemah and His Son by James Berry (Harper)

FICTION HONOR BOOK

The Giver by Lois Lowry (Houghton)

PICTURE BOOK

The Fortune Tellers by Lloyd Alexander, illustrated by Trina Schart Hyman (Dutton)

PICTURE BOOK HONOR BOOKS

Komodo! byPeter Sis (Greenwillow)

Raven: A Trickster Tale from the Pacific Northwest by Gerald McDermott (Harcourt)

NONFICTION

Sojourner Truth: Ain't I a Woman? by Patricia C. and Frederick McKissack (Scholastic)

NONFICTION HONOR BOOKS

Lives of the Musicians: Good Times, Bad Times (and What the Neighbors Thought) by Kathleen Krull, illustrated by Kathryn Hewitt (Harcourt)

1992

FICTION

Missing May by Cynthia Rylant (Orchard)

FICTION HONOR BOOKS

Nothing but the Truth by Avi (Orchard)

Somewhere in the Darkness by Walter Dean Myers (Scholastic)

NONFICTION

Talking with Artists by Pat Cummings (Bradbury)

NONFICTION HONOR BOOKS

Red Leaf, Yellow Leaf by Lois Ehlert (Harcourt)

The Handmade Alphabet by Laura Rankin (Dial)

PICTURE BOOK

Seven Blind Mice by Ed Young (Philomel)

PICTURE BOOK HONOR BOOK

In the Tall, Tall Grass by Denise Fleming (Holt)

1991

FICTION

The True Confessions of Charlotte Doyle by Avi (Orchard/Jackson)

FICTION HONOR BOOKS

Paradise Cafe and Other Stories by Martha Brooks (Joy Street)

Judy Scuppernong by Brenda Seabrooke (Cobblehill)

NONFICTION

Appalachia: The Voices of Sleeping Birds by Cynthia Ryland, illustrated by Barry Moser (Harcourt)

NONFICTION HONOR BOOKS

The Wright Brothers: How They Invented the Airplane by Russell Freedman (Holiday)

Good Queen Bess: The Story of Queen Elizabeth I of England by Diane Stanley and Peter Vennema, illustrated by Diane Stanley (Four Winds)

PICTURE BOOK

The Tale of the Mandarin Ducks, retold by Katherine Paterson, illustrated by Leo and Diane Dillon (Lodestar)

PICTURE BOOK HONOR BOOKS

Aardvarks, Disembark! by Ann Jonas (Greenwillow)

Sophie and Lou by Petra Mathers (HarperCollins)

1990

FICTION

Maniac Magee by Jerry Spinelli (Little)

FICTION HONOR BOOKS

Stonewords by Pam Conrad (Harper)

Saturnalia by Paul Fleischman (Harper/Zolotow)

NONFICTION

The Great Little Madison by Jean Fritz (Putnam)

NONFICTION HONOR BOOKS

Insect Metamorphosis by Ron and Nancy Goor, illustrated with photos by Ron Goor (Atheneum)

Shadows and Reflections photographed by Tana Hoban (Greenwillow)

PICTURE BOOK

Lon Po, Po: A Red Riding Hood Story from China trans, and illustrated by Ed Young (Philomel)

PICTURE BOOK HONOR BOOKS

Chicka Chicka Boom Boom by Bill Martin Jr. and John Archambault, illustrated by Lois Ehlert (Simon)

Special Award for Excellence in Bookmaking: Valentine and Orson, written and illustrated by Nancy Ekholm Burkert (Farrar)

1989

FICTION

The Village by the Sea by Paula Fox (Orchard)

FICTION HONOR BOOKS

Eva by Peter Dickinson (Delacorte)

Gideon Ahoy! by William Mayne (Delacorte)

NONFICTION

The Way Things Work by David Macaulay (Houghton)

NONFICTION HONOR BOOKS

The Rainbow People by Laurence Yep (HarperCollins)

Round Buildings, Square Buildings, & Buildings that Wiggle Like a Fish by Philip M. Isaacson (Knopf)

PICTURE BOOK

Shy Charles by Rosemary Wells (Dial)

PICTURE BOOK HONOR BOOKS

The Nativity illustrated by Julie Vivas (Gulliver/Harcourt)

Island Boy by Barbara Cooney (Viking Kestrel)

1988

FICTION

The Friendship by Mildred Taylor, illustrated by Max Ginsburg (Dial)

FICTION HONOR BOOKS

Granny Was a Buffer Girl by Berlie Doherty (Orchard)

Joyful Noise: Poems for Two Voices by Paul Fleischman, illustrated by Eric Beddows (Harper)

Memory by Margaret Mahy (McElderry)

NONFICTION

Anthony Burns: The Defeat and Triumph of a Fugitive Slave by Virginia Hamilton (Knopf)

NONFICTION HONOR BOOKS

African Journey by John Chiasson (Bradbury)

Little by Little: A Writer's Education by Jean Little (Viking Kestrel)

PICTURE BOOK

The Boy of the Three-Year Nap by Dianne Snyder, illustrated by Allen Say (Houghton)

PICTURE BOOK HONOR BOOKS

Where the Forest Meets the Sea by Jeannie Baker (Greenwillow)

Stringbean 's Trip to the Shining Sea by Vera B. Williams, illustrated by Jennifer and Vera B. Williams (Greenwillow)

1987

FICTION

Rabble Starkey by Lois Lowry (Houghton)

FICTION HONOR BOOKS

Georgia Music by Helen Griffith, illustrated by James Stevenson (Greenwillow)

Isaac Campion by Janni Howker (Greenwillow)

NONFICTION

Pilgrims of Plimoth by Marcia Sewall (Atheneum)

NONFICTION HONOR BOOKS

Being Born by Sheila Kitzinger, photos by Lennart Nilsson (Grosset)

The Magic School Bus at the Waterworks by Joanna Cole, illustrated by Bruce Degen (Scholastic)

Steamboat in a Cornfield by John Hartford (Crown)

PICTURE BOOK

Mufaro's Beautiful Daughters: An African Tale by John Steptoe (Lothrop)

PICTURE BOOK HONOR BOOKS

In Coal Country by Judith Hendershot, illustrated by Thomas B. Allen (Knopf)

Cherries and Cherry Pits by Vera B. Williams (Greenwillow)

Old Henry by Joan W. Bios, illustrated by Stephen Gammell (Morrow)

1986

FICTION

In Summer Light by Zibby Oneal (Viking Kestrel)

FICTION HONOR BOOKS

Prairie Songs by Pam Conrad (Harper)

Howl's Moving Castle by Diana Wynne Jones (Greenwillow)

NONFICTION

Auks, Rocks and the Odd Dinosaur: Inside Stories from the Smithsonian's Museum of Natural History by Peggy Thomson (Crowell)

NONFICTION HONOR BOOKS

Dark Harvest: Migrant Farmworkers in America by Brent Ashabranner (Dodd)

The Truth About Santa Claus by James Cross Giblin (Crowell)

PICTURE BOOK

The Paper Crane by Molly Bang (Greenwillow)

PICTURE BOOK HONOR BOOKS

Gorilla by Anthony Browne (Knopf)

The Trek by Ann Jonas (Greenwillow)

The Polar Express by Chris Van Allsburg (Houghton)

1985

FICTION

The Moves Make the Man by Bruce Brooks (Harper)

FICTION HONOR BOOKS

The Changeover: A Supernatural Romance by Margaret Mahy (Atheneum/McElderry)

Babe: The Gallant Pig by Dick King-Smith, illustrated by Mary Rayner (Crown)

NONFICTION

Commodore Perry in the Land of the Shogun by Rhoda Blumberg (Lothrop)

NONFICTION HONOR BOOKS

Boy by Roald Dahl (Farrar)

1812: The War Nobody Won by Albert Martin (Atheneum)

PICTURE BOOK

Mama Don't Allow by Thacher Hurd (Harper)

PICTURE BOOK HONOR BOOKS

Like Jake and Me by Mavis Jukes, ill. by Lloyd Bloom (Knopf)

How Much Is a Million? by David Schwartz, ill. by Steven Kellog (Lothrop)

The Mysteries of Harris Burdick by Chris Van Allsburg (Houghton)

Special Award: 1, 2, 3 by Tana Hoban (Greenwillow)

1984

FICTION

A Little Fear by Patricia Wrightson (McElderry/Atheneum)

FICTION HONOR BOOKS

A Solitary Blue by Cynthia Voight (Atheneum)

Archer's Goon by Diana Wynne Jones (Greenwillow)

Unclaimed Treasures by Patricia MacLachlan (Harper)

NONFICTION

The Double Life of Pocahontas by Jean Fritz (Putnam)

NONFICTION HONOR BOOKS

Children of the Wild West by Russell Freedman (Clarion)

Queen Eleanor: Independent Spirit of the Medieval World by Polly Schoyer Brooks (Lippincott)

The Tipi: A Center of Native American Life by David and Charlotte Yue (Knopf)

PICTURE BOOK

Jonah and the Great Fish retold and illustrated by Warwick Hutton (McElderry/Atheneum)

PICTURE BOOK HONOR BOOKS

Dawn by Molly Bang (Morrow)

The Guinea Pig ABC by Kate Duke (Dutton)

The Rose in My Garden by Arnold Lobel, illustrated by Anita Lobel (Greenwillow)

1983

FICTION

Sweet Whispers, Brother Rush by Virginia Hamilton (Philomel)

FICTION HONOR BOOKS

Homesick: My Own Story by Jean Fritrz, illustrated by Margot Tomes (Putnam)

The Road to Camlann by Rosemary Sutcliff (Dutton)

Dicey's Song by Cynthia Voigt (Atheneum)

NONFICTION

Behind Barbed Wire: The Imprisonment of Japanese Americans During World War II by Daniel S. Davis (Dutton)

NONFICTION HONOR BOOKS

Hiroshima No Pika by Toshi Maruki (Lothrop)

The Jewish Americans: A History in their Own Words, 1650-1950 by Milton Meltzer (Crowell)

PICTURE BOOK

A Chair for My Mother by Vera B. Williams (Greenwillow)

PICTURE BOOK HONOR BOOKS

Friends by Helme Heine (Atheneum/McElderry)

Yeh-Shen: A Cinderella Story from China by Ai-Ling Louie, illustrated by Ed Young (Philomel)

Doctor De Soto by William Steig (Farrar)

1982

FICTION

Playing Beatie Bow by Ruth Park (Atheneum)

FICTION HONOR BOOKS

The Voyage Begun by Nancy Bond (Atheneum)

Ask Me No Questions by Ann Schlee (Holt)

The Scarecrows by Robert Westall (Greenwillow)

NONFICTION

Upon the Head of the Goat: a Childhood in Hungary 1939–1944 by Aranka Siegal (Farrar)

NONFICTION HONOR BOOKS

Lobo of the Tasaday by John Nance (Pantheon)

Dinosaurs of North America by Helen Roney Sadler, ill. by Anthony Rao (Lothrop)

PICTURE BOOK

A Visit to William Blake's Inn: Poems for Innocent and Experienced Travelers by Nancy Willard, ill. by Alice and Martin Provensen (HBJ)

PICTURE BOOK HONOR BOOK

The Friendly Beasts: An Old English Christmas Carol by Tomie de Paola (Putnam)

1981

FICTION

The Leaving by Lynn Hall (Scribner)

FICTION HONOR BOOKS

Flight of the Sparrow by Julia Cunningham (Pantheon)

Footsteps by Leon Garfield (Delacorte)

Ida Early Comes Over the Mountain by Robert Burch (Viking)

NONFICTION

The Weaver's Gift by Kathryn Lasky (Warner)

NONFICTION HONOR BOOKS

The Hospital Book by James Howe, ill. with photos by Maj Warshaw (Crown)

Junk Food, Fast Food, Health Food: What America Eats and Why by Lila Perl (Clarion)

You Can't Be Timid with a Trumpet: Notes from the Orchestra by Betty Lou English (Lothrop)

PICTURE BOOK

Outside Over There by Maurice Sendak (Harper)

PICTURE BOOK HONOR BOOKS

Jumanjii by Chris Van Allsburg (Houghton)

On Market Street by Arnold Lobel, ill. by Anita Lobel (Greenwillow)

Where the Buffaloes Begin by Olaf Baker, ill. by Stephen Gammell (Warner)

1980

FICTION

Conrad's War by Andrew Davies (Crown)

FICTION HONOR BOOKS

The Alfred Summer by Jan Slepian (Macmillan)

Me and My Million by Clive King (Crowell)

The Night Swimmers by Betsy Byars, illustrated by Troy Howell (Delacorte)

NONFICTION

Building: The Fight Against Gravity by Mario Salvadori (McElderry/Atheneum)

NONFICTION HONOR BOOKS

Childtimes: A Three-Generation Memoir by Eloise Greenfield, illustrated by Jerry Pinkney (Crowell)

How the Forest Grew by William Jaspersohn, ill. by Chuck Eckart (Greenwillow)

Stonewall by Jean Fritz, illustrated by Stephen Gammell (Putnam)

PICTURE BOOK

The Garden of Abdul Gasazi by Chris Van Allsburg (Houghton)

PICTURE BOOK HONOR BOOKS

The Grey Lady and the Strawberry Snatcher by Molly Bang (Four Winds)

Why the Tides Ebb and Flow by John Chase Bowden, illustrated by Marc Brown (Houghton Mifflin)

Special Citation (Illustration): Graham Oakley's Magical Changes by Graham Oakley (Atheneum)

1979

FICTION

Humbug Mountain by Sid Fleischman (Atlantic-Little)

FICTION HONOR BOOKS

All Together Now by Sue Ellen Bridgers (Knopf)

Silas and Ben-Godik by Cecil Bodker (Delacorte)

NONFICTION

The Road from Home: The Story of an Armenian Girl by David Kherdian (Greenwillow)

NONFICTION HONOR BOOKS

The Iron Road: A Portrait of American Railroading by Richard Snow, illustrated with photos by David Plowden (Four Winds)

Self-Portrait: Margot Zemach by Margot Zemach (Addison-Wesley)

The Story of American Photography: An Illustrated History for Young People by Martin Sandler (Little Brown)

PICTURE BOOK

The Snowman by Raymond Briggs (Random)

PICTURE BOOK HONOR BOOKS

Ben's Trumpet by Rachel Isadora (Greenwillow)

Cross-Country Cat by Mary Calhoun, illustrated by Erik Ingraham (Morrow)

1978

FICTION

The Westing Game by Ellen Raskin (Dutton)

FICTION HONOR BOOKS

Ramona and Her Father by Beverly Cleary (Morrow)

Anpao: An American Indian Odyssey by James Highwater (Lippincott)

Alan and Naomi by Myron Levoy (Harper)

NONFICTION

Mischling, Second Degree: My Childhood in Nazi Germany by Ilse Koehn (Greenwillow)

NONFICTION HONOR BOOKS

Settlers and Strangers: Native Americans of the Desert Southwest and History as they Saw It by Betty Baker (Macmillan)

Castle by David Macaulay (Houghton)

PICTURE BOOKS
Anno's Journey by Mitsumasa Anno (Philomel)

PICTURE BOOK HONOR BOOKS
The Story of Edward by Philippe Dumas (Parents)
On to Widecombe Fair by Patricia Lee Gauch, illustrated by Trina Schart Hyman (Putnam)
What Do You Feed Your Donkey On? Rhymes from a Belfast Childhood by Collette O'Hare, illustrated by Jenny Rodwell (Collins-World)

1977

FICTION
Child of the Owl by Laurence Yep (Harper)

FICTION HONOR BOOKS
Blood Feud by Rosemary Sutcliff (Dutton)
The Machine Gunners by Robert Westall (Greenwillow)
Roll of Thunder, Hear My Cry by Mildred Taylor (Dial)

NONFICTION
Chance, Luck, and Destiny by Peter Dickinson (Atlantic-Little)

NONFICTION HONOR BOOKS
From Slave to Abolitionist by Lucille Schulberg Warner (Dial)
The Colonial Cookbook by Lucille Recht Penner (Hastings)
Watching the Wild Apes by Betty Ann Kevles (Dutton)

PICTURE BOOK
Granfa Grig Had a Pig and Other Rhymes Without Reason from Mother Goose by Wallace Tripp (Little)

PICTURE HONOR BOOKS
Anno 's Counting Book by Mitsumasa Anno (Crowell)
Ashanti to Zulu: African Traditions by Margaret Musgrove, illustrated by **Leo** and Diane Dillon (Dial)
The Amazing Bone by William Steig (Farrar)

SPECIAL HONORABLE MENTION FOR NONBOOK ILLUSTRATION:
The Changing City and the Changing Countryside by Jorg Miller (Atheneum/McElderry)

1976

FICTION
Unleaving by Jill Paton Walsh (Farrar)

FICTION HONOR BOOKS
A String in the Harp by Nancy Bond (Atheneum/McElderry)
A Stranger Came Ashore by Mollie Hunter (Harper)
Dragonwings by Laurence Yep (Harper)

NONFICTION
Voyaging to Cathay: Americans in the China Trade by Alfred Tamarin and Shirley Glubok (Viking)

NONFICTION HONOR BOOKS
Will You Sign Here, John Hancock? by Jean Fritz (Coward)
Never to Forget: The Jews of the Holocaust by Milton Meltzer (Harper)

Pyramid by David Macaulay (Houghton)

PICTURE BOOK
Thirteen by Remy Charlip and Jerry Joyner (Four Winds)

PICTURE BOOK HONOR BOOKS
The Desert Is Theirs by Byrd Baylor, illustrated by Peter Parnall (Scribner)
Six Little Ducks by Chris Conover (Crowell)
Song of the Boat by Lorenz Graham, illustrated by Leo and Diane Dillon (Crowell)

1975

FICTION
Transport 7-451-R by T. Degens (Viking)

FICTION HONOR BOOKS
The Hundred Penny Box by Sharon Bell Mathis, illustrated by Leo and Diane Dillon (Viking)

PICTURE BOOK
Anno's Alphabet by Mitsumasa Anno (Harper)

PICTURE BOOK HONOR BOOKS
She Come Bringing Me That Little Baby Girl by Eloise Greenfield, illustrated by John Steptoe (Lippincott)
Scram, Kid by Ann McGovern, illustrated by Nola Lanner (Viking)
The Bear's Bicycle by Emilie Warren McLeod, illustrated by David McPhail (Little)

1974

FICTION
M. C. Higgins, The Great by Virginia Hamilton (Macmillan)

FICTION HONOR BOOKS
And Then What Happened Paul Revere? by Jean Fritz, illustrated by Margot Tomes (Coward)
The Summer After the Funeral by Jane Gardam (Macmillan)
Tough Chauncey by Doris Buchanan Smith (Morrow)

PICTURE BOOK
Jambo Means Hello by Muriel Feelings, illustrated by Tom Feelings (Dial)

PICTURE BOOK HONOR BOOKS
All Butterflies by Marcia Brown (Scribners)
Herman the Helper by Robert Kraus, illustrated by Jose Aruego and Ariane Dewey (Windmill)
A Prairie Boy's Winter by William Kurelek (Houghton)

1973

FICTION
The Dark Is Rising by Susan Cooper (Atheneum/McElderry)

FICTION HONOR BOOKS
The Cat Who Wished to Be a Man by Lloyd Alexander (Dutton)
An Island in a Green Sea by Mabel Esther Allan (Atheneum)

No Way of Telling by Emma Smith (Atheneum/ McElderry)

PICTURE BOOK

King Stork by Howard Pyle, illustrated by Trina Schart Hyman (Little)

PICTURE BOOK HONOR BOOKS

The Magic Tree by Gerald McDermott (Holt)
Who, Said Sue, Said Whool by Ellen Raskin (Atheneum)
The Silver Pony by Lynd Ward (Houghton)

1972

FICTION

Tristan and Isold by Rosemary Sutcliff (Dutton)

PICTURE BOOK

Mr. Gumpy 's Outing by John Burningham (Holt)

1971

FICTION

A Room Made of Windows by Eleanor Cameron (Atlantic Little)

FICTION HONOR BOOKS

Beyond the Weir Bridge by Herster Burton (Crowell)
Come by Here by Olivia Coolidge (Houghton)
Mrs. Frisby and the Rats of NIMH by Robert O'Brien (Atheneum)

PICTURE BOOK

If I Built a Village by Kazue Mizumura (Harper)

PICTURE BOOK HONOR BOOKS

If All the Seas Were One Sea by Janina Domanska (Macmillan)
The Angry Moon retold by William Sleator, illustrated by Blair Lent (Atlantic Little)
A Firefly Named Torchy by Bernard Waber (Houghton)

1970

FICTION

The Intruder by John Rowe Townsend (Lippincott)

FICTION HONOR BOOK

Where the Lillies Bloom by Vera and Bill Cleaver (Lippincott)

PICTURE BOOK

Hi, Cat! by Ezra Jack Keats (Macmillan)

PICTURE BOOK HONOR BOOK

A Story, A Story by Gail Haley (Atheneum)

1969

FICTION

A Wizard of Earthsea by Ursula K. Le Guin (Parnassus) (Houghton)

FICTION HONOR BOOKS

Flambards by K. M. Peyton (World)
Turi's Poppa by Elizabeth de Trevino (Farrar)
The Pigman by Paul Zindel (Harper)

PICTURE BOOK

The Adventures of Paddy Pork by John Goodall (Harcourt)

PICTURE BOOK HONOR BOOKS

New Moon Cove written by Ann Atwood (Scribners)
Monkey in the Jungle by Edna Mitchell Preston, illustrated by Clement Hurd (Viking)
Thy Friend Obadiah by Brinton Turkle (Viking)

1968

FICTION

The Spring Rider by John Lawson (Crowell)

FICTION HONOR BOOKS

Young Mark by E. M. Almedingen (Farrar)
Dark Venture by Audrey White Beyer (Knopf)
Smith by Leon Garfield (Pantheon)
The Endless Steppe by Esther Hautiz (Crowell)

PICTURE BOOK

Tikki Tikki Tembo by Arlene Mosel, illustrated by Blair Lent (Holt)

PICTURE BOOK HONOR BOOKS

Gilgamesh: Man's First Story retold and illustrated by Bernarda Bryson (Holt)
Rosie 's Walk by Pat Hutchins (Macmillan)
Jorinda and Joringel by the Brothers Grimm, illustrated by Adrienne Adams (Scribners)
All in Free but Janey by Elizabeth Johnson, illustrated by Trina Hyman (Little)

1967

FICTION

The Little Fishes by Erik Christian Haugaard (Houghton Mifflin)

PICTURE BOOK:

London Bridge Is Falling Down by Peter Spier (Doubleday)

THE LEE BENNETT HOPKINS POETRY AWARD

The Lee Bennett Hopkins Poetry Award was established in 1993 by Penn State University to honor a living American poet who has published an original collection or an anthology of poetry for children that is outstanding. It is presented annually and, since 1999, has included honor books as well. In 2007 the award was presented by The Pennsylvania Center for the Book, the University Libraries, and the Pennsylvania School Librarians' Association.

2007

Jazz written by Walter Dean Myers (Holiday House)

HONOR BOOKS

Behold the Bold Umbrellaphant and Other Poems by Jack Prelutsky (Greenwillow)
The Braid by Helen Frost (Farrar, Straus, & Giroux)
Tour America by Diane Siebert (Chronicle Books)

2006

Song of the Water Boatman & Other Pond Poems by Joyce Sidman (Houghton Mifflin)

HONOR BOOKS

A Maze Me by Naomi Shihab Nye (HarperCollins)
A Wreath for Emmett Till by Marilyn Nelson (Houghton Mifflin)

2005

Here in Harlem by Walter Dean Myers (Holiday House)

HONOR BOOKS

Is This Forever or What? Poems and Paintings from Texas by Naomi Shihab Nye (Greenwillow)
Creature Carnival by Marilyn Singer (Hyperion)

2004

The Wishing Bone and Other Poems by Stephen Mitchell (Candlewick)

HONOR BOOKS

Animal Sense by Diane Ackerman (Knopf)
Blues Journey by Walter Dean Myers (Holiday House)
The Pond God and Other Stories by Samuel Jay Keyser (Front Street)
The Way a Door Closes by Anita Smith (Henry Holt)

2003

Splash! Poems of Our Watery World by Constance Levy (Orchard Books)

HONOR BOOKS

Girl Coming In for a Landing—A Novel in Poems by April Halprin Wayland (Knopf)
Becoming Joe DiMaggio by Maria Testa (Candlewick)
The Song Shoots Out of My Mouth by Jaime Adolf (Dutton)

2002

HONOR BOOKS

Pieces: A Year in Poems and Quilts by Anna Grossnickle Hines (Greenwillow)
A Humble Life: Plain Poems by Linda Oatman High (Eerdmans)
A Poke in the I: A collection of Concrete Poems by Paul Janeczko (Candlewick)
Skort Takes: Fastbreaking Basketball Poetry by Charles R. Smith Jr. (Dutton)

2001

Light-Gathering Poems by Liz Rosenberg (Henry Holt)

HONOR BOOK

Stone Bench in an Empty Park by Paul Janeczko (Orchard)

2000

What Have You Lost? by Naomi Shihab Nye (Greenwillow)

HONOR BOOK

An Old Shell by Tony Johnston (Farrar, Straus, & Giroux)
The Rainbow Hand by Janet Wong (McElderry)

1999

The Other Side: Shorter Poems by Angela Johnson (Orchard)

HONOR BOOK

A Crack in the Clouds by Constance Levy (McElderry)

1998

The Great Frog Race by Kristen O'Connell George (Clarion)

1997

Voices from the Wild by David Bouchard (Chronicle Books)

1996

Dance with Me by Barbara Juster Esbensen (HarperCollins)

1995

Beast Feast by Douglas Florian (Greenwillow)

1994

Spirit Walker by Nancy Wood (Doubleday)

1993

Sing to the Sun by Ashley Bryan (McElderry)

ORBIS PICTUS AWARD AND HONOR BOOKS

The Orbis Pictus Award, established in 1990 by the National Council of Teachers of English, is named in honor of the work of Johann Amos Comenius's, Orbis Pictus: The World in Pictures, *published in 1657. It is presented annually to an outstanding work of nonfiction for children that incorporates accuracy, organization, design, and style (Zarnowski,* The Best in Children's Nonfiction, *2001).*

2007

Quest for the Tree Kangaroo: An Expedition to the Cloud Forest of New Guinea by Sy Montgomery (Houghton Mifflin)

HONOR BOOKS

Gregor Mendel: The Friar Who Grew Peas by Cheryl Bardoe (Abrams)
Freedom Walkers: The Story of the Montgomery Bus Boycott by Russell Freedman (Holiday House)
John Muir: America's First Environmentalist by Kathryn Lasky (Candlewick)
Something Out of Nothing: Marie Curie and Radium by Carla Killough McClafferty (Farrar, Straus, & Giroux)
Team Moon: How 400,000 People Landed Apollo 11 on the Moon by Catherine Thimmesh (Houghton Mifflin)

2006

Children of the Great Depression by Russell Freedman (Clarion)

HONOR BOOKS

ER Vets: Life in an Animal Emergency Room by Donna Jackson (Houghton Mifflin)
Forbidden Schoolhouse: The True and Dramatic Story of Prudence Crandall and Her Students by Suzanne Jurmain (Houghton Mifflin)
Genius: A Photobiography of Albert Einstein by Marfe Ferguson Delano (National Geographic Society)
Hitler Youth: Growing Up in Hilter's Shadow by Susan Campbell Bartoletti (Scholastic)
Mosquito Bite by Alexandra Sly (Charlesbridge Publishing)

2005

York's Adventures with Lewis and Clark: An African-American's Part in the Great Expedition by Rhonda Blumberg (HarperCollins)

HONOR BOOKS

Actual Size by Steve Jenkins (Houghton Mifflin)
The Race to Save the Lord God Bird by Philip Hoose (Farrar, Straus, & Giroux)
Secrets of the Sphinx by James Cross Giblin (Scholastic)
Seurat and La Grande Jatte: Connecting the Dots by Robert Burleigh (HNA Books)
The Voice that Challenged a Nation: Marian Anderson and the Struggle for Equal Rights by Russell Freedman (Clarion)

2004

An American Plague: The True and Terrifying Story of the Yellow Fever Epidemic of 1793 by Jim Murphy (Clarion)

HONOR BOOKS

Empire State Building: When New York Reached for the Skies by Elizabeth Mann (Mikaya Press)
In Defense of Liberty: The Story of America's Bill of Rights by Russell Freedman (Holiday House)
Leonardo: Beautiful Dreamer by Robert Byrd (Dutton)
The Man Who Made Time Travel by Kathryn Lasky (Farrar, Straus, & Giroux)
Shutting Out the Sky: Life in the Tenements of New York, 1880–1924 by Deborah Hopkinson (Orchard)

2003

When Marian Sang: The True Recital of Marian Anderson: The Voice of a Century by Pam Munoz Ryan (Scholastic)

HONOR BOOKS

Tenement: Immigrant Life on the Lower East Side by Raymond Bial (Houghton Mifflin)
Phineas Gage: A Gruesome but True Story About Brain Science by John Fleischman (Houghton Mifflin)
Confucius: The Golden Rule, Russell Freedman (Arthur A. Levine)
The Emperor's Silent Army: Terracotta Warriors of Ancient China by Jane O'Connor (Viking)

To Fly: The Story of the Wright Brothers by Wendie Old (Clarion)

2002

Black Potatoes: The Story of the Great Irish Famine, 1845-1850 by Susan Campbell Bartoletti (Houghton Mifflin)

HONOR BOOKS

The Dinosaurs of Waterhouse Hawkins: An Illuminating History of Mr. Waterhouse Hawkins, Artist and Lecturer by Barbara Kerley (Scholastic)
The Cod's Tale by Mark Kurlansky (Putnam)
Martin's Big Words: The Life of Dr. Martin Luther King, Jr. by Doreen Rappaport (Hyperion)

2001

Hurry Freedom: African American in Gold Rush California by Jerry Stanley (Crown)

HONOR BOOKS

America's Champion Swimmer: Gertrude Ederle by David A. Adler (Voyager)
Wild and Swampy by Jim Arnosky (HarperCollins)
The Amazing Life of Benjamin Franklin by James Cross Giblin (Scholastic)
Osceola: Memories of a Sharecropper's Daughter by Alan B. Govenar (Jump At The Sun)
Michelangelo by Diane Stanley (HarperCollins)

2000

Through My Eyes by Ruby Bridges (Scholastic)

HONOR BOOKS

At Her Majesty's Request: An African Princess in Victorian England by Walter Dean Myers (Scholastic)
Clara Schumann: Piano Virtuoso by Susanna Reich (Clarion)
Mapping the World by Sylvia Johnson (Atheneum)
The Snake Scientist by Sy Montgomery (Houghton Mifflin)
The Top of the World by Steve Jenkins (Houghton Mifflin)

1999

Shipwreck at the Bottom of the World: The Extraordinary True Story of Shackleton and the Endurance by Jennifer Armstrong (Crown)

HONOR BOOKS

Black Whiteness: Admiral Byrd Alone in the Antarctic by Robert Burleigh (Atheneum)
Fossil Feud: The Rivalry of the First American Dinosaur Hunters by Thom Holmes (Messner)
Hottest, Coldest, Highest, Deepest by Steve Jenkins (Houghton Mifflin)
No Pretty Pictures: A Child of War by Anita Lobel (Greenwillow)

1998

An Extraordinary Life: The Story of a Monarch Butterfly by Laurence Pringle (Orchard)

HONOR BOOKS

A Tree Is Growing by Artur Dorros (Scholastic)

Charles Lindbergh: A Human Hero by James Cross Giblin (Clarion)

Kennedy Assassinated! The World Mourns: A Reporter's Story by Wilborn Hampton (Candlewick)

Digger: The Tragic Fate of the California Indians from the Missions to the Gold Rush by Jerry Stanley (Crown)

A Drop of Water: A Book of Science and Wonder by Walter Wick (Scholastic)

1997

Leonardo da Vinci by Diane Stanley (Morrow Junior Books)

HONOR BOOKS

Full Steam Ahead: The Race to Build a Transcontinental Railroad by Rhoda Blumberg (National Geographic Society)

The Life and Death of Crazy Horse by Russell Freedman (Holiday House)

One World, Many Religions: The Ways We Worship by Mary Pope Osborne (Knopf)

1996

The Great Fire by Jim Murphy (Scholastic)

HONOR BOOKS

Rosie the Riveter; Women Working on the Home Front in World War II by Penny Colman (Crown)

Dolphin Man: Exploring the World of Dolphins by Laurence Pringle (Atheneum)

1995

Safari Beneath the Sea: The Wonder World of the North Pacific Coast by Diane Swanson (Sierra Books For Children)

HONOR BOOKS

Wildlife Rescue: The Work of Dr. Kathleen Ramsay by Jennifer Owings Dewey (Boyds Mill Press)

Kids at Work: Lewis Hine and the Crusade against Child Labor by Russell Freedman (Clarion)

Christmas in the Big House, Christmas in the Quarters by Patricia C. McKissack (Scholastic)

1994

Across America on an Emigrant Train by Jim Murphy (Clarion Books)

HONOR BOOKS

To the Top of the World: Adventures with Arctic Wolves by Jim Brandenburg (Walker)

Making Sense: Animal Perception and Comunication by Bruce Brooks (Farrar, Straus, & Giroux)

1993

Children of the Dust Bowl: The True Story of the School at Weedpatch Camp by Jerry Stanley (Crown)

HONOR BOOKS

Come Back, Salmon: How a Group of Dedicated Kids Adoped Pigeon Creek and Brought It Back to Life by Molly Cone (San Francisco Sierra Club)

Talking to Artists by Pat Cummings (Bradbury Press)

1992

Flight: The Journey of Charles Lindbergh by Robert Burleigh (Philomel Books)

HONOR BOOKS

Prairie Vision: The Life and Times of Solomon Butcher by Pam Conrad (HarperCollins)

Now Is Your Time! The African American Struggle for Freedom by Walter Dean Myers (Harper Trophy)

1991

Franklin Delano Roosevelt by Russell Freedman (Clarion)

HONOR BOOKS

Arctic Memories by Normee Ekoomiak (Henry Holt)

Seeing Earth from Space by Patricia Lauber (Orchard Books)

1990

The Great Little Madison by Jean Fritz (G. P. Putnam's Sons)

HONOR BOOKS

The Great American Gold Rush by Rhoda Blumberg (Bradbury Press)

The News About Dinosaurs by Patricia Lauber (Bradbury Press)

THE ROBERT F. SIBERT AWARD AND HONOR BOOKS

The Robert F. Sibert Award was established in 2001 by The Association of Library Service to Children division of the American Library Association and the Bound to Stay Bound Books Inc., in honor of its president, Robert F. Sibert. It recognizes an American author who has written an outstanding informational book the previous year.

2007

Team Moon: How 40,000 People Landed Apollo 11 on the Moon by Catherine Thimmesh (Houghton)

HONOR BOOKS

Freedom Riders: John Lewis and Jim Zwerg on the Front Lines of the Civil Rights Movement by Ann Bausum (National Geographic)

Quest for the Tree Kangaroo: An Expedition to the Cloud Forest of New Guinea by Sy Montgomery (Houghton)

To Dance by Siena Cherson Siegal (Jackson/Atheneum)

2006

Secrets of a Civil War Submarine: Solving the Mysteries of the H. L. Hunley by Sally M. Walker (Carolrhoda)

HONOR BOOKS

Hitler Youth: Growing Up in Hitler's Shadow by Susan Campbell Bartoletti (Scholastic)

2005

The Voice that Challenged a Nation: Marian Anderson and the Struggle for Equal Rights by Russell Freedman (Clarion)

HONOR BOOKS

Sequoyah: The Cherokee Man Who Gave His People Writing by James Rumford (Houghton Mifflin)
The Tarantula Scientist by Sy Montgomery (Houghton Mifflin)
Walt Whitman: Words for America by Barbara Kerley (Scholastic)

2004

An American Plague: The True and Terrifying Story of the Yellow Fever Epidemic of 1793 by Jim Murphy (Clarion)

HONOR BOOKS

I Face the Wind by Vicki Cobb (HarperCollins)

2003

The Life and Death of Adolf Hitler by James Cross Giblin (Clarion)

HONOR BOOKS

Six Days in October: The Stock Market Crash of 1929 by Karen Blumenthal (Atheneum)
Hole in My Life by Jack Gantos (Farrar, Straus, & Giroux)
Action Jackson by Jan Greenberg and Sandra Jordan (Roaring Brook Press)
When Marian Sang by Pam Munoz Ryan (Scholastic)

2002

Black Potatoes: The Story of the Great Irish Famine, 1845–1850 by Susan Campbell Bartoletti (Houghton Mifflin)

HONOR BOOKS

Surviving Hitler: A Boy in the Nazi Death Camps by Andrea Warren (HarperCollins)
Vincent van Gogh by Jan Greenberg and Sandra Jordan (Delacorte Press)
Brooklyn Bridge by Lynn Curlee (Atheneum)

2001

Sir Walter Ralegh and the Quest for El Dorado by Marc Aronson (Clarion)

HONOR BOOKS

The Longitude Prize by Joan Dash (Farrar, Straus, & Giroux)
Blizzard! by Jim Murphy (Scholastic)
My Season with Penguins: An Antarctic Journal by Sophie Webb (Houghton Mifflin)

THE MICHAEL L. PRINTZ AWARD AND HONOR BOOKS

The Michael L. Printz Award was established in 2000 by the Young Adult Library Services Association of the American Library Association, to honor Michael Printz, an active young adult librarian from Kansas. It is presented annually to an author whose book written the previous year epitomizes literary excellence in young adult literature.

2007

American Born Chinese by Gene Luen Yang (First Second/Roaring Brook)

HONOR BOOK

The Astonishing Life of Octavian Nothing, Traitor to the Nation; Volume I by M. T. Anderson (Candlewick)
An Abundance of Katherines by John Green (Dutton)
Surrender by Sonya Hartnett (Candlewick)
The Book Thief by Markus Zusak (Knopf)

2006

Looking for Alaska by John Green (Dutton)

HONOR BOOK

Black Juice by Margo Lanagan (HarperCollins)
A Wreath for Emmet Till by Marilyn Nelson (Houghton Mifflin)
John Lennon: All I Want Is the Truth, A Photographic Biography by Elizabeth Patridge (Viking)
I Am the Messenger by Markus Zusak (Knopf)

2005

How I Live Now by Meg Rosoff (Random House)

HONOR BOOKS

Airborn by Kenneth Oppel (EOS)
Chanda's Secrets by Allan Straton (Annick)
Lizzie Bright and the Buckminster Boy by Gary Schmidt (Clarion)

2004

The First Part Last by Angela Johnson (Simon & Schuster)

HONOR BOOKS

A Northern Light by Jennifer Donnelly (Harcourt)
Keesha's House by Helen Frost (Farrar, Straus, & Giroux)
Fat Kid Rules the World by K. L. Going (Putnam)
The Earth, My Butt, and Other Big Round Things by Carolyn Mackler (Candlewick)

2003

Postcards from No Man's Land by Aidan Chambers (Dutton)

HONOR BOOKS

The House of the Scorpion by Nancy Farmer (Atheneum)
My Heartbeat by Garret Freymann-Weyr (Houghton Mifflin)
Hole in My Life by Jack Gantos (Farrar, Straus, & Giroux)

2002

A Step From Heaven by An Na (Speak)

HONOR BOOKS

The Ropemaker by Peter Dickinson (Delacorte)
Heart to Heart: New Poems Inspired by Twentieth-Century American Art by Jan Greenberg (ed) (HNA Books)

Freewill by Chris Lynch (HarperCollins)
True Believer by Virginia Euwer Wolf (Atheneum)

2001
Kit's Wilderness by David Almond (Delacorte)

HONOR BOOKS
Many Stones by Carolyn Coman (Front Street)
The Body of Christopher Creed by Carol Plum-Ucci (Harcourt)

Angus, Thongs, and Full Frontal Snogging by Louise Rennison (HarperCollins)
Stuck in Neutral by Terry Trueman (HarperCollins)

2000
Monster by Walter Dean Myers (HarperCollins)

HONOR BOOKS
Skellig by David Almond (Delacorte)
Speak by Laurie Halse Anderson (Farrar, Straus, & Giroux)
Hard Love by Ellen Wittlinger (Simon & Schuster)

MULTICULTURAL AWARDS IN CHILDREN'S LITERATURE

CORETTA SCOTT KING AWARDS AND HONOR BOOKS

The Coretta Scott King Award, established in 1970 by the Social Responsibilities Round Table, a division of the American Library Association, is named in honor of Coretta Scott King and dedicated to the life and work of her husband, Martin Luther King. It is presented annually to an African American author whose book published the previous year promotes the world peace and unity that exemplified the Kings' work. Since 1974 the Coretta Scott King Award has also been given annually to an African American illustrator whose work promotes world peace and unity.

2007
Author Award Winner
Copper Sun by Sharon Draper (Atheneum)

HONOR BOOKS
The Road to Paris by Nikki Grimes (G. P. Putnam's Sons)

ILLUSTRATOR HONOR BOOKS
Jazz illus. by Christopher Myers, written by Walter Dean Myers (Holiday House)
Poetry for Young People: Langston Hughes illus. by Benny Andrews, edited by David Roessel and Arnold Rampersad (Sterling Publishing)

Illustrator Award Winner
Moses: When Harriet Tubman Led Her People to Freedom illustrated by Kadir Nelson, written by Carole Boston Weatherford (Jump at the Sun/Hyperion)

2006
Author Award Winner
Day of Tears: A Novel in Dialogue by Julius Lester (Jump at the Sun/Hyperion)

HONOR BOOKS
Maritcha: A Nineteenth Century American Girl by Tonya Bolden (Harry Abrams Publishers)
Dark Sons by Nikki Grimes (Jump at the Sun/Hyperion)
A Wreath for Emmet Till by Marilyn Nelson, illus. by Philippe Lardy (Henry Holt)

Illustrator Award Winner
Rosa by Nikki Giovanni, illus. by Bryan Collier (Henry Holt)

ILLUSTRATOR HONOR BOOK
Brothers in Hope: The Story of the Lost Boys of Sudan by R. Gregory Christie, illus. by R. Gregory Christie (Lee & Low)

2005
Author Award Winner
Remember: The Journey to School Integration by Toni Morrison (Houghton Mifflin)

HONOR BOOKS
The Legend of Buddy Bush by Shelia P. Moses (Margaret K. McElderry)
Who Am I Without Him? Short Stories about Girls and the Boys in Their Lives by Sharon Flake (Jump at the Sun/Hyperion Books for Children)
Fortune's Bones: The Manumission Requiem by Marilyn Nelson (Front Street)

ILLUSTRATOR AWARD BOOK
Ellington Was Not a Street illus. by Kadir Nelson, text by Ntozake Shange (Simon & Schuster Books for Young Readers)

ILLUSTRATOR HONOR BOOKS
God Bless the Child illus. by Jerry Pinkney, text by Billie Holiday and Arthur Herzog Jr. (Amistad)
The People Could Fly: The Picture Book illus. by Leo and Diane Dillon, text by Virginia Hamilton (Alfred Knopf)

2004
Author Award Winner
The First Part Last by Angela Johnson (Simon & Schuster Books for Young Readers)

HONOR BOOKS
Days of Jubilee: The End of Slavery in the United States by Patricia C. and Frederick L. McKissack (Scholastic)
Locomotion by Jacqueline Woodson (Grosset & Dunlap)
The Battle of Jericho by Sharon Draper (Atheneum Books for Young Readers)

ILLUSTRATOR AWARD BOOK
Beautiful Blackbird by Ashley Bryan (Atheneum Books for Young Readers)

ILLUSTRATOR HONOR BOOKS
Almost to Freedom illus. by Colin Bootman, text by Vaunda Micheaux Nelson (Carolrhoda)

Thunder Rose illustrated by Kadir Nelson, text by Jerdine Nolen (Silver Whistle)

2003
Author Award Winner
Bronx Masquerade by Nikki Grimes (Dial Books for Young Readers)

AUTHOR HONOR BOOKS
The Red Rose Box by Brenda Woods (G. P. Putnam's Sons)
Talkin' About Bessie: The Story of Aviator Elizabeth Coleman illus. by Nikki Grimes (Orchard Books/Scholastic)

Illustrator Award Winner
Talkin' About Bessie: The Story of Aviator Elizabeth Coleman illus. by E. B. Lewis, text by Nikki Grimes (Orchard Books/Scholastic)

ILLUSTRATED HONOR BOOKS
Rap a Tap Tap: Here's Bojangles—Think of That illus. and written by Leo and Diane Dillon (Blue Sky Press/Scholastic)
Visiting Langston illus. by Bryan Collier, text by Willie Perdomo (Henry Holt)

2002
Author Award Winner
The Land by Mildred Taylor (Phyllis Fogelman Books/Penguin Putnam)

AUTHOR HONOR BOOKS
Money-Hungry by Sharon Flake (Jump at the Sun/Hyperion)
Carver: A Life in Poems by Marilyn Nelson (Front Street)

Illustrator Award Winner
Goin' Someplace Special illus. by Jerry Pinkney, text by Patricia McKissack (Anne Schwartz Book/Atheneum)

ILLUSTRATOR HONOR BOOK
Martin's Big Words illus. by Bryan Collier, text by Doreen Rappaport (Jump at the Sun/Hyperion)

2001
Author Award Winner
Miracle's Boys by Jacqueline Woodson (G. P. Putnam's Sons)

AUTHOR HONOR BOOK
Let It Shine! Stories of Black Women Freedom Fighters by Andrea Davis Pinkney, illus. by Stephen Alcorn (Gulliver Books, Harcourt)

Illustrator Award Winner
Uptown by Bryan Collier (Henry Holt)

ILLUSTRATOR HONOR BOOKS
Freedom River illus. by Bryan Collier, text by Doreen Rappaport (Jump at the Sun Hyperion)
Only Passing Through: The Story of Sojourner Truth illus. by R. Gregory Christie, text by Anne Rockwell (Random House)

Virgie Goes to School with Us Boys illus. by E, B. Lewis, text by Elizabeth Fitzgerald Howard (Simon & Schuster)

2000
Author Award Winner
Bud, Not Buddy by Christopher Paul Curtis (Delacorte)

AUTHOR HONOR BOOKS
Francie by Karen English (Farrar, Straus, & Giroux)
Black Hands, White Sails: The Story of African American Whalers by Patricia and Frederick McKissack (Scholastic)
Monster by Walter Dean Myers (HarperCollins)

Illustrator Award Winner
In the Time of the Drums illus. by Brian Pinkney, text by Kim Siegelson (Jump at the Sun/Hyperion)

ILLUSTRATOR HONOR BOOKS
My Rows and Piles of Coins illus. by E. B. Lewis, text by Tololwa Mollel (Clarion)
Black Cat by Christopher Myers (Scholastic)

1999
Author Award Winner
Heaven by Angela Johnson (Simon & Schuster)

AUTHOR HONOR BOOKS
Jazmin's Notebook by Nikki Grimes (Dial Books)
Breaking Ground, Breaking Silence: The Story of New York's African Burial Ground by Joyce Hansen and Gary McGowan (Henry Holt)
The Other Side: Shorter Poems by Angela Johnson (Orchard)

Illustrator Award Winner
I See the Rhythm illus. by Michele Wood, text by Toyomi Igus (Children's Book Press)

ILLUSTRATOR HONOR BOOKS
I Have Heard of a Land illus. by Floyd Cooper, text by Joyce Carol Thomas (Joanna Cotler Books/HarperCollins)
The Bat Boy and His Violin illus. by E. B. Lewis, text by Gavin Curtis (Simon & Schuster)
Duke Ellington: The Piano Prince and His Orchestra illus. by Brian Pinkney, text by Andrea Davis Pinkney (Hyperion Books for Children)

1998
Author Award Winner
Forged by Fire by Sharon Draper (Atheneum)

AUTHOR HONOR BOOKS
Bayard Rustin: Behind the Scenes of the Civil Rights Movement by James Haskins (Hyperion)
I Thought My Soul Would Rise and Fly: The Diary of Patsy, a Freed Girl by Joyce Hansen (Scholastic)

Illustrator Award Winner
In Daddy's Arms I Am Tall: African Americans Celebrating Fathers illus. by Javaka Steptoe, text by Alan Schroeder (Lee & Low)

ILLUSTRATOR HONOR BOOKS

Ashley Bryan's ABC of African American Poetry by Ashley Bryan (Jean Karl/Atheneum)

Harlem illus. by Christopher Myers, text by Walter Dean Myers (Scholastic)

The Hunterman and the Crocodile by Baba Wague Diakite (Scholastic)

1997

Author Award Winner

Slam by Walter Dean Myers (Scholastic)

AUTHOR HONOR BOOK

Rebels Against Slavery: American Slave Revolts by Patricia and Frederick McKissack (Scholastic)

Illustrator Award Winner

Minty: A Story of Young Harriet Tubman illus. by Jerry Pinkney, text by Alan Schroeder (Dial Books for Young Readers)

ILLUSTRATOR HONOR BOOKS

The Palm of My Heart: Poetry by African American Children illus. by Gregorie Christie, edited by Davida Adedjouma (Lee & Low)

Running the Road to ABC illus. by Reynolds Ruffins, text by Denize Lauture (Simon & Schuster)

Neeny Coming, Neeny Going illus. by Synthia Saint James, text by Karen English (Bridgewater Books)

1996

Author Award Winner

Her Stories by Virginia Hamilton (Scholastic/Blue Sky Press)

AUTHOR HONOR BOOKS

The Watsons Go to Birmingham—1963 by Christopher Paul Curtis (Delacorte)

Like Sisters on the Homefront by Rita Williams-Garcis (Delacorte)

From the Notebooks of Melanin Sun by Jacqueline Woodson (Scholastic/Blue Sky Press)

Illustrator Award Winner

The Middle Passage: White Ships Black Cargo illus. by Tom Feelings (Dial Books for Young Readers)

ILLUSTRATOR HONOR BOOKS

Her Stories illus. by Leo and Diane Dillon, text by Virginia Hamilton (Scholastic/BlueSky Press)

The Faithful Friend illus. by Brian Pinkney, text by Robert San Souci (Simon & Schuster)

1995

Author Award Winner

Christmas in the Big House, Christmas in the Quarters by Patricia and Frederick McKissack (Scholastic)

AUTHOR HONOR BOOKS

The Captive by Joyce Hansen (Scholastic)

I Hadn't Meant to Tell You This by Jacqueline Woodson (Delacorte)

Black Diamond: Story of the Negro Baseball League by Patricia and Frederick McKissack (Scholastic)

Illustrator Award Winner

The Creation illus. by James Ransome, text by James Weldon Johnson (Holiday House)

ILLUSTRATOR HONOR BOOKS

The Singing Man illus. by Terea Schaffer, text by Angela Shelf Medearis (Holiday House)

Meet Danitra Brown illus. by Floyd Cooper, text by Nikki Grimes (Lothrop, Lee & Shepard)

1994

Author Award Winner

Toning the Sweep by Angela Johnson (Orchard)

AUTHOR HONOR BOOKS

Brown Honey in Broom Wheat Tea by Joyce Carol Thomas (HarperCollins)

Malcolm X: byAny Means Necessary by Walter Dean Myers (Scholastic)

Illustrator Award Winner

Soul Looks Back in Wonder illus. by Tom Feelings, text edited by Phyllis Fogelman (Dial Books for Young Readers)

ILLUSTRATOR HONOR BOOKS

Brown Honey in Broom Wheat Tea illus. by Floyd Cooper, text by Joyce Carol Thomas (HarperCollins)

Uncle Jed's Barbershop illus. by James Ransome, text by Margaret King Mitchell (Simon & Schuster)

1993

Author Award Winner

Dark Thirty: Southern Tales of the Supernatural by Patricia McKissack (Knopf)

AUTHOR HONOR BOOKS

Mississippi Challenge by Mildred Pitts Walter (Bradbury)

Sojourner Truth: Ain't I a Woman? by Patricia and Frederick McKissack (Scholastic)

Somewhere in the Darkness by Walter Dean Myers (Scholastic)

Illustrator Award Winner

The Origin of Life on Earth: An African Creation Myth illus. by Kathleen Atkins Wilson, retold by David Anderson/SANKOFA (Sights)

ILLUSTRATOR HONOR BOOKS

Little Eight John illus. by Wil Clay, text by Jan Wahl (Lodestar)

Sukey and the Mermaid illus. by Brian Pinkney, text by Robert San Souci (Four Winds)

Working Cotton illus. by Carole Byard, text by Sherley Williams (Harcourt)

1992

Author Award Winner

Now Is Your Time: The African American Struggle for Freedom by Walter Dean Myers (HarperCollins)

AUTHOR HONOR BOOK

Night on Neighborhood Street by Eloise Greenfield (Dial)

Illustrator Award Winner

Tar Beach by Faith Ringgold (Crown)

ILLUSTRATOR HONOR BOOKS

All Night, All Day/A Child's First Book of African American Spirituals illus. and selected by Ashley Bryan (Atheneum)

Night on Neighborhood Street illus. by Jan Spivey Gilchrist, text by Eloise Greenfield (Dial)

1991

Author Award Winner

The Road to Memphis by Mildred Tyler (Dial)

AUTHOR HONOR BOOKS

Black Dance in America by James Haskins (Crowell)

When I Am Old with You by Angela Johnson (Orchard)

Illustrator Award Winner

Aida illus. by Leo and Diane Dillon, text by Leontyne Price (Harcourt)

1990

Author Award Winner

A Long Hard Journey: The Story of the Pullman Porter by Patricia and Frederick McKissack (Walker)

AUTHOR HONOR BOOKS

Nathaniel Talking by Eloise Greenfield (Black Butterfly)

The Bells of Christmas by Virginia Hamilton (Harcourt)

Martin Luther King, Jr. and the Freedom Movement by Lillie Patterson (Facts on File)

Illustrator Award Winner

Nathaniel Talking illus. by Jan Spivey Gilchrist, text by Eloise Greenfield (Black Butterfly)

ILLUSTRATOR HONOR BOOK

The Talking Eggs illus. by Jerry Pinkney, text by Robert San Souci (Dial)

1989

Author Award Winner

Fallen Angels by Walter Dean Myers (Scholastic

AUTHOR HONOR BOOKS

A Thief in the Village and Other Stories by James Berry (Orchard)

Anthony Burns: The Defeat and Triumph of a Fugitive Slave by Virginia Hamilton (Knopf)

Illustrator Award Winner

Mirandy and Brother Wind illus. by Jerry Pinkney (Knopf)

ILLUSTRATOR HONOR BOOKS

Under the Sunday Tree illus. by Amos Ferguson (Harper)

Storm in the Night illus. by Pat Cummings (Harper)

1988

Author Award Winner

The Friendship by Mildred Taylor (Dial)

AUTHOR HONOR BOOKS

An Enchanted Hair Tale by Alexis De Veaux (Harper)

The Tales of Uncle Remus: The Adventures of Brer Rabbit by Julius Lester (Dial)

Illustrator Award Winner

Mufaro's Beautiful Daughters: An African Tale illus. by John Steptoe (Lothrop)

ILLUSTRATOR HONOR BOOKS

What a Morning! The Christmas Story in Black Spirituals illus. by Ashley Bryan (Macmillan)

The Invisible Hunters: A Legend from the Miskito Indians of Nicaragua illus. by Joe Sam (Children's Press)

1987

Author Award Winner

Justin and the Best Biscuits in the World by Mildred Pitts Walker (Lothrop)

AUTHOR HONOR BOOKS

Lion and the Ostrich Chicks and Other African Folk Tales by Ashley Bryan (Atheneum)

Which Way Freedom by Joyce Hansen (Walker)

Illustrator Award Winner

Half a Moon and One Whole Star illus. by Jerry Pinkney (Macmillan)

ILLUSTRATOR HONOR BOOKS

Lion and the Ostrich Chicks and Other African Folk Tales illus. by Ashley Bryan (Atheneum)

C.L.O.U.D.S. illus. by Pat Cummings (Lothrop)

1986

Author Award Winner

The People Could Fly: American Black Folktales by Virginia Hamilton (Knopf)

AUTHOR HONOR BOOKS

Junius Over Far by Virginia Hamilton (Harper)

Trouble's Child by Mildred Pitts Walker (Lothrop)

Illustrator Award Winner

The Patchwork Quilt illus. by Jerry Pinkney (Dial)

ILLUSTRATOR HONOR BOOK

The People Could Fly: American Black Folktales illus. by Leo and Diane Dillon (Knopf)

1985

Author Award Winner

Motown and Didi by Walter Dean Myers (Viking)

AUTHOR HONOR BOOKS

Circle of Gold by Candy Dawson Boyd (Scholastic)

A Little Love by Virginia Hamilton (Philomel)

Illustrator Award Winner

None

1984

Author Award Winner

Everett Anderson's Good-bye by Lucile Clifton (Holt)

Special Citation

The Words of Martin Luther King Jr., compiled by Coretta Scott King (Newmarket Press)

AUTHOR HONOR BOOKS

The Magical Adventures of Pretty Pearl by Virginia Hamilton (Harper)

Lena Horne by James Haskins (Coward-McCann)

Bright Shadow by Joyce Carol Thomas (Avon)

Because We Are by Mildred Pitts Walker (Lothrop)

Illustrator Award Winner

My Mama Needs Me illus. by Pat Cummings (Lothrop)

1983

Author Award Winner

Sweet Whispers, Brother Rush by Virginia Hamilton (Philomel)

AUTHOR HONOR BOOK

This Strange New Feeling by Julius Lester (Dial)

Illustrator Award Winner

Black Child by Peter Mugabane (Knopf)

ILLUSTRATOR HONOR BOOKS

All the Colors of the Race illus. by John Steptoe (Lothrop)

I'm Going To Sing: Black American Spirituals illus. by Ashley Bryan (Atheneum)

Just Us Women illus. by Pat Cummings (Harper)

1982

Author Award Winner

Let the Circle Be Unbroken by Mildred Taylor (Dial)

AUTHOR HONOR BOOKS

Rainbow Jordan by Alice Childress (Coward McCann)

Lou in the Limelight by Kristen Hunter (Scribner)

Mary: An Autobiography by Mary E. Mebane (Viking)

Illustrator Award Winner

Mother Crocodile: An Uncle Amadou Tale from Senegal illus. by John Steptoe, text by Rosa Guy (Delacorte)

ILLUSTRATOR HONOR BOOK

Daydreamers illus. by Tom Feelings, text by Eloise Greenfield (Dial)

1981

Author Award Winner

This Life by Sidney Poitier (Knopf)

AUTHOR HONOR BOOK

Don't Explain: A Song of Billie Holiday by Alexis De Veaux (Harper)

Illustrator Award Winner

Beat the Story Drum, Pum-Pum by Ashley Bryan (Atheneum)

ILLUSTRATOR HONOR BOOKS

Grandmama's Joy illus. by Carole Byard, text by Eloise Greenfield (Collins)

Count on Your Fingers African Style illus. by Jerry Pinkney, text by Claudia Zaslavsky (Crowell)

1980

Author Award Winner

The Young Landlords by Walter Dean Myers (Viking)

AUTHOR HONOR BOOKS

Movin' Up by Betty Gordy (Harper)

Childtimes: A Three-Generation Memoir by Eloise Greenfield and Lessie Jones Little (Harper)

Andrew Young: Young Man with a Mission by James Haskins (Lothrop)

James Van Der Zee: The Picture Takin' Man by James Haskins (Dodd)

Let the Lion Eat Straw by Ellease Southerland (Scribner)

Illustrator Award Winner

Cornrows illus. by Carole Byard, text by Camille Yarborough (Coward McCann)

1979

Author Award Winner

Escape to Freedom by Ossie Davis (Viking)

AUTHOR HONOR BOOKS

Benjamin Banneker by Lillie Patterson (Abington)

I Have a Sister, My Sister Is Deaf by Jeanne Peterson (Harper)

Justice and Her Brothers by Virginia Hamilton (Greenwillow)

Skates of Uncle Richard by Carol Fenner (Random)

Illustrator Award Winner

Something On My Mind illus. by Tom Feelings, text by Nikki Grimes (Dial)

1978

Author Award Winner

Africa Dream by Eloise Greenfield (Crowell)

AUTHOR HONOR BOOKS

The Days When the Animals Talked: Black Folk Tales and How They Came to Be by William J. Faulkner (Follett)

Marvin and Tige by Frankcina Glass (St. Martin's)

Mary McCleod Bethune by Eloise Greenfield (Crowell)

Barbara Jordan by James Haskins (Dial)

Coretta Scott King by Lillie Patterson (Garrard)

Portia: The Life of Portia Washington Pittman, the Daughter of Booker T. Washington by Ruth Ann Stewart (Doubleday)

Illustrator Award Winner

Africa Dream illus. by Carole Bayard, text by Eloise Greenfield (Crowell)

1977

Author Award Winner

The Story of Stevie Wonder by James Haskins (Lothrop)

Illustrator Award Winner

None

1976

Author Award Winner

Duey's Tale by Pearl Bailey (Harcourt)

Illustrator Award Winner
None

1975

Author Award Winner
The Legend of Africana by Dorothy Robinson (Johnson Publishing)
Illustrator Award Winner
None

1974

Author Award Winner
Ray Charles by Sharon Bell Mathis (Crowell)
Illustrator Award Winner
Ray Charles illus. by George Ford, text by Sharon Bell Mathis (Crowell)
(Prior to 1974 the CSK Award was given to authors only)

1973

I Never Had It Made: The Autobiography of Jackie Robinson, as told to Alfred Duckett (Putnam)

1972

17 Black Artists by Elton Fax (Dodd)

1971

Black Troubador: Langston Hughes by Charlemae Rollins (Rand McNally)

1970

Martin Luther King, Jr.: Man of Peace by Lillie Patterson (Garrard)

THE PURA BELPRÉ AWARD AND HONOR BOOKS

The Pura Belpré Award was established in 1996 by the National Association to Promote Library Services to the Spanish Speaking (REFORMA), a division of the American Library Association, and named in honor of Pura Belpré, the first Latina librarian at the New York Public Library. It is presented biannually to an outstanding Latino or Latina author and illustrator whose work demonstrates for children the best of the Latino culture.

2006

Author
The Tequila Worm by Viola Canales (Random House)
HONOR BOOKS
Cesar: Si, Se Puede! Yes, We Can! by Carmen T. Bernier-Grand (Marshall Cavendish).
Dona Flor: A Tall Tale about a Giant Woman with a Great Big Heart by Pat Mora (Knopf)
Becoming Naomi Leon by Pam Nunoz Ryan (Scholastic)
Illustrator
Dona Flor: A Tall Tale about a Giant Woman with a Great Big Heart illus. by Raul Colon, written by Pat Mora (Knopf)

HONOR BOOKS
Arrorro, Mi Nino: Latino Lullabies and Gentle Games selected and illus. by Lulu Delacre (Lee & Low)
My Name Is Celia/Me Llamo Celia: The Life of Celia Cruz La Vida de Celia Cruz illus. by Rafael Lopez, written by Monica Brown (Rising Moon)

2004

Author
Before We Were Free by Julia Alvarez (Knopf)
HONOR BOOKS
Cuba 15 by Nancy Osa (Delacorte)
My Diary from Here to There /Mi Diario de Aqui Hasta Allia by Amada Irma Perez (Children's Book Press)
Illustrator
Just a Minute: a Trickster Tale and Counting Book illus. by Yuyi Morales (Chronicle Books).
HONOR BOOKS
First Day in Grapes illus. by Robert Casilla, written by L. King Perez (Lee & Low Books, 2002)
The Pot that Juan Built illus. by David Diaz, written by Nancy Andrews-Goebel (Lee & Low)
Harvesting Hope: The Story of Cesar Chavez illus. by Yuyi Morales, written by Kathleen Krull (Harcourt)

2002

Author
Esperanza Rising by Pam Munoz Ryan (Scholastic)
HONOR BOOKS
Breaking Through by Francisco Jimenez (Houghton Mifflin)
Iguanas in the Snow by Francisco X. Alarcon (Children's Book Press)
Illustrator
Chato and the Party Animals illus. by Susan Guevara, written by Gary Soto (G. P. Putnam's Sons)
HONOR BOOKS
Juan Bobo Goes to Work illus. by Joe Cepeda, retold by Marisa Montes (HarperCollins)

2000

Author
Under the Royal Palms: A Childhood in Cuba by Alma Flor Ada (Atheneum)
HONOR BOOKS
From the Bellybutton of the Moon and Other Summer Poems/Del Ombligo de la Luna y Otro Poemas de Verana by Francisco X. Alarcon (Children's Books Press)
Laughing Out Loud, I Fly: Poems in English and Spanish by Juan Felipe Herrera (HarperCollins,)
Illustrator
Magic Windows by Carmen Lomas Garza (Children's Book Press)
HONOR BOOKS
Barrio: Jose's Neighborhood by George Ancona (Harcourt)

The Secret Stars illus. by Felipe Davalos, written by Joseph Slate (Marshall Cavendish)
Mama & Papa Have a Store by Amelia Lau Carling (Dial Books)

1998
Author
Parrot in the Oven Mi Vida by Victor Martinez (Harper-Collins)

HONOR BOOKS

Laughing Tomatoes and Other Spring Poems/Jitomates Risuelnos y otros Poemas de Primavera by Francisco Alarcon (Children's Book Press)
Spirit of the High Mesa by Floyd Martinez (Arte Publico Press)

Illustrator
Snapshots from the Wedding illus. by Susan Guevara, written by Gary Soto (Putnam)

HONOR BOOKS

In My Family/En Mi Familia by Carmen Lomas Garza (Children's Book Press)
The Golden Flower: a Taino Myth from Puerto Rico illus. by Enrique O. Sanchez, written by Nina Jaffe (Simon & Schuster)
Gathering the Sun: An Alphabet in Spanish and English illus. by Simon Silva, written by Alma Flor Ada (Lothrop)

1996
Author
An Island Like You: Stories of the Barrio by Judith Ortiz Cofer (Orchard Books, 1995)

HONOR BOOKS

The Bossy Gallito/En Gallo de Bodas: A Traditional Cuban Folktale by Lucia Gonzalez (Scholastic)
Baseball in April and Other Stories by Gary Soto (Harcourt)

Illustrator
Chato's Kitchen illus. by Susan Guevara, written by Gary Soto (Putnam)

HONOR BOOKS

Pablo Remembers: The Fiesta of the Day of the Dead by George Ancona (Lothrop)
The Bossy Gallito/El Gallo de Bodas: A Traditional Cuban Folktale illus. by Lulu Delacre, written by Lucia Gonzalez (Scholastic)
Family Pictures/Cuadros de Familia illus. by Carmen Lomas Garza (Children's Book Press)

AMERICAS AWARD

Americas Award was established in 1993 by the Consortium of Latin American Studies Programs (CLASP) to recognize books, in English or Spanish that were written in the United States the previous year for children and young adults. The books are selected for their "distinctive literary quality, cul-tural contextualization, exceptional integration of text, il-lustration and design, and potential for classroom use" (Yokota, 2001, p. 161).

2005
Cinnamon Girl: Letters Found Inside a Cereal Box by Juan Felipe Herrera (HarperCollins)

2004
My Name Is Celia/Me llamo Celia by Monica Brown (Luna Rising)
Sammy & Juliana in Hollywood by Benjamin Alire Saenz (Cinco Puntos)

2003
Just a Minute by Yuyi Morales (Chronicle)
The Meaning of Consuelo by Judith Ortiz Cofer (Farrar, Straus, & Giroux)

2002
Before we Were Free by Julia Alvarez (Knopf)

2001
A Movie in My Pillow/Una pelicula en mi almohada by Jorge Argueta (Children's Book Press)

2000
The Composition by Antonio Skarmeta (Groundwood)
The Color of My Words by Lynn Joseph (HarperCollins)

1999
Crashboomlove by Juan Felipe Herrera (University of New Mexico Press)

1998
Barrio: Jose's Neighborhood by George Ancona (Harcourt Brace)
Mama and Papa Have a Store by Amelia Lau Carling (Dial)

1997
The Circuit by Francisco Jimenez (University of New Mexico Press)
The Face at the Window by Regina Hanson illus. by Linda Saport (Clarion)

1996
In My Family/En Mi Familia by Carmen Lomas Garza (Children's Book Press)
Parrot in the Oven by Victor Martinez (HarperCollins)

1995
Tonight, by Sea by Frances Temple (Orchard)

1994
The Mermaid's Twin Sister by Lynn Joseph (Clarion)

1993
Vejigante Masquerader by Lulu Delacre (Scholastic)

INTERNATIONAL AWARDS

MILDRED L. BATCHELDER AWARD AND HONOR BOOKS

The Mildred L. Batchelder Award was established by the Association for Library Service for Children, a division of the American Library Association, to honor former executive director Mildred L. Batchelder. Originally presented for a book published during the previous two years, it is now presented annually to an American publisher for a book written for children and published the previous year in a foreign language in a foreign country, and then published in the United States.

2007
The Pull of the Ocean by Jean-Claude Mourievat, trans. by Y, Maudet (Delacorte)

HONOR BOOK
The Killer's Tears by Anne-Laure Bondoux (Delacorte)
The Last Dragon by Silvana De Mari, trans. by Shaun Whiteside (Hyperion)

2006
An Innocent Soldier by Josef Holub, trans. by Michael Hoffmann (Arthur Levine Books)

HONOR BOOK
Nicholas by Rene Goscinny, trans. by Anthea Bell (Phaidon Press)
When I Was a Soldier by Valerie Zenatti, trans. by Adriana Hunter (Bloomsbury)

2005
The Shadows of Ghadames by Joelle Stolz, trans. by Catherine Temerson (Delacorte)

HONOR BOOK
The Crow-Girl: The Children of Crow Cove by Bodil Bredsdorff, trans. by Faith Ingwersen (Farrar, Straus, & Giroux)
Daniel Half Human and the Good Nazi by David Chotjewitz, trans. by Doris Orgel (Atheneum)

2004
Run, Boy, Run by Uri Orlev, trans. by Hillel Halkin (Houghton Mifflin)

HONOR BOOK
The Man Who Went to the Far Side of the Moon: The Story of Apollo 11 Astronaut Michael Collins by Bea Uusma Schyffert, trans. by Emi Guner (Chronicle Books)

2003
The Thief Lord by Cornelia Funke, trans. by Oliver Latsch (Scholastic)

HONOR BOOK
Henrietta and the Golden Eggs by Hanna Johansen, illus. by Kathi Bhend, trans. by John Barrett (David Godine)

2002
How I Became an American by Karin Gundisch, trans. by James Skofield (Cricket/Carus Publishing)

HONOR BOOK
A Book of Coupons by Susie Morgenstern, trans. by Gil Rosner (Viking)

2001
Samir and Yonatan by Daniella Carmi, trans. by Yael Lotan (Scholastic)

HONOR BOOK
Ultimate Game by Christian Lehmann, trans. by William Rodarmor (David Godine)

2000
The Baboon King by Anton Quintana, trans. by John Nieuwenhuzen (Walker & Co.)

HONOR BOOKS
Collector of Moments by Quint Buchholz, trans. by Peter Neumeyer (Farrar, Straus, & Giroux)
Vendela in Venice by Chriistina Bjork, illus. by Inga Karin Eriksson, trans. by Patricia Crampton
Asphalt Angels by Ineke Holtwijk, trans. by Wanda Boeke (Front Street)

1999
Thanks to My Mother by Schoschana Rabinovici, trans. by James Skofield (Dial)

HONOR BOOK
Secret Letters from 0 to 10 by Susie Morgenstern, trans. by Gill Rosner (Viking)

1998
The Robber and Me by Josef Holub, trans. by Elizabeth Crawford (Henry Holt)

HONOR BOOKS
Hostage to War: A True Story by Tatjana Wassiljewa, trans. by Anna Trenter (Scholastic)
Nero Corleone: A Cat's Story by Elke Heidenrich, trans. by Doris Orgel (Viking)

1997
The Friends by Kazumi Yumoto, trans. by Cathy Hirano (Farrar, Straus, & Giroux)

1996
The Lady with the Hat by Uri Orlev, trans. by Hillel Halkin (Houghton Mifflin)

HONOR BOOK
Damned Strong Love: The True Story of Willi G. and Stephan K. by Lutz Van Dijk, trans. by Elizabeth Crawford

Star of Fear, Star of Hope by Jo Hoestlandt, trans. by Matk Polizzotti (Walker & Co.)

1995
The Boys from St. Petri by Bjarne Reuter, trans. by Anthea Bell (Dutton)

HONOR BOOK
Sister Shako and Kolo the Goat: Memories of My Childhood in Turkey by Vedat Dalokay, trans. by Guner Ener (Lothrop, Lee & Shepard)

1994
The Apprentice by Pilar Molina Llorente, trans. by Robin Longshaw (Farrar, Straus, & Giroux)

HONOR BOOK
The Princess in the Kitchen Garden by Annemie & Margriet Heymans, trans. by Johanna Prins (Farrar, Straus, & Giroux)
Anne Frank Beyond the Diary: A Photographic Remembrance by Rudd van der Rol & Rian Verhoeven, trans. by Tony Langham and Plym Peters (Viking)

1993
None

1992
The Man from the Other Side by Uri Orlev, trans. by Hillel Halkin (Houghton Mifflin)

1991
A Hand Full of Stars by Rafik Schami, trans. by Rika Lesser (Dutton)

1990
Buster's World by Bjarne Reuter, trans. by Anthea Bell (Dutton)

1989
Crutches by Peter Hartling, trans. by Elizabeth Crawford (Lothrop, Lee & Shepard)

1988
If You Didn't Have Me by Ulf Nilsson, trans. by Lone Thygesen Blecher and George Blecher (McElderry Books)

1987
No Hero for the Kaiser by Rudolph Frank, trans. by Patricia Crampton (Lothrop, Lee & Shepard)

1986
Rose Blanche by Christophe Gallaz & Robert Innocenti, trans. by Martha Coventry and Richard Craglia (Creative Education)

1985
The Island on Bird Street by Uri Orlev, trans. by Hillel Halkin (Houghton Mifflin)

1984
Ronia, The Robber's Daughter by Astrid Lindgren, trans. by Patricia Crampton (Viking)

1983
Hiroshima No Pika by Toshi Maruki, trans. through Kurita-Bando Literary Agency (Lothrop, Lee & Shepard)

1982
The Battle Horse by Harry Kullman, trans. by George Blecher and Lone Thygesen Blecher (Bradbury Press)

1981
The Winter When Time Was Frozen by Els Pelgrom, trans. Maryka & Raphael Rudnik (William Morrow)

1980
The Sound of the Dragon's Feet by Aliki Zei, trans. by Edward Fenton (Dutton)

1979 (Two Awards)
Rabbit Island by Jorg Steiner, trans. by Ann Conrad Lammers (Harcourt Brace Jovanovich)
Konrad by Christine Nostlinger, trans. by Anthea Bell (Franklin Watts)

1978
None

1977
The Leopard by Cecil Bodker. trans. by Gunnar Poulson (Atheneum)

1976
The Cat and Mouse Who Shared a House by Ruth Hurlimann, trans. by Anthea Bell (Henry Z. Walck)

1975
An Old Tale Carved Out of Stone by A. Linevskii, trans. by Maria Polushkin (Crown)

1974
Petros' War by Aliki Zei, trans. by Edward Fenton (E. P. Dutton)

1973
Pulga by S. R. Van Iterson, trans. by Alexander & Alison Gode (Wm. Morrow)

1972
Friedrich by Hans Peter Richter, trans. by Edith Kroll (Holt)

1971
In the Land of Ur, the Discovery of Ancient Mesopotamia by Hans Baumann, trans. by Stella Humphries (Pantheon)

1970
Wildcat Under Glass by Aliki Zei, trans. by Edward Fenton (Holt)

1969

Don't Take Teddy by Babbis Friis-Baastad, trans. by Lise Somme McKinnon (Scribner)

1968

The Little Man by Erich Kastner, trans. by James Kirkup (Knopf)

HANS CHRISTIAN ANDERSEN AWARD

The Hans Christian Andersen Award was first given to an author in 1956 and to an illustrator in 1966. The International Board on Books for Young People selects the award winners biennially based on the contribution that their complete works have made to children's literature.

Year	Author	Country
2006	Margaret Mahy	New Zealand
2004	Martin Waddell	Ireland
2002	Aidan Chambers	United Kingdom
2000	Ana Maria Machado	Brazil
1998	Katherine Paterson	USA
1996	Uri Orlev	Israel
1994	Michio Mado	Japan
1992	Virginia Hamilton	USA
1990	Tormod Haugen	Norway
1988	Annie M.G. Schmidt	Netherlands
1986	Patricia Wrightson	Australia
1984	Christine Nostlinger	Austria
1982	Lygia Bojunga Nunes	Brazil
1980	Bohumil Riha	Czechoslovakia
1978	Paula Fox	USA
1976	Cecil Bodker	Denmark
1974	Marcia Gripe	Sweden

Year	Author	Country
1972	Scott O'Dell	USA
1970	Gianni Rodari	Italy
1968	James Kraus	Germany
	Jose Maria Sanchez-Silva	Spain
1966	Tove Jansson	Finland
1964	Rene Guillot	France
1962	Meindert DeJong	USA
1960	Erich Kastner	Germany
1958	Astrid Lindgren	Sweden
1956	Eleanor Farjeon	United Kingdom

Year	Illustrator	Country
2006	Wolf Erlbruch	Germany
2004	Max Velthuijs	Netherlands
2002	Quentin Blake	United Kingdom
2000	Anthony Browne	United Kingdom
1998	Tomi Ungerer	France
1996	Klaus Ensikat	Germany
1994	Jorg Muller	Switzerland
1992	Kveta Pacovska	Czechoslovakia
1990	Lisbeth Zwerger	Austria
1988	Dusan Kallay	Czechoslovakia
1986	Robert Ingpen	Australia
1984	Mitsumasa Anno	Japan
1982	Zbigniew Rychlicki	Poland
1980	Suekichi Akaba	Japan
1978	Otto S. Svend	Denmark
1976	Tatjana Mawrina	USSR
1974	Farshid Mesghali	Iran
1972	Ib Spang Olsen	Denmark
1970	Maurice Sendak	USA
1968	Jiri Trnka	Czechoslovakia
1966	Alois Carigiet	Switzerland

A

Aesthetic reading   Reading for emotional content.

Alphabet book   Contains letters of the alphabet and pictures corresponding to each letter.

Americas Award   Up to two awards given to U. S. publications that recognize the multicultural heritages within the hemispheres.

Anthropomorphism   Attributing human characteristics to animals.

Audiobook   A book that is transcribed into an audiotape.

Autonomy versus shame and doubt   Erikson's second stage of psychosocial development (13 years) during which children begin to demonstrate a sense of independence.

B

Banned books   Books that are proven unacceptable for specific reasons and may sometimes be removed from library shelves.

Beast tale   A traditional folktale in which animals are the main characters.

Bibliography   Procedure for documenting works cited.

Big6   An information problem-solving strategy.

Biography and autobiography   A true account of a person's life written by or about that person.

Biopsychosocial interactions   Belief that development proceeds by the interactions among biological, psychological, and social forces.

Board book   A cardboard book that is comfortable for a small child to handle.

Bodily-kinesthetic intelligence   Coordinated development of bodily movements and adaptations.

Boston Globe/Horn Book Award   The Boston Globe—Horn Book Awards are given in three categories: Fiction and Poetry, Picture Book, and Nonfiction. Books must be published in the United States but they may be written and/or illustrated by citizens of any country. The selections are made by a panel of three independent judges.

Bullying   Physical, emotional, verbal, and racial tormenting of another child. (See also cyberbullying.)

C

Caldecott Award   An award presented annually to an American illustrator for the most distinguished picture book published the previous year.

Celebrity book   A children's book written by well-known actors and actresses and other famous people.

Censorship   The process whereby adults seek to remove books from library shelves.

Chapbooks   Cheap editions of fairy tales and folktales.

Characters   As an important literary element, characters must be fully developed and not stereotypical in a well-constructed book.

Chick lit   Originally written for adults, it has been adapted for teenage girls who relate to the independence of its characters.

Children's Internet Protection Act (CIPA)   Public libraries and public school libraries are required to filter online workstations if they receive e-rate monies.

Classification   Grouping objects on the basis of a set of characteristics.

Cognitive structures   Piaget's term to describe the basic building blocks of intellectual development.

Concept book   Teaches children how to organize their world by grouping together different characteristics based on a particular similarity.

Concrete operational period   The third of Piaget's stages of cognitive development.

Conflict   When characters with different motives, some external, some internal, compete with one another.

Contemporary realistic fiction   Stories that *could* be true in the here and now.

Coretta Scott King Awards   Presented annually to an outstanding African American author and illustrator.

Counting book   Presents each number with a picture of an equivalent number of objects.

Crossover   A book that is published for the adult reader but considered more appropriate for the young adult reader, and vice versa.

Cultural literacy   Knowledge of and appreciation of the diversity of peoples and cultures.

Culture   The customs, values, and traditions inherent in one's environment.

Cumulative tale   A story that is based on repetitive elements.

Cyberbullying   Abuse through the use of the Internet.

D

Dewey decimal classification system   Melvil Dewey's classic means of organizing knowledge into ten specific categories.

Dialogic reading   A strategy that stresses the value of shared reading as adults ask children open-ended questions and encourage children to expand their answers.

Drama   A play that contains all the elements of a story but is written to be performed.

E

Easy reader   Specifically written for the beginning reader that contains short words and a controlled vocabulary.

Efferent reading   Reading for information.

Emergent literacy   A term coined by New Zealand educator Marie Clay referring to a young child's ability to learn to read and write by observing and using materials that encourage those skills.

Episodic plot   A minor plot within one chapter or a few chapters of the main story that contains its own resolution.

Esteem needs   The fourth of Maslow's needs that refers to a child's need to have a deserved sense of worth based on the opinion of others and the child's own self-evaluation.

F

Fable   Stories in which animals speak and act like humans.

Fairy tale   A type of folktale that weaves a story of magic and fairies.

Fantasy   Written by a known author and best described as the concept of what *might* be, e.g. journeys into imaginative worlds.

"Five to Seven" shift   A child's thinking after age 7 differs from thinking before age 5.

Folktale   Universal in nature, having no known author, and belonging to the oral tradition, it relates events in the lives of humans and nonhumans alike.

Formal operational period   The fourth and final stage of Piaget's stages of cognitive development.

Fractured fairy tale   An author or authors' humorous version of a traditional fairy tale.

Free verse   Unrhymed poetry with no regular pattern.

G

Gender   Psychosocial aspects of maleness and femaleness.

Genres   Characteristics that distinguish one kind of literature from another.

Global literacy   Knowledge and appreciation of the diversity of peoples and cultures.

Goodness-of-fit   The match between a child's developmental level and appropriate literature. Based on the concept devised by child psychiatrists Stella Chess and Alexander Thomas.

Grand conversation   Originally called *literature circles*, children in small groups talk about a book while the teacher offers open-ended questions to further discussion.

Graphic novel   A graphically illustrated book whose origin is the comic book.

Haiku   A single stanza, three line lyric poem of seventeen syllables about a single subject of Japanese origin.

Hans Christian Andersen award   Given by the International Board on Books for Young People to an author and illustrator whose complete works have made a lasting contribution to children's literature throughout the world.

Historical fiction   Stories that *could* have happened in the past.

I

Identity versus identity confusion   The fifth of Erikson's stages of psychosocial development during which adolescents face the task of discovering who they are; this is the final stage of the childhood years.

Industry versus inferiority   Erikson's fourth stage of psychosocial development during which children are immersed in the task of acquiring the needed information and skills of their culture (the elementary school years).

Information literacy   Ability to find, evaluate, and use information effectively.

Informational books   Books containing verifiable facts.

Inhibited children   Children who are shy and frightened when facing anything unknown.

Initiative versus guilt   Erikson's third stage of psychosocial development during which children demonstrate responsibility and a sense of purpose (the preschool years).

Interactive book   Mechanical devices within the book that are used to advance the story.

Interpersonal intelligence   Ability to work with others and understand them.

Intrapersonal intelligence   Ability to be aware of inner feelings, intentions, goals, etc.

Intuitive thought   A child's ability to reason logically occurs; typically appears in the 5- to 7-year age period.

K

Kamishabai   The portable stage once used by itinerant storytellers in Japan.

Kohlberg's moral stages   A psychological explanation of a child's moral development.

L

Lee Bennett Hopkins Poetry Award   Presented annually to an American poet or anthologist for the most outstanding book of children;s poetry published the previous year.

Legend   Story based on history but not always verifiable.

Leveling   Classifying books according to specific reading skills of the child.

Linear plot.   Another term for a progressive plot.

Linguistic intelligence   Organizing thoughts for verbal tasks.

Literacy   Ability to read, write, speak, and understand a language.

Literary awards   Local, national, or international recognition to authors and illustrators of outstanding children's literature.

Literary devices   Various means by which authors develop the plots for their stories.

Literary elements   The setting, plot, characters, point of view, style, and theme of a well-made story.

Literary fairy tale   A modern tale written by a known author as contrasted to the traditional fairy tale that has no known author.

Literary lunch bunch   Adults and students meet together for refreshments and discussion of a book.

Literary theme   The selection and development of one theme across the curriculum using various genres.

Logical-mathematical intelligence   Understanding the components of thinking and problem solving, probably best represented in scientific, mathematical, and logical abilities.

Love and belonging needs   The third of Maslow's needs that refer to children's need to be wanted and accepted.

Lyric poetry   Short, expressive, nonnarrative poems.

M

Manga   Japanese comic books, often read from right to left.

Memoir   A form of biography, relating one or more incidents in the life of the person who is writing the story.

Michael L. Printz Award   Presented annually by the ALA to an American author whose book written the previous year epitomizes literary excellence in young adult literature.

Mildred Batchelder Award   Presented annually to an American publisher for a book written for children and published the previous year in a foreign language in a foreign country and then published in the United States.

Multiple intelligences   Howard Gardner's belief that humans possess eight types of intelligences.

Musical intelligence   Recognizing the themes in musical works and distinguishing melody.

Mythology   The study of the lives of gods and goddesses in ancient times.

Myths   Universal and timeless religious stories based on the lives of supernatural beings, the gods and goddesses.

N

Narrative poetry   Long story-telling poems.

Naturalistic intelligence   Ability to be aware of the environment and the means to protect it.

Needs theory   Abraham Maslow's contention that humans possess five basic needs that must be satisfied for satisfactory development to occur.

Newbery Medal   Named in honor of John Newbery, an English publisher and bookseller, and presented to an American author who has written the most distinguished children's book the previous year.

Noodlehead tale   Often called a droll, merry, or numbskull tale, it is a humorous folktale.

O

Object permanence   Infants come to realize that objects continue to exist even if they can't be seen, heard, or touched.

Observational learning   Bandura's belief that learning occurs by observing others without actively imitating their responses. (Also known as social cognitive learning.)

Orbis Pictus award   Given annually by the National Council of Teachers of English to the most outstanding nonfiction or informational book published in the United States the previous year.

Outstanding International Booklist   Founded in 2006 to recognize the most outstanding books throughout the world that counteract cultural stereotypes, bridge cultural gaps, and build connections.

P

Parable   Short moralistic story.

Parallel cultures   A phrase that pertains to minorities who are uneasy because of the ideological difference they feel from the majority.

Parental monitors   Parents seriously concerned with their young adults' well being.

Penny dreadfuls   Books about boys' schools that appeared in inexpensive periodicals.

Phonological development   The acquisition of speech sounds.

Physiological needs   The first of Maslow's needs such as hunger and thirst.

Picture book   Usually, the integration of words with pictures; some picture books, however, are wordless.

Picture storybook   A story told by the integration of words with pictures.

Plagiarism   Taking another's work and passing it off as one's own.

Plot   The action of a book beginning with a problem, rising to a climax or turning point, and descending to a solution or outcome.

Poetry   Poetry has many forms. It is frequently written in rhyme but is also written in free verse. It is often written in stanzas but never in paragraphs.

Point of view   The perspective from which the story is told.

Pop-Up book   A paper engineered book whose individual pages open up to reveal three-dimensional images.

Porquoi tale   Explains why natural events occur.

Postmodernism   Often termed *metafiction*, it is a kind of experimental or avant-garde writing and illustration.

Pragmatic development   Understanding the conversational rules of a language.

Preoperational period   The second of Piaget's stages of cognitive development.

Printing press   Invented by Gutenberg about the year 1455, the printing press was responsible for the initial proliferation of books.

Progressive plot   A plot that proceeds chronologically with a beginning, a middle, and an end.

Psychosocial stages   Erik Erikson's belief that humans pass through eight stages of psychosocial development.

Puberty   Physical and psychological changes that occur during the teen years (age is not a precise indicator).

Pura Belpré award   Presented biannually to a writer or illustrator from any one of the Spanish speaking cultures of the Western Hemisphere who has written or illustrated an outstanding book.

R

Readers Theatre   A dramatic reading of a book by a group of students.

Reissues   Books previously out-of-print that are again being published.

Response theory   Another term for Louise Rosenblatt's Transactional theory about how a child responds to a book.

S

Safety needs   The second of Maslow's needs that refer to a child's need to be free from fear and anxiety to achieve their potential.

Scaffolding   Children move from initial difficulty with a topic when they're working independently to a point where, with help, they learn to perform the task successfully.

School phobia   Apprehension about attending school; may be accompanied by such physical symptoms of illness as nausea, dizziness, etc., which disappear when the child is not at school.

Science fiction   The creation of a situation that *could* happen in the future. It is often based on scientific fact.

Scientific literacy   Knowledge of science, scientific thinking, and mathematics.

Self-actualization   Maslow's fifth and final need that refers to the need to do what we think we are capable of doing.

Self-efficacy   Children's beliefs that they have the ability to achieve and obtain their goals.

Semantic development   Understanding the meaning of language (words, phrases, sentences).

Sensorimotor period   The first of Piaget's cognitive stages of development.

Series   A group of books, often numbered, that contain many of the same characters in each book.

Shonen   Boys' manga.

Shoujo   Girls' manga.

Snack-brand book   Book that uses food—candy, cereals—to attract children's attention; children insert food into holes on the pages, identify colors, and count the number of pieces on a page.

Social perspective-taking   Children's views on how to relate to others emerge from their personal ideas about the traits of others.

Sonnet   Consists of fourteen lines and is of three types: Italian, Shakespearean, and Spensorian.

Spatial intelligence   Forming mental representations to aid thinking and remembering.

Storytelling   Passing on children's literature from generation to generation by oral means.

Stranger anxiety   An infant's fear of strangers; peaks at about one year.

Stratemeyer syndicate   Edward Stratemeyer, during the 1930s and 1940s, planned and assigned over forty different series to a variety of writers.

Style   The author's unique manner of creating a story by using words, images, and figures of speech, that is, how a writer says things.

Symbolic function   Piaget's term to describe a child's ability to represent an object not present; appears during the 2- to 4-age period.

Symbolic setting   Found predominantly in traditional literature where the setting is vague and general.

Synergy   A marketing term for the cross-promotion of a book into a successful brand.

Syntactic development   Understanding the structure of a language.

T

Tabula rasa   The mind as a blank slate or, as defined by John Locke, a "white paper void of all characters."

Tall tale   Exaggerated retelling of daring exploits of men and women who become legend.

Technological literacy   Ability to understand and work with computers, networks, and software.

TESOL   Teaching English to Speakers of Other Languages.

Theme   The lesson that the story tells, the central idea of the story.

Theory of mind   Children's growing understanding of how the human mind works.

Time travel   A story that takes the reader who suspends disbelief back to another time.

Toy books   Engineered, interactive, press-the-button, pop-up, open the flap, etc., books.

Traditional literature   Stories and songs emerging from the oral tradition whose authors are unknown.

Transactional theory   Describes the active role of the reader in the interaction between child and book. (Also known as Reader Response Theory.)

Transformational tale   Stories that change an animal into a human or a human into an animal.

Transitional books   Books that are written to help children make the leap from reading easy readers to reading chapter books.

Trust versus mistrust   Erikson's first stage of psychosocial development that is based on feelings of comfort and safety that develop in the first year of life.

U

Uninhibited children   Children who are cautious but unafraid when faced with unknown circumstances.

V

Visual literacy   Ability to decipher, interpret, and express ideas using images, charts, graphs, and video.

W

Word spurt   Explosion of words and ideas that occur in a child's life from 18 months to 3 years.

Wordless book   Tells a story without a written word.

Z

Zone of proximal development   Vygotsky's description of the distance between a child's actual developmental level and what that child could achieve with help.

Author/Illustrator Name and Book Index